# DAVID BUSCH'S
# CANON® EOS®
# REBEL T5i/700D

## GUIDE TO DIGITAL SLR PHOTOGRAPHY

David D. Busch

**Cengage Learning PTR**

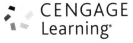

Professional • Technical • Reference

Australia, Brazil, Japan, Korea, Mexico, Singapore, Spain, United Kingdom, United States

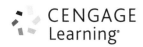

# CENGAGE
## Learning

Professional • Technical • Reference

**David Busch's Canon® EOS® Rebel T5i/700D Guide to Digital SLR Photography**
**David D. Busch**

**Pu blisher and General Manager, Cengage Learning PTR:**
Stacy L. Hiquet

**Associate Director of Marketing:**
Sarah Panella

**Manager of Editorial Services:**
Heather Talbot

**Senior Marketing Manager:**
Mark Hughes

**Executive Editor:**
Kevin Harreld

**Project Editor:**
Jenny Davidson

**Series Technical Editor:**
Michael D. Sullivan

**Interior Layout Tech:**
Bill Hartman

**Cover Designer:**
Mike Tanamachi

**Indexer:**
Katherine Stimson

**Proofreader:**
Michael Beady

© 2014 David D. Busch

For product information and technology assistance, contact us at
**Cengage Learning Customer & Sales Support, 1-800-354-9706**

For permission to use material from this text or product, submit all requests online at **cengage.com/permissions**
Further permissions questions can be emailed to
**permissionrequest@cengage.com**

Library of Congress Control Number: 2013942737

ISBN-13: 978-1-285-78113-6

ISBN-10: 1-285-78113-9

**Cengage Learning PTR**
20 Channel Center Street
Boston, MA 02210
USA

Cengage Learning is a leading provider of customized learning solutions with office locations around the globe, including Singapore, the United Kingdom, Australia, Mexico, Brazil, and Japan. Locate your local office at: **international.cengage.com/region**

Cengage Learning products are represented in Canada by Nelson Education, Ltd.

For your lifelong learning solutions, visit **cengageptr.com**

Visit our corporate website at **cengage.com**

Printed in the United States of America
1 2 3 4 5 6 7 15 14 13

*For Cathy*

# Acknowledgments

Once again thanks to the folks at Cengage Learning PTR, who have pioneered publishing digital imaging books in full color at a price anyone can afford. Special thanks to executive editor Kevin Harreld, who always gives me the freedom to let my imagination run free with a topic, as well as my veteran production team including project editor Jenny Davidson and series technical editor Mike Sullivan. Also thanks to Bill Hartman, layout; Katherine Stimson, indexing; Mike Beady, proofreading; Mike Tanamachi, cover design; and my agent, Carole Jelen, who has the amazing ability to keep both publishers and authors happy. I'd also like to thank the Continent of Europe, without which this book would have a lot of blank spaces where illustrations are supposed to go.

Also, big thanks to the folks at Campus Camera (www.campuscamera.net), who obtained one of the first Rebel T5i's available for me when even Canon had none to provide. Their help made it possible for me to be using this great camera and putting together this book while most Canonphiles were still waiting for delivery.

Thanks again to master photographer Nancy Balluck (www.nancyballuckphotography.com) for the back cover photo of yours truly.

# About the Author

With more than a million books in print, **David D. Busch** is one of the bestselling authors of books on digital photography and imaging technology, and the originator of popular series like *David Busch's Pro Secrets* and *David Busch's Quick Snap Guides*. He has written dozens of hugely successful guidebooks for Canon digital camera models, including all-time #1 bestsellers for many of them, additional user guides for other camera models, as well as many popular books devoted to dSLRs, including *Mastering Digital SLR Photography, Third Edition* and *Digital SLR Pro Secrets*. As a roving photojournalist for more than 20 years, he illustrated his books, magazine articles, and newspaper reports with award-winning images. He's operated his own commercial studio, suffocated in formal dress while shooting weddings-for-hire, and shot sports for a daily newspaper and upstate New York college. His photos and articles have been published in *Popular Photography, Rangefinder, Professional Photographer*, and hundreds of other publications. He's also reviewed dozens of digital cameras for Ziff-Davis online and print publications.

When About.com named its top five books on Beginning Digital Photography, debuting at the #1 and #2 slots were Busch's *Digital Photography All-In-One Desk Reference for Dummies* and *Mastering Digital Photography*. During the past year, he's had as many as five of his books listed in the Top 20 of Amazon.com's Digital Photography Bestseller list—simultaneously! Busch's 150 other books published since 1983 include bestsellers like *David Busch's Quick Snap Guide to Using Digital SLR Lenses*. His advice has been featured on National Public Radio's *All Tech Considered*.

Busch is a member of the Cleveland Photographic Society (www.clevelandphoto.org), which has operated continuously since 1887. Visit his website at http://www.dslrguides.com/blog.

# Contents

## PART I: GETTING STARTED WITH YOUR CANON EOS REBEL T5i/700D

# Chapter 3
# Canon EOS Rebel T5i/700D Roadmap     39

# PART II: MASTERING YOUR TOOLS

# Chapter 4
# Nailing the Right Exposure     61

# Chapter 5
# Mastering the Mysteries of Autofocus    103

# Chapter 6
# Movies and Live View                                        127

# Chapter 7
# Advanced Shooting                                           157

# PART III: CONFIGURING YOUR CANON EOS REBEL T5i/700D

## Chapter 8
## Customizing with the Shooting and Playback Menus    179

# Chapter 9
# Customizing with the Set-up Menu and My Menu    237

## PART IV: ENHANCING YOUR CANON EOS REBEL T5i/700D

# Chapter 10
# Working with Lenses                                      263

# Chapter 11
# Working with Light 297

# Chapter 12
# Working with Wireless Flash                                    341

# Chapter 13
## Downloading, Editing, and Printing Your Images    371

# Chapter 14
## Troubleshooting and Prevention    385

# Index    405

# Preface

You don't want good pictures from your new Canon EOS Rebel T5i/700D—you demand *outstanding* photos. After all, the T5i/700D is one of the most advanced entry-level cameras that Canon has ever introduced. It boasts 18 megapixels of resolution, blazing-fast automatic focus, and cool features like the real-time preview system called Live View, full high-definition movie shooting, a touch screen that allows you to make many settings with a tap of the LCD, and an amazing new wireless flash capability. But your gateway to pixel proficiency is dragged down by the slim little book included in the box as a manual. You know everything you need to know is in there, somewhere, but you don't know where to start. In addition, the camera manual doesn't offer much information on photography or digital photography. Nor are you interested in spending hours or days studying a comprehensive book on digital SLR photography that doesn't necessarily apply directly to your T5i.

What you need is a guide that explains the purpose and function of the T5i's basic controls, how you should use them, and *why*. Ideally, there should be information about file formats, resolution, exposure, and other special autofocus modes available, but you'd prefer to read about those topics only after you've had the chance to go out and take a few hundred great pictures with your new camera. Why isn't there a book that summarizes the most important information in its first two or three chapters, with lots of illustrations showing what your results will look like when you use this setting or that?

Now there is such a book. If you want a quick introduction to the T5i's focus controls, wireless flash synchronization options, how to choose lenses, or which exposure modes are best, this book is for you. If you can't decide on what basic settings to use with your camera because you can't figure out how changing ISO or white balance or focus defaults will affect your pictures, you need this guide.

# Introduction

Although the Canon EOS Rebel T5i/700D is a modest upgrade from its predecessor, the T4i, the company has continued its campaign to package many of the most alluring capabilities of its most advanced digital SLRs (such as wireless flash capabilities), added a touch screen for making settings with a tap on the swiveling LCD, and stuffed them into a compact, highly affordable body. Your new 18-megapixel camera is loaded with capabilities that few would have expected to find in a dSLR in the sub-$1,000 price range. Indeed, the T5i eases the transition for those new to digital photography. For those just dipping their toes into the digital pond, the experience is warm and inviting.

Nor will you easily outgrow this camera. The T5i upgrade can be purchased with one of two STM (stepper technology motor) autofocus lenses that are smooth and quiet, and ideal for the burgeoning interest in video shooting. It's got resolution that's more than 85 percent of what you get with the 22-megapixel Canon EOS 5D Mark III "pro" camera and lots of customization options. Its wireless flash capabilities, which allow the camera's built-in electronic flash to control off-camera flash units remotely, is a most welcome addition. Canon must love serious photographers, because it seems to work extra hard to give them incredible value for their money.

But once you've confirmed that you made a wise purchase decision, the question comes up, *how do I use this thing?* All those cool features can be mind-numbing to learn, if all you have as a guide is the manual furnished with the camera. Help is on the way. I sincerely believe that this book is your best bet for learning how to use your new camera, and for learning how to use it well.

If you're a Canon EOS Rebel T5i owner who's looking to learn more about how to use this great camera, you've probably already explored your options. There are DVDs and online tutorials—but who can learn how to use a camera by sitting in front of a television or computer screen? Do you want to watch a movie or click on HTML links, or do you want to go out and take photos with your camera? Videos are fun, but not the best answer.

There's always the manual furnished with the T5i. It's compact and filled with information, but there's really very little about *why* you should use particular settings or features, and its organization may make it difficult to find what you need. Multiple cross-references may send you flipping back and forth between two or three sections of the book to find what you want to know. The basic manual is also hobbled by black-and-white line drawings and tiny monochrome pictures that aren't very good examples of what you can do.

Also available are third-party guides to the T5i, like this one. I haven't been happy with some of these guidebooks, which is why I wrote this one. The existing books range from skimpy and illustrated by black-and-white photos to lushly illustrated in full color but too generic to do much good. Photography instruction is useful, but it needs to be related directly to the Canon EOS T5i as much as possible.

I've tried to make *David Busch's Canon EOS Rebel T5i/700D Guide to Digital SLR Photography* different from your other T5i learn-up options. The roadmap sections use larger, color pictures to show you where all the buttons and dials are, and the explanations of what they do are longer and more comprehensive. I've tried to avoid overly general advice, including the two-page checklists on how to take a "sports picture" or a "portrait picture" or a "travel picture." Instead, you'll find tips and techniques for using all the features of your Canon EOS Rebel T5i to take *any kind of picture* you want. If you want to know where you should stand to take a picture of a quarterback dropping back to unleash a pass, there are plenty of books that will tell you that. This one concentrates on teaching you how to select the best autofocus mode, shutter speed, f/stop, or flash capability to take, say, a great sports picture under any conditions.

*David Busch's Canon EOS Rebel T5i/700D Guide to Digital SLR Photography* is aimed at both Canon and dSLR veterans as well as newcomers to digital photography and digital SLRs. Both groups can be overwhelmed by the options the T5i offers, while underwhelmed by the explanations they receive in their user's manual. The manuals are great if you already know what you don't know, and you can find an answer somewhere in a booklet arranged by menu listings and written by a camera vendor employee who last threw together instructions on how to operate a camcorder.

Of course, once you've read this book and are ready to learn more, you might want to pick up one of my other guides to digital SLR photography. I'm listing them here not to hawk my other books, but because a large percentage of the e-mails I get are from readers who want to know if I've got a book on this topic or that. In the chapters that follow, I also may mention another one of my books that covers a particular subject in more depth than is possible in a camera-specific guide. Again, that's only for the benefit of those who want to delve more deeply into a topic. *Most* of what you need to know to use and enjoy your T5i is contained right here in this book. Some of my other guides offered by Cengage Learning PTR include:

### *David Busch's Compact Field Guide for the Canon EOS Rebel T5i/700D*
While most readers enjoy poring over the wealth of information I provide in my full-size guides, many of you have asked for a condensed version with just the basic operational and settings information, in a compact size that can be slipped in a camera bag. Well, you can throw away your cheat sheets and command cards. My *Compact Field Guide* for your T5i is a spiral-bound, lay-flat, full-color book with all the information you need when on the go. Unlike a laminated command card, my field guide tells you what each control, menu item, and option does—and why you should or should not use it. If you like my "big book" and want to get the most from your T5i, you need this compact guide, too.

### David Busch's Guide to Canon Flash Photography

Although I cover photography with Canon Speedlites in several chapters of this book, those who are looking for more detailed instructions for using the latest Canon strobes will want to check out my new guide to Canon flash photography. It provides tips on using wireless flash, multiple units, and lists the steps you need to follow to activate the essential features of the most recent Canon Speedlites, including the new 600EX-RT.

### Quick Snap Guide to Digital SLR Photography

Consider this a prequel to the book you're holding in your hands. It might make a good gift for a spouse or friend who may be using your T5i, but who lacks even basic knowledge about digital photography, digital SLR photography, and Canon EOS photography. It serves as an introduction that summarizes the basic features of digital SLR cameras in general (not just the T5i), and what settings to use and when, such as continuous autofocus/single autofocus, aperture/shutter priority, EV settings, and so forth. The guide also includes recipes for shooting the most common kinds of pictures, with step-by-step instructions for capturing effective sports photos, portraits, landscapes, and other types of images.

### David Busch's Quick Snap Guide to Using Digital SLR Lenses

A bit overwhelmed by the features and controls of digital SLR lenses, and not quite sure when to use each type? This book explains lenses, their use, and lens technology in easy-to-access two- and four-page spreads, each devoted to a different topic, such as depth-of-field, lens aberrations, or using zoom lenses.

### David Busch's Quick Snap Guide to Lighting

This book tells you everything you need to know about using light to create the kind of images you'll be proud of. It's not Canon-specific, and doesn't include any details on using any of the Canon-dedicated flash units, but the information you'll find applies to any digital SLR photography.

### Mastering Digital SLR Photography, Third Edition

This book is an introduction to digital SLR photography, with nuts-and-bolts explanations of the technology, more in-depth coverage of settings, and whole chapters on the most common types of photography. While not specific to the T5i, this book can show you how to get more from its capabilities. I've added six brand new chapters and the latest technology secrets in this new version.

### David Busch's dSLR Movie Shooting Compact Field Guide

Although this book is not specific to Canon cameras, it takes up where my T5i guidebooks leave off in offering additional techniques and tips for shooting your best video ever. Movie shooting is an entirely different discipline from still photography, and deserves an entire book—or two—of its own. My movie-oriented *Compact Field Guide* belongs in your camera bag.

# Why the Canon EOS Rebel T5i/700D Needs Special Coverage

When I started writing digital photography books in 1995, digital SLRs cost $30,000 and few people other than certain professionals could justify them. Most of my readers a dozen years ago were stuck using the point-and-shoot, low-resolution digital cameras of the time—even if they were advanced photographers. I myself took countless digital pictures with an Epson digital camera with 1024 × 768 (less than 1 megapixel!) resolution, and which cost $500.

Less than a decade ago (before the original Digital Rebel was introduced), the lowest-cost dSLRs were priced at $3,000 or more. Today, anyone with around $600 can afford one of those basic cameras, and roughly $1,000 buys you a sophisticated model like the Canon EOS T5i (with lens). The digital SLR is no longer the exclusive bailiwick of the professional, the wealthy, or the serious photography addict willing to scrimp and save to acquire a dream camera. Digital SLRs have become the favored camera for anyone who wants to go beyond point-and-shoot capabilities. And Canon cameras have enjoyed a dominating position among digital SLRs because of Canon's innovation in introducing affordable cameras with interesting features and outstanding performance (particularly in the area of high ISO image quality). It doesn't hurt that Canon also provides both full-frame and smaller format digital cameras and a clear migration path between them (if you stick to the Canon EF lenses that are compatible with both).

You've selected your camera of choice, and you belong in the Canon camp if you fall into one of the following categories:

- Individuals who want to get better pictures, or perhaps transform their growing interest in photography into a full-fledged hobby or artistic outlet with a Canon T5i and advanced techniques.

- Those who want to produce more professional-looking images for their personal or business website, and feel that the T5i will give them more control and capabilities.

- Small business owners with more advanced graphics capabilities who want to use the T5i to document or promote their business.

- Corporate workers who may or may not have photographic skills in their job descriptions, but who work regularly with graphics and need to learn how to use digital images taken with a Canon EOS T5i for reports, presentations, or other applications.

- Professional webmasters with strong skills in programming (including Java, JavaScript, HTML, Perl, etc.) but little background in photography, but who realize that the T5i can be used for sophisticated photography.

- Graphic artists and others who already may be adept in image editing with Photoshop or another program, and who may already be using a simple camera (Canon or otherwise), but who need to learn more about digital photography and the special capabilities of the T5i dSLR.

# Who Am I?

After spending years as the world's most successful unknown author, I've become slightly less obscure in the past few years, thanks to a horde of camera guidebooks and other photographically oriented tomes. You may have seen my photography articles in *Popular Photography* magazine. I've also written about 2,000 articles for magazines like *Petersen's PhotoGraphic* (which is now defunct through no fault of my own), plus *Rangefinder*, *Professional Photographer*, and dozens of other photographic publications. But, first, and foremost, I'm a photojournalist and made my living in the field until I began devoting most of my time to writing books.

Although I love writing, I'm happiest when I'm out taking pictures, which is why I invariably spend several days each week photographing landscapes, people, close-up subjects, and other things. I spend a month or two each year traveling to events, such as Native American "powwows," Civil War re-enactments, county fairs, ballet, and sports (baseball, basketball, football, and soccer are favorites). Recently, I spent a full two weeks in Salamanca, Spain. I went there to shoot photographs of the people, landscapes, and monuments that I've grown to love, with about five hours a day set aside for study at a *colegio* located in an ancient monastery in the old part of the city, just steps from the cathedral. I can offer you my personal advice on how to take photos under a variety of conditions because I've had to meet those challenges myself on an ongoing basis.

Like all my digital photography books, this one was written by someone with an incurable photography bug. My first Canon SLR was a now-obscure model called the Pellix back in the 1960s, and I've used a variety of newer models since then. I've worked as a sports photographer for an Ohio newspaper and for an upstate New York college. I've operated my own commercial studio and photo lab, cranking out product shots on demand and then printing a few hundred glossy 8 × 10s on a tight deadline for a press kit. I've served as a photo-posing instructor for a modeling agency. People have actually paid me to shoot their weddings and immortalize them with portraits. I even prepared press kits and articles on photography as a PR consultant for a large Rochester, N.Y., company, which shall remain nameless. My trials and travails with imaging and computer technology have made their way into print in book form an alarming number of times.

Like you, I love photography for its own merits, and I view technology as just another tool to help me get the images I see in my mind's eye. But, also like you, I had to master this technology before I could apply it to my work. This book is the result of what I've learned, and I hope it will help you master your T5i digital SLR, too.

In closing, I'd like to ask a special favor: let me know what you think of this book. If you have any recommendations about how I can make it better, visit my website at www.dslrguides.com/blog, click on the E-Mail Me tab, and send your comments, suggestions on topics that should be explained in more detail, or, especially, any typos. (The latter will be compiled on the Errata page you'll also find on my website.) I really value your ideas, and appreciate it when you take the time to tell me what you think! Some of the content of the book you hold in your hands came from suggestions I received from readers like yourself. If you found this book especially useful, tell others about it. Visit http://www.amazon.com/dp/1285781139 and leave a positive review. Your feedback is what spurs me to make each one of these books better than the last. Thanks!

# Part I

# Getting Started with Your Canon EOS Rebel T5i/700D

This first part of the book, consisting of just three short chapters, is designed to familiarize you with the basics of your Canon EOS Rebel T5i/700D as quickly as possible, even though I have no doubt that you've already been out shooting a few hundred (or thousand) photographs with your pride and joy.

After all, inserting a memory card, mounting a lens, stuffing a charged battery into the base, and removing the lens cap to fire off a shot or two isn't rocket science. Even the rawest neophyte can rotate the Mode Dial (located at top right on the camera body) to the P (Programmed auto) position or select Scene Intelligent Auto (marked with a green A+ icon) and then point the T5i at something interesting and press the shutter release. Presto! A pretty good picture will pop up on the color LCD on the back of the camera. It's easy!

But in digital photography, there is such a thing as *too* easy. If you bought a T5i, you certainly had no intention of using the camera as a point-and-shoot snapshooter. After all, the T5i is a tool suitable for the most advanced photographic pursuits, with an extensive array of customization possibilities. As such, you don't want the camera's operation to be brainless; you want *access* to the advanced features to be easy.

You get that easy access with the Canon T5i. However, you'll still need to take the time to learn how to use these features, and I'm going to provide everything you need to know in these first three chapters to begin shooting:

- **Chapter 1, "Thinking Outside of the Box":** This is a "Meet Your T5i" introduction, where you'll find information about what came in the box with your camera and, more importantly, what *didn't* come with the camera that you seriously should consider adding to your arsenal. I'll also cover some things you might not have known about charging the T5i's battery, choosing a memory card, setting the time and date, and a few other pre-flight tasks. This is basic stuff, and if you're a Canon veteran, you can skim over it quickly. A lot of this first chapter is intended for EOS newbies, and even if you personally don't find it essential, you'll probably agree that there was some point during your photographic development (so to speak) that you would have wished this information was spelled out for you. There's no extra charge!

- **Chapter 2, "Canon EOS Rebel T5i/700D Quick Start":** Here, you'll find a Quick Start aimed at those who may not be old hands with Canon cameras having this level of sophistication. The T5i has some interesting new features, including one of the most advanced autofocus systems ever seen in a mid-level camera body (and which deserves an entire chapter of its own later in this book). But even with all the goodies to play with and learning curve still to climb, you'll find that Chapter 2 will get you shooting quickly with a minimum of fuss.

■ **Chapter 3, "Canon EOS Rebel T5i/700D Roadmap":** This is a Streetsmart Roadmap to the Canon EOS Rebel T5i/700D. Confused by the tiny little diagrams and multiple cross-references for each and every control that send you scurrying around looking for information you know is buried somewhere in the small and inadequate manual stuffed in the box? This chapter uses multiple large full-color pictures that show every dial, knob, and button, and explain the basics of using each in clear, easy-to-understand language. I'll give you the basics up front, and, even if I have to send you deeper into the book for a full discussion of a complex topic, you'll have what you need to use a control right away.

Once you've finished (or skimmed through) these three chapters, you'll be ready for Part II, which explains how to use the most important basic features, such as the T5i's exposure controls, nifty new autofocus system (originally introduced with the predecessor T4i model), and the related tools that put live view and movie-making tools at your fingertips. Then, you can visit Part III, the advanced tools section, which explains all the dozens of setup options that can be used to modify the capabilities you've learned to use so far, how to choose and use lenses, and introduces the EOS Rebel T5i/700D's built-in flash and external flash capabilities. I'll wind up this book with Part IV, which covers image software, printing, and transfer options and includes some troubleshooting that may help you when good cameras (or film cards) go bad.

# 1

# Thinking Outside of the Box

Whether you subscribe to the "my camera is just a tool" theory, or belong to the "an exquisite camera adds new capabilities to my shooting arsenal" camp, picking up a new Canon EOS Rebel T5i/700D is a special experience. Those who simply wield tools will find this camera as comforting as an old friend, a solid piece of fine machinery ready and able to do their bidding as part of the creative process.

Other photographers see the low-light capabilities (up to H, the equivalent of ISO 25600), the 5 frames-per-second continuous shooting, commendable ruggedness, and 18-megapixel resolution of the T5i, and gain a sense of empowerment. *Here* is a camera with fewer limitations and more capabilities for exercising renewed creative vision. In either case, using less mawkish terms, the T5i is one of the coolest cameras Canon has ever offered. Whether you're upgrading from another brand, from another Canon model (like one of the "lesser" Rebel models), or your T5i is your first digital camera and/or single lens reflex, welcome to the club.

But, now that you've unwrapped and recharged the beast, mounted a lens, and fueled it with a memory card, what do you *do* with it? That's where this chapter—and the chapters that follow—should come in handy. Like many of you, I am a Canon user of long standing. And, like other members of our club, I had to learn at least some aspects of my newest EOS camera for the very first time at some point. Experienced pro, or Canon newbie, you bought this book because you wanted to get the most from a very powerful tool, and I'm here to help.

Depending on your path to the camera, the Canon EOS T5i is either the company's most ambitious beginner camera, or most affordable advanced camera, which are both distinctions that I find almost meaningless in the greater scheme of things. I know consummate professionals who produced amazing images with an original Digital Rebel and experienced wedding photographers who evoke the most romantic photos from an ancient Canon 30D. In the right hands, the T5i is a professional camera capable of professional photographs. But whether your *images* are of professional quality, both technically and inspirationally, depends on what's between your ears, and how you apply it. The goal of this book is to provide you with the information you need to put your brain cells together with Canon's electro-mechanical components to work productively.

There's a lot to learn, but you don't have to master every detail all at once. Some of the other camera guides I've seen winnow this information down to about one-third as many pages. Indeed, I find it odd that those guidebooks use the same basic template for more advanced cameras as for a resolutely amateur-level model like the very basic Rebel T3. A camera like the T5i has a lot more depth than that, and deserves the in-depth coverage you'll find here.

Whether you've already taken a dozen or twelve hundred photos with your new camera, now that you've got that initial creative burst out of your system, you'll want to take a more considered approach to operating the camera. This chapter and the next are designed to get your camera fired up and ready for shooting as quickly as possible. After all, the T5i is not a point-and-shoot camera, even though it does boast easy-to-use "Basic Zone" options with icons on a handy dial representing various fully automatic modes, plus "scene" modes with icons for a person (for portraits), flower (close-ups), mountain scene (landscapes), or runner (sports activity).

So I'm going to provide a basic pre-flight checklist that you need to complete before you really spread your wings and take off. You won't find a lot of detail in these first two chapters. Indeed, I'm going to tell you just what you absolutely *must* understand, accompanied by some interesting tidbits that will help you become acclimated to your T5i. I'll go into more depth and even repeat some of what I explain here in later chapters, so you don't have to memorize everything you see. Just relax, follow a few easy steps, and then go out and begin taking your best shots—ever.

Even if you're a long-time Canon shooter, I hope you won't be tempted to skip this chapter or the next one. I realize that you probably didn't purchase this book the same day you bought your camera and that, even if you did, the urge to go out and take a few hundred—or thousand—photos with your new camera is enticing. As valuable as a book like this one is, nobody can suppress their excitement long enough to read the instructions before initiating play with a new toy.

No matter how extensive your experience level is, you don't need to fret about wading through a manual to find out what you must know to take those first few tentative snaps. I'm going to help you hit the ground running with this chapter, which will help you set up your camera and begin shooting in minutes. Because I realize that some of you may already have experience with Canon cameras similar to the T5i, each of the major sections in this chapter will begin with a brief description of what is covered in that section, so you can easily jump ahead to the next if you are in a hurry to get started.

# First Things First

This section helps get you oriented with all the things that come in the box with your Canon EOS Rebel T5i/700D, including what they do. I'll also describe some optional equipment you might want to have. If you want to get started immediately, skim through this section and jump ahead to "Initial Setup" later in the chapter.

The Canon EOS Rebel T5i/700D comes in an impressive gray-and-red box filled with stuff, including connecting cords, booklets, CDs, and lots of paperwork. The most important components are the camera and lens (if you purchased your T5i with a lens), battery, battery charger, and, if you're the nervous type, the neck strap. You'll also need a memory card, as one is not included. If you purchased your EOS Rebel T5i/700D from a camera shop, as I did, the store personnel probably attached the neck strap for you, ran through some basic operational advice that you've already forgotten, tried to sell you a memory card, and then, after they'd given you all the help you could absorb, sent you on your way with a handshake.

Perhaps you purchased your T5i from one of those mass merchandisers that also sell washing machines and vacuum cleaners. In that case, you might have been sent on your way with only the handshake, or, maybe, not even that if you resisted the efforts to sell you an extended warranty. You save a few bucks, but don't get the personal service a professional photo retailer provides. It's your choice. There's a third alternative, of course. You might have purchased your camera from a mail order or Internet source, and your T5i arrived in a big brown (or purple/red) truck. Your only interaction when you took possession of your camera was to scrawl your signature on an electronic clipboard.

In all three cases, the first thing to do is carefully unpack the camera and double-check the contents with the checklist on one end of the box, helpfully designated with a CONTENTS heading. The box should include a Digital Camera EOS Rebel T5i/700D, Wide Strap EW-100DB IV, Battery Charger LC-E8 or LC-E8E, Battery Pack LP-E8, Interface Cable IFC-200U, and two software/instructional CD-ROMs, all described in more detail below. You also got an instruction manual and some other paperwork. It's likely that the camera was accompanied by a lens, as well, and that the contents I've listed above will vary slightly depending on when and where you bought the camera.

While this level of setup detail may seem as superfluous as the instructions on a bottle of shampoo, checking the contents *first* is always a good idea. No matter who sells a camera, it's common to open boxes, use a particular camera for a demonstration, and then repack the box without replacing all the pieces and parts afterward. Someone might actually have helpfully checked out your camera on your behalf—and then mispacked the box. It's better to know *now* that something is missing so you can seek redress immediately, rather than discover two months from now that the video cable you thought you'd never use (but now *must* have) was never in the box.

At a minimum, the box should have the following:

- **Canon EOS Rebel T5i/700D digital camera.** This is hard to miss. The camera is the main reason you laid out the big bucks, and it is tucked away inside a nifty bubble-wrap envelope you should save for protection in case the T5i needs to be sent in for repair.
- **Rubber eyecup Ef.** This slide-on soft-rubber eyecup should be attached to the viewfinder when you receive the camera. It helps you squeeze your eye tightly against the window, excluding extraneous light, and also protects your eyeglasses (if you wear them) from scratching.

- **Body cap.** The twist-off body cap keeps dust from entering the camera when no lens is mounted. Even with automatic sensor cleaning built into the T5i, you'll want to keep the amount of dust to a minimum. The body cap belongs in your camera bag if you contemplate the need to travel with the lens removed.

- **Lens (if purchased).** The Rebel T5i may come in a kit with the Canon Zoom Lens EF-S 18-135mm f/3.5-5.6 IS STM lens, or the new EF-S 18-55mm f/3.5-56 IS STM lens introduced at the same time as the camera. You may purchase it with another lens. I would have purchased mine as a body only, because I already have an extensive collection of Canon lenses, but I wanted to check out the new STM version of the venerable 18-55mm kit lens. (The pioneering Digital Rebel came with the original version in 2003—more than a decade ago!) The lens will come with a lens cap on the front, and a rear lens cap aft.

- **Battery pack LP-E8 (with cover).** The power source for your Rebel T5i is packaged separately. You'll need to charge this 7.2V, 1120mAh (milliampere hour) battery before using it. It should be charged as soon as possible (as described next) and inserted in the camera. Save the protective cover. If you transport a battery outside the camera, it's a good idea to re-attach the cover to prevent the electrical contacts from shorting out.

- **Battery charger LC-E8 or LC-E8E.** One of these two battery chargers will be included.

- **Wide strap EW-100DB IV.** Canon provides you with a suitable neck strap, emblazoned with Canon advertising. While I am justifiably proud of owning a fine Canon camera, I prefer a low-key, more versatile and secure strap from UPstrap (www.upstrap.com). If you carry your camera over one shoulder, as many do, I particularly recommend the UPstrap shown in Figure 1.1. That patented non-slip pad offers reassuring traction and eliminates the contortions we sometimes go through to keep the camera from slipping off. I know several photographers who refuse to use anything else. If you do purchase an UPstrap, be sure you mention to photographer-inventor Al Stegmeyer that I sent you hence. You won't get a discount, but Al will get yet another confirmation of how much I like his neck straps.

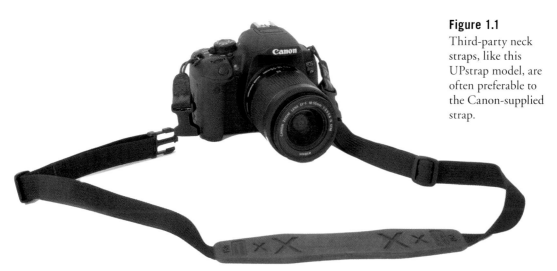

**Figure 1.1**
Third-party neck straps, like this UPstrap model, are often preferable to the Canon-supplied strap.

- **Interface cable IFC-130U.** You can use this USB cable to transfer photos from the camera to your computer, although I don't recommend that mode, because direct transfer uses a lot of battery power. You can also use the cable to upload and download settings between the camera and your computer (highly recommended), and to operate your camera remotely using the software included on the CD-ROM. It can also be used to link the camera to PictBridge compatible printers. This cable is a standard one that works with the majority of digital cameras—Canon and otherwise—so if you already own one, now you have a spare.

- **EOS Digital Solution Disc CD.** The disc contains useful software that will be discussed in more detail in Chapter 13.

- **Software instruction manual CD.** While the software itself is easy to use, if you need more help you'll find it in the PDF manuals included on this CD.

- **Printed instruction manuals.** These include the 388-page instruction manual. Even if you have this book, you'll probably want to check the printed user's guide that Canon provides, if only to check the actual nomenclature for some obscure accessory, or to double-check an error code. Google "Canon T5i manual PDF" to find a downloadable version that you can store on your laptop, a CD-ROM, or other media in case you want to access this reference when the paper version isn't handy. If you have an old SD card that's too small to be usable on a modern dSLR (I still have some 128MB and 256MB cards), you can store the PDF on that. But an even better choice is to put the manual on a low-capacity USB "thumb" drive, which you can buy for less than $10. You'll then be able to access the reference anywhere you are, because you can always find someone with a computer that has a USB port and Adobe Acrobat Reader available. You might not be lucky enough to locate a computer with an SD card reader.

- **Warranty and registration card.** Don't lose these! You can register your Canon T5i by mail, although you don't really need to in order to keep your warranty in force, but you may need the information in this paperwork (plus the purchase receipt/invoice from your retailer) should you require Canon service support.

Don't bother rooting around in the box for anything beyond what I've listed previously. There are a few things Canon classifies as optional accessories, even though you (and I) might consider some of them essential. Here's a list of what you *don't* get in the box, but might want to think about as an impending purchase. I'll list them roughly in the order of importance:

- **Memory card.** First-time digital camera buyers are sometimes shocked that their new tool doesn't come with a memory card. Why should it? The manufacturer doesn't have the slightest idea of how much storage you require, or whether you want a slow/inexpensive card or one that's faster/more expensive, so why should they pack one in the box and charge you for it? For an 18-megapixel camera, you really need one that's a minimum of 8GB in size.

- **Extra LP-E8 battery.** Even though you might get 440 shots from a single battery, it's easy to exceed that figure in a few hours of shooting sports at 5 fps. Batteries can unexpectedly fail, too, or simply lose their charge from sitting around unused for a week or two. Buy an extra (I own four, in total), keep it charged, and free your mind from worry.

- **Add-on Speedlite.** One of the best uses for your Canon T5i's built-in electronic flash is as a remote trigger for an off-camera Speedlite such as the 600EX-RT, or the more affordable 320EX and 270EX II strobes, which were designed especially for cameras in this class. Your built-in flash can function as the main illumination for your photo, or softened and used to fill in shadows. If you do much flash photography at all, consider an add-on Speedlite as an important accessory.

- **Stereo AV Cable AVC-DC400ST.** Use this cable to view your camera's LCD output on a larger television screen, monitor, or other device with a yellow RCA composite input jack. Unlike the cables for previous Rebel models, this one allows stereo sound output. Canon stopped providing it in the box with the camera, so it's now an optional purchase, for about $25.

- **AC Adapter Kit ACK-E8.** This includes the Compact Power Adapter CA-PS700 and DC Coupler DR-E8, which are used together to power the T5i independently of the batteries. There are several typical situations where this capability can come in handy: when you're cleaning the sensor manually and want to totally eliminate the possibility that a lack of juice will cause the fragile shutter and mirror to spring to life during the process; when indoors shooting tabletop photos, portraits, class pictures, and so forth for hours on end; when using your T5i for remote shooting as well as time-lapse photography; for extensive review of images on your television; or for file transfer to your computer. These all use prodigious amounts of power, which can be provided by this AC adapter. (Beware of power outages and blackouts when cleaning your sensor, however!)

- **Angle Finder C right angle viewer.** This handy accessory fastens in place of the standard rubber eyecup and provides a 90-degree view for framing and composing your image at right angles to the original viewfinder, useful for low-level (or high-level) shooting. (Or, maybe, shooting around corners!)

- **HDMI cable HTC-100.** You'll need this optional cable if you want to connect your camera directly to an HDTV for viewing your images. Not everyone owns a high-def television, and Canon saved the holdouts a few bucks (actually, close to $80) by not including one (or charging for it).

- **Battery Grip BG-E8.** This add-on vertical grip/battery pack can be outfitted with two LP-E8 batteries or six AA batteries for longer shooting life, and an extra shutter release and control dial for convenient shooting with the camera in a vertical orientation.

# Initial Setup

This section helps you become familiar with the important controls most used to make adjustments. You'll also find information on charging the battery, setting the clock, mounting a lens, and making diopter vision adjustments. If you're comfortable with all these things, skim through and skip ahead to "Activating Your EOS Rebel T5i/700D" in the next section.

The initial setup of your Canon EOS Rebel T5i/700D is fast and easy. Basically, you just need to charge the battery, attach a lens, and insert a memory card. I'll address each of these steps separately, but if you already feel you can manage these setup tasks without further instructions, feel free to skip this section entirely. You should at least skim its contents, however, because I'm going to list a few options that you might not be aware of.

## Battery Included

Your Canon EOS Rebel T5i/700D is a sophisticated hunk of machinery and electronics, but it needs a charged battery to function, so rejuvenating the LP-E8 lithium-ion battery pack furnished with the camera should be your first step. A fully charged power source should be good for approximately 440 shots, based on standard tests defined by the Camera & Imaging Products Association (CIPA) document DC-002.

### A BATTERY AND A SPARE

My experience is that the CIPA figures are often a little optimistic, so it's probably a good idea to have a spare battery on hand. I always recommend purchasing Canon-brand batteries (for less than $50) over less-expensive third-party packs. My reasoning is that it doesn't make sense to save $20 on a component for an advanced camera, especially since batteries (from Canon as well as other sources) have been known to fail in potentially harmful ways. Canon, at least, will stand behind its products, issue a recall if necessary, and supply a replacement if a Canon-brand battery is truly defective. A third-party battery supplier that sells under a half-dozen or more different product labels and brands may not even have an easy way to get the word out that a recall has been issued.

If your pictures are important to you, always have at least one spare battery available, and make sure it is an authentic Canon product.

All rechargeable batteries undergo some degree of self-discharge just sitting idle in the camera or in the original packaging. Lithium-ion power packs of this type typically lose a small amount of their charge every day, even when the camera isn't turned on. Li-ion cells lose their power through a chemical reaction that continues when the camera is switched off. So, it's very likely that the battery purchased with your camera is at least partially pooped out, so you'll want to revive it before going out for some serious shooting.

There are many situations in which you'll be glad you have that spare battery:

■ **Remote locales.** If you like to backpack and will often be far from a source of electricity, rechargeable cells won't be convenient. They tend to lose some charge over time, even if not used, and will quickly become depleted as you use them. You'll have no way to recharge the cells, lacking a solar-powered charger that might not be a top priority for your backpacking kit.

- **Unexpected needs.** Perhaps you planned to shoot landscapes one weekend, and then are given free front-row tickets to a Major League Baseball game. Instead of a few dozen pictures of trees and lakes, you find yourself shooting hundreds of images of Nick Swisher and company, which may be beyond the capacity of the single battery you own. If you have a spare battery, you're in good shape.

- **Unexpected failures.** I've charged up batteries and then discovered that they didn't work when called upon, usually because the rechargeable cells had past their useful life, the charger didn't work, or because of human error. (I *thought*, I'd charged them!) That's one reason why I always carry three times as many batteries as I think I will need.

- **Long shooting session.** Perhaps your niece is getting married, and you want to photograph the ceremony, receiving line, and reception. Several extra batteries will see you through the longest shooting session.

## Power Options

Several battery chargers are available for the Canon EOS Rebel T5i/700D. Purchasing an additional charging device offers more than some additional features: You gain a spare that can keep your camera running until you can replace your primary power rejuvenator. Here's a list of your power options:

- **LC-E8E.** This is the standard charger for the T5i and charges a single battery, but requires a cord (see Figure 1.2). That can be advantageous in certain situations. For example, if your power outlet is behind a desk or in some other semi-inaccessible location, the cord can be plugged in and routed so the charger sits on your desk or another more convenient spot. The cord itself is a standard one that works with many different chargers and devices (including the power supply for my laptop), so I purchased several of them and leave them plugged into the wall in various

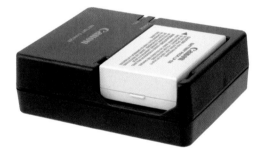

**Figure 1.2** A flashing status light (not shown) indicates that the battery is being charged.

locations. I can connect my T5i's charger, my laptop computer's charger, and several other electronic components to one of these cords without needing to crawl around behind the furniture. The cord itself draws no "phantom" power when it's not plugged in to a charger.

- **LC-E8.** This charger may be the most convenient for some, because of its compact size and built-in wall plug prongs that connect directly into your power strip or wall socket and require no cord. This charger, as well as the LC-E8E, has a switching power module that is fully compatible with 100V to 240V 50/60 Hz AC power, so you can use it outside the U.S. with no problems. When I travel to Europe, for example, I take my charger and an adapter to convert the plug shape for the European sockets. No voltage converter is needed.

- **AC Adapter Kit ACK-E8.** This device consists of Compact Power Adapter CA-PS700 and DC Couple DR-E8, and allows you to operate your Rebel T5i directly from AC power, with no battery required. Studio photographers need this capability because they often snap off hundreds of pictures for hours on end and want constant, reliable power. The camera is probably plugged into a flash sync cord (or radio device), and the studio flash are plugged into power packs or AC power, so the extra tether to this adapter is no big deal in that environment. You also might want to use the AC adapter when viewing images on a TV connected to your T5i, or when shooting remote or time-lapse photos.

- **Car Battery Charger CBC-E8.** This is a charger that can juice up your battery when connected to your auto's 12V power source. The vehicle battery option allows you to keep shooting when in remote locations that lack AC power.

- **Battery Grip BG-E8.** This accessory holds two LP-E8 batteries (another reason to own a spare, or two). It can also be equipped with six AA cells with the BGM-E8A battery holder. You can potentially increase your shooting capacity to 1,200 shots, while adding an additional shutter release, Main Dial, AE Lock/FE Lock, and AF point selection controls for vertically oriented shooting.

## Charging the Battery

When the battery is inserted into the LC-E8 charger properly (it's impossible to insert it incorrectly), a Charge light begins glowing orange-red. When the battery completes the charge, the Full Charge lamp glows green, approximately two hours later. When the battery is charged, remove it from the charger, flip the lever on the bottom of the camera, and slide the battery in. (See Figure 1.3.) To remove the battery, you must press a white lever, which prevents the pack from slipping out when the door is opened.

**Figure 1.3**
Insert the battery in the camera; it only fits one way. Press the white button to release the battery when you want to remove it.

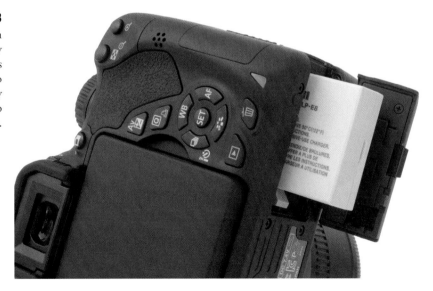

# Final Steps

Your Canon EOS Rebel T5i is almost ready to fire up and shoot. You'll need to select and mount a lens, adjust the viewfinder for your vision, and insert a memory card. Each of these steps is easy, and if you've used any Canon EOS camera in the past, you already know exactly what to do. I'm going to provide a little extra detail for those of you who are new to the Canon or digital SLR worlds.

## Mounting the Lens

As you'll see, my recommended lens mounting procedure emphasizes protecting your equipment from accidental damage, and minimizing the intrusion of dust. If your T5i has no lens attached, select the lens you want to use and loosen (but do not remove) the rear lens cap. I generally place the lens I am planning to mount vertically in a slot in my camera bag, where it's protected from mishaps, but ready to pick up quickly. By loosening the rear lens cap, you'll be able to lift it off the back of the lens at the last instant, so the rear element of the lens is covered until then.

After that, remove the body cap by rotating the cap toward the shutter release button. You should always mount the body cap when there is no lens on the camera, because it helps keep dust out of the interior of the camera, where it can settle on the mirror, focusing screen, the interior mirror box, and potentially find its way past the shutter onto the sensor. (While the T5i's sensor cleaning mechanism works fine, the less dust it has to contend with, the better.) The body cap also protects the vulnerable mirror from damage caused by intruding objects (including your fingers, if you're not cautious).

Once the body cap has been removed, remove the rear lens cap from the lens, set it aside, and then mount the lens on the camera by matching the alignment indicator on the lens barrel (red for EF lenses and white for EF-S lenses) with the corresponding indicator on the camera's lens mount (see Figure 1.4). Rotate the lens away from the shutter release until it seats securely. (You can find out more about the difference between EF and EF-S lenses in Chapter 10.) Set the focus mode switch on the lens to AF (autofocus). If the lens hood is bayoneted on the lens in the reversed position (which makes the lens/hood combination more compact for transport), twist it off and remount with the edge facing outward (see Figure 1.5). A lens hood protects the front of the lens from

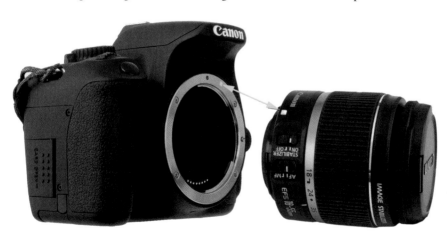

**Figure 1.4**

Match the the raised white square on EF-S lenses with the raised white square on the camera mount to properly align the lens with the bayonet mount. For EF lenses, use the red dots.

**Figure 1.5**
A lens hood
protects the lens
from extraneous
light and accidental
bumps.

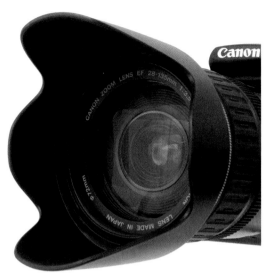

accidental bumps, stray fingerprints, and reduces flare caused by extraneous light arriving at the front element of the lens from outside the picture area.

## Adjusting Diopter Correction

Those of us with less than perfect eyesight can often benefit from a little optical correction in the viewfinder. Your contact lenses or glasses may provide all the correction you need, but if you are a glasses wearer and want to use the EOS Rebel T5i/700D without your glasses, you can take advantage of the camera's built-in diopter adjustment, which can be varied from –3 to +1 correction. Press the shutter release halfway to illuminate the indicators in the viewfinder, then rotate the diopter adjustment knob next to the viewfinder (see Figure 1.6) while looking through the viewfinder until the indicators appear sharp.

**Figure 1.6**
Viewfinder diopter
correction from
–3 to +1 can be
dialed in.

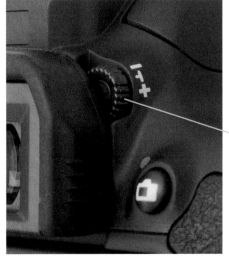

*Diopter adjustment
knob*

If the available correction is insufficient, Canon offers 10 different Dioptric Adjustment Lens Series E correction lenses for the viewfinder window. If more than one person uses your T5i, and each requires a different diopter setting, you can save a little time by noting the number of clicks and direction (clockwise to increase the diopter power; counterclockwise to decrease the diopter value) required to change from one user to the other. There are 18 detents in all.

## Inserting a Memory Card

You can't take photos without a memory card inserted in your EOS Rebel T5i/700D (although there is a Release Shutter without Card entry in Shooting 1 menu that enables/disables shutter release functions when a memory card is absent—learn about that in Chapter 8). So, your final step will be to insert a memory card. Slide the door on the right side of the body toward the back of the camera to release the cover, and then open it. (You should only remove the memory card when the camera is switched off, but the T5i will remind you if the door is opened while the camera is still writing photos to the memory card.)

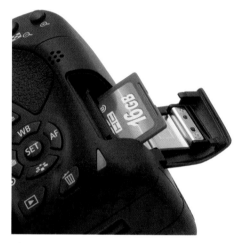

Insert the memory card with the label facing the back of the camera, as shown in Figure 1.7, oriented so the edge with the connectors goes into the slot first. Close the door, and your pre-flight checklist is done! (I'm going to assume you remember to remove the lens cap when you're ready to take a picture!) When you want to remove the memory card later, push it inward to make the memory card pop out.

**Figure 1.7** Insert the memory in the slot with the label facing the back of the camera.

## Formatting a Memory Card

There are three ways to create a blank memory card for your T5i, and two of them are at least partially wrong. Here are your options, both correct and incorrect:

- **Transfer (move) files to your computer.** When you transfer (rather than copy) all the image files to your computer from the memory card (either using a direct cable transfer or with a card reader, as described later in this chapter), the old image files are erased from the card, leaving the card blank. Theoretically. This method does *not* remove files that you've labeled as Protected (choosing the Protect Images function in the Playback menu) nor does it identify and lock out parts of your memory card that have become corrupted or unusable since the last time you formatted the card. Therefore, I recommend always formatting the card, rather than simply moving the image files, each time you want to make a blank card. The only exception is when you *want* to leave the protected/unerased images on the card for a while longer, say, to share with friends, family, and colleagues.

■ **(Don't) Format in your computer.** With the memory card inserted in a card reader or card slot in your computer, you can use Windows or Mac OS to reformat the memory card. Don't! The operating system won't necessarily arrange the structure of the card the way the T5i likes to see it (in computer terms, an incorrect *file system* may be installed). The only way to ensure that the card has been properly formatted for your camera is to perform the format in the camera itself. The only exception to this rule is when you have a seriously corrupted memory card that your camera refuses to format. Sometimes it is possible to revive such a corrupted card by allowing the operating system to reformat it first, then trying again in the camera.

■ **Set-up menu format.** To use the recommended method to format a memory card, turn on the camera, press the MENU button, rotate the Main Dial (located on top of the camera, just behind the shutter release button), choose the Set-up 1 menu (which is represented by a wrench icon with a single dot next to it), use the up/down cross keys (the buttons immediately above and below the SET button in the center of the cross key control pad) to navigate to the Format entry, and press the SET button in the center of the cross key pad to access the Format screen. Press the left/right cross keys (located to the left and right of the SET button) again to select OK and press the SET button one final time to begin the format process.

---

## LOW LEVEL FORMAT

You can also press the Trash button, located in the lower-right corner of the back of the camera, to mark the Low level format box on the Format screen. This tells the T5i to perform an additional, more thorough, formatting of the card after the initial format is finished. The low level format serves to remove data from all writable portions of your memory card while locking out "bad" sectors, and can be used to restore a memory card that is slowing down as it "trips" over those bad sectors. This extra step takes a bit longer than a standard reformat, and need not be used every time you format your card.

---

### Powering Up/Setting Date and Time

Rotate the On/Off switch on top of the camera to the On position. Automatic sensor cleaning takes place (unless you specifically disable this action) as the T5i powers up. The camera will remain on or in a standby mode until you manually turn it off. After 30 seconds of idling, the T5i goes into standby mode to save battery power. Just tap the shutter release button to bring it back to life. The automatic sensor cleaning operation does not occur when exiting standby mode.

The first time you use the Rebel T5i, it may ask you to enter the time and date. (This information may have been set by someone checking out your camera on your behalf prior to sale.) Just follow these steps, using the cross key control pad shown in Figure 1.8:

1. Press the MENU button, located in the upper-left corner of the back of the T5i.

2. Rotate the Main Dial (near the shutter release button on top of the camera) until the Set-up 2 menu is highlighted. It's marked by a wrench with two dots next to it, as shown in Figure 1.9.

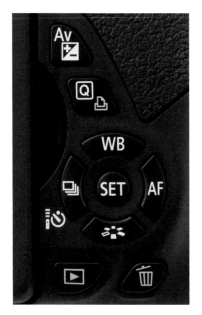

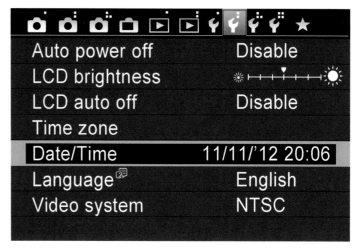

**Figure 1.8** The four buttons above, below, and to either side of the SET button are used to navigate menus and for direct setting of their marked functions.

**Figure 1.9** Choose the Date/Time entry from the Set-up 2 menu.

3. Use the up/down cross keys to move the highlighting down to the Time Zone entry, and press the SET button.

4. When the Time Zone screen appears, if the currently selected time zone is not correct for your location, use the left/right cross keys to highlight the zone and press the SET button. Then, use the up/down cross keys to scroll through a list of alternate time zones.

5. When you see the zone you want to use, press SET to it lock in, then press the right cross key to highlight OK, and press SET again to confirm.

6. Next, scroll down to the Date/Time entry and press the SET button in the center of the keypad to access the Date/Time setting screen, shown in Figure 1.10.

7. Use the left/right cross keys to select the value you want to change. When the gold box highlights the month, day, year, hour, minute, or second format (using a 24-hour clock) you want to adjust, press the SET button to activate that value. A pair of up/down pointing triangles appears above the value.

8. Press the up/down cross keys to adjust the value up or down. Press the SET button to confirm the value you've entered.

**Figure 1.10**
Adjust the date, time, and format used to display the date.

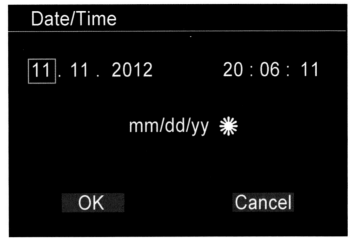

9. Repeat steps 7 and 8 for each of the other values you want to change. The date format can be switched from the default mm/dd/yy to yy/mm/dd or dd/mm/yy.

10. When finished, navigate with the right cross key to select either OK (if you're satisfied with your changes) or Cancel (if you'd like to return to the Set-up 2 menu screen without making any changes). Press SET to confirm your choice.

11. When finished setting the date and time, press the MENU button to exit.

Your Canon EOS Rebel T5i/700D is ready to go. If you need a quick start for its basic operation, jump ahead to Chapter 2.

## REACH OUT AND TOUCH SOMETHING

The EOS T5i/700D is one of the first advanced cameras with a touch-screen LCD. When menus are on the screen, you can tap choices to select them, slide your finger across the screen to scroll among menus and change sliding scales, and perform other functions. I'll explain how to use the touch screen in more detail in Chapter 2.

# 2

# Canon EOS Rebel T5i/700D Quick Start

Now it's time to fire up your EOS T5i and take some photos. The easy part is turning on the power—that Off-On switch on the right side, just east of the Mode Dial. Turn on the camera, and, if you mounted a lens and inserted a fresh battery and memory card—as I prompted you in the last chapter—you're ready to begin. You'll need to select a shooting mode, metering mode, focus mode, and, if need be, elevate the T5i's built-in flash.

## Navigating the Menus

While you'll find complete instructions for using every menu option the T5i offers in Chapters 8 and 9, the next few chapters will often ask you to use the camera's menu system to make adjustments. The T5i often provides several different ways of performing an action, and menu navigation is one of them. The traditional way is to use the physical controls:

- **Access menus.** You can produce the T5i's main menus by pressing the MENU button, located at the far-left corner of the back of the camera (and shown at left in Figure 2.1).

- **Navigate among menus.** Use the up/down/left right cross keys (seen at center in Figure 2.1) to move within the menu system. Note that each of these buttons has a secondary function, such as setting white balance, that I'll explain in Chapter 3.

- **Main Dial.** This dial (shown at right in Figure 2.1) can often be used to move highlighting left and right, say, to scroll among the main menu heading tabs.

- **Quick Control button.** The Quick Control button (Q button) (shown in upper center in Figure 2.1) produces a Quick Control menu (described later), which offers fast access to many adjustments.

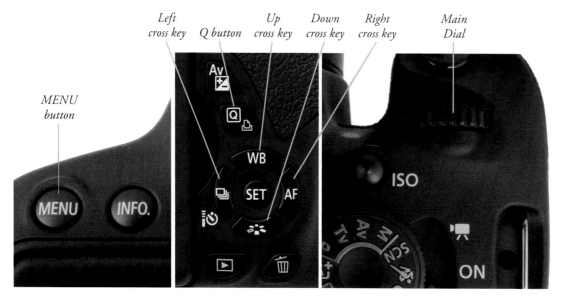

**Figure 2.1**  Your basic controls include the MENU button (left), cross keys and Q button (center), and Main Dial (right).

## Mastering the Touch Screen

When a main menu, adjustment screen, or the Quick Control menu is displayed, you will probably elect to use the T5i's touch screen to make your changes. Optionally, you can resort to the physical controls that provide the equivalent functions, including the available buttons and cross key navigational buttons. However, I think that once you become familiar with the speed with which the touch screen allows you to make these adjustments, you'll be reluctant to go back to the "old" way of doing things.

The T5i's touch screen is *capacitive* rather than *resistive*, making it more like the current generation of smart phones than earlier computer touch-sensitive screens. The difference is that your camera's LCD responds to the electrical changes that result from *contact* rather than the force of *pressure* on the screen itself. That means that the screen is able to interpret your touches and taps in more complex ways. It "knows" when you're using two fingers instead of one, and can react to multi-touch actions and gestures, such as swiping (to scroll in any direction), and pinching/spreading of fingers to zoom in and out. Since you probably have been using a smart phone for a while, these actions have become ingrained enough to be considered intuitive. Virtually every main and secondary function or menu operation can be accessed from the touch screen. However, if you want to continue using the buttons and dials, the T5i retains that method of operation.

**TIP: YOUR CHOICE**

Throughout this book, I may not explicitly say "tap the screen (or use the button)" for every single operation, in order to simplify descriptions and avoid extra verbiage. I'm assuming that once you master the touch screen using the information in this section, you'll make your own choice and use whichever method you prefer.

Here's what you need to know to get started:

- **Tap to select.** Tap (touch the LCD screen briefly) to select an item, including a menu heading or icon. Any item you can tap will have a frame or box around it. Figure 2.2 shows the taps needed to select a menu tab and specific entry within that menu.

- **Drag/swipe to select.** Many functions can be selected by touching the screen and then sliding your finger to the right or left until the item you want is highlighted. For example, instead of tapping you can slide horizontally along the main menu's tabs to choose any Shooting, Playback, Custom, or My Menu tab, and slide vertically to choose an individual menu entry.

- **Drag/swipe to adjust scales.** Screens that contain a sliding scale (say, to make an image brighter or darker) can be adjusted by dragging. Figure 2.3 shows how you can drag along the LCD Brightness scale to select a value or, alternatively, tap the left/right arrow icons to either side of the scale. (Note that you can also press the left/right cross keys if you prefer.)

- **Drag/swipe to scroll among images.** In Playback mode, as you review your images you can drag your finger left and right to advance from one image to another, much as you might do with a smart phone or tablet computer. This is probably the coolest use for the touch screen. Figure 2.4 shows you can use either one finger to scroll, or two fingers to jump among playback images.

**Figure 2.2**
Tap menu tabs or entries to select them.

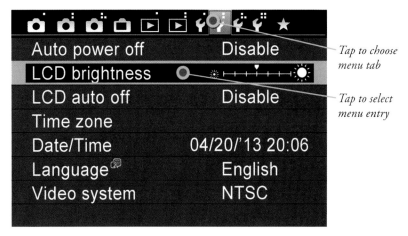

*Tap to choose menu tab*

*Tap to select menu entry*

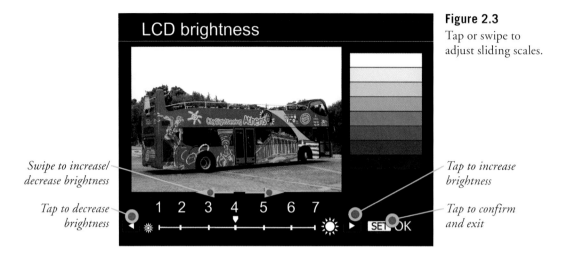

**Figure 2.3**
Tap or swipe to adjust sliding scales.

Swipe to increase/decrease brightness

Tap to decrease brightness

Tap to increase brightness

Tap to confirm and exit

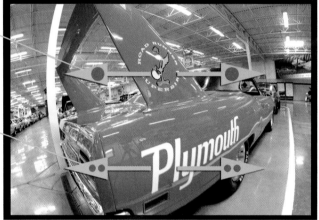

**Figure 2.4**
Swipe left or right with one finger to scroll among images; swipe with two fingers to jump.

Swipe with one finger to scroll among images

Swipe with two fingers to jump among images

- **Pinch to reduce/enlarge.** During playback, you can use two fingers to "pinch" the screen to zoom out from single-frame display to multiple thumbnails, and spread those two fingers apart to zoom in again to a single frame and magnified image—also very cool and intuitive. (See Figure 2.5.)

- **Enable/Disable touch features.** As I'll explain in Chapter 9, you can enable or disable touch operation in the Set-up 3 menu under the Touch Control entry, and turn the click sound the touch feature makes on or off using the Beep setting in the Shooting 1 menu.

- **Avoid "protective" sheets, moisture, sharp implements.** The LCD uses capacitive technology to sense your touch, rather than pressure sensitivity. LCD protectors or moisture can interfere with the touch functions, and styluses or sharp objects (such as pens) won't produce the desired results. I have, in fact, used "skins" on my T5i's LCD with good results (even though the screen is quite rugged and really doesn't need protection from scratches), but there is no guarantee that all such protectors will work for you.

**Figure 2.5**
Spread two fingers apart to enlarge/zoom in, or pinch two fingers together to zoom out/view thumbnails.

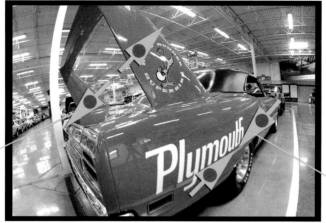

*Spread two fingers apart to enlarge/zoom in*

*Pinch two fingers together to reduce/zoom out*

As I noted, the choice of whether to use the traditional buttons or touch screen is up to you. I've found that the with some screens, the controls are too close together to be easily manipulated with my wide fingers. The touch screen can be especially dangerous when working with some functions, such as card formatting. In screens where the icons are large and few in number, such as the screen used to adjust LCD brightness, touch control works just fine. Easiest of all is touch operation during playback. It's a no-brainer to swipe your finger from side to side to scroll among images and pinch/spread to zoom out and in.

## Selecting a Shooting Mode

> The following sections show you how to choose Scene, semi-automatic, or automatic shooting (exposure) modes; select a metering mode (which tells the camera what portions of the frame to evaluate for exposure); and set the basic autofocus functions. If you understand how to do these things, you can skip ahead to "Other Functions."

You can choose a shooting method from the Mode Dial located on the top right of the Canon EOS Rebel T5i. There are ten Basic Zone/Image Zone shooting modes, in which the camera makes virtually all the decisions for you (except when to press the shutter). Canon has started referring to the true scene settings (Portrait, Landscape, Close-up, Sports, and Night Portrait) as "Image Zone" modes, a subset of the Basic Zone modes that also includes three additional automatic modes (Scene Intelligent Auto, Flash Off, and Creative Auto). Because these automatic modes share many characteristics, I'm going to stick with the original Basic Zone nomenclature after I've explained the functions of each in this chapter.

The camera also offers four Creative Zone modes, which allow you to provide input over the exposure and settings the camera uses. You'll find a complete discussion of both Basic/Image Zone and Creative Zone modes in Chapter 4.

Turn your camera on by flipping the power switch (located to the right of the Mode Dial) to On. Next, you need to select which shooting mode to use. If you're very new to digital photography, you might want to set the camera to Auto (the green frame on the Mode Dial) or P (Program mode) and start snapping away. Either mode will make all the appropriate settings for you for many shooting situations. If you have a specific type of picture you want to shoot, you can try out one of the other Basic Zone modes indicated on the Mode Dial with appropriate icons, as shown in Figure 2.6.

- **Scene Intelligent Auto/Full Auto.** In this mode, marked with a green A+ icon, the EOS T5i makes all the exposure decisions for you, and will pop up the flash if necessary under low-light conditions.

- **Flash Off.** This mode is like Scene Intelligent Auto with the flash disabled. You'll want to use it in museums and other locations where flash is forbidden or inappropriate. It otherwise operates exactly like the Auto setting but disables the pop-up internal flash unit.

- **CA.** This Creative Auto mode is basically the same as the Full Auto option, but, unlike the other Basic Zone modes, allows you to change the brightness and other parameters of the image. The T5i still makes most of the decisions for you, but you can make some simple adjustments using the Creative Auto setting screen that appears when you press the Quick Control button (located just above the WB/up cross key in Figure 2.1). You can find instructions for using this mode and the other shooting modes in Chapter 4, and a brief summary below.

- **Portrait.** Use this mode when you're taking a portrait of a subject standing relatively close to the camera and want to de-emphasize the background, maximize sharpness, and produce flattering skin tones.

- **Landscape.** Select this mode when you want extra sharpness and rich colors of distant scenes.

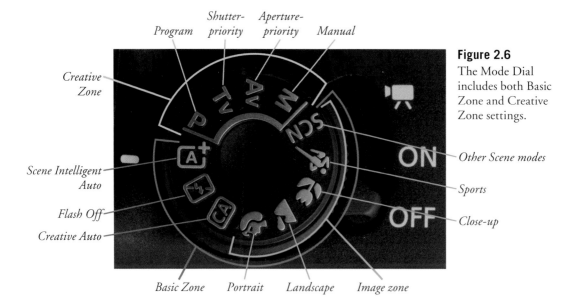

**Figure 2.6**
The Mode Dial includes both Basic Zone and Creative Zone settings.

- **Close-up.** This mode is helpful when you are shooting close-up pictures of a subject from about one foot away or less.
- **Sports.** Use this mode to freeze fast-moving subjects.

With the dial in the SCN position, you can also select any of three additional Special Scene modes:

- **Night Portrait.** Choose this mode when you want to illuminate a subject in the foreground with flash, but still allow the background to be exposed properly by the available light. Be prepared to use a tripod or an image-stabilized (IS) lens to reduce the effects of camera shake. (You'll find more about IS and camera shake in Chapter 10.)
- **Handheld Night Scene.** The T5i takes four continuous shots and combines them to produce a well-exposed image with reduced camera shake.
- **HDR Backlight Control.** The T5i takes three continuous shots at different exposures and combines them to produce a single image with improved detail in the highlights and shadows.

If you have more photographic experience, you might want to opt for one of the Creative Zone modes. These, too, are described in more detail in Chapter 4. These modes let you apply a little more creativity to your camera's settings. These modes are indicated on the Mode Dial by letters M, Av, Tv, and P.

- **M (Manual).** Select when you want full control over the shutter speed and lens opening, either for creative effects or because you are using a studio flash or other flash unit not compatible with the T5i's automatic flash metering.
- **Av (Aperture-priority).** Choose when you want to use a particular lens opening, especially to control sharpness or how much of your image is in focus. The T5i will select the appropriate shutter speed for you. Av stands for *aperture value.*
- **Tv (Shutter-priority).** This mode (Tv stands for *time value*) is useful when you want to use a particular shutter speed to stop action or produce creative blur effects. The T5i will select the appropriate f/stop for you.
- **P (Program).** This mode allows the T5i to select the basic exposure settings, but you can still override the camera's choices to fine-tune your image.

You can change some settings when the shooting settings display is shown on the screen (press the INFO. button to the left of the viewfinder window if you want to make the display visible). Press the Quick Control button and then tap the touch screen or use the cross keys to navigate to the setting you'd like to adjust. (See Figure 2.7.) The available adjustments change, depending on what Basic Zone or Creative Zone exposure mode you're using. (See Figure 2.8 for a typical Creative Zone shooting settings display.)

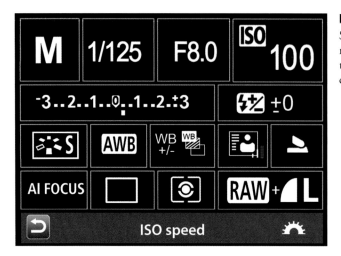

**Figure 2.7**
Some settings can be made quickly when the shooting settings display is visible.

## TWEAKING SETTINGS WITH CREATIVE AUTO

"Ambience" is a new, Picture-Style-like feature, available to let you tweak settings when using Basic Zone modes, including Creative Auto. I'll explain all the options in Chapter 4, but you can begin using Ambience now.

If you've set the Mode Dial to CA, when you press the Quick Control button, a screen like the one shown in Figure 2.8 appears. One of nine "ambience" options can be selected by pressing the left/right/up/down cross keys. Your choices are Standard Setting, Vivid, Soft, Warm, Intense, Cool, Brighter, Darker, or Monochrome, plus Standard Setting. Once your ambience is selected, the up/down cross keys let you highlight an intensity for that kind of ambience (for example, more vivid or less vivid), plus background/foreground blur, and drive/flash settings. Choose the parameter you want to modify, and press the left/right buttons to make the change.

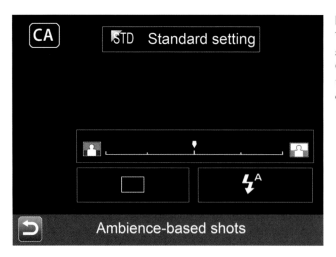

**Figure 2.8**
You can tweak the settings of the Creative Auto mode using this screen of options.

# Choosing a Metering Mode

You might want to select a particular metering mode for your first shots, although the default Evaluative metering (which is set automatically when you choose a Basic Zone mode) is probably the best choice as you get to know your camera. To change metering modes when using a Creative Zone mode, you'll need to use the Q button or the T5i's menu system (navigated using the cross keys or the touch screen, as described at the beginning of this chapter).

Press the MENU button and navigate to the Shooting 2 menu (a camera icon with two dots next to it). Tap or press the down cross key to highlight Metering Mode and select SET. A screen pops up on the LCD offering four choices. Highlight the choice you want. Then select SET to confirm your choice. The options are shown in Figure 2.9. You can also use the Quick Control button to access these settings.

- **Evaluative metering.** The standard metering mode; the T5i attempts to intelligently classify your image and choose the best exposure based on readings from 63 different zones in the frame, with emphasis on the autofocus points.
- **Partial metering.** Exposure is based on a central spot, roughly nine percent of the image area.
- **Spot metering.** Exposure is calculated from a smaller central spot, about 4 percent of the image area.
- **Center-weighted averaging metering.** The T5i meters the entire scene, but gives the most emphasis to the central area of the frame.

You'll find a detailed description of each of these modes in Chapter 4.

**Figure 2.9**
Metering modes (left to right): Evaluative, Partial, Spot, Center-weighted.

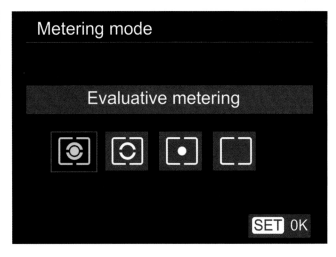

# Choosing a Focus Mode

You can easily switch between automatic and manual focus by moving the AF/MF switch on the lens mounted on your camera. However, if you're using a Creative Zone shooting mode, you'll still need to choose an appropriate focus mode. (You can read more on selecting focus parameters in Chapter 5.) If you're using a Basic Zone mode, the focus method is set for you automatically.

To set the focus mode, you must first have set the lens to the AF position (instead of the manual focus MF position). Then press the AF button (it's the right cross key) on the back of the camera to produce the selection screen shown in Figure 2.10. Choose the focus mode you want and select SET to confirm your focus mode. The three choices available in Creative Zone modes are as follows:

- **One-Shot.** This mode, sometimes called *single autofocus*, locks in a focus point when the shutter button is pressed down halfway, and the focus confirmation light glows in the viewfinder. The focus will remain locked until you release the button or take the picture. If the camera is unable to achieve sharp focus, the focus confirmation light will blink. This mode is best when your subject is relatively motionless. Portrait, Night Portrait, and Landscape Basic Zone modes use this focus method exclusively.

- **AI Servo.** This mode, sometimes called *continuous autofocus*, sets focus when you partially depress the shutter button, but continues to monitor the frame and refocuses if the camera or subject is moved. This is a useful mode for photographing sports and moving subjects. The Sports Basic Zone mode uses this focus method exclusively.

- **AI Focus.** In this mode, the T5i switches between One-Shot and AI Servo as appropriate. That is, it locks in a focus point when you partially depress the shutter button (One-Shot mode), but switches automatically to AI Servo if the subject begins to move. This mode is handy when photographing a subject, such as a child at quiet play, that might move unexpectedly. The Flash Off Basic Zone mode uses this focus method.

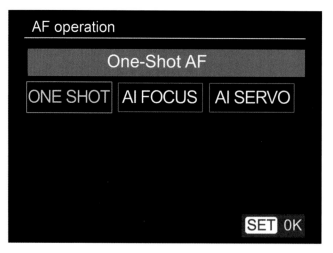

**Figure 2.10**
Set AF mode.

# Selecting a Focus Point

The Canon EOS Rebel T5i uses nine different focus points to calculate correct focus. In any of the Basic Zone shooting modes, the focus point is selected automatically by the camera. In the other Creative Zone modes, you can allow the camera to select the focus point automatically, or you can specify which focus point should be used.

There are several methods to set the focus point manually. You can press the AF point selection button on the back of the camera (it's in the upper-right corner) and choose a zone from the AF point selection screen that pops up. (Press the INFO. button if this screen is not visible.) Select SET to toggle between automatic focus point selection (the camera does it for you) or manual focus point selection (you need to specify the point yourself). In manual selection mode, tap the point you want to use, use the cross keys, or you can rotate the Main Dial to cycle among the available points. SET returns the focus point to the center. (See Figure 2.11.) Press the AF point selection button again (or just tap the shutter release button) to confirm your choice and exit.

Or, you can look through the viewfinder, press the AF point selection button, and rotate the Main Dial to move the focus point to the zone you want to use (see Figure 2.12). The focus point will cycle among the edge points counterclockwise (if you turn the Main Dial to the left) or clockwise (if you spin the Main Dial to the right), ending/starting with the center focus point/all nine focus points.

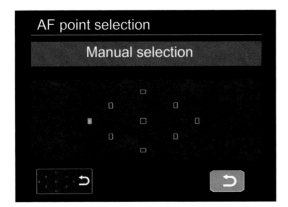

**Figure 2.11** Select a focus point and selection mode from the AF point selection screen.

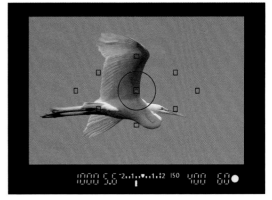

**Figure 2.12** Or choose the focus point while looking through the viewfinder.

# Other Settings

There are a few other options, such as ISO, using the self-timer, or working with flash. Use these right away if you're feeling ambitious, but don't feel ashamed if you postpone using these features until you've racked up a little more experience with your EOS T5i.

## Adjusting White Balance and ISO

If you like, you can custom-tailor your white balance (color balance) and ISO sensitivity settings. To start out, it's best to set white balance (WB) to Auto, and ISO to ISO 100 or ISO 200 for daylight photos, and ISO 400 for pictures in dimmer light. You can adjust either one now by pressing the WB button (the up cross key) (for white balance) or the ISO button (just southwest of the Main Dial) and then navigating with the touch screen or cross keys until the setting you want appears on the LCD.

If you've been playing with your camera's settings, or your T5i has been used by someone else, you can restore the factory defaults by selecting Clear Settings from the Set-up 3 menu. Just press the MENU button (located at the upper-left corner of the back of the camera), and highlight the yellow wrench icon with three dots, then select Clear Settings. A screen will pop up asking whether you'd like to Clear All Camera Settings, or Clear All Custom Func. (C.Fn). Choose the one you'd like to reset, and choose SET.

## Using the Self-Timer

If you want to set a short delay before your picture is taken, you can use the self-timer. Press the drive/left cross key and then press the right cross key to select from the Self-timer: 10-sec/Remote control (which also can be used with the optional RC-1, RC-5, and RC-6 infrared remote controls), Self-timer: 2 sec, or Self-timer: Continuous, which allows you to press the up/down cross keys to specify a number of shots to be taken (from 2 to 10) once the timer runs its course (see Figure 2.13). Select SET to confirm your choice, and a self-timer icon will appear on the shooting settings display on the back of the Rebel T5i. Press the shutter release to lock focus and start the timer. The self-timer lamp will blink and the beeper will sound (unless you've silenced it in the menus) until the final two seconds, when the lamp remains on and the beeper beeps more rapidly.

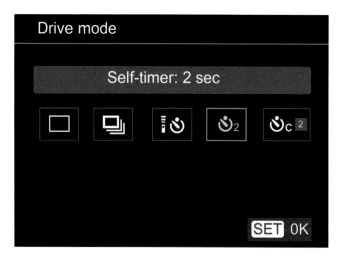

**Figure 2.13**
The drive modes include (left to right) Single shooting, Continuous shooting, Self-timer: 10-sec/Remote control, Self-timer: 2 sec, and Self-timer: Continuous (which takes multiple shots when the self-timer's delay has elapsed).

Canon recommends slipping off the eyepiece cup and replacing it with the viewfinder cap, in order to keep extraneous light from reaching the exposure meter through the viewfinder "back door." I usually just shade the viewfinder window with my hand (if I'm using the self-timer to reduce camera shake for a long exposure) or drape a jacket or sweater over the back of the camera (if I'm scurrying to get into the picture myself).

# Using the Built-in Flash

Working with the EOS T5i's built-in flash as well as external flash units like the Canon 430EX II deserves a chapter of its own, and I'm providing it (see Chapter 11). But the built-in flash is easy enough to work with that you can begin using it right away, either to provide the main lighting of a scene or as supplementary illumination to fill in the shadows. The T5i will automatically balance the amount of light emitted from the flash so that it illuminates the shadows nicely, without over-whelming the highlights and producing a glaring "flash" look. (Think *Baywatch* when they're using too many reflectors on the lifeguards!)

The T5i's flash has a power rating of 13/43 (meters/feet) at ISO 100, using the GN (guide number) system that dates back to the film era and before electronic flash units had any sort of automatic features. In plain terms, the flash's rating means that the unit is powerful enough to allow proper illumination of a subject that's 10 feet away at f/4 at the *lowest* ISO (sensitivity) setting of your camera. Boost the ISO (or use a wider f/stop) and you can shoot subjects that are located at a great distance. For example, at ISO 800, the T5i's flash is good enough for a subject at 20 feet using f/5.6 or, alternatively, you can expose that scene at the original 10 feet distance at f/11. Ordinarily, the T5i takes care of all these calculations for you. If you need a bigger blast of light, you can add one of the Canon external flash units, described in Chapter 11.

The flash will pop up automatically when using any of the Basic Zone modes except for Landscape, Sports, or No Flash modes. In Creative Zone modes, just press the flash button (marked with a lighting bolt as shown in Figure 2.14). When using these modes, the flash functions in the following way:

- **P (Program mode).** The T5i selects a shutter speed from 1/60th to 1/200th second and appropriate aperture automatically.

- **Tv (Shutter-priority mode).** You choose a shutter speed from 30 seconds to 1/200th second, and the T5i chooses the lens opening for you, while adjusting the flash output to provide the correct exposure.

- **Av (Aperture-priority mode).** You select the aperture you want to use, and the camera will select a shutter speed from 30 seconds to 1/200th second, and adjust the flash output to provide the correct exposure. In low light levels, the T5i may select a very slow shutter speed to allow the flash and background illumination to balance out, so you should use a tripod.

- **M (Manual mode).** You choose both shutter speed (up to 1/200th second) and aperture, and the camera will adjust the flash output to produce a good exposure based on the aperture you've selected.

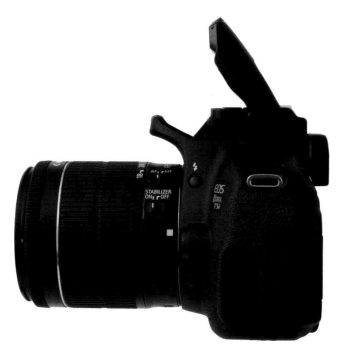

**Figure 2.14**
The pop-up electronic flash can be used as the main light source, or for supplemental illumination.

You can read about flash exposure compensation, red-eye reduction options, and other built-in flash features in Chapter 11.

# Taking a Picture

This final section of the chapter guides you through taking your first pictures, reviewing them on the LCD, and transferring your shots to your computer.

Just press the shutter release button halfway to lock in focus at the selected autofocus point. (Remember that you can select a focus point manually when using Creative Zone modes, whereas the camera always chooses the focus point in Basic Zone modes.) When the shutter button is in the half-depressed position, the exposure, calculated using the shooting mode you've selected, is also locked.

Press the button the rest of the way down to take a picture. At that instant, the mirror flips up out of the light path to the optical viewfinder (assuming you're not using Live View mode, discussed in Chapter 6), the shutter opens, the electronic flash (if enabled) fires, and your T5i's sensor absorbs a burst of light to capture an exposure. In fractions of a moment, the shutter closes, the mirror flips back down restoring your view, and the image you've taken is escorted off the CMOS sensor chip very quickly into an in-camera store of memory called a buffer, and the EOS T5i is ready to take another photo. The buffer continues dumping your image onto the Secure Digital card as you keep snapping pictures without pause (at least until the buffer fills and you must wait for it to get ahead of your continuous shooting, or your memory card fills completely).

# Reviewing the Images You've Taken

The Canon EOS Rebel T5i has a broad range of playback and image review options, including the ability to jump ahead 10 or 100 images at a time. I'll cover them in more detail in Chapter 3. For now, you'll want to learn just the basics. Here is all you really need to know at this time, as shown in Figure 2.15, with the touch screen options shown earlier in Figures 2.4 and 2.5.

■ **Display image.** Press the Playback button (marked with a blue right-pointing triangle just southeast of the color LCD) to display the most recent image on the LCD in full-screen Single Image mode. If you last viewed your images using the thumbnail mode (described later in this list), the Index display appears instead.

■ **View additional images.** Use the left and right cross keys or swipe the touch screen left or right to view the next or previous image. Use a two-finger swipe to jump quickly among the images.

■ **View image information.** Press the INFO. button repeatedly to cycle among overlays of basic image information, detailed shooting information, or no information at all.

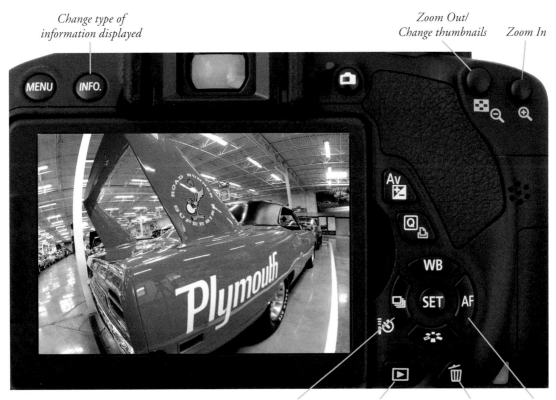

*Change type of information displayed*

*Zoom Out/ Change thumbnails*   *Zoom In*

**Figure 2.15** Review your images.

*View previous image*   *Display last image captured/Exit image display*   *Erase image displayed on screen*   *View next image*

- **Zoom in on an image.** When an image is displayed full-screen on your LCD, magnify the image by spreading two fingers apart on the touch screen, or reduce the image to thumbnails by pinching two fingers together on the touch screen. You can also press the Zoom In button repeatedly to zoom in. The Zoom In button is located in the upper-right corner of the back of the camera, marked with a blue magnifying glass with a plus sign in it. The Zoom Out button, located to the right of the Zoom In button, zooms back out. Press the Playback button to exit magnified display.

- **Scroll around in a magnified image.** Use the left/right/up/down cross keys or swipe the touch screen to scroll around within a magnified image. If you're using the touch screen, tap the "Return" arrow icon to go back to a single-image display.

- **View thumbnail images.** You can also rapidly move among a large number of images using the Index mode described in the section that follows this list. The Zoom Out button in full-frame view switches from single image display to display of four or nine reduced-size thumbnails. To change from a larger number of thumbnails to a smaller number (from nine to four to single image, for example), press the Zoom In button until the display you want appears. You can also tap the highlighted image on the touch screen to view a full screen rendition of that thumbnail.

- **Jump forward or back.** You can set the jump increment in the Playback 2 menu. (I'll explain all the jump options in Chapter 3.) Once a jump increment has been selected, you can leap forward or back that number of pictures by rotating the Main Dial or by swiping the touch screen from left to right with *two* fingers. If using the Main Dial, turn it counterclockwise to review images from most recent to oldest, or clockwise to start with the first image on the memory card and cycle forward to the newest, using the jump size you've selected.

## Cruising Through Index Views

You can navigate quickly among thumbnails representing a series of images using the T5i's Index mode. Here are your options.

- **Display thumbnails.** Press the Playback button to display an image on the color LCD. If you last viewed your images using Index mode, an Index array of four or nine reduced-size images appears automatically (see Figure 2.16). If an image pops up full-screen in single-image mode, press the Zoom Out button once to view four thumbnails, or twice to view nine thumbnails. You can switch between four, nine, and single images by pressing the Zoom Out button to see more/smaller versions of your images, and the Zoom In button to see fewer/larger versions of your images.

- **Navigate within a screen of index images.** In Index mode, use the up/down/left/right cross keys or the touch screen to move the blue highlight box around within the current Index display screen. Swipe the scroll bar at the right of the touch screen to scroll down or up.

**Figure 2.16**
Review thumbnails of four or nine images using Index review.

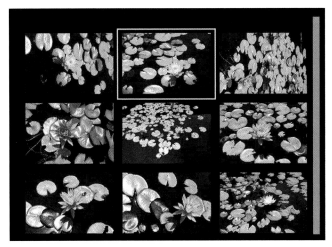

- **View more Index pages.** To view additional Index pages, rotate the Main Dial. The display will leap ahead or back by the Jump increment you've set in the Playback 2 menu (as described in Chapter 8), 10 or 100 images, by index page, by date, or by folder.
- **Check image.** When an image you want to examine more closely is highlighted, press the Zoom In button or tap the thumbnail on the touch screen until the single image version appears full-screen on your LCD.

# Transferring Photos to Your Computer

The final step in your picture-taking session will be to transfer the photos you've taken to your computer for printing, further review, or image editing. Your T5i allows you to print directly to PictBridge-compatible printers and to create print orders right in the camera, plus you can select which images to transfer to your computer.

For now, you'll probably want to transfer your images either by using a cable transfer from the camera to the computer or by removing the memory card from the T5i and transferring the images with a card reader. The latter option is usually the best, because it's typically much faster and doesn't deplete the battery of your camera. However, you can use a cable transfer when you have the cable and a computer, but no card reader (perhaps you're using the computer of a friend or colleague, or at an Internet café).

To transfer images from the camera to a Mac or PC computer using the USB cable:

1. Turn off the camera.
2. Pry back the rubber cover that protects the Rebel T5i's USB port (located closest to the LCD monitor), and plug the USB cable furnished with the camera into the USB port. (See Figure 2.17.)

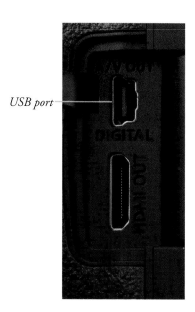

*USB port*

**Figure 2.17**
Images can be transferred to your computer using a USB cable.

3. Connect the other end of the USB cable to a USB port on your computer.

4. Turn the camera on. Your installed software usually detects the camera and offers to transfer the pictures, or the camera appears on your desktop as a mass storage device, enabling you to drag and drop the files to your computer.

To transfer images from a memory card to the computer using a card reader:

1. Turn off the camera.

2. Slide open the memory card door, and press on the card, which causes it to pop up so it can be removed from the slot.

3. Insert the memory card into your memory card reader. Your installed software detects the files on the card and offers to transfer them. The card can also appear as a mass storage device on your desktop, which you can open, and then drag and drop the files to your computer.

# 3

# Canon EOS Rebel T5i/700D Roadmap

One thing that surprises new owners of the Canon EOS Rebel T5i is that the camera has a total of 496 buttons, dials, switches, levers, latches, and knobs bristling from its surface. Okay, I lied. Actually, the real number is closer to two dozen controls and adjustments, just among the physical components and not counting the virtual controls on the touch screen. But that's still a lot of components to master, especially when you consider that many of these controls serve double-duty to give you access to multiple functions.

Traditionally, there have been two ways of providing a roadmap to guide you through this maze of features. One approach uses two or three tiny 2 × 3–inch black-and-white line drawings or photos impaled with dozens of callouts labeled with cross-references to the actual pages in the book that tell you what these components do. You'll find this tactic used in the pocket-sized manual Canon provides with the Rebel T5i, and most of the other third-party guidebooks as well. Deciphering one of these miniature camera layouts is a lot like being presented with a world globe when what you really want to know is how to find the capital of Belgium.

I originated a more useful approach in my field guides, providing you, instead of a satellite view, a street-level map that includes close-up, full-color photos of the camera from several angles (see Figure 3.1), with a smaller number of labels clearly pointing to each individual feature. And, I don't force you to flip back and forth among dozens of pages to find out what a particular component does. Each photo is accompanied by a brief description that summarizes the control, so you can begin using it right away. Only when a particular feature deserves a lengthy explanation do I direct you to a more detailed write-up later in the book.

So, if you're wondering what the depth-of-field preview does, I'll tell you up front, rather than have you flip to Page 114. This book is not a scavenger hunt. But after I explain how to use the ISO button to change the sensitivity of the T5i, I *will* provide a cross-reference to a longer explanation later in the book that clarifies noise reduction, ISO, and its effects on exposure. I think this kind of organization works best for a camera as sophisticated as the Rebel T5i.

By the time you finish this chapter, you'll have a basic understanding of every control and what it does. I'm not going to delve into menu functions here—you'll find a discussion of your Set-up, Shooting, and Playback menu options in Chapters 8 and 9. Everything here is devoted to the button pusher and dial twirler in you.

# Front View

When we picture a given camera, we always imagine the front view. That's the view that your subjects see as you snap away, and the aspect that's shown in product publicity and on the box. The frontal angle is, for all intents and purposes, the "face" of a camera like the Rebel T5i. But, not surprisingly, most of the "business" of operating the camera happens *behind* it, where the photographer resides. The front of the T5i actually has very few controls and features to worry about. Five of them are readily visible in Figure 3.1:

- **Shutter release.** Angled on top of the hand grip is the shutter release button. Press this button down halfway to lock exposure and focus (in One-Shot mode and AI Focus with nonmoving subjects). The T5i assumes that when you tap or depress the shutter release, you are ready to take a picture, so the release can be tapped to activate the exposure meter or to exit from most menus.

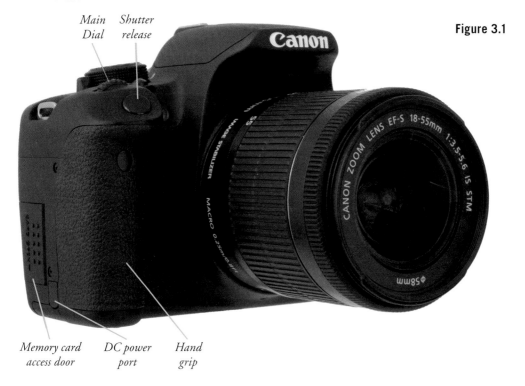

*Main Dial*   *Shutter release*

Figure 3.1

*Memory card access door*   *DC power port*   *Hand grip*

- **Main Dial.** This dial is used to change shooting settings. When settings are available in pairs (such as shutter speed/aperture), this dial will be used to make one type of setting, such as shutter speed. The other setting, say, the aperture, is made using an alternate control, such as spinning the Main Dial while holding down an additional button like the exposure compensation button (which resides conveniently under the thumb on the back of the camera).

- **Memory card access door.** Slide this panel toward the back of the camera to gain access to the memory card.

- **Hand grip.** This provides a comfortable handhold, and also contains the T5i's battery.

- **DC power port.** You'll find an opening to allow the cable from the DC power pack to pass through to the battery compartment under this small rubber door in the side of the camera.

When viewed from the front with the lens removed, you can see more components, as shown in Figure 3.2:

- **Red-eye reduction/Self-timer lamp.** This LED provides a blip of light shortly before a flash exposure to cause the subjects' pupils to close down, reducing the effect of red-eye reflections off their retinas. When using the self-timer, this lamp also flashes to mark the countdown until the photo is taken.

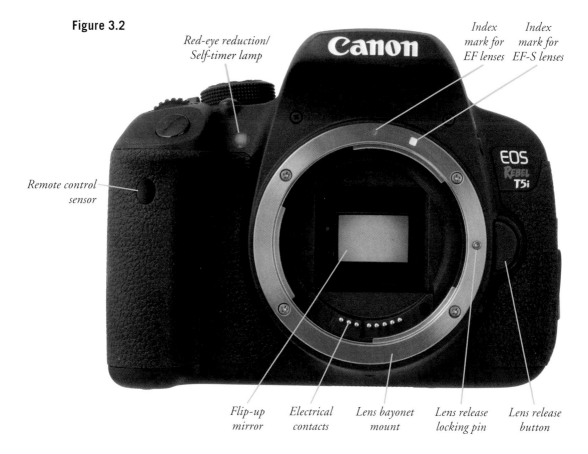

**Figure 3.2**

- **Remote control sensor.** The sensor behind this window receives signals from the optional Canon RC-1, RC-5, and RC-6 infrared remote controls. The RC-1 trips the shutter immediately or after a two-second delay, while the RC-5 always initiates a two-second delay before taking the picture. The RC-6 release gives the choice of triggering the camera immediately, or with the two-second delay. Note that the sensor is on the hand grip and thus would be blocked if you happened to be holding the T5i when trying to take a picture. In practice, of course, the camera will be mounted on a tripod or supported in some other way when using the remote control. The remote control generally must be used from in front of the camera for the sensor to detect its signal.

- **Lens bayonet mount.** This sturdy component mates with the matching bayonet mount on the lens to secure it to the camera body.

- **Index mark for EF lenses.** Match the round red bump on the lens with this mark to align EF-series lenses for mounting.

- **Index mark for EF-S lenses.** Match the raised white square on the lens with this mark to align EF-S-series lenses for mounting.

- **Lens release button/locking pin.** Press this button to retract the lens release locking pin so the lens can be rotated toward the shutter release and removed.

- **Flip-up mirror.** This partially silvered reflective component directs most of the light that passes through the lens upward toward the focus screen, exposure metering system, and viewfinder eyepiece. Some illumination is directed downward to the 9-point autofocus system in the floor of the mirror chamber.

You'll find more controls on the other side of the T5i, shown in Figure 3.3.

- **Flash button.** This button releases the built-in flash in Creative Zone modes so it can flip up (see Figure 3.4) and start the charging process. If you decide you do not want to use the flash, you can turn it off by pressing the flash head back down.

- **Depth-of-field preview button.** This button, adjacent to the lens mount, stops down the lens to the aperture that will be used to take the picture, so you can see in the viewfinder how much of the image is in focus. The view grows dimmer as the aperture is reduced.

- **Lens switches.** Canon autofocus lenses have a switch to allow changing between automatic focus and manual focus, and, in the case of IS lenses, another switch to turn image stabilization on and off.

- **Neck strap mount.** This is one of two neck strap mounts (the other is on the other side of the camera).

- **Port covers.** These flip-away panels protect the connector ports underneath.

**Figure 3.3**

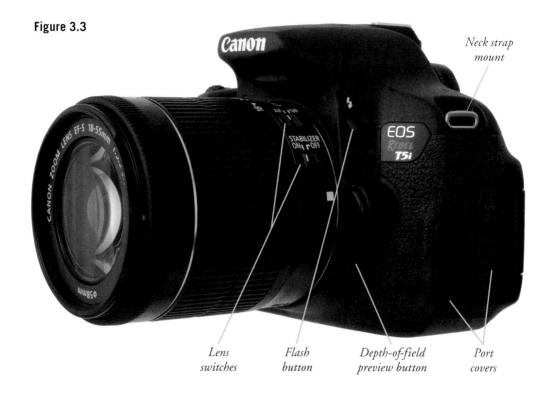

Neck strap
mount

Lens
switches

Flash
button

Depth-of-field
preview button

Port
covers

**Figure 3.4**
Pressing the Flash
button (which has
an arrow/lightning
bolt symbol) pops
up the built-in flash
unit and starts the
charging process.

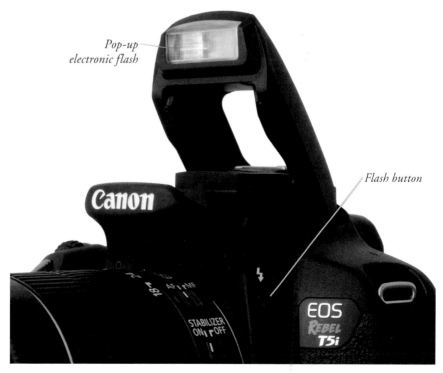

Pop-up
electronic flash

Flash button

The main feature on this side of the Rebel T5i is a pair of flexible covers that protect the four connector ports underneath from dust and moisture. The four connectors, shown in Figure 3.5, are as follows:

- **Microphone input.** Plug a stereo microphone into this jack.
- **Remote control terminal.** You can plug various Canon remote release switches, timers, and wireless controllers into this connector.
- **USB/Video out port.** Plug in the USB cable furnished with your Rebel T5i and connect the other end to a USB port in your computer to transfer photos. Or, connect the AV cable and connect your camera to a television to view your photos on a large screen. Note that some previous Rebel models used two separate ports with different connectors for this pair of functions. They were combined to make room for the HDMI port.
- **HDMI port.** Use a Type C HDMI cable (not included in the box with your camera) to direct the video and audio output of the T5i to a high-definition television (HDTV) or HD monitor.

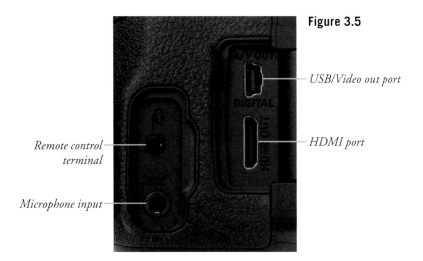

**Figure 3.5**

*USB/Video out port*

*HDMI port*

*Remote control terminal*

*Microphone input*

# The Canon EOS Rebel T5i's Business End

The back panel of the Rebel T5i (see Figure 3.6) bristles with nearly a dozen different controls, buttons, and knobs. That might seem like a lot of controls to learn, but you'll find, as I noted earlier, that it's a lot easier to press a dedicated button and spin a dial than to jump to a menu every time you want to change a setting.

You can see the controls clustered on the top back edge of the T5i in the figure. The key buttons and components and their functions are as follows:

- **MENU button.** Summons/exits the menu displayed on the rear LCD of the T5i. When you're working with submenus, this button also serves to exit a submenu and return to the main menu.

**Figure 3.6**

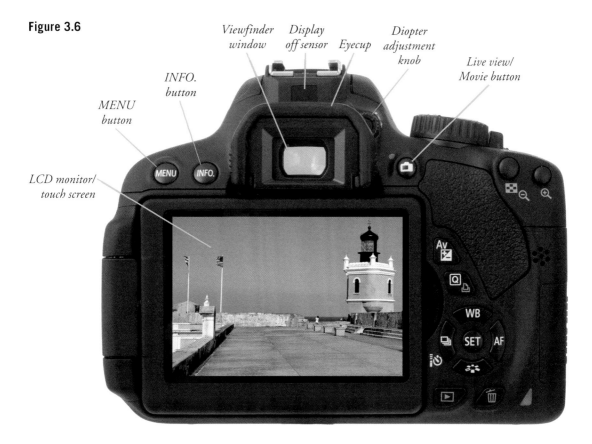

- **INFO. button.** When pressed repeatedly, changes the amount of picture information displayed in Shooting and Playback modes. In Playback mode, pressing the INFO. button cycles among basic display of the image; a detailed display with a thumbnail of the image, shooting parameters, and a brightness histogram; and a display with less detail but with separate histograms for brightness, red, green, and blue channels. (I'll show you what these look like later in the chapter.) When setting Picture Styles, the INFO. button is used to select a highlighted Picture Style for modification. In Live View mode, the INFO. button adjusts the amount of information overlaid on the live image that appears on the LCD screen. When the camera is connected to a printer, you can trim an image; in Direct Printing mode, the INFO. button selects the orientation.

- **Viewfinder eyepiece.** You can frame your composition by peering into the viewfinder. It's surrounded by a soft rubber frame that seals out extraneous light when pressing your eye tightly up to the viewfinder, and it also protects your eyeglass lenses (if worn) from scratching.

- **Display off sensor.** When your eye (or anything else) approaches the eyepiece, the Display Off sensor will detect that and turn off the LCD display, saving power. You can disable this behavior using the LCD Auto Off entry in the Set-up 2 menu, as described in Chapter 9. Note that the Display Off sensor has no effect when using live view. (It's unlikely you'd be peering through the viewfinder in live view in any case.)

- **Diopter adjustment knob.** Use of this knob to adjust the viewfinder sharpness was explained in Chapter 1.

- **Live view/Movie button.** Press this button, marked with a red dot above it, to activate/deactivate live view. To shoot movies, turn the power switch on top of the camera to the Movie position, and then press this button to start/stop video/audio recording.

- **LCD.** This is the three-inch display that shows your live view preview image review after the picture is taken, shooting settings display before the photo is snapped, and all the menus used by the Rebel T5i. A significant feature is the swiveling LCD, which can be folded with the display screen facing inward to protect it or reversed into the normal position, flipped out, swiveled, or even turned around to allow you to view yourself while shooting self portraits. (See Figure 3.7.)

**Figure 3.7**

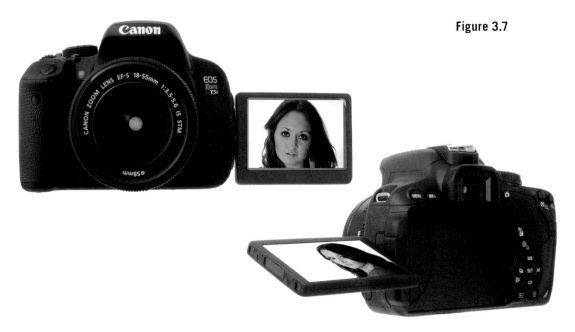

The most-used controls reside on the right side of the Rebel T5i (see Figure 3.8). There are 11 buttons in all, many of which do double-duty to perform several functions. I've divided them into two groups; here's the first set of controls, found in the upper half of the panel:

- **AE/FE (Autoexposure/Flash exposure) lock/Index/Zoom Out button.** This button, which has a * label above it, has several functions, which differ depending on the AF point and metering mode. You can find more about these variations, available in Creative Zone modes only, in Chapter 4.

    **Shooting mode:** The button locks the exposure or flash exposure that the camera sets when you partially depress the shutter button. In Evaluative exposure mode, exposure is locked at the AF point that achieved focus. In Partial, Spot, or Center-weighted modes, exposure is locked at the AF center point. The exposure lock indication (*) appears in the viewfinder and on the shooting settings display. If you want to recalculate exposure with the shutter button still partially depressed, press the * button again. The exposure will be unlocked when you release the shutter button or take the picture. To retain the exposure lock for subsequent photos, keep the * button pressed while shooting.

When using flash, pressing the * button fires an extra pre-flash that allows the unit to calculate and lock exposure prior to taking the picture. The characters FEL will appear momentarily in the viewfinder, and the exposure lock indication and a flash indicator appear. (See the description of the viewfinder display later in this chapter.)

**Playback mode:** Press this button to switch from single-image display to nine-image thumbnail index. (See Figure 3.9.) Move highlighting among the thumbnails with the touch screen, cross keys, or Main Dial. To view a highlighted image, press the Zoom In button.

In Playback mode, when an image is zoomed in, press this button to zoom out, or use the touch screen.

■ **AF point selection/Zoom In button.** In Shooting mode, this button activates autofocus point selection. (See Chapter 4 for information on setting autofocus/exposure point selection when using Creative Zone exposure modes.) In Playback mode, if you're viewing a single image, this button zooms in on the image that's displayed. If thumbnail indexes are shown, pressing this button switches from nine thumbnails to four thumbnails, or from four thumbnails to a full-screen view of a highlighted image.

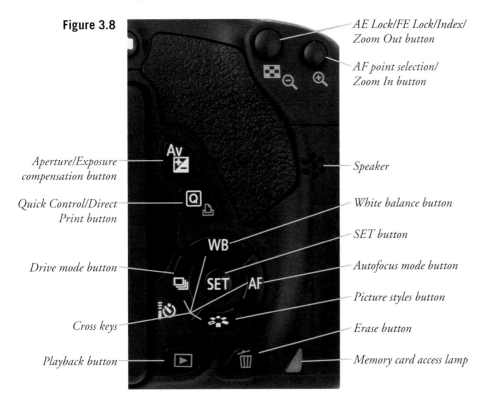

Figure 3.8

AE Lock/FE Lock/Index/
Zoom Out button

AF point selection/
Zoom In button

Aperture/Exposure
compensation button

Speaker

Quick Control/Direct
Print button

White balance button

SET button

Autofocus mode button

Drive mode button

Picture styles button

Cross keys

Erase button

Playback button

Memory card access lamp

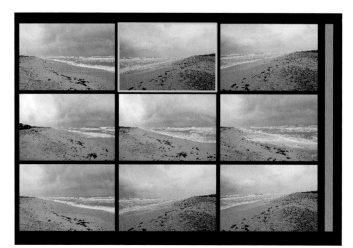

**Figure 3.9**
The Index/Zoom Out button changes the playback display from single image to four or nine thumbnails.

- **Quick Control/Direct Print button.** This button activates the Quick Control screen (described later in this chapter), which allows you to set image recording quality and switch between single shot and self-timer/remote settings when using Basic Zone exposure modes, and to set a full range of controls when using Creative Zone exposure modes. The button can also be used when the T5i is connected to a printer or personal computer to initiate transfer.

- **Aperture value (AV)/Exposure compensation button.** When using manual exposure mode, hold down this button and rotate the Main Dial to specify a lens aperture; rotate the Main Dial alone to choose the shutter speed. In other Creative Zone exposure modes—Aperture-priority (Av), Shutter-priority (Tv), or Program (P)—hold down this button and rotate the Main Dial to the right to add exposure compensation (EV) to an image (making it brighter), or rotate to the left to subtract EV and make the image darker.

Some of the controls in the lower half of the panel perform dual functions, one for navigation and one for making various settings. I'll describe both.

- **Cross keys.** This array of four-directional keys provides those who aren't using the touch screen an alternate method for left/right/up/down movement to navigate menus, and is used to cycle among various options (usually with the left/right buttons) and to choose amounts (with the up/down buttons). The four cross keys also have secondary functions to adjust white balance, autofocus mode, Picture Styles, and drive mode (I'll describe these separately).

- **SET button.** Located in the center of the cross key cluster, this button is used to confirm a selection or activate a feature, similarly to the SET icon on the touch screen.

- **Playback button.** Displays the last picture taken. Thereafter, you can move back and forth among the available images by pressing the left/right cross keys to advance or reverse one image at a time, or the Main Dial, to jump forward or back using the jump method you've selected. (See the section below for more on jumping.) To quit playback, press this button again.

The T5i also exits playback mode automatically when you press the shutter button (so you'll never be prevented from taking a picture on the spur of the moment because you happened to be viewing an image).

- **Erase button.** Press to erase the image shown on the LCD during Playback mode. A menu will pop up displaying Cancel and Erase choices. Use the left/right cross keys to select one of these actions, then press the SET button to activate your choice.

- **Memory card access lamp.** When lit or blinking, this lamp indicates that the memory card is being accessed.

The cross keys also each have a secondary function:

- **White balance button.** The up cross key also serves to access the white balance function. Press this WB button when using one of the Creative Zone modes (M, Av, Tv, or P) to produce the White Balance screen. Then, use the touch screen or left/right cross keys to select a white balance, and choose SET to confirm.

- **AF mode button.** Press the right cross key when using a Creative Zone mode to produce a screen that allows choosing autofocus mode from among One-Shot, AI Focus, and AI Servo. Use the touch screen or press the button repeatedly until the focus mode you want is selected. Then select SET to confirm your focus mode.

- **Drive mode button.** Press the left cross key to produce a screen that allows choosing a drive mode, in both Creative Zone and Basic Zone modes. Then use the touch screen or press the right cross key to select the 10-second self-timer (which also can be used with the optional IR remote controls), 2-second self-timer, or Self-timer: Continuous, which allows you to specify a number of shots to be taken (from 2 to 10) with the up/down keys. Choose SET to confirm your choice.

- **Picture Styles selection button.** When in Shooting mode using a Creative Zone exposure setting, press the down cross key to pop up the Picture Styles menu on the LCD, so you can select a given style, or gain access to user-defined styles. To modify a Picture Style, you'll need to use the Shooting 2 menu, as described in Chapter 8.

## Jumping Around

When a photo you've taken is displayed on the color LCD, you can move forward or backward one image at a time or "jump" ahead or back in different increments by rotating the Main Dial. As you jump, an overlay appears on the screen briefly showing the size of the leap you're making. (See Figure 3.10.)

As I'll describe in Chapter 8, you can specify the exact increment using the Image Jump with Dial entry in the Playback 2 menu. Your options are as follows:

- **1 image.** Rotating the Main Dial one click or swiping jumps forward or back one image.

- **10 images.** Rotating the Main Dial one click or swiping jumps forward or back ten images.

- **100 images.** Rotating the Main Dial one click or swiping jumps forward or back one hundred images.

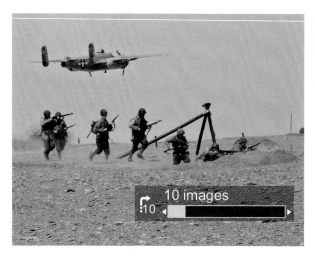

**Figure 3.10**
Rotate the Main Dial to jump ahead or back during image playback.

- **Display by Date.** Rotating the Main Dial one click or swiping jumps forward or back to the first image taken on the next or previous calendar date.

- **Display by Folder.** Rotating the Main Dial one click or swiping jumps to the next folder on your memory card.

- **Display Movies only.** Tells the T5i to jump only among movie images when using a card that contains both video clips and still images. This option is useful when you prefer to view only one kind of file.

- **Display Stills only.** Specifies jumping only between still images when using a card that has both video clips and still images.

- **Display by Image Rating.** As explained in Chapter 8, you can rate a particular movie or still photo by applying from one to five stars, using the Rating menu entry in the Playback 2 menu. This Jump choice allows you to select a rating rank, and then jump among photos with that rating applied.

# Going Topside

The top surface of the Canon EOS Rebel T5i has a few frequently accessed controls of its own. The key controls, shown in Figure 3.11, are as follows:

- **Mode Dial.** Rotate this dial to switch among Basic Zone and Creative Zone modes. Unlike the dial installed on the previous T4i, this Mode Dial rotates a complete 360 degrees. You'll find the various modes and options described in more detail in Chapter 4.

- **Sensor focal plane.** Precision macro and scientific photography sometimes requires knowing exactly where the focal plane of the sensor is. The symbol on the top side of the camera, to the left of the viewfinder, marks that plane.

Figure 3.11

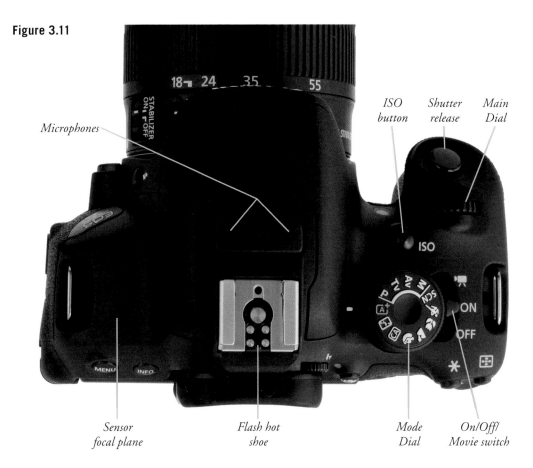

Microphones

ISO button    Shutter release    Main Dial

Sensor focal plane    Flash hot shoe    Mode Dial    On/Off/ Movie switch

■ **Flash hot shoe.** Slide an electronic flash into this mount when you need a more powerful speedlite. A dedicated flash unit, like those from Canon, can use the multiple contact points shown to communicate exposure, zoom setting, white balance information, and other data between the flash and the camera. There's more on using electronic flash in Chapter 11.

■ **ISO button.** Press this button and use the touch screen or cross keys to navigate until the setting you want appears on the LCD. Choose SET to confirm your choice. You'll find more about ISO options in Chapter 4, and flash EV settings in Chapter 11.

■ **Main Dial.** This dial is used to make many shooting settings. When settings come in pairs (such as shutter speed/aperture in Manual shooting mode), the Main Dial is used for one (for example, shutter speed), while some other control, such as the Av button (when shooting in manual exposure mode) is used for the other (aperture).

■ **Shutter release button.** Partially depress this button to lock in exposure and focus. Press all the way to take the picture. Tapping the shutter release when the camera has turned off the autoexposure and autofocus mechanisms reactivates both. When a review image is displayed on the back-panel color LCD, tapping this button removes the image from the display and reactivates the autoexposure and autofocus mechanisms.

■ **Microphones.** The stereo microphones record the audio track of your HDTV movies. You can plug an external stereo mic into a port on the side.

■ **On/Off/Movie switch.** Flip forward one click to turn the Rebel T5i on in still photography mode, and one additional click to activate movie mode. Flip back to the off position again to power down.

## Underneath Your Rebel T5i

There's not a lot going on with the bottom panel of your Rebel T5i. You'll find a tripod socket, which secures the camera to a tripod, and is also used to lock on the optional BG-E8 battery grip, which provides more juice to run your camera to take more exposures with a single charge. It also adds a vertically oriented shutter release, and Main Dial, AE Lock/FE Lock, and AF point selection controls for easier vertical shooting. To mount the grip, slide the battery door latch to open the door, then push gently toward the outside edge of the camera to free the hinge pins from their sockets. That will let you remove the battery door. Then slide the grip into the battery cavity, aligning the pin on the grip with the small hole on the other side of the tripod socket. Tighten the grip's tripod socket screw to lock the grip onto the bottom of your T5i. Figure 3.12 shows the underside view of the camera.

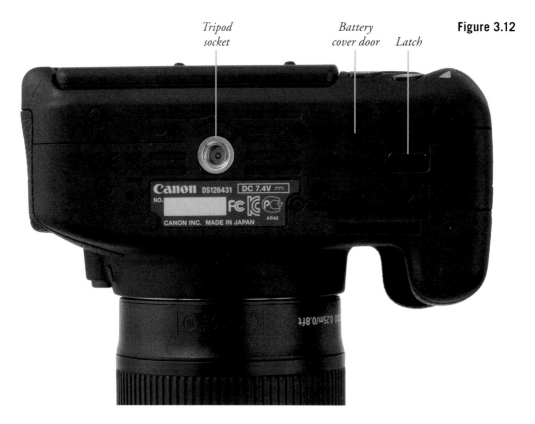

*Tripod socket*      *Battery cover door*    *Latch*      **Figure 3.12**

# Lens Components

The typical lens, like the ones shown in Figures 3.13 and 3.14, has seven or eight common features. Not every component appears on every lens. The lens on the left in Figure 3.13, for example, lacks the distance scale and distance indicator that the lens on the right has. Lenses that lack image stabilization will not have a stabilization switch.

- **Filter thread.** Lenses have a thread on the front for attaching filters and other add-ons. Some also use this thread for attaching a lens hood (you screw on the filter first, and then attach the hood to the screw thread on the front of the filter).
- **Lens hood.** Shields the front element of the lens from extraneous light arriving from outside the image area, and serves as protection.
- **Lens hood bayonet.** This is used to mount the lens hood for lenses that don't use screw-mount hoods (the majority).

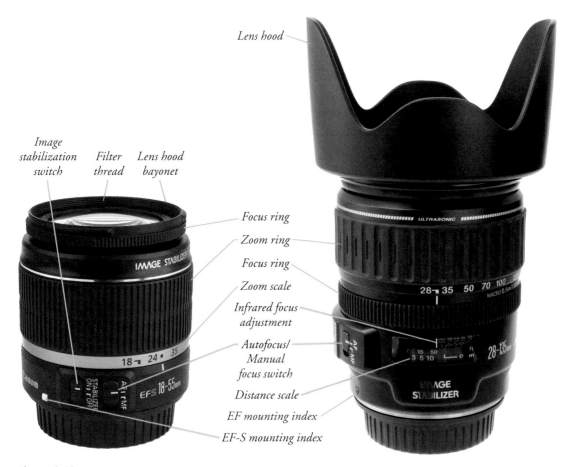

**Figure 3.13**

- **Zoom ring.** Turn this ring to change the zoom setting.
- **Zoom scale.** These markings on the lens show the current focal length selected.
- **Focus ring.** This is the ring you turn when you manually focus the lens.
- **Distance scale.** This is a readout that rotates in unison with the lens's focus mechanism to show the distance at which the lens has been focused. It's a useful indicator for double-checking autofocus, roughly evaluating depth-of-field, and for setting manual focus guesstimates.
- **Infrared focus adjustment.** IR illumination doesn't focus at the exact same plane as visible light, so if you're shooting infrared photos, move the focus ring to line up to the appropriate focal length opposite the distance determined by normal focusing.
- **Autofocus/manual focus switch.** Allows you to change from automatic focus to manual focus.
- **Image stabilization switch.** Lenses with IS include a separate switch for adjusting the stabilization feature.
- **EF-S/EF mounting index.** EF-S lenses have a raised white square, while EF lenses have a raised red bump; line up these indexes with the matching white and red indicators on the camera lens mount to attach the lens.
- **Electrical contacts.** On the back of the lens (see Figure 3.14) are electrical contacts that the camera uses to communicate focus, aperture setting, and other information.
- **Lens mount.** This mount is used to attach the lens to a matching bayonet on the camera body.

**Figure 3.14**

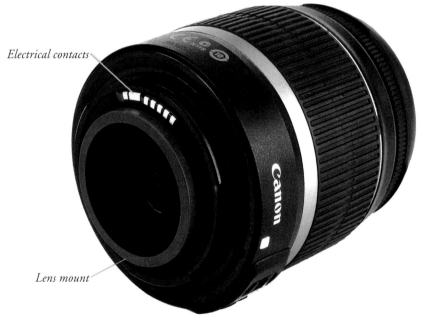

*Electrical contacts*

*Lens mount*

# LCD Monitor Readouts

The Rebel T5i does not have a monochrome status LCD like the one found on the top panel of the mid- and upper-level EOS cameras, such as the 5D Mark III. Nor does it have such a monochrome panel underneath the color LCD on the back, as the original Digital Rebel and Rebel XT did. Lacking this auxiliary information display, the T5i uses the generously expansive three-inch color LCD to show you everything you need to see, from images to a collection of informational data displays. Here's an overview of these displays, and how to access them:

■ **Image playback displays.** When the T5i shows you a picture for review, you can select from among four different information overlays. To switch among them, press the INFO. button while the image is on the screen. The LCD will cycle among the single-image display (Figure 3.15); single-image display with recording quality (Figure 3.16); histogram display, which shows basic shooting information as well as a brightness histogram at bottom right, with individual histograms for the red, green, and blue channels above (Figure 3.17); and a complete shooting information display (Figure 3.18), which includes most of the relevant shooting settings, plus a brightness histogram. I'll explain how to work with histograms in Chapter 4.

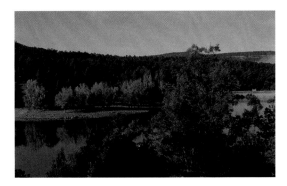

**Figure 3.15**

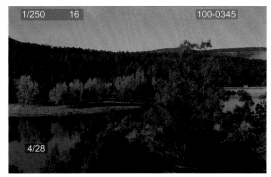

**Figure 3.16**

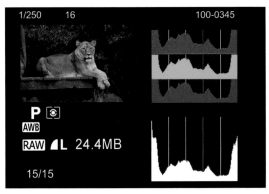

**Figure 3.17**

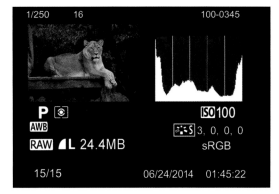

**Figure 3.18**

Image playback displays include single image, single image with recording quality, histogram, and shooting information.

■ **Shooting settings display.** While you are taking pictures, this screen will be shown, with information like that shown in Figure 3.19. Not all of the data pictured will be seen at one time; only the settings that are appropriate for the current shooting mode will be displayed. I'll explain how to make and use each of these settings later in this book. You can turn this display off by pressing the INFO. button, and restore it again by pressing the INFO. button a second time. When the shooting settings display is active, you can return to it when there is a menu screen or image review on the LCD by tapping the shutter release button. If you want to make adjustments, press the Quick Control button to activate the Quick Control screen, and use the cross keys to navigate to the setting you want to change. As I mentioned in Chapter 1, when using Basic Zone modes other than Creative Auto, you can change only the drive mode and image quality. When using Creative Auto, you can adjust additional settings, such as flash modes, Picture Styles (or image effects), brightness, and depth-of-field (range of sharpness), and Ambience. With Creative Zone modes, you can change any of the settings visible in the Quick Control screen.

■ **Camera function settings.** When Shooting Settings is displayed, you can switch to the Camera Functions settings screen by pressing the INFO. button. A screen like the one shown in Figure 3.20 will appear, with key camera function settings arrayed.

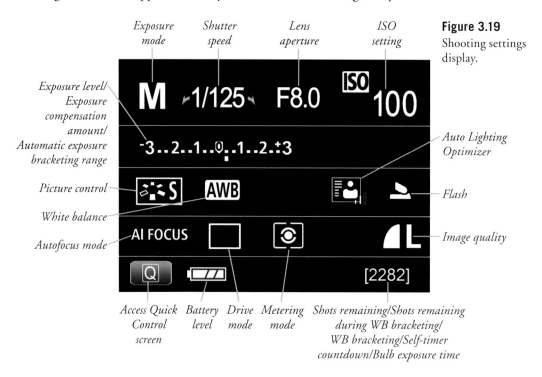

**Figure 3.19**
Shooting settings display.

**Figure 3.20**
Camera functions
display.

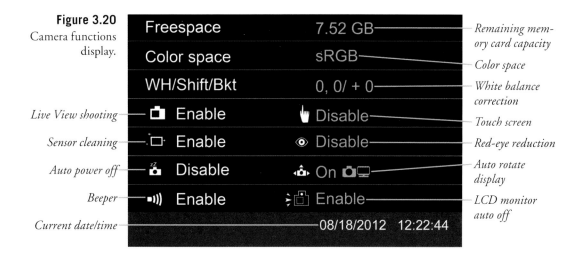

# Looking Inside the Viewfinder

Much of the important shooting status information is shown inside the viewfinder of the Rebel T5i. As with the displays shown on the color LCD, not all of this information will be shown at any one time. Figure 3.21 shows what you can expect to see. I'll explain all of these readouts later in this book, with those pertaining to exposure in Chapter 4, and those relating to flash in Chapter 11. These readouts include:

■ **Spot metering reference circle.** Shows the circle that delineates the metered area when Spot metering is activated. (The reference circle is visible at all times, even when you're not using Spot metering.)

■ **Autofocus zones.** Shows the nine areas used by the T5i to focus. The camera can select the appropriate focus zone for you, or you can manually select one or all of the zones, as described in Chapters 1 and 4.

■ **Autoexposure lock.** Shows that exposure has been locked. This icon also appears when an automatic exposure bracketing sequence is in process.

■ **Flash-ready indicator.** This icon appears when the flash is fully charged. It also shows when the flash exposure lock has been applied for an inappropriate exposure value.

■ **Flash status indicator.** Appears along with the flash-ready indicator. The H is shown when high-speed (focal plane) flash sync is being used. The * appears when flash exposure lock or a flash exposure bracketing sequence is underway.

■ **Flash exposure compensation.** Appears when flash EV changes have been made.

■ **Shutter speed/aperture readouts.** Most of the time, these readouts show the current shutter speed and aperture. This pair can also warn you of memory card conditions (full, error, or missing), ISO speed, flash exposure lock, and a buSY indicator when the camera is busy doing other things (including flash recycling).

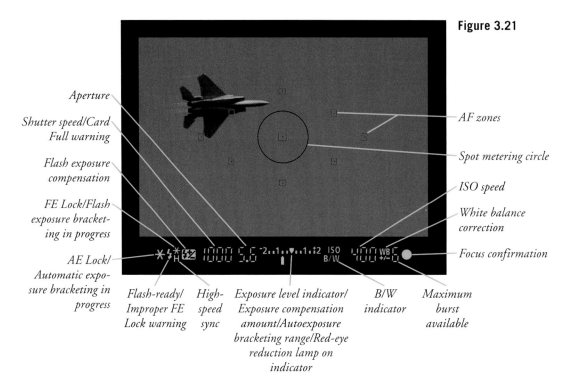

Figure 3.21

*Aperture*

*Shutter speed/Card Full warning*

*Flash exposure compensation*

*FE Lock/Flash exposure bracketing in progress*

*AE Lock/ Automatic exposure bracketing in progress*

*Flash-ready/ Improper FE Lock warning*

*High-speed sync*

*Exposure level indicator/ Exposure compensation amount/Autoexposure bracketing range/Red-eye reduction lamp on indicator*

*B/W indicator*

*Maximum burst available*

*AF zones*

*Spot metering circle*

*ISO speed*

*White balance correction*

*Focus confirmation*

- **Exposure level indicator.** This scale shows the current exposure level, with the bottom indicator centered when the exposure is correct as metered. The indicator may also move to the left or right to indicate under- or overexposure (respectively). The scale is also used to show the amount of EV and flash EV adjustments and the number of stops covered by the current automatic exposure bracketing range, and is used as a red-eye reduction lamp indicator.

- **ISO sensitivity.** This useful indicator shows the current ISO setting value. Those who have accidentally taken dozens of shots under bright sunlight at ISO 1600 because they forgot to change the setting back after some indoor shooting will treasure this addition.

- **B/W indicator.** Illuminates when the Monochrome Picture Style is being used. There's no way to restore color when you're shooting JPEGs without RAW, so this indicator is another valuable warning.

- **White balance correction.** Shows that white balance has been tweaked.

- **Maximum burst available.** Changes to a number to indicate the number of frames that can be taken in continuous mode using the current settings.

- **Focus confirmation.** This green dot appears when the subject covered by the active autofocus zone is in sharp focus.

# Part II

# Mastering Your Tools

Even if you've learned the fundamentals and controls of the Canon EOS T5i, there is lots of room to learn more and master the features of the camera so you can use them to their fullest. Even if you're getting great exposures a high percentage of the time, you can fine-tune tonal values and use your shutter speed, aperture, and ISO controls creatively. Your camera's high-performance autofocus system may zero in on your subject in most situations—but you still need to be able to tell the camera *what* to focus on, and *when*. Other tools at your disposal let you freeze an instant of time, create multiple exposures on a single frame, and improve your images in other imaginative ways. The chapters in this part will help you move your photography to the next level by understanding exposure, mastering the mysteries of autofocus, and using the T5i's advanced features.

This part of the book contains the core chapters that will help you improve your images by nailing the best exposure every time, using the (often confusing, sometimes conflicting) features of the camera's advanced autofocus system and exploring some advanced techniques like trap focus, stacked focus, and in-camera HDR. I'll also clear up any questions you might have about which lenses are best suited for the T5i when it comes time to add to your collection.

- **Chapter 4, "Nailing the Right Exposure":** This chapter explores all your options for fine-tuning exposure with the Canon T5i. You'll learn when to use—and not use—each of the camera's metering modes, how to work with histograms, and the rationale for choosing the built-in HDR feature—or whether to capture high dynamic range images "manually." I'm also going to explode the myth of the 18 percent gray card.

- **Chapter 5, "Mastering the Mysteries of Autofocus":** As autofocus features like the T5i's new "hybrid" AF system are added, this useful capability often becomes more confusing, even for veteran photographers. I'm going to show you exactly how autofocus works so you can better understand the strengths and limitations of each mode. You'll discover how to select the mode that will give you tack-sharp focus time after time, and learn how to use fine-tuning (with the included focus chart) to correct lenses with front- and back-focus problems.

- **Chapter 6, "Movies and Live View":** This is your introduction to shooting in Live View mode and capturing movies, with complete descriptions of the T5i's shooting features, along with tips on better video.

- **Chapter 7, "Advanced Shooting":** Here you'll find discussions of some more advanced techniques, including how to make people "invisible" with long exposures, getting the most from the T5i's continuous shooting capabilities, and some clever ways to create multiple exposures.

# 4

# Nailing the Right Exposure

As you learn to use your T5i creatively, you're going to find that the right settings—as determined by the camera's exposure meter and intelligence—need to be *adjusted* to account for your creative decisions or to fine-tune the image for special situations.

For example, when you shoot with the main light source behind the subject, you end up with *backlighting*, which results in an overexposed background and/or an underexposed subject. The Rebel T5i recognizes backlit situations nicely, and can properly base exposure on the main subject, producing a decent photo. Features like Highlight Tone Priority and the Auto Lighting Optimizer can fine-tune exposure to preserve detail in the highlights and shadows.

But what if you *want* to underexpose the subject, to produce a silhouette effect? Or, perhaps, you might want to flip up the T5i's built-in flash unit to fill in the shadows on your subject. The more you know about how to use your T5i, the more you'll run into situations where you want to creatively tweak the exposure to provide a different look than you'd get with a straight shot.

This chapter shows you the fundamentals of exposure, so you'll be better equipped to override the Rebel T5i's default settings when you want to, or need to. After all, correct exposure is one of the foundations of good photography, along with accurate focus and sharpness, appropriate color balance, freedom from unwanted noise and excessive contrast, as well as pleasing composition.

The Rebel T5i gives you a great deal of control over all of these, although composition is entirely up to you. You must still frame the photograph to create an interesting arrangement of subject matter, but all the other parameters are basic functions of the camera. You can let your T5i set them for you automatically, you can fine-tune how the camera applies its automatic settings, or you can make them yourself, manually. The amount of control you have over exposure, sensitivity (ISO settings), color balance, focus, and image parameters like sharpness and contrast make the T5i a versatile tool for creating images.

In the next few pages, I'm going to give you a grounding in one of those foundations, and explain the basics of exposure, either as an introduction or as a refresher course, depending on your current level of expertise. When you finish this chapter, you'll understand most of what you need to know to take well-exposed photographs creatively in a broad range of situations.

# Getting a Handle on Exposure

This section explains the fundamental concepts that go into creating an exposure. If you already know about the role of f/stops, shutter speeds, and sensor sensitivity in determining an exposure, you might want to skip to the next section, which explains how the T5i calculates exposure.

In the most basic sense, exposure is all about light. Exposure can make or break your photo. Correct exposure brings out the detail in the areas you want to picture, providing the range of tones and colors you need to create the desired image. Poor exposure can cloak important details in shadow, or wash them out in glare-filled featureless expanses of white. However, getting the perfect exposure requires some intelligence—either that built into the camera or the smarts in your head—because digital sensors can't capture all the tones we are able to see. If the range of tones in an image is extensive, embracing both inky black shadows and bright highlights, we often must settle for an exposure that renders most of those tones—but not all—in a way that best suits the photo we want to produce.

As the owner of a Canon T5i, you're probably well aware of the traditional "exposure triangle" of aperture (quantity of light, light passed by the lens), shutter speed (the amount of time the shutter is open), and the ISO sensitivity of the sensor—all working proportionately and reciprocally to produce an exposure. The trio is itself affected by the amount of illumination that is available to work with. So, if you double the amount of light, increase the aperture by one stop, make the shutter speed twice as long, or boost the ISO setting 2X, you'll get twice as much exposure. Similarly, you can increase any of these factors while decreasing one of the others by a similar amount to keep the same exposure.

Working with any of the three controls involves trade-offs. Larger f/stops provide less depth-of-field, while smaller f/stops increase depth-of-field (and potentially at the same time can *decrease* sharpness through a phenomenon called *diffraction*). Shorter shutter speeds do a better job of reducing the effects of camera/subject motion, while longer shutter speeds make that motion blur more likely. Higher ISO settings increase the amount of visual noise and artifacts in your image, while lower ISO settings reduce the effects of noise. (See Figure 4.1.)

Exposure determines the look, feel, and tone of an image, in more ways than one. Incorrect exposure can impair even the best-composed image by cloaking important tones in darkness, or by washing them out so they become featureless to the eye. On the other hand, correct exposure brings out the detail in the areas you want to picture, and provides the range of tones and colors you need to create the desired image. However, getting the perfect exposure can be tricky, because digital sensors can't capture all the tones we are able to see. If the range of tones in an image is extensive,

**Figure 4.1**

The traditional exposure triangle includes aperture, shutter speed, and ISO sensitivity.

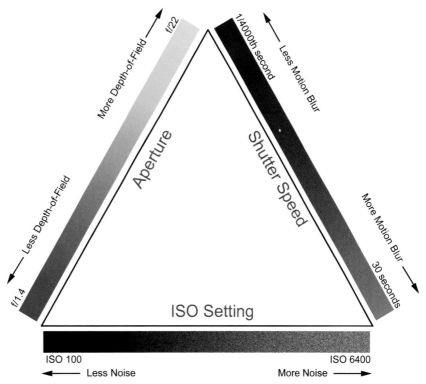

embracing both inky black shadows and bright highlights, the sensor may not be able to capture them all. Sometimes, we must settle for an exposure that renders most of those tones—but not all—in a way that best suits the photo we want to produce. You'll often need to make choices about which details are important, and which are not, so that you can grab the tones that truly matter in your image. That's part of the creativity you bring to bear in realizing your photographic vision.

For example, look at two bracketed exposures presented in Figure 4.2. For the image at the left, the highlights (chiefly the clouds at upper left and the top-left edge of the skyscraper) are well exposed, but everything else in the shot is seriously underexposed. The version at the right, taken an instant later with the tripod-mounted camera, shows detail in the shadow areas of the buildings, but the highlights are completely washed out. The camera's sensor simply can't capture detail in both dark areas and bright areas in a single shot.

With digital camera sensors, it's tricky to capture detail in both highlights and shadows in a single image, because the number of tones, the *dynamic range* of the sensor, is limited. The solution, in this particular case, was to resort to a technique called High Dynamic Range (HDR) photography, in which the two exposures from Figure 4.2 were combined in an image editor such as Photoshop, or a specialized HDR tool like Photomatix (about $100 from www.hdrsoft.com). The resulting shot is shown in Figure 4.3. I'll explain more about HDR photography later in this chapter. For now, though, I'm going to concentrate on showing you how to get the best exposures possible without resorting to such tools, using only the features of your Canon Rebel T5i.

To understand exposure, you need to understand the six aspects of light that combine to produce an image. Start with a light source—the sun, an interior lamp, or the glow from a campfire—and trace its path to your camera, through the lens, and finally to the sensor that captures the illumination.

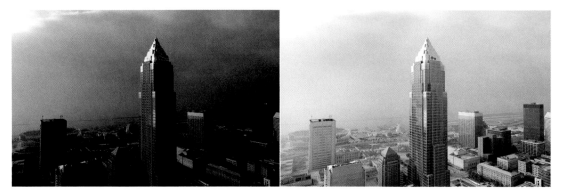

**Figure 4.2**  At left, the image is exposed for the highlights, losing shadow detail. At right, the exposure captures detail in the shadows, but the background highlights are washed out.

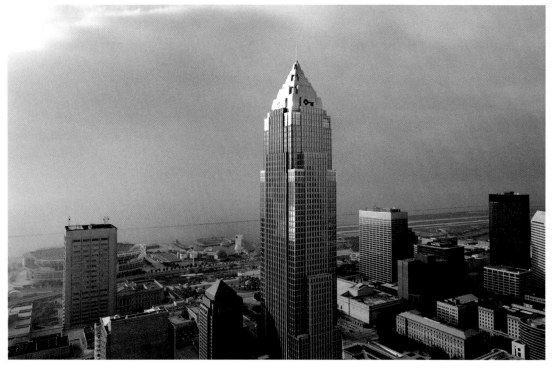

**Figure 4.3**  Combining the two exposures produces the best compromise image.

Here's a brief review of the things within our control that affect exposure.

- **Light at its source.** Our eyes and our cameras—film or digital—are most sensitive to that portion of the electromagnetic spectrum we call *visible light*. That light has several important aspects that are relevant to photography, such as color and harshness (which is determined primarily by the apparent size of the light source as it illuminates a subject). But, in terms of exposure, the important attribute of a light source is its *intensity*. We may have direct control over intensity, which might be the case with an interior light that can be brightened or dimmed. Or, we might have only indirect control over intensity, as with sunlight, which can be made to appear dimmer by introducing translucent light-absorbing or reflective materials in its path.

- **Light's duration.** We tend to think of most light sources as continuous. But, as you'll learn in Chapter 11, the duration of light can change quickly enough to modify the exposure, as when the main illumination in a photograph comes from an intermittent source, such as an electronic flash.

- **Light reflected, transmitted, or emitted.** Once light is produced by its source, either continuously or in a brief burst, we are able to see and photograph objects by the light that is reflected from our subjects toward the camera lens; transmitted (say, from translucent objects that are lit from behind); or emitted (by a candle or television screen). When more or less light reaches the lens from the subject, we need to adjust the exposure. This part of the equation is under our control to the extent we can increase the amount of light falling on or passing through the subject (by adding extra light sources or using reflectors), or by pumping up the light that's emitted (by increasing the brightness of the glowing object).

- **Light passed by the lens.** Not all the illumination that reaches the front of the lens makes it all the way through. Filters can remove some of the light before it enters the lens. Inside the lens barrel is a variable-sized diaphragm that dilates and contracts to vary the size of the aperture and control the amount of light that enters the lens. You, or the T5i's autoexposure system, can control exposure by varying the size of the aperture. The relative size of the aperture is called the *f/stop* (see Figure 4.4).

**Figure 4.4**
Top row
(left to right):
f/2, f/2.8, f/4, f/5.6;
bottom row:
f/8, f/11, f/16, f/22.

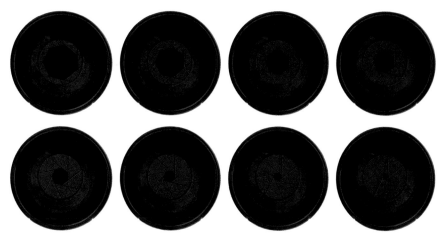

- **Light passing through the shutter.** Once light passes through the lens, the amount of time the sensor receives it is determined by the T5i's shutter, which can remain open for as long as 30 seconds (or even longer if you use the Bulb setting) or as briefly as 1/4,000th second.

- **Light captured by the sensor.** Not all the light falling onto the sensor is captured. If the number of photons reaching a particular photosite doesn't pass a set threshold, no information is recorded. Similarly, if too much light illuminates a pixel in the sensor, then the excess isn't recorded or, worse, spills over to contaminate adjacent pixels. We can modify the minimum and maximum number of pixels that contribute to image detail by adjusting the ISO setting. At higher ISOs, the incoming light is amplified to boost the effective sensitivity of the sensor.

These factors—the quantity of light produced by the light source, the amount reflected or transmitted toward the camera, the light passed by the lens, the amount of time the shutter is open, and the sensitivity of the sensor—all work proportionately and reciprocally to produce an exposure. That is, if you double the amount of light that's available, increase the aperture by one stop, make the shutter speed twice as long, or boost the ISO setting 2X, you'll get twice as much exposure. Similarly, you can increase any of these factors while decreasing one of the others by a similar amount to keep the same exposure.

Most commonly, exposure settings are made using the aperture and shutter speed, followed by adjusting the ISO sensitivity if it's not possible to get the preferred exposure; that is, the one that uses the "best" f/stop or shutter speed for the depth-of-field (range of sharp focus) or action stopping we want (produced by short shutter speeds, as I'll explain later). Table 4.1 shows equivalent exposure settings using various shutter speeds and f/stops.

## F/STOPS AND SHUTTER SPEEDS

If you're *really* new to more advanced cameras (and I realize that many soon-to-be-ambitious photographers do purchase the T5i as their first digital SLR), you might need to know that the lens aperture, or f/stop, is a ratio, much like a fraction, which is why f/2 is larger than f/4, just as 1/2 is larger than 1/4. However, f/2 is actually *four times* as large as f/4. (If you remember your high school geometry, you'll know that to double the area of a circle, you multiply its diameter by the square root of two: 1.4.)

Lenses are usually marked with intermediate f/stops that represent a size that's twice as much/half as much as the previous aperture. So, a lens might be marked f/2, f/2.8, f/4, f/5.6, f/8, f/11, f/16, f/22, with each larger number representing an aperture that admits half as much light as the one before, as shown in Figure 4.4.

Shutter speeds are actual fractions (of a second), but the numerator is omitted, so that 60, 125, 250, 500, 1,000, and so forth represent 1/60th, 1/125th, 1/250th, 1/500th, and 1/1,000th second. To avoid confusion, Canon uses quotation marks to signify longer exposures: 2", 2"5, 4", and so forth representing 2.0-, 2.5-, and 4.0-second exposures, respectively.

## Table 4.1 Equivalent Exposures

| Shutter Speed | f/stop | Shutter Speed | f/stop |
|---|---|---|---|
| 1/30th second | f/22 | 1/500th second | f/5.6 |
| 1/60th second | f/16 | 1/1,000th second | f/4 |
| 1/125th second | f/11 | 1/2,000th second | f/2.8 |
| 1/250th second | f/8 | 1/4,000th second | f/2 |

When the T5i is set for P (Program) mode, the metering system selects the correct exposure for you automatically, but you can change quickly to an equivalent exposure by locking the current exposure, and then spinning the Main Dial until the desired *equivalent* exposure combination is displayed. You can use this standard Program Shift feature more easily if you remember that you need to rotate the dial toward the *left* when you want to increase the amount of depth-of-field or use a slower shutter speed; rotate to the *right* when you want to reduce the depth-of-field or use a faster shutter speed. The need for more/less DOF and slower/faster shutter speed are the primary reasons you'd want to use Program Shift. I'll explain Program mode exposure shifting options in more detail later in this chapter.

In Aperture-priority (Av) and Shutter-priority (Tv) modes, you can change to an equivalent exposure using a different combination of shutter speed and aperture, but only by either adjusting the aperture in Aperture-priority mode (the camera then chooses the shutter speed) or shutter speed in Shutter-priority mode (the camera then selects the aperture). I'll cover all these exposure modes and their differences later in the chapter.

# How the Rebel T5i Calculates Exposure

Your Canon T5i calculates exposure by measuring the light that passes through the lens and is bounced up by the mirror to sensors located near the focusing surface, using a pattern you can select (more on that later) and based on the assumption that each area being measured reflects about the same amount of light as a neutral gray card that reflects a "middle" gray of about 12- to 18-percent reflectance. (The photographic "gray cards" you buy at a camera store have an 18-percent gray tone, which does represent middle gray; however, your camera is calibrated to interpret a somewhat darker 12-percent gray; I'll explain more about this later.) That "average" 12- to 18-percent gray assumption is necessary, because different subjects reflect different amounts of light. In a photo containing, say, a white cat and a dark gray cat, the white cat might reflect five times as much light as the gray cat. An exposure based on the white cat will cause the gray cat to appear to be black, while an exposure based only on the gray cat will make the white cat washed out.

This is more easily understood if you look at some photos of subjects that are dark (they reflect little light), those that have predominantly middle tones, and subjects that are highly reflective. The next few figures show some images of actual cats (actually, the *same* cat rendered in black, gray, and white varieties through the magic of Photoshop), with each of the three strips exposed using a different cat for reference.

## Correctly Exposed

The three pictures shown in Figure 4.5 represent how the black, gray, and white cats would appear if the exposure were calculated by measuring the light reflecting from the middle, gray cat, which, for the sake of illustration, we'll assume reflects approximately 12 to 18 percent of the light that strikes it. The exposure meter sees an object that it thinks is a middle gray, calculates an exposure based on that, and the feline in the center of the strip is rendered at its proper tonal value. Best of all, because the resulting exposure is correct, the black cat at left and white cat at right are rendered properly as well.

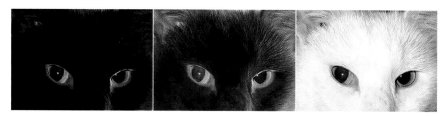

**Figure 4.5**
When exposure is calculated based on the middle-gray cat in the center, the black-and-white cats are rendered accurately, too.

When you're shooting pictures with your T5i, and the meter happens to base its exposure on a subject that averages that "ideal" middle gray, then you'll end up with similar (accurate) results. The camera's exposure algorithms are concocted to ensure this kind of result as often as possible, barring any unusual subjects (that is, those that are backlit, or have uneven illumination). The T5i has four different metering modes (described next), each of which is equipped to handle certain types of unusual subjects, as I'll outline.

## Overexposed

The strip of three images in Figure 4.6 shows what would happen if the exposure were calculated based on metering the leftmost, black cat. The light meter sees less light reflecting from the black cat than it would see from a gray middle-tone subject, and so figures, "Aha! I need to add exposure to brighten this subject up to a middle gray!" That lightens the black cat, so it now appears to be gray.

But now, the cat in the middle that was *originally* middle gray is overexposed and becomes light gray. And the white cat at right is now seriously overexposed, and loses detail in the highlights, which have become a featureless white.

**Figure 4.6**
When exposure is calculated based on the black cat at the left, the black cat looks gray, the gray cat appears to be a light gray, and the white cat is seriously overexposed.

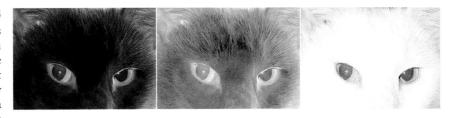

# Underexposed

The third possibility in this simplified scenario is that the light meter might measure the illumination bouncing off the white cat, and try to render that feline as a middle gray. A lot of light is reflected by the white kitty, so the exposure is *reduced*, bringing that cat closer to a middle gray tone. The cats that were originally gray and black are now rendered too dark. Clearly, measuring the gray cat—or a substitute that reflects about the same amount of light—is the only way to ensure that the exposure is precisely correct. (See Figure 4.7.)

As you can see, the ideal way to measure exposure is to meter from a subject that reflects 12 to 18 percent of the light that reaches it. If you want the most precise exposure calculations, if you don't have a gray cat handy, the solution is to use a stand-in, such as the evenly illuminated gray card I mentioned earlier. But, because the standard Kodak gray card reflects 18 percent of the light that reaches it and, as I said, your camera is calibrated for a somewhat darker 12-percent tone, you would need to add about one-half stop *more* exposure than the value metered from the card.

Another substitute for a gray card is the palm of a human hand (the backside of the hand is too variable). But a human palm, regardless of ethnic group, is even brighter than a standard gray card, so instead of one-half stop more exposure, you need to add one additional stop. That is, if your meter reading is 1/500th of a second at f/11, use 1/500th second at f/8 or 1/250th second at f/11 instead. (Both exposures are equivalent.) You can use exposure compensation (described later in this chapter) to add the half or full stop of exposure in either case.

If you actually wanted to use a gray card, place it in your frame near your main subject, facing the camera, and with the exact same even illumination falling on it that is falling on your subject. Then, use the Spot metering function (described in the next section) to calculate exposure. Of course, in most situations, it's not necessary to make the (technically correct) adjustment from the gray card/

**Figure 4.7**
When exposure is calculated based on the white cat on the right, the other two cats are underexposed.

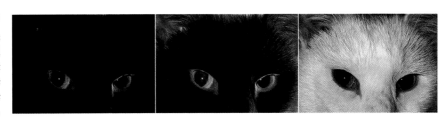

human hand reading. Your camera's light meter will do a good job of calculating the right exposure that's close enough for practical purposes, especially if you use the exposure tips in the next section. But, I felt that explaining exactly what is going on during exposure calculation would help you understand how your T5i's metering system works.

---

## WHY THE GRAY CARD CONFUSION?

Why are so many photographers under the impression that cameras and meters are calibrated to the 18-percent "standard," rather than the true value, which may be 12 to 14 percent, depending on the vendor? The most common explanation is that during a revision of Kodak's instructions for its gray cards in the 1970s, the advice to open up an extra half stop was omitted, and a whole generation of shooters grew up thinking that a measurement off a gray card could be used as-is. The proviso returned to the instructions by 1987, it's said, but by then it was too late. Next to me is a (c)2006 version of the instructions for KODAK Gray Cards, Publication R-27Q, and the current directions read (with a bit of paraphrasing from me in italics):

- For subjects of normal reflectance increase the indicated exposure by 1/2 stop.

- For light subjects use the indicated exposure; for very light subjects, decrease the exposure by 1/2 stop. (*That is, you're measuring a cat that's lighter than middle gray.*)

- If the subject is dark to very dark, increase the indicated exposure by 1 to 1-1/2 stops. (*You're shooting a black cat.*)

---

# Choosing a Metering Method

To calculate exposure automatically, you need to tell the T5i *where* in the frame to measure the light (this is called the *metering method*) and *what controls* should be used (aperture, shutter speed, or both) to set the exposure. That's called *exposure mode* (and includes Program (P), Shutter-priority (Tv), Aperture-priority (Av), or Manual (M) options, plus Auto and Creative Auto. I'll explain all these next).

But first, I'm going to introduce you to the four metering methods. You can select any of the four if you're working with P, Tv, Av, or M exposure modes; if you're using Auto or Creative Auto, Evaluative metering is selected automatically and cannot be changed.

1. Press the MENU button and navigate to the Shooting 2 menu (a camera icon with two dots next to it).

2. Use the Quick Control key (Q button) to access the Quick Control screen and navigate to the metering mode section. Select SET, and a screen pops up on the LCD offering four choices. (The screen was shown earlier in Chapter 2.) You can also change metering method using the Shooting 2 menu.

3. Use the touch screen or left/right cross keys to highlight Evaluative, Partial, Spot, or Center-weighted.

■ **Evaluative.** The T5i slices up the frame into 63 different zones, shown as blue rectangles in Figure 4.8. The zones used are linked to the autofocus system (the 9 autofocus zones are also shown in the figure). The camera evaluates the measurements, giving extra emphasis to the metering zones that indicate sharp focus to make an educated guess about what kind of picture you're taking, based on examination of thousands of different real-world photos. For example, if the top sections of a picture are much lighter than the bottom portions, the algorithm can assume that the scene is a landscape photo with lots of sky. This mode is the best all-purpose metering method for most pictures. I'll explain how to choose an autofocus/exposure zone in the section on autofocus operation later in this chapter. See Figure 4.9 for an example of a scene that can be easily interpreted by the Evaluative metering mode.

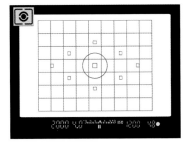

**Figure 4.8** Evaluative metering uses 63 zones marked by blue rectangles, linked to the autofocus points shown as red brackets.

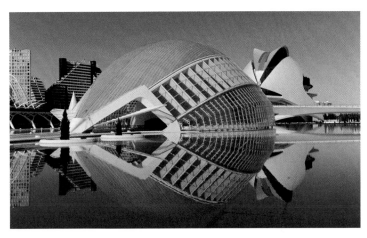

**Figure 4.9** An evenly lit scene like this one can be metered effectively using the Evaluative metering setting.

■ **Partial.** This is a *faux* spot mode, using roughly 9 percent of the image area to calculate exposure, which, as you can see in Figure 4.10, is a rather large spot, represented by the larger blue circle. The status LCD icon is shown in the upper-left corner. Use this mode if the background is much brighter or darker than the subject, as in Figure 4.11.

■ **Spot.** This mode confines the reading to a limited area in the center of the viewfinder, as shown in Figure 4.12, making up only 4 percent of the image. This mode is useful when you want to base exposure on a small area in the frame, such as a spotlight performer on stage (see Figure 4.13), surrounded by a black background. If that area is in the center of the frame, so much the better. If not, you'll have to make your meter reading and then lock exposure by pressing the shutter release halfway, or by pressing the AE Lock button.

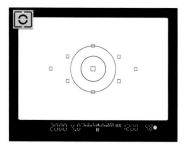

**Figure 4.10** Partial metering uses a center spot that's roughly 9 percent of the frame area.

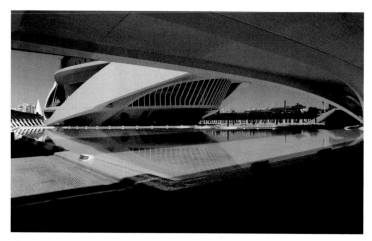

**Figure 4.11** Partial metering allowed measuring exposure from the central area of the image, while giving less emphasis to the darker areas at top and bottom.

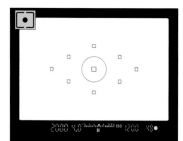

**Figure 4.12** Spot metering calculates exposure based on a center spot that's only 4 percent of the image area.

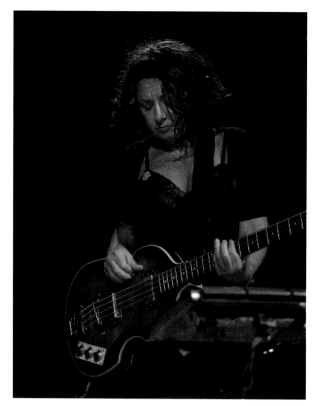

**Figure 4.13** Spot metering allowed calculating exposure exclusively from the performer's face.

■ **Center-weighted.** In this mode, the exposure meter emphasizes a zone in the center of the frame to calculate exposure, as shown in Figure 4.14, on the theory that, for most pictures, the main subject will be located in the center. Center-weighting works best for portraits, architectural photos, and other pictures in which the most important subject is located in the middle of the frame, as in Figure 4.15. As the name suggests, the light reading is *weighted* toward the central portion, but information is also used from the rest of the frame. If your main subject is surrounded by very bright or very dark areas, the exposure might not be exactly right. However, this scheme works well in many situations if you don't want to use one of the other modes.

4. Choose SET to confirm your choice.

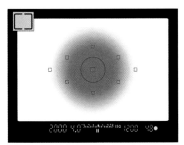

**Figure 4.14** Center-weighted metering calculates exposure based on the full frame, but emphasizes the center area.

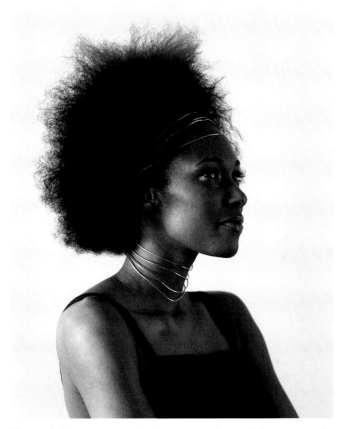

**Figure 4.15** Center-weighted metering calculated the exposure for this shot from the large area in the center of the frame, with less emphasis on the bright, window-lit area behind the subject.

# Choosing an Exposure Method

You'll find four Creative Zone methods for choosing the appropriate shutter speed and aperture: Program (P), Shutter-priority (Tv), Aperture-priority (Av), and Manual (M). To select one of these modes, just spin the Mode Dial (located at the top-right side of the camera) to choose the method you want to use. You can also select from the Basic Zone exposure methods, which provide much less control.

Your choice of which exposure method is best for a given shooting situation will depend on things like your need for lots of (or less) depth-of-field, a desire to freeze action or allow motion blur, or how much noise you find acceptable in an image. Each of the Rebel T5i's exposure methods emphasizes one of those aspects of image capture or another. This section introduces you to all of them.

## Basic Zone Exposure Methods

When using Basic Zone modes, you have little control over exposure. In any of these modes, the T5i sets Evaluative metering for you, and chooses the shutter speed and aperture automatically. Indeed, when using scene modes, you can't change any of the other shooting settings (other than image quality).

In Scene Intelligent Auto mode, the T5i selects an appropriate ISO sensitivity setting, color (white) balance, Picture Style, color space, noise reduction features, and use of the Auto Lighting Optimizer. (All of these will be discussed in Chapter 8.)

In Creative Auto mode, the T5i makes most of the exposure decisions for you (just as in Scene Intelligent Auto mode), but allows you to make some adjustments, in a round-about way. In terms of exposure adjustments, what you can do is adjust the f/stop used by telling the T5i whether you want the background more blurred or less blurred. Because the Basic Zone modes don't provide extensive exposure control, I'll continue the description of the adjustments you *can* make at the end of this chapter.

## Aperture-Priority

In Av mode, you specify the lens opening used, and the T5i selects the shutter speed. Aperture-priority is especially good when you want to use a particular lens opening to achieve a desired effect. Perhaps you'd like to use the smallest f/stop possible to maximize depth-of-field in a close-up picture. Or, you might want to use a large f/stop to throw everything except your main subject out of focus, as in Figure 4.16. Maybe you'd just like to "lock in" a particular f/stop smaller than the maximum aperture because it's the sharpest available aperture with that lens. Or, you might prefer to use, say, f/2.8 on a lens with a maximum aperture of f/1.4, because you want the best compromise between speed and sharpness.

Aperture-priority can even be used to specify a *range* of shutter speeds you want to use under varying lighting conditions, which seems almost contradictory. But think about it. You're shooting a soccer game outdoors with a telephoto lens and want a relatively high shutter speed, but you don't

**Figure 4.16**
Use Aperture-priority to "lock in" a large f/stop when you want to blur the background.

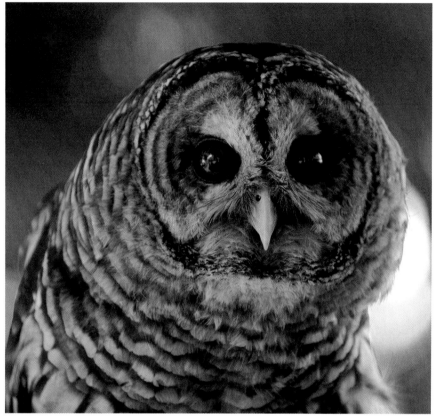

care if the speed changes a little should the sun duck behind a cloud. Set your T5i to Av, and adjust the aperture until a shutter speed of, say, 1/1,000th second is selected at your current ISO setting. (In bright sunlight at ISO 400, that aperture is likely to be around f/11.) Then, go ahead and shoot, knowing that your T5i will maintain that f/11 aperture (for sufficient DOF as the soccer players move about the field), but will drop down to 1/750th or 1/500th second if necessary should the lighting change a little.

A blinking 30 or 4000 shutter speed in the viewfinder indicates that the T5i is unable to select an appropriate shutter speed at the selected aperture and that over- and underexposure will occur at the current ISO setting. That's the major pitfall of using Av: you might select an f/stop that is too small or too large to allow an optimal exposure with the available shutter speeds. For example, if you choose f/2.8 as your aperture and the illumination is quite bright (say, at the beach or in snow), even your camera's fastest shutter speed might not be able to cut down the amount of light reaching the sensor to provide the right exposure. Or, if you select f/8 in a dimly lit room, you might find yourself shooting with a very slow shutter speed that can cause blurring from subject movement or camera shake. Aperture-priority is best used by those with a bit of experience in choosing settings. Many seasoned photographers leave their T5i set on Av all the time.

When to use Aperture-priority:

- **General landscape photography.** The T5i is a great camera for landscape photography, of course, because its 18MP of resolution allows making huge, gorgeous prints, as well as smaller prints that are filled with eye-popping detail. Aperture-priority is a good tool for ensuring that your landscape is sharp from foreground to infinity, if you select an f/stop that provides maximum depth-of-field.

  If you use Av mode and select an aperture like f/11 or f/16, it's your responsibility to make sure the shutter speed selected is fast enough to avoid losing detail to camera shake, or that the T5i is mounted on a tripod. One thing that new landscape photographers fail to account for is the movement of distant leaves and tree branches. When seeking the ultimate in sharpness, go ahead and use Aperture-priority, but boost ISO sensitivity a bit, if necessary, to provide a sufficiently fast shutter speed, whether shooting handheld or with a tripod.

- **Specific landscape situations.** Aperture-priority is also useful when you have no objection to using a long shutter speed, or, particularly, *want* the T5i to select one. Waterfalls are a perfect example. You can use A mode, set your camera to ISO 100, use a small f/stop, and let the camera select a longer shutter speed that will allow the water to blur as it flows. Indeed, you might need to use a neutral-density filter to get a sufficiently long shutter speed. But Aperture-priority mode is a good start.

- **Portrait photography.** Portraits are the most common applications of selective focus. A medium large aperture (say, f/5.6 or f/8) with a longer lens/zoom setting (in the 85mm–135mm range) will allow the background behind your portrait subject to blur. A *very* large aperture (I frequently shoot wide open with my 85mm f/1.2 lens) lets you apply selective focus to your subject's *face*. With a three-quarters view of your subject, as long as their eyes are sharp, it's okay if the far ear or their hair is out of focus.

- **When you want to ensure optimal sharpness.** All lenses have an aperture or two at which they perform best, providing the level of sharpness you expect from a camera with the resolution of the T5i. That's usually about two stops down from wide open, and thus will vary depending on the maximum aperture of the lens. My 85mm f/1.2 is good wide open, but it's even sharper at f/2.8 or f/4; I shoot my 70-200mm f/2.8 wide open at concerts, but, if I can use f/4 instead, I'll get better results. Aperture-priority allows me to use each lens at its very best f/stop.

- **Close-up/Macro photography.** Depth-of-field is typically very shallow when shooting macro photos, and you'll want to choose your f/stop carefully. Perhaps you need the smallest aperture you can get away with to maximize DOF. Or, you might want to use a wider stop to emphasize your subject, as I did with the photo of the owl in Figure 4.16. A mode comes in very useful when shooting close-up pictures. Because macro work is frequently done with the T5i mounted on a tripod, and your close-up subjects, if not living creatures, may not be moving much, a longer shutter speed isn't a problem. Aperture-priority (Av mode) can be your preferred choice.

# Shutter-Priority

Shutter-priority (Tv) is the inverse of Aperture-priority: you choose the shutter speed you'd like to use, and the camera's metering system selects the appropriate f/stop. Perhaps you're shooting action photos and you want to use the absolute fastest shutter speed available with your camera; in other cases, you might want to use a slow shutter speed to add some blur to a ballet photo that would be mundane if the action were completely frozen (see Figure 4.19, later in this section). Shutter-priority mode gives you some control over how much action-freezing capability your digital camera brings to bear in a particular situation, as you can see in Figure 4.17.

You'll also encounter the same problem as with Aperture-priority when you select a shutter speed that's too long or too short for correct exposure under some conditions. I've shot outdoor soccer games on sunny fall evenings and used Shutter-priority mode to lock in a 1/1,000th second shutter speed, which triggered the blinking warning, even with the lens wide open.

Like Av mode, it's possible to choose an inappropriate shutter speed. If that's the case, the maximum aperture of your lens (to indicate underexposure) or the minimum aperture (to indicate overexposure) will blink.

When to use Shutter-priority:

■ **To reduce blur from subject motion.** Set the shutter speed of the T5i to a higher value to reduce the amount of blur from subjects that are moving. The exact speed will vary depending on how fast your subject is moving and how much blur is acceptable. You might want to freeze a basketball player in mid-dunk with a 1/1000th second shutter speed, or use 1/250th second to allow the spinning wheels of a motocross racer to blur a tiny bit to add the feeling of motion.

**Figure 4.17**
Lock the shutter at a slow speed to introduce a little blur into an action shot, seen here in the sticks, hands, and faces of the hockey players.

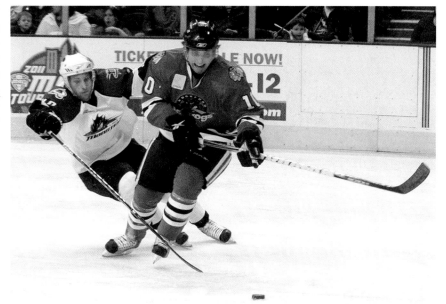

■ **To add blur from subject motion.** There are times when you want a subject to blur, say, when shooting waterfalls with the camera set for a one- or two-second exposure in Shutter-priority mode.

■ **To add blur from camera motion when *you* are moving.** Say you're panning to follow a pair of relay runners. You might want to use Shutter-priority mode and set the T5i for 1/60th second, so that the background will blur as you pan with the runners. The shutter speed will be fast enough to provide a sharp image of the athletes.

■ **To reduce blur from camera motion when *you* are moving.** In other situations, the camera may be in motion, say, because you're shooting from a moving train or auto, and you want to minimize the amount of blur caused by the motion of the camera. Shutter-priority is a good choice here, too.

■ **Landscape photography handheld.** If you can't use a tripod for your landscape shots, you'll still probably want the sharpest image possible. Shutter-priority can allow you to specify a shutter speed that's fast enough to reduce or eliminate the effects of camera shake. Just make sure that your ISO setting is high enough that the T5i will select an aperture with sufficient depth-of-field, too.

■ **Concerts, stage performances.** I shoot a lot of concerts with my 70-200mm f/2.8 lens, and have discovered that, when image stabilization is taken into account, a shutter speed of 1/180th second is fast enough to eliminate the effects of camera shake from handholding the T5i with this lens, and also to avoid blur from the movement of all but the most energetic performers. I use Shutter-priority and set the ISO so the camera will select an aperture in the f/4-5.6 range.

## Program Mode

Program mode (P) uses the T5i's built-in smarts to select the correct f/stop and shutter speed using a database of picture information that tells it which combination of shutter speed and aperture will work best for a particular photo. If the correct exposure cannot be achieved at the current ISO setting, the shutter speed or aperture indicator in the viewfinder will blink, indicating under- or overexposure. You can then boost or reduce the ISO to increase or decrease sensitivity.

The T5i's recommended exposure can be overridden if you want. Use the EV setting feature (described later, because it also applies to Tv and Av modes) to add or subtract exposure from the metered value. And, as I mentioned earlier in this chapter, you can change from the recommended setting to an equivalent setting (as shown in Table 4.1) that produces the same exposure, but using a different combination of f/stop and shutter speed. To accomplish this:

1. Press the shutter release halfway to lock in the current base exposure, or press the AE Lock button (*) on the back of the camera (in which case the * indicator will illuminate in the viewfinder to show that the exposure has been locked).

2. Spin the Main Dial to change the shutter speed (the T5i will adjust the f/stop to match).

Your adjustment remains in force for a single exposure; if you want to change from the recommended settings for the next exposure, you'll need to repeat those steps.

When to use Program mode priority:

- **When you're in a hurry to get a grab shot.** The T5i will do a pretty good job of calculating an appropriate exposure for you, without any input from you.
- **When you hand your camera to a novice.** Set the T5i to P, hand the camera to your friend, relative, or trustworthy stranger you meet in front of the Eiffel Tower, point to the shutter release button and viewfinder, and say, "Look through here, and press this button."
- **When no special shutter speed or aperture settings are needed.** If your subject doesn't require special anti- or pro-blur techniques, and depth-of-field or selective focus aren't important, use P as a general-purpose setting. You can still make adjustments to increase/decrease depth-of-field or add/reduce motion blur with a minimum of fuss.

## Manual Exposure

Part of being an experienced photographer comes from knowing when to rely on your Rebel T5i's automation (including Scene Intelligent Auto, Creative Auto, or P mode), when to go semi-automatic (with Tv or Av), and when to set exposure manually (using M). Some photographers actually prefer to set their exposure manually, as the T5i will be happy to provide an indication of when its metering system judges your settings provide the proper exposure, using the analog exposure scale at the bottom of the viewfinder and on the status LCD.

Manual exposure can come in handy in some situations. You might be taking a silhouette photo and find that none of the exposure modes or EV correction features give you exactly the effect you want. For example, when I shot the ballet dancer in Figure 4.18 in front of a mostly dark background highlighted by an illuminated curtain off to the right, there was no way any of my Rebel T5i's exposure modes would be able to interpret the scene the way I wanted to shoot it, even with Spot metering, which didn't have a narrow enough field-of-view from my position. So, I took a couple test exposures, and set the exposure manually using the exact shutter speed and f/stop I needed. You might be working in a studio environment using multiple flash units. The additional flash are triggered by slave devices (gadgets that set off the flash when they sense the light from another flash, or, perhaps from a radio or infrared remote control). Your camera's exposure meter doesn't compensate for the extra illumination, and can't interpret the flash exposure at all, so you need to set the aperture manually.

Because, depending on your proclivities, you might not need to set exposure manually very often, you should still make sure you understand how it works. Fortunately, the Rebel T5i makes setting exposure manually very easy. Just set the Mode Dial to M, turn the Main Dial to set the shutter speed, and hold down the Av button while rotating the Main Dial to adjust the aperture. Press the shutter release halfway or press the AE Lock button, and the exposure scale in the viewfinder shows you how far your chosen setting diverges from the metered exposure.

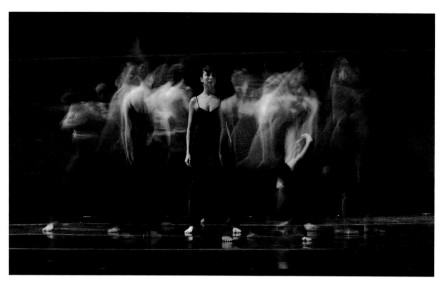

**Figure 4.18**
Manual exposure allows selecting both f/stop and shutter speed, especially useful when you're experimenting, as with this shot of ballet dancers.

When to use manual exposure:

■ **When working in the studio.** If you're working in a studio environment, you generally have total control over the lighting and can set exposure exactly as you want. The last thing you need is for the T5i to interpret the scene and make adjustments of its own. Use M, and shutter speed, aperture, and (as long as you don't use ISO-Auto) the ISO setting are totally up to you.

■ **When using non-dedicated flash.** External Canon dedicated flash units are cool, and can even be used to coordinate use of your T5i's internal flash. But if you're working with a non-compatible flash unit, particularly studio flash plugged into a PC/X sync adapter mounted on the hot shoe, the camera has no clue about the intensity of the flash, so you'll have to dial in the appropriate aperture manually.

■ **If you're using a handheld light meter.** Determining that appropriate aperture, both for flash exposures and shots taken under continuous lighting, can be determined by a handheld light meter, flash meter, or combo meter that measures both kinds of illumination. With an external meter, you can measure highlights, shadows, backgrounds, or additional subjects separately, and use Manual exposure to make your settings.

■ **When you want to outsmart the metering system.** Your T5i's metering system is "trained" to react to unusual lighting situations, such as backlighting, extra bright illumination, or low-key images with murky shadows. In many cases, it can counter these "problems" and produce a well-exposed image. But what if you don't *want* a well-exposed image? Manual exposure allows you to produce silhouettes in backlit situations, wash out all the middle tones to produce a luminous look, or underexpose to create a moody or ominous dark-toned photograph.

# Adjusting Exposure with ISO Settings

Another way of adjusting exposures is by changing the ISO sensitivity setting. Sometimes photographers forget about this option, because the common practice is to set the ISO once for a particular shooting session (say, at ISO 100 or 200 for bright sunlight outdoors, or ISO 800 when shooting indoors) and then forget about ISO. ISOs higher than ISO 100 or 200 are seen as "bad" or "necessary evils." However, changing the ISO is a valid way of adjusting exposure settings, particularly with the Canon EOS Rebel T5i, which produces good results at ISO settings that create grainy, unusable pictures with some other camera models.

Indeed, I find myself using ISO adjustment as a convenient alternate way of adding or subtracting EV when shooting in Manual mode, and as a quick way of choosing equivalent exposures when in Auto or semi-automatic modes. For example, I've selected a Manual exposure with both f/stop and shutter speed suitable for my image using, say, ISO 200. I can change the exposure in full-stop increments by pressing the ISO button on top of the camera, and spinning the Main Dial one click at a time. The difference in image quality/noise at the base setting of ISO 200 is negligible if I dial in ISO 100 to reduce exposure a little, or change to ISO 400 to increase exposure. I keep my preferred f/stop and shutter speed, but still adjust the exposure.

Or, perhaps, I am using Tv mode and the metered exposure at ISO 200 is 1/500th second at f/11. If I decide on the spur of the moment I'd rather use 1/500th second at f/8, I can press the ISO button and spin the Main Dial to switch to ISO 100. Of course, it's a good idea to monitor your ISO changes, so you don't end up at ISO 1600 accidentally. ISO settings can, of course, also be used to boost or reduce sensitivity in particular shooting situations. The Rebel T5i can use ISO settings from ISO 100 up to 6400. When Custom Function 2: ISO Expansion is set to 1: On, then ISO can be set manually to H (ISO 25600 equivalent).

The camera can adjust the ISO automatically as appropriate for various lighting conditions. In Basic Zone modes, ISO is normally set between ISO 100 and ISO 3200. When you choose the Auto ISO setting, the T5i adjusts the sensitivity dynamically to suit the subject matter. In Basic Zone Scene Intelligent Auto, Landscape, Close-Up, Sports, Night Portrait, and Flash Off modes, the T5i adjusts ISO between ISO 100 and ISO 3200 as required. In Portrait mode, ISO is fixed at ISO 100, because the T5i attempts to use larger f/stops to blur the background, and the lower ISO setting lends itself to those larger stops.

When Auto ISO is chosen when using Creative Zone modes, sensitivity will be generally set to ISO 100 to ISO 6400 in Program and Av exposure modes.

When using flash, Auto ISO produces a setting of ISO 400 automatically, except when overexposure would occur (as when shooting subjects very close to the camera), in which case a lower setting (down to ISO 100) will be used. If you have an external dedicated flash attached, the T5i can set ISO in the range of 400 to 1600 automatically. That capability can be useful when shooting outdoor field sports at night and other "long distance" flash pictures, particularly with a telephoto lens, because you want to extend the "reach" of your external flash as far as possible (to dozens of feet or more), and boosting the ISO does that. Remember that if the Auto ISO ranges aren't suitable for you, individual ISO values can also be selected in any of the Creative Zone modes.

**Tip**

Find yourself locked out of ISO settings lower than 200 or higher than 6400? Check C.Fn I-03: Highlight Tone Priority, located in the Set-up 4 menu. When set to 1: Enable, only ISO 200 to 6400 can be selected.

# Dealing with Visual Noise

Visual image noise is that random grainy effect that some like to use as a special effect, but which, most of the time, is objectionable because it robs your image of detail even as it adds that "interesting" texture. Noise is caused by two different phenomena: high ISO settings and long exposures.

High ISO noise commonly first appears when you raise your camera's sensitivity setting above ISO 800. With Canon cameras, which are renown for their good ISO noise characteristics, noise may become visible at ISO 1600, and is usually fairly noticeable at ISO 3200. At the H setting (ISO 25600 equivalent), noise is usually quite bothersome, which is why that lofty sensitivity rating is disabled by default and must be activated with ISO expansion using Custom Function I-02. This kind of noise appears as a result of the amplification needed to increase the sensitivity of the sensor. While higher ISOs do pull details out of dark areas, they also amplify non-signal information randomly, creating noise.

A similar noisy phenomenon occurs during long time exposures, which allow more photons to reach the sensor, increasing your ability to capture a picture under low-light conditions. However, the longer exposures also increase the likelihood that some pixels will register random phantom photons, often because the longer an imager is "hot," the warmer it gets, and that heat can be mistaken for photons. There's also a special kind of noise that CMOS sensors like the one used in the T5i are potentially susceptible to. With a CCD, the entire signal is conveyed off the chip and funneled through a single amplifier and analog-to-digital conversion circuit. Any noise introduced there is, at least, consistent. CMOS imagers, on the other hand, contain millions of individual amplifiers and A/D converters, all working in unison. Because all these circuits don't necessarily process in precisely the same way all the time, they can introduce something called fixed-pattern noise into the image data.

Fortunately, Canon's electronics geniuses have done an exceptional job minimizing noise from all causes in the T5i. Even so, you might still want to apply the optional long exposure noise reduction. This type of noise reduction involves the T5i taking a second, blank exposure, and comparing the random pixels in that image with the photograph you just took. Pixels that coincide in the two represent noise and can safely be suppressed. This noise reduction system, called *dark frame subtraction,* effectively doubles the amount of time required to take a picture, and is used only for exposures longer than one second. Noise reduction can reduce the amount of detail in your picture, as some image information may be removed along with the noise. So, you might want to use this feature with moderation. Some types of images don't require noise reduction, because the grainy pattern tends to blend into the overall scene.

To activate your T5i's long exposure noise reduction features, go to the Shooting 3 menu, as explained further in Chapter 8.

You can also apply noise reduction to a lesser extent using Photoshop, and when converting RAW files to some other format, using your favorite RAW converter, or an industrial-strength product like Noise Ninja (www.picturecode.com) to wipe out noise after you've already taken the picture.

# Making EV Changes

Sometimes you'll want more or less exposure than indicated by the T5i's metering system. Perhaps you want to underexpose to create a silhouette effect, or overexpose to produce a high-key look. It's easy to use the T5i's Exposure Compensation system to override the exposure recommendations, available in any Creative Zone mode except Manual. There are two ways to make exposure value (EV) changes with the Rebel T5i. One method is fast and a bit clumsy to use, especially if your fingers aren't well coordinated. The other method takes a few seconds longer, but can be done smoothly by the most fumble-fingered among us.

## Fast EV Changes

Activate the exposure meters by tapping the shutter release button. Then, just hold down the AV button (located on the back, next to the upper-right corner of the LCD) and rotate the Main Dial to the right to make the image brighter (add exposure), and to the left to make the image darker (subtract exposure). The exposure scale in the viewfinder and on the LCD indicates the EV change you've made. The EV change you've made remains for the exposures that follow, until you manually zero out the EV setting with the AV button + Main Dial. EV changes are ignored when using M or any of the Basic Zone modes.

## Slower EV Changes

If you find yourself not turning the Main Dial quickly enough after you tap the shutter release button, try the second method for making EV changes with the T5i. It can be a little slower, but gives you more time to dial in your EV adjustment. You also have the option of setting exposure bracketing at the same time:

1. Press the MENU button and navigate to the Expo. Comp./AEB entry on the Shooting 2 menu.

2. When the screen appears, use the touch screen or press the left/right cross keys to add or subtract EV adjustment. The screen has helpful labels (Darker on the left and Brighter on the right) to make sure you're adding/subtracting when you really want to. (See Figure 4.19.) Note that you can also set exposure bracketing, as discussed in Chapter 8, by rotating the Main Dial while viewing this screen. (See Figure 4.20.)

3. Choose SET to confirm your choice.

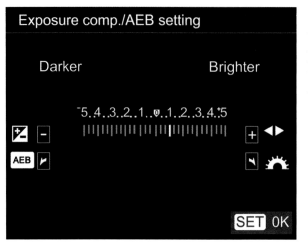

**Figure 4.19**
EV changes are displayed on the scale in the LCD when using the Shooting 2 menu.

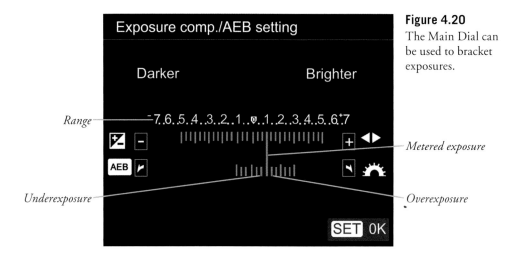

**Figure 4.20**
The Main Dial can be used to bracket exposures.

# Bracketing

Bracketing is a method for shooting several consecutive exposures using different settings, as a way of improving the odds that one will be exactly right. Before digital cameras took over the universe, it was common to bracket exposures, shooting, say, a series of three photos at 1/125th second, but varying the f/stop from f/8 to f/11 to f/16. In practice, smaller than whole-stop increments were used for greater precision. Plus, it was just as common to keep the same aperture and vary the shutter speed, although in the days before electronic shutters, film cameras often had only whole increment shutter speeds available. Figure 4.21 shows a typical bracketed series.

Today, cameras like the T5i can bracket exposures much more precisely, and bracket white balance as well (using the WB Shift/Bkt entry found in the Shooting 2 menu and described in Chapter 8). While WB bracketing is sometimes used when getting color absolutely correct in the camera is

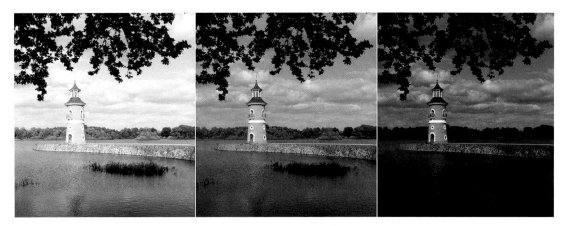

**Figure 4.21** In this bracketed series you can see overexposure (left), metered exposure (center), and underexposure (right).

important, autoexposure bracketing (AEB) is used much more often. When this feature is activated, the T5i takes three (and only three) consecutive photos: one at the metered "correct" exposure, one with less exposure, and one with more exposure, using an increment of your choice up to plus 2/minus 2 stops. (Choose between increments by setting Custom Function I-01 to 0 [1/3 stop] or 1 [1/2 stop].) In Av mode, the shutter speed will change, while in Tv mode, the aperture speed will change.

Using AEB is trickier than it needs to be, but has been made more flexible than with some earlier Rebel models. With the T5i you can now choose to bracket only overexposures or underexposures—a very useful improvement! Just follow these steps:

1. **Activate the Expo. Comp./AEB screen.** Press the MENU button and navigate to the Shooting 2 menu, where you'll find the Expo. Comp./AEB option. Choose SET to select this choice.

2. **Set the bracket range.** Rotate the Main Dial to spread out or contract the three bars to include the desired range you want to cover. For example, in Figure 4.22 (top), the red highlighted bars are separated from the center bar by a full f/stop, so the bracketing will produce one image at one stop *less* than the zero point (the large center bar), one at the zero point, and one at one stop more than that. Figure 4.22 (bottom) shows the bars more widely separated, for a bracketed set two stops under and two stops over the midpoint.

3. **Adjust zero point.** By default, the bracketing is zeroed around the center of the scale, which represents the correct exposure as metered by the T5i. But you might want to have your three bracketed shots all biased toward overexposure or underexposure. Perhaps you feel that the metered exposure will be too dark or too light, and you want the bracketed shots to lean in the other direction. Use the left/right cross keys to move the bracket spread toward one end of the scale or the other. Figure 4.22 (top) shows the bracketing biased toward overexposure, while in 4.22 (bottom), the zero point is clustered around underexposure. (Actually, the exposure bar at left will be four stops under the metered exposure, the center bar two stops under, and the right bar at the metered value.)

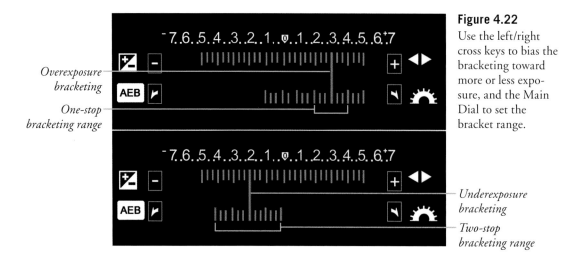

*Overexposure bracketing*

*One-stop bracketing range*

**Figure 4.22**
Use the left/right cross keys to bias the bracketing toward more or less exposure, and the Main Dial to set the bracket range.

*Underexposure bracketing*

*Two-stop bracketing range*

## NON-BRACKETING IS EXPOSURE COMPENSATION

When the three bracket indicators aren't separated, using the left/right cross keys simply, in effect, adds or subtracts exposure compensation. You'll be shooting a "bracketed" set of one picture, with the zero point placed at the portion of the scale you indicated. Until you rotate the Main Dial to separate the three bracket indicators by at least one indicator, this screen just supplies EV adjustment. Also keep in mind that the increments shown will be either 1/3 stop or 1/2 stop, depending on how you've set C.Fn I-01.

4. **Confirm your choice.** Choose SET to enter the settings.

5. **Take your three photos.** You can use Single shooting mode to take the trio of pictures yourself, use the self-timer (which will expose all three pictures after the delay), or switch to Continuous shooting mode to take the three pictures in a burst.

6. **Monitor your shots.** As the images are captured, three indicators will appear on the exposure scale in the viewfinder, with one of them flashing for each bracketed photo, showing when the base exposure, underexposure, and overexposure are taken.

7. **Turn bracketing off when done.** Bracketing remains in effect when the set is taken so you can continue shooting bracketed exposures until you use the electronic flash, turn off the camera, or return to the menu to cancel bracketing.

## NOTE

AEB is disabled when you're using Multi Shot Noise Reduction, taking long time exposures with the Bulb setting, or have enabled the Auto Lighting Optimizer in the Shooting 2 menu (in which case the optimizer will probably override and nullify bracketing).

# Working with HDR

High dynamic range (HDR) photography is quite the rage these days, and entire books have been written on the subject. It's not really a new technique—film photographers have been combining multiple exposures for ages to produce a single image of, say, an interior room while maintaining detail in the scene visible through the windows.

Suppose you wanted to photograph a dimly lit room that had a bright window showing an outdoors scene. Proper exposure for the room might be on the order of 1/60th second at f/2.8 at ISO 200, while the outdoors scene probably would require f/11 at 1/400th second. That's almost a 7 EV step difference (approximately 7 f/stops) and well beyond the dynamic range of any digital camera, including the Canon T5i.

Until camera sensors gain much higher dynamic ranges (which may not be as far into the distant future as we think), special tricks like Active D-Lighting and HDR photography will remain basic tools. With the Canon T5i, you can create in-camera HDR exposures, or shoot HDR the old-fashioned way—with separate bracketed exposures that are later combined in a tool like Photomatix or Adobe's Merge to HDR Pro image editing feature. I'm going to show you how to use both.

## HDR Backlight Control

The T5i's in-camera HDR feature, available as a Special Scene option when the Mode dial is in the SCN position, is simple, not particularly flexible, but still surprisingly effective in creating high dynamic range images. It's also remarkably easy to use. Although it combines only three images to create a single HDR photograph, and while it's not as good as the manual HDR method I'll describe in the section after this one, it's a *lot* faster.

Figure 4.23 (left) shows you a typical situation in which you might want to use this setting. When the exposure is set for the interior of the cathedral, the beautiful backlit stained glass windows are washed out and have no detail. When the exposure is adjusted to produce detail in the glass panes, the rest of the cathedral goes dark. The quickie solution is to use the T5i's HDR Backlight Control. It captures three consecutive images and then merges them to preserve both highlight and shadow detail, as you can see in Figure 4.24, which has a much fuller range of tones.

Here are some tips for using this feature (these also apply to the Handheld Night Scene mode, which also merges multiple shots to create a single improved image):

- **Use a tripod if possible.** Because there may be some camera movement between the continuous shots, you'll get better results if you mount the T5i on a tripod.

- **Moving objects may produce ghosts.** In this case, there may be some *subject* motion between shots, producing "ghost" effects.

- **Misalignment.** If you *don't* use a tripod, this scene mode does a good job of realigning your multiple images when they are merged. However, it can't do a perfect job, particularly with repetitive patterns that are difficult for the camera's "brains" to sort out. Some misalignment is possible.

- **Unwanted cropping.** Because the processor needs to be able to shift each individual image slightly in any (or all) of four directions, it needs to crop the image slightly to trim out any non-image areas that result. Your final image will be slightly smaller than one shot in other modes.

- **Can't use RAW or RAW+L.** Your image will be recorded as a Large JPEG only.

- **The process takes time.** Forget about firing off a large number of HDR Backlight Control shots in a row. After the T5i captures its three images, it takes a few seconds to process them and save your final image. Be patient.

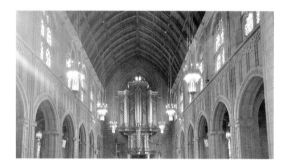 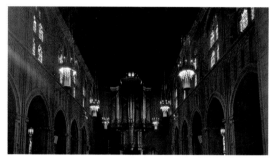

**Figure 4.23** Exposing for the cathedral interior produces overexposed backlit stained glass windows (left), while exposing for the windows captures a murky cathedral interior.

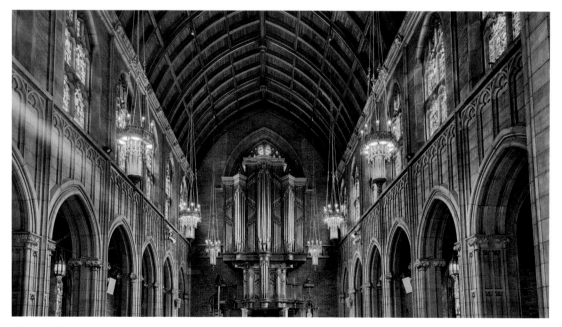

**Figure 4.24** The T5i's HDR Backlight Control mode captures a full range of tones.

# Bracketing and Merge to HDR

As I mentioned, HDR photography involves shooting two or three or more images at different bracketed exposures, giving you an "underexposed" version with lots of detail in highlights that would otherwise be washed out; an "overexposed" rendition that preserves detail in the shadows; and several intermediate shots. These are combined to produce a single image that has an amazing amount of detail throughout the scene's entire tonal range.

I call this technique a fad because the reason it exists in the first place is due to a (temporary, I hope) defect in current digital camera sensors. It's presently impossible to capture the full range of brightness that we perceive; digital cameras, including the EOS T5i, can't even grab the full range of brightness that *film* can see, as I showed you in Figures 4.2 and 4.3 at the beginning of this chapter.

But as the megapixel race slows down, sensor designers have already begun designing capture electronics that have larger density (dynamic) ranges, and cameras like the T5i with its HDR Backlight Control feature, will eventually produce images similar to what we're getting now with HDR manipulation in image editors.

When you're using Merge to HDR Pro, a feature found in Adobe Photoshop (similar functions are available in other programs, including the Mac/PC utility Photomatix [www.hdrsoft.com; free to try, $99 to buy]), you'd take several pictures. As I mentioned earlier, one would be exposed for the shadows, one for the highlights, and perhaps one for the midtones. Then, you'd use the Merge to HDR command (or the equivalent in other software) to combine all of the images into one HDR image that integrates the well-exposed sections of each version. You can use the EOS T5i's bracketing feature to produce those images.

The next steps show you how to combine the separate exposures into one merged high dynamic range image. The sample images in Figure 4.25 show the results you can get from a four-shot (manually) bracketed sequence.

The images should be as identical as possible, except for exposure. So, it's a good idea to mount the T5i on a tripod, use a remote release, and take all the exposures at once. Just follow these steps:

1. **Set up the camera.** Mount the T5i on a tripod.
2. **Choose an f/stop.** Set the camera for Manual exposure and select an aperture that will provide a correct exposure at your initial settings for the series of manually bracketed shots. *And then leave this adjustment alone!* You don't want the aperture to change for your series, as that would change the depth-of-field. You want the T5i to adjust exposure *only* using the shutter speed.
3. **Choose manual focus.** You don't want the focus to change between shots, so set the T5i to manual focus, and carefully focus your shot.
4. **Choose RAW exposures.** Set the camera to take RAW files, which will give you the widest range of tones in your images.

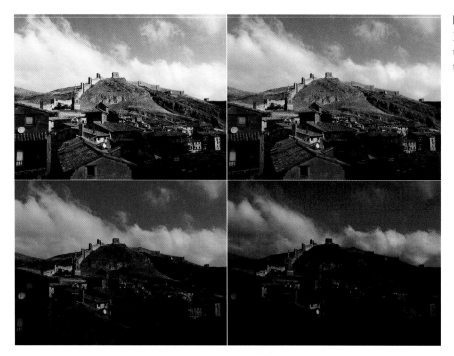

**Figure 4.25**
Four bracketed photos should look like this.

5. **Take your bracketed set.** Press the button on the remote (or carefully press the shutter release or use the self-timer) and take the set of bracketed exposures, adjusting the shutter speed manually. Try spacing your four shots one f/stop apart.

6. **Continue with the Merge to HDR Pro steps listed next.** You can also use a different program, such as Photomatix, if you know how to use it.

The next steps show you how to combine the separate exposures into one merged high dynamic range image.

1. **Copy your images to your computer.** If you use an application to transfer the files to your computer, make sure it does not make any adjustments to brightness, contrast, or exposure. You want the real raw information for Merge to HDR Pro to work with.

2. **Activate Merge to HDR Pro.** Choose File > Automate > Merge to HDR Pro.

3. **Select the photos to be merged.** Use the Browse feature to locate and select your photos to be merged. You'll note a checkbox that can be used to automatically align the images if they were not taken with the camera mounted on a rock-steady support. This will adjust for any slight movement of the camera that might have occurred when you changed exposure settings.

4. **Choose parameters (optional).** The first time you use Merge to HDR Pro, you can let the program work with its default parameters. Once you've played with the feature a few times, you can read the Adobe help files and learn more about the options than I can present in this non-software-oriented camera guide.

**Figure 4.26**
You'll end up with an extended dynamic range photo like this one.

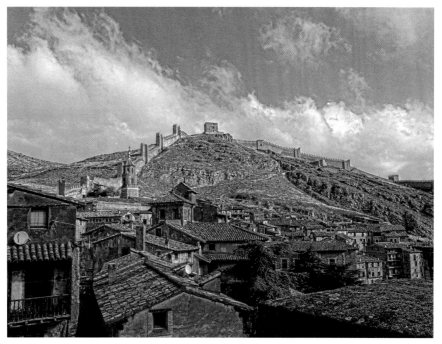

5. **Click OK.** The merger begins.

6. **Save.** Once HDR merge has done its thing, save the file to your computer.

If you do everything correctly, you'll end up with a photo like the one shown in Figure 4.26.

What if you don't have the opportunity, inclination, or skills to create several images at different exposures, as described? If you shoot in RAW format, you can still use Merge to HDR, working with a *single* original image file. What you do is import the image into Photoshop several times, using Adobe Camera Raw to create multiple copies of the file at different exposure levels.

For example, you'd create one copy that's too dark, so the shadows lose detail, but the highlights are preserved. Create another copy with the shadows intact and allow the highlights to wash out. Then, you can use Merge to HDR to combine the two and end up with a finished image that has the extended dynamic range you're looking for. (This concludes the image-editing portion of the chapter. We now return you to our alternate sponsor: photography.)

# Fixing Exposures with Histograms

Your T5i's histograms are a simplified display of the numbers of pixels at each of 256 brightness levels, producing an interesting mountain range effect. Although separate charts may be provided for brightness and the red, green, and blue channels, when you first start using histograms, you'll want to concentrate on the brightness histogram.

Each vertical line in the graph represents the number of pixels in the image for each brightness value, from 0 (black) on the left to 255 (white) on the right. The vertical axis measures that number of pixels at each level. The T5i provides a "live" histogram on the screen when using Live View mode, and offers two different histogram views in Playback mode when using the shooting information display (Figure 4.27, left) and histogram display (Figure 4.28, right). The former shows a simple brightness/luminance histogram, while the histogram display allows you to see brightness as well as separate red, green, and blue channel histograms.

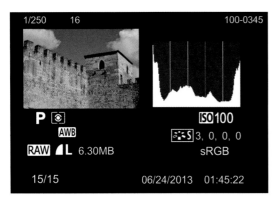
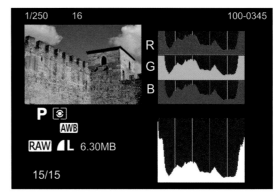

**Figure 4.27**                     **Figure 4.28**

Shooting information display, with luminance histogram (left); Histogram display with luminance, red, green, and blue histograms (right).

## Histograms and Contrast

Although histograms are most often used to fine-tune exposure, you can glean other information from them, such as the relative contrast of the image. Figure 4.29 shows a histogram representing an image having normal contrast. In such an image, most of the pixels are spread across the image, with a healthy distribution of tones throughout the midtone section of the graph. That large peak at the right side of the graph represents all those light tones in the sky. A normal-contrast image you shoot may have less sky area, and less of a peak at the right side, but notice that very few pixels hug the right edge of the histogram, indicating that the lightest tones are not being clipped because they are off the chart.

With a lower-contrast image, like the one shown in Figure 4.30, the basic shape of the previous histogram will remain recognizable, but gradually will be compressed together to cover a smaller area of the gray spectrum. The squished shape of the histogram is caused by all the grays in the original image being represented by a limited number of gray tones in a smaller range of the scale.

Instead of the darkest tones of the image reaching into the black end of the spectrum and the whitest tones extending to the lightest end, there is a small gap at either end. Consequently, the blackest areas of the scene are now represented by a light gray, and the whites by a somewhat lighter gray. The overall contrast of the image is reduced. Because all the darker tones are actually a middle gray or lighter, the scene in this version of the photo appears lighter as well.

Going in the other direction, increasing the contrast of an image produces a histogram like the one shown in Figure 4.31. In this case, the tonal range is now spread over the entire width of the chart, but, except for the bright sky (which you can see peaks at right), there is not much variation in the middle tones; the mountain "peaks" are not very high. When you stretch the grayscale in both directions like this, the darkest tones become darker (that may not be possible) and the lightest tones become lighter (ditto). In fact, shades that might have been gray before can change to black or white as they are moved toward either end of the scale.

**Figure 4.29**
This image has fairly normal contrast, even though there is a peak of light tones at the right side representing the sky.

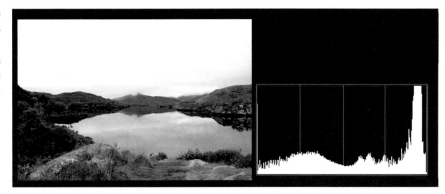

**Figure 4.30**
This low-contrast image has all the tones squished into one section of the grayscale.

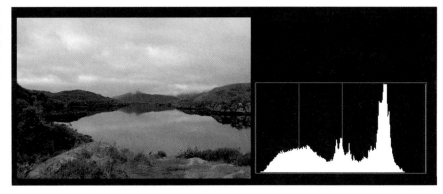

**Figure 4.31**
A high-contrast image produces a histogram in which the tones are spread out.

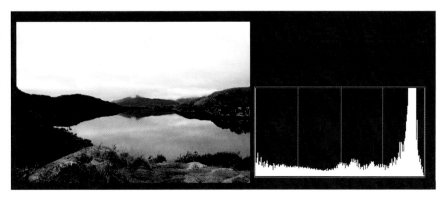

The effect of increasing contrast may be to move some tones off either end of the scale altogether, while spreading the remaining grays over a smaller number of locations on the spectrum. That's exactly the case in the example shown. The number of possible tones is smaller and the image appears harsher.

## Understanding Histograms

The important thing to remember when working with the histogram display in your T5i is that changing the exposure does *not* change the contrast of an image. The curves illustrated in the previous three examples remain exactly the same shape when you increase or decrease exposure. I repeat: The proportional distribution of grays shown in the histogram doesn't change when exposure changes; it is neither stretched nor compressed. However, the tones as a whole are moved toward one end of the scale or the other, depending on whether you're increasing or decreasing exposure. You'll be able to see that in some illustrations that follow.

So, as you reduce exposure, tones gradually move to the black end (and off the scale), while the reverse is true when you increase exposure. The contrast within the image is changed only to the extent that some of the tones can no longer be represented when they are moved off the scale.

To change the *contrast* of an image, you must do one of four things:

- **Change the T5i's contrast setting** using the menu system. You'll find these adjustments in your camera's Picture Styles, as explained in Chapter 8.
- **Use your camera's tone "booster."** The Highlight Tone Priority and Auto Lighting Optimizer features, described in Chapter 8, can also adjust contrast.
- **Alter the contrast of the scene itself,** for example, by using a fill light or reflectors to add illumination to shadows that are too dark.
- **Attempt to adjust contrast in post-processing** using your image editor or RAW file converter. You may use features such as Levels or Curves (in Photoshop, Photoshop Elements, and many other image editors), or work with HDR software to cherry-pick the best values in shadows and highlights from multiple images.

Of the four of these, the third—changing the contrast of the scene—is the most desirable, because attempting to fix contrast by fiddling with the tonal values is unlikely to be a perfect remedy. However, adding a little contrast can be successful because you can discard some tones to make the image more contrasty. However, the opposite is much more difficult. An overly contrasty image rarely can be fixed, because you can't add information that isn't there in the first place.

What you *can* do is adjust the exposure so that the tones *that are already present in the scene* are captured correctly. Figure 4.32 shows the histogram for an image that is badly underexposed. You can guess from the shape of the histogram that many of the dark tones to the left of the graph have been clipped off. There's plenty of room on the right side for additional pixels to reside without having them become overexposed. So, you can increase the exposure (either by changing the f/stop or shutter speed, or by adding an EV value) to produce the corrected histogram shown in Figure 4.33.

Conversely, if your histogram looks like the one shown in Figure 4.34, with bright tones pushed off the right edge of the chart, you have an overexposed image, and you can correct it by reducing exposure. In addition to the histogram, the T5i has its Highlights feature, which shows areas that are overexposed with flashing tones (often called "blinkies") in the review screen. Depending on the importance of this "clipped" detail, you can adjust exposure or leave it alone. For example, if all the dark-coded areas in the review are in a background that you care little about, you can forget about them and not change the exposure, but if such areas appear in facial details of your subject, you may want to make some adjustments.

**Figure 4.32**
A histogram of an underexposed image may look like this.

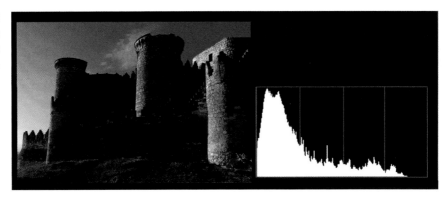

**Figure 4.33**
Adding exposure will produce a histogram like this one.

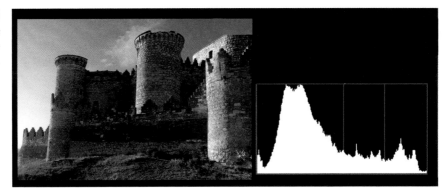

**Figure 4.34**
A histogram of an overexposed image will show clipping at the right side.

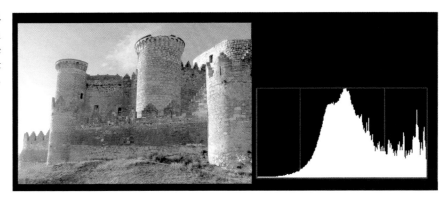

In working with histograms, your goal should be to have all the tones in an image spread out between the edges, with none clipped off at the left and right sides. Underexposing (to preserve highlights) should be done only as a last resort, because retrieving the underexposed shadows in your image editor will frequently increase the noise, even if you're working with RAW files. A better course of action is to expose for the highlights, but, when the subject matter makes it practical, fill in the shadows with additional light, using reflectors, fill flash, or other techniques rather than allowing them to be seriously underexposed.

The more you work with histograms, the more useful they become. One of the first things that histogram veterans notice is that it's possible to overexpose one channel even if the overall exposure appears to be correct. For example, flower photographers soon discover that it's really, really difficult to get a good picture of a rose. The exposure and luminance histogram may look okay—but there's no detail in the rose's petals. Looking at the RGB histograms can show why: the red channel is probably blown out. If you look at the red histogram, you'll probably see a peak at the right edge that indicates that highlight information has been lost. In fact, the green channel may be blown, too, and so the green parts of the flower also lack detail. Only the blue channel's histogram would typically be entirely contained within the boundaries of the chart, and, on first glance, the white luminance histogram at top of the column of graphs seems fairly normal.

Any of the primary channels, red, green, or blue, can blow out all by themselves, although bright reds seem to be the most common problem area. More difficult to diagnose are overexposed tones in one of the "in-between" hues on the color wheel. Overexposed yellows (which are very common) will be shown by blowouts in *both* the red and green channels. Too-bright cyans will manifest as excessive blue and green highlights, while overexposure in the red and blue channels reduces detail in magenta colors. As you gain experience, you'll be able to see exactly how anomalies in the RGB channels translate into poor highlights and murky shadows.

The only way to correct for color channel blowouts is to reduce exposure. As I mentioned earlier, you might want to consider filling in the shadows with additional light to keep them from becoming too dark when you decrease exposure. In practice, you'll want to monitor the red channel most closely, followed by the blue channel, and slightly decrease exposure to see if that helps. Because of the way our eyes perceive color, we are more sensitive to variations in green, so green channel blowouts are less of a problem, unless your main subject is heavily colored in that hue. If you plan on photographing a frog hopping around on your front lawn, you'll want to be extra careful to preserve detail in the green channel, using bracketing or other exposure techniques outlined in this chapter.

While you can often recover poorly exposed photos in your image editor, your best bet is to arrive at the correct exposure in the camera, minimizing the tweaks that you have to make in post-processing.

# Basic Zone Modes

The final factor in the exposure equation is one that your T5i offers little control over: Basic Zone modes. Your Canon Rebel T5i includes Basic Zone shooting modes that can automatically make all the basic settings needed for certain types of shooting situations, such as Portraits, Landscapes, Close-ups, Sports, Night Portraits, and "No-Flash zone" pictures. They are especially useful when you suddenly encounter a picture-taking opportunity and don't have time to decide exactly which Creative Zone mode you want to use. Instead, you can spin the Mode Dial to the appropriate Basic Zone mode and fire away, knowing that, at least, you have a fighting chance of getting a good or usable photo.

Basic Zone modes are also helpful when you're just learning to use your T5i. Once you've learned how to operate your camera, you'll probably prefer one of the Creative Zone modes that provide more control over shooting options. The Basic Zone scene modes may give you few options or none at all. The AF mode, drive mode, and metering mode are all set for you. Here are the modes available directly from the Mode Dial:

- **Scene Intelligent Auto.** All the photographer has to do in this mode is press the shutter release button. Every other decision is made by the camera's electronics.

- **Flash Off.** Absolutely prevents the flash from flipping up and firing, which you might want in some situations, such as religious ceremonies, museums, classical music concerts, and your double-naught spy activities.

- **Creative Auto.** Similar to Scene Intelligent Auto, Creative Auto, like the scene modes described next, allows you to change some parameters.

- **Portrait.** This mode tends to use wider f/stops and faster shutter speeds, providing blurred backgrounds and images with no camera shake. If you hold down the shutter release, the T5i will take a continuous sequence of photos, which can be useful in capturing fleeting expressions in portrait situations.

- **Landscape.** The T5i tries to use smaller f/stops for more depth-of-field, and boosts saturation slightly for richer colors.

- **Close-Up.** This mode is similar to the Portrait setting, with wider f/stops to isolate your close-up subjects, and high shutter speeds to eliminate the camera shake that's accentuated at close focusing distances. However, if you have your camera mounted on a tripod or are using an image-stabilized (IS) lens, you might want to use the Creative Zone Aperture-priority (Av) mode instead, so you can specify a smaller f/stop with additional depth-of-field.

- **Sports.** In this mode, the T5i tries to use high shutter speeds to freeze action, switches to continuous shooting to allow taking a quick sequence of pictures with one press of the shutter release, and uses AI Servo AF to continually refocus as your subject moves around in the frame. You can find more information on autofocus options in Chapter 5.

With the Mode Dial in the SCN position, you can also choose:

- **Night Portrait.** Combines flash with ambient light to produce an image that is mainly illuminated by the flash, but the background is exposed by the available light. This mode uses longer exposures, so a tripod, monopod, or IS lens is a must.
- **Handheld Night Scene.** This mode, like HDR Backlight Control, takes multiple shots and combines them into one improved image.
- **HDR Backlight Control.** This mode combines three shots to improve both highlight and shadow detail, as described earlier in this chapter.

# That Quick Control Screen Again

I've previously described how to use the Quick Control screen when working with Creative Zone modes, to change many settings, such as ISO, shutter speed, aperture, and other parameters. When using Basic Zone modes, your options are different. In each case, you can activate the Quick Control screen by pressing the Quick Control button. Then, one of several different screens will appear on your LCD.

## Scene Intelligent Auto/ Auto (No Flash)

In either of these modes, your only choices are Single shooting and Self-timer/10-second remote control. Press the INFO. button to exit.

## Creative Auto Mode

When the Mode Dial is set to Creative Auto, a screen like the one shown in Figure 4.35 appears.

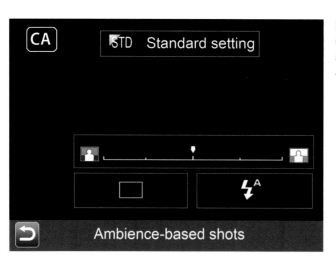

**Figure 4.35**
Quick Control screen in Creative Auto mode.

You can then do one of three things:

- **Change shooting parameters by Ambience.** Press the Quick Control button and then the up cross key to select the ambience box. When the top box on the screen is highlighted, it will display the most recent "ambience" setting you've selected (Standard, unless you've made a change). Ambience is a type of picture style that adjusts parameters like sharpness or color richness to produce a particular look.

  - Press the left/right cross keys or rotate the Main Dial and select from among: Vivid, Soft, Warm, Intense, Cool, Brighter, Darker, or Monochrome.

  - Once you've selected your ambience, if you want to change its intensity, press the down cross key to highlight Effect.

  - You can then rotate the Main Dial to change the Effect to Low, Standard, or Strong. Press the Quick Control button to exit.

- **Press the down cross key to highlight Background: Blurredfl> Sharp.** Then, rotate the Main Dial to adjust the amount of background blurring. The T5i will try to use a larger f/stop to reduce depth-of-field and blur the background, or a smaller f/stop and increased depth-of-field to sharpen the background.

- **Press the down cross key to highlight Drive mode/Flash firing.** Then press the SET button to pop up the Drive mode/Flash firing screen. In this screen, you can rotate the Main Dial to change among the various drive modes, or use the cross keys to switch among flash modes.

## Other Basic Zone Modes

When you select one of the other Basic Zone modes, your options are similar to those in Creative Auto mode:

- **Change shooting parameters by Ambience.** After you've pressed the Q button, when the top box on the screen is highlighted, it will display the most recent "ambience" setting you've selected.

  - Press the left/right cross keys or rotate the Main Dial and select from among: Vivid, Soft, Warm, Intense, Cool, Brighter, Darker, or Monochrome, the same choices available in Creative Auto mode.

  - Once you've selected your Ambience, if you want to change its intensity, press the down cross key to highlight Effect.

  - You can then rotate the Main Dial to change the Effect to Low, Standard, or Strong. Press the Quick Control button to exit.

- **Press the down cross key to highlight Default Settings.** This option is available only if you're using Portrait, Landscape, Close-up, and Sports modes. The prompt in the blue box at the bottom of the screen will change to Shoot by Lighting or Scene Type. You can then rotate the Main Dial to cycle through Default setting, Daylight, Shade, Cloudy, Tungsten Light, Fluorescent Light, or Sunset. You can also press the SET button and see a menu listing each of these options simultaneously.

■ **Press the down cross key to highlight Drive mode/Self-timer.** In this screen, you can press the left/right cross keys or rotate the Main Dial to switch between the available drive mode (either Single shot, or Continuous shooting, depending on the Basic Zone mode selected) and 10-second Self-timer/Remote.

Find your desired ambience in Table 4.2.

## Table 4.2  Selecting Ambience

| Ambience Setting | Effect |
| --- | --- |
| Standard | This is the customized set of parameters for each Basic Zone mode, each tailored specifically for Portrait, Landscape, Close-Up, Sports, or other mode. |
| Vivid | Produces a look that is slightly sharper and with richer colors for the relevant Basic Zone mode. |
| Soft | Reduced sharpness for adult portraits, flowers, children, and pets. |
| Warm | Warmer, soft tones. An alternative setting for portraits and other subjects that you want to appear both soft and warm. |
| Intense | Darker tones with increased contrast to emphasize your subject. This setting is great for portraits of men. |
| Cool | Darker, cooler tones. Use with care on human subjects, which aren't always flattered by the icier look this setting can produce. |
| Brighter | Overall lighter image with less contrast. |
| Darker | Produces a darker image. |
| Monochrome | Choose from black-and-white, sepia, or blue (cyanotype) toning. |

## PREVIEW AMBIENCE

If you set ambience in Live View mode, the T5i will provide a preview image that simulates the effect your ambience setting will have on the finished image. Examples of each ambience setting can be seen in Figure 4.36.

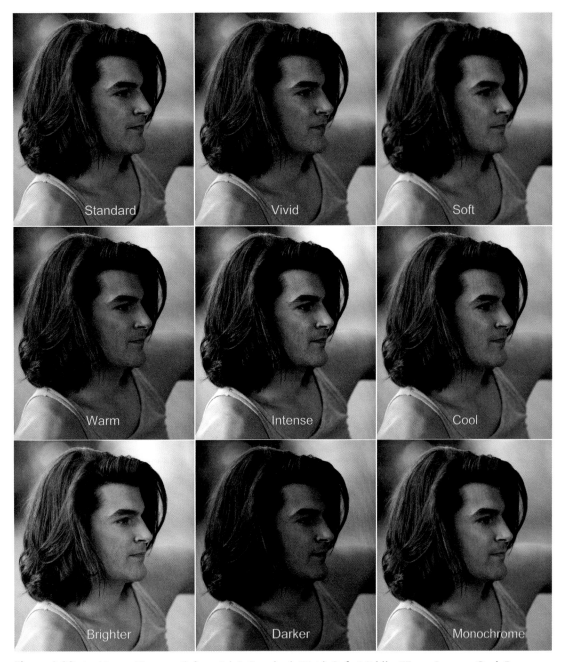

**Figure 4.36** Ambience: Top row (left to right): Standard, Vivid, Soft; Middle: Warm, Intense, Cool; Bottom: Brighter, Darker, Monochrome.

# 5

# Mastering the Mysteries
# of Autofocus

Great things are happening in the world of Canon autofocus! Your new EOS Rebel T5i/700D, in fact, is one of the first to boast a new "hybrid" AF system that goes a long way toward enhancing live view and movie-shooting focus to the same levels of precision applied when you're using the traditional optical viewfinder. And your camera's conventional AF system has been improved, too, with each of the focus points now upgraded to the same more versatile type found in some more upscale Canon cameras. Most exciting, the ability of the T5i to provide continuous autofocus when shooting movies, using the new "hybrid" autofocus that combines elements of the traditional, slower *contrast detection* system with a specialized sensor-embedded *phase detection* process (both described in detail later in this chapter).

The improvements will help you get better photographs—as long as you understand how to use them. After all, capturing a compelling photograph involves a lot more than just correct exposure. The right tonal range, proper white balance, good color, and other factors all can help elevate your image from good to exceptional. But one of the most important and, sometimes, the most frustrating aspects of shooting with a highly automated—yet fully adjustable—camera like the T5i is achieving sharp focus. Your camera has lots of AF controls and options—some of them completely new to the Canon lineup—and new users and veterans alike can quickly become confused. In this chapter, I'm going to clear up the mysteries of autofocus and show you exactly how to use your T5i's AF features to their fullest. I'll even tell you when to abandon the autofocus system and turn to the ancient art of manual focus, too.

# How Focus Works

Although Canon added autofocus capabilities in the 1980s, back in the day of film cameras, prior to that focusing was always done manually. Honest. Even though viewfinders were bigger and brighter than they are today, special focusing screens, magnifiers, and other gadgets were often used to help the photographer achieve correct focus. Imagine what it must have been like to focus manually under demanding, fast-moving conditions such as sports photography.

I don't have to imagine it. I did it for many years. I started my career as a sports photographer, and then traveled the country as a roving photojournalist for more years than I like to admit. (Okay, eighteen years. You forced it out of me.) Indeed, I was a holdout for manual focus right through the film era, even as AF lenses became the norm and autofocus systems in cameras were (gradually) perfected. I purchased my first autofocus lens back in 2004, at the same time I switched from non-SLR digital cameras and my film cameras to digital SLR models.

Manual focusing was problematic because our eyes and brains have poor memory for correct focus, which is why your eye doctor must shift back and forth between sets of lenses and ask "Does that look sharper—or was it sharper before?" in determining your correct prescription. Similarly, manual focusing involves jogging the focus ring back and forth as you go from almost in focus, to sharp focus, to almost focused again. The little clockwise and counterclockwise arcs decrease in size until you've zeroed in on the point of correct focus. What you're looking for is the image with the most contrast between the edges of elements in the image.

The camera also looks for these contrast differences among pixels to determine relative sharpness. There are two ways that sharp focus is determined: phase detection and contrast detection.

## Phase Detection

Like all digital SLRs that use an optical viewfinder and mirror system to preview an image (that is, when not in Live View mode), the Canon EOS T5i calculates focus using what is called a *passive phase detection* system. It's passive in the sense that the ambient illumination in a scene (or that illumination augmented with a focus-assist beam) is used to determine correct focus. (An *active* phase detection system might use a laser, sonar, or other special signal.)

Parts of the image from two opposite sides of the lens are directed down to the floor of the camera's mirror box, where an autofocus sensor array resides; the rest of the illumination from the lens bounces upward toward the optical viewfinder system and the autoexposure sensors. Figure 5.1 is a wildly over-simplified illustration that may help you visualize what is happening.

As light emerges from the rear element of the lens, most of it is reflected upward toward the focusing screen, where the relative sharp focus (or lack of it) is displayed (and which can be used to evaluate manual focus). It then bounces off two more reflective surfaces in the pentamirror (a lighter-weight, less expensive version of the solid-glass *pentaprism* system used in more expensive Canon EOS models, including the 5D Mark III) emerging at the optical viewfinder correctly oriented left/right and up/down. (The image emerges from the lens reversed.) Some of the illumination is directed to the autoexposure sensor at the top of the pentamirror housing.

A small portion of the illumination passes through the partially silvered center of the main mirror, and is directed downward to the autofocus sensor array, which includes nine separate autofocus "detectors." In the interests of arrow-clutter reduction (ACR), the diagram doesn't show that parts of the image from opposite sides of the lens surface are directed through separate microlenses, producing two half-images. These images are compared with each other, much like (actually, *exactly* like) a two-window rangefinder used in surveying, weaponry, and non-SLR cameras like the venerable Leica M film models.

## SIMPLIFICATION MADE OVERLY SIMPLE

To reduce the complexity of the diagram, it doesn't show the actual path of the light passing through the lens, as it converges to the point of focus—on the viewfinder screen when the mirror is down, and on the sensor plane when the mirror is flipped up and the shutter has opened. Nor does it show the path of the light directed to the autoexposure sensor. Only two of the nine pairs of autofocus microlenses are shown, and greatly enlarged so you can see their approximate position. All we're concerned about here is *how* light reaches the autofocus sensor.

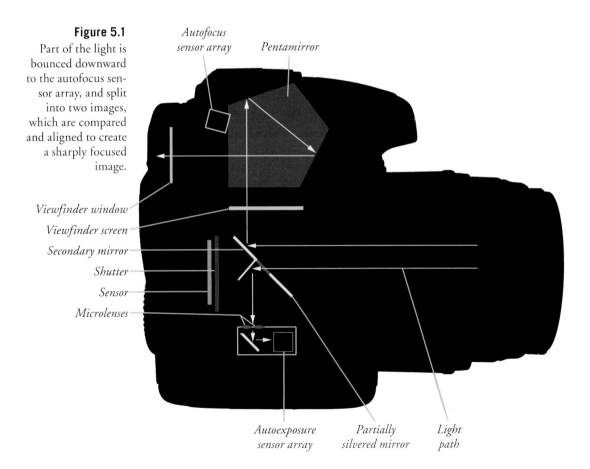

**Figure 5.1**
Part of the light is bounced downward to the autofocus sensor array, and split into two images, which are compared and aligned to create a sharply focused image.

*Autofocus sensor array*

*Pentamirror*

*Viewfinder window*
*Viewfinder screen*
*Secondary mirror*
*Shutter*
*Sensor*
*Microlenses*

*Autoexposure sensor array*

*Partially silvered mirror*

*Light path*

When the image is out of focus—or out of phase—as in Figure 5.2, the two halves, each representing a slightly different view from opposite sides of the lens, don't line up. Sharp focus is achieved when the images are "in phase," and aligned, as in Figure 5.3. The two figures, which represent the simplest type of AF sensor, the *line* sensor, don't show exactly what happens. That's because all nine of the AF sensors in the T5i have been upgraded to the more versatile *cross* variety. But to understand how cross sensors work, you first need to see how the line sensor (found in the predecessor T3i model) operates. I'll explain cross-type sensors after you see the basic phase detection process.

As with any rangefinder-like function, accuracy is better when the "base length" between the two images is larger. (Think back to your high school trigonometry; you could calculate a distance more accurately when the separation between the two points where the angles were measured was greater.) For that reason, phase detection autofocus is more accurate with larger (wider) lens openings than with smaller lens openings, and may not work at all when the f/stop is smaller than f/5.6. Obviously, the "opposite" edges of the lens opening are farther apart with a lens having an f/2.8 maximum aperture than with one that has a smaller, f/5.6 maximum f/stop, and the base line is much longer. The T5i is able to perform these comparisons and then move the lens elements directly to the point of correct focus very quickly, in milliseconds.

Unfortunately, while the T5i's focus system finds it easy to measure degrees of apparent focus at each of the focus points in the viewfinder, it doesn't really know with any certainty *which* object should be in sharpest focus. Is it the closest object? The subject in the center? Something lurking *behind* the closest subject? A person standing over at the side of the picture? Many of the techniques for using autofocus effectively involve telling the EOS T5i exactly what it should be focusing on,

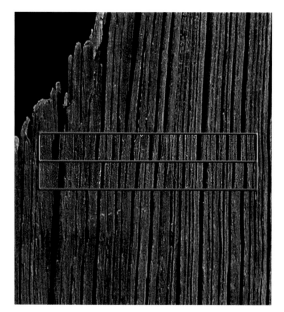 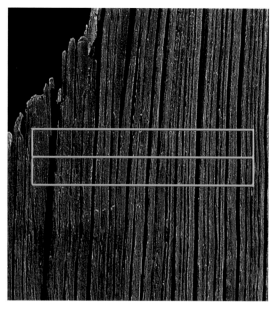

**Figure 5.2** In phase detection, parts of an image are split in two and compared.

**Figure 5.3** When the image is in focus, the two halves of the image align, as with a rangefinder.

by choosing a focus zone or by allowing the camera to choose a focus zone for you. I'll address that topic shortly.

## Cross-Type Focus Points

So far, we've only looked at focus sensors that calculate focus in a single direction. (Canon often calls them *AF points*, but I use the term *sensors* to avoid confusion, because they aren't really "points" at all.) Figures 5.2 and 5.3 illustrate a horizontally oriented focus sensor evaluating a subject that is made up, predominantly, of vertical lines. But what does such a sensor do when it encounters a subject that isn't conveniently aligned at right angles to the sensor array, so that the defining lines are parallel to the line sensor? You can see the problem in Figure 5.4, which pictures the same weathered wood siding rotated 90 degrees. The horizontal grain of the wood isn't divided as neatly by the split image, so focusing using phase detection is more difficult.

In the past, the "solution" was to include a sprinkling of vertically oriented AF sensors in with horizontally oriented sensors. The vertical sensors could detect differences in horizontal lines, while the horizontal sensors took care of the vertical lines. Both types were equally adept at handling *diagonal* lines, which crossed each type at a 45-degree angle. Earlier Canon entry-level digital SLRs were limited to a single "multi-function" sensor (in the center of the array) that has a cross-type arrangement. However, with the T5i, Canon has upgraded all nine sensors to cross sensors, which operate with any lens having a maximum aperture of f/5.6 or larger. The center sensor is especially sensitive when used with lenses having a maximum aperture of at least f/2.8.

The value of cross-type focus sensors in phase detection is that such sensors can line up edges and interpret image contrast in both horizontal and vertical directions, as shown in Figure 5.5. The horizontal lines are still more difficult to interpret with the horizontal arm of the cross, but they

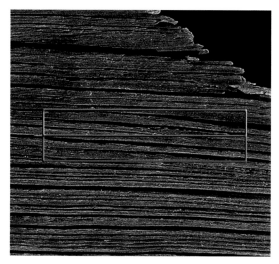

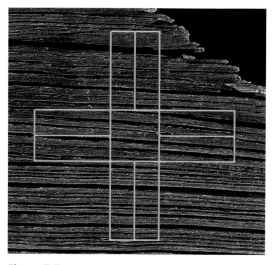

**Figure 5.4** Horizontal focus sensors do a poor job of interpreting the alignment of horizontal lines; they work better with vertical lines or diagonals.

**Figure 5.5** Cross-type sensors can achieve sharp focus with both horizontal and vertical lines.

stand out in sharp contrast in the vertical arms, and allow the camera to align the edges and snap the image into focus easily, as you can see at lower right. In lower light levels, with subjects that were moving, or with subjects that have no pattern and less contrast to begin with, the cross-type sensor not only works faster but can focus subjects that a horizontal- or vertical-only sensor can't handle at all. (Note that the actual horizontal, vertical, and cross-type sensors don't look like the illustrations—we're still in over-simplification mode, so you can understand the *concept* rather than the actual engineering.) The location of the T5i's sensors in the viewfinder is shown in Figure 5.6, where they appear as nine highlighted spots arranged in a diamond pattern.

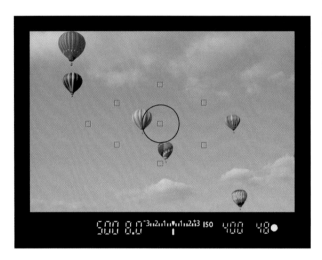

**Figure 5.6**
The AF sensors in the T5i are arranged like this.

## Contrast Detection

Contrast detection is a slower mode and used, at least part of the time, by the Rebel T5i with Live View and Movie modes. That's because to allow live viewing of the sensor image, the camera's mirror has to be flipped up out of the way so that the illumination from the lens can continue through the open shutter to the sensor. Your view through the viewfinder is obstructed, of course, and there is no partially silvered mirror to reflect some light down to the autofocus sensors. So, an alternate means of autofocus must be used, and that method has traditionally been *contrast detection.* The T5i does have pixels in the sensor dedicated to a form of phase detection to locate the main subject of your image, at which point contrast detection takes over the AF functions using the identified area of the sensor, making it a *hybrid* autofocus system.

The T5i in Live View mode also includes a Quick Mode feature that temporarily flips the mirror back down to allow phase detection autofocus, but unless you use that mode, which I'll discuss later, focus must be achieved manually (with the color LCD live view as a focusing screen), by contrast detection, or using the hybrid phase detection/contrast detection AF tandem.

Contrast detection is a bit easier to understand and is illustrated by Figure 5.7. At top in the extreme enlargement of the wood siding, the transitions between pixels are soft and blurred. When the image is brought into focus (bottom), the transitions are sharp and clear. Although this example is

**Figure 5.7**

Focus in contrast detection mode evaluates the increase in contrast in the edges of subjects, starting with a blurry image (top) and producing a sharp, contrasty image (bottom).

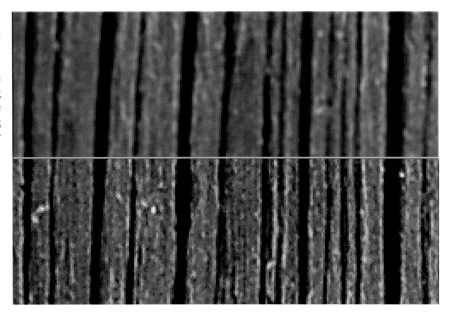

a bit exaggerated so you can see the results on the printed page, it's easy to understand that when maximum contrast in a subject is achieved, it can be deemed to be in sharp focus.

Contrast detection is used as the primary focus mode in live view, and may be the only focus mode possible with point-and-shoot cameras that doesn't offer a through-the-lens optical viewfinder as found in a digital SLR like the EOS T5i. Contrast detection works best with static subjects, because it is inherently slower and not well suited for tracking moving objects. Contrast detection works less well than phase detection in dim light, because its accuracy is determined not by the length of the baseline of a rangefinder focus system, but by its ability to detect variations in brightness and contrast. You'll find that contrast detection works better with faster lenses, too, not as with phase detection (which gains accuracy because the diameter of the lens is simply wider) but because larger lens openings admit more light that can be used by the sensor to measure contrast.

We'll look at contrast detection again when we explore live view modes.

# Focus Modes

Focus modes tell the camera *when* to evaluate and lock in focus. They don't determine *where* focus should be checked; that's the function of other autofocus features. Focus modes tell the camera whether to lock in focus once, say, when you press the shutter release halfway (or use some other control, such as the AF-ON button), or whether, once activated, the camera should continue tracking your subject and, if it's moving, adjust focus to follow it.

The T5i has three AF modes: One-Shot AF (also known as single autofocus), AI Servo (continuous autofocus), and AI Focus AF (which switches between the two as appropriate). I'll explain all of these in more detail later in this section. But first, some confusion…

**MANUAL FOCUS**

With manual focus activated by sliding the AF/MF switch on the lens, your T5i lets you set the focus yourself. There are some advantages and disadvantages to this approach. While your batteries will last longer in manual focus mode, it will take you longer to focus the camera for each photo, a process that can be difficult. Modern digital cameras, even dSLRs, depend so much on autofocus that the viewfinders of models that have less than full-frame-sized sensors are no longer designed for optimum manual focus. Pick up any film camera and you'll see a bigger, brighter viewfinder with a focusing screen that's a joy to focus on manually.

# Adding Circles of Confusion

You know that increased depth-of-field brings more of your subject into focus. But more depth-of-field also makes autofocusing (or manual focusing) more difficult because the contrast is lower between objects at different distances. This is an added factor *beyond* the rangefinder aspects of lens opening size in phase detection. An image that's dimmer is more difficult to focus with any type of focus system, phase detection, contrast detection, or manual focus.

So, focus with a 200mm lens (or zoom setting) may be easier in some respects than at a 28mm focal length (or zoom setting) because the longer lens has less apparent depth-of-field. By the same token, a lens with a maximum aperture of f/1.8 will be easier to autofocus (or manually focus) than one of the same focal length with an f/4 maximum aperture, because the f/4 lens has more depth-of-field *and* a dimmer view. That's yet another reason why lenses with a maximum aperture smaller than f/5.6 can give your T5i's autofocus system fits—increased depth-of-field joins forces with a dimmer image that's more difficult to focus using phase detection.

To make things even more complicated, many subjects aren't polite enough to remain still. They move around in the frame, so that even if the T5i is sharply focused on your main subject, it may change position and require refocusing. An intervening subject may pop into the frame and pass between you and the subject you meant to photograph. You (or the T5i) have to decide whether to lock focus on this new subject, or remain focused on the original subject. Finally, there are some kinds of subjects that are difficult to bring into sharp focus because they lack enough contrast to allow the T5i's AF system (or our eyes) to lock in. Blank walls, a clear blue sky, or other subject matter may make focusing difficult.

If you find all these focus factors confusing, you're on the right track. Focus is, in fact, measured using something called a *circle of confusion.* An ideal image consists of zillions of tiny little points, which, like all points, theoretically have no height or width. There is perfect contrast between the point and its surroundings. You can think of each point as a pinpoint of light in a darkened room. When a given point is out of focus, its edges decrease in contrast and it changes from a perfect point to a tiny disc with blurry edges (remember, blur is the lack of contrast between boundaries in an image). (See Figure 5.8.)

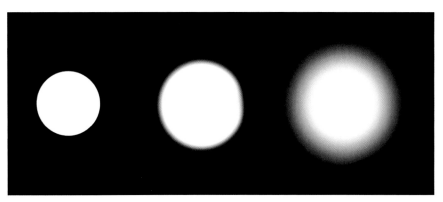

If this blurry disc—the circle of confusion—is small enough, our eye still perceives it as a point. It's only when the disc grows large enough that we can see it as a blur rather than a sharp point that a given point is viewed as out of focus. You can see, then, that enlarging an image, either by displaying it larger on your computer monitor or by making a large print, also enlarges the size of each circle of confusion. Moving closer to the image does the same thing. So, parts of an image that may look perfectly sharp in a 5 × 7–inch print viewed at arm's length, might appear blurry when blown up to 11 × 14 and examined at the same distance. Take a few steps back, however, and it may look sharp again.

To a lesser extent, the viewer also affects the apparent size of these circles of confusion. Some people see details better at a given distance and may perceive smaller circles of confusion than someone standing next to them. For the most part, however, such differences are small. Truly blurry images will look blurry to just about everyone under the same conditions.

Technically, there is just one plane within your picture area, parallel to the back of the camera (or sensor, in the case of a digital camera), that is in sharp focus. That's the plane in which the points of the image are rendered as precise points. At every other plane in front of or behind the focus plane, the points show up as discs that range from slightly blurry to extremely blurry until, as you can see in Figure 5.9, the out-of-focus areas become one large blur that de-emphasizes the background.

In practice, the discs in many of these planes will still be so small that we see them as points, and that's where we get depth-of-field. Depth-of-field is just the range of planes that include discs that we perceive as points rather than blurred splotches. The size of this range increases as the aperture is reduced in size and is allocated roughly one-third in front of the plane of sharpest focus, and two-thirds behind it. The range of sharp focus is always greater behind your subject than in front of it.

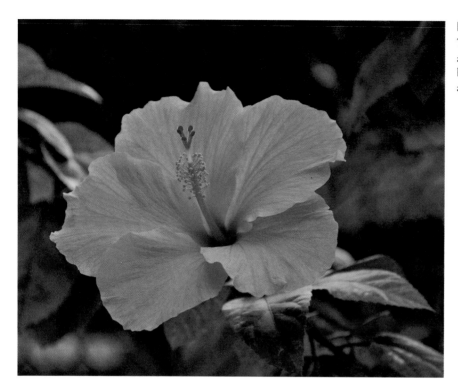

**Figure 5.9**
The background is almost totally blurred, thanks to a wide f/stop.

# Making Sense of Sensors

The number and type of autofocus sensors can affect how well the system operates. As I mentioned, the Canon EOS T5i has nine AF points or zones. Other EOS cameras may have from seven to 61 AF points. These focus sensors can consist of vertical or horizontal lines of pixels, cross-shapes (including both + and X orientations), and often a mixture of these types within a single camera, although, as I mentioned, the EOS T5i includes only cross-type sensors at all positions. The more AF points available, the more easily the camera can differentiate among areas of the frame, and the more precisely you can specify the area you want to be in focus if you're manually choosing a focus spot.

As the camera collects focus information from the sensors, it then evaluates it to determine whether the desired sharp focus has been achieved. The calculations may include whether the subject is moving, and whether the camera needs to "predict" where the subject will be when the shutter release button is fully depressed and the picture is taken. The speed with which the camera is able to evaluate focus and then move the lens elements into the proper position to achieve the sharpest focus determines how fast the autofocus mechanism is. Although your T5i will almost always focus more quickly than a human, there are types of shooting situations where that's not fast enough. For example, if you're having problems shooting sports because the T5i's autofocus system manically follows each moving subject, a better choice might be to switch autofocus modes or shift into manual and prefocus on a spot where you anticipate the action will be, such as a goal line or soccer net. At night football games, for example, when I am shooting with a telephoto lens almost wide open, I often focus manually on one of the referees who happens to be standing where I expect the action to be taking place (say, a halfback run or a pass reception). When I am less sure about what is going to happen, I may switch to AI Servo autofocus and let the camera decide.

## Your Autofocus Mode Options

Choosing the right autofocus mode and the way in which focus points are selected is your key to success. Using the wrong mode for a particular type of photography can lead to a series of pictures that are all sharply focused—on the wrong subject. When I first started shooting sports with an autofocus SLR (back in the film camera days), I covered one game alternating between shots of base runners and outfielders with pictures of a promising young pitcher, all from a position next to the third-base dugout. The base runner and outfielder photos were great, because their backgrounds didn't distract the autofocus mechanism. But all my photos of the pitcher had the focus tightly zeroed in on the fans in the stands behind him. Because I was shooting film instead of a digital camera, I didn't know about my gaffe until the film was developed. A simple change, such as locking in focus or focus zone manually, or even manually focusing, would have done the trick.

To save battery power, your T5i doesn't start to focus the lens until you partially depress the shutter release. But, autofocus isn't some mindless beast out there snapping your pictures in and out of focus with no feedback from you after you press that button. There are several settings you can modify that return at least a modicum of control to you. Your first decision should be whether you set the T5i to One-Shot, AI Servo AF, or AI Focus AF. With the camera set for one of the Creative Zone modes, press the AF button (the right cross key) and use the Main Dial or left/right cross keys to select the focus mode you want (see Figure 5.10). Press SET to confirm your choice. (The AF/M switch on the lens must be set to AF before you can change autofocus mode.)

**Figure 5.10**
Press the left/right cross keys or rotate the Main Dial until the AF choice you want is selected.

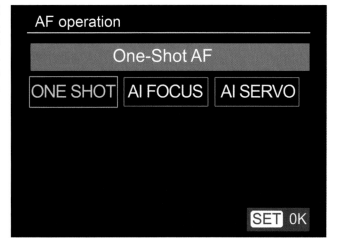

# One-Shot AF

In this mode, also called *single autofocus*, focus is set once and remains at that setting until the button is fully depressed, taking the picture, or until you release the shutter button without taking a shot. For non-action photography, this setting is usually your best choice, as it minimizes out-of-focus pictures (at the expense of spontaneity). The drawback here is that you might not be able to take a picture at all while the camera is seeking focus; you're locked out until the autofocus mechanism is happy with the current setting. One-Shot AF/Single Autofocus is sometimes referred to as *focus priority* for that reason. Because of the small delay while the camera zeroes in on correct focus, you might experience slightly more shutter lag. This mode uses less battery power.

When sharp focus is achieved, the selected focus point will flash red in the viewfinder, and the focus confirmation light at the lower right will illuminate and remain lit as long as focus is maintained and you continue to hold down the shutter release. If you're using Evaluative metering, the exposure will be locked at the same time. By keeping the shutter button depressed halfway, you'll find you can reframe the image while retaining the focus (and exposure) that's been set. With other metering methods, you can use the AE Lock/FE Lock button to retain the exposure calculated from the center AF point while reframing.

# AI Servo AF

This mode, also known as *continuous autofocus* is the mode to use for sports and other fast-moving subjects. In this mode, once the shutter release is partially depressed, the camera sets the focus but continues to monitor the subject, so that if it moves or you move, the lens will be refocused to suit. Focus and exposure aren't really locked until you press the shutter release down all the way to take the picture. You'll often see continuous autofocus referred to as *release priority*. If you press the shutter release down all the way while the system is refining focus, the camera will go ahead and take a picture, even if the image is slightly out of focus. You'll find that AI Servo AF produces the least amount of shutter lag of any autofocus mode: press the button and the camera fires. It also uses the most battery power, because the autofocus system operates as long as the shutter release button is partially depressed.

AI Servo AF uses a technology called *predictive AF*, which allows the T5i to calculate the correct focus if the subject is moving toward or away from the camera at a constant rate. It uses either the automatically selected AF point or the point you select manually to set focus.

# AI Focus AF

This setting is actually a combination of the first two. When selected, the camera focuses using One-Shot AF and locks in the focus setting. But, if the subject begins moving, it will switch automatically to AI Servo AF and change the focus to keep the subject sharp. AI Focus AF is a good choice when you're shooting a mixture of action pictures and less dynamic shots and want to use One-Shot AF when possible. The camera will default to that mode, yet switch automatically to AI Servo AF when it would be useful for subjects that might begin moving unexpectedly, such as children or pets.

# Setting AF Point

You can change which of the nine focus points the Canon EOS Rebel T5i uses to calculate correct focus, or allow the camera to select the point for you. In any of the Basic Zone shooting modes, the focus point is always selected automatically by the camera. In the Creative Zone modes, you can allow the camera to select the focus point automatically, or you can specify which focus point should be used.

To review, there are several methods to set the focus point manually. You can press the AF point selection button on the back of the camera (at the upper-right edge of the back), look through the viewfinder, and use the cross keys to move the focus point to the zone you want to use. It is not necessary to *hold* the AF point selection button down. Just press it once, and the cross keys become active for about four seconds, or until you stop moving the focus point around. For example, press the cross keys straight up or down, and the top or bottom focus points are selected. To the left or right, and the side points are selected. Press the SET button, and the center focus point becomes active. Press the SET button twice, and automatic focus is selected with all focus points active.

You can also choose a focus point by pressing the AF point selection button and then rotating the Main Dial. The focus point will cycle among the edge points counterclockwise (if you turn the Main Dial to the left) or clockwise (if you spin the Main Dial to the right). At each end of the cycle the center focus point and then all nine focus points will be active. When all nine are "live," auto point selection will be switched back on.

When you press the AF point selection button, the screen shown in Figure 5.11 appears on the LCD. You can then use the touch screen, rotate the Main Dial, or use the cross keys to select the focus point. This method may be easier under dark conditions, when the viewfinder focus points are not as easily seen, or when you're photographing a subject that has many red hues (it happens!) and the viewfinder image, awash in red, doesn't show the red-highlighted focus points readily.

**Figure 5.11**
When selecting focus points manually, rotate the Main Dial to select specific points. Continue rotating until all nine points are visible, and the T5i switches back to automatic AF point selection mode.

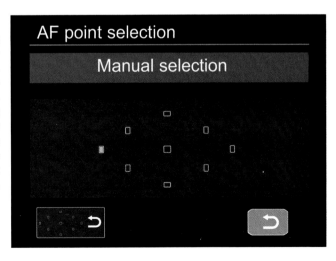

# Focusing in Live View/Movie Modes

When using Live View/Movie modes, the Rebel T5i performs its autofocusing chores in quite a different manner, one that, for the first time, offers improved AF speed when shooting movies and live view stills. The enhancements are important compared to AF when working with the optical viewfinder, and *especially* different when contrasted with live view/movie shooting with previous EOS models. That's because the T5i is able to use a *hybrid* system that uses both traditional contrast detection technology (as the main AF tool), as well as a specialized application of phase detection.

Another autofocus innovation has been Canon's use of *stepping motor technology* (STM) in lenses such as new 18-55mm and 18-135mm STM kit lenses, or the 40mm f/2.8 "pancake" lens. STM has smooth, ultra-quiet autofocus, used by the T5i's Movie Servo AF mode.

Figure 5.12 will help you understand how the hybrid system works. Note that the illustration is just a color-coded conceptual guide to the layout of the hybrid focus components, and does *not* in any way represent what you will see through the viewfinder. Here are the major considerations:

- **Image frame (green).** The outer box represents the full image frame in its 3:2 aspect ratio (proportions). This is the area that will be captured when shooting a live view still image.
- **Video frame (white).** The area between the white bars represents the image that will be captured in video mode when using the HD 16:9 aspect ratio.
- **Phase detection search area (yellow).** The T5i's sensor includes pixels that can use phase detection to quickly achieve focus tracking on what the camera deems to be the main subjects of the image. I'll explain why this capability is important next.
- **Contrast detect focus area (blue).** The area inside the blue box is the focus area for the contrast detection system, which finalizes focus after the phase detection pixels finish their work.

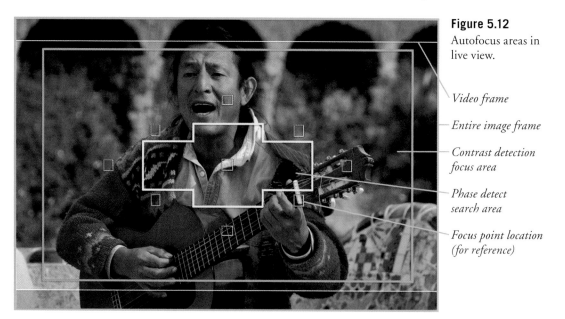

**Figure 5.12**
Autofocus areas in live view.

*Video frame*

*Entire image frame*

*Contrast detection focus area*

*Phase detect search area*

*Focus point location (for reference)*

■ **Focus point locations (red).** These are shown to help you visualize the boundaries of the other elements. They are the nine focus points used when working with the optical viewfinder in non-Live View mode, and in live view when you've activated Quick mode (which flips the mirror back down briefly to use the optical system's phase detection). The focus points do *not* appear on the live view screen, except when you are using Quick mode, as described later in this section.

Canon says that this hybrid AF system was designed to *improve* focusing when shooting video, acknowledging that this rudimentary live phase detection process hasn't been developed enough to serve as a stand-alone full-time autofocus feature. Now that you know the position of all the components, I can explain why that's true. Here's how it works:

1. **Select zone.** In live focus modes that let you choose the focus zone (FlexiZone—Single and FlexiZone—Multi, described next), you can use the cross keys to move an indicator box around the screen to choose the part of the frame you're primarily interested in.

2. **Phase detect activates.** If the focus zone you select is within the area bounded by the yellow box in the figure, when you press the shutter release halfway to activate focus, the phase detect pixels in the sensor examine the selected focus zone. Unlike contrast detection AF, which must often "hunt" near and far, phase detection knows exactly which direction the camera needs to focus, and by how much. That avoids the sudden blurry moments that contrast detection produces when the camera focuses in the wrong direction (and which are particularly nasty during the continuous capture of video shooting). We've all viewed an almost-sharp image that suddenly blurs completely as the camera focuses in the wrong direction, then snaps back into focus when it reverses itself.

3. **Hand-off to contrast detection.** If your focus zone is *within* the phase detection area, once focus has been initiated, the hybrid process hands off AF duties to the contrast detection. (If your selected zone is *outside* the phase detection area, contrast detection is used from the very start.)

4. **Fine-tuning.** The contrast detection algorithms fine-tune the focus, with, perhaps, a slight amount of focus wobbling during the focus confirmation step. The hybrid system lets you use fast phase detection for the initial focus when that's possible, and rely on slower contrast detection only for the final adjustments.

Autofocus works a bit differently in Face+Tracking and Quick mode. I'll describe all the live view focus modes next.

## Live View/Movie Focus Modes

You can select the autofocus method used in live modes from the Live Shooting menu, which is also outlined in Chapter 8. Navigate to AF method, and press SET to access the menu shown in Figure 5.13. Or, you can press the Q button and use the screen shown in Figure 5.14. (Note: you can't select a live focusing mode by pressing the AF button/right cross key. That's for non-live focusing only.) Select one of the following autofocus modes.

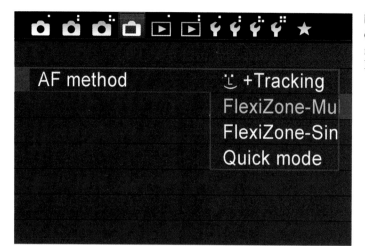

**Figure 5.13**
Choose a live AF method from the Live menu…

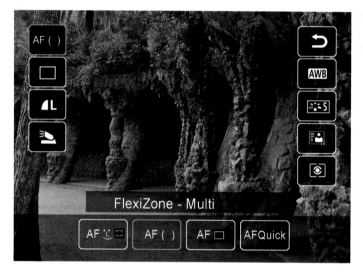

**Figure 5.14**
…or use this Q menu screen.

## Face Detection+Tracking Mode

This mode uses contrast detection, using the relative sharpness of the image as it appears on the sensor to determine focus. The T5i will search the frame for a human face and attempt to focus on the face. To autofocus using Face Detection+Tracking mode, follow these steps:

1. **Set lens to autofocus.** Make sure the focus switch on the lens is set to AF.

2. **Activate live view.** If you're shooting stills, press the Live View button, located to the immediate right of the viewfinder window to activate live view. If movie capture is in your plans, flip the On/Off/Movie button to the movie position.

3. **Face detection.** If you've selected Face Detection using the Live menu or Quick Control screen, a frame will appear around a face found in the image. If more than one face is found, a frame with notches that look like "ears" appears. (See Figure 5.15, left.) In that case, use the cross keys to move the frame to the face you want to use for focus. You can also tap the LCD monitor to select a face. If no face is detected or you tap the LCD monitor on a non-face subject, the T5i will switch to FlexiZone—Multi and select the AF point automatically.

4. **Troubleshoot (if necessary).** If you experience problems in Face Detection+Tracking mode, use another mode. Face Detection is far from perfect. The AF system may fail to find a face if the person's visage is too large/small or light/dark in the frame, tilted, or located near an edge of the picture. It may classify a non-face as a face. If you switch to FlexiZone—Single Live mode, you can always select another AF point and press the cross keys button again to toggle back to Face Detection+Tracking mode.

5. **Press and hold the shutter release halfway.** When focus is achieved, the AF point turns green, as shown in Figure 5.15, right, and you'll hear a beep. If the T5i is unable to focus, the AF point turns orange instead.

6. **Take picture.** Press the shutter release all the way down to take the picture.

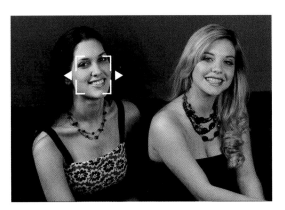 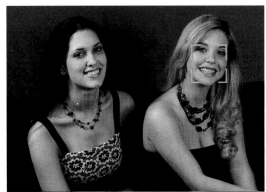

**Figure 5.15** If more than one face is located (left), use the cross keys to choose one. When focus is achieved, the frame turns green (right).

## FlexiZone—Multi

In this mode, the T5i can automatically select the focus *area* from up to 31 different AF positions in the frame, or any of nine different *zones* you select. The nine manual zones are difficult to illustrate without resorting to a Venn diagram, because they overlap. So, for clarity, I show the position of the four corner zones in Figure 5.16 (the boxes are *not* colored on the screen). The individual boxes represent focus *areas* that may be selected once you've zeroed in on the *zone* you want to emphasize. The other five zones you can select include one each at the top and bottom middle (overlapping the magenta and blue zones, and yellow and red zones), plus three middle zones that overlap both each other and the zones above and below them.

■ **Switch between automatic and manual select.** Press the SET or Trash buttons to toggle between automatic area selection and manual zone selection, if you're not using a Basic Zone mode. (Basic Zone always uses automatic area selection.) When in either mode, tap the SET or TRASH buttons to switch to the center focus zone.

■ **Automatic selection.** With auto selection active, the T5i will choose one or more focus areas from a wide area of the frame, as shown in Figure 5.17.

■ **Zone selection.** In zone selection mode, the T5i will still select the exact focus area, but will use one or more focus areas that reside within the specified overlapping zone you choose. You can also tap the LCD monitor screen to choose a particular zone. Tap the Return icon to switch back to automatic selection.

■ **Focus.** With the selected AF zone superimposed on your subject, press the shutter button halfway. The AF areas will turn green and a beep will sound when focus is achieved. The zone will turn orange, instead, if the T5i is unable to achieve sharp focus.

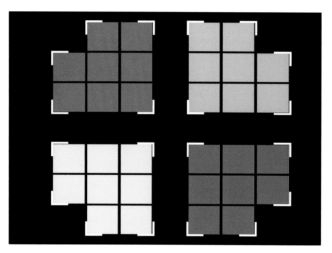

**Figure 5.16**
Manual zone selection.

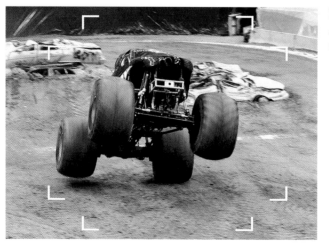

**Figure 5.17**
Automatic selection area.

**TIP**

The exact number of automatic AF areas will vary, depending on the aspect ratio of your frame. At the default 3:2 proportions, a maximum of 31 areas are available. If you choose 1:1 or 4:3 aspect ratios, there will be 25 AF areas. When shooting HD movies, you'll have 21 AF points allocated among three zones. I'm not going to illustrate all the combinations or variations. You can experiment to see how your autofocus options fluctuate.

## FlexiZone—Single

In this mode, a single AF area appears on the screen, in both Still and Movie modes.

- **Choose zone.** Use the cross keys or tap the LCD screen to select the specific zone you want to use.
- **Focus.** With the selected AF zone superimposed on your subject, press the shutter button halfway. The AF zone will turn green and a beep will sound when focus is achieved. The zone will turn orange, instead, if the T5i is unable to achieve sharp focus.

## Quick Mode

This mode temporarily interrupts Live View mode to allow the EOS T5i to focus the same AF sensor used when you focus through the viewfinder. Because the step takes a second or so, you may get better results using this autofocus mode when the camera is mounted on a tripod. If you hand-hold the T5i, you may displace the point of focus achieved by the autofocus system. It also simplifies the operation if you use One-Shot focus and center the focus point. You can use AI Servo and AF or Manual focus point selection, but if the focus point doesn't coincide with the subject you want to focus on, you'll end up with an out-of-focus image. Just follow these steps.

1. **Set lens to autofocus.** Make sure the focus switch on the lens is set to AF. You can press the SET or Trash buttons to toggle between automatic and manual selection.
2. **Activate live view.** Press the Start/Stop button.
3. **Choose AF point.** Use the cross keys to move the active AF focus point around on the screen.
4. **Select subject.** Compose the image on the LCD so the selected focus point is on the subject.
5. **Press and hold the shutter release halfway.** The LCD will go blank as the mirror flips down, reflecting the view of the subject to the phase detection AF sensor.
6. **Wait for focus.** When the T5i is able to lock in focus using phase detection, a beep (if activated) will sound. If you are handholding the T5i, you may hear several beeps as the AF system focuses and refocuses with each camera movement. Then, the mirror will flip back up, and the live view image reappears. The AF focus point will be highlighted in green on the LCD.
7. **Take picture.** Press the shutter release *all* the way down to take the picture. (You can't take a photo while Quick mode AF is in process, until the mirror flips back up.)

## Manual Mode

You can also use manual focusing, regardless of what live focusing mode you've chosen, by flipping the A/M switch on your lens to the M position. Focusing manually on an LCD screen isn't as difficult as you might think, but Canon has made the process even easier by providing a magnified view. Just follow these steps to focus manually:

1. **Set lens to manual focus and activate live view.** Make sure the focus switch on the lens is set to MF.

2. **Press the Zoom In (AF Point Selection/Magnify) button.** The area of the image inside the focus frame will be magnified 1X. Press the Zoom In button a second time, and the magnification will increase to 5X, and a navigation box will appear at the lower-right corner, along with arrows at the boundaries of the frame, indicating you can move the zoomed area around within the image. Press the Zoom In button a third time to increase the magnification to 10X. A fourth press will return you to the full-frame view. The enlarged area is artificially sharpened to make it easier for you to see the contrast changes, and simplify focusing. When zoomed in, press the shutter release halfway and the current shutter speed and aperture are shown in orange. If no information at all appears, press the INFO. button.

3. **Move magnifying frame.** Use the cross keys to move the focus frame that's superimposed on the screen to the location where you want to focus. You can press the cross keys to center the focus frame in the middle of the screen.

4. **Focus manually.** Use the focus ring on the lens to focus the image. When you're satisfied, you can zoom back out by pressing the Zoom In button. (See Figure 5.18.)

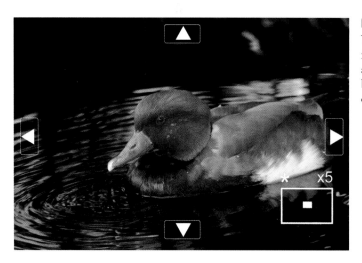

**Figure 5.18**
You can manually focus the center area, which can be zoomed in 5X or 10X.

# Focus Stacking

If you are doing macro (close-up) photography of flowers, or other small objects at short distances, the depth-of-field often will be extremely narrow. In some cases, it will be so narrow that it will be impossible to keep the entire subject in focus in one photograph. Although having part of the image out of focus can be a pleasing effect for a portrait of a person, it is likely to be a hindrance when you are trying to make an accurate photographic record of a flower, or small piece of precision equipment. One solution to this problem is focus stacking, a procedure that can be considered like HDR translated for the world of focus—taking multiple shots with different settings, and, using software as explained below, combining the best parts from each image in order to make a whole that is better than the sum of the parts. Focus stacking requires a non-moving object, so some subjects, such as flowers, are best photographed in a breezeless environment, such as indoors.

For example, see Figures 5.19 through 5.21, in which I took photographs of three colorful crayons. As you can see from these images, the depth-of-field was extremely narrow, and only a small part of the subject was in focus for each shot.

Now look at Figure 5.22, in which the entire subject is in reasonably sharp focus. This image is a composite, made up of the three shots above, as well as 10 others, each one focused on the same scene, but at very gradually increasing distances from the camera's lens. All 13 images were then combined in Adobe Photoshop using the focus stacking procedure. Here are the steps you can take to combine shots for the purpose of achieving sharp focus in this sort of situation:

1. **Set the camera firmly on a solid tripod.** A tripod or other equally firm support is absolutely essential for this procedure.

2. **Attach a remote release.** You want to be able to trigger the camera without moving it.

3. **Set the camera to manual focus mode.** Use the procedure described in the previous section to activate manual focus.

4. **Set the exposure, ISO, and white balance manually.** Use test shots if necessary to determine the best values. This step in the Shooting menu will help prevent visible variations from arising among the multiple shots that you'll be taking. You don't want the camera to change the ISO setting or white balance between shots.

5. **Set the quality of the images to RAW.** Use the Shooting 1 menu to make this adjustment. Having both formats will give you flexibility when combining the images.

6. **Turn off Image Stabilization.** If your lens has IS, turn it off. You don't need it when the camera is securely mounted on a tripod, and disabling image stabilization will keep the T5i from making any sort of image adjustment between exposures.

7. **Focus manually on the very closest point of the subject to the lens.** Use the focus ring on the lens.

8. **Trip the shutter.** Use the remote.

9. **Carefully refocus.** Gently rotate the focus ring on the lens to focus on a point slightly farther away from the lens and trip the shutter again.

10. **Continue taking photographs** in this way until you have covered the entire subject with in-focus shots.

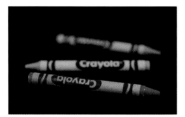
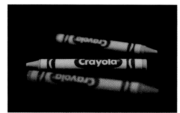
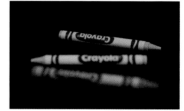

**Figure 5.19**          **Figure 5.20**          **Figure 5.21**

These three shots were all focused on different distances within the same scene. No single shot could bring the entire subject into sharp focus.

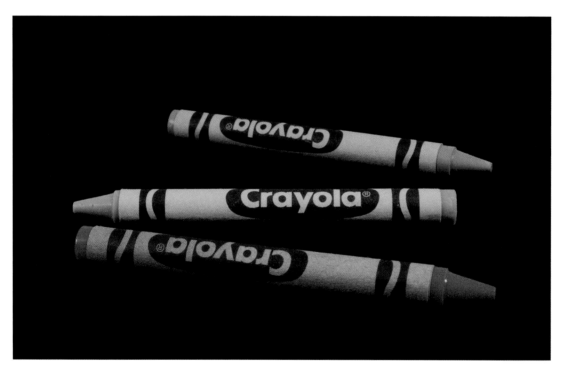

**Figure 5.22** Three partially out-of-focus shots have been merged, along with ten others, through a focus stacking procedure in Adobe Photoshop, to produce a single image with the entire subject in focus.

The next step is to process the images you've taken in Photoshop. Transfer the images to your computer, and then follow these steps:

1. In Photoshop, select File > Scripts > Load Files into Stack. In the dialog box that then appears, navigate on your computer to find the files for the photographs you have taken, and highlight them all.

2. At the bottom of the next dialog box that appears, check the box that says, "Attempt to Automatically Align Source Images," then click OK. The images will load; it may take several minutes for the program to load the images and attempt to arrange them into layers that are aligned based on their content.

3. Once the program has finished processing the images, go to the Layers panel and select all of the layers. You can do this by clicking on the top layer and then Shift-clicking on the bottom one.

4. While the layers are all selected, in Photoshop go to Edit > Auto-Blend Layers. In the dialog box that appears, select the two options, Stack Images and Seamless Tones and Colors, then click OK. The program will process the images, possibly for a considerable length of time.

5. If the procedure worked well, the result will be a single image made up of numerous layers that have been processed to produce a sharply focused rendering of your subject. If it did not work well, you may have to take additional images the next time, focusing very carefully on small slices of the subject as you move progressively farther away from the lens.

Although this procedure can work very well in Photoshop, you also may want to try it with programs that were developed more specifically for focus stacking and related procedures, such as Helicon Focus (www.heliconsoft.com), PhotoAcute (www.photoacute.com), or CombineZM (www.hadleyweb.pwp.blueyonder.co.uk).

# 6

# Movies and Live View

Cameras like the Canon EOS T5i are loaded with killer features. And, by killer, I mean that new capabilities found in digital SLRs have virtually killed off whole categories of cameras, such as high-end, point-and-shoot cameras that lack interchangeable lenses or superzoom optics, and, in the future, camcorders. Who needs a camcorder when your digital SLR can shoot full HD 1080p video *and* stills?

Live View has been around long enough that it's becoming old hat for some, but, we have learned, it was really just a precursor to one of the T5i's deadliest killer features—full HD video shooting. Indeed, the opening montages of *Saturday Night Live* were all shot using Canon cameras, so you can see that movie shooting with your camera has a lot of potential. You can now buy fancy harnesses, rigs, and Steadycam setups for Canon digital cameras, turning the more ambitious among us into one-person motion picture studios, ready and able to shoot everything from family vacation movies suitable for broadcasting on PBS during pledge week to full-length feature films. It's mind-boggling to see how far movie-shooting dSLRs have progressed in the past several years.

Although this is a fairly hefty chapter that emphasizes a broad range of video techniques, movie shooting is an entirely separate discipline from still photography, and the things you can do with the T5i deserve an entire book of their own. I've expanded the number of pages devoted to movie shooting, but this is, after all, my *Guide to Digital SLR Photography*, not *Digital SLR Photography and Movie Shooting,* and an extra 100 or so pages stuffed into this tome is not in the offing. What I hope to accomplish in this chapter is to spark your interest in learning more about the T5i's video capabilities and give you enough information to get you started.

## Working with Live View

Of course, Live View is tightly integrated with movie shooting, so we'll start with that. Live View (and to a lesser extent movie shooting) is one of those features that, despite increasing evidence to the contrary, experienced SLR users (especially those dating from the film era) sometimes think they don't need—until they try it. But Live View and movie shooting have become a permanent fixture, even for latecomers to the party. Indeed, many point-and-shoot models don't even *have* optical viewfinders, and my favorite compact camera, the Canon PowerShot G1 X, has only a marginally useful vestigial optical finder. So, we have an entire generation of amateur photographers who think the only way to frame and compose an image is to hold the camera out at arm's length so the back-panel LCD can be viewed more easily.

While dSLR veterans are finally warming up to Live View, many still underuse the video capture capabilities of cameras like the T5i. After all, who needs to shoot home movies, and why would you eschew a big, bright, magnified through-the-lens optical view that showed depth-of-field fairly well, and which was easily visible under virtually all ambient light conditions? LCD displays, after all, were small, tended to wash out in bright light, and didn't really provide you with an accurate view of what your picture was going to look like.

Today, however, the Canon EOS Rebel T5i has a gorgeous 3-inch LCD that can be viewed under a variety of lighting conditions and from wide-ranging angles, so you don't have to be exactly behind the display to see it clearly. (See Figure 6.1.) It offers a 95-percent view of the sensor's capture area. It's large enough to allow manual focusing. If you want to use automatic focus, you have several options. You can opt for Quick mode, described in Chapter 5, which briefly flips the mirror back down for autofocusing, interrupting Live View, and then restoring the sensor preview image after focus is achieved. Or, you can use the T5i's combination contrast detection/phase detection hybrid mode for automatic focus (also described in detail in the last chapter).

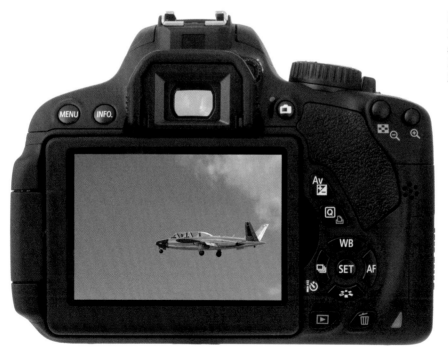

**Figure 6.1**
Live View really shines on the Canon EOS T5i's large 3-inch LCD.

# Live View Essentials

You may not have considered just what you can do with Live View, because the capability is so novel. But once you've played with it, you'll discover dozens of applications for this capability. Here's a list of things to think about:

- **Preview your images on a TV.** Connect your EOS T5i to an HDTV with the optional HDMI cable, and you can preview your image on a large screen.
- **Preview remotely.** Extend the cable between the camera and TV screen, and you can preview your images some distance away from the camera.
- **Shoot from your computer.** Canon gives you the software you need to control your camera from your computer, so you can preview images and take pictures or movies without physically touching the EOS T5i.
- **Shoot from tripod or handheld.** Of course, holding the camera out at arm's length to preview an image is poor technique, and will introduce a lot of camera shake. If you want to use Live View for handheld images, use an image-stabilized lens and/or a high shutter speed. A tripod is a better choice if you can use one.
- **Watch your power.** Live View uses a lot of juice and will deplete your battery rapidly. Canon estimates that you can get 310 to 350 shots per battery when using Live View, depending on the temperature. Expect slightly fewer exposures when using flash. The optional AC adapter is a useful accessory.

# Enabling Live View

You need to take some steps before using Live View. This workflow prevents you from accidentally using Live View when you don't mean to, thus potentially losing a shot, and it also helps ensure that you've made all the settings necessary to successfully use the feature efficiently. Here are the steps to follow:

1. **Choose a shooting mode.** Live View works with any exposure mode, including Scene Intelligent Auto and Creative Auto. You can even switch from one Basic Zone mode to another or from one Creative Zone mode to another while Live View is activated. (If you change from Basic to Creative, or vice versa while Live View is on, it will be deactivated and must be restarted.)
2. **Enable Live View.** You'll need to activate Live View by choosing Live View Shoot. setting from the Live View Shooting menu (when the Mode Dial is set to a Creative Zone mode; if you're using a Basic Zone mode, an abbreviated list of Live View options is found in the Live View Shooting menu). Press SET and use the up/down cross keys to select Enable and press the SET button again to exit.

> **TIP**
>
> Note that even if you've disabled Live View, you can still flip the On/Off/Movie switch to Movie and shoot video.

3. **Choose other Live View functions.** Select from the other Live View functions in the Live View Shooting menu (described next), then press the MENU button to exit from the Live View Function Settings menu. Make sure you're using a Creative Zone mode if you want to view the full array of Live View function options.

4. **Select Live View or Movie shooting.** Press the Live View button on the right side of the viewfinder to begin or end Live View, or rotate the On/Off/Movie switch to the Movie position if you want to shoot video instead of stills.

There are seven choices in the Live View Shooting menu when using a Creative Zone mode. (See Figure 6.2.) Only the first five choices of those listed below are available when using a Basic Zone mode. The array of options include:

- **Live View shoot.** Enable/disable Live View shooting here. As I mentioned, disabling Live View does not affect movie shooting, which is activated by rotating the On/Off/Movie switch to the Movie position.

- **AF method (Face+Tracking, FlexiZone—Multi, FlexiZone—Single, Quick Mode).** This option lets you choose between AF with face recognition, manual zone selection, single zone selection, and Quick mode (all described in Chapter 5).

- **Continuous AF (Enable/Disable).** When enabled, the T5i will constantly refocus during Live View if you've specified Face+Tracking, FlexiZone—Multi, or FlexiZone—Single modes. This provides faster AF when you finally take a picture, but consumes more battery power. If you want to maximize the number of possible shots, disable the continuous AF feature, at the cost of some focusing speed. Because Continuous AF is not possible if you select Quick mode focus (remember, the camera flips down the mirror and uses the optical viewing system's phase detection AF mechanism), this setting is set to Disable. When you switch to one of the other three Live View focus modes, your original setting for this entry is restored.

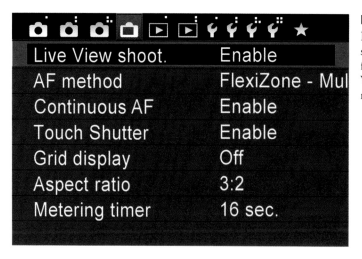

**Figure 6.2**
Live View function settings can be found in the Live View Shooting menu.

■ **Touch Shutter (Enable/Disable).** In all Live View shooting modes, when Touch Shutter is enabled, you can tap the subject on the screen to initiate focus on that subject and take a picture. The focus point will turn green and the image will be captured. If the T5i is unable to achieve focus, the point where you tapped will turn orange and the picture will not be taken. Tap the subject once more to try again. If you don't want to use this menu entry, the Touch Shutter can be enabled/disabled by tapping the Touch Shutter icon in the lower-left corner of the touch screen. If you don't see the icon on the screen, press the INFO. button until it appears.

■ **Grid display (Off, Grid 1, Grid 2).** Overlays Grid 1, a "rule of thirds" grid, on the screen to help you compose your image and align vertical and horizontal lines; or Grid 2, which consists of four rows of six boxes, which allow finer control over placement of images in your frame.

■ **Aspect ratio (3:2, 4:3, 16:9, or 1:1).** Selecting proportions other than the 3:2/18-megapixel default results in a cropped image. At the Large or RAW size setting, you end up with images that measure $4608 \times 3456$ pixels/16 MP (4:3 ratio); $5184 \times 2912$ pixels/15.1 MP (16:9 ratio); and $3456 \times 3456$ pixels/11.9 MP (1:1 ratio). At Medium (M), Small 1 (S1), Small 2 (S2), and Small 3 (S3), the images are proportionately smaller. (See Figure 6.3.) This choice is not available when using a Basic Zone mode.

■ **Metering timer (4 sec. to 30 min.).** This option allows you to specify how long the EOS T5i's metering system will remain active before switching off. Tap the shutter release to start the timer again after it switches off. This choice is not available when using a Basic Zone mode.

**Figure 6.3**
Aspect ratios, clockwise from top left: 3:2 (standard/ uncropped); 4:3; 16:9; 1:1.

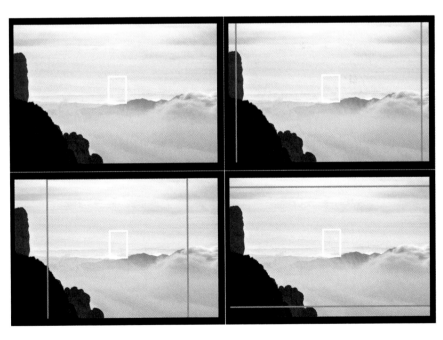

# Activating Live View

Once you've enabled Live View for later use, you can continue taking pictures normally through the T5i's viewfinder. When you're ready to activate Live View, press the Live View button on the back of the camera, to the immediate right of the viewfinder window (and marked with a red dot). The mirror will flip up, and the sensor image will appear on the LCD. Press the INFO. button to cycle among a display that is blank (except for the image), one that contains basic shooting information, a full display with settings, and one that adds a live histogram. (See Figure 6.4 for the view with histogram.)

In addition to the icons shown in the figure, additional information may be shown on the screen, depending on what focus or other mode you are working with, or optional accessories you are using:

- **Focus points.** If you've set focus to Quick mode, the same nine focus points visible in the viewfinder will be shown on the LCD for reference. You can select any of these points with the cross keys, and when the T5i activates autofocus by flipping down the mirror, the selected point in the optical system will be used to focus. In focus modes other than Quick mode, the active focus point will be shown.

- **Switch to Auto Selection.** In Quick mode, an icon will appear at the lower-left side of the touch screen that can be tapped to change to autofocus point selection.

- **Digital Compass/GPS/Eye-Fi Transmission.** If you're using these optional features, an icon will appear just above the bottom line to show their status.

- **AEB/FEB.** These icons will appear next to the Exp. Sim indicator when you're using autoexposure bracketing or flash exposure bracketing with an external flash unit.

- **Highlight Tone Priority.** If activated, a D+ will be shown next to the ISO indicator.

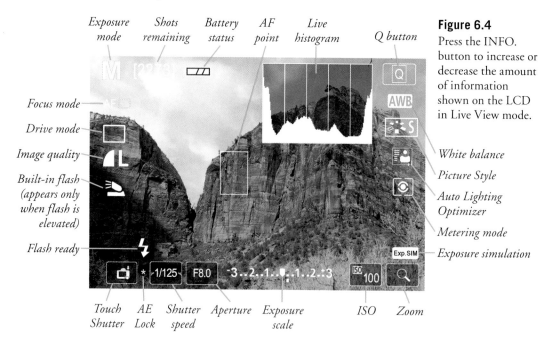

**Figure 6.4**
Press the INFO. button to increase or decrease the amount of information shown on the LCD in Live View mode.

# Using Simulated Exposure/Final Image Simulation

When Exp. Sim. is displayed in white on the Live View screen, it indicates that the LCD screen image brightness is an approximation of the brightness of the image that will be captured. If the Exp. Sim. display is blinking, it shows that the screen image does *not* represent the appearance of the final image because the light level is too dim or too bright. When using flash or bulb exposure, or night scene modes, the Exp. Sim. indicator is dimmed out to show you that the LCD image is not being adjusted to account for the actual exposure.

The T5i applies any active Picture Style settings to the LCD image, so you can have a rough representation of the image as it will appear when modified. Sharpness, contrast, color saturation, and color tone will all be applied. In addition, the camera applies the following parameters to the Live View image shown:

- White balance/white balance correction
- Shoot by ambience/lighting/scene choices
- Auto lighting optimization
- Peripheral illumination correction
- Highlight Tone Priority
- Aspect ratio
- Depth-of-field when DOF button is pressed

# Quick Control

Press the Q button or tap the Q icon at the upper right of the touch screen while using a Creative Zone in Live View, and you can adjust any of the values shown in the left- and right-hand columns. These include AF mode, Drive mode, White Balance, Picture Style, Auto Lighting Optimizer settings, Image quality settings, and Built-in flash functions. Figure 6.5 shows the focus mode adjustment screen that appears. If you're using a Basic Zone mode, you can change AF mode, Self-timer settings, and several other settings, depending on the Basic Zone mode you are using:

- **Shoot by ambience.** Can be changed when using Creative Auto, Portrait, Landscape, Close-Up, Sports, and Night Portrait modes.
- **Shoot by lighting or scene type.** Can be changed in Portrait, Landscape, Close-Up, and Sports modes.
- **Blurring/Sharpening the background.** Can be changed in Creative Auto mode.
- **Automatic Flash Firing.** Can be changed in Creative Auto mode; it is set automatically in Scene Intelligent Auto, Auto (Flash Off), Portrait, Close-Up, and Night Portrait modes.
- **Flash on at all times (Fill flash).** Can be set in Creative Auto mode.
- **Flash Off.** Can be set in Creative Auto mode; it is set automatically in Auto (Flash Off), Landscape, and Sports modes.
- **Drive mode, continuous shooting.** Can be set in Creative Auto, Portrait, and Sports modes.

**CREATIVE FILTERS LIVE**

Canon has added the ability to apply Creative Filters (described in Chapter 8) as you shoot images—and preview their looks before snapping a photo—when using Live View. You'll find the Creative Filters options in the lower-right corner of the live Quick Control screen, as seen in Figure 6.5.

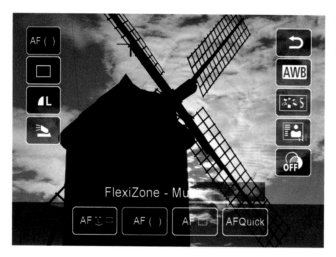

**Figure 6.5**
Focus mode adjustment screen.

# Shooting Movies

The Canon EOS T5i can shoot full HD movies with stereo sound at 1920 × 1080 resolution, or Standard HD video at 1280 × 720 resolution. VGA movies can also be shot at 640 × 480 resolution.

In some ways, the camera's Movie mode is closely related to the T5i's Live View still mode. In fact, the T5i uses Live View type imaging to show you the video clip on the LCD as it is captured. Many of the functions and setting options are the same, so the information in the previous sections will serve you well as you branch out into shooting movies with your camera. See Figure 6.6 for a typical live view presented during movie shooting.

To shoot in Movie mode, just rotate the On/Off/Movie switch to the Movie position. Press the Start/Stop button to begin/end capture. That's quite simple, but there are some additional things you need to keep in mind before you start:

- **Choose your resolution.** The T5i can capture movies in Full High Definition (1920 × 1080 pixel) resolution at 30, 25, or 24 fps; Standard High Definition (1280 × 720 at 60/50 fps); and 640 × 480 resolution at 30 or 25 fps. I'll show you how to specify resolution in the next section.

- **You can still shoot stills.** Press the shutter release all the way down at any time while filming movies in order to capture a still photo. Movie capture will stop for about one second while a still image is captured, leaving a gap in your clip, but will resume automatically after the picture is taken. The T5i will use the Image Quality settings you specify in the Shooting 1 menu, and will operate only in Single shooting drive mode (Continuous shooting or Self-timer delays are not possible). The flash is disabled. You can also extract a 2MP, 1MP, or .3MP image from your movie clips using ZoomBrowser. Still photos are stored as separate files.

- **Use the right card.** You'll want to use a fast memory card, at least a Class 6 SDHC card; a Class 10 card is even better. Slower cards may not work properly. Choose a memory card with at least 4GB capacity (8GB or 16GB are preferable). If the card you are working with is too slow, a five-level thermometer-like "buffer" indicator may appear at the right side of the LCD, showing the status of your camera's internal memory. If the indicator reaches the top level because the buffer is full, movie shooting will stop automatically.

- **Use a fully charged battery.** Canon says that a fresh battery will allow about one hour of filming at normal (non-Winter) temperatures.

- **Image stabilizer uses extra power.** If your lens has an image stabilizer, it will operate at all times (not just when the shutter button is pressed halfway, which is the case with still photography) and use a considerable amount of power, reducing battery life. You can switch the IS feature off to conserve power. Mount your camera on a tripod, and you don't need IS anyway.

- **Silent running.** You can connect your T5i to a television or video monitor while shooting movies, and see the video portion on the bigger screen as you shoot. However, the sound will not play—that's a good idea, because, otherwise, you could likely get a feedback loop of sound going. The sound will be recorded properly and will magically appear during playback once shooting has concluded.

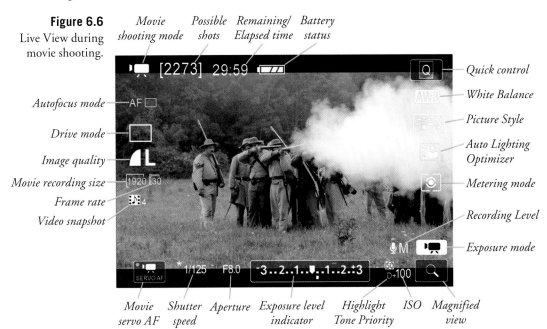

**Figure 6.6**
Live View during movie shooting.

*Movie shooting mode*  *Possible shots*  *Remaining/ Elapsed time*  *Battery status*

*Autofocus mode*
*Drive mode*
*Image quality*
*Movie recording size*
*Frame rate*
*Video snapshot*

*Quick control*
*White Balance*
*Picture Style*
*Auto Lighting Optimizer*
*Metering mode*
*Recording Level*
*Exposure mode*

*Movie servo AF*  *Shutter speed*  *Aperture*  *Exposure level indicator*  *Highlight Tone Priority*  *ISO*  *Magnified view*

# Resolution and Frame Rates

Even intermediate movie shooters can be confused by the number of different choices for resolution and frame rates. This section will help clarify things for you. First, resolution:

- **1920 × 1080.** This resolution is so-called "full HD" and is the maximum resolution displayed when using the HDTV format. Many monitors and most HD televisions can display this resolution, and you'll have the best image quality when you use it. Use this resolution for your "professional" productions, especially those you'll be editing and converting to nifty-looking DVDs. However, the top-of-the line resolution requires the most storage space, approximately 330 megabytes per minute, yielding about 44 minutes of "shooting time" on a 16GB memory card. (Of course the maximum length of a single continuous clip is nearly 30 minutes.)

- **1280 × 720.** "Standard HD" provides less resolution, and can be displayed on any monitor or television that claims HDTV compatibility. If your production will appear only on computer monitors with 1280 × 720 resolution, or on HDTVs that max out at 720p, this resolution will be fine.

- **640 × 480.** This is so-called VGA resolution, suitable for display on computer monitors and, possibly, old standard-definition televisions. (Remember the ones with CRT tubes instead of LCD, LED, or plasma displays?) This lower-resolution format is less demanding of your storage, too, requiring about 82 megabytes per minute capture, and providing more than three hours of video clips on a single 16GB card. You'll use this resolution for productions destined for display on the Internet, and other similar uses.

Frame rates are a trickier proposition. Fortunately, one seemingly confusing set of alternatives can be dispensed with quickly: The 50/25 fps and 60/30 fps options can be considered as pairs of *video*-oriented frame rates. The 60/30 fps rates are used only where the NTSC television standard is in place, such as North America, Japan, Korea, Mexico, and a few other places. The 50/25 frame rates are used where the PAL standard reigns, such as Europe, Russia, China, Africa, Australia, and other places. For simplicity, I'll refer just to the 60/30 frame rates in this section; if you're reading this in India, just convert to 50/25.

The third possibility is 24 fps, which is a standard frame rate used for motion pictures. Keep in mind that the rates are *nominal.* A 24 fps setting actually yields 23.976 frames per second; 30 fps gives you 29.97 actual "frames" per second.

The difference lies in the two "worlds" of motion images: film and video. The standard frame rate for motion picture film is 24 fps, while the video rate, at least in the United States, Japan, and those other places using the NTSC standard is 30 fps (actually 60 interlaced *fields* per second, which is why we can choose either 30 frames/fields per second or 60 frames/fields per second). Computer-editing software can handle either type, and convert between them. The choice between 24 fps and 30 fps is determined by what you plan to do with your video.

The short explanation is that, for technical reasons I won't go into here, shooting at 24 fps gives your movie a "film" look, excellent for showing fine detail. However, if your clip has moving subjects, or you pan the camera, 24 fps can produce a jerky effect called "judder." A 30 or 60 fps rate produces a home-video look that some feel is less desirable, but which is smoother and less jittery when displayed on an electronic monitor. I suggest you try both and use the frame rate that best suits your tastes and video-editing software.

## Movie Settings

The Movie Settings menus can be summoned by the MENU button only when the T5i has been set to Movie mode (rotate the On/Off/Movie switch to the Movie position). The five settings on the Movie 1 menu (see Figure 6.7) include:

- **AF method.** This option, explained in Chapter 5, lets you choose between AF with face recognition, manual zone selection, single zone selection, and Quick mode (all described in Chapter 5).

- **Movie Servo AF.** Set to enable if you want to activate continuous autofocus by pressing the shutter release halfway, even if One-Shot AF is active. This allows following focus with moving objects. Remember to turn off the camera before switching the lens's switch to Manual focus. Choose Disable to always use the focus mode you've selected. You can temporarily activate/deactivate Movie Servo AF by tapping the Servo/AF icon at lower left of the screen, or by pressing the Flash button. You can also redefine the * button to stop/start this feature, as described in Chapter 9. Resume Movie Servo AF by pressing the MENU or Playback buttons.

- **AF w/shutter button during movie recording.** You can choose Enable to allow refocusing during movie shooting or Disable to prevent it. Refocusing after you've begun capturing a movie clip can be a good thing or a bad thing, so you want to be able to control when it happens. If you select Enable, then you can refocus during capture by pressing the shutter button. Refocusing will take place *only* when you press the shutter button; the T5i is not able to refocus continually as you shoot.

  Changing the focus during capture can be dangerous—your image is likely to go out of focus for a fraction of a second while the camera refocuses. That might not be bad if you plan on

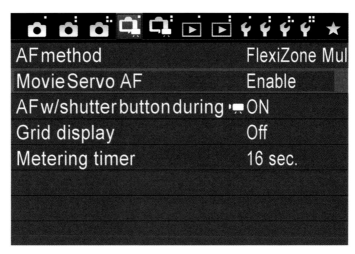

**Figure 6.7**
The Movie 1 menu has five entries.

| AF method | FlexiZone Mul |
| Movie Servo AF | Enable |
| AF w/shutter button during | ON |
| Grid display | Off |
| Metering timer | 16 sec. |

editing your movie and can remove the out-of-focus part of the clip. But refocusing during a shot can be disconcerting. Note that even if you've set the T5i to Quick mode focus, it will use phase detection only at the beginning of the clip; subsequent refocusing will be performed using the live mode. Most of the time, I set this parameter to Disable to avoid accidentally refocusing during a shot.

- **Grid display.** You can select Off, Grid #1, or Grid #2.
- **Metering timer (4 sec. to 30 min.).** This option allows you to specify how long the EOS T5i's metering system will remain active before switching off.

The Movie 2 menu has three entries (see Figure 6.8):

- **Movie rec. size.** Choose 1920 × 1080 (Full HD) at 30 or 24 fps; 1280 × 720 (HD) at 60 fps; or 640 × 480 pixel (Standard resolution) at 60 fps. The frame rates are for NTSC television mode; for the PAL system, the camera will substitute 50 fps for 60 fps, and 25 fps for 30 fps. (The motion picture standard, 24 fps, remains constant.)

  Single movie clips can be no more than 4GB in size, and shooting will stop automatically at that point. So, the maximum *length* of your videos is determined by the resolution you choose. At either HD setting, your movie will max out at about 29 minutes for a single clip. With either of the 640 × 480–pixel settings, you can shoot about 24 minutes continuously. The number of multiple clips you can fit on a single memory card depends on the size of the card. You can record about 44 minutes of video/sound (in 12-minute max clips) on a 16GB memory card in HD format, or 92 minutes (in maximum 24-minute clips) in 640 × 480–pixel format.

- **Sound recording.** Choose Auto, Manual, or Disable; plus enable or disable wind filter:

  - **Auto.** The T5i sets the audio level for you.

  - **Manual.** Choose from 64 different sound levels. Select Rec Level and rotate the QCD while viewing the decibel meter at the bottom of the screen to choose a level that averages –12 dB for the loudest sounds.

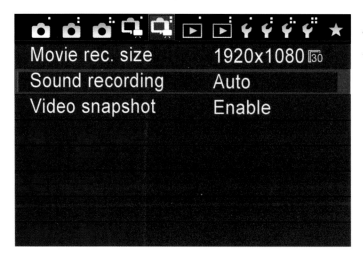

**Figure 6.8**
The Movie 2 menu has three entries.

- **Disable.** Shoot silently, and add voice over, narration, music, or other sound later in your movie-editing software.

  You can use your T5i's built-in stereo microphone or plug in a stereo microphone into the 3.5mm jack on the side of the camera. An external microphone is a good idea because the built-in microphone can easily pick up camera operation, such as the autofocus motor in a lens.

- **Wind filter.** Enable to reduce the effects of wind noise on the microphone. This also reduces low tones in the sound recording. If wind is not a problem, you'll get better quality audio with this option disabled. Even better is to use an external microphone with a wind shield.

- **Video snapshot.** This is an easy way to create a set of movie clips, each lasting 2, 4, or 8 seconds. The T5i saves your snapshots to an album, each giving you a short movie that can be played back along with background music. Select Video Snapshot from the Movie 2 menu, and choose 2 Sec. Movie, 4 Sec. Movie, or 8 Sec. Movie (or Disable). Press SET to confirm your choice.

## Capturing Video/Sound

To shoot movies with your camera, just follow these steps:

1. **Change to Movie mode.** Rotate the On/Off/Movie switch to the Movie setting.
2. **Focus.** Use the autofocus or manual focus techniques described in the preceding sections to achieve focus on your subject.
3. **Begin filming.** Press the Live View button to begin shooting. A red dot appears in the upper-right corner of the screen to show that video/sound are being captured. The access lamp also flashes during shooting.
4. **Changing shooting functions.** As with Live View, you can change settings or review images normally when shooting video.
5. **Lock exposure.** You can lock in exposure by pressing the Zoom Out button on top of the T5i, located just aft of the Main Dial. Unlock exposure again by pressing the button once more.
6. **Stop filming.** Press the Live View button again to stop filming.
7. **View your clip.** Press the Playback button (located to the bottom right of the LCD). You will see a still frame with the clip timing and a symbol telling you to press the SET button to see the clip. A series of video controls appear at the bottom of the frame. Press SET again and the clip begins. A blue thermometer bar progresses in the upper-left corner as the timing counts down. Press SET to stop at any time.

**GETTING INFO**

The information display shown on the LCD screen when shooting movies is almost identical to the one displayed during live view shooting. The settings icons in the left column show the same options, which can be changed in Movie mode, too, except that the Drive mode choice is replaced by an indicator that shows the current movie resolution and time remaining on your memory card.

# Video Snapshots

Video snapshots are movie clips, all the same length, assembled into video albums as a single movie. You can choose a fixed length of 2, 4, or 8 seconds for all clips in a particular album. I use the 2-second length to compile mini-movies of fast-moving events, such as parades, giving me a lively album of clips that show all the things going on without lingering too long on a single scene. The 8-second length is ideal for landscapes and many travel clips, because the longer scenes give you time to absorb all the interesting things to see in such environments. The 4-second clips are an excellent way to show details of a single subject, such as a cathedral or monument when traveling, or an overview of the action at a sports event.

Activate the video snapshot feature in the Movie 2 menu, as described above. Then, follow these steps:

1. **Begin an album.** In Movie mode, press the Live View/Movie button. The T5i will begin shooting a clip, and a set of blue bars will appear at the bottom of the frame showing you how much time remains before shooting stops automatically.

2. **Save your clip as a video snapshot album.** A confirmation appears at the bottom of the LCD. Press the left/right cross keys to choose the left-most icon, Save as Album.

3. **Press SET.** Your first clip will be saved as the start of a new album.

4. **Shoot additional clips.** Press the Movie button to shoot more clips of the length you have chosen, and indicated by the blue bars at the bottom of the frame. At the end of the specified time, the confirmation screen will appear again. (See Figure 6.9.)

5. **Add to album or create new album.** Select the left-most icon again if you want to add the most recent clip to the album you just started. Alternatively, you can press the left/right cross keys to choose the second icon from the left, Save as a New Album. That will complete your previous album, and start a new one with the most recent clip.

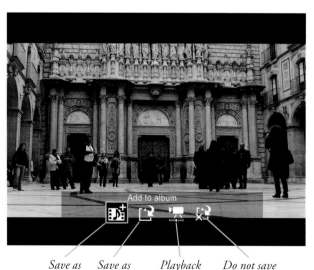

**Figure 6.9**
Save your clip as a video snapshot album.

*Save as       Save as       Playback        Do not save*
*album     new album   video snapshot    to album*

Or, if you'd like to review the most recent clip first to make sure it's worth adding to an album, select the Playback Video Snapshot icon (second from the right) and review the clip you just shot. You can then Add to Album, Create New Album, or Delete the Clip.

6. **Delete most recent clip.** If you decide the most recent clip is not one you'd like to add to your current album, you can select Do Not Save to Album/Delete without Saving to Album (the right-most icon).

7. **Switch from Video Snapshots to conventional movie clips.** If you want to stop shooting video snapshots and resume shooting regular movie clips (of a variable length), navigate to the Movie 2 menu again, and disable Video Snapshot.

## Playback and Editing

You can play back your video snapshots from the confirmation screen. Or, you can exit Movie mode and review your stills and images and play any of them back by pressing the playback button located to the lower right of the LCD. A movie or album will be marked with an icon in the upper-left corner. If you're viewing thumbnails, the movies will be identified by a sprocket hole marking. Press the SET button to play back a movie or album when you see this icon.

As a movie or album is being played back, a screen of options appears at the bottom of the screen, as shown in Figure 6.10. When the icons are shown, use the left/right cross keys to highlight one, and then press the SET button to activate that function:

- **Exit.** Exits playback mode.
- **Playback.** Begins playback of the movie or album. To pause playback, press the SET button again. That restores the row of icons so you can choose a function.
- **Slow motion.** Displays the video in slow motion.

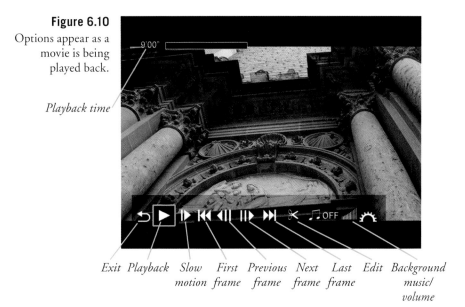

**Figure 6.10**
Options appear as a movie is being played back.

*Playback time*

*Exit  Playback  Slow      First    Previous  Next    Last    Edit  Background*
*                motion   frame    frame    frame   frame          music/*
*                                                                   volume*

- **First frame.** Jumps to the first frame of the video, or the first scene of an album's first video snapshot.
- **Previous frame.** Press SET to view previous frame; hold down SET to rewind movie.
- **Next frame.** Press SET to view next frame; hold down SET to fast forward movie.
- **Last frame.** Jumps to last frame of the video, or the last scene of the album's last video snapshot.
- **Edit.** Summons an editing screen (see Figure 6.11).
- **Background music/volume.** Select to turn background music on/off. Rotate the Main Dial to adjust the volume of the background music.

While reviewing your video, you can trim from the beginning or end of your video clip by selecting the scissors symbol. The icons that appear have the following functions:

- **Cut beginning.** Trims off all video prior to the current point.
- **Cut end.** Removes video after the current point.
- **Play video.** Play back your video to reach the point where you want to trim the beginning or end.
- **Save.** Saves your video to the memory card. A screen appears offering to save the clip as a New File, or to Overwrite the existing movie with your edited clip.
- **Exit.** Exits editing mode.
- **Adjust volume.** Modifies the volume of the background music.

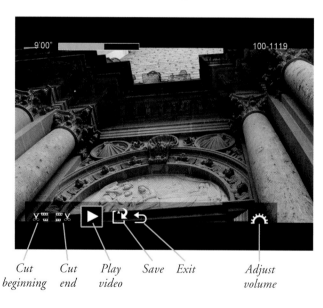

**Figure 6.11**
The editing screen allows you to snip off the beginning or end of a video clip.

*Cut       Cut    Play    Save   Exit        Adjust*
*beginning  end   video                      volume*

# Tips for Shooting Better Movies

Producing high-quality movies can be a real challenge for amateur photographers. After all, by comparison we're used to watching the best productions that television, video, and motion pictures can offer. Whether it's fair or not, our efforts are compared to what we're used to seeing produced by experts. While this chapter can't make you into a pro videographer, it can help you improve your efforts.

There are a number of different things to consider when planning a video shoot, and when possible, a shooting script and storyboard can help you produce a higher quality video.

# Lens Craft

I cover the use of lenses with the T5i in more detail in Chapter 10, but a discussion of lens selection when shooting movies may be useful at this point. In the video world, not all lenses are created equal. The two most important considerations are depth-of-field, or the beneficial lack thereof, and zooming. I'll address each of these separately.

## Depth-of-Field and Video

Have you wondered why professional videographers have gone nuts over still cameras that can also shoot video? As I mentioned, the producers of *Saturday Night Live* could afford to have Alex Buono, their director of photography, use the niftiest, most expensive high-resolution video cameras to shoot the opening sequences of the program. Instead, Buono opted for a pair of digital SLR cameras. One thing that makes digital still cameras so attractive for video is that they have relatively large sensors, which provides improved low-light performance and results in the oddly attractive reduced depth-of-field, compared with most professional video cameras.

*But wait!* you say. No matter what size sensor is used to capture a full HD video frame, isn't the number of pixels in that frame exactly the same—1920 × 1080 pixels? That's true—the final resolution of the video image is exactly 1920 × 1080 pixels, whether you're capturing that frame with a point-and-shoot camera, a professional video camera, or a digital SLR like the T5i. But that's only the *final* resolution. The number of pixels used to capture each video frame varies by sensor size.

For example, your T5i does *not* use only its central 1920 × 1080 pixels to capture a full HD video frame. Instead, the T5i captures a video frame using the proportions of a 16:9 area of its sensor, measuring roughly 5184 × 2912 pixels. Your wide-angle and telephoto lenses retain their same fields of view, and you can frame and compose your video through the viewfinder normally, with only the top and bottom of the frame cropped off to account for the wider video aspect ratio.

The roughly 15 million pixels used to *capture* the image are processed to create the 2,073,600 pixels of the final video frame. That's why the T5i gives you such great video quality, and why your video images retain roughly the same field of view and exact same depth-of-field you get with full-frame still images.

Figure 6.12 provides a comparison of the relative size of sensors. The typical size of a professional video camera sensor is shown at lower right. The sensor of the typical point-and-shoot camera like the PowerShot G15 is shown just northeast of it, and the proportions of the PowerShot G1 X are shown at the lower-left corner. In comparison, the T5i's image-grabber at upper left is *much* larger when compared with the sensors used in many pro video cameras and the even smaller sensors found in the typical consumer camcorder.

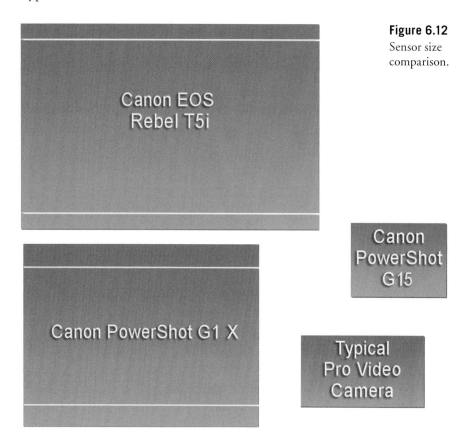

**Figure 6.12**
Sensor size comparison.

A larger sensor calls for the use of longer focal lengths to produce the same field of view, so, in effect, a larger sensor has reduced depth-of-field. And *that's* what makes cameras like the T5i attractive from a creative standpoint. Less depth-of-field means greater control over the range of what's in focus. Your T5i, with its larger sensor, has a distinct advantage over consumer camcorders in this regard, and even does a better job than many professional video cameras.

## Zooming and Video

When shooting still photos, a zoom is a zoom is a zoom. The key considerations for a zoom lens used only for still photography are the maximum aperture available at each focal length ("How *fast* is this lens?"), the zoom range ("How far can I zoom in or out?"), and its sharpness at any given f/stop ("Do I lose sharpness when I shoot wide open?").

When shooting video, the priorities may change, and there are two additional parameters to consider. The first two I listed, lens speed and zoom range, have roughly the same importance in both still and video photography. Zoom range gains a bit of importance in videography, because you can always/usually move closer to shoot a still photograph, but when you're zooming during a shot most of us don't have that option (or the funds to buy/rent a dolly to smoothly move the camera during capture). But, oddly enough, overall sharpness may have slightly less importance under certain conditions when shooting video. That's because the image changes in some way many times per second, so any given frame doesn't hang around long enough for our eyes to pick out every single detail. You want a sharp image, of course, but your standards don't need to be quite as high when shooting video.

Here are the remaining considerations:

- **Zoom lens maximum aperture.** The speed of the lens matters in several ways. A zoom with a relatively large maximum aperture lets you shoot in lower light levels, and a big f/stop allows you to minimize depth-of-field for selective focus. Keep in mind that the maximum aperture may change during zooming. A lens that offers an f/3.5 maximum aperture at its widest focal length may provide only f/5.6 worth of light at the telephoto position.

- **Zoom range.** Use of zoom during actual capture should not be an everyday thing, unless you're shooting a kung-fu movie. However, there are effective uses for a zoom shot, particularly if it's a "long" one from extreme wide angle to extreme close-up (or vice versa). Most of the time, you'll use the zoom range to adjust the perspective of the camera *between* shots, and a longer zoom range can mean less trotting back and forth to adjust the field of view. Zoom range also comes into play when you're working with selective focus (longer focal lengths have less depth-of-field), or want to expand or compress the apparent distance between foreground and background subjects. A longer range gives you more flexibility.

- **Linearity.** Interchangeable lenses may have some drawbacks, as many photographers who have been using the video features of their digital SLRs have discovered. That's because, unless a lens is optimized for video shooting, zooming with a particular lens may not necessarily be linear. Rotating the zoom collar manually at a constant speed doesn't always produce a smooth zoom. There may be "jumps" as the elements of the lens shift around during the zoom. Keep that in mind if you plan to zoom during a shot, and are using a lens that has proved, from experience, to provide a non-linear zoom. (Unfortunately, there's no easy way to tell ahead of time whether you own a lens that is well suited for zooming during a shot.)

## Keeping Things Stable and on the Level

Camera shake's enough of a problem with still photography, but it becomes even more of a nuisance when you're shooting video. The image-stabilization feature found in many lenses (and some third-party optics) can help minimize this. That's why these lenses make an excellent choice for video shooting if you're planning on going for the handheld cinema verité look.

Just realize that while handheld camera shots—even image stabilized—may be perfect if you're shooting a documentary or video that intentionally mimics traditional home movie-making, in other contexts it can be disconcerting or annoying. And even IS can't work miracles. As I'll point out in the next section, it's the camera movement itself that is distracting—not necessarily any blur in our subject matter.

If you want your video to look professional, putting the T5i on a tripod will give you smoother, steadier video clips to work with. It will be easier to intercut shots taken from different angles (or even at different times) if everything was shot on a tripod. Cutting from a tripod shot to a handheld shot, or even from one handheld shot to another one that has noticeably more (or less) camera movement can call attention to what otherwise might have been a smooth cut or transition.

Remember that telephoto lenses and telephoto zoom focal lengths magnify any camera shake, even with IS, so when you're using a longer focal length, that tripod becomes an even better idea. Tripods are essential if you want to pan from side to side during a shot, dolly in and out, or track from side to side (say, you want to shoot with the camera in your kid's coaster wagon). A tripod and (for panning) a fluid head built especially for smooth video movements can add a lot of production value to your movies.

## Shooting Script

A shooting script is nothing more than a coordinated plan that covers both audio and video and provides order and structure for your video when you're in planned, storytelling mode. A detailed script will cover what types of shots you're going after, what dialogue you're going to use, audio effects, transitions, and graphics. A good script needn't constrain you: as the director you are free to make changes on the spot during actual capture. But, before you change the route to your final destination, it's good to know where you were headed, and how you originally planned to get there.

When putting together your shooting script, plan for lots and lots of different shots, even if you don't think you'll need them. Only amateurish videos consist of a bunch of long, tedious shots. You'll want to vary the pace of your production by cutting among lots of different views, angles, and perspectives, so jot down your ideas for these variations when you put together your script.

If you're shooting a documentary rather than telling a story that's already been completely mapped out, the idea of using a shooting script needs to be applied more flexibly. Documentary filmmakers often have no shooting script at all. They go out, do their interviews, capture video of people, places, and events as they find them, and allow the structure of the story to take shape as they learn more about the subject of their documentary. In such cases, the movie is typically "created" during editing, as bits and pieces are assembled into the finished piece.

## Storyboards

A storyboard makes a great adjunct to a detailed shooting script. It is a series of panels providing visuals of what each scene should look like. While the ones produced by Hollywood are generally of very high quality, there's nothing that says drawing skills are important for this step. Stick figures work just fine if that's the best you can do. The storyboard just helps you visualize locations, placement of actors/actresses, props and furniture, and also helps everyone involved get an idea of

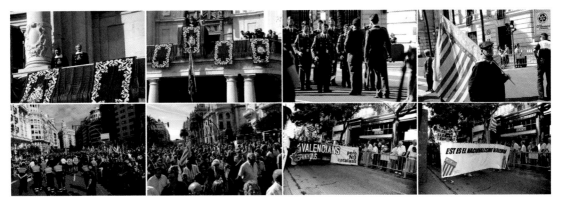

**Figure 6.13** A storyboard is a series of simple sketches or photos to help visualize a segment of video.

what you're trying to show. It also helps show how you want to frame or compose a shot. You can even shoot a series of still photos and transform them into a "storyboard" if you want, such as in Figure 6.13.

# Storytelling in Video

Today's audience is used to fast-paced, short-scene storytelling. In order to produce interesting video for such viewers, it's important to view video storytelling as a kind of shorthand code for the more leisurely efforts print media offers. Audio and video should always be advancing the story. While it's okay to let the camera linger from time to time, it should only be for a compelling reason and only briefly.

Above all, look for movement in your scene as you shoot. You're not taking still photographs! Perhaps your ideal still picture of an old castle in Segovia, Spain might be to show the edifice in its modern-day surroundings, but a movie needs to show something *moving,* like the hang glider who soared overhead when I captured the image shown in Figure 6.14.

It only takes a second or two for an establishing shot to impart the necessary information. For example, many of the scenes for a video documenting a model being photographed in a Rock and Roll music setting might be close-ups and talking heads, but an establishing shot showing the studio where the video was captured helps set the scene.

Provide variety too. If you put your shooting script together correctly, you'll be changing camera angles and perspectives often and never leave a static scene on the screen for a long period of time. (You can record a static scene for a reasonably long period and then edit in other shots that cut away and back to the longer scene with close-ups that show each person talking.)

When editing, keep transitions basic! I can't stress this one enough. Watch a television program or movie. The action "jumps" from one scene or person to the next. Fancy transitions that involve exotic "wipes," dissolves, or cross fades take too long for the average viewer and make your video ponderous.

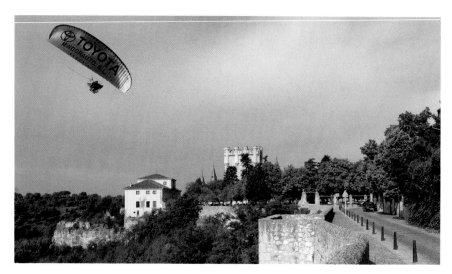

**Figure 6.14**
Movies need motion to come alive.

# Composition

In movie shooting, several factors restrict your composition, and impose requirements you just don't always have in still photography (although other rules of good composition do apply). Here are some of the key differences to keep in mind when composing movie frames:

- **Horizontal compositions only.** Some subjects, such as basketball players and tall buildings, just lend themselves to vertical compositions. But movies are shown in horizontal format only. So if you're interviewing a local basketball star, you can end up with a worst-case situation like the one shown in Figure 6.15. If you want to show how tall your subject is, it's often impractical to move back far enough to show him full-length. You really can't capture a vertical composition. Tricks like getting down on the floor and shooting up at your subject can exaggerate the perspective, but aren't a perfect solution.

- **Wasted space at the sides.** Moving in to frame the basketball player as outlined by the yellow box in Figure 6.15 means that you're still forced to leave a lot of empty space on either side. (Of course, you can fill that space with other people and/or interesting stuff, but that defeats your intent of concentrating on your main subject.) So when faced with some types of subjects in a horizontal frame, you can be creative, or move in *really* tight. For example, if I was willing to give up the "height" aspect of my composition, I could have framed the shot as shown by the green box in the figure, and wasted less of the image area at either side.

- **Seamless (or seamed) transitions.** Unless you're telling a picture story with a photo essay, still pictures often stand alone. But with movies, each of your compositions must relate to the shot that preceded it, and the one that follows. It can be jarring to jump from a long shot to a tight close-up unless the director—you—is very creative. Another common error is the "jump cut" in which successive shots vary only slightly in camera angle, making it appear that the main subject has "jumped" from one place to another. (Although everyone from French New Wave director Jean-Luc Goddard to Guy Ritchie—Madonna's ex—have used jump cuts effectively

**Figure 6.15**
Movie shooting requires you to fit all your subjects into a horizontally oriented frame.

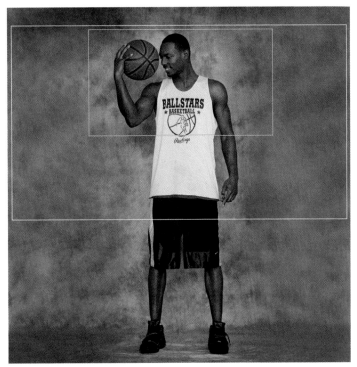

in their films.) The rule of thumb is to vary the camera angle by at least 30 degrees between shots to make it appear to be seamless. Unless you prefer that your images flaunt convention and appear to be "seamy."

■ **The time dimension.** Unlike still photography, with motion pictures there's a lot more emphasis on using a series of images to build on each other to tell a story. Static shots where the camera is mounted on a tripod and everything is shot from the same distance are a recipe for dull videos. Watch a television program sometime and notice how often camera shots change distances and directions. Viewers are used to this variety and have come to expect it. Professional video productions are often done with multiple cameras shooting from different angles and positions. But many professional productions are shot with just one camera and careful planning, and you can do just fine with your T5i.

Here's a look at the different types of commonly used compositional tools:

■ **Establishing shot.** Much like it sounds, this type of composition, as shown in Figure 6.16, left, establishes the scene and tells the viewer where the action is taking place. Let's say you're shooting a video of your offspring's move to college; the establishing shot could be a wide shot of the campus with a sign welcoming you to the school in the foreground. Another example would be for a child's birthday party; the establishing shot could be the front of the house decorated with birthday signs and streamers or a shot of the dining room table decked out with party favors and a candle-covered birthday cake. Or, in Figure 6.16, I wanted to show the studio where the video was shot.

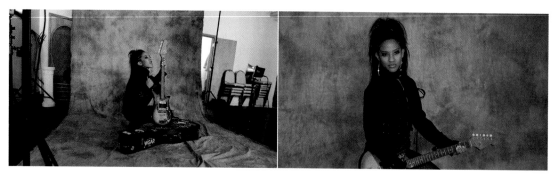

**Figure 6.16** An establishing shot sets the stage for your video scene (left). A medium shot is used to introduce a character and provide context via their surroundings (right).

- **Medium shot.** This shot is composed from about waist to head room (some space above the subject's head). It's useful for providing variety from a series of close-ups and also makes for a useful first look at a speaker. (See Figure 6.16, right.)

- **Close-up.** The close-up, usually described as "from shirt pocket to head room," provides a good composition for someone talking directly to the camera. Although it's common to have your talking head centered in the shot, that's not a requirement. In Figure 6.17, left, the subject was offset to the right. This would allow other images, especially graphics or titles, to be superimposed in the frame in a "real" (professional) production. But the compositional technique can be used with T5i videos, too, even if special effects are not going to be added.

- **Extreme close-up.** When I went through broadcast training back in the '70s, this shot was described as the "big talking face" shot and we were actively discouraged from employing it. Styles and tastes change over the years and now the big talking face is much more commonly used (maybe people are better looking these days?) and so this view may be appropriate. Just remember, the T5i is capable of shooting in high-definition video and you may be playing the video on a high-def TV; be careful that you use this composition on a face that can stand up to high definition. (See Figure 6.17, right.)

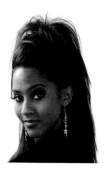 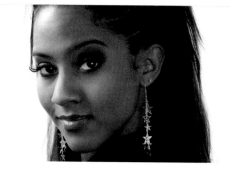

**Figure 6.17** A close-up generally shows the full face with a little head room at the top and down to the shoulders at the bottom of the frame (left). An extreme close-up is a very tight shot that cuts off everything above the top of the head and below the chin (or even closer!).

- **"Two" shot.** A two shot shows a pair of subjects in one frame. They can be side by side or one in the foreground and one in the background. (See Figure 6.18, left.) This does not have to be a head-to-ground composition. Subjects can be standing or seated. A "three shot" is the same principle except that three people are in the frame.

- **Over-the-shoulder shot.** Long a composition of interview programs, the "over-the-shoulder shot" uses the rear of one person's head and shoulder to serve as a frame for the other person. This puts the viewer's perspective as that of the person facing away from the camera. (See Figure 6.18, right.)

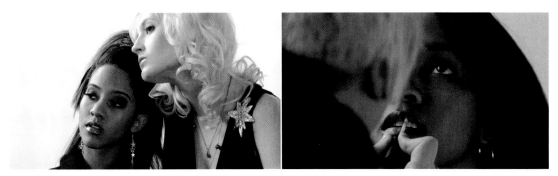

**Figure 6.18** A "two shot" features two people in the frame. This version can be framed at various distances such as medium or close up (left). An "over-the-shoulder" shot is a popular shot for interview programs, making viewers feel like they're asking the questions.

# Lighting for Video

Much like in still photography, how you handle light pretty much can make or break your videography. Lighting for video can be more complicated than lighting for still photography, since both subject and camera movement is often part of the process.

Lighting for video presents several concerns. First off, you want enough illumination to create a useable video. Beyond that, you want to use light to help tell your story or increase drama. Let's take a better look at both.

## Illumination

You can significantly improve the quality of your video by increasing the light falling in the scene. This is true indoors or out, by the way. While it may seem like sunlight is more than enough, it depends on how much contrast you're dealing with. If your subject is in shadow (which can help them from squinting) or wearing a ball cap, a video light can help make them look a lot better.

Lighting choices for amateur videographers are a lot better these days than they were a decade or two ago. An inexpensive incandescent video light, which will easily fit in a camera bag, can be found for $15 or $20. You can even get a good-quality LED video light for less than $100.

(See Figure 6.19.) Work lights sold at many home improvement stores can also serve as video lights since you can set the camera's white balance to correct for any color casts. You'll need to mount these lights on a tripod or other support, or, perhaps, to a bracket that fastens to the tripod socket on the bottom of the camera.

Much of the challenge depends upon whether you're just trying to add some fill light on your subject versus trying to boost the light on an entire scene. A small video light will do just fine for the former. It won't handle the latter.

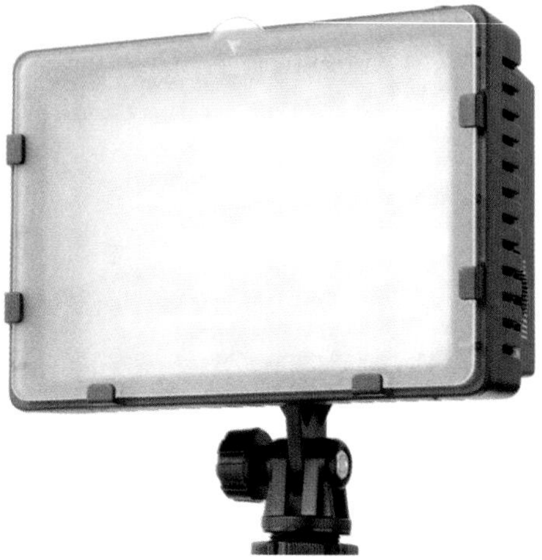

## Creative Lighting

While ramping up the light intensity will produce better technical quality in your video, it won't necessarily improve the artistic quality of it. Whether we're out-

**Figure 6.19** This inexpensive LED video light cost $35.

doors or indoors, we're used to seeing light come from above. Videographers need to consider how they position their lights to provide even illumination while up high enough to angle shadows down low and out of sight of the camera.

When considering lighting for video, there are several factors. One is the quality of the light. It can either be hard (direct) or soft (diffused). Hard light is good for showing detail, but can also be very harsh and unforgiving. "Softening" the light, but diffusing it somehow, can reduce the intensity of the light but make for a kinder, gentler light as well.

While mixing light sources isn't always a good idea, one approach is to combine window light with supplemental lighting. Position your subject with the window to one side and bring in either a supplemental light or a reflector to the other side for reasonably even lighting.

## Lighting Styles

Some lighting styles are more heavily used than others. Some forms are used for special effects, while others are designed to be invisible. At its most basic, lighting just illuminates the scene, but when used properly it can also create drama. Let's look at some types of lighting styles:

- **Three-point lighting.** This is a basic lighting setup for one person. A main light illuminates the strong side of a person's face, while a fill light lights up the other side. A third light is then positioned above and behind the subject to light the back of the head and shoulders. (See Figure 6.20.)

- **Flat lighting.** Use this type of lighting to provide illumination and nothing more. It calls for a variety of lights and diffusers set to raise the light level in a space enough for good video reproduction, but not to create a particular mood or emphasize a particular scene or individual.

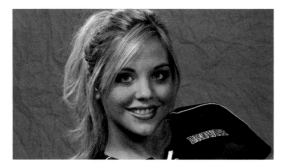

**Figure 6.20** With three-point lighting, two lights are placed in front and to the side of the subject (45-degree angles are ideal) and positioned about a foot higher than the subject's head. Another light is directed on the background in order to separate the subject and the background.

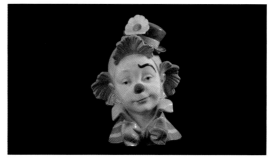

**Figure 6.21** Flat lighting is another approach for creating even illumination. Here the lights can be bounced off of a white ceiling and walls to fill in shadows as much as possible. It is a flexible lighting approach since the subject can change positions without needing a change in light direction.

With flat lighting, you're trying to create even lighting levels throughout the video space and minimize any shadows. Generally, the lights are placed up high and angled downward (or possibly pointed straight up to bounce off of a white ceiling). (See Figure 6.21.)

- **"Ghoul lighting."** This is the style of lighting used for old horror movies. The idea is to position the light down low, pointed upward. It's such an unnatural style of lighting that it makes its targets seem weird and "ghoulish."

- **Outdoor lighting.** While shooting outdoors may seem easier because the sun provides more light, it also presents its own problems. As a general rule of thumb, keep the sun behind you when you're shooting video outdoors, except when shooting faces (anything from a medium shot and closer) since the viewer won't want to see a squinting subject. When shooting another human this way, put the sun behind her and use a video light to balance light levels between the foreground and background. If the sun is simply too bright, position the subject in the shade and use the video light for your main illumination. Using reflectors (white board panels or aluminum foil covered cardboard panels are cheap options) can also help balance light effectively.

# Audio

When it comes to making a successful video, audio quality is one of those things that separates the professionals from the amateurs. We're used to watching top-quality productions on television and in the movies, yet the average person has no idea how much effort goes in to producing what seems to be "natural" sound. Much of the sound you hear in such productions is actually recorded on carefully controlled sound stages and "sweetened" with a variety of sound effects and other recordings of "natural" sound.

## Tips for Better Audio

Since recording high-quality audio is such a challenge, it's a good idea to do everything possible to maximize recording quality. Here are some ideas for improving the quality of the audio your camera records:

- **Get the camera and its microphone close to the speaker.** The farther the microphone is from the audio source, the less effective it will be in picking up that sound. While having to position the camera and its built-in microphone closer to the subject affects your lens choices and lens perspective options, it will make the most of your audio source. Of course, if you're using a very wide-angle lens, getting too close to your subject can have unflattering results, so don't take this advice too far. It's important to think carefully about what sounds you want to capture. If you're shooting video of an acoustic combo that's not using a PA system, you'll want the microphone close to them, but not so close that, say, only the lead singer or instrumentalist is picked up, while the players at either side fade off into the background.

- **Use an external microphone.** You'll recall the description of the camera's external microphone port in Chapter 3. As noted, this port accepts a stereo mini-plug from a standard external microphone, allowing you to achieve considerably higher audio quality for your movies than is possible with the camera's built-in microphones (which are disabled when an external mic is plugged in). An external microphone reduces the amount of camera-induced noise that is picked up and recorded on your audio track. (The action of the lens as it focuses can be audible when the built-in microphones are active.)

The external microphone port can provide plug-in power for microphones that can take their power from this sort of outlet rather than from a battery in the microphone. You may find suitable microphones from companies such as Shure and Audio-Technica. If you are on a quest for really superior audio quality, you can even obtain a portable mixer that can plug into this jack, such as the affordable Rolls MX124 (around $150) (www.rolls.com), letting you use multiple high-quality microphones (up to four) to record your soundtrack.

An exciting new option designed specifically for still cameras like the T5i is the Beachtek DXA-SLR PRO HDSLR Audio Adapter. It's more expensive, at around $450, but has even more professional sound options and clips right onto the bottom of your camera using the tripod mounting socket. (See Figure 6.22.)

One advantage that a sound mixing device like the DSX-SLR PRO offers over the stock T5i is that it adds a headphone output jack to your camera, so you can monitor the sound being recorded (you can also listen to your soundtrack through the headphones during playback, which is *way* better than using the T5i's built-in speaker). The adapter has two balanced XLR microphone inputs and can also accept line input (from another audio source), and provides

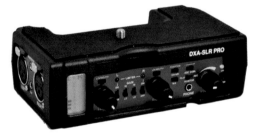

**Figure 6.22** The Beachtek DXA-SLR PRO HDSLR Audio Adapter offers professional sound mixing options.

cool features like AGC (automatic gain control), built-in limiting, and VU meters you can use to monitor sound input.

- **Hide the microphone.** Combine the first few tips by using an external mic, and getting it as close to your subject as possible. If you're capturing a single person, you can always use a lapel microphone (described in the next section). But if you want a single mic to capture sound from multiple sources, your best bet may be to hide it somewhere in the shot. Put it behind a vase, using duct tape to fasten the microphone and fix the mic cable out of sight (if you're not using a wireless microphone).

- **Turn off any sound makers you can.** Little things like fans and air handling units aren't obvious to the human ear, but will be picked up by the microphone. Turn off any machinery or devices that you can plus make sure cell phones are set to silent mode. Also, do what you can to minimize sounds such as wind, radio, television, or people talking in the background.

- **Make sure to record some "natural" sound.** If you're shooting video at an event of some kind, make sure you get some background sound that you can add to your audio as desired in postproduction.

- **Consider recording audio separately.** Lip-syncing is probably beyond most of the people you're going to be shooting, but there's nothing that says you can't record narration separately and add it later. It's relatively easy if you learn how to use simple software video-editing programs like iMovie (for the Macintosh) or Windows Movie Maker (for Windows PCs). Any time the speaker is off-camera, you can work with separately recorded narration rather than recording the speaker on-camera. This can produce much cleaner sound.

## External Microphones

The single most important thing you can do to improve your audio quality is to use an external microphone. The T5i's internal stereo microphones mounted on the front of the camera will do a decent job, but have some significant drawbacks, partially spelled out in the previous section:

- **Camera noise.** There are plenty of noise sources emanating from the camera, including your own breathing and rustling around as the camera shifts in your hand. Manual zooming is bound to affect your sound, and your fingers will fall directly in front of the built-in mics as you change focal lengths. An external microphone isolates the sound recording from camera noise.

- **Distance.** Anytime your T5i is located more than 6 to 8 feet from your subjects or sound source, the audio will suffer. An external unit allows you to place the mic right next to your subject.

- **Improved quality.** Obviously, Canon wasn't able to install a super-expensive, super high-quality microphone. Not all owners of the T5i would be willing to pay the premium, especially if they didn't plan to shoot much video themselves. An external microphone will almost always be of better quality.

- **Directionality.** The T5i's internal microphones generally record only sounds directly in front of them. An external microphone can be either of the directional type or omnidirectional, depending on whether you want to "shotgun" your sound or record more ambient sound.

You can choose from several different types of microphones, each of which has its own advantages and disadvantages. If you're serious about movie making with your T5i, you might want to own more than one. Common configurations include:

- **Shotgun microphones.** These can be mounted directly on your T5i. I prefer to use a bracket, which further isolates the microphone from any camera noise. One thing to keep in mind is that while the shotgun mic will generally ignore any sound coming from *behind* it, it will pick up any sound it is pointed at, even *behind* your subject. You may be capturing video and audio of someone you're interviewing in a restaurant, and not realize you're picking up the lunchtime conversation of the diners seated in the table behind your subject. Outdoors, you may record your speaker, as well as the traffic on a busy street or freeway in the background.

- **Lapel microphones.** Also called *lavalieres*, these microphones attach to the subject's clothing and pick up their voice with the best quality. You'll need a long enough cord or a wireless mic (described later). These are especially good for video interviews, so whether you're producing a documentary or grilling relatives for a family history, you'll want one of these.

- **Handheld microphones.** If you're capturing a singer crooning a tune, or want your subject to mimic famed faux newscaster Wally Ballou, a handheld mic may be your best choice. They serve much the same purpose as a lapel microphone, and they're more intrusive—but that may be the point. A handheld microphone can make a great prop for your fake newscast! The speaker can talk right into the microphone, point it at another person, or use it to record ambient sound. If your narrator is not going to appear on-camera, one of these can be an inexpensive way to improve sound.

- **Wired and wireless external microphones.** This option is the most expensive, but you get a receiver and a transmitter (both battery-powered, so you'll need to make sure you have enough batteries). The transmitter is connected to the microphone, and the receiver is connected to your T5i. In addition to being less klutzy and enabling you to avoid having wires on view in your scene, wireless mics let you record sounds that are physically located some distance from your camera. Of course, you need to keep in mind the range of your device, and be aware of possible signal interference from other electronic components in the vicinity.

## WIND NOISE REDUCTION

Always use the windscreen provided with an external microphone to reduce the effect of noise produced by even light breezes blowing over the microphone. Many mics include a low-cut filter to further reduce wind noise. However, these can also affect other sounds. External mics often have their own low-cut filter switch.

# 7

# Advanced Shooting

You can happily spend your entire shooting career using the techniques and features already explained in this book. Great exposures, sharp pictures, and creative compositions are all you really need to produce great shot after great shot. But, those with enough interest in getting the most out of their Canon EOS T5i who buy this book probably will be interested in going beyond those basics to explore some of the more advanced techniques and capabilities of the camera. Capturing the briefest instant of time, transforming common scenes into the unusual with lengthy time exposures, and working with new tools like Wi-Fi are all tempting avenues for exploration. So, in this chapter, I'm going to offer longer discussions of some of the more advanced techniques and capabilities that I like to put to work.

## Continuous Shooting

The Canon EOS T5i's Continuous shooting mode reminds me how far digital photography has brought us. The first accessory I purchased when I worked as a sports photographer some years ago was a motor drive for my film SLR. It enabled me to snap off a series of shots in rapid succession, which came in very handy when a fullback broke through the line and headed for the end zone. Even a seasoned action photographer can miss the decisive instant when a crucial block is made, or a baseball superstar's bat shatters and pieces of cork fly out. Continuous shooting simplifies taking a series of pictures, either to ensure that one has more or less the exact moment you want to capture or to capture a sequence that is interesting as a collection of successive images.

The T5i's "motor drive" capabilities are, in many ways, much superior to what you got with a film camera. For one thing, a motor-driven film camera can eat up film at an incredible pace, which is why many of them were used with cassettes that hold hundreds of feet of film stock. At three frames per second (typical of film cameras), a short burst of a few seconds burned up as much as half of an ordinary 36 exposure roll of film. Digital cameras, in contrast, have reusable "film," so if you waste a few dozen shots on non-decisive moments, you can erase them and shoot more. Save only the best shots, like the series shown in Figure 7.1.

To use the T5i's Continuous shooting mode, when using one of the Creative Zone modes, press the Drive button (the left cross key) and use the touch screen or cross keys to select the Continuous shooting icon. Alternatively, you can press the Q button to pop up the Quick Control screen and use the touch screen or physical controls to specify the drive mode. When you partially depress the shutter button, the viewfinder will display a number representing the maximum number of shots you can take at the current quality settings. (If your battery is low, this figure will be lower.)

Continuous shooting can be affected by the speed with which your T5i is able to focus. So, in AI Servo AF mode, the frames-per-second rate may be lower. Lenses that inherently focus more slowly (see Chapter 10 for information on the various types of autofocus motors built into Canon lenses), and scenes that are poorly lit can also affect the frame rate. The buffer in the T5i will generally allow you to take as many as 30 JPEG shots at 5 frames per second in a single burst (when using an UHS-I, or Ultra High Speed I compatible memory card), or 6 RAW photos at the 18MP resolution setting. To increase this number, reduce the image-quality setting by switching to JPEG only (from JPEG+RAW), to a lower JPEG quality setting, or by reducing the T5i's resolution from L to M or S.

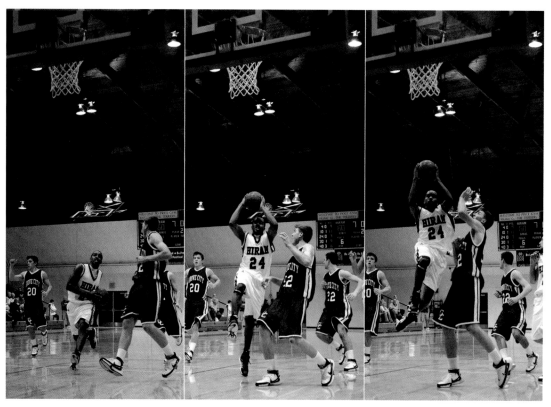

**Figure 7.1** Continuous shooting allows you to capture an entire sequence of exciting moments as they unfold.

The reason the size of your bursts is limited by the buffer is that continuous images are first shuttled into the T5i's internal memory, then doled out to the memory card as quickly as they can be written to the card. Technically, the T5i takes the RAW data received from the digital image processor and converts it to the output format you've selected—either JPG or CR2 (RAW) or both—and deposits it in the buffer ready to store on the card.

This internal "smart" buffer can suck up photos much more quickly than the memory card and, indeed, some memory cards are significantly faster or slower than others. You'll get the best results when using a shutter speed of 1/500th second, the widest lens opening of the lens, One-Shot auto-focus, and when, image stabilization is turned off. However, when One-Shot AF is active, the T5i will focus only once at the beginning of the sequence, and then use that focus setting for the rest of the shots in the burst. If your subject is moving, you can use AI Servo AF instead, at a slightly slower continuous frame rate.

Setting High ISO Speed Noise Reduction to High or Multi Shot Noise Reduction in the Shooting 3 menu also limits the length of your continuous burst. You'll also see a decrease if Chromatic Aberration is enabled in the Shooting 1 menu's Lens Aberration Correction entry, or you have the camera set to do white balance bracketing. (In such cases, the T5i stores three copies of each image snapped, slowing down the burst rate.) While you can use flash in Continuous mode, the camera will wait for the flash to recycle between shots, slowing down the continuous shooting rate.

When the buffer fills, you can't take any more continuous shots (a buSY indicator appears in the viewfinder) until the T5i has written some of them to the card, making more room in the buffer. (You should keep in mind that faster memory cards write images more quickly, freeing up buffer space faster.)

## BURSTS NOT JUST FOR ACTION

I often use Continuous shooting mode even when I'm not busy shooting action. As I've mentioned before, bursts make sense when you're shooting HDR or bracketing. But here's a technique you might not have thought of—continuous shooting can give you sharper images!

When I'm photographing concerts, I most frequently use my 70-200mm f/2.8 IS zoom, handheld, with image stabilization turned on, and using the highest continuous frame rate at my disposal. I enjoy greater mobility by not using a monopod (and a tripod would be even more of a ball-and-chain, even if not forbidden by the venue). I'm generally shooting at around 1/180th second, which is usually fast enough to eliminate blur from the performers' motion. IS has no effect on stopping *their* movement, of course, and it does a fairly good job of eliminating camera/photographer shake. However, I invariably find that if I shoot in Continuous, one of the middle frames in a sequence will be sharpest. Even the most seasoned photographer will add a little bump to the camera when they squeeze (not stab) the shutter release.

# More Exposure Options

In Chapter 4, you learned techniques for getting the *right* exposure, but I haven't explained all your exposure options just yet. You'll want to know about the *kind* of exposure settings that are available to you with the Canon EOS T5i. There are options that let you control when the exposure is made, or even how to make an exposure that's out of the ordinary in terms of length (time or bulb exposures). The sections that follow explain your camera's special exposure features, and even discuss a few it does not have (and why it doesn't).

# A Tiny Slice of Time

Exposures that seem impossibly brief can reveal a world we didn't know existed. In the 1930s, Dr. Harold Edgerton, a professor of electrical engineering at MIT, pioneered high-speed photography using a repeating electronic flash unit he patented called the *stroboscope*. As the inventor of the electronic flash, he popularized its use to freeze objects in motion, and you've probably seen his photographs of bullets piercing balloons and drops of milk forming a coronet-shaped splash.

Electronic flash freezes action by virtue of its extremely short duration—as brief as 1/50,000th second or less. Although the EOS T5i's built-in flash unit can give you these ultra-quick glimpses of moving subjects, an external flash, such as one of the Canon Speedlites, offers even more versatility. You can read more about using electronic flash to stop action in Chapter 11.

Of course, the T5i is fully capable of immobilizing all but the fastest movement using only its shutter speeds, which range all the way up to 1/4,000th second. Indeed, you'll rarely have need for such a brief shutter speed in ordinary shooting. If you wanted to use an aperture of f/2.8 at ISO 100 outdoors in bright sunlight, for some reason, a shutter speed of 1/4,000th second would more than do the job. You'd need a faster shutter speed only if you moved the ISO setting to a higher sensitivity (but why would you do that?). Under less than full sunlight, 1/4,000th second is more than fast enough for any conditions you're likely to encounter.

Most sports action can be frozen at 1/2,000th second or slower, and for many sports a slower shutter speed is actually preferable—for example, to allow the wheels of a racing automobile or motorcycle, or the propeller on a classic aircraft to blur realistically.

But if you want to do some exotic action-freezing photography without resorting to electronic flash, the T5i's top shutter speed is at your disposal. Here are some things to think about when exploring this type of high-speed photography:

- **You'll need a lot of light.** High shutter speeds cut very fine slices of time and sharply reduce the amount of illumination that reaches your sensor. To use 1/4,000th second at an aperture of f/6.3, you'd need an ISO setting of 800—even in full daylight. To use an f/stop smaller than f/6.3 or an ISO setting lower than 800, you'd need *more* light than full daylight provides. (That's why electronic flash units work so well for high-speed photography when used as the sole illumination; they provide both the effect of a brief shutter speed and the high levels of illumination needed.)

■ **Forget about reciprocity failure.** If you're an old-time film shooter, you might recall that very brief shutter speeds (as well as very high light levels and very *long* exposures) produced an effect called *reciprocity failure,* in which given exposures ended up providing less than the calculated value because of the way film responded to very short, very intense, or very long exposures of light. Solid-state sensors don't suffer from this defect, so you don't need to make an adjustment when using high shutter speeds (or brief flash bursts).

■ **Don't combine high shutter speeds with electronic flash.** You might be tempted to use an electronic flash with a high shutter speed. Perhaps you want to stop some action in daylight with a brief shutter speed and use electronic flash only as supplemental illumination to fill in the shadows. Unfortunately, under most conditions you can't use flash in subdued illumination with your T5i at any shutter speed faster than 1/200th second. That's the fastest speed at which the camera's focal plane shutter is fully open: at shorter speeds, the "slit" described above comes into play, so that the flash will expose only the small portion of the sensor exposed by the slit during its duration. (Check out "Avoiding Sync Speed Problems" in Chapter 11 if you want to see how you *can* use shutter speeds shorter than 1/200th second with certain Canon Speedlites, albeit at much-reduced effective power levels.)

## Working with Short Exposures

You can have a lot of fun exploring the kinds of pictures you can take using very brief exposure times, whether you decide to take advantage of the action-stopping capabilities of your built-in or external electronic flash or work with the Canon EOS T5i's faster shutter speeds. Here are a few ideas to get you started:

■ **Take revealing images.** Fast shutter speeds can help you reveal the real subject behind the façade, by freezing constant motion to capture an enlightening moment in time. Legendary fashion/portrait photographer Philippe Halsman used leaping photos of famous people, such as the Duke and Duchess of Windsor, Richard Nixon, and Salvador Dali to illuminate their real selves. Halsman said, *"When you ask a person to jump, his attention is mostly directed toward the act of jumping and the mask falls so that the real person appears."* Try some high-speed portraits of people you know in motion to see how they appear when concentrating on something other than the portrait. (See Figure 7.2.)

■ **Create unreal images.** High-speed photography can also produce photographs that show your subjects in ways that are quite unreal. A helicopter in mid-air with its rotors frozen makes for an unusual picture. Figure 7.3 shows a pair of pictures. At top, a shutter speed of 1/1000th second virtually stopped the rotation of the chopper's rotors, while the bottom image, shot at 1/200th second, provides a more realistic view of the blurry blades as they appeared to the eye.

■ **Capture unseen perspectives.** Some things are *never* seen in real life, except when viewed in a stop-action photograph. Edgerton's balloon bursts were only a starting point. Freeze a hummingbird in flight for a view of wings that never seem to stop. Or, capture the splashes as liquid falls into a bowl, as shown in Figure 7.4. No electronic flash was required for this image (and wouldn't have illuminated the water in the bowl as evenly). Instead, a clutch of high-intensity lamps and an ISO setting of 1600 allowed the EOS T5i to capture this image at 1/2,000th second.

■ **Vanquish camera shake and gain new angles.** Here's an idea that's so obvious it isn't always explored to its fullest extent. A high enough shutter speed can free you from the tyranny of a tripod, making it easier to capture new angles, or to shoot quickly while moving around, especially with longer lenses. I tend to use a monopod or tripod for almost everything when I'm not using an image-stabilized lens, and I end up missing some shots because of a reluctance to adjust my camera support to get a higher, lower, or different angle. If you have enough light and can use an f/stop wide enough to permit a high shutter speed, you'll find a new freedom to choose your shots. I have a favored 170mm-500mm lens that I use for sports and wildlife photography, almost invariably with a tripod, as I don't find the "reciprocal of the focal length" rule particularly helpful in most cases. (I would *not* handhold this hefty lens at its 500mm setting with a 1/500th second shutter speed under most circumstances.) However, at 1/2,000th second or faster, and with a sufficiently high ISO setting (I recommend ISO 800–1600) to allow such a speed, it's entirely possible for a steady hand to use this lens without a tripod or monopod's extra support, and I've found that my whole approach to shooting animals and other elusive subjects changes in high-speed mode. Selective focus allows dramatically isolating my prey wide open at f/6.3, too.

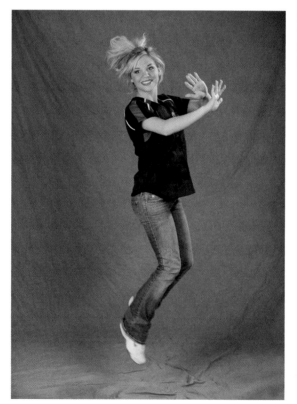

**Figure 7.2**
When your subjects leap, the real person inside emerges.

**Figure 7.3**
Top: the chopper's blades are frozen at 1/1,000th second; bottom: a more realistic blurry rendition at 1/200th second shutter speed.

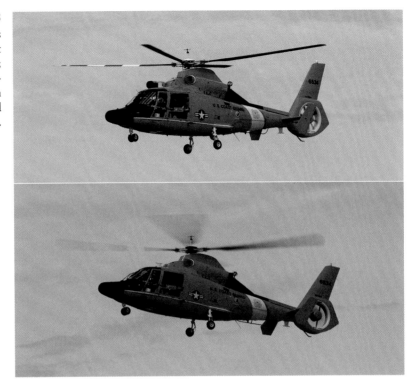

**Figure 7.4**
A large amount of artificial illumination and an ISO 1600 sensitivity setting allowed capturing this shot at 1/2,000th second without use of an electronic flash.

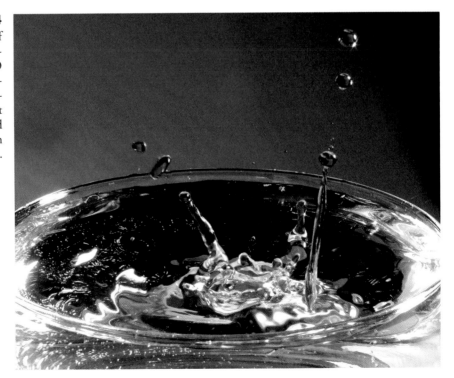

# Long Exposures

Longer exposures are a doorway into another world, showing us how even familiar scenes can look much different when photographed over periods measured in seconds. At night, long exposures produce streaks of light from moving, illuminated subjects like automobiles or amusement park rides. Extra-long exposures of seemingly pitch-dark subjects can reveal interesting views using light levels barely bright enough to see by. At any time of day, including daytime (in which case you'll often need the help of neutral-density filters, which reduce the amount of light passing through the lens, to make the long exposure practical), long exposures can cause moving objects to vanish entirely, because they don't remain stationary long enough to register in a photograph.

## Three Ways to Take Long Exposures

There are actually three common types of lengthy exposures: *timed exposures*, *bulb exposures*, and *time exposures*. The EOS T5i offers only the first two, but once you understand all three, you'll see why Canon made the choices it did. Because of the length of the exposure, all of the following techniques should be used with a tripod to hold the camera steady.

- **Timed exposures.** These are long exposures from 1 second to 30 seconds, measured by the camera itself. To take a picture in this range, simply use Manual or Tv modes and use the Main Dial to set the shutter speed to the length of time you want, choosing from preset speeds of 1.0, 1.5, 2.0, 3.0, 4.0, 6.0, 8.0, 10.0, 15.0, 20.0, or 30.0 seconds (if you've specified 1/2 stop increments for exposure adjustments), or 1.0, 1.3, 1.6, 2.0, 2.5, 3.2, 4.0, 5.0, 6.0, 8.0, 10.0, 13.0, 15.0, 20.0, 25.0, and 30.0 seconds (if you're using 1/3 stop increments). The advantage of timed exposures is that the camera does all the calculating for you. There's no need for a stop-watch. If you review your image on the LCD and decide to try again with the exposure doubled or halved, you can dial in the correct exposure with precision. The disadvantage of timed exposures is that you can't take a photo for longer than 30 seconds.

- **Bulb exposures.** This type of exposure is so-called because in the olden days the photographer squeezed and held an air bulb attached to a tube that provided the force necessary to keep the shutter open. Traditionally, a bulb exposure is one that lasts as long as the shutter release button is pressed; when you release the button, the exposure ends. To make a bulb exposure with the T5i, set the camera on M using the Mode Dial, then rotate the Main Dial all the way past the longest available shutter speeds to the Bulb position. Then, press the shutter to start the exposure, and press it again to close the shutter.

- **Time exposures.** This is a setting found on some cameras to produce longer exposures. With cameras that implement this option, the shutter opens when you press the shutter release button, and remains open until you press the button again. Usually, you'll be able to close the shutter using a mechanical cable release or, more commonly, an electronic release cable. The advantage of this approach is that you can take an exposure of virtually any duration without the need for special equipment (the tethered release is optional). You can press the shutter release button, go off for a few minutes, and come back to close the shutter (assuming your camera is still there). The disadvantages of this mode are exposures must be timed manually, and with shorter exposures, it's possible for the vibration of manually opening and closing the shutter to register in the photo. For longer exposures, the period of vibration is relatively brief and not usually a problem—and there is always the release cable option to eliminate photographer-caused camera shake entirely. While the T5i does not have a built-in time exposure capability, you can simulate it with the bulb exposure technique, described previously, or use a remote control with the facility.

## WATCH OUT FOR AMP NOISE

When exposures extend past 30 seconds into the realm of several minutes—or more—all digital cameras are theoretically susceptible to a phenomenon called *amp noise*, which manifests itself as a purplish glow, often around the edges of an image, creating an aurora borealis–style ghost effect. Amp noise happens when the sensor heats up during a long exposure, and some cameras fall victim more readily than others. The EOS T5i resists this phenomenon better than most dSLRs, but you should be aware it exists, even if you'd need to use an uncommon exposure (on the order of 30 minutes or so) to create the effect with your camera.

# Working with Long Exposures

Because the EOS T5i produces such good images at longer exposures, and there are so many creative things you can do with long-exposure techniques, you'll want to do some experimenting. Get yourself a tripod or another firm support and take some test shots with long exposure noise reduction both enabled and disabled using the entry in the Shooting 3 menu, as explained in Chapter 8 (to see whether you prefer low noise or high detail) and get started. Here are some things to try:

- **Make people invisible.** One very cool thing about long exposures is that objects that move rapidly enough won't register at all in a photograph, while the subjects that remain stationary are portrayed in the normal way. That makes it easy to produce people-free landscape photos and architectural photos at night or, even, in full daylight if you use a neutral-density filter (or two or three) to allow an exposure of at least a few seconds. At ISO 100, f/22, and a pair of 8X (three-stop) neutral-density filters, you can use exposures of nearly two seconds; overcast days and/or more neutral-density filtration would work even better if daylight people-vanishing is your goal. They'll have to be walking *very* briskly and across the field of view (rather than directly toward the camera) for this to work. At night, it's much easier to achieve this effect with the 20- to 30-second exposures that are possible, as you can see in Figures 7.5 and 7.6.

- **Create streaks.** If you aren't shooting for total invisibility, long exposures with the camera on a tripod or monopod can produce some interesting streaky effects, as you can see in Figure 7.7. You don't need to limit yourself to indoor photography, however. Even a single 8X ND filter will let you shoot at f/22 and 1/6th second in full daylight at ISO 100.

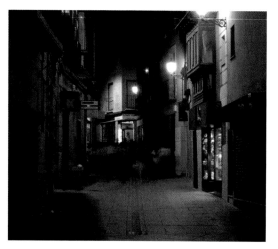

**Figure 7.5** This alleyway is thronged with people, as you can see in this two-second exposure using only the available illumination.

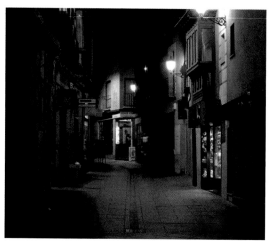

**Figure 7.6** With the camera still on a tripod, a 30-second exposure rendered the passersby almost invisible.

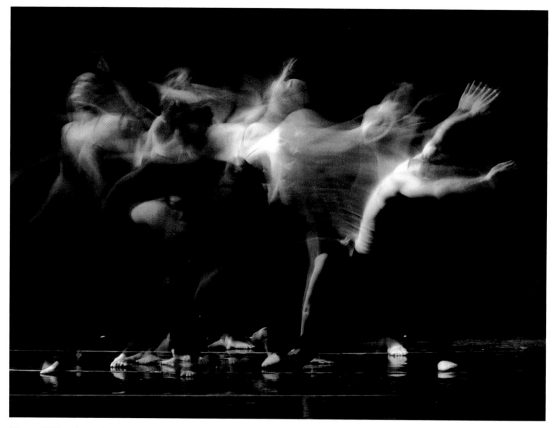

**Figure 7.7** These dancers produced a swirl of movement during the 1/8th second exposure.

- **Produce light trails.** At night, car headlights and taillights and other moving sources of illumination can generate interesting light trails. Your camera doesn't even need to be mounted on a tripod; handholding the T5i for longer exposures adds movement and patterns to your trails. If you're shooting fireworks, a longer exposure of several seconds may allow you to combine several bursts into one picture, as shown in Figure 7.8, which was shot with a tripod-mounted camera.

- **Blur waterfalls, etc.** You'll find that waterfalls and other sources of moving liquid produce a special type of long exposure blur, because the water merges into a fantasy-like veil that looks different at different exposure times, and with different waterfalls. Cascades with turbulent flow produce a rougher look at a given longer exposure than falls that flow smoothly. Although blurred waterfalls have become almost a cliché, there are still plenty of variations for a creative photographer to explore, as you can see in Figure 7.9.

- **Show total darkness in new ways.** Even on the darkest nights, there is enough starlight or glow from distant illumination sources to see by, and, if you use a long exposure, there is enough light to take a picture, too. Figure 7.10 shows San Juan, Puerto Rico late at night.

**Figure 7.8** A long exposure and a tripod allows capturing several bursts of fireworks in one image.

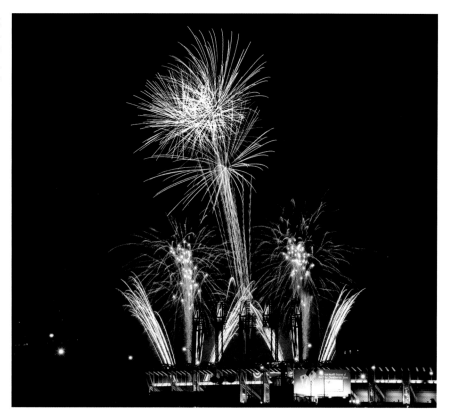

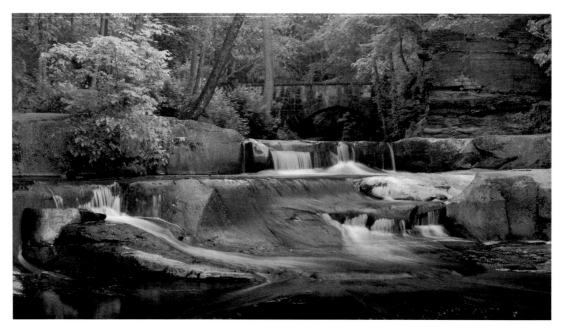

**Figure 7.9** A 1/4-second exposure blurred the falling water.

**Figure 7.10** A 20-second exposure revealed this view of San Juan, Puerto Rico.

# Delayed Exposures

Sometimes it's desirable to have a delay of some sort before a picture is actually taken. Perhaps you'd like to get in the picture yourself, and would appreciate it if the camera waited 10 seconds after you press the shutter release to actually take the picture. Maybe you want to give a tripod-mounted camera time to settle down and damp any residual vibration after the release is pressed to improve sharpness for an exposure with a relatively slow shutter speed. It's possible you want to explore the world of time-lapse photography. The next sections present your delayed exposure options.

## Self-Timer

The EOS T5i has a built-in self-timer with 10-second and 2-second delays. Activate the timer by pressing the DRIVE button and press the left cross keys until the drive modes appear on the LCD status panel. Press the shutter release button halfway to lock in focus on your subjects (if you're taking a self-portrait, focus on an object at a similar distance and use focus lock). When you're ready to take the photo, continue pressing the shutter release the rest of the way. The lamp on the front of the camera will blink slowly for eight seconds (when using the 10-second timer) and the beeper will chirp (if you haven't disabled it in the Shooting menu, as described in Chapter 8). During the final two seconds, the beeper sounds more rapidly and the lamp remains on until the picture is taken. The top-panel LCD displays a countdown while all this is going on.

Another way to use the self-timer is with the mirror lockup feature (which can be enabled using Custom Function C.Fn III-05, as explained in Chapter 9). This is something you might want to do if you're shooting close-ups, landscapes, or other types of pictures using the self-timer, to trip the shutter in the most vibration-free way possible. Forget to bring along your tripod, but still want to take a close-up picture with a precise focus setting? Set your digital camera to the self-timer function, then put the camera on any reasonably steady support, such as a fence post or a rock. When you're ready to take the picture, press the shutter release. The camera might teeter back and forth for a second or two, but it will settle back to its original position before the self-timer activates the shutter. The self-timer remains active until you turn it off—even if you power down the T5i, so remember to turn it off when finished.

## Time-Lapse/Interval Photography

Who hasn't marveled at a time-lapse photograph of a flower opening, a series of shots of the moon marching across the sky, or one of those extreme time-lapse picture sets showing something that takes a very, very long time, such as a building under construction.

You probably won't be shooting such construction shots, unless you have a spare T5i you don't need for a few months (or are willing to go through the rigmarole of figuring out how to set up your camera in precisely the same position using the same lens settings to shoot a series of pictures at intervals). However, other kinds of time-lapse photography are entirely within reach.

Although the EOS T5i can't take time-lapse/interval photographs all by itself, if you're willing to tether the camera to a computer (a laptop will do) using the USB cable, you can take time-lapse photos using EOS Utility software furnished with your camera.

Here are some tips for effective time-lapse photography:

■ **Use AC power.** If you're shooting a long sequence, consider connecting your camera to an AC adapter, as leaving the T5i on for long periods of time will rapidly deplete the battery.

■ **Make sure you have enough storage space.** Unless your memory card has enough capacity to hold all the images you'll be taking, you might want to change to a higher compression rate or reduced resolution to maximize the image count.

■ **Make a movie.** While time-lapse stills are interesting, you can increase your fun factor by compiling all your shots into a motion picture using your favorite desktop movie-making software.

■ **Protect your camera.** If your camera will be set up for an extended period of time (longer than an hour or two), make sure it's protected from weather, earthquakes, animals, young children, innocent bystanders, and theft.

■ **Vary intervals.** Experiment with different time intervals. You don't want to take pictures too often or less often than necessary to capture the changes you hope to image.

# Wi-Fi and Geotagging

These days, Wi-Fi and GPS capabilities work together with your EOS T5i in interesting new ways. Wireless capabilities allow you to upload photos directly from your T5i to your computer at home or in your studio, or, through a hotspot at your hotel or coffee shop back to your home computer or to a photo-sharing service like Facebook or Flickr. A special Wi-Fi-enabled memory card that you slip in the SD slot of your camera performs the magic. GPS capabilities—built right into some of those Wi-Fi cards—allow you to mark your photographs with location information, so you don't have to guess where a picture was taken.

Both capabilities are very cool. Wi-Fi uploads can provide instant backup of important shots and sharing. Geotagging is most important as a way to associate the geographical location where the photographer was when a picture was taken, with the actual photograph itself. It can be done with the location-mapping capabilities of the Wi-Fi card, or through add-on devices that third parties make available for your T5i.

Geotagging can also be done by attaching geographic information to the photo after it's already been taken. This is often done with online sharing services, such as Flickr, which allow you to associate your uploaded photographs with a map, city, street address, or postal code. When properly geotagged and uploaded to sites like Flickr, users can browse through your photos using a map, finding pictures you've taken in a given area, or even searching through photos taken at the same location by other users.

Canon offers an affordable GP-E2 GPS receiver that can be purchased for less than $400, and connects through the T5i's hot shoe. It records locational data such as latitude, longitude, and altitude, and saves it to the EXIF metadata in your image files, where it can be retrieved by compatible software to plot to maps or insert into your uploads to Flickr or other sites. You can even track your trajectory of movement with the receiver's logging function, and there is a built-in electric compass that logs the camera's orientation for each shot.

If you're looking for an even less-expensive GPS solution, with Wi-Fi to boot, try one of the memory cards offered by Transcend or Eye-Fi (www.eye.fi). Eye-Fi cards have been around longer and offer a wider choice of models. Each Eye-Fi card is an SDHC memory card with a wireless transmitter built in. You insert it in your camera just as with any ordinary card (see Figure 7.11), and then specify which networks to use. You can add as many as 32 different networks. The next time your camera is on within range of a specified network, your photos and videos can be uploaded to your computer and/or to your favorite sharing site. During setup, you can customize where you want your images uploaded. The Eye-Fi card will only send them to the computer and to the sharing site you choose.

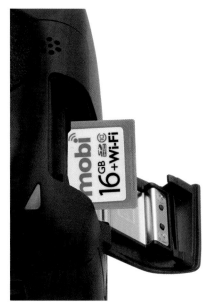

Uploads over these networks can go to your own destinations or to any of 25 popular sharing websites, including Flickr, Facebook, Costco, Adorama, Smugmug, YouTube, Shutterfly, or Walmart. Online Sharing is included as a lifetime, unlimited service with all X2 cards. Although the Eye-Fi card does not have a GPS receiver, it uses information

**Figure 7.11** The Eye-Fi card is a memory card with built-in Wi-Fi and GPS capabilities.

from connected Wi-Fi networks to determine the current location, and embeds that in the image files stored on the card. Your EOS T5i has an Eye-Fi Settings entry with two entries at the bottom of the Setup 1 menu that appear when you have an Eye-Fi card inserted:

- **Eye-Fi trans.** This setting has two options: Enable and Disable. Because the Eye-Fi card draws its power from the T5i, you might want to disable the capability when you don't want it, in order to save some juice. I tend to leave it on all the time, and allow the card to upload information to the networks I've specified. When enabled, the card can also draw location information from the hotspots it accesses, associating geographical information with each shot, too.
- **Connection info.** This displays current information about your Eye-Fi card's link to your network or hotspot, and other data, such as the firmware version. (See Figure 7.12.)

You'll want to turn off Eye-Fi when traveling on an airplane (just as you disable your cell phone, tablet, or laptop's wireless capabilities when required to do so). In addition, use of Wi-Fi cards may be restricted or banned outside the United States, because the telecommunications laws differ in other countries.

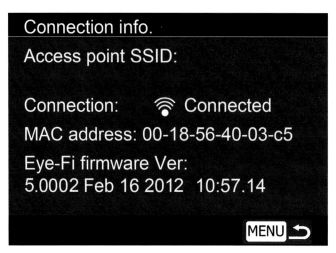

**Figure 7.12**
The EOS T5i has built-in support for Eye-Fi cards.

When uploading to online sites, you can specify not just where your images are sent, but how they are organized, by specifying preset album names, tags, descriptions, and even privacy preferences on certain sharing sites. (You should be cautious about sharing your location when using social media sites.) Some Eye-Fi cards also include geotagging service, which help you view uploaded photos on a map, and sort them by location. Eye-Fi's geotagging uses Wi-Fi Positioning System (WPS) technology. Using built-in Wi-Fi, the Eye-Fi card senses surrounding Wi-Fi networks as you take pictures. When photos are uploaded, the Eye-Fi service then adds the geotags to your photos. You don't need to have the password or a subscription for the Wi-Fi networks the card accesses; it can grab the location information directly without the need to "log in." You don't need to set up or control the Eye-Fi card from your camera. Software on your computer manages all the parameters.

If you frequently travel outside the range of your home (or business) Wi-Fi network, an optional service called Hotspot Access is available, allowing you to connect to any AT&T Wi-Fi hotspot in the USA. In addition, you can use your own Wi-Fi accounts from commercial network providers, your city, even organizations you belong to such as your university.

The card has another interesting feature called Endless Memory. When pictures have been safely uploaded to an external site, the card can bet set to automatically erase the oldest images to free up space for new pictures. You choose the threshold where the card starts zapping your old pictures to make room.

Eye-Fi currently offers several models, from about $50 to $100. The most sophisticated options are found in the Eye-Fi X2 cards, available in capacities up to 8GB, and which can add geographic location labels to your photo (so you'll know where you took it), and frees you from your own computer network by allowing uploads from more than 10,000 Wi-Fi hotspots around the USA. Very cool, and the ultimate in picture backup. Eye-Fi has added the ability to upload from your camera to your smartphone, too, using an Android or iOS application.

In June 2013, the company introduced the latest wrinkle in its lineup, the Mobi, available in 8GB and 16GB Class 10 forms for $49 and $79, respectively. The Mobi was shown in Figure 7.11, earlier. The other Eye-Fi cards can be used to upload only when you're located near a Wi-Fi connection, either a local area network (say, at work or your home) or a nearby Wi-Fi hotspot. The Mobi has its own specialized "hot spot" built right into the tiny card. That is, you can go to your phone or tablet's settings screen and, if your camera is powered up and has the Mobi card in the slot, you'll be able to select the memory card's network just as you would any Wi-Fi hotspot.

However, the Mobi's network can be used only to communicate between the memory card and your phone/tablet. All you need to do is download the free Eye-Fi app from the Apple or Android app store, and "pair" the card with your device using a unique access code supplied with the card itself. You can use the same code with any device that needs to communicate with the Mobi card, so you can pair it with any number of smart phones or tablets that you use.

My biggest beef with any of the Eye-Fi cards is slow uploads, whether to my network, to online destinations, to a smart phone, or to an iPad. You can't really shoot "tethered" with them because you'll invariably shoot faster than the uploads can take place. And, for sure, avoid instant upload of *everything* to social networking sites (specify automatic upload of images marked with Protect only) if you're using public settings and don't want everyone to see and comment on every picture you take. Let's keep the clunkers to ourselves!

## Tablets, Smart Phones, and the Canon T5i

Although tablets and smart phones are still in their infancies, in the future, your iPhone, iPad/tablet computer, iPod Touch/MP3 player, smart phone, or Google Android portable device will be one of the most important accessories you can have for your T5i (or other) digital camera. We're only now seeing the beginnings of the trend. The relevant platforms are these:

- **Old-style smart phones.** I include in this category all smart phones that are *not* iPhones or phones based on Google's Android operating system. You can buy lots of interesting apps for these phones, although not many applications specifically for photography. This type of phone should be on its way out, too, with iPhone and Android smart phones dominating, simply because it's easier to write applications for the iPhone's iOS and Android than to create them for multiple "old" smart phone platforms.

- **Android smart phones.** There are already more Android-based smart phones on the market than for all other types, including iOS. Although Apple had a head start, the number of Android applications is rapidly catching up.

- **iPhones.** To date, iOS has a commanding lead in number of applications, especially for photography apps. When my first app was developed as a guide for cameras, it appeared for the iOS platform first.

■ **iPod Touch.** Basically, the latest iPod Touch is an iPhone that can't make phone calls. (Although there are some hacks around that limitation.) Virtually all of the apps that run on the iPhone under iOS also run on the iPod Touch. You need a Wi-Fi connection to access features that use network capabilities, but, these days, Wi-Fi hot spots aren't that difficult to find. Tethering and Mi-Fi (which allow another device to serve as a hot spot for non-connected gadgets like the Touch), and *automobiles* that include built-in Wi-Fi (!) make connectivity almost universal. In my travels through Europe in the last year, I found free Wi-Fi connections in the smallest towns. (Indeed, the only time I was asked to pay for it was when staying in an upscale hotel.) So, for many who are tied to a non-iPhone cell phone, the iPod Touch is a viable alternative.

■ **Tablet computers.** I've been welded to my iPad (shown alongside my iPhone in Figure 7.13) since I bought it the first day they became available. I use it to access e-mail, useful apps, and as a portable portfolio. Today, there are alternative tablet computers running Android. I recently picked up an Amazon Kindle Fire, which also does e-mail and a limited number of apps, and which has a Gallery feature (see Figure 7.14) that transforms it into a compact portfolio almost as useful for that purpose as an iPad. However, only 6 of the original Kindle Fire's 8GB of storage are available to the user, so you'll have to limit the size of your portfolio. Later Kindle tablets have as much as 32GB of memory. During the life of this book, I expect to see the Microsoft Surface, Google Nexus, the Nook, and Samsung Galaxy carve out their own little niches in this market.

I use the Kindle Fire and both an iPhone and iPad. (If I'm traveling overseas where my iPhone can't be used, I usually take along the iPod Touch instead.) The iPhone/iPod slips in a pocket and can be used anywhere. I don't even have to think about taking it with me, because I always have one or the other. I have to remember to tote along the iPad or Kindle Fire, and, I do, to an extent you'd probably find surprising. (After the movie finally starts in the theater, I fold them into their cases and use them as a tray for my popcorn bucket.) Tablet computers can do everything a pocket-sized device can do, and are easier to read/view/type on. When I am out shooting, I prefer to have all my apps in a smaller device that I can put in the camera bag, but if there's room, the iPad goes along instead. Because my iPad (unlike the Kindle Fire) has 3G connectivity, I don't need a Wi-Fi connection to use it almost anywhere. I do have a Wi-Fi hot spot built into my iPhone that I can use to connect the Kindle Fire to the net if I need to.

## What Else Can You Do with Them?

Many of these devices can serve as a backup for your T5i's memory cards. I've got Apple's camera connection kit, and can offload my pictures to my iPad's 64GB of memory, then upload them to Flickr or Facebook, or send to anyone through e-mail. My iPad also makes a perfect portable portfolio, too. I have hundreds of photos stored on mine, arranged into albums ready for instant display, either individually, or in slide shows. I have the same photo library on my iPhone and iPod Touch, and more than a few pictures available for showing on my Kindle Fire.

**Figure 7.13**
The iPad, iPod, and other devices open a whole world of useful apps to the photographer.

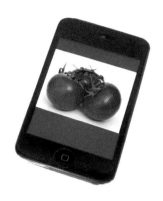

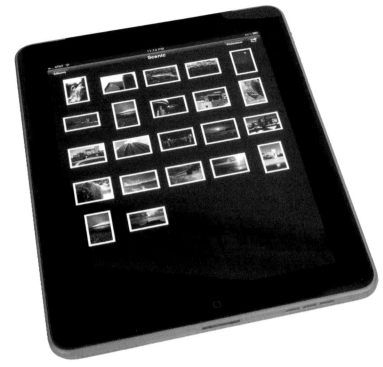

**Figure 7.14**
The Kindle Fire is a smaller, more affordable alternative to the iPad.

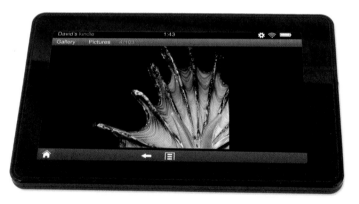

But the real potential for using these devices comes from specialized apps written specifically to serve photographic needs. Here are some of the kinds of apps you can expect in the future. (I'm working on more than a few of them myself.)

■ **Camera guides.** Even the inadequate manual that came with your camera is too large to carry around in your camera bag all day. I'm converting many of my own camera-specific guides to app form, while adding interactive elements, including hyperlinks and videos. You can already put a PDF version of your camera manual on your portable device and read it, if you like. In the future, you should be able to read any of the more useful third-party guides anywhere, anytime.

- **Lens selector.** Wonder what's the best lens to use in a specific situation? Enter information about your scene, and your app will advise you.

- **Exposure estimator.** Choose a situation and the estimated exposure will be provided. Useful as a reality check and in difficult situations, such as fireworks, where the camera's meters may falter.

- **Shutter speed advisor.** The correct shutter speed for a scene varies depending on whether you want to freeze action, or add a little blur to express motion. Other variables include whether the subject is crossing the frame, moving diagonally, or headed toward you. The photographer also needs to consider the focal length of the lens, and presence/absence of image stabilization features, tripod, monopod, etc. This app will allow you to tap in all the factors and receive advice about what shutter speed to use.

- **Hyperfocal length calculator.** In any given situation, set the focus point at the distance specified for your lens's current focal length setting, and everything from half that distance to infinity will be in focus. But the right setting differs at various focal lengths. This app tells you, and is a great tool for grab shots.

- **Accessory selector.** Confused about what flash, remote control, battery grip, lens hood, filter, or other accessory to use with your camera or lens? This selector lists the key gadgets, which ones fit which cameras, and explains how to use them.

- **Before and after.** Images showing before/after versions of dozens of situations with and without corrective/in-camera special effects applied.

- **Fill light.** Pesky shadows on faces from overhead lighting indoors? This turns your iPod/ iPhone or (best of all) iPad into a bright, diffuse fill light panel. Choose from white fill light, or *colors* for special effects. Makes good illumination for viewing your camera's buttons and dials in dark locations, too. Some of these apps use the iPhone's flash for an especially bright light.

- **Gray card.** Turn your i-device into a gray card for metering and color balance.

- **Super links.** If you don't find your answer in the Toolkit, you can link to websites, including mine, with more information.

- **How It's Made.** A collection of inspiring photos, with details on how they were taken in camera—or manipulated in Photoshop (if that's your thing).

- **Quickie guides.** Small apps that lead you, step-by-step, through everything you need to photograph lots of different types of scenes. Typical subjects would be sports, landscape photography, macro work, portraits, concerts/performances, flowers, wildlife, and nature.

As you can see, the potential for apps is virtually unlimited. You can expect your smart phone, tablet computer, or other device to be a mainstay in your camera bag within a very short time.

# Part III

# Configuring Your Canon EOS Rebel T5i/700D

The next two chapters are devoted to helping you dig deeper into the customization capabilities of your EOS T5i, so you can exploit all those cool features that your previous camera might have lacked. Chapters 8 and 9 list every setting and option found in the Shooting, Playback, Set-up, and My Menu tabs. I explained your options with the single Live View and two Movie menus in Chapter 6.

- **Chapter 8, "Customizing with the Shooting and Playback Menus:"** In this chapter, you'll learn some easy stuff——like how to turn your T5i's Beep on or off, along with some very important capabilities, like using the camera's lens aberration correction facility to banish vignetted corners and color fringes. I explain Picture Styles, recap the most important Live View/Movie options originally discussed in Chapter 6, and show you how to apply creative filters and assemble your own photo books.

- **Chapter 9, "Customizing with the Set-up Menu and My Menu:"** A broad array of setup options are discussed here. You'll learn how to format memory cards, adjust LCD brightness and screen colors, and enter time zones and dates. You'll even discover how to set up your own command listings with the My Menus option.

# Customizing with the Shooting and Playback Menus

The Canon Rebel T5i is undoubtedly the most customizable, tweakable, fine-tunable camera Canon has offered non-professional users. In fact, this versatility has made the T5i surprisingly popular among professional photographers as well. If your camera doesn't behave in exactly the way you'd like, chances are you can make a small change in the Shooting, Playback, and Set-up menus that will tailor the T5i to your needs. In fact, if you don't like the *menus*, you can create your own using the clever My Menu system.

This chapter and the next will help you sort out the settings you can make to customize how your Canon Rebel T5i uses its features, shoots photos, displays images, and processes the pictures after they've been taken. As I've mentioned before, this book isn't intended to replace the manual you received with your T5i, nor have I any interest in rehashing its contents. You'll still find the original manual useful as a standby reference that lists every possible option in exhaustive (if mindnumbing) detail—without really telling you how to use those options to take better pictures. There is, however, some unavoidable duplication between the Canon manual and this chapter, because I'm going to explain the key menu choices and the options you may have in using them. You should find, though, that this chapter gives you the information you need in a much more helpful format, with plenty of detail on why you should make some settings that are particularly cryptic.

I'm not going to waste a lot of space on some of the more obvious menu choices. For example, you can probably figure out that the Beep option in the Shooting 1 menu deals with the solid-state beeper in your camera that sounds off during various activities (such as the self-timer countdown). You can certainly decipher the import of the two options available for the Red-Eye Reduc. entry

(Enable, Disable), assuming you know what red-eye reduction is. (I'll explain it if you don't.) So, in this chapter, I'll devote no more than a sentence or two to the blatantly obvious settings and concentrate on the more confusing aspects of T5i setup, such as Automatic Exposure Bracketing. I'll cover the Shooting menus (including Live View shooting) and Playback menus in this chapter, and turn to the Set-up, Custom Functions, and My Menu options in Chapter 9. Movie options were explained in Chapter 6.

Let's start off with an overview of the T5i's menus themselves.

## Anatomy of the Rebel T5i's Menus

If you have jumped directly to the Canon Rebel T5i from an ancient model like the EOS 30D, you're in for a pleasant surprise from a menu perspective. Like all recent EOS cameras, this model abandons the time-consuming scrolling through one endless menu in favor of 11 individually tabbed menus, each with a single screen of options (so you won't need to scroll within a menu to see all the entries). The menus are much cleaner, too.

If you've used another EOS model, you'll find the T5i's menu system familiar, but with a more attractive look that includes "shaded" menu tabs (see Figure 8.1). Some menu items have been moved around and/or renamed. With the current system, just press the MENU button, spin the Main Dial to highlight the menu tab you want to access, and then scroll up and down within a menu with the cross keys. If you have small enough fingers, you can use the touch screen, too. What could be easier?

Tapping the MENU button brings up a typical menu like the one shown in the figure. (If the camera goes to "sleep" while you're reviewing a menu, you may need to wake it up again by tapping the shutter release button.)

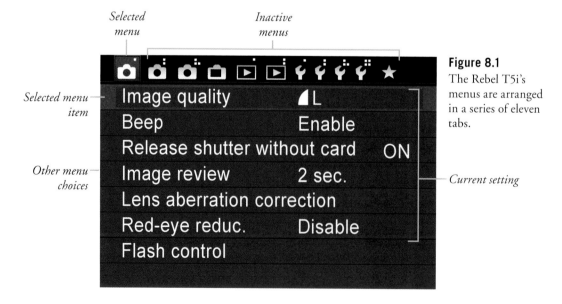

**Figure 8.1**
The Rebel T5i's menus are arranged in a series of eleven tabs.

Different menu tabs are provided, depending on the shooting mode:

### Table 8.1 Available Menus

| Modes | Available Menus tabs |
|---|---|
| M, Tv, Av, P Modes | Shooting 1, Shooting 2, Shooting 3, Live View Shooting, Playback 1, Playback 2, Set-up 1, Set-up 2, Set-up 3, Set-up 4, My Menu |
| Scene, Scene Intelligent Auto, Flash Off, Creative Auto Modes | Shooting 1, Live View Shooting, Playback 1, Playback 2, Set-up 1, Set-up 2, Set-up 3 |
| Movie mode | Shooting 1, Movie Shooting 1, Movie Shooting 2, Playback 1, Playback 2, Set-up 1, Set-up 2, Set-up 3 |

In this chapter, I'm going to explain all the tabs and all the menu entries, and not take the time to mention which of those are not available when using scene and other modes. The automatic modes are intended for situations when you don't want full control over your T5i's operation, anyway, and menu limitations go with the territory. The Movie menus were previously discussed in Chapter 6 and won't be repeated here.

The T5i's tabs are color-coded: red for Shooting, Live View Shooting, and Movie Shooting menus; blue for Playback menus; amber for Set-up menus; and green for the My Menu tab. The currently selected menu's icon is white within a background corresponding to its color code. All the inactive menus are dimmed.

### MENU NAVIGATION

Remember: you can use the touch screen to move from menu to menu, or, alternatively, you can work with the Main Dial and the cross keys to highlight a particular menu entry. Press SET to select a menu item. That procedure is probably the best way to start out, because those controls are used to make so many settings with the Rebel T5i that they quickly become almost intuitive.

You can jump from tab to tab even if you've highlighted a particular menu setting on another tab—and the T5i will remember which menu entry you've highlighted when you return to that menu. The memorization works even if you leave the menu system or turn off your camera. The T5i always remembers the last menu entry you used with a particular tab. So, if you generally use the Format command each time you access the Set-up 1 menu, that's the entry that will be highlighted when you choose that tab. The camera remembers which tab was last used, too, so, potentially, formatting your memory card might take just a couple of presses (the MENU button, SET to select the highlighted Format command, then a tap, or a press of the cross keys to choose OK, and another SET to start the format process).

Here are the things to watch for as you navigate the menus:

- **Menu tabs.** In the top row of the menu screen, the menu that is currently active will be highlighted as described earlier. One, two, three, or four dots in the tab lets you know if you are in, say Set-up 1, Set-up 2, Set-up 3, or Set-up 4. Just remember that the red camera icons stand for still, live view, and movie shooting options; the two blue right-pointing triangles represent playback options; the four yellow wrench icons stand for set-up options; and the green star stands for personalized menus defined for the star of the show—you.

- **Selected menu item.** The currently selected menu entry within a given tab will have a black background and will be surrounded by a box the same hue as its color code.

- **Other menu choices.** The other menu items visible on the screen will have a dark gray background.

- **Current setting.** The current settings for visible menu items are shown in the right-hand column, until one menu item is selected (by choosing SET). At that point all the settings vanish from the screen except for those dealing with the active menu choice.

When you've moved the menu highlighting to the menu item you want to work with, choose the SET button to select it. The current settings for the other menu items in the list will be hidden, and a list of options for the selected menu item (or a submenu screen) will appear. Within the menu choices, you can scroll up or down with the touch screen or cross keys; choose SET to select the choice you've made; and choose MENU again to exit.

# Shooting Menu Options

The various direct setting buttons on the back panel of the camera for white balance (the up cross key), Picture Styles (down cross key), drive mode (left cross key), AF mode (right cross key), and ISO (the top panel button southwest of the Main Dial) are likely to be the most common settings changes you make, with changes during a particular session fairly common. You'll find that the Shooting menu options are those that you access second most frequently when you're using your Rebel T5i. You might make such adjustments as you begin a shooting session, or when you move from one type of subject to another. Canon makes accessing these changes very easy.

This section explains the options of the three Shooting menus and how to use them. The options you'll find in these red-coded menus include:

- Quality Settings
- Beep
- Release Shutter without Card
- Image Review
- Lens Aberration Correction
- Red-Eye Reduction

- Flash Control
- Exposure Compensation/Automatic Exposure Bracketing (AEB)
- Auto Lighting Optimizer
- Custom White Balance
- WB Shift/BKT
- Color Space

- Picture Style
- Metering Mode
- Dust Delete Data
- ISO Auto
- Long Exposure Noise Reduction
- High ISO Speed Noise Reduction

## Quality Settings

You can choose the image quality settings used by the T5i to store its files. You have three choices when selecting a quality setting:

- **Resolution.** The number of pixels captured determines the absolute resolution of the photos you shoot with your T5i. Your choices range from 18 megapixels (Large or L), measuring 5184 × 3456 pixels; 8 megapixels (Medium or M), measuring 3456 × 2304 pixels; 4.5 megapixels (Small 1 or S1), 2592 × 1728 pixels; 2.5 megapixels (Small 2 or S2), 1920 × 1280 pixels; and 350,000 pixels (Small 3 or S3), 720 × 480 pixels.

- **JPEG compression.** To reduce the size of your image files and allow more photos to be stored on a given memory card, the T5i uses JPEG compression to squeeze the images down to a smaller size. This compacting reduces the image quality a little, so you're offered your choice of Fine compression and Normal compression. The symbols help you remember that Fine compression (represented by a quarter-circle) provides the smoothest results, while Normal compression (signified by a stair-step icon) provides "jaggier" images.

- **JPEG, RAW, or both.** You can elect to store only JPEG versions of the images you shoot (6.4MB each at the Large Fine resolution setting) or you can save your photos as uncompressed, loss-free RAW files, which consume about four times as much space on your memory card (up to 20MB per file). Or, you can store both at once as you shoot. Many photographers elect to save *both* a JPEG and a RAW file, so they'll have a JPEG version that might be usable as-is, as well as the original "digital negative" RAW file in case they want to do some processing of the image later. You'll end up with two different versions of the same file: one with a JPG extension, and one with the CR2 extension that signifies a Canon RAW file.

To choose the combination you want, access the menus, scroll to Quality, and choose SET. A screen similar to the one shown in Figure 8.2 will appear with two rows of choices. The top row and first two entries on the second row are JPEG-only settings, two Large and Medium options (at Fine and Normal compression), and four Small choices, representing S1 Fine, S1 Normal, S2, and S3, at the

**Figure 8.2**
Choose your resolution, JPEG compression, and file format from this screen.

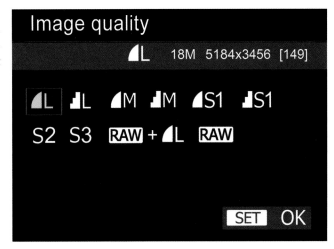

resolutions listed above. A red box appears around the currently selected choice. You can also select RAW+JPEG Large Fine and RAW only. Both produce full-resolution versions of the image.

Why so many choices? There are some limited advantages to using the Medium and Small resolution settings, Normal JPEG compression setting, and the two lower resolution RAW formats. They all allow stretching the capacity of your memory card so you can shoehorn quite a few more pictures onto a single memory card. That can come in useful when on vacation and you're running out of storage, or when you're shooting non-critical work that doesn't require full resolution. The Small 2 and Small 3 settings can be useful for photos taken for real estate listings, web page display, photo ID cards, or similar non-critical applications.

For most work, using lower resolution and extra compression is often false economy. You never know when you might actually need that extra bit of picture detail. Your best bet is to have enough memory cards to handle all the shooting you want to do until you have the chance to transfer your photos to your computer or a personal storage device.

However, reduced image quality can sometimes be beneficial if you're shooting sequences of photos rapidly, as the T5i is able to hold more of them in its internal memory buffer before transferring to the memory card. Still, for most sports and other applications, you'd probably rather have better, sharper pictures than longer periods of continuous shooting.

## JPEG vs. RAW

You'll sometimes be told that RAW files are the "unprocessed" image information your camera produces, before it's been modified. That's nonsense. RAW files are no more unprocessed than your camera film is after it's been through the chemicals to produce a negative or transparency. A lot can happen in the developer that can affect the quality of a film image—positively and negatively— and, similarly, your digital image undergoes a significant amount of processing before it is saved as a RAW file. Canon even applies a name (DIGIC 5) to the digital image processing (DIP) chip used to perform this magic.

A RAW file is more similar to a film camera's processed negative. It contains all the information, captured in 14-bit channels per color (and stored in a 16-bit space), with no compression, no sharpening, no application of any special filters or other settings you might have specified when you took the picture. Those settings are *stored* with the RAW file so they can be applied when the image is converted to a form compatible with your favorite image editor. However, using RAW conversion software such as Adobe Camera Raw or Canon's Digital Photo Professional, you can override those settings and apply settings of your own. You can select essentially the same changes there that you might have specified in your camera's picture-taking options.

RAW exists because sometimes we want to have access to all the information captured by the camera, before the camera's internal logic has processed it and converted the image to a standard file format. RAW doesn't save as much space as JPEG. What it does do is preserve all the information captured by your camera after it's been converted from analog to digital form. Of course, the T5i's RAW format preserves the *settings* information.

So, why don't we always use RAW? Although some photographers do save only in RAW format, it's more common to use either RAW plus one of the JPEG options or just shoot JPEG and avoid RAW altogether. That's because having only RAW files to work with can significantly slow down your workflow. While RAW is overwhelmingly helpful when an image needs to be fine-tuned, in other situations working with a RAW file, when all you really need is a good quality, untweaked JPEG image, consumes time that you may not want to waste. For example, RAW images take longer to store on the memory card, and require more post-processing effort, whether you elect to go with the default settings in force when the picture was taken, or just make minor adjustments.

As a result, those who depend on speedy access to images or who shoot large numbers of photos at once may prefer JPEG over RAW. Wedding photographers, for example, might expose several thousand photos during a bridal affair and offer hundreds to clients as electronic proofs for possible inclusion in an album or transfer to a CD or DVD. These wedding shooters, who want JPEG images as their final product, take the time to make sure that their in-camera settings are correct, minimizing the need to post-process photos after the event. Given that their JPEGs are so good (in most cases thanks, in large part, to the pro photographer's extensive experience), there is little need to get bogged down shooting RAW.

Sports photographers also eschew RAW files. I visited a local Division III college one sunny September afternoon and managed to cover a football game, trot down a hill to shoot a women's soccer match later that afternoon, and ended up in the adjacent field house shooting a volleyball invitational tournament an hour later. I managed to shoot 1,920 photos, most of them at a 3.7 fps clip, in about four hours. I certainly didn't have any plans to do post-processing on very many of those shots, and firing the T5i at its maximum frame rate didn't allow RAW shooting, so carefully exposed and precisely focused JPEG images were my file format of choice that day.

JPEG was invented as a more compact file format that can store most of the information in a digital image, but in a much smaller size. JPEG predates most digital SLRs, and was initially used to squeeze down files for transmission over slow dialup connections. Even if you were using an early dSLR with 1.3 megapixel files for news photography, you didn't want to send them back to the office over a modem (Google it) at 1,200 bps.

But, as I noted, JPEG provides smaller files by compressing the information in a way that loses some image data. JPEG remains a viable alternative because it offers several different quality levels. At the highest quality Fine level, you might not be able to tell the difference between the original RAW file and the JPEG version, even though the 18-megapixel RAW file occupies, by Canon's estimate, 25.1MB on your memory card, while the Fine JPEG at the same resolution takes up only 6.6MB of space. You've squeezed the image significantly without losing much visual information at all.

In my case, I shoot virtually everything at RAW+JPEG Fine. Most of the time, I'm not concerned about filling up my memory cards, as I usually have a minimum of five fast 8GB memory cards with me. I also have some 32GB SD cards that are a little slower (so I don't use them for sports), but with even more capacity. If I think I may fill up all those cards, I have Apple's Camera Connection Kit for my iPad, and can transfer photos to that device. As I mentioned earlier, when shooting sports I'll shift to JPEG Fine (with no RAW file) to squeeze a little extra speed out of my

T5i's Continuous shooting mode, and to reduce the need to wade through eight-photo bursts taken in RAW format. On the other hand, on my last trip to Europe, I took only RAW (instead of my customary RAW+JPEG) photos to fit more images onto my iPad, as I planned on doing at least some post-processing on many of the images for a travel book I was working on.

## MANAGING LOTS OF FILES

The only long-term drawback to shooting everything in RAW+JPEG is that it's easy to fill up your computer's hard drive if you are a prolific photographer. Here's what I do. My most recent photos are stored on my working hard drive in a numbered folder, say T5i-01, with subfolders named after the shooting session, such as 110501Trees, for pictures of trees taken on May 1, 2011. An automatic utility, TrueImage Home, copies new and modified photos to a different hard drive for temporary backup four times daily.

When the top-level folder accumulates about 30GB of images, I back it up to DVDs and then move the folder to a 2000GB (2 terabyte) drive dedicated solely for storage of folders that have already been backed up onto DVD. Then I start a new folder, such as T5i-02, on the working hard drive and repeat the process. I always have at least one backup of every image taken, either on another hard drive or on a DVD.

# Beep

The Rebel T5i's internal beeper provides a helpful chirp to signify various functions, such as the countdown of your camera's self-timer. You can switch it off if you want to avoid the beep because it's annoying, impolite, or distracting (at a concert or museum), or undesired for any other reason. It's one of the few ways to make the T5i a bit quieter, other than Live View's "silent shoot" mode. (I've actually had new dSLR owners ask me how to turn off the "shutter sound" the camera makes; such an option was available in the point-and-shoot camera they'd used previously.) Select Beep from the menu, choose SET, and use the touch screen or cross keys to choose Enable or Disable, or Touch To Screen (which silences the beep only during touch screen operations), as you prefer, as shown in Figure 8.3. Use SET again to activate your choice.

# Release Shutter without Card

This entry in the Set-up 1 menu (see Figure 8.4) gives you the ability to snap off "pictures" without a memory card installed—or to lock the camera shutter release if that is the case. It is sometimes called Play mode, because you can experiment with your camera's features or even hand your T5i to a friend to let him fool around, without any danger of pictures actually being taken. Back in our film days, we'd sometimes finish a roll, rewind the film back into its cassette surreptitiously, and then hand the camera to a child to take a few pictures—without actually wasting any film. It's hard to waste digital film, but Release Shutter without Card mode is still appreciated by some, especially camera vendors who want to be able to demo a camera at a store or trade show, but don't want to

**Figure 8.3**
Silence your camera's beep when it might prove distracting.

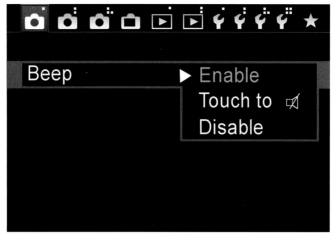

**Figure 8.4**
You can enable triggering the shutter even when no memory card is present.

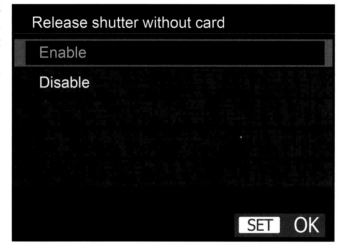

have to equip each and every demonstrator model with a memory card. Choose this menu item, invoke SET, select Enable or Disable, and SET again to turn this capability on or off.

## Image Review

You can adjust the amount of time an image is displayed for review on the LCD after each shot is taken. You can elect to disable this review entirely (Off), or choose display times of 2, 4, or 8 seconds. You can also select Hold, an indefinite display, which will keep your image on the screen until you use one of the other controls, such as the shutter button, Main Dial, or cross keys. Turning the review display off or choosing a brief duration can help preserve battery power. However, the T5i will always override the review display when the shutter button is partially or fully depressed, so you'll never miss a shot because a previous image was on the screen. Choose Review Time from the Shooting 1 menu, and select Off, 2 sec., 4 sec., 8 sec., or Hold, as shown in Figure 8.5. If you want

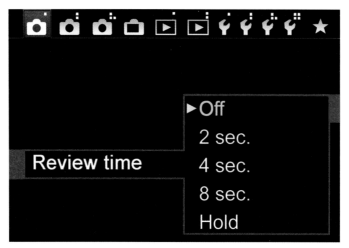

**Figure 8.5**
Adjust the time an image is displayed on the LCD for review after a picture is taken.

to retain an image on the screen for a longer period, but don't want to use Hold as your default, press the Erase button under the LCD monitor. The image will display until you choose Cancel or Erase from the menu that pops up at the bottom of the screen. A longer review time gives you an opportunity to delete a non-keeper without a visit to the menu system.

# Lens Aberration Correction

With certain lenses, under certain conditions, your images might suffer from one of two aberrations, both of which can be partially corrected by activating the correction items offered in this menu entry.

## Peripheral Illumination Correction

One defect is caused by a phenomenon called *vignetting*, which is a darkening of the four corners of the frame because of a slight amount of fall-off in illumination at those nether regions. This menu option allows you to activate Peripheral Illumination Correction, a clever feature built in to the Rebel T5i that partially (or fully) compensates for this effect. Depending on the f/stop you use, the lens mounted on the camera, and the focal length setting, vignetting can be non-existent, slight, or may be so strong that it appears you've used a too-small hood on your camera. (Indeed, the wrong lens hood can produce a vignette effect of its own.) Vignetting can be affected by the use of a telephoto converter (more on those in Chapter 10).

Peripheral illumination drop-off, even if pronounced, may not be much of a problem. I actually *add* vignetting, sometimes, when shooting portraits and some other subjects. Slightly dark corners tend to focus attention on a subject in the middle of the frame. On the other hand, vignetting with subjects that are supposed to be evenly illuminated, such as landscapes, is seldom a benefit.

To minimize the effects of corner light fall-off, you can process RAW files using Digital Photo Professional (described in Chapter 13), or, if you want your JPEG files fixed as you shoot them, by using this menu option. Figure 8.6 shows an image without peripheral illumination correction at top, and a corrected image at the bottom. I've exaggerated the vignetting a little to make it more evident on the printed page. Keep in mind that the amount of correction available with Digital Photo Pro can be a little more intense than that applied in the camera. In addition, the higher the ISO speed, the less correction is applied. If you see severe vignetting with a particular lens, focal length, or ISO setting, you might want to turn off this feature, shoot RAW, and apply correction using DPP instead (see Figure 8.7).

When you select this menu option from the Shooting 1 menu, the screen shown in Figure 8.7 appears. The lens currently attached to the camera is shown, along with a notation whether correction data needed to brighten the corners is already registered in the camera. (Information about 25

**Figure 8.6**
Vignetting (top) is undesirable in a landscape photo. You can correct this defect in the camera or by using Digital Photo Pro software.

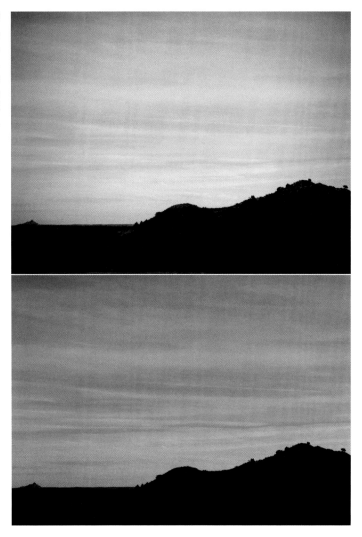

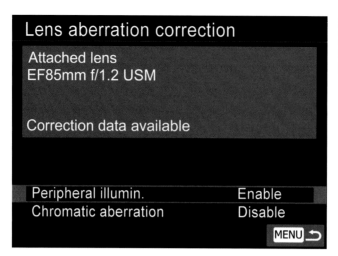

**Figure 8.7**
Peripheral illumination correction can fix dark corners.

of the most popular lenses is included in the T5i's firmware.) If so, you can use the touch screen or cross keys to choose Enable to activate the feature, or Disable to turn it off. Select SET to confirm your choice. Note that in-camera correction must be specified *before* you take the photo, so that the magical DIGIC 5 processing engine can lighten the corners of your photo before it is saved to the memory card.

## Chromatic Aberration

The second defect involves fringes of color around backlit objects, produced by *chromatic aberration*, which comes in two forms: *longitudinal/axial*, in which all the colors of light don't focus in the same plane; and *lateral/transverse*, in which the colors are shifted to one side. (See Figure 8.8.) Your T5i has a database of information about certain lenses, similar to the one provided for peripheral illumination correction.

When this feature is enabled, the T5i will automatically correct images taken with one of the supported lenses to reduce or eliminate the amount of color fringing seen in the final photograph. (See Figure 8.9.)

If lens aberration correction information for your lens is not registered in the camera, you can remedy that deficit using the EOS Utility (also described in Chapter 13). Just follow these steps:

1. **Link up your camera.** Connect your T5i to your computer using the USB cable supplied with the camera.

2. **Launch the EOS Utility.** Load the utility and click on Camera Settings/Remote Shooting from the splash screen that appears.

3. **Select the Shooting menu.** It's located on the menu bar about midway in the control panel that appears on your computer display. The Shooting menu icon is the white camera on a red background.

4. **Click on the Lens Aberration Correction choice.** The selection screen will appear.

5. **Choose your lens.** Select the category containing the lens you want to register from the panels at the top of the new screen; then place a check mark next to all the lenses you'd like to register in the camera.

6. **Confirm your choice.** Click OK to send the data from your computer to the T5i and register your lenses.

7. **Activate correction.** When a newly registered lens is mounted on the camera, you will be able to activate the anti-vignetting feature for that lens from the Set-up 1 menu.

**Figure 8.8**
Lateral chromatic aberration, which shows as color fringes, can be corrected using the lens aberration correction feature.

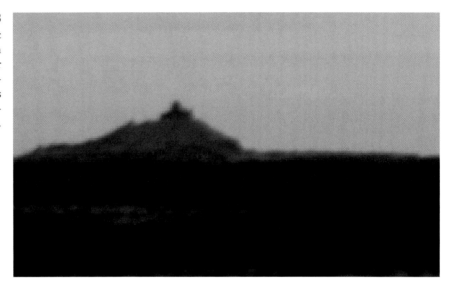

**Figure 8.9**
The corrected image displays much less fringing.

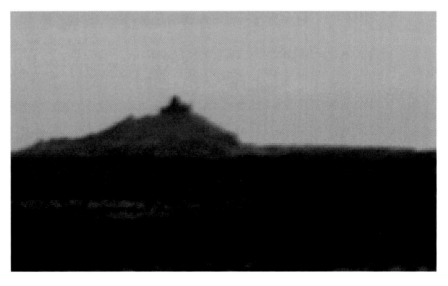

The Lens Aberration Correction feature is a more versatile fixer-upper than the Peripheral Illumination Correction feature found in earlier cameras. Once you've registered a lens as described above, you can use the Raw Image Processing entry in the Playback 1 menu to enable or disable peripheral illumination correction, chromatic aberration correction, general lens distortion correction, and make other changes to the RAW file—after it's been shot—right in the camera. I'll describe this capability later in this chapter.

## Red-Eye Reduction

Your Rebel T5i has a fairly effective Red-Eye Reduction flash mode. Unfortunately, your camera is unable, on its own, to *eliminate* the red-eye effects that occur when an electronic flash (or, rarely, illumination from other sources) bounces off the retinas of the eye and into the camera lens. Animals seem to suffer from yellow or green glowing pupils, instead; the effect is equally undesirable. The effect is worst under low-light conditions (exactly when you might be using a flash) as the pupils expand to allow more light to reach the retinas. The most you can hope for is to *reduce* or minimize the red-eye effect.

The best way to truly eliminate red-eye is to raise the flash up off the camera so its illumination approaches the eye from an angle that won't reflect directly back to the retina and into the lens. The extra height of the built-in flash may not be sufficient, however. That alone is a good reason for using an external flash. If you're working with your T5i's built-in flash, your only recourse may be to switch on the Red-Eye Reduction feature with the menu choice shown in Figure 8.10. It causes a lamp on the front of the camera to illuminate with a half-press of the shutter release button, which may cause your subjects' pupils to contract, decreasing the amount of the red-eye effect. (You may have to ask your subject to look at the lamp to gain maximum effect.) Figure 8.11 shows the effects of wider pupils (left) and those that have been contracted using the T5i's Red-Eye Reduction feature.

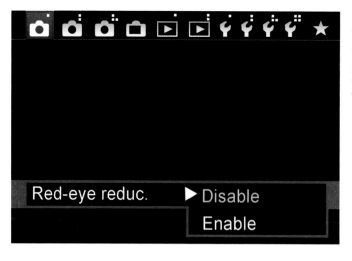

**Figure 8.10**
Turn on your camera's Red-Eye Reduction feature to help eliminate demon-red pupils.

**Figure 8.11**
Red-eye (left) is tamed (right), thanks to the Rebel T5i's red-eye reduction lamp.

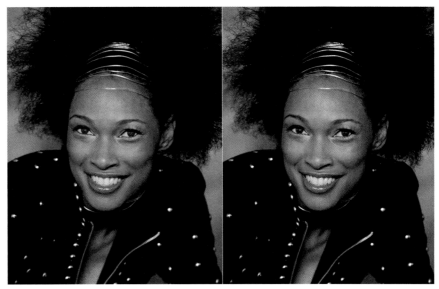

# Flash Control

This multi-level menu entry includes six settings for controlling the Canon Rebel T5i's built-in, pop-up electronic flash unit, as well as accessory flash units you can attach to the camera (see Figure 8.12). I'll provide in-depth coverage of how you can use these options in Chapter 11, but will list the main options here for reference.

## Flash Firing

Use this option to enable or disable the built-in electronic flash. You might want to totally disable the T5i's flash (both built-in and accessory flash) when shooting in sensitive environments, such as concerts, in museums, or during religious ceremonies. When disabled, the flash cannot fire even if

**Figure 8.12**
The Flash Control menu entry has six setting submenus.

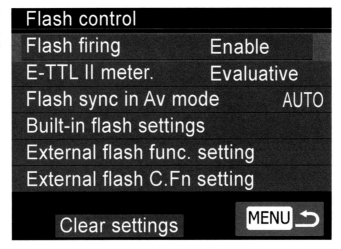

you accidentally elevate it, or have an accessory flash attached and turned on. If you turn off the flash here, it is disabled in any exposure mode. You can also select Flash Off from the Mode Dial.

## E-TTL II Metering

You can choose Evaluative (Matrix) or Average metering modes for the electronic flash exposure meter. Evaluative looks at selected areas in the scene to calculate exposure, and is the best choice for most images because it attempts to interpret the type of scene being shot; Average calculates flash exposure by reading the entire scene, and it is possibly a good option if you want exposure to be calculated for the overall scene.

## Flash Sync in AV mode

You can select the flash synchronization speed that will be used when working in Aperture-priority mode; choose from Auto (the T5i selects the shutter speed from 30 seconds to 1/200th second), to a range embracing only the speeds from 1/200th to 1/60th second, or fixed at 1/200th second.

Normally, in Aperture-priority mode when using flash, you specify the f/stop to be locked in. The exposure is then adjusted by varying the output of the electronic flash. Because the primary exposure comes from the flash, the main effect of the shutter speed selected is on the secondary exposure from the ambient light on the scene.

As I'll explain in Chapter 11, Auto is your best choice under most conditions. The T5i will choose a shutter speed that balances the flash exposure and available, ambient light. The 1/200th to 1/60th second setting locks out slower shutter speeds, preventing blur from camera/subject movement in the secondary ("ghost") exposure. However, the background may be rendered dark, if the flash is not strong enough to illuminate it. The 1/200th second (fixed) setting further reduces the chance of getting those blurry ghosts, but there is more of a chance the background will be dark. You'll find a more detailed explanation of these options in Chapter 11.

## Built-in Flash Function Setting

There are a total of five possible choices for this menu screen, plus Clear Settings. The additional options are grayed out unless you're working in wireless flash mode. All these are explained in Chapters 11 and 12.

- **Built-in flash.** Your choices here are Normal Firing, Easy Wireless, and Custom Wireless. The first choice is used when you're working with the built-in flash only; the two other options are used when you are syncing your camera with a wireless external flash, as explained in detail in Chapters 11 and 12.
- **Flash mode.** This entry is available only if you've selected Custom Wireless (above), and allows you to choose from automatic exposure calculation (E-TTL II) or manual flash exposure.
- **Shutter sync.** Available only in Normal Firing mode, you can choose 1st curtain sync, which fires the pre-flash used to calculate the exposure before the shutter opens, followed by the main flash as soon as the shutter is completely open. This is the default mode, and you'll generally

perceive the pre-flash and main flash as a single burst. Alternatively, you can select 2nd curtain sync, which fires the pre-flash as soon as the shutter opens, and then triggers the main flash in a second burst at the end of the exposure, just before the shutter starts to close. (If the shutter speed is slow enough, you may clearly see both the pre-flash and main flash as separate bursts of light.) This action allows photographing a blurred trail of light of moving objects with sharp flash exposures at the beginning and the end of the exposure. This type of flash exposure is slightly different from what some other cameras produce using 2nd curtain sync. I'll explain how it works in Chapter 11.

If you have an external compatible Speedlite attached, you can also choose Hi-speed sync, which allows you to use shutter speeds faster than 1/200th second, using the External Flash Function Setting menu, described next and explained in Chapter 11.

■ **Flash exposure compensation.** If you'd rather adjust flash exposure using a menu than with the ISO/Flash exposure compensation button, you can do that here. Select this option with the SET button, then dial in the amount of flash EV compensation you want using the cross keys. The EV that was in place before you started to make your adjustment is shown as a blue indicator, so you can return to that value quickly. Use SET again to confirm your change, then tap MENU or press the MENU button twice to exit.

■ **Wireless functions.** These choices appear when you've selected Custom Wireless, and include Mode, Channel, Firing Group, and other options used only when you're working in wireless mode to control an external flash. If you've disabled wireless functions, the other options don't appear on the menu. I'm going to leave the explanation of these options for Chapter 12, which is an entire chapter dedicated to using the Rebel T5i's wireless shooting capabilities, first introduced in the EOS 7D.

■ **Clear flash settings.** When the Built-in Flash Func. setting (or External Flash Func. setting) screen is shown, you can press the INFO. button to produce a screen that allows you to clear all the flash settings.

## External Flash Function Setting

You can access this menu only when you have a compatible electronic flash attached and switched on. If you press the INFO. button while adjusting flash settings, both the changes made to the settings of an attached external flash and to the built-in flash will be cleared. These options are quite complex, so I'm going to save the description of them for Chapters 11 and 12.

## External Flash Custom Function Setting

Many external Speedlites from Canon include their own list of Custom Functions, which can be used to specify things like flash metering mode and flash bracketing sequences, as well as more sophisticated features, such as modeling light/flash (if available), use of external power sources (if attached), and functions of any slave unit attached to the external flash. This menu entry allows you to set an external flash unit's Custom Functions from your T5i's menu.

## Clear External Flash Custom Function Setting

This entry allows you to zero-out any changes you've made to your external flash's Custom Functions, and return them to their factory default settings.

# Exposure Compensation/Automatic Exposure Bracketing

The first entry on the Shooting 2 menu is Expo. Comp./AEB, or exposure compensation and automatic exposure bracketing. (See Figure 8.13.) As you learned in Chapter 4, exposure compensation (added/subtracted by pressing the cross keys while this menu screen is visible) increases or decreases exposure from the metered value.

Exposure bracketing using the T5i's AEB feature is a way to shoot several consecutive exposures using different settings, to improve the odds that one will be exactly right. Automatic exposure bracketing is also an excellent way of creating the base exposures you'll need when you want to combine several shots to create a high dynamic range (HDR) image. (You'll find a discussion of HDR photography—one of the latest rages—in Chapter 4, too.)

To activate automatic exposure bracketing, select this menu choice, then rotate the Main Dial to spread or contract the three dots beneath the scale until you've defined the range you want the bracket to cover, shown as full-stop jumps in Figure 8.14. Then, use the touch screen or cross keys to move the brackets right or left, biasing the bracketing toward underexposure (move left) or over-exposure (move right).

When AEB is activated, the three bracketed shots will be exposed in this sequence: metered exposure, decreased exposure, increased exposure. You'll find more information about exposure bracketing in Chapter 4.

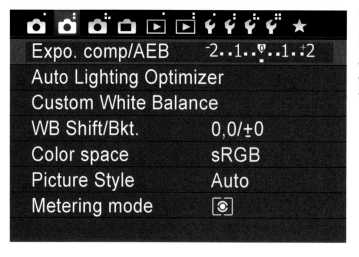

**Figure 8.13**
Exposure compensation/exposure bracketing is the first entry in the Shooting 2 menu.

**Figure 8.14**
Set the range of the three bracketed exposures.

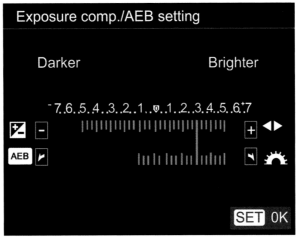

Exposure comp./AEB setting

Darker                                    Brighter

‾7.6.5.4.3.2.1.ᵥ.1.2.3.4.5.6.⁺7

SET OK

# Auto Lighting Optimizer

The Auto Lighting Optimizer provides a partial fix for images that are too dark or flat. Such photos typically have low contrast, and the Auto Lighting Optimizer improves them—as you shoot—by increasing both the brightness and contrast as required. The feature can be activated in Program, Aperture-priority, and Shutter-priority modes. You can select from four settings: Standard (the default value, which is always selected when using Scene Intelligent Auto and Creative Auto modes, and used for Figure 8.15), plus Low, Strong, and Disable. Press the INFO. button to add/remove a

**Figure 8.15**
Auto Lighting Optimizer can brighten dark, low-contrast images (top), giving them a little extra snap and brightness (bottom).

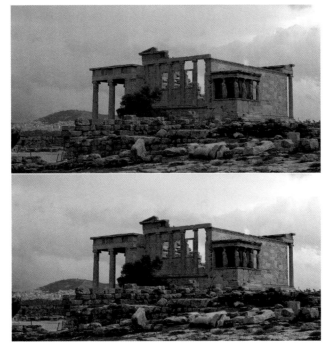

check mark icon that indicates the Auto Lighting Optimizer is disabled during manual exposure. Since you're likely to be specifying a particular exposure in Manual mode, you probably don't want the optimizer to interfere with your settings, so disabling the feature is the default.

## Custom White Balance

If automatic white balance or one of the seven preset settings available (Auto, Daylight, Shade, Cloudy/Twilight/Sunset, Tungsten, White Fluorescent, or Flash) aren't suitable, you can set a custom white balance using this menu option. The custom setting you establish will then be applied whenever you select Custom using the White Balance menu that pops up when you press the WB button (the up cross key). (See Figure 8.16.)

To set the white balance to an appropriate color temperature under the current ambient lighting conditions, focus manually (with the lens set on MF) on a plain white or gray object, such as a card or wall, making sure the object fills the spot metering circle in the center of the viewfinder. Then, take a photo. Next press the MENU button and select Custom WB from the Shooting 2 menu. Use the cross keys until the reference image you just took appears and choose SET to store the white balance of the image as your Custom setting. Only compatible images that can be used to specify a custom white balance will be shown on the screen. Custom white balance images are marked with a custom icon, and cannot be removed (although they can be replaced with a new custom white balance image).

### A WHITE BALANCE LIBRARY

Shoot a selection of blank-card images under a variety of lighting conditions on a spare memory card. If you want to "recycle" one of the color temperatures you've stored, insert the card and set the Custom white balance to that of one of the images in your white balance library, as described above.

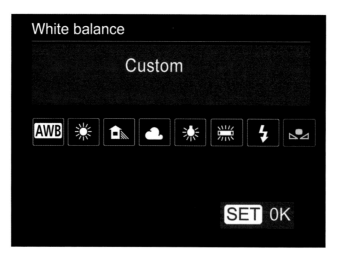

**Figure 8.16**
Preset white balance settings can be chosen from this menu, which appears when you press the WB button.

# White Balance Shift and Bracketing

White balance shift allows you to dial in a white balance color bias along the blue-yellow/amber dimensions, and/or magenta/green scale. In other words, you can set your color balance so that it is a little bluer or yellower (only), a little more magenta or green (only), or a combination of the two bias dimensions. You can also bracket exposures, taking several consecutive pictures each with a slightly different color balance biased in the directions you specify.

The process is a little easier to visualize if you look at Figure 8.17. The center intersection of lines BA and GM (remember high school geometry!) is the point of zero bias. Move the point at that intersection using the cross keys to locate it at any point on the graph using the blue-yellow/amber and green-magenta coordinates. The amount of shift will be displayed in the SHIFT box to the right of the graph.

White balance bracketing is like white balance shifting, only the bracketed changes occur along the bias axis you specify. The three squares in Figure 8.17 show that the white balance bracketing will occur in two-stop steps along the blue-yellow/amber axis. The amount of the bracketing is shown in the lower box to the right of the graph.

This form of bracketing is similar to exposure bracketing, but with the added dimension of hue. Bias bracketing can be performed in any JPEG-only mode. You can't use any RAW format or RAW+JPEG format because the RAW files already contain the information needed to fine-tune the white balance and white balance bias.

When you select WB SHIFT/BKT, the adjustment screen appears. First, you press the cross keys to set the range of the shift in either the green/magenta dimension (move to the left to change the vertical separation of the three dots representing the separate exposures) or in the blue-yellow/amber dimension by pressing the right cross key. Use all four cross keys to move the bracket set around within the color space, and outside the green-magenta or blue-yellow/amber axes.

**Figure 8.17**
Use the touch screen or cross keys to specify color balance bracketing using green-magenta bias or to specify blue-yellow/amber bias.

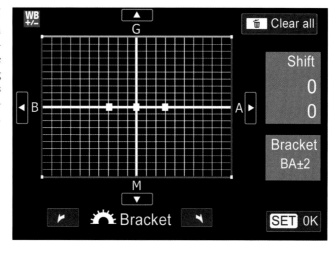

In most cases, it's fairly easy to determine if you want your image to be more green, more magenta, more blue, or more yellow, although judging your current shots on the LCD screen can be tricky unless you view the screen in a darkened location so it will be bright and easy to see. Bracketing is covered in Chapter 4.

## Color Space

When you are using one of the Creative Zone modes, you can select one of two different color spaces (also called *color gamuts*) using this menu entry, shown previously among the other menu choices in Figure 8.13. One color space is named *Adobe RGB* (because it was developed by Adobe Systems in 1998), while the other is called *sRGB* (supposedly because it is the *standard* RGB color space). These two color gamuts define a specific set of colors that can be applied to the images your T5i captures.

The Color Space menu choice applies directly to JPEG images shot using P, Tv, Av, and M exposure modes. When you're using Scene Intelligent Auto or Creative Auto modes, the T5i uses the sRGB color space for all the JPEG images you take. RAW images are a special case. They have the information for *both* sRGB and Adobe RGB, but when you load such photos into your image editor, it will default to sRGB (with Scene Intelligent Auto or Creative Auto shots) or the color space specified here unless you change that setting while importing the photos. (See the "Best of Both Worlds" sidebar that follows for more information.)

You may be surprised to learn that the Rebel T5i doesn't automatically capture *all* the colors we see. Unfortunately, that's impossible because of the limitations of the sensor and the filters used to capture the fundamental red, green, and blue colors, as well as that of the elements used to display those colors on your camera and computer monitors. Nor is it possible to *print* every color our eyes detect, because the inks or pigments used don't absorb and reflect colors perfectly. In short, your sensor doesn't capture all the colors that we can see, your monitor can't display all the colors that the sensor captures, and your printer outputs yet another version.

On the other hand, the T5i does capture quite a few more colors than we need. The original 14-bit RAW image contains a possible 4.4 *trillion* different hues, which are condensed down to a mere 16.8 million possible colors when converted to a 24-bit (eight bits per channel) image. While 16.8 million colors may seem like a lot, it's a small subset of 4.4 trillion captured, and an even smaller subset of all the possible colors we can see. The set of colors, or gamut, that can be reproduced or captured by a given device (scanner, digital camera, monitor, printer, or some other piece of equipment) is represented as a color space that exists within the larger full range of colors.

That full range is represented by the odd-shaped splotch of color shown in Figure 8.18, as defined by scientists at an international organization called the International Commission on Illumination (usually known as the CIE for its French name *Commission internationale de l'éclairage*) back in 1931. The colors possible with Adobe RGB are represented by the larger, black triangle in the figure, while the sRGB gamut is represented by the smaller white triangle.

**Figure 8.18**
The outer figure shows all the colors we can see; the two inner outlines show the boundaries of Adobe RGB (black triangle) and sRGB (white triangle).

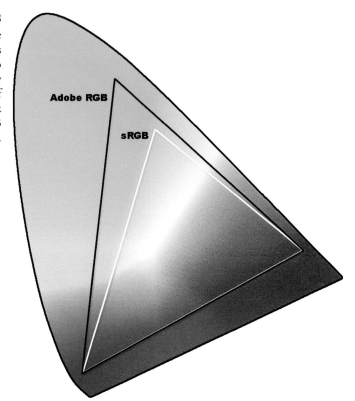

Regardless of which triangle—or color space—is used by the T5i, you end up with some combination of 16.8 million different colors that can be used in your photograph. (No one image will contain all 16.8 million! If each and every pixel in a 15-megapixel photo were a different color—which is extremely unlikely—you'd need only 15 million different colors.) But, as you can see from the figure, the colors available will be *different*.

Adobe RGB is what is often called an *expanded* color space, because it can reproduce a range of colors that is spread over a wider range of the visual spectrum. Adobe RGB is useful for commercial and professional printing. You don't need this range of colors if your images will be displayed primarily on your computer screen or output by your personal printer.

The other color space, sRGB, is recommended for images that will be output locally on the user's own printer, as this color space matches that of the typical inkjet printer fairly closely. While both Adobe RGB and sRGB can reproduce the exact same 16.8 million absolute colors, Adobe RGB spreads those colors over a larger portion of the visible spectrum, as you can see in the figure. Think of a box of crayons (the jumbo 16.8 million crayon variety). Some of the basic crayons from the original sRGB set have been removed and replaced with new hues not contained in the original box. Your "new" box contains colors that can't be reproduced by your computer monitor, but which work just fine with a commercial printing press.

## BEST OF BOTH WORLDS

As I mentioned, if you're using a Basic Zone mode, the T5i selects the sRGB color space automatically. In addition, you may choose to set the sRGB color space with this menu entry to apply that gamut to all your other photos as well. But, in either case, you can still easily obtain Adobe RGB versions of your photos if you need them. Just shoot using RAW+JPEG. You'll end up with sRGB JPEGs suitable for output on your own printer, but you can still extract an Adobe RGB version from the RAW file at any time. It's like capturing two different color spaces at once—sRGB and Adobe RGB—and getting the best of both worlds.

Of course, choosing the right color space doesn't solve the problems that result from having each device in the image chain manipulating or producing a slightly different set of colors. To that end, you'll need to investigate the wonderful world of *color management*, which uses hardware and software tools to match or *calibrate* all your devices, as closely as possible, so that what you see more closely resembles what you capture, what you see on your computer display, and what ends up on a printed hardcopy. Entire books have been devoted to color management, and most of what you need to know doesn't directly involve your Canon Rebel T5i, so I won't detail the nuts and bolts here.

To manage your color, you'll need, at the bare minimum, some sort of calibration system for your computer display, so that your monitor can be adjusted to show a standardized set of colors that is repeatable over time. (What you see on the screen can vary as the monitor ages, or even when the room light changes.) I use the Spyder4 monitor color correction system from Datacolor (www.datacolor.com) for my computer's dual 26-inch wide screen LCD displays. The Huey checks room light levels every five minutes, and reminded me to recalibrate every week or two using the small sensor device shown in Figure 8.19, which attaches temporarily to the front of the screen and interprets test patches that the software displays during calibration. The rest of the time, the sensor sits in its stand, measuring the room illumination, and adjusting my monitors for higher or lower ambient light levels.

If you're willing to make a serious investment in equipment to help you produce the most accurate color and make prints, you'll want a more advanced system (up to $500) like the various other Spyder products from Datacolor or Colormunki from X-Rite (www.colormunki.com).

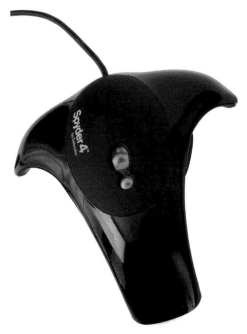

**Figure 8.19** Datacolor's Spyder4 monitor color correction system is an inexpensive device for calibrating your display.

# Picture Style

The Picture Style feature is one of the most important tools for customizing the way your Canon Rebel T5i renders its photos. It carries the "ambience" idea of tweaking images as they are shot to a new level. Picture Styles are a type of fine-tuning you can apply to your photos to change certain characteristics of each image taken using a particular Picture Style setting. The parameters you can specify for full-color images include the amount of sharpness, degree of contrast, the richness of the color, and the hue of skin tones. For black-and-white images, you can tweak the sharpness and contrast, but the two color adjustments (meaningless in a monochrome image) are replaced by controls for filter effects (which I'll explain shortly), and sepia, blue, purple, or green tone overlays.

The Canon Rebel T5i has five preset color Picture Styles, for Standard, Portrait, Landscape, Neutral, and Faithful pictures, plus Auto, and three user-definable settings called User Def. 1, User Def. 2, and User Def. 3, which you can define to apply to any sort of shooting situation you want, such as sports, architecture, or baby pictures. There is also a sixth, Monochrome, Picture Style that allows you to adjust filter effects or add color toning to your black-and-white images. See Figure 8.20 for the main Picture Style menu.

Picture Styles are extremely flexible. Canon has set the parameters for the five predefined color Picture Styles and the single monochrome Picture Style to suit the needs of most photographers. But you can adjust any of those "canned" Picture Styles to settings you prefer. Better yet, you can use those three User Definition files to create brand-new styles that are all your own. If you want rich, bright colors to emulate Velvia film or the work of legendary photographer Pete Turner, you can build your own color-soaked style. If you want soft, muted colors and less sharpness to create a romantic look, you can do that, too. Perhaps you'd like a setting with extra contrast for shooting outdoors on hazy or cloudy days.

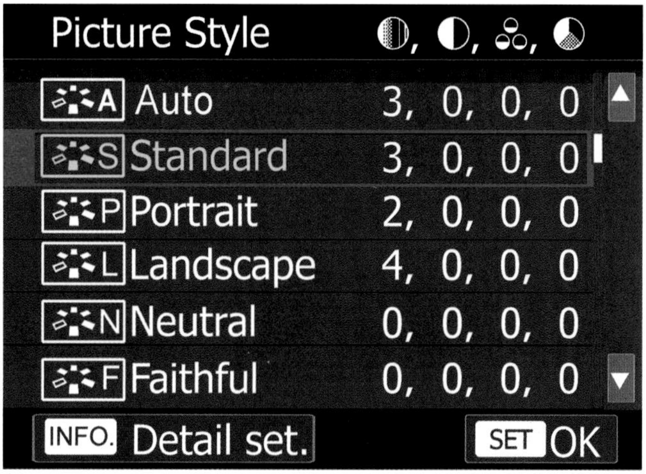

**Figure 8.20**
Ten different Picture Styles are available from this scrolling menu; these six plus Monochrome and three User Def. styles not shown.

The parameters applied when using Picture Styles follow. Figure 8.21 shows exaggerated examples of the first four (color photo) attributes, as applied by Picture Styles (your real-world tweaks may not be quite this drastic, but are more difficult to represent on the printed page):

- **Sharpness.** This parameter determines the apparent contrast between the outlines or edges in an image, which we perceive as image sharpness. You can adjust the sharpness of the image between values of 0 (no sharpening added) to 7 (dramatic additional sharpness). When adjusting sharpness, remember that more is not always a good thing. A little softness is necessary (and is introduced by a blurring "anti-alias" filter in front of the sensor) to reduce or eliminate the moiré effects that can result when details in your image form a pattern that is too close to the pattern, or frequency, of the sensor itself. The default levels of sharpening (which are, for most

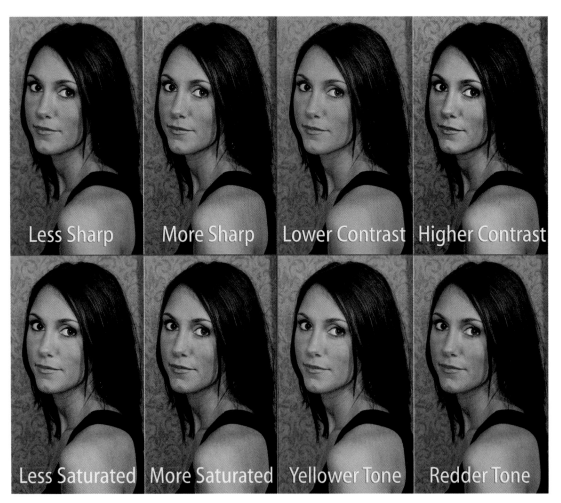

**Figure 8.21** These sets of photos represent the main color image Picture Styles parameters: sharpness (upper-left pair); contrast (upper-right pair); saturation (lower-left pair); and color tone (lower-right pair).

Picture Styles, not 0) were chosen by Canon to allow most moiré interference to be safely blurred to invisibility, at the cost of a little sharpness. As you boost sharpness (either using a Picture Style or in your image editor), moiré can become a problem, plus, you may end up with those noxious "halos" that appear around the edges of images that have been oversharpened. Use this adjustment with care.

■ **Contrast.** Use this control, with values from −4 (low contrast) to +4 (higher contrast), to change the number of middle tones between the deepest blacks and brightest whites. Low contrast settings produce a flatter-looking photo, while high contrast adjustments may improve the tonal rendition while possibly losing detail in the shadows or highlights.

■ **Saturation.** This parameter, adjustable from −4 (low saturation) to +4 (high saturation) controls the richness of the color, making, say, a red tone appear to be deeper and fuller when you increase saturation, and tend more toward lighter, pinkish hues when you decrease saturation of the reds. Boosting the saturation too much can mean that detail may be lost in one or more of the color channels, producing what is called "clipping." You can detect this phenomenon when using the RGB histograms, as described in Chapter 4.

■ **Color tone.** This adjustment has the most effect on skin tones, making them either redder (0 to −4) or yellower (0 to +4).

■ **Filter effect (Monochrome only).** Filter effects do not add any color to a black-and-white image. Instead, they change the rendition of gray tones as if the picture were taken through a color filter. I'll explain this distinction more completely in the sidebar "Filters vs. Toning" later in this section.

■ **Toning effect (Monochrome only).** Using toning effects preserves the monochrome tonal values in your image, but adds a color overlay that gives the photo a sepia, blue, purple, or green cast.

The predefined Picture Styles are as follows:

■ **Auto.** Adjusts the color to make outdoor scenes look more vivid, with richer colors.

■ **Standard.** This Picture Style applies a set of parameters, including boosted sharpness, that are useful for most picture taking, and which are applied automatically when using Basic Zone modes other than Portrait or Landscape.

■ **Portrait.** This style boosts saturation for richer colors when shooting portraits, which is particularly beneficial for women and children, while reducing sharpness slightly to provide more flattering skin texture. The Basic Mode Portrait setting uses this Picture Style. You might prefer the Faithful style for portraits of men when you want a more rugged or masculine look, or when you want to emphasize character lines in the faces of older subjects of either gender.

■ **Landscape.** This style increases the saturation of blues and greens, and increases both color saturation and sharpness for more vivid landscape images. The Basic Zone Landscape mode uses this setting.

- **Neutral.** This Picture Style is a less-saturated and lower-contrast version of the Standard style. Use it when you want a more muted look to your images, or when the photos you are taking seem too bright and contrasty (say, at the beach on a sunny day).

- **Faithful.** The goal of this style is to render the colors of your image as accurately as possible, roughly in the same relationships as seen by the eye.

- **Monochrome.** Use this Picture Style to create black-and-white photos in the camera. If you're shooting JPEG only, the colors are gone forever. But if you're shooting JPEG+RAW you can convert the RAW files to color as you import them into your image editor, even if you've shot using the Monochrome Picture Style. Your T5i displays the images in black-and-white on the screen during playback, but the colors are there in the RAW file for later retrieval.

> **Tip**
>
> You can use the Monochrome Picture Style even if you are using one of the RAW formats alone, without a JPEG version. The Rebel T5i displays your images on the screen in black-and-white, and marks the RAW image as monochrome so it will default to that style when you import it into your image editor. However, the color information is still present in the RAW file and can be retrieved, at your option, when importing the image.

## Selecting Picture Styles

Canon makes selecting a Picture Style for use very easy, and, to prevent you from accidentally changing an existing style when you don't mean to, divides *selection* and *modification* functions into two separate tasks. There are actually two different ways to choose from among your existing Picture Styles.

One way is to choose Picture Styles from the Shooting 2 menu and press SET to produce the main Picture Style menu screen. Use the cross keys to rotate among the nine choices. (Neutral, Faithful, Monochrome, and User Def. 1, User Def. 2, and User Def. 3 are shown in Figure 8.22; the rest appear when you scroll using the cross keys.) The current settings for each Picture Style are shown on the right half of the screen. Choose SET to activate your choice. Then select MENU to exit the menu system. You can see that even with this method, switching among Picture Styles is fast and easy enough to allow you to shift gears as often as you like during a shooting session.

But your T5i offers an even simpler way to activate a Picture Style. Press the Picture Style button (the down cross key) or press the Q button and navigate to the Picture Styles section, and choose SET. Then use the cross keys to scroll through the list of available styles on the screen that appears, shown in Figure 8.23. When you use this method, the current settings for a particular style are shown *only* when you've highlighted that style. Select SET to activate the style of your choice.

**Figure 8.22**
You can select a style from the the Picture Style menu in Set-up 2 menu.

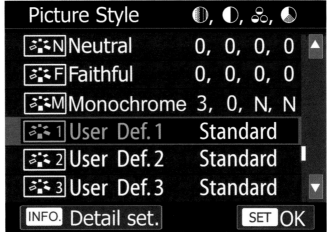

**Figure 8.23**
Choose Picture Style from the Quick Control menu to choose a style from this fast-access screen.

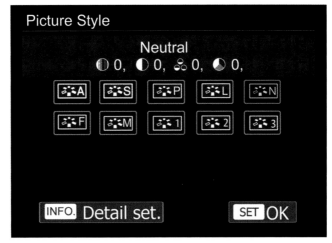

## Defining Picture Styles

Canon makes interpreting current Picture Style settings and applying changes very easy. As you saw in Figures 8.22 and 8.23, the current settings of the visible Picture Style options are shown as numeric values on the menu screen. Some camera vendors use word descriptions, like Sharp, Extra Sharp, or Vivid, More Vivid that are difficult to relate to. The T5i's settings, on the other hand, are values on uniform scales, with seven steps (from 1 to 7) for sharpness, and plus/minus four steps clustered around a zero (no change) value for contrast and saturation (so you can change from low contrast/low saturation, –4, to high contrast/high saturation, +4), as well as color tone (–4/reddish to +4/yellowish). The individual icons at the top of Figure 8.22 represent (left to right) Sharpness, Contrast, Saturation, and Color Tone.

You can change one of the existing Picture Styles or define your own whenever the Shooting 2 menu version of the Picture Styles menu, or the pop-up selection screen shown in Figure 8.23, is visible. Just press the INFO. button when either screen is on the LCD. Follow these steps:

1. **Choose a style to modify.** Use the touch screen or cross keys to scroll to the style you'd like to adjust.

2. **Activate adjustment mode.** Press the INFO. button to choose Detail Set. If you're coming from the Shooting 2 menu, the screen that appears next will look like the one shown in Figure 8.20 for the five color styles or three User Def. styles. If you've accessed the adjustment screen by pressing the Picture Styles button first, the screen looks much the same, but has blue highlighting instead of red.

3. **Choose a parameter to change.** Use the touch screen or cross keys to scroll among the four parameters, plus Default Set. at the bottom of the screen, which restores the values to the preset numbers.

4. **Activate changes.** Choose SET to change the values of one of the four parameters. If you're redefining one of the default presets, the menu screen will look like Figure 8.24, which represents the Landscape Picture Style.

5. **Adjust values.** Use the touch screen or cross keys to move the triangle to the value you want to use. Note that the previous value remains on the scale, represented by a gray triangle. This makes it easy to return to the original setting if you want.

6. **Confirm changes.** Choose SET to lock in that value, then press the MENU button three times to back out of the menu system.

Any Picture Style that has been changed from its defaults will be shown in the Picture Style menu with blue highlighting the altered parameter. You don't have to worry about changing a Picture Style and then forgetting that you've modified it. A quick glance at the Picture Style menu will show you which styles and parameters have been changed.

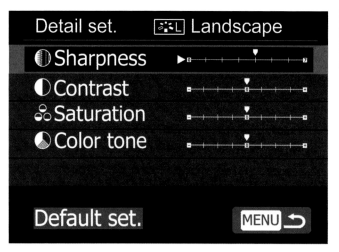

**Figure 8.24**
Each parameter can be changed separately.

Making changes in the Monochrome Picture Style is slightly different, as the Saturation and Color Tone parameters are replaced with Filter Effect and Toning Effect options. (See Figure 8.25.) (Keep in mind that once you've taken a photo using a Monochrome Picture Style, you can't convert the image back to full color.) You can choose from Yellow, Orange, Red, or Green filters, or None, and specify Sepia, Blue, Purple, or Green toning, or None. You can still set the Sharpness and Contrast parameters that are available with the other Picture Styles. Figure 8.26 shows filter effects being applied to the Monochrome Picture Style.

**Figure 8.25**
Apply changes to the Monochrome Picture Style.

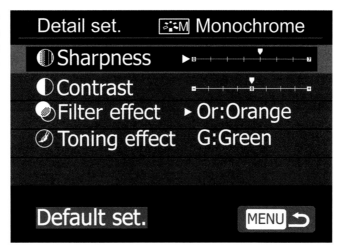

**Figure 8.26**
No filter (upper left); Yellow filter (upper right); Green filter (lower left); and Red filter (lower right).

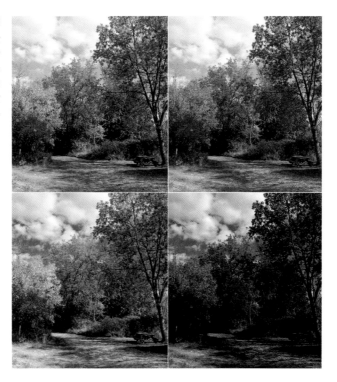

## FILTERS VS. TONING

Although some of the color choices overlap, you'll get very different looks when choosing between Filter Effects and Toning Effects. Filter Effects add no color to the monochrome image. Instead, they reproduce the look of black-and-white film that has been shot through a color filter. That is, Yellow will make the sky darker and the clouds will stand out more, whereas Orange makes the sky even darker and sunsets more full of detail. The Red filter produces the darkest sky of all and darkens green objects, such as leaves. Human skin may appear lighter than normal. The Green filter has the opposite effect on leaves, making them appear lighter in tone. Figure 8.26 shows the same scene shot with no filter, then Yellow, Green, and Red filters.

The Sepia, Blue, Purple, and Green Toning Effects, on the other hand, all add a color cast to your monochrome image. Use these when you want an old-time look or a special effect, without bothering to recolor your shots in an image editor. Figure 8.27 shows the various Toning Effects available.

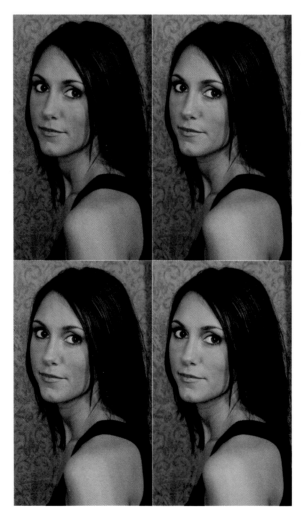

**Figure 8.27**
Select from among four color filters in the Monochrome Picture Style, including Sepia (top left); Blue (top right); Purple (lower left); and Green (lower right).

## Adjusting Styles with the Picture Style Editor

If you'd rather edit Picture Styles in your computer, the Picture Style Editor supplied for your camera in versions for both Windows and Macs, allows you to create your own custom Picture Styles, or edit existing styles, including the Standard, Landscape, Faithful, and other predefined settings already present in your Rebel T5i. You can change sharpness, contrast, color saturation, and color tone—and a lot more—and then save the modifications as a PF2 file that can be uploaded to the camera, or used by Digital Photo Professional (described in Chapter 13) to modify a RAW image as it is imported.

To create and load your own Picture Style, just follow these steps:

1. **Load the editor.** Launch the Picture Style Editor (PSE, not to be confused with the *other* PSE, Photoshop Elements).

2. **Access a RAW file.** Load a RAW CR2 image you'd like to use as a reference into PSE. You can drag a file from a folder into the editor's main window, or use the Open command in the File menu.

3. **Choose an existing style to base your new style on.** Select any of the base styles except for Standard. Your new style will begin with all the attributes of the base style you choose, so start with one that already is fairly close to the look you want to achieve ("tweaking" is easier than building a style from the ground up).

4. **Split the screen.** You can compare the appearance of your new style with the base style you are working from. Near the lower-left edge of the display pane are three buttons you can click to split the old/new styles vertically, horizontally, or return to a single image.

5. **Dial in basic changes.** Click the Advanced button in the Tool palette to pop up the Advanced Picture Style Settings dialog box that appears at left in the figure. These are the same parameters you can change in the camera. Click OK when you're finished.

6. **Make advanced changes.** The Tool palette has additional functions for adjusting hue, tonal range, and curves. Use of these tools is beyond the scope of a single chapter, let alone a notation in a list, but if you're familiar with the advanced tools in Photoshop, Photoshop Elements, Digital Photo Pro, or another image editor, you can experiment to your heart's content. Note that these modifications go way beyond what you can do with Picture Styles in the camera itself, so learning how to work with them is worth the effort. Figure 8.28 shows an image taken using the Standard Picture Style (left) and a custom User Def. style with enhanced saturation, sharpness, and contrast (right).

7. **Save your Picture Style.** When you're finished, choose Save Picture Style File from the File menu to store your new style as a PF2 file on your hard disk. Add a caption and copyright information to your style in the boxes provided. If you click Disable Subsequent Editing, your style will be "locked" and protected from further changes, and the modifications you did make will be hidden from view (just in case you dream up your own personal, "secret" style). But you'll be unable to edit that style later on. If you think you might want to change your custom Picture Style, save a second copy without marking the Disable Subsequent Editing box.

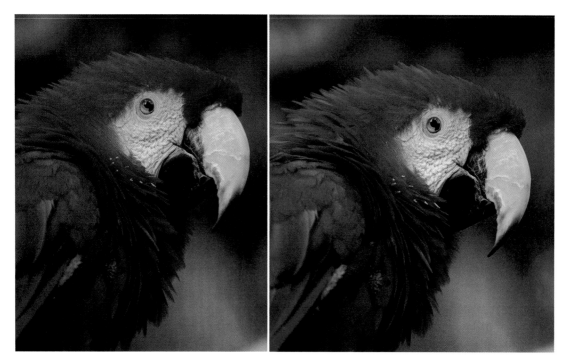

**Figure 8.28** Image taken using Standard Picture Style (left) and custom User Def. Picture Style with enhanced saturation, sharpness, and contrast (right).

## Uploading a Picture Style to the Camera

Now it's time to upload your new style to your Canon Rebel T5i into one of your three User Def. slots in the Picture Style array. Just follow these steps:

1. **Link your camera for upload.** Connect your camera to your computer using the USB cable, turn the T5i on, launch the EOS Utility, and click the Camera Settings/Remote Shooting choice in the splash screen.

2. **Choose the Shooting menu.** It's marked with an icon of a white camera on a red background, from the menu bar located about midway in the control panel that appears on your computer display.

3. **Select Register User Defined Style.** Click on the box, outlined in red in the figure, to produce the Register Picture Style dialog box.

4. **Choose a User Def. tab.** Click on one of the three tabs, labeled User Def. 1, User Def. 2, or User Def. 3. Each tab will include the name of the current Picture Style active in that tab.

5. **Click the Open File button and choose the Picture Style file to load.** The Picture Styles you've saved (or downloaded from another source) will appear with a PF2 extension. Click on the one you want to use, and then click the Open button in the Open dialog box.

**Figure 8.29**
The new style will appear in the menu.

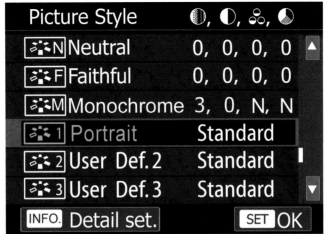

6. **Upload Picture Style to the camera.** The Register Picture Style File dialog box will return. Click OK and the Picture Style will be uploaded to the camera in the User Def. "slot" represented by the tab you've chosen. The name of the Picture Style will appear in the T5i's menu in place of User Def. 1 (or User Def. 2/User Def. 3). (See Figure 8.29.)

## Changing a Picture Style's Settings from the EOS Utility

You can modify the settings of a Picture Style that's already loaded into your camera from the EOS Utility when your camera is linked to your computer. Just follow these steps:

1. **Link your camera to the computer.** Connect your camera to your computer using the USB cable, turn the T5i on, launch the EOS Utility, and click the Camera Settings/Remote Shooting choice in the splash screen.

2. **Choose the Shooting menu.** It's marked with an icon of a white camera on a red background, from the menu bar located about midway in the control panel that appears on your computer display.

3. **Access the Picture Style.** Click on the Picture Style choice to produce the screen shown at upper right in Figure 8.30. The currently active Picture Style in the camera will be shown, along with its detail settings.

4. **Choose a Picture Style to modify.** Click the Picture Style box (highlighted with a red box at upper left in Figure 8.30) to produce a listing of all the available Picture Styles, which you can see at right in Figure 8.30. For this illustration, I clicked on Landscape, which is highlighted with a red box.

5. **Click Detail Set**. At lower left Landscape is now highlighted. When you click on Detail Set., the dialog box shown at lower right in Figure 8.30 appears. You can move the sliders to change the settings, as described earlier. You can also click the Default Set. button to return the settings to their original values.

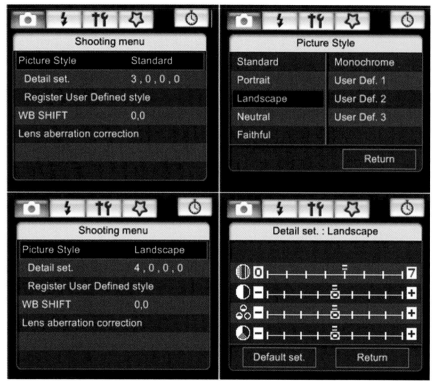

**Figure 8.30**
Adjust the settings of a Picture Style in your camera.

6. **Confirm choice.** Click Return when you've finished making changes, and the Picture Style you've modified will be changed in the camera.

7. **Exit EOS Utility.** Disconnect your camera from your computer, and your modified style is ready to use.

## Getting More Picture Styles

I've found that careful Googling can unearth other Picture Styles that helpful fellow EOS owners have made available, and even a few from the helpful Canon company itself. My own search turned up this link: http://web.canon.jp/imaging/picturestyle/file/index.html, where Canon offers a half dozen or more useful PF2 files you can download and install on your own. Remember that Picture Style files are compatible between various Canon EOS camera models (that is, you can use a style created for the Canon 40D with your T5i), but you should be working with the latest software versions to work with the latest cameras and Picture Styles. If you installed your software from the CDs that came with your Rebel T5i, you're safe. If you owned an earlier EOS and haven't re-installed the software since your camera upgrade, you might need to re-install the software. It's available for download from the Canon website.

Try the additional styles Canon offers. They include:

■ **Studio Portrait.** Compared to the Portrait style built into the camera, this one, Canon says, expresses translucent skin in smooth tones, but with less contrast. (Similar to films in the pre-digital age that were intended for studio portraiture.)

■ **Snapshot Portrait.** This is another "translucent skin" style, but with increased contrast with enhanced contrast indoors or out.

■ **Nostalgia.** This style adds an amber tone to your images, while reducing the saturation of blue and green tones.

■ **Clear.** This style adds contrast for what Canon says is additional "depth and clarity."

■ **Twilight.** Adds a purple tone to the sky just before and after sunset or sunrise.

■ **Emerald.** Emphasizes blues and greens.

■ **Autumn Hues.** Increases the richness of browns and red tones seen in fall colors.

■ **Metering Mode.** This menu entry provides an additional way to select from among Evaluative, Partial, Spot, and Center-weighted average metering.

## Dust Delete Data

This menu choice is the first of four that appear in the Shooting 3 menu. (See Figure 8.31.) It lets you "take a picture" of any dust or other particles that may be adhering to your sensor. The T5i will then append information about the location of this dust to your photos, so that the Digital Photo Professional software can use this reference information to identify dust in your images and remove it automatically. You should capture a Dust Delete Data photo from time to time as your final line of defense against sensor dust.

To use this feature, select Dust Delete Data to produce the screen shown in Figure 8.32. Select OK and choose SET. The camera will first perform a self-cleaning operation by applying ultrasonic vibration to the low-pass filter that resides on top of the sensor. Then, a screen will appear asking

**Figure 8.31**
Dust Delete Data is the first choice in the Shooting 3 menu.

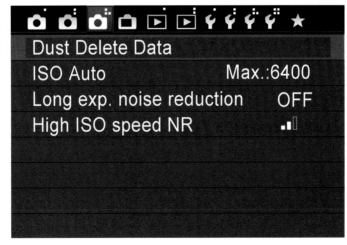

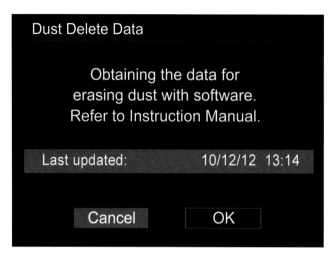

**Figure 8.32**
Capture updated dust data for your sensor to allow Digital Photo Professional to remove it automatically.

you to press the shutter button. Point the T5i at a solid-white card with the lens set on manual focus and rotate the focus ring to infinity. When you press the shutter release, the camera takes a photo of the card using Aperture-priority and f/22 (which provides enough depth-of-field [actually, in this case, *depth-of-focus*] to image the dust sharply). The "picture" is not saved to your memory card but, rather, is stored in a special memory area in the camera. Finally, a "Data obtained" screen appears.

The Dust Delete Data information is retained in the camera until you update it by taking a new "picture." The T5i adds the information to each image file automatically.

# ISO Auto

Fixed ISO speeds can be set by pressing the ISO button on top of the camera, and choosing ISO 100, 200, 400, 800, 1600, 3200, 6400, or 12800. You can also choose Auto, which allows the T5i to adjust the ISO setting to suit your scene. You can also make ISO settings from the Quick Control screen using the touch screen.

Fortunately, if you do select Auto, that doesn't necessarily mean that ISO settings are totally beyond your control. With this menu entry, you can choose the *maximum* ISO setting that will be used when working in Auto ISO mode. That will help you avoid unpleasant surprises, which can happen when the T5i opts for an ISO setting that's high enough to produce more visual noise than you might find acceptable.

You can choose a maximum ISO of 400, 800, 1600, 3200, or 6400, and the camera will honor your wishes. When you've chosen ISO 6400 as the max rating, though, that doesn't mean that the T5i will necessarily adjust sensitivity all the way up to that lofty level. Instead, it will choose an ISO appropriate for the amount of illumination available; that is, a higher ISO in dimmer conditions, and a lower ISO for brighter scenes, but within the limitations shown in Table 8.2.

The actual ISO in use will be displayed on the top-panel LCD when you press the shutter button halfway, so you aren't necessarily in the dark (so to speak) about the ISO setting being applied. The

| Table 8.2  Automatic ISO Ranges | |
| --- | --- |
| **Shooting Mode** | **ISO Range** |
| Scene Intelligent Auto, No Flash, Creative Auto, Landscape, Close-Up, Sports, Night Portrait, HDR Backlight Control modes | ISO 100–6400 (Auto) |
| Portrait mode | ISO 100 (Fixed) |
| Handheld Night Scene | ISO 100–12800 (Auto) |
| Bulb | ISO 400 (Fixed) |
| All modes, direct flash | ISO 400 (Fixed, except if overexposure results, then ISO 100–400) |
| Program, Tv, Av, M modes | ISO 100–6400 (Auto) |
| Movie shooting | ISO 100–6400 |

range used depends on the shooting mode you're working with, and the maximum you set using this menu entry. This menu entry allows you to place a limitation on the ranges selected in certain shooting modes, as outlined in Table 8.2.

# Long Exposure Noise Reduction

This entry allows you to enable or disable long exposure noise reduction, or allow the T5i to evaluate your scene and decide whether to use this noise-canceling adjustment. Visual noise is that graininess that shows up as multicolored specks in images, and this setting helps you manage it. In some ways, noise is like the excessive grain found in some high-speed photographic films. However, while photographic grain is sometimes used as a special effect, it's rarely desirable in a digital photograph.

The visual noise-producing process is something like listening to a CD in your car, and then rolling down all the windows. You're adding sonic noise to the audio signal, and while increasing the CD player's volume may help a bit, you're still contending with an unfavorable signal to noise ratio that probably mutes tones (especially higher treble notes) that you really want to hear.

The same thing happens when the analog signal is amplified: You're increasing the image information in the signal, but boosting the background fuzziness at the same time. Tune in a very faint or distant AM radio station on your car stereo. Then turn up the volume. After a certain point, turning up the volume further no longer helps you hear better. There's a similar point of diminishing returns for digital sensor ISO increases and signal amplification as well.

These processes create several different kinds of noise. Noise can be produced from high ISO settings. As the captured information is amplified to produce higher ISO sensitivities, some random noise in the signal is amplified along with the photon information. Increasing the ISO setting of your camera raises the threshold of sensitivity so that fewer and fewer photons are needed to register as an exposed pixel. Yet, that also increases the chances of one of those phantom photons being counted among the real-life light particles, too.

Fortunately, the Rebel T5i's sensor and its digital processing chip are optimized to produce the low noise levels, so ratings as high as ISO 800 can be used routinely (although there will be some noise, of course), and even ISO 3200 can generate good results.

A second way noise is created is through longer exposures. Extended exposure times allow more photons to reach the sensor, but increase the likelihood that some photosites will react randomly even though not struck by a particle of light. Moreover, as the sensor remains switched on for the longer exposure, it heats, and this heat can be mistakenly recorded as if it were a barrage of photons. This entry can be used to tailor the amount of noise-canceling performed by the digital signal processor.

- **Off.** Disables long exposure noise reduction. Use this setting when you want the maximum amount of detail present in your photograph, even though higher noise levels will result. This setting also eliminates the extra time needed to take a picture caused by the noise reduction process. If you plan to use only lower ISO settings (thereby reducing the noise caused by ISO amplification), the noise levels produced by longer exposures may be acceptable. For example, you might be shooting a river spilling over rocks at ISO 100 with the camera mounted on a tripod, using a neutral-density filter and long exposure to cause the pounding water to blur slightly. To maximize detail in the non-moving portions of your photos, you can switch off long exposure noise reduction. Because the noise-reduction process used with Auto and On can effectively double the time required to take a picture, Off is a good setting to use when you want to avoid this delay when possible.

- **Auto.** The Rebel T5i examines your photo taken with an exposure of one second or longer, and if long exposure noise is detected, a second, blank exposure is made and compared to the first image. Noise found in the "dark frame" image is subtracted from your original picture, and only the noise-corrected image is saved to your memory card.

- **On.** When this setting is activated, the T5i applies dark frame subtraction to all exposures longer than one second. You might want to use this option when you're working with high ISO settings (which will already have noise boosted a bit) and want to make sure that any additional noise from long exposures is eliminated, too. Noise reduction will be applied to some exposures that would not have caused it to kick in using the Auto setting.

**Tip**

While the "dark frame" is being exposed, the LCD screen will be blank during Live View mode, and the number of shots you can take in Continuous shooting mode will be reduced. White balance bracketing is disabled during this process.

# High ISO Speed Noise Reduction

The other type of noise results from using higher ISO settings. This entry allows you to specify just how much or how little of this noise reduction to apply, which can be a valuable option because noise reduction does eliminate detail while blurring the amount of noise. The default is Standard noise reduction, but you can specify Low or Strong noise reduction, or disable noise reduction entirely. At lower ISO values, noise reduction improves the appearance of shadow areas without affecting highlights; at higher ISO settings, noise reduction is applied to the entire photo. Note that when the Strong option is selected, the maximum number of continuous shots that can be taken will decrease significantly, because of the additional processing time for the images.

- **Standard.** At lower ISO values, noise reduction is applied primarily to shadow areas; at higher ISO settings, noise reduction affects the entire image.

- **Low.** A smaller amount of noise reduction is used. This will increase the grainy appearance, but preserve more fine image detail.

- **Strong.** More aggressive noise reduction is used, at the cost of some image detail, adding a "mushy" appearance that may be noticeable and objectionable. Because of the image processing applied by this setting, your continuous shooting maximum burst will decrease significantly.

- **Disable.** No additional noise reduction will be applied.

# Live View Shooting Menu Options

This menu tab is color-coded red like the three previous Shooting menu tabs, but contains only options that apply to photography in Live View mode (see Figure 8.33). All of the settings on this tab pertain to the T5i's Live View functions, which I explained in detail in Chapter 6. The available entries are as follows:

- Live View Shooting
- AF Method
- Continuous AF
- Touch Shutter
- Grid Display
- Aspect Ratio
- Metering Timer

# Live View Shooting

This menu entry is the first in the Live View Shooting menu (see Figure 8.33). It enables/disables live view shooting and the Live View button here. Disabling live view does not affect movie shooting, which is activated by rotating the On/Off/Movie switch to the Movie position.

# AF Method

Here you can select the autofocus mode, Face Detection+Tracking Mode, FlexiZone—Multi, FlexiZone—Single, and Quick mode, all explained at length in Chapter 5.

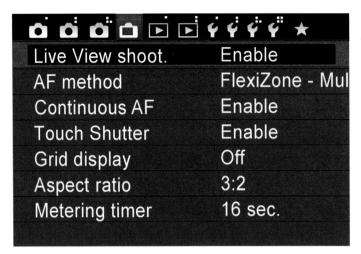

**Figure 8.33**
All the settings on the Live View Shooting menu involve live view functions.

## Continuous AF

This menu entry enables and disables the Continuous AF feature, which is the live view equivalent of the AI Servo mode explained in Chapter 5. When activated, the T5i will refocus on objects as their distance from the camera changes. The feature is automatically disabled when you choose Quick mode focus.

## Touch Shutter

Enables and disables the Touch Shutter feature, which allows you to initiate focus and take a picture automatically just by tapping your subject as it appears on the touch screen.

## Grid Display

When enabled, overlays Grid 1, a "rule of thirds" grid, on the screen to help you compose your image and align vertical and horizontal lines; or Grid 2, which consists of four rows of six boxes, which allow finer control over placement of images in your frame.

## Aspect Ratio

Allows you to choose an aspect ratio, or proportions of your image, from 3:2, 4:3, 16:9, or 1:1 when working in PSAM exposure modes. Selecting proportions other than the 3:2 default results in a cropped image, and the live view display provides a black border on the LCD to show the limits of the image area (see Figure 8.34). At the Large or RAW size setting, you end up with images that measure 5184 × 3456 pixels/18MP (3:2 ratio); 4608 × 3456 pixels/16MP (4:3 ratio); 5184 × 2912 pixels/15.1MP (16:9 ratio); and 3456 × 3456 pixels/11.9MP (1:1 ratio). At Medium (M), Small 1 (S1), Small 2 (S2), and Small 3 (S3), the images are proportionately smaller. This choice is not available when using a Basic Zone mode.

**Figure 8.34**
You can choose the proportions of your image.

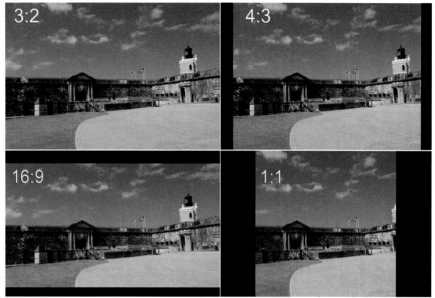

## Metering Timer

This option allows you to specify how long the EOS T5i's metering system will remain active before switching off. Tap the shutter release to start the timer again after it switches off. This choice is not available when using a Basic Zone mode (the timer is fixed at 16 seconds). In Creative Zone modes, you can select 4, 16, or 30 seconds, plus 1, 10, or 30 minutes.

## Movie Shooting Menu Options

The two red-coded Movie Shooting menus are available only when the T5i has been switched to Movie mode by rotating the On/Off/Movie Switch to the Movie position. The choices you'll find include:

- AF Method
- Movie Servo AF
- AF with Shutter Button During Movie Shooting
- Grid Display
- Metering Timer
- Movie Recording Size
- Sound Recording
- Video Snapshot

## AF Method

This is the first entry in the first of the two Movie Shooting menus (see Figure 8.35). Here you can select the autofocus mode, Face Detection+Tracking Mode, FlexiZone—Multi, and FlexiZone—Single, all explained at length in Chapter 5. When shooting movies, Quick mode is not available.

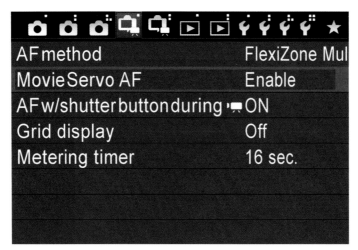

**Figure 8.35**
This is the first Movie Shooting menu.

## Movie Servo AF

This menu entry enables and disables the Movie Servo AF feature, which is the live view equivalent of the AI Servo mode explained in Chapter 5. Initiate autofocus by pressing the shutter release halfway, whether you've selected Face Detection+Tracking, FlexiZone—Multi, or FlexiZone—Single autofocus modes. You can then release the shutter button, and autofocus will continue.

When activated, the T5i will refocus on objects as their distance from the camera changes. Using one of Canon's new nearly silent STM focus lenses (described in Chapter 10), such as the EF-S 18-55mm f/3.5-5.6 IS STM or EF-S 18-135mm f/3.5-5.6 IS STM kit lenses or the 40mm f/2.8 STM lens virtually eliminates autofocus noise while shooting video. When using this mode, remember to turn off the T5i before switching to manual focus mode to avoid damage to the continuously focusing lens.

If you choose Disable for this feature, autofocus is active only when the shutter release is held down halfway. You might want to disable Movie Servo AF when you don't want focus to change while capturing video.

## AF with Shutter Button During Movie Shooting

Movie shooting is stopped/started by pressing the Live View/Movie button on the back of the camera to the right of the viewfinder window. However, you can take a still photo by pressing the shutter release down all the way. Enable this option to tell the T5i to refocus when you press the shutter release halfway as you take that still picture. One-Shot (single autofocus) is used. Select Disable instead, and pressing the shutter release button has no effect on autofocus. In effect, turning the feature off gives priority to taking the still picture, rather than to autofocus, so it's possible to shoot a still that's out of focus. As you might expect, this feature works best with subjects that are not moving.

# Grid Display

When enabled, this setting overlays Grid 1 on the screen to help you compose your image and align vertical and horizontal lines, or Grid 2, which consists of four rows of six boxes, which allows finer control over placement of images in your frame. The grids are similar to those shown in live view, except that the top and bottom of the frame are masked off on the LCD to show the 16:9 movie proportions. (See Figure 8.36.)

**Figure 8.36**
Two grids are available when shooting movies to help you align horizontal and vertical subjects.

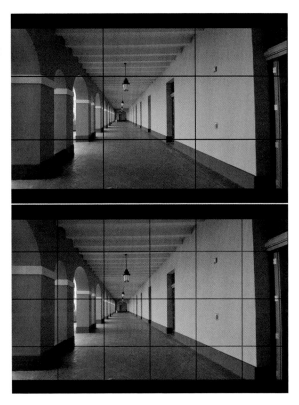

# Metering Timer

This corresponds to Live View's metering timer, and allows you to specify how long the EOS T5i's metering system will remain active before switching off. Tap the shutter release to start the timer again after it switches off. You can select 4, 16, or 30 seconds, plus 1, 10, or 30 minutes.

# Movie Recording Size

This option, the first on the second Movie Shooting menu, allows you to choose the movie image size and frame rate. You can select full HD (1920 × 1080 pixels) at either 30 or 24 frames per second, standard HD (1280 × 720 pixels) at 60 frames per second, or VGA resolution movies (640 × 480 pixels) at 30 frames per second. I explained the reasons for choosing a particular frame rate in Chapter 6.

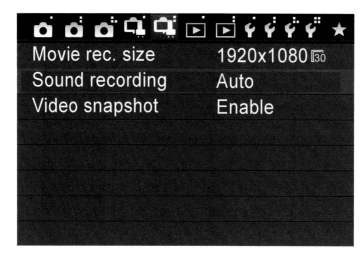

**Figure 8.37**
All the settings on the Live View Shooting menu involve live view functions.

## Sound Recording

This option allows you to choose the sound level for recording movies, either Auto (the T5i adjusts the audio level) or Manual (you can choose 64 different recording levels). Use this feature to evaluate the noise levels in a room prior to beginning serious video capture. Select Disable to record silent movies. You may also turn the wind filter on or off to mask wind noise outdoors that might be recorded by the built-in microphone (but also reducing the bass levels). The Attenuator control can be set to Enable to reduce sound distortion from sudden very loud sounds, or Disable when you don't expect or don't mind such distortion. I explained all these sound options in Chapter 6.

## Video Snapshot

Video snapshots are short clips lasting 2, 4, or 8 seconds (your choice) and assembled into video snapshot "albums" for playback as a continuous movie. You can enable or disable the feature, create new albums, add to old albums, and specify the length of your clips. I explained how to manage all these options in Chapter 6.

## Playback Menu Options

The two blue-coded Playback menus are where you select options related to the display, review, and printing of the photos you've taken. The choices you'll find include:

- Protect Images
- Rotate Images
- Erase Images
- Print Order
- Photobook Setup
- Creative Filters

- Resize
- Histogram Display
- Image Jump with Main Dial
- Slide Show
- Rating
- Ctrl over HDMI

# Protect Images

This is the first entry in the Playback 1 menu (see Figure 8.38). If you want to keep an image from being accidentally erased (either with the Erase button or by using the Erase Images menu entry), you can mark that image for protection. To protect one or more images, press the MENU button while viewing an image and choose Protect. Then, select from the following options:

- Select Images
- All Images in Folder
- Unprotect All Images in Folder
- All Images on Card
- Unprotect All Images on Card

If you choose the first option, you can view and select individual images by pressing the SET button when they are displayed on the screen. A key icon will appear at the upper edge of the information display while still in the protection screen, and when reviewing that image later. To remove protection, repeat the process. You can scroll among the other images on your memory card and protect/unprotect them in the same way. Image protection will not save your images from removal when the card is reformatted.

# Rotate Images

While you can set the Rebel T5i to automatically rotate images taken in a vertical orientation using the Auto Rotate option in the Set-up 1 menu (as described in Chapter 9), you can manually rotate an image during playback using this menu selection. Select Rotate from the Playback 1 menu, use the touch screen or cross keys to page through the available images on your memory card until the one you want to rotate appears, then choose SET. The image will appear on the screen rotated 90 degrees, as shown in Figure 8.39. Select SET again, and the image will be rotated 270 degrees.

**Figure 8.38**
The Playback 1 menu.

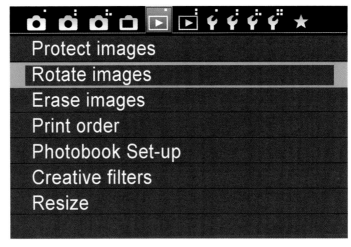

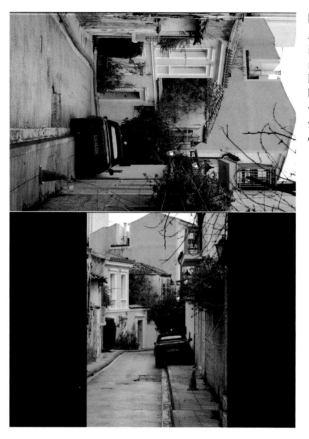

**Figure 8.39**
A vertically oriented image that isn't rotated appears larger on the LCD, but rotation allows viewing the photo without turning the camera.

# Erase Images

Choose this menu entry and you'll be given three choices: Select and Erase Images, All Images in Folder, and All Images on Card. You can use the first two to selectively remove images, while the third option deletes all the pictures on a card. But, using the Format command is usually faster and more thorough.

- **Select and Erase Images.** View the images on your card by pressing the left/right cross keys to scroll through them. To mark an image for deletion or to remove a checkmark, press the up/down cross keys. When you're finished selecting, press the Trash button (to the left of the viewfinder window) and you'll be asked to confirm. Choose Cancel or OK and SET to finish.

- **All Images in Folder.** You'll be shown a list of the available folders on your memory card. Select SET, and a prompt will appear asking you to confirm, and reminding you that Protected images will not be removed.

- **All Images on Card.** A prompt will ask you to confirm this step. The All Images on Card choice removes all the pictures on the card, except for those you've marked with the Protect command, and does not reformat the memory card.

# Print Order

The Rebel T5i supports the DPOF (Digital Print Order Format) that is now almost universally used by digital cameras to specify which images on your memory card should be printed, and the number of prints desired of each image. This information is recorded on the memory card, and can be interpreted by a compatible printer when the camera is linked to the printer using the USB cable, or when the memory card is inserted into a card reader slot on the printer itself. Photo labs are also equipped to read this data and make prints when you supply your memory card to them.

While marking images for printing is similar to the Erase procedure described earlier, you can read more about assembling print orders and printing photobooks in Chapter 13.

# Photobook Setup

You can select up to 998 images on your memory card, and then use the EOS Utility to copy them all to a specific folder on your computer. This is a handy way to transfer only specific images to a particular folder, and is especially useful when you're collecting photos to assemble in a photobook. Your choices include:

■ **Select images.** You can mark individual images from any folder on your memory card.

■ **All images in folder.** Mark all the images in a particular folder for transfer.

■ **Clear all in folder.** Unmark all the images in a folder.

■ **All images on card.** Mark all the images on the memory card for transfer to the specific folder.

■ **Clear all on card.** Unmark all the images on the card.

Once you marked the images you want to transfer to the specified folder, use the EOS Utility to copy them, as described in Chapter 13.

# Creative Filters

One new feature of the T5i is the ability to apply Creative Filters to images as you take the picture, and preview their effect before shooting during live view. However, the original method of applying interesting effects to images you've already taken remains available. You can process an image using one of these filters, and save a copy alongside the original. When you select this menu entry, you'll be taken to a screen that allows you to choose an image to modify. You can scroll through the available images with the touch screen or cross keys or press the Thumbnail/Reduce Image button to view thumbnails and select from those. Only images that can be edited are shown. Then, select SET, and choose the filter you want to apply from a list at the bottom of the screen using the left/right cross keys. Choose SET to activate the filter, then use the touch screen or left/right cross keys again to adjust the amount of the effect (or select the area to be adjusted using the miniature effect). Choose SET once more to save your new image.

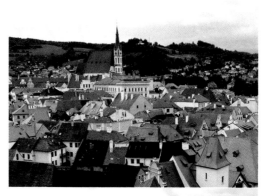

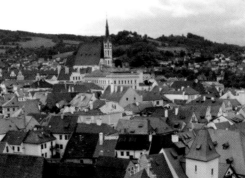

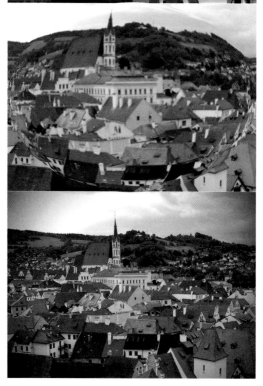

**Figure 8.40**
Top to bottom:
Grainy B/W, Soft
Focus, Fish-Eye, Toy
Camera Effect.

The seven effects include the following. Four of them (Grainy B/W, Soft Focus, Fish-Eye, Toy Camera Effect) are shown in Figure 8.40, and the Miniature Effect is shown in Figures 8.41 and 8.42.

- **Grainy B/W.** Creates a grainy monochrome image. You can adjust contrast among Low, Normal, and Strong settings.

- **Soft Focus.** Blur your image using Low, Normal, and Strong options.

- **Fish-eye Effect.** Creates a distorted, curved image.

- **Art Bold Effect.** Produces a three-dimensional oil painting effect. You can adjust contrast and saturation.

- **Water Painting Effect.** Gives you soft colors like a watercolor painting, and allows you to adjust color density.

- **Toy Camera Effect.** Darkens the corners of an image, much as a toy camera does, and adds a warm or cool tone (or none), as you wish.

- **Miniature Effect.** This is a clever effect, and it's hampered by a misleading name and the fact that its properties are hard to visualize (which is not a great attribute for a visual effect). This tool doesn't create a "miniature" picture, as you might expect. What it does is mimic tilt/shift lens effects that angle the lens off the axis of the sensor plane to drastically change the plane of focus, producing the sort of look you get when viewing some photographs of a diorama, or miniature scene. Confused yet? All you need to do is specify the area of the image that you want to remain sharp (see Figure 8.41) and you'll end up with a version like the one shown in Figure 8.42.

**Figure 8.41**
Choose the area for sharp focus by moving the white box within the frame.

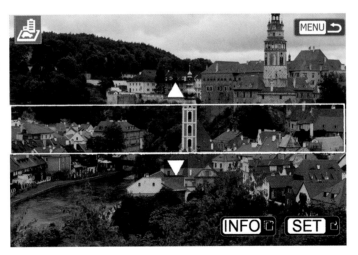

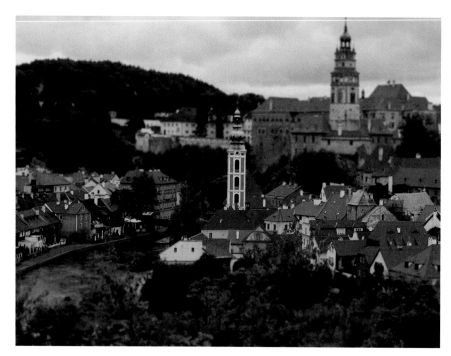

**Figure 8.42**
The resulting image looks like a miniature town, perhaps for a toy train layout.

# Resize

If you've already taken an image and would like to create a smaller version (say, to send by e-mail), you can create one from this menu entry. Just follow these steps:

1. **Choose Resize.** Select this menu entry from the Playback 1 menu.

2. **View images to resize.** You can scroll through the available images with the touch screen or cross keys, or press the Thumbnail/Reduce Image button to view thumbnails and select from those. Only images that can be resized are shown. They include JPEG Large, Medium, Small 1, and Small 2 images. Small 3 and RAW images of any type cannot be resized.

3. **Select an image.** Choose SET to select an image to resize. A pop-up menu will appear on the screen offering the choice of reduced size images. These include M (Medium: 8MP, 3456 × 2304 pixels); S1 (Small 1: 4.5MP, 2592 × 1728 pixels); S2 (Small 2: 2.5MP, 1920 × 1280 pixels); or S3 (Small 3, .3MP, 720 × 480 pixels). You cannot resize an image to a size that is larger than its current size; that is, you cannot save a JPEG Medium image as JPEG Large.

4. **Resize and save.** Choose SET to save as a new file, and confirm your choice by selecting OK from the screen that pops up, or cancel to exit without saving a new version. The old version of the image is untouched.

# Histogram Display

The T5i can show either a brightness histogram or set of three separate Red, Green, and Blue histograms in the full information display during picture review, or, it can show you both types of histogram in the partial information display. This entry, the first on the Playback 2 menu, gives you those options. (See Figure 8.43.)

Brightness histograms give you information about the overall tonal values present in the image. The RGB histograms can show more advanced users valuable data about specific channels that might be "clipped" (details are lost in the shadows or highlights). This menu choice determines only how they are displayed during picture review. The amount of information displayed cycles through the following list as you repeatedly press the INFO. button in Playback mode:

- **Single image display.** Only the image itself is shown, with basic shooting information displayed in a band across the top of the image, as you can see at upper left in Figure 8.44.

- **Single image display+Image-recording quality.** Identical to Single image display, except that the image size, RAW format (if selected), and JPEG compression (if selected) are overlaid on the image in the lower-left corner of the frame.

- **Histogram display.** Both RGB and brightness histograms are shown, along with partial shooting information. This menu choice has no effect on which histograms are shown in this display, which you can see at upper right in Figure 8.44.

- **Shooting information display.** Full shooting data is shown, along with either a brightness histogram (bottom left in Figure 8.44) or RGB histogram (bottom right in Figure 8.44). The type of histogram on view in this screen is determined by the setting you make in this menu choice. Select Histogram from the Playback 2 menu and choose Brightness or RGB. You can read more about *using* histograms in Chapter 4.

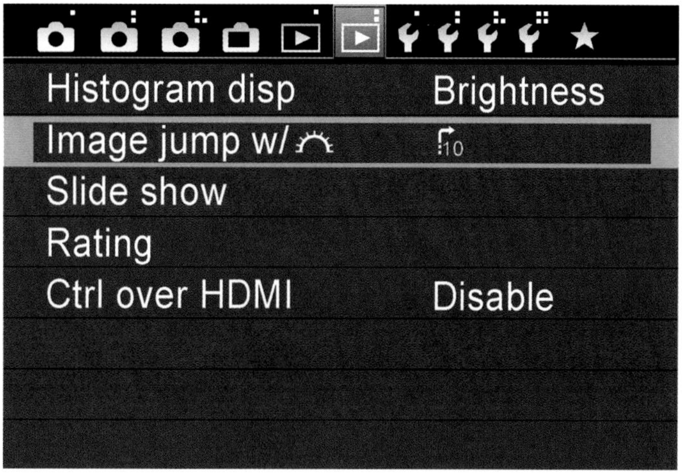

**Figure 8.43**
The Playback 2 menu.

| Histogram disp | Brightness |
| Image jump w/ ⌒ | 10 |
| Slide show | |
| Rating | |
| Ctrl over HDMI | Disable |

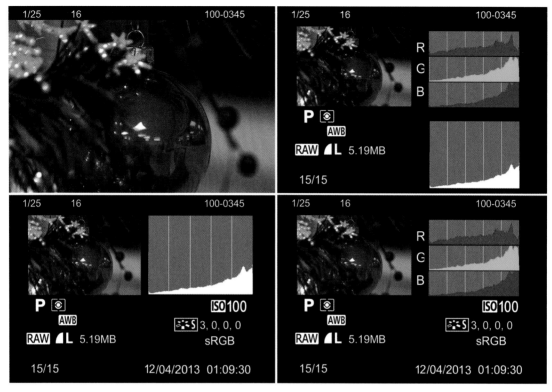

**Figure 8.44** Press the INFO. button to cycle between Single image display (upper left); Single image display+Image-recording quality (not shown); Histogram display (upper right); Shooting information display with brightness histogram (bottom left); or RGB histogram (bottom right).

## Image Jump with Main Dial

As first described in Chapter 2, you can leap ahead or back during picture review by swiping across the touch screen with two fingers, or by rotating the Main Dial. You can select from a variety of increments that will be used with this menu entry. The Jump method is shown briefly on the screen as you leap ahead to the next image displayed, as shown in Figure 8.45. Your options are as follows:

- **1 image.** Rotating the Main Dial one click or swiping jumps forward or back 1 image.
- **10 images.** Rotating the Main Dial one click or swiping jumps forward or back 10 images.
- **100 images.** Rotating the Main Dial one click or swiping jumps forward or back 100 images.
- **Date.** Rotating the Main Dial one click or swiping jumps forward or back to the first image taken on the next or previous calendar date.
- **Folder.** Rotating the Main Dial one click or swiping jumps forward or back to the first image in the next folder available on your memory card (if one exists).

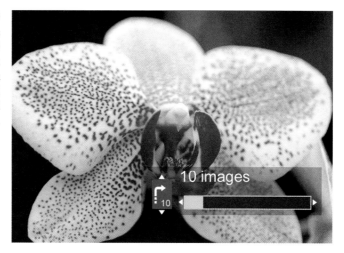

**Figure 8.45**
The Jump method is shown on the LCD briefly when you leap forward or back using the Main Dial or a two-fingered touch screen swipe.

- **Movies.** Rotating the Main Dial one click or swiping jumps forward or back, displaying movies you captured only.
- **Stills.** Rotating the Main Dial one click or swiping jumps forward or back, displaying still images only.
- **Rating.** Rotating the Main Dial one click or swiping jumps forward or back, displaying images by the ratings you've applied (as described next). Tap the touch screen or rotate the Main Dial to choose the rating parameter.

# Slide Show

Slide Show is a convenient way to review images one after another, without the need to manually switch between them. To activate, just choose Slide Show from the Playback 2 menu. During playback, you can press the SET button to pause the "slide show" (in case you want to examine an image more closely), or the INFO. button to change the amount of information displayed on the screen with each image. For example, you might want to review a set of images and their histograms to judge the exposure of the group of pictures. To set up your slide show, follow these steps:

1. **Begin setup.** Choose Slide Show from the Playback 2 menu, choosing SET to display the screen shown in Figure 8.46.
2. **Choose image selection method.** Navigate to All Images, and choose SET. Then use the touch screen or rotate the cross keys to choose from All Images, Folder, or Date. Choose SET to activate that selection mode. If you selected All Images, skip to Step 4.
3. **Choose images.** If you've selected Folder or Date, press the INFO. button to produce a screen that allows you to select from the available folders, or the available image creation dates on your memory card. When you've chosen a folder or date, choose SET to confirm your choice.

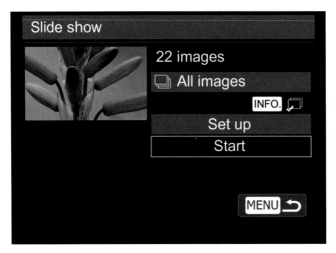

**Figure 8.46**
Set up your slide show using this screen.

4. **Choose Play Time and Repeat Options.** Highlight Setup and choose SET to produce a screen with playing time (1, 2, 3, or 5 seconds per image), and repeating options (On or Off). When you've specified either value, select MENU to confirm your choice, and then MENU once more to go back to the main Slide Show screen.

5. **Start the show.** Highlight Start and choose SET to begin your show. (If you'd rather cancel the show you've just set up, select MENU.)

6. **Use show options during display.** Press SET to pause/restart; INFO. to cycle among the four information displays described in the section before this one; MENU to stop the show.

# Rating

If you want to apply a quality rating to images or movies you've shot (or use the rating system to represent some other criteria), you can use this entry to give particular images one, two, three, four, or five stars, or turn the rating system off. The Image Jump function can display only images with a given rating. Suppose you were photographing a track meet with multiple events. You could apply a one-star rating to jumping events, two-stars to relays, three-stars to throwing events, four-stars to hurdles, and five-stars to dashes. Then, using the Image Jump feature, you could review only images of one particular type.

With a little imagination you can apply the rating system to all sorts of categories. At a wedding, you could classify pictures of the bride, the groom, guests, attendants, and parents of the couple. If you were shooting school portraits, one rating could apply to First Grade, another to Second Grade, and so on. Given a little thought, this feature has many more applications than you might think.

To use it, just follow these steps:

1. Choose the Rating menu item.

2. Use the touch screen or cross keys to select an image or movie. Press the Thumbnail/Reduce Image/Zoom Out button to display three images at once. Press the AF point/Magnify/Zoom In button to return to a single image.

3. When an image or movie is visible, press the up/down buttons to apply a one- to five-star rating. The display shows how many images have been assigned each rating so far.

4. When finished rating, choose MENU to exit.

## Ctrl over HDMI

When your camera is connected to a TV that is compatible with the HDMI CEC standard, you can use the remote control to activate playback functions. You'll need a compatible TV, remote control, and an HDMI cable to connect your camera to the television. Then, choose Enable in this menu entry, and then follow the directions that came with your television and remote for selecting still photo and movie playback features. If your TV does not allow use of the remote, return to the menu selection and chose Disable to give the camera control of playback.

# 9

# Customizing with the Set-up Menu and My Menu

In the last chapter, I introduced you to the layout and general functions of the Canon EOS T5i's menu system, with specifics on how to customize your camera with the Shooting 1, Shooting 2, Shooting 3, Live View, and Movie Shooting menus, as well as the Playback 1 and Playback 2 menus. In this chapter, you'll learn how to work with the four Set-up menus, and how to assemble your own roster of favorite menu listings with the My Menu feature.

If you're jumping directly to this chapter and need some guidance in how to navigate the T5i's menu system, review the first few pages of Chapter 8. Otherwise, you're welcome to dive right in.

## Set-up Menu Options

There are four amber-coded set-up menus where you make adjustments on how your camera *behaves* during your shooting session, as differentiated from the Shooting menu, which adjusts how the pictures are actually taken. Your choices include:

- Select Folder
- File Numbering
- Auto Rotate
- Format Card
- Eye-Fi Settings
- Auto Power Off
- LCD Brightness
- LCD Auto Off

- Time Zone
- Date/Time
- Language
- Video System
- Screen Color
- Feature Guide
- Touch Control
- Sensor Cleaning

- GPS Device Settings
- Certification Logo Display
- Custom Functions (C.Fn)
- Copyright Information
- Clear Settings
- Firmware Version

# Select Folder

Choose this menu option, the first on the Set-up 1 menu (see Figure 9.1) to create a folder where the images you capture will be stored on your memory card, or to switch between existing folders. Just follow these steps:

1. **Choose Select Folder.** Access the option from the Set-up 1 menu.

2. **View list of available folders.** The Select Folder screen pops up with a list of the available folders on your memory card, with names like 100CANON, 101CANON, etc.

3. **Choose a different folder.** To store subsequent images in a different existing folder, use the touch screen or cross keys to highlight the label for the folder you want to use. When a folder that already has photos is selected, two thumbnails representing images in that folder are displayed at the right side of the screen.

4. **Confirm the folder.** Choose SET to confirm your choice of an existing folder.

5. **Create new folder.** If you'd rather create a new folder, highlight Create Folder in the Select Folder screen and choose SET. The name of the folder that will be created is displayed, along with a choice to Cancel or OK creating the folder. Choose SET to confirm your choice.

6. **Exit.** Press MENU to return to the Set-up 1 menu.

The folders your T5i create always follow the *nnn*CANON convention. You can also use your computer to create folders with names that depart from this arrangement, as long as you adhere to the camera's general rules for memory card folder names. Here's how to create folders with personalized names:

1. **Access the memory card from your computer.** There are two ways to do this:

   a. **USB link.** Plug the USB cable into the port on the left side of the T5i and connect to a USB connector on your computer. In Windows, the T5i will appear as a generic digital camera icon. A similar icon will appear on the Mac OS X desktop.

   b. **Use a card reader.** Remove the card from the T5i and insert it in a card reader attached to your computer. A typical card reader is shown in Figure 9.2.

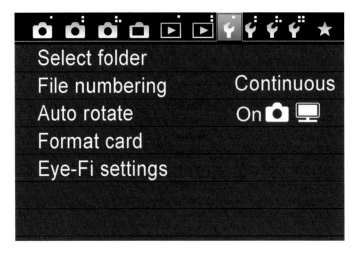

**Figure 9.1**
The Set-up 1 menu.

2. **Open the camera/memory card in your computer.** A folder called DCIM will appear at the top level. All the folders your T5i can access must be located inside the DCIM folder.

3. **Create a new folder within the DCIM folder.** Although you're not limited to the *nnn*CANON arrangement, you must adhere to the rules in the steps that follow.

4. **Type in a three-digit folder number.** You can use any three numbers from 100 to 999, as long as those numbers are not already in use on that memory card. In other words, you can't have folders named 101CANON and 101SPAIN.

5. **Add a five-character description of your choice.** You can use any uppercase or lowercase letters from A to z, plus the underscore character (to represent a space). You cannot use an actual space, nor any other characters, even if your computer allows them in a file name. An invalid folder name will end up being "invisible" to the T5i, even if it actually exists on your memory card.

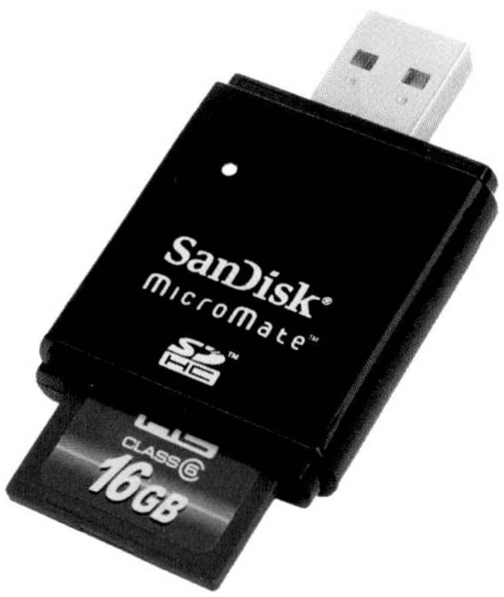

**Figure 9.2** Access your memory cards using a card reader.

With a little imagination (and caution, to avoid creating "bad" folder names), you can develop some useful folder names, and switch among them at will. I find this capability especially useful when working with very large (32GB or 64GB) cards, because I can do a great deal of organizing right on the card itself. Perhaps I have some images in a particular folder that I use as a "slide show" for display on my T5i's back panel LCD. Or, I might want to sort images by location or date. For example, I could use 104_USA_, 105SPAIN, 106FRANC, or 107GBRIT to indicate the location where the images were shot.

# File Numbering

The EOS T5i will automatically apply a file number to each picture you take, using consecutive numbering for all your photos over a long period of time, spanning many different memory cards, starting over from scratch when you insert a new card, or when you manually reset the numbers. Numbers are applied from 0001 to 9999, at which time the camera creates a new folder on the card (100, 101, 102, and so forth), so you can have 0001 to 9999 in folder 100, then numbering will start over in folder 101.

The camera keeps track of the last number used in its internal memory. That can lead to a few quirks you should be aware of. For example, if you insert a memory card that had been used with a different camera, the T5i may start numbering with the next number after the highest number used by the previous camera. (I once had a brand-new T5i start numbering files in the 8,000 range.) I'll explain how this can happen next.

On the surface, the numbering system seems simple enough: In the menu, you can choose Continuous, Automatic Reset, or Manual Reset. Here is how each works:

- **Continuous.** If you're using a blank/reformatted memory card, the T5i will apply a number that is one greater than the number stored in the camera's internal memory. If the card is not blank and contains images, then the next number will be one greater than the highest number on the card *or* in internal memory. (In other words, if you want to use continuous file numbering consistently, you must always use a card that is blank or freshly formatted.) Here are some examples:
  - You've taken 4,235 shots with the camera, and you insert a blank/reformatted memory card. The next number assigned will be 4,236, based on the value stored in internal memory.
  - You've taken 4,235 shots with the camera, and you insert a memory card with a picture numbered 2,728. The next picture will be numbered 4,236.
  - You've taken 4,235 shots with the camera, and you insert a memory card with a picture numbered 8,281. The next picture will be numbered 8,282, and that value will be stored in the camera's menu as the "high" shot number (and will be applied when you next insert a blank card).
- **Automatic reset.** If you're using a blank/reformatted memory card, the next photo taken will be numbered 0001. If you use a card that is not blank, the next number will be one greater than the highest number found on the memory card. Each time you insert a memory card, the next number will either be 0001 or one higher than the highest already on the card.
- **Manual reset.** The T5i creates a new folder numbered one higher than the last folder created, and restarts the file numbers at 0001. Then, the camera uses the numbering scheme that was previously set, either Continuous or Automatic Reset, each time you subsequently insert a blank or non-blank memory card.

## Auto Rotate

You can turn this feature On or Off. When activated, the EOS T5i rotates pictures taken in vertical orientation on the LCD screen so you don't have to turn the camera to view them comfortably. However, this orientation also means that the longest dimension of the image is shown using the shortest dimension of the LCD, so the picture is reduced in size. (You have three options, shown in Figure 9.3.) The image can be autorotated when viewing in the camera *and* on your computer screen using your image editing/viewing software. The image can be marked to autorotate *only* when reviewing your image in your image editor or viewing software. This option allows you to have rotation applied when using your computer, while retaining the ability to maximize the image on your LCD in the camera. The third choice is Off. The image will not be rotated when displayed in the camera or with your computer. Note that if you switch Auto Rotate off, any pictures shot while the feature is disabled will not be automatically rotated when you turn Auto Rotate back on; information embedded in the image file when the photo *is taken* is used to determine whether autorotation is applied.

**Figure 9.3**

Choose auto rotation both in the camera and on your computer display (top); only on your computer display (middle); or no automatic rotation (bottom).

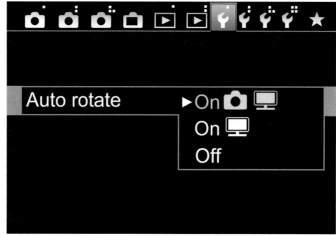

# Format Card

Use this item to erase everything on your memory card and set up a fresh file system ready for use. When you select Format, you'll see a display like Figure 9.4, showing the capacity of the card, how much of that space is currently in use, and two choices at the bottom of the screen to Cancel or OK (proceed with the format). Press the Trash button if you'd like to do a low-level format. That's a more basic format that removes all sectors from the card and creates new ones, which can help speed up a card that seems to be slow (because the camera must skip over "bad" sectors left behind from previous uses). An orange bar appears on the screen to show the progress of the formatting step.

**Figure 9.4**

You must confirm the format step before the camera will erase a memory card.

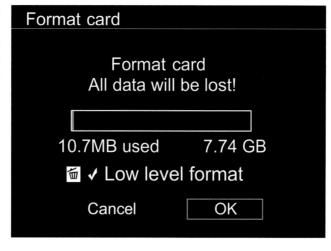

# Eye-Fi Settings

This menu item appears when you have an Eye-Fi card inserted in the camera. You can enable and disable Eye-Fi wireless functions, and view connection information. I explained the T5i's Eye-Fi options in detail in Chapter 7. The pair of entries allows you to Enable or Disable the card, and view current connection information. Because the Eye-Fi card draws power from the camera even when it's switched off, you might want to Disable the card (or remove it from the camera) when you don't need to use its features.

# Auto Power Off

This setting, the first in the Set-up 2 menu (see Figure 9.5), allows you to determine how long the EOS T5i remains active before shutting itself off. As you can see in Figure 9.6, you can select 30 seconds, 1, 2, 4, 8, or 15 minutes, or Disable, which leaves the camera turned on indefinitely. However, even if the camera has shut itself off, if the power switch remains in the On position, you can bring the camera back to life by pressing the shutter button.

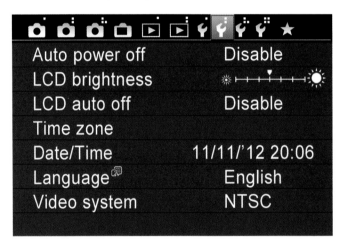

**Figure 9.5**
The Set-up 2 menu has seven options.

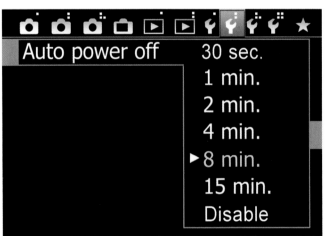

**Figure 9.6**
Select an automatic shut-off period to save battery power.

# LCD Brightness

Choose this menu option and a thumbnail image with a grayscale strip appears on the LCD, as shown in Figure 9.7. You can use the touch screen, cross keys, or the Main Dial to adjust the brightness to a comfortable viewing level. Use the gray bars as a guide; you want to be able to see both the lightest and darkest steps at top and bottom, and not lose any of the steps in the middle. Brighter settings use more battery power, but can allow you to view an image on the LCD outdoors in bright sunlight. When you have the brightness you want, select SET to lock it in and return to the menu.

**Figure 9.7**
Adjust LCD brightness for easier viewing under varying ambient lighting conditions.

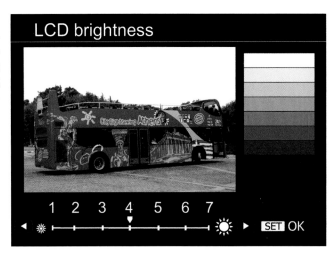

# LCD Auto Off

If you don't want the display-off sensor located above the viewfinder eyepiece to turn off the shooting setting display when your eye (or any other object) nears the viewfinder, you can disable the LCD Auto Off feature. At times you may want to keep the display active no matter what. Choose Disable to keep the display from turning off, or select Enable to retain automatic shutoff.

# Time Zone

Use this menu entry to set the current time zone used by the camera. Canon assigned a separate menu item to this setting so that you can quickly change time zones with no risk of adjusting any of the other date/time settings by accident.

When the screen appears, highlight the time zone and choose SET, and then press the up/down cross keys to switch to a different zone, represented by a major city name within that time zone (e.g., New York, London, Moscow). Choose SET again to lock it in. Use the left/right cross keys to switch between time zone and the Daylight Savings fields. You can specify whether the camera honors Daylight Savings Time. When you're finished adjusting the time zone information, press the right cross key to advance to the bottom row, and then choose OK to confirm or Cancel to return to the last settings specified.

# Date/Time

Use this option to set the date and time, which will be embedded in the image file along with exposure information and other data. As first outlined in Chapter 1, you can set the date and time by following these steps:

1. Access this menu entry from the Set-up 2 menu.

2. Use the cross keys to move the highlighting down to the entries, as seen in Figure 9.8.

3. Use the cross keys to select the value you want to change. When the gold box highlights the month, day, year, hour, minute, or second format you want to adjust, or the daylight savings time setting, press the SET button to activate that value. A pair of up/down pointing triangles appears above the value.

4. Use the cross keys to adjust the value up or down. Press SET to confirm the value you've entered.

5. Repeat steps 3 and 4 for each of the other values you want to change. The date format can be switched from the default mm/dd/yy to yy/mm/dd or dd/mm/yy.

6. When finished, use the touch screen or cross keys to select either OK (if you're satisfied with your changes) or Cancel (if you'd like to return to the Set-up 2 menu without making any changes). Choose SET to confirm your choice.

7. When finished setting the date and time, press MENU to exit, or just tap the shutter release.

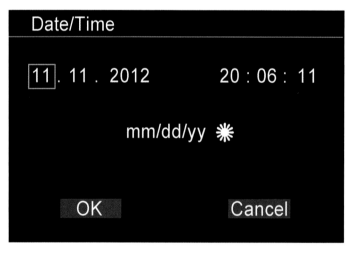

**Figure 9.8**
Adjust the time and date.

# Language

Choose from 25 languages for menu display, rotating the cross keys until the language you want to select is highlighted. Press the SET button to activate. Your choices include English, German, French, Dutch, Danish, Portuguese, Finnish, Italian, Ukrainian, Norwegian, Swedish, Spanish, Greek, Russian, Polish, Czech, Magyar, Romanian, Turkish, Arabic, Thai, Simplified Chinese, Traditional Chinese, Korean, and Japanese.

If you accidentally set a language you don't read and find yourself with incomprehensible menus, don't panic. Just choose the sixth option from the top of the Set-up 2 menu, and select the idioma, sprache, langue, or kieli of your choice. English is the first selection in the list.

# Video System

This setting controls the output of the T5i through the AV cable when you're displaying images on an external monitor. You can select either NTSC, used in the United States, Canada, Mexico, many Central American, South American, and Caribbean countries, much of Asia, and other countries, or PAL, used in the UK, much of Europe, Africa, India, China, and parts of the Middle East.

## VIEWING ON A TELEVISION

Canon makes it quite easy to view your images on a standard television screen, and not much more difficult on a high-definition television (HDTV). (You have to buy a separate cable for HDTV.) For regular TV, just open the port cover on the left side of the camera, plug in the optional AVC-DC400ST cable into the socket labeled A/V-digital, and connect the other end to the yellow VIDEO RCA composite jack on your television or monitor.

For HDTV display, purchase the optional HDMI Cable HTC-100 and connect it to the HDMI OUT terminal just below the microphone input on the left side of the camera.

Connect the other end to an HDMI input port on your television or monitor (my 42-inch HDTV has three of them; my 26-inch monitor has just two). Then turn on the camera and press the Playback button. The image will appear on the external TV/HDTV/monitor and will not be displayed on the camera's LCD. HDTV systems automatically show your images at the appropriate resolution for that set.

# Screen Color

Here in the first entry of the Set-up 3 menu, you can select one of five different shooting information screen color schemes, which are helpfully displayed in the setup screen so you can decide which looks best.

# Feature Guide

The Feature Guide is an easy pop-up description of a function or option that appears when you change the shooting mode or use the Quick Control screen to select a function, switch to Live View, Movie mode, or playback. The instructional screen quickly vanishes in a few seconds. You can use this setting to enable or disable the Feature Guide.

# Touch Control

Use this entry to totally disable or enable the LCD touch screen feature. If you find yourself accidentally triggering commands by touching the screen or frequently touch the wrong settings and want to turn it off, you can do so. I often disable touch screen control when I am wearing gloves.

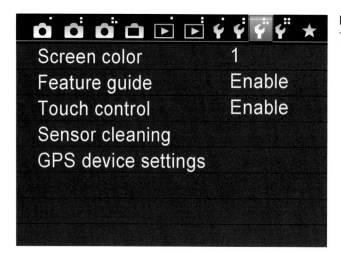

**Figure 9.9**
The Set-up 3 menu.

## Sensor Cleaning

One of the Canon EOS T5i's most useful features is the automatic sensor cleaning system that reduces or eliminates the need to clean your camera's sensor manually. Canon has applied anti-static coatings to the sensor and other portions of the camera body interior to counter charge build-ups that attract dust. A separate filter over the sensor vibrates ultrasonically each time the T5i is powered on or off, shaking loose any dust, which is captured by a sticky strip beneath the sensor.

Use this menu entry (see Figure 9.10) to enable or disable automatic sensor cleaning on power up (select Auto Cleaning to choose) or to activate automatic cleaning during a shooting session (select Clean Now). You can also choose the Clean Manually option to flip up the mirror and clean the sensor yourself with a blower, brush, or swab, as described in Chapter 14. If the battery level is too low to safely carry out the cleaning operation, the T5i will let you know and refuse to proceed, unless you use the optional AC Adapter Kit ACK-E6.

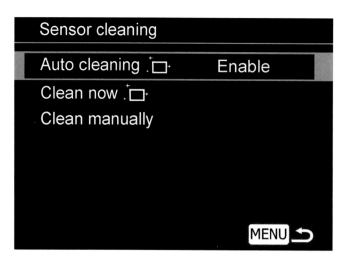

**Figure 9.10**
Use this menu choice to activate automatic sensor cleaning or enable/disable it on power up.

## GPS Device Settings

Although this menu item appears in the Set-up 4 menu all the time, its adjustments can be displayed only if the optional Canon GPS Receiver GP-E2 (about $270) is attached.

## Certification Logo Display

This cryptic entry, the first on the fourth page of the Set-up menu (shown in Figure 9.11) , is used by Canon to display the logos of some of the certification organizations that have approved the T5i's specifications. You'll find others on the bottom of the camera itself. As a camera user, you don't really care about certifications, but Canon added this entry as a way of updating any new credentials through a firmware update, thus avoiding the need to change the labels/engravings on the camera body itself. So now you know.

## Custom Functions

Custom Functions let you customize the behavior of your camera in eight different ways. If you don't like the default way the camera carries out certain tasks, you just may be able to do something about it. You can find the Custom Functions in their own screen with eight choices, divided into four groups of settings: Exposure (I, C.Fn 01, and 02); Image (II, C.Fn 03); Autofocus/Drive (III, C.Fn 04 and 05); and Operation/Others (IV, C.Fn 06, 07, and 08). The Roman numeral divisions within a single screen with a single line of choices seem odd until you realize that some other more upscale Canon EOS models separate each of these groups into separate screens (with larger numbers of options). For example, my 5D Mark III has four separate C.Fn menus with a total of 14 different adjustable functions.

Each of the Custom Functions is set in exactly the same way, so I'm not going to bog you down with a bunch of illustrations showing how to make this setting or that. One quick run-through using Figure 9.12 should be enough.

**Figure 9.11**
The fourth Set-up menu page.

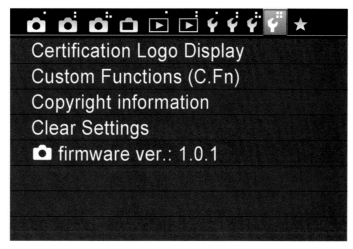

Here are the key parts of the Custom Functions screen.

- **Custom Functions category.** At the top of the settings screen is a label that tells you which category that screen represents.

- **Current Function name.** Use the touch screen or left/right cross keys to select the function you want to adjust. The name of the function currently selected appears at the top of the screen, and its number is marked with an overscore in the row of numbers at the bottom of the screen. You don't need to memorize the function numbers.

- **Function currently selected.** The function number appears in two places. In the upper-right corner you'll find a box with the current function clearly designated. In the lower half of the screen are two lines of numbers. The top row has numbers from 1 to 8, representing the Custom Function. The second row shows the number of the current setting. If the setting is other than the default value (a zero), it will be colored blue, so you can quickly see which Custom Functions have been modified. The currently selected function will have a gold line above it.

- **Available settings.** Within the alternating medium gray/dark gray blocks appear numbered setting options. The current setting is highlighted in blue. You can use the up/down cross keys to scroll to the option you want and then choose SET to select it; then press MENU to back out of the Custom Functions menus.

- **Current setting.** Underneath each Custom Function is a number from 0 to 5 that represents the current setting for that function.

- **Option selection.** When a function is selected, the currently selected option appears in a highlighted box. As you scroll up and down the option list, the setting in the box changes to indicate an alternate value.

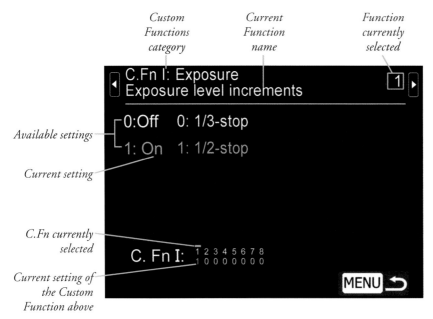

**Figure 9.12**
Each C.Fn screen has two to six settings, represented by the numbers at the bottom of the screen. The currently selected function has a gold line above it.

In the listings that follow, I'm going to depart from the sometimes-cryptic labels Canon assigns to each Custom Function in the menu, and instead categorize them by what they actually do. I'm also going to provide you with a great deal more information on each option and what it means to your photography.

## C.Fn I-01: Size of Exposure Adjustments

**Exposure level increments.** This setting tells the Rebel T5i the size of the "jumps" it should use when making exposure adjustments—either one-third or one-half stop. The increment you specify here applies to f/stops, shutter speeds, EV changes, and autoexposure bracketing.

- **0: 1/3 stop.** Choose this setting when you want the finest increments between shutter speeds and/or f/stops. For example, the T5i will use shutter speeds such as 1/60th, 1/80th, 1/100th, and 1/125th second, and f/stops such as f/5.6, f/6.3, f/7.1, and f/8, giving you (and the autoexposure system) maximum control.

- **1: 1/2 stop.** Use this setting when you want larger and more noticeable changes between increments, as when you're shooting HDR images. The T5i will apply shutter speeds such as 1/60th, 1/125th, 1/250th, and 1/500th second, and f/stops including f/5.6, f/6.7, f/8, f/9.5, and f/11. These coarser adjustments are useful when you want more dramatic changes between different exposures.

## C.Fn I-02: Whether ISO 25600 Is Available or Disabled

**ISO expansion.** Ordinarily, only ISO settings from 100 to 12800 are available (ISO 200–12800 if Highlight Tone Priority [C.Fn II-3] is enabled). The ISO Expansion function is disabled by default to prevent you from unintentionally using ISO settings higher than ISO 12800. If you want to use the H (ISO 25600; ISO 12800 for movies) setting, it must be activated using this Custom Function. I've found the noise produced at the ISO 12800 setting on my EOS T5i to be quite acceptable under certain situations, and ISO 25600/12800 can sometimes be useable. That's particularly so with images of subjects that have a texture of their own that tends to hide or mask the noise. Figure 9.13 is an example of this type of shot. It was taken indoors at a jellyfish exhibit, with the back illumination so dim and ethereal that I needed a high ISO setting to provide a shutter speed fast enough to freeze the pulsating motion of the creature. Although there is a fair amount of noise in the image, the speckles are not objectionable.

---

**CAUTION**

Be aware that if you've activated Highlight Tone Priority (described later), the H setting (and ISO values less than ISO 200) will not be available even if you have enabled ISO expansion.

- **0: Off.** The H (ISO 25600 still images/12800 for movies) setting is locked out and not available when using the ISO button or menu options.
- **1: On.** The H settings can be selected.

---

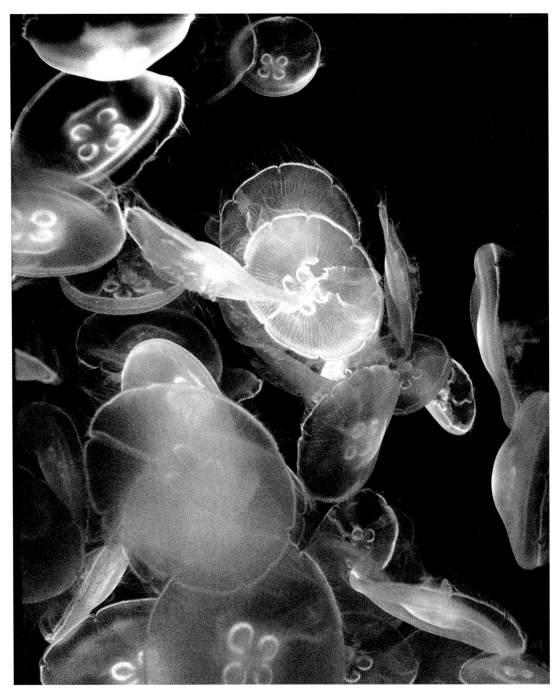

**Figure 9.13** This enlargement shows that noise levels can be acceptable even at a high ISO 3200 setting.

## C.Fn II-03: Improving Detail in Highlights

**Highlight Tone Priority.** This setting concentrates the available tones in an image from the middle grays up to the brightest highlights, in effect expanding the dynamic range of the image at the expense of shadow detail. You'd want to activate this option when shooting subjects in which there is lots of important detail in the highlights, and less detail in shadow areas. Highlight tones will be preserved, while shadows will be allowed to go dark more readily (and may exhibit an increase in noise levels). Bright beach or snow scenes, especially those with few shadows (think high noon, when the shadows are smaller) can benefit from using Highlight Tone Priority.

- **0: Disable.** The Rebel T5i's normal dynamic range is applied.

- **1: Enable.** Highlight areas are given expanded tonal values, while the tones available for shadow areas are reduced. The ISO 100 sensitivity setting is disabled and only ISO 200 to ISO 12800 are available. You can tell that this restriction is in effect by viewing the D+ icon shown in the viewfinder, on the ISO Selection screen, and in the shooting information display for a particular image.

## C.Fn III-04: Activation of the Autofocus Assist Lamp

**Autofocus assist beam.** This setting determines when the built-in flash or an external flash is activated to emit a pulse of light prior to the main exposure that helps provide enough contrast for the Rebel T5i to focus on a subject.

- **0: Emits.** The AF-assist light is emitted by the camera's built-in flash whenever light levels are too low for accurate focusing using the ambient light.

- **1: Does not emit.** The AF-assist illumination is disabled. You might want to use this setting when shooting at concerts, weddings, or darkened locations where the light might prove distracting or discourteous.

- **2: Only external flash emits.** The built-in AF-assist light is disabled, but if a Canon EX dedicated flash unit is attached to the camera, its AF-assist feature (a flash pulse) will be used when needed. Because the flash unit's AF-assist is more powerful, you'll find this option useful when you're using flash and are photographing objects in dim light that are more than a few feet away from the camera (and thus not likely to be illuminated usefully by the Rebel T5i's built-in light source). Note that if AF-assist beam firing is disabled within the flash unit's own Custom Functions, this setting will not override that.

- **3: IR AF-assist beam only.** Canon dedicated Speedlites with an infrared assist beam can be set to use only the IR assist burst. That will keep other flash bursts from triggering the AF-assist beam.

## C.Fn III-05: Whether It Is Possible to Lock Up the Viewing Mirror Prior to an Exposure

**Mirror lockup.** The Mirror Lockup function determines whether the reflex viewing mirror will be flipped up out of the way in advance of taking a picture, thereby eliminating any residual blurring effects caused by the minuscule amount of camera shake that can be produced if (as is the case normally) the mirror is automatically flipped up an instant before the actual exposure. When shooting telephoto pictures with a very long lens, or close-up photography at extreme magnifications, even this tiny amount of vibration can have an impact.

You'll want to make this adjustment immediately prior to needing the mirror lockup function, because once it's been enabled, the mirror *always* flips up, and picture taking becomes a two-press operation. That is, you press the shutter release once to lock exposure and focus, and to swing the mirror out of the way. Your viewfinder goes blank (of course, the mirror's blocking it). Press the shutter release a second time to actually take the picture. Because the goal of mirror lockup is to produce the sharpest picture possible, and because of the viewfinder blackout, you can see that the camera should be mounted on a tripod prior to taking the picture, and, to avoid accidentally shaking the camera yourself, using an off-camera shutter release mechanism is a good idea.

- **0: Disable.** Mirror lockup is not possible.
- **1: Enable.** Mirror lockup is activated and will be used for every shot until disabled.

Canon lists some important warnings and techniques related to using mirror lockup in the Rebel T5i manual, and I want to emphasize them here and add a few of my own, even if it means a bit of duplication. Better safe than sorry!

- **Don't use ML for sensor cleaning.** Though locked up, the mirror will flip down again automatically after 30 seconds, which you don't want to happen while you're poking around the sensor with a brush, swab, or air jet. There's a separate menu item—Sensor Cleaning—for sensor housekeeping. You can find more about this topic in Chapter 14.

- **Avoid long exposure to extra-bright scenes.** The shutter curtain, normally shielded from incoming light by the mirror, is fully exposed to the light being focused on the focal plane by the lens mounted on the T5i. When the mirror is locked up, you certainly don't want to point the camera at the sun, and even beach or snow scenes may be unsafe if the shutter curtain is exposed to their illumination for long periods. (This advice also applies to Live View, of course, because the sensor is similarly exposed while you're previewing the image on the LCD.)

- **ML can't be used in continuous shooting modes.** The Rebel T5i will use single shooting mode for mirror lockup exposures, regardless of the sequence mode you've selected.

- **Use self-timer to eliminate second button press.** If you've activated the self-timer, the mirror will flip up when you press the shutter button down all the way, and then the picture will be taken two seconds later. This technique can help reduce camera shake further if you don't have a remote release available and have to use a finger to press the shutter button. You can also use the Remote Controller RC-5 or RC-6. With the RC-5, press the transmit button to lock up the mirror; the shot will be taken automatically two seconds later. With the RC-6, set the remote for a two-second delay to produce the same effect.

## C.Fn IV-06: What Happens When You Partially Depress the Shutter Release/Press the AE Lock Button

**Shutter button/AE Lock button (*).** This setting controls the behavior of the shutter release and the AE Lock button (*) when you are using Creative Zone exposure modes. With Basic Zone modes, the Rebel T5i always behaves as if it has been set to Option 0, described below. Options 1, 2, and 3 are designed to work with AI Servo mode, which locks focus as it is activated, but refocuses if the subject begins to move. The options allow you to control exactly when focus and exposure are locked when using AI Servo mode.

In the option list, the first action in the pair represents what happens when you press the shutter release; the second action says what happens when the AE Lock button is pressed.

- **0: AF/AE Lock.** With this option, pressing the shutter release halfway locks in focus; pressing the * button locks exposure. Use this when you want to control each of these actions separately.

- **1: AE Lock/AF.** Pressing the shutter release halfway locks exposure; pressing the * button locks autofocus. This setting swaps the action of the two buttons compared to the default 0 option.

- **2: AF/AF Lock, no AE Lock.** Pressing the AE Lock button interrupts the autofocus and locks focus in AI Servo mode. Exposure is not locked at all until the actual moment of exposure when you press the shutter release all the way. This mode is handy when moving objects may pass in front of the camera (say, a tight end crosses your field of view as you focus on the quarterback) and you want to be able to avoid change of focus. Note that you can't lock in exposure using this option.

- **3: AE/AF, no AE Lock.** Pressing the shutter release halfway locks in autofocus, except in AI Servo mode, in which you can use the * button to start or stop autofocus. Exposure is always determined at the moment the picture is taken, and cannot be locked.

## C.Fn IV-07: Using the SET Button as a Function Key

**Assign SET button.** You already know that the physical SET button can be used to select a choice or option when navigating the menus. However, when you're taking photos, the button has no function at all. You can easily remedy that with this setting. This setting allows you to assign one of five different actions to the SET key. Because the button is within easy reach of your right thumb, that makes it quite convenient for accessing a frequently used function. When this Custom Function is set to 5, the SET button has no additional function during shooting mode (except to activate Live View when it is turned on), and options 0 through 4 assign an action to the button during shooting.

- **0: Normal (disabled).** This is the default during shooting; no action is taken. (If you have used the T1i, you know that this choice activated the Quick Control screen; the T5i now has a Q/Print button to perform the same function.)

- **1: Image quality.** Pressing the SET button produces the Shooting 1 menu's Quality menu screen on the color LCD. You can cycle among the various quality options with the up/down and left/right cross keys. Choose SET again to lock in your choice.

- **2: Flash exposure comp.** The SET button summons the flash exposure compensation screen. Use the left/right cross keys to adjust flash exposure plus or minus two stops. If you're using an external flash unit, its internal flash exposure compensation settings override those set from the camera. Choose SET to confirm your choice.

- **3: LCD monitor On/Off.** Assigns to the SET button the same functions as the DISP. button. Because the SET button can be accessed with the thumb, you may find it easier to use when turning the LCD monitor on or off.

- **4: Menu display.** Pressing SET produces the T5i's menu screen on the LCD, with the last menu entry you used highlighted. Choose SET again to work with that menu normally, or press the MENU button to cancel and back out of the menus. This setting duplicates the MENU button's function, but some find it easier to locate the SET button with their thumb.

- **5: ISO speed.** This assigns the SET button the same function as the ISO button. Use it if you'd rather not grope for the ISO button on top of the camera.

---

### CAUTION

One thing to keep in mind when redefining the behavior of controls (including other controls that can be modified within the Custom Functions menus) is that any non-standard customization you do will definitely be confusing to others who use your camera, and may even confuse you if you've forgotten that you've changed a control from its default function.

---

## C.Fn IV-08: LCD Display When Power On

**LCD display when power on.** Controls the behavior of the LCD when the Rebel T5i is switched on. There are two options:

- **0: Display on.** When the T5i is powered on, the shooting settings screen will be shown. You can turn this screen on and off by pressing the DISP. button. Use this option if you always want the settings screen to be displayed when the camera is turned on.

- **1: Previous display status.** When the Rebel T5i is turned on, the LCD monitor will display the shooting settings screen if it was turned on when the camera was last powered down. If the screen had been turned off (by pressing the DISP. button), it will not be displayed when the T5i is next powered up. Use this option if you frequently turn off the settings screen, and want the camera to "remember" whether the screen was on display when the T5i was last powered down.

## Copyright Information

You can embed your name (as "author" or *auteur* of the image) and copyright information in the Exif (Exchangeable Image File format) data appended to each photo that you take.

When you choose this menu entry (see Figure 9.14), you have four options:

- **Display copyright info.** Shows the current author and copyright data.
- **Enter author's name.** Produces a text entry screen like the one shown in Figure 9.15. See "Entering Text" for instructions on how to type in text for this screen and the Copyright Details screen.
- **Enter copyright details.** Produces the same text entry screen, allowing you to enter copyright details. Oddly enough, no copyright symbol is available (although the @ sign is provided so you can type in your e-mail address!). Many just use the parentheses and a lowercase c: (c). However, you should know that this is, strictly speaking, not legal. The legit substitute for the actual copyright symbol are the characters *Copr.* or the full term *Copyright.*
- **Delete copyright information.** Removes the current copyright information (both author and copyright data). Once you delete the data, or if you haven't entered it yet, this option and the Display Copyright Info. option are grayed out and unavailable.

**Figure 9.14**

Access text entry screens for entering the name of the photographer and copyright details here.

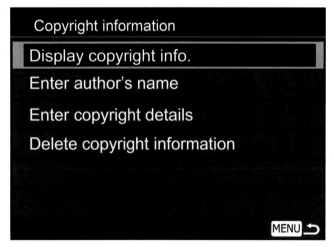

Copyright information

Display copyright info.

Enter author's name

Enter copyright details

Delete copyright information

MENU

## Entering Text

Entering text into the Author's Name or Copyright Details screens is done in the same way, using a screen like the one shown in Figure 9.15. Just use these instructions:

- **Choose areas.** Either the text area (at top left) or available characters area (bottom half of the screen) will be highlighted with a blue outline. Switch between them by pressing the Q button on the right side of the back of the camera.
- **Scroll among text.** When the text area is highlighted, you can scroll among the text using the cross keys. Up to 63 alphanumeric characters can be entered/displayed.

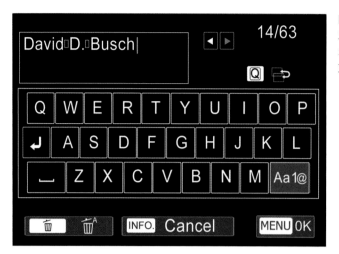

**Figure 9.15**
Select the alphanumeric characters for your text entry.

- **Enter characters.** When the available characters list is highlighted, use the touch screen, or the cross keys to move among the alphanumeric characters shown. Press the SET button to enter that character at the cursor position in the text area above. You can delete the current character by pressing the Delete/Trash button.

- **Finish/Cancel.** When finished entering text, press the MENU button to confirm your choice, or press the INFO. button to cancel and return to the Copyright Information screen.

# Clear Settings

This menu choice has provisions for resetting all the settings to their default values. Regardless of how you've set up your EOS T5i, it will be adjusted for One-Shot AF mode, Automatic AF point selection, Evaluative metering, JPEG Fine Large image quality, Automatic ISO, sRGB color mode, Automatic white balance, and Standard Picture Style. Any changes you've made to exposure compensation, flash exposure compensation, and white balance will be canceled, and any bracketing for exposure or white balance nullified. Custom white balances and Dust Delete Data will be erased. The Clear Setting screen has two options: Clear All Camera Settings, and Clear All Custom Func (C.Fn).

Table 9.1 shows the settings defaults after using this menu option.

# Firmware Version

You can see the current firmware release in use in the menu listing. If you want to update to a new firmware version for either the camera or a lens, press the SET button to select which type of firmware you want to upgrade. Then insert a memory card containing the binary file, and press the SET button to begin the process. You can read more about firmware updates in Chapter 14.

## Table 9.1  Camera Setting Defaults

| Shooting Settings | Default Value |
| --- | --- |
| AF mode | One-Shot AF |
| AF point selection | Auto selection |
| Drive mode | Single shooting |
| Metering mode | Evaluative |
| ISO speed | Auto |
| ISO Auto | Maximum 6400 |
| Exposure Compensation/AEB | Canceled |
| Flash exposure compensation | 0 |
| Custom functions | Unchanged |
| External flash function settings | Unchanged |

| Image-Recording Settings | Default Value |
| --- | --- |
| Quality | JPEG Large/Fine |
| Picture Style | Auto |
| Auto Lighting Optimizer | Standard |
| Peripheral illumination correction | Enable/Correction data retained |
| Chromatic aberration correction | Disable/Correction data retained |
| Color space | sRGB |
| White balance | Auto |
| Custom white balance | Canceled |
| White balance correction | Canceled |
| WB-BKT | Canceled |
| Long exposure NR | Disable |
| High ISO NR | Standard |
| File numbering | Continuous |
| Auto cleaning | Enable |
| Dust Delete Data | Erased |

| Camera Settings | Default Value |
| --- | --- |
| Auto power off | 30 seconds |
| Beep | Enable |
| Release shutter without card | Enable |
| Image Review | 2 seconds |
| Histogram | Brightness |
| Image jump with Main Dial | 10 images |

## Table 9.1  Camera Setting Defaults (continued)

| Camera Settings | Default Value |
| --- | --- |
| Auto rotate | On/Camera/Computer |
| LCD brightness | Centered |
| LCD Auto Off | Enable |
| Time Zone | Unchanged |
| Date/Time | Unchanged |
| Language | Unchanged |
| Video system | Unchanged |
| Screen Color | 1 |
| Video system | Unchanged |
| Feature Guide | Enable |
| Touch control | Enable |
| Copyright information | Unchanged |
| Control over HDMI | Disable |
| Eye-Fi transmission | Disable |
| My Menu settings | Unchanged |
| Display from My Menu | Disable |

| Live View Settings | Default Value |
| --- | --- |
| Live view shooting | Enable |
| AF Method | Face+Tracking |
| Continuous AF | Enable |
| Touch Shutter | Disable |
| Grid display | Off |
| Aspect Ratio | 3:2 |
| Metering timer | 16 seconds |

| Movie Shooting | Default Value |
| --- | --- |
| AF Method | Face+Tracking |
| Movie Servo AF | Enable |
| AF with Shutter button during movie shooting | ONE SHOT |
| Grid Display | Off |
| Metering timer | 16 seconds |
| Movie-recording size | 1920 × 1080 |
| Sound recording | Auto |
| Video snapshot | Disable |

# My Menu

The Canon EOS T5i has a great feature that allows you to define your own menu, with just the items listed that you want. Remember that the T5i always returns to the last menu and menu entry accessed when you press the MENU button. So you can set up My Menu to include just the items you want, and jump to those items instantly by pressing the MENU button. Or, you can set your camera so that My Menu appears when the MENU button has been pressed, regardless of what other menu entry you accessed last.

To create your own My Menu, you have to *register* the menu items you want to include. Just follow these steps:

1. Press the MENU button and use the touch screen or Main Dial to select the My Menu tab. When you first begin, the personalized menu will be empty except for the My Menu Settings entry. Choose SET to select it. You'll then see a screen like the one shown in Figure 9.16.

2. Use the touch screen or cross keys to select Register; then press SET.

3. Use the touch screen or cross keys to scroll down through the continuous list of menu entries to find one you would like to add. Choose SET.

4. Confirm your choice by selecting OK in the next screen and choosing SET again.

5. Continue to select up to six menu entries for My Menu.

6. When you're finished, press the MENU button twice to return to the My Menu screen to see your customized menu, which might look like Figure 9.17.

**Figure 9.16**
In the My Menu Settings screen you can add menu items, delete them, and specify whether My Menu always pops up when the MENU button is pressed.

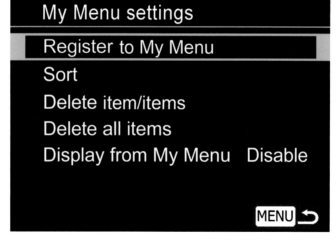

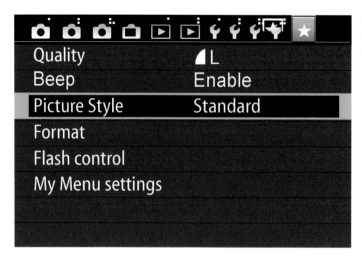

**Figure 9.17**
You can add one to
six menu entries to
My Menu.

In addition to registering menu items, you can perform other functions at the My Menu Settings screen:

■ **Changing the order.** Choose Sort to reorder the items in My Menu. Select the menu item and choose SET. Rotate the cross keys to move the item up and down within the menu list. When you've placed it where you'd like it, press MENU to lock in your selection and return to the previous screen.

■ **Delete/Delete All Items.** Use these to remove an individual menu item or all menu items you've registered in My Menu.

■ **Display from My Menu.** As I mentioned earlier, the T5i (almost) always shows the last menu item accessed. That's convenient if you used My Menu last, but if you happen to use another menu, then pressing the MENU button will return to that item instead. If you enable the Display from My Menu option, pressing the MENU button will *always* display My Menu first. You are free to switch to another menu tab if you like, but the next time you press the MENU button, My Menu will come up again. Use this option if you work with My Menu a great deal and make settings with other menu items less frequently.

# Part IV

# Enhancing Your Canon EOS Rebel T5i/700D

The next five chapters are devoted to helping you dig deeper into the capabilities of your Canon EOS Rebel T5i, so you can exploit all those cool features that your previous camera may have lacked. Here's what you can expect:

- **Chapter 10, "Working with Lenses":** Working with lenses is the goal of this chapter, where I'll show you how to select the best lenses for the kinds of photography you want to do, with my recommendations for starter lenses as well as more advanced optics for specialized applications.

- **Chapter 11, "Working with Light":** This chapter is devoted to the magic of light—your fundamental tool in creating any photograph. There are entire books devoted to working with electronic flash, but I hope to get you started with plenty of coverage of the EOS T5i's capabilities. I'll show you how to master your camera's built-in flash—and avoid that "built-in flash" look, and offer an introduction to the use of external flash units.

- **Chapter 12, "Working with Wireless Flash":** This chapter goes a little more deeply into the use of flash, and covers working with the T5i's wireless flash capabilities.

- **Chapter 13, "Downloading, Editing, and Printing Your Images":** This chapter covers downloading and editing your images and will help you understand the software tools available to you.

- **Chapter 14, "Troubleshooting and Prevention":** Troubleshooting, updating your firmware, and cleaning your sensor are all covered in this chapter.

# 10

# Working with Lenses

In mid-2013, Canon announced that it had produced its 90 millionth EF-series lens. Considering that it took 11 years for Canon to sell its first 10 million copies of its EF lens line, but only nine months to peddle its most recent 10 million lenses, it's easy to see that the digital photography revolution can take credit for the most recent explosion.

With nearly six dozen lenses in its current lineup, Canon is catering to the wide-ranging needs of a broad user base, from novice photo enthusiasts to advanced amateur and professional photographers. It's this mind-bending assortment of high-quality lenses available to enhance the capabilities of cameras like the Canon EOS T5i that make the product line so appealing. Thousands of current and older lenses introduced by Canon and third-party vendors since 1987 can be used to give you a wider view, bring distant subjects closer, let you focus closer, shoot under lower-light conditions, or provide a more detailed, sharper image for critical work. Other than the sensor itself, the lens you choose for your dSLR is the most important component in determining image quality and perspective of your images.

The most exciting development in recent months has been the introduction of Canon's first STM (Stepper Motor) lenses, which, when coupled with a new diaphragm mechanism, provides especially fast and quiet autofocus that's perfect for video capture (where camera noises can be recorded while shooting).

This chapter explains how to select the best lenses for the kinds of photography you want to do.

## But Don't Forget the Crop Factor

From time to time you've heard the term *crop factor*, and you've probably also heard the term *lens multiplier factor*. Both are misleading and inaccurate terms used to describe the same phenomenon: the fact that cameras like the T5i (and most other affordable digital SLRs) provide a field of view that's smaller and narrower than that produced by certain other (usually much more expensive) cameras, when fitted with exactly the same lens.

Figure 10.1 quite clearly shows the phenomenon at work. The outer rectangle, marked 1X, shows the field of view you might expect with a 28mm lens mounted on a Canon EOS 5D Mark III camera, a so-called "full-frame" model. The rectangle marked 1.3X shows the effective field of view from the same vantage point with the exact same lens mounted on the discontinued Canon EOS 1D Mark III camera, while the area marked 1.6X shows the field of view you'd get with that 28mm lens installed on a T5i. It's easy to see from the illustration that the 1X rendition provides a wider, more expansive view, while the other two are, in comparison, *cropped*.

The cropping effect is produced because the sensors of the latter two cameras are smaller than the sensors of the 5D Mark III. The "full-frame" camera has a sensor that's the size of the standard 35mm film frame, 24mm × 36mm. Your T5i's sensor does *not* measure 24mm × 36mm; instead, it specs out at 22.3mm × 14.9mm, or about 62.5 percent of the area of a full-frame sensor, as shown by the yellow boxes in the figure. You can calculate the relative field of view by dividing the focal length of the lens by .625. Thus, a 100mm lens mounted on a T5i has the same field of view as a 160mm lens on the 5D Mark III. We humans tend to perform multiplication operations in our heads more easily than division, so such field of view comparisons are usually calculated using the reciprocal of .625—1.6—so we can multiply instead. (100 / .625=160; 100 × 1.6=160)

This translation is generally useful only if you're accustomed to using full-frame cameras (usually of the film variety) and want to know how a familiar lens will perform on a digital camera. I strongly prefer *crop factor* over *lens multiplier*, because nothing is being multiplied; a 100mm lens doesn't "become" a 160mm lens—the depth-of-field and lens aperture remain the same. (I'll explain more about these later in this chapter.) Only the field of view is cropped. But *crop factor* isn't much

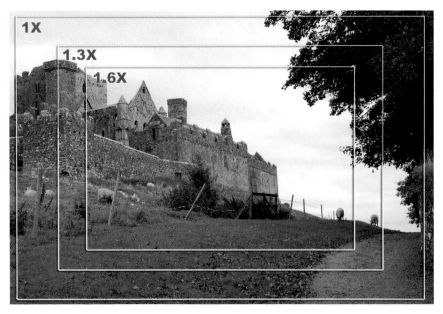

**Figure 10.1**
Canon offers digital SLRs with full-frame (1X) crops, as well as 1.3X and 1.6X crops.

better, as it implies that the 24 × 36mm frame is "full" and anything else is "less." I get e-mails all the time from photographers who point out that they own full-frame cameras with 36mm × 48mm sensors (like the Mamiya 645ZD or Hasselblad H3D-39 medium-format digitals). By their reckoning, the "half-size" sensors found in cameras like the 1Ds Mark III and 5D Mark II are "cropped."

If you're accustomed to using full-frame film cameras, you might find it helpful to use the crop factor "multiplier" to translate a lens's real focal length into the full-frame equivalent, even though, as I said, nothing is actually being multiplied. Throughout most of this book, I've been using actual focal lengths and not equivalents, except when referring to specific wide-angle or telephoto focal length ranges and their fields of view.

# Your First Lens

Back in ancient times (the pre-zoom, pre-autofocus era before the mid-1980s), choosing the first lens for your camera was a no-brainer: you had few or no options. Canon cameras (which used a different lens mount in those days) were sold with a 50mm f/1.4, a 50mm f/1.8, or, if you had deeper pockets, a super-fast 50mm f/1.2 lens. It was also possible to buy a camera as a body alone, which didn't save much money back when a film SLR like the Canon A-1 sold for $435—*with lens.* (Thanks to the era of relatively cheap optics, I still own a total of *eight* 50mm f/1.4 lenses; I picked one up each time I purchased a new or used body.)

Today, your choices are more complicated, and Canon lenses, which now include zoom, autofocus, and, more often than not, built-in image stabilization (IS) features, tend to cost a lot more compared to the price of a camera. (Adjusted for inflation, that $435 A-1 cost $879 in today's dollars.)

The Canon EOS T5i is frequently purchased with a lens, even now. I could have purchased mine as a body-only rather than in a kit, because I already own a nice collection of Canon lenses, but I wanted to try out the new Canon EF-S 18-55mm f/3.5-5.6 IS STM autofocus lens. It adds only about $100 to the price tag of the body alone, and is thus an irresistible bargain. You might opt instead for the EF-S 18-135mm f/3.5-5.6 IS STM lens, which adds about $350 to the price of the body. Those looking for a longer zoom range might opt to pay an additional $700 for the older Canon EF-S 18-200mm f/3.5-5.6 IS lens, which provides a very useful 11X zoom range. Some buyers don't need quite that zoom range, and save a few dollars by purchasing the Canon EF 28-135mm f/3.5-5.6 IS USM lens ($480). The latter lens has one advantage. *EF* lenses like the 28-135mm zoom can also be used with any *full-frame* camera you add/migrate to at a later date. You'll learn the difference later in this chapter.

So, depending on which category you fall into, you'll need to make a decision about what kit lens to buy, or decide what other kind of lenses you need to fill out your existing complement of Canon optics. This section will cover "first lens" concerns, while later in the chapter we'll look at "add-on lens" considerations.

When deciding on a first lens, there are several factors you'll want to consider:

- **Cost.** You might have stretched your budget a bit to purchase your T5i, so you might want to keep the cost of your first lens fairly low. Fortunately, as I've noted, there are excellent lenses available that will add from $100 to $600 to the price of your camera if purchased at the same time.

- **Zoom range.** If you have only one lens, you'll want a fairly long zoom range to provide as much flexibility as possible. Fortunately, the two most popular basic lenses for the T5i have 3X to 5X zoom ranges, extending from moderate wide-angle/normal out to medium telephoto. These are fine for everyday shooting, portraits, and some types of sports.

- **Adequate maximum aperture.** You'll want an f/stop of at least f/3.5 to f/4 for shooting under fairly low-light conditions. The thing to watch for is the maximum aperture when the lens is zoomed to its telephoto end. You may end up with no better than an f/5.6 maximum aperture. That's not great, but you can often live with it.

- **Image quality.** Your starter lens should have good image quality, befitting a camera with 18MP of resolution, because that's one of the primary factors that will be used to judge your photos. Even at a low price, the several different lenses sold with the T5i as a kit include extra-low dispersion glass and aspherical elements that minimize distortion and chromatic aberration; they are sharp enough for most applications. If you read the user evaluations in the online photography forums, you know that owners of the kit lenses have been very pleased with their image quality.

- **Size matters.** A good walking-around lens is compact in size and light in weight.

- **Fast/close focusing.** Your first lens should have a speedy autofocus system (which is where the ultrasonic motor/USM and new STM system found in nearly all moderately priced lenses is an advantage). Close focusing (to 12 inches or closer) will let you use your basic lens for some types of macro photography.

You can find comparisons of the lenses discussed in the next section, as well as third-party lenses from Sigma, Tokina, Tamron, and other vendors, in online groups and websites. I'll provide my recommendations, but obtaining more information from these additional sources is always helpful when making a lens purchase, because, while camera bodies come and go, lenses may be a lifetime addition to your kit.

## Buy Now, Expand Later

The T5i is commonly available with several good, basic lenses that can serve you well as a "walk-around" lens (one you keep on the camera most of the time, especially when you're out and about without your camera bag). The number of options available to you is actually quite amazing, even if your budget is limited to about $100–$500 for your first lens. One other vendor, for example, offers only 18mm-70mm and 18mm-55mm kit lenses in that price range, plus a 24mm-85mm zoom. Two popular starter lenses Canon offers are shown in Figures 10.2 and 10.3.

Canon's best-bet first lenses are as follows:

- **Canon EF-S 18-55mm f/3.5-5.6 IS STM autofocus lens.** This lens, shown in Figure 10.2, replaces the old "II" version, and is a bit larger than the older optic. It boasts the new STM stepper motor technology that Canon video fans have found to be so useful. It has image stabilization that can counter camera shake by providing the vibration-stopping capabilities of a shutter speed four stops faster than the one you've dialed in. That is, with image stabilization activated, you can shoot at 1/30th second and eliminate camera shake as if you were using a shutter speed of 1/250th second. (At least, that's what Canon claims; I usually have slightly less impressive results.) Of course, IS doesn't freeze subject motion—that basketball player driving for a layup will still be blurry at 1/30th second, even though the effects of camera shake will be effectively nullified. But this lens is an all-around good choice if your budget is tight.

- **Canon EF-S 18-135mm f/3.5-5.6 IS STM autofocus lens.** This one, priced at about $350 when purchased in a kit, is an upgrade from a similar earlier lens without the stepper motor technology. It's also light, compact (you can see it mounted on the T5i in Figure 10.3), and covers a useful range from true wide-angle to intermediate telephoto. As with Canon's other affordable zoom lenses, image stabilization partially compensates for the slow f/5.6 maximum aperture at the telephoto end, by allowing you to use longer shutter speeds to capture an image under poor lighting conditions. I'll explain the advantages of the STM autofocus later in this chapter.

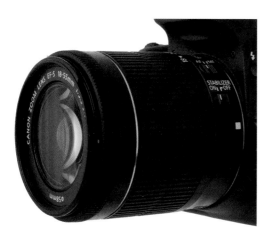

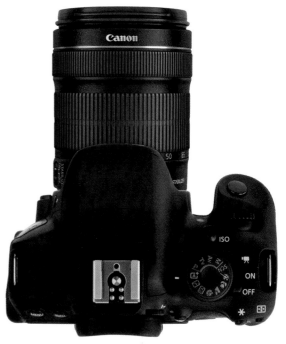

**Figure 10.2** The Canon EF-S 18-55mm f/3.5-5.6 IS STM autofocus lens ships as a basic kit lens for entry-level Canon cameras.

**Figure 10.3** The new EF-S 18-135 f/3.5-5.6 IS STM lens is affordable and features near-silent autofocus that's perfect for video shooting.

■ **Canon EF-S 18-200mm f/3.5-5.6 IS autofocus lens.** This one, priced at about $700, has been popular as a basic lens for the T5i, because it's light, compact, and covers a full range from true wide-angle to long telephoto. Image stabilization keeps your pictures sharp at the long end of the zoom range, allowing the longer shutter speeds that the f/5.6 maximum aperture demands at 200mm. Automatic panning detection turns the IS feature off when panning in both horizontal and vertical directions. An improved "Super Spectra Coating" minimizes flare and ghosting, while optimizing color rendition.

■ **Canon EF-S 17-85mm f/4-5.6 IS USM autofocus lens.** This older lens (introduced in 2004 with the EOS 20D) is a very popular "basic" lens still sold for the T5i. The allure here with this $600 lens is the longer telephoto range, coupled with the built-in image stabilization, which allows you to shoot rock-solid photos at shutter speeds that are at least two or three notches slower than you'd need normally (say, 1/8th second instead of 1/30th or 1/60th second), as long as your subject isn't moving. It also has a quiet, fast, reliable ultrasonic motor (more on that later, too). This is another lens designed for the 1.6X crop factor; all but one of the remaining lenses in this list can also be used on full-frame cameras. (I'll tell you why later in this chapter.) This lens is shown in Figure 10.4.

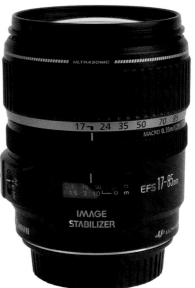

**Figure 10.4** The Canon EF-S 17-85mm f/4-5.6 IS USM autofocus lens is another popular starter lens for the T5i.

■ **Canon EF 55-200mm f/4.5-5.6 II USM autofocus lightweight compact telephoto zoom lens.** If you bought the 18-55mm kit lens, this one picks up where that one leaves off, going from short telephoto to medium long (88mm-320mm full-frame equivalent). It features a desirable ultrasonic motor. Best of all, it's very affordable at around $300. If you can afford only two lenses, the 18-55mm and this one make a good basic set.

■ **EF-S 55-250mm f/4-5.6 IS telephoto zoom lens.** This is an image-stabilized EF-S lens (which means it can't be used with Canon's 1.3X and 1.0X crop-factor pro cameras), providing the longest focal range in the EF-S range to date, and that 4-stop Image Stabilizer. It's about $300, but it's worth the cost for the stabilization.

■ **Canon EF 24-85mm f/3.5-4.5 USM autofocus wide-angle telephoto zoom lens.** If you can get by with normal focal length to medium telephoto range, Canon offers four affordable lenses, plus one more expensive killer lens that's worth the extra expenditure. All of them can be used on full-frame or cropped-frame digital Canons, which is why they include "wide angle" in their product names. They're really wide-angle lenses only when mounted on a full-frame camera. This one, priced in the $300 range, offers a useful range of focal lengths, extending from the equivalent of 38mm to 136mm.

- **Canon EF 28-105mm f/3.5-4.5 II USM autofocus wide-angle telephoto zoom lens.** If you want to save about $100 and gain a little reach compared to the 24-85mm zoom, this 45mm-168mm (equivalent lens) might be what you are looking for.

- **Canon EF 28-200mm f/3.5-5.6 USM autofocus wide-angle telephoto zoom lens.** If you want one lens to do everything except wide-angle photography, this 7X zoom lens costs less than $400 and takes you from the equivalent of 45mm out to a long 320mm.

- **Canon EF 24-70mm f/2.8L II USM autofocus zoom wide-angle-telephoto lens.** I couldn't leave this premium lens out of the mix, even though it costs well over $2,000. As part of Canon's L-series (Luxury) lens line, it offers the best sharpness over its focal range than any of the other lenses in this list. Best of all, it's fast (for a zoom), with an f/.2.8 maximum aperture that *doesn't change* as you zoom out. Unlike the other lenses, which may offer only an f/5.6 maximum f/stop at their longest zoom setting, this is a *constant aperture* lens, which retains its maximum f/stop. The added sharpness, constant aperture, and ultra-smooth USM motor are what you're paying for with this lens. Another version with an f/4 maximum aperture with image stabilization can be purchased for less than $1,400.

# What Lenses Can You Use?

The previous section helped you sort out what lens you need to buy with your T5i (assuming you already didn't own any Canon lenses). Now, you're probably wondering what lenses can be added to your growing collection (trust me, it will grow). You need to know which lenses are suitable and, most importantly, which lenses are fully compatible with your T5i.

With the Canon T5i, the compatibility issue is a simple one: It accepts any lens with the EF or EF-S designation, with full availability of all autofocus, autoaperture, autoexposure, and image-stabilization features (if present). It's comforting to know that any EF (for full-frame or cropped sensors) or EF-S (for cropped sensor cameras only) will work as designed with your camera. As I noted at the beginning of the chapter, that's more than 70 million lenses!

But wait, there's more. You can also attach Nikon F mount, Leica R, Olympus OM, and M42 ("Pentax screw mount") lenses with a simple adapter, if you don't mind losing automatic focus and aperture control. If you use one of these lenses, you'll need to focus manually (even if the lens operates in Autofocus mode on the camera it was designed for), and adjust the f/stop to the aperture you want to use to take the picture. That means that lenses that don't have an aperture ring (such as Nikon G-series lenses) must be used only at their maximum aperture if you use them with a simple adapter. However, Novoflex makes expensive adapter rings (the Nikon-Lens-on-Canon-Camera version is called EOS/NIK NT) with an integral aperture control that allows adjusting the aperture of lenses that do not have an old-style aperture ring. Expect to pay as much as $300 for an adapter of this type. Should you decide to pick up a new Canon EOS-M mirrorless camera, you'll be able to get double-duty with your EF and EF-S lenses, too, with an adapter that will allow you to use the same lenses on your T5i and companion EOS-M cameras.

Because of the limitations imposed on using "foreign" lenses on your T5i, you probably won't want to make extensive use of them, but an adapter can help you when you really, really need to use a particular focal length but don't have a suitable Canon-compatible lens. For example, I occasionally use an older 400mm lens that was originally designed for the Nikon line on my T5i. The lens needs to be mounted on a tripod for steadiness, anyway, so its slower operation isn't a major pain. Another good match is the 105mm Micro-Nikkor I sometimes use with my Canon T5i. Macro photos, too, are most often taken with the camera mounted on a tripod, and manual focus makes a lot of sense for fine-tuning focus and depth-of-field. Because of the contemplative nature of close-up photography, it's not much of an inconvenience to stop down to the taking aperture just before exposure.

The restrictions on use of lenses within Canon's own product line (as well as lenses produced for earlier Canon SLRs by third-party vendors) are fairly clear-cut. The T5i cannot be used with any of Canon's earlier lens mounting schemes for its film cameras, including the immediate predecessor to the EF mount, the FD mount (introduced with the Canon F1 in 1964 and used until the Canon T60 in 1990), FL (1964–1971), or the original Canon R mount (1959–1964). That's really all you need to know. While you'll find FD-to-EF adapters for about $40, you'll lose so many functions that it's rarely worth the bother.

In retrospect, the switch to the EF mount seems like a very good idea, as the initial EOS film cameras can now be seen as the beginning of Canon's rise to eventually become the leader in film and (later) digital SLR cameras. By completely revamping its lens mounting system, the company was able to take advantage of the latest advances in technology without compromise.

For example, when the original EF bayonet mount was introduced in 1987, the system incorporated new autofocus technology (EF actually stands for "electro focus") in a more rugged and less complicated form. A tiny motor was built into the lens itself, eliminating the need for mechanical linkages with the camera. Instead, electrical contacts are used to send power and the required focusing information to the motor. That's a much more robust and resilient system that made it easier for Canon to design faster and more accurate autofocus mechanisms just by redesigning the lenses.

## WHY SO MANY LENS MOUNTS?

Four different lens mounts in 40-plus years (five, if you count the EF-M mount for the new EOS M cameras) might seem like a lot of different mounting systems, especially when compared to the Nikon F mount of 1959, which retained quite a bit of compatibility with that company's film and digital camera bodies during that same span. However, in digital photography terms, the EF mount itself is positively ancient, having remained reasonably stable for more than 25 years. Lenses designed for the EF system work reliably with every EOS film and digital camera ever produced.

However, at the time, yet another lens mount switch, especially a change from the traditional breech system to a more conventional bayonet-type mount, was indeed a daring move by Canon. One of the reasons for staying with a particular lens type is to "lock" current users into a specific camera system. By introducing the EF mount, Canon in effect cut loose every photographer in its existing user base. If they chose to upgrade, they were free to choose another vendor's products and lenses. Only satisfaction with the previous Canon product line and the promise of the new system would keep them in the fold.

# EF vs. EF-S

Today, in addition to its EF lenses, Canon offers lenses that use the EF-S (the S stands for "short back focus") mount, with the chief difference being (as you might expect) lens components that extend farther back into the camera body of some of Canon's latest digital cameras (specifically those with smaller than full-frame sensors), such as the T5i. As I'll explain next, this refinement allows designing more compact, less-expensive lenses especially for those cameras, but not for models that include current cameras like the EOS 5D Mark III, 1D X, or 1D Mark III (even though the latter camera does have a sensor that is slightly smaller than full frame).

Canon's EF-S lens mount variation was born in 2003, when the company virtually invented the consumer-oriented digital SLR category by introducing the original EOS 300D/Digital Rebel, a dSLR that cost less than $1,000 *with lens* at a time when all other interchangeable lens digital cameras (including the T5i's "grandparent," the original EOS 10D) were priced closer to $2,000 with a basic lens. Like the EOS 10D, the EOS T5i features a smaller than full-frame sensor with a 1.6X crop factor (Canon calls this format APS-C). But the EOS Digital Rebel accepted lenses that took advantage of the shorter mirror found in APS-C cameras, with elements of shorter focal length lenses (wide angles) that extended *into* the camera, space that was off limits in other models because the mirror passed through that territory as it flipped up to expose the shutter and sensor. (Canon even calls its flip-up reflector a "half mirror.")

In short (so to speak), the EF-S mount made it easier to design less-expensive wide-angle lenses that could be used *only* with 1.6X-crop cameras, and featured a simpler design and reduced coverage area suitable for those non-full-frame models. The new mount made it possible to produce lenses like the ultrawide EF-S 10-22mm f/3.5-4.5 USM lens, which has the equivalent field of view as a 16mm-35mm zoom on a full-frame camera. (See Figure 10.5.)

Suitable cameras for EF-S lenses include all recent non-full-frame models. The EF-S lenses cannot be used on the APS-C-sensor EOS 10D, the 1D Mark II N/Mark III (which have a 28.7mm × 19.1mm APS-H sensor with a 1.3X crop factor), or any of the full-frame digital or film EOS models, such as the EOS 1D X, EOS 1Ds Mark III, or EOS 5D Mark III. It's easy to tell an EF lens from an EF-S lens: The latter incorporate EF-S into their name! Plus, EF lenses have a raised red dot on the barrel that is used to align the lens with a matching dot on the camera when attaching the lens. EF-S lenses and compatible bodies use a white square instead. Some EF-S lenses also have a rubber ring at the attachment end that provides a bit of weather/dust sealing and protects the back components of the lens if a user attempts to mount it on a camera that is not EF-S compatible.

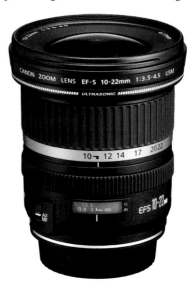

**Figure 10.5** The EF-S 10-22mm ultrawide lens was made possible by the shorter back focus difference offered by the original Digital Rebel and subsequent Canon 1.6X "cropped sensor" models.

# Ingredients of Canon's Alphanumeric Soup

The actual product names of individual Canon lenses are fairly easy to decipher; they'll include either the EF or EF-S designation, the focal length or focal length range of the lens, its maximum aperture, and some other information. Additional data may be engraved or painted on the barrel or ring surrounding the front element of the lens, as shown in Figure 10.6. Here's a decoding of what the individual designations mean:

- **EF/EF-S.** If the lens is marked EF, it can safely be used on any Canon EOS camera, film or digital. If it is an EF-S lens, it should be used only on an EF-S compatible camera.

- **Focal length.** Given in millimeters or a millimeter range, such as 60mm in the case of a popular Canon macro lens, or 17-55mm, used to describe a medium-wide to short-telephoto zoom.

- **Maximum aperture.** The largest f/stop available with a particular lens is given in a string of numbers that might seem confusing at first glance. For example, you might see 1:1.8 for a fixed-focal length (prime) lens, and 1:4.5-5.6 for a zoom. The initial 1: signifies that the f/stop given is actually a ratio or fraction (in regular notation, f/ replaces the 1:), which is why a 1:2 (or f/2) aperture is larger than an 1:4 (or f/4) aperture—just as 1/2 is larger than 1/4. With most zoom lenses, the maximum aperture changes as the lens is zoomed to the telephoto position, so a range is given instead: 1:4.5-5.6. (Some zooms, called *constant aperture* lenses, keep the same maximum aperture throughout their range.)

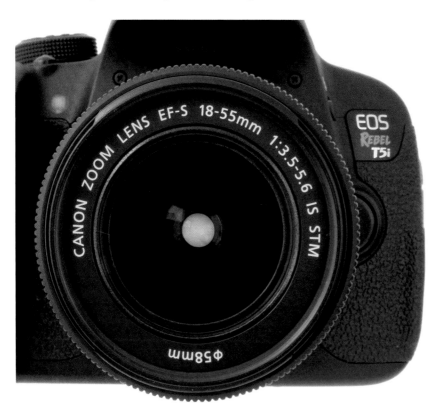

**Figure 10.6**
Most of the key specifications of the lens are marked on the ring around the front element.

■ **Autofocus type.** Most newer Canon lenses that aren't of the bargain-basement type use Canon's *ultrasonic motor* autofocus system (more on that later) and are given the USM designation. Several of the company's newest optics use the Stepper Motor (STM) technology. If USM or STM does not appear on the lens or its model name, the lens uses the less sophisticated AFD (arc-form drive) autofocus system or the micromotor (MM) drive mechanism.

■ **Series.** Canon adds a Roman numeral to many of its products to represent an updated model with the same focal length or focal length range, so some lenses will have a II or III added to their name.

■ **Pro quality.** Canon's more expensive lenses with more rugged construction and higher optical quality, intended for professional use, include the letter L (for "luxury") in their product name. You can further differentiate these lenses visually by a red ring around the lens barrel and the off-white color of the metal barrel itself in virtually all telephoto L-series lenses. (Some L-series lenses have shiny or textured black plastic exterior barrels.) Internally, every L lens includes at least one lens element that is built of ultra-low dispersion glass, is constructed of expensive fluorite crystal, or uses an expensive ground (not molded) aspheric (non-spherical) lens component.

■ **Filter size.** You'll find the front lens filter thread diameter in millimeters included on the lens, preceded by a Ø symbol, as in Ø67 or Ø72.

■ **Special-purpose lenses.** Some Canon lenses are designed for specific types of work, and they include appropriate designations in their names. For example, close-focusing lenses such as the Canon EF-S 60mm f/2.8 Macro USM lens incorporate the word *Macro* into their name. Lenses with perspective control features preface the lens name with T-S (for tilt-shift). Lenses with built-in image-stabilization features, such as the nifty EF 28-300mm f/3.5-5.6L IS USM telephoto zoom include *IS* in their product names.

## SORTING THE MOTOR DRIVES

Incorporating the autofocus motor inside the lens was an innovative move by Canon, and this allowed the company to produce better and more sophisticated lenses as technology became available to upgrade the focusing system. As a result, you'll find four different types of motors in Canon-designed lenses, each with cost and practical considerations. Most newer lenses use only the latest USM motor, and incorporate that designation in their names.

■ **AFD (Arc-form drive)** and **Micromotor (MM)** drives are built around tiny versions of electromagnetic motors, which generally use gear trains to produce the motion needed to adjust the focus of the lens. Both are slow, noisy, and not particularly effective with larger lenses. Manual focus adjustments are possible only when the motor drive is disengaged.

■ **Micromotor ultrasonic motor (USM)** drives use high-frequency vibration to produce the motion used to drive the gear train, resulting in a quieter operating system at a cost that's not much more than that of electromagnetic motor drives. With the exception of a couple lenses that have a slipping clutch mechanism, manual focus with this kind of system is possible only when the motor drive is switched off and the lens is set in manual mode. This is the kind of USM system you'll find in lower-cost lenses.

- **Ring ultrasonic motor (USM)** drives, available in two different types (*electronic focus ring USM* and *ring USM*), also use high-frequency movement, but generate motion using a pair of vibrating metal rings to adjust focus. Both variations allow a feature called Full Time Manual (FTM) focus, which lets you make manual adjustments to the lens's focus even when the autofocus mechanism is engaged. With electronic focus ring USM, manual focus is possible only when the lens is mounted on the camera and the camera is turned on; the focus ring of lenses with ring USM can be turned at any time.

- **Stepper motor (STM) drives.** In autofocus mode, the precision motor of STM lenses, along with a new aperture mechanism, allows lenses equipped with this technology to focus quickly, accurately, silently, and with smooth continuous increments. If you think about video capture, you can see how these advantages pay off. Silent operation is a plus, especially when noise from autofocusing can easily be transferred to the camera's built-in microphones through the air or transmitted through the body itself. In addition, because autofocus is often done *during* capture, it's important that the focus increments are continuous. USM motors are not as smooth, but are better at jumping quickly to the exact focus point. You can adjust focus manually, using a focus-by-wire process. As you rotate the focus ring, that action doesn't move the lens elements; instead, your rotation of the ring sends a signal to the motor to change the focus. Figure 10.7 shows the new Canon EF-S 40mm f/2.8 STM lens.

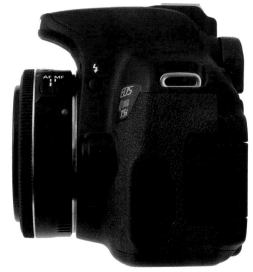
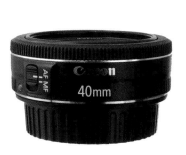

**Figure 10.7**
Canon's 40mm f/2.8 lens, with an STM motor, is designed for video capture.

# Your Second (and Third...) Lens

There are really only two advantages to owning just a single lens. One of them is creative. Keeping one set of optics mounted on your T5i all the time forces you to be especially imaginative in your approach to your subjects. I once visited Europe with only a single camera body and a 35mm f/2 lens. The experience was actually quite exciting, because I had to use a variety of techniques to allow that one lens to serve for landscapes, available light photos, action, close-ups, portraits, and other kinds of images. Canon makes an excellent 35mm f/2 lens (which focuses down to 9.6 inches) that's perfect for that kind of experiment; although, today, my personal choice would be the sublime (and expensive) Canon Wide-Angle EF 35mm f/1.4L USM autofocus lens. I also own the Canon EF 50mm f/1.8 II lens, which I favor as a very compact and light walkaround/short telephoto/portrait lens, especially indoors. It makes a great close-up/macro lens, too, and, at less than $125, is my choice as a very good second lens.

Of course, it's more likely that your "single" lens is actually a zoom, which is, in truth, many lenses in one, taking you from, say, 17mm to 85mm (or some other range) with a rapid twist of the zoom ring. You'll still find some creative challenges when you stick to a single zoom lens's focal lengths.

The second advantage of the unilens camera is only a marginal technical benefit since the introduction of the T5i. If you don't exchange lenses, the chances of dust and dirt getting inside your T5i and settling on the sensor is reduced (but *not* eliminated entirely). Although I've known some photographers who minimized the number of lens changes they made for this very reason, reducing the number of lenses you work with is not a productive or rewarding approach for most of us. The T5i's automatic sensor cleaning feature has made this "advantage" much less significant than it was in the past.

It's more likely that you'll succumb to the malady known as *Lens Lust*, which is defined as an incurable disease marked by a significant yen for newer, better, longer, faster, sharper, anything-er optics for your camera. (And, it must be noted, this disease can *cost* you significant yen—or dollars, or whatever currency you use.) In its worst manifestations, sufferers find themselves with lenses that have overlapping zoom ranges or capabilities, because one or the other offers a slight margin in performance or suitability for specific tasks. When you find yourself already lusting after a new lens before you've really had a chance to put your latest purchase to the test, you'll know the disease has reached the terminal phase.

## What Lenses Can Do for You

A saner approach to expanding your lens collection is to consider what each of your options can do for you and then choosing the type of lens that will really boost your creative opportunities. Here's a general guide to the sort of capabilities you can gain by adding a lens to your repertoire.

■ **Wider perspective.** Your 18-55mm f/3.5-5.6 or 17-85mm f/4-5.6 or 18-200mm lens has served you well for moderate wide-angle shots. Now you find your back is up against a wall and you *can't* take a step backwards to take in more subject matter. Perhaps you're standing on the rim of the Grand Canyon, and you want to take in as much of the breathtaking view as you can. You might find yourself just behind the baseline at a high school basketball game and want an interesting shot with a little perspective distortion tossed in the mix. There's a lens out there that will provide you with what you need, such as the EF-S 10-22mm f/3.5-4.5 USM zoom. If you want to stay in the sub-$800 price category, you'll need something like the Sigma Super Wide-Angle 10-20mm f/4-5.6 EX DC HSM autofocus lens. The two lenses provide the equivalent of a 16mm to 32/35mm wide-angle view. For a distorted view, there is the Canon Fisheye EF 15mm f/2.8 autofocus, with a similar lens available from Sigma, which offers an extra-wide circular fisheye, and the Sigma Fisheye 8mm f/3.5 EX DG Circular Fisheye. Your extra-wide choices may not be abundant, but they are there. Figure 10.8 shows the perspective you get from an ultrawide-angle, non-fisheye lens.

- **Bring objects closer.** A long lens brings distant subjects closer to you, offers better control over depth-of-field, and avoids the perspective distortion that wide-angle lenses provide. They compress the apparent distance between objects in your frame. In the telephoto realm, Canon is second to none, with a dozen or more offerings in the sub-$650 range, including the Canon EF 100-300mm f/4.5-5.6 USM autofocus and Canon EF 70-300mm f/4-5.6 IS USM autofocus telephoto zoom lenses, and a broad array of zooms and fixed-focal length optics if you're willing to spend up to $1,000 or a bit more. Don't forget that the T5i's crop factor narrows the field of view of all these lenses, so your 70-300mm lens looks more like a 112mm-480mm zoom through the viewfinder. Figures 10.9 and 10.10 were taken from the same position as Figure 10.8, but with an 85mm and 500mm lens, respectively.

- **Bring your camera closer.** Macro lenses allow you to focus to within an inch or two of your subject. Canon's best close-up lenses are all fixed focal length optics in the 50mm to 180mm range (including the well-regarded Canon EF-S 60mm f/2.8 compact and Canon EF 100mm f/2.8 USM macro autofocus lenses). But you'll find macro zooms available from Sigma and others. They don't tend to focus quite as close, but they provide a bit of flexibility when you want to vary your subject distance (say, to avoid spooking a skittish creature).

- **Look sharp.** Many lenses, particularly Canon's luxury "L" line, are prized for their sharpness and overall image quality. While your run-of-the-mill lens is likely to be plenty sharp for most applications, the very best optics are even better over their entire field of view (which means no fuzzy corners), are sharper at a wider range of focal lengths (in the case of zooms), and have better correction for various types of distortion.

- **More speed.** Your Canon EF 100-300mm f/4.5-5.6 telephoto zoom lens might have the perfect focal length and sharpness for sports photography, but the maximum aperture won't cut it for night baseball or football games, or, even, any sports shooting in daylight if the weather is cloudy or you need to use some unusually fast shutter speed, such as 1/4,000th second. You might be happier with the Canon EF 100mm f/2 medium telephoto for close-range stuff, or even the pricier Canon EF 135mm f/2L. If money is no object, you can spring for Canon's 400mm f/2.8 and 600mm f/4 L-series lenses (both with image stabilization and priced in the four- and five-figure stratosphere). Or, maybe you just need the speed and can benefit from an

**Figure 10.8**
An ultrawide-angle lens provided this view of a castle in Prague, Czech Republic.

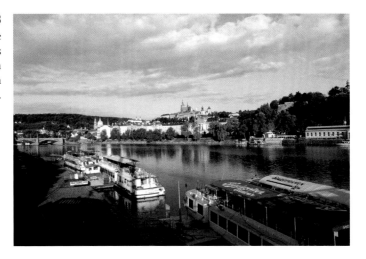

**Figure 10.9**
This photo, taken from roughly the same distance, shows the view using a short telephoto lens.

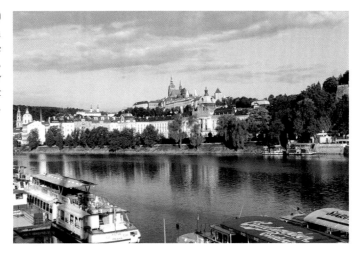

**Figure 10.10**
A longer telephoto lens captured this closer view of the castle from approximately the same shooting position.

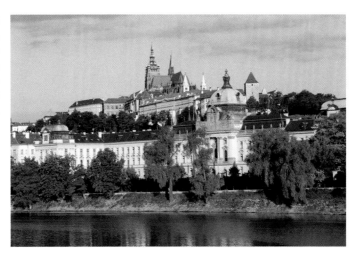

f/1.8 or f/1.4 lens in the 20mm-85mm range. They're all available in Canon mounts (there's even an 85mm f/1.2 and 50mm f/1.2 for the real speed demons). With any of these lenses you can continue photographing under the dimmest of lighting conditions without the need for a tripod or flash.

- **Special features.** Accessory lenses give you special features, such as tilt/shift capabilities to correct for perspective distortion in architectural shots. Canon offers four of these TS-E lenses in 17mm, 24mm, 45mm, and 90mm focal lengths, at more than $1,300–$2,000 (and up) each. You'll also find macro lenses, including the MP-E 65mm f/2.8 1-5x macro photo lens, a manual focus lens which shoots *only* in the 1X to 5X life-size range. If you want diffused images, check out the EF 135mm f/2.8 with two soft-focus settings. The fisheye lenses mentioned earlier and all IS (image-stabilized) lenses also count as special-feature optics. The recent Canon EF 8-15mm f/4L Fisheye USM ultrawide zoom lens is highly unusual in offering a *zoomable* fisheye range. Tokina's 10-17mm fisheye zoom is its chief competitor; I've owned one and it is not in the same league in terms of sharpness and speed.

## Zoom or Prime?

Zoom lenses have changed the way serious photographers take pictures. One of the reasons that I own 12 SLR film bodies is that in ancient times it was common to mount a different fixed focal length prime lens on various cameras and take pictures with two or three cameras around your neck (or tucked in a camera case) so you'd be ready to take a long shot or an intimate close-up or wide-angle view on a moment's notice, without the need to switch lenses. It made sense (at the time) to have a half dozen or so bodies (two to use, one in the shop, one in transit, and a couple backups). Zoom lenses of the time had a limited zoom range, were heavy, and not very sharp (especially when you tried to wield one of those monsters handheld).

That's all changed today. Lenses like the razor-sharp Canon EF 28-300mm f/3.5-5.6L IS USM can boast 10X or longer zoom ranges, in a package that's about 7 inches long, and while not petite at 3.7 pounds, it is quite usable handheld (especially with IS switched on). Although such a lens might seem expensive at $2,600-plus, it's actually much less costly than the six or so lenses it replaces.

When selecting between zoom and prime lenses, there are several considerations to ponder. Here's a checklist of the most important factors. I already mentioned image quality and maximum aperture earlier, but those aspects take on additional meaning when comparing zooms and primes.

- **Logistics.** As prime lenses offer just a single focal length, you'll need more of them to encompass the full range offered by a single zoom. More lenses mean additional slots in your camera bag, and extra weight to carry. Just within Canon's line alone you can select from about a dozen general-purpose prime lenses in 28mm, 35mm, 50mm, 85mm, 100mm, 135mm, 200mm, and 300mm focal lengths, all of which are overlapped by the 28-300mm zoom I mentioned earlier. Even so, you might be willing to carry an extra prime lens or two in order to gain the speed or image quality that lens offers.

■ **Image quality.** Prime lenses usually produce better image quality at their focal length than even the most sophisticated zoom lenses at the same magnification. Zoom lenses, with their shifting elements and f/stops that can vary from zoom position to zoom position, are in general more complex to design than fixed focal length lenses. That's not to say that the very best prime lenses can't be complicated as well. However, the exotic designs, aspheric elements, low-dispersion glass, and Canon's diffraction optics (DO) technology (a three-layer diffraction grating to better control how light is captured by a lens) can be applied to improving the quality of the lens, rather than wasting a lot of it on compensating for problems caused by the zoom process itself.

■ **Maximum aperture.** Because of the same design constraints, zoom lenses usually have smaller maximum apertures than prime lenses, and the most affordable zooms have a lens opening that grows effectively smaller as you zoom in. The difference in lens speed verges on the ridiculous at some focal lengths. For example, the 18mm-55mm basic zoom gives you a 55mm f/5.6 lens when zoomed all the way out, while prime lenses in that focal length commonly have f/1.8 or faster maximum apertures. Indeed, the fastest f/2, f/1.8, f/1.4, and f/1.2 lenses are all primes, and if you require speed, a fixed focal length lens is what you should rely on. Figure 10.11 shows an image taken with a Canon 85mm f/1.8 Series EF USM telephoto lens.

**Figure 10.11**
An 85mm f/1.8 lens was perfect for this handheld photo of a musician.

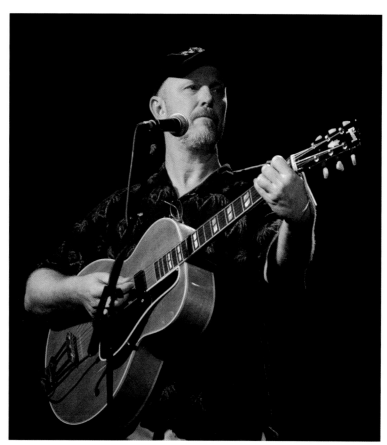

■ **Speed.** Using prime lenses takes time and slows you down. It takes a few seconds to remove your current lens and mount a new one, and the more often you need to do that, the more time is wasted. If you choose not to swap lenses, when using a fixed focal length lens you'll still have to move closer or farther away from your subject to get the field of view you want. A zoom lens allows you to change magnifications and focal lengths with the twist of a ring and generally saves a great deal of time.

■ **Special features.** Prime lenses often have special features not found in zoom lenses. For example, the new EF 40mm f/2.8 STM lens boasts that smooth, silent autofocus motor described earlier in this chapter. It functions as a wide-angle lens on a full-frame camera like the 5D Mark III, and as a short telephoto, portrait lens on cameras like the T5i. You'll also find close-focusing capabilities and perspective control features on prime lenses.

---

### TIP

Early copies of the EF 40mm f/2.8 STM lens (including the one I purchased), had suffered from a defect that caused autofocusing to cease functioning when pressure was applied to the lens barrel. In my case, gripping the barrel while removing the UV filter I use as a lens cap was enough. Until Canon issued a product advisory, I was really puzzled by this phenomenon. When I removed the lens and tried it on my 5D Mark III to see if the problem was in the lens or the camera body, it went away (temporarily). Before a firmware fix was issued in August, 2012, Canon advised the workaround of removing and reattaching the lens, or removing and reinserting the battery. If you own this lens, make sure your T5i firmware updates are all current.

---

## Categories of Lenses

Lenses can be categorized by their intended purpose—general photography, macro photography, and so forth—or by their focal length. The range of available focal lengths is usually divided into three main groups: wide-angle, normal, and telephoto. Prime lenses fall neatly into one of these classifications. Zooms can overlap designations, with a significant number falling into the catch-all, wide-to-telephoto zoom range. This section provides more information about focal length ranges, and how they are used.

Any lens with an equivalent focal length of 10mm to 20mm is said to be an *ultrawide-angle lens*; from about 20mm to 40mm (equivalent) is said to be a *wide-angle lens. Normal lenses* have a focal length roughly equivalent to the diagonal of the film or sensor, in millimeters, and so fall into the range of about 45mm to 60mm (on a full-frame camera). *Telephoto lenses* usually fall into the 75mm and longer focal lengths, while those from about 300mm to 400mm and longer often are referred to as *super-telephotos*.

# Using Wide-Angle and Wide-Zoom Lenses

To use wide-angle prime lenses and wide zooms, you need to understand how they affect your photography. Here's a quick summary of the things you need to know.

- **More depth-of-field.** Practically speaking, wide-angle lenses offer more depth-of-field at a particular subject distance and aperture. (But see the sidebar below for an important note.) You'll find that helpful when you want to maximize sharpness of a large zone, but not very useful when you'd rather isolate your subject using selective focus (telephoto lenses are better for that).

- **Stepping back.** Wide-angle lenses have the effect of making it seem that you are standing farther from your subject than you really are. They're helpful when you don't want to back up, or can't because there are impediments in your way.

- **Wider field of view.** While making your subject seem farther away, as implied above, a wide-angle lens also provides a larger field of view, including more of the subject in your photos. Table 10.1 shows the diagonal field of view offered by an assortment of lenses, taking into account the crop factor introduced by the T5i's smaller-than-full-frame sensor.

- **More foreground.** As background objects retreat, more of the foreground is brought into view by a wide-angle lens. That gives you extra emphasis on the area that's closest to the camera. Photograph your home with a normal lens/normal zoom setting, and the front yard probably looks fairly conventional in your photo (that's why they're called "normal" lenses). Switch to a wider lens and you'll discover that your lawn now makes up much more of the photo. So, wide-angle lenses are great when you want to emphasize that lake in the foreground, but problematic when your intended subject is located farther in the distance.

## Table 10.1  Field of View at Various Focal Lengths

| Diagonal Field of View | Focal Length at 1X Crop | Focal Length Needed to Produce Same Field of View at 1.6X Crop |
| --- | --- | --- |
| 107 degrees | 16mm | 10mm |
| 94 degrees | 20mm | 12mm |
| 84 degrees | 24mm | 15mm |
| 75 degrees | 28mm | 18mm |
| 63 degrees | 35mm | 22mm |
| 47 degrees | 50mm | 31mm |
| 28 degrees | 85mm | 53mm |
| 18 degrees | 135mm | 85mm |
| 12 degrees | 200mm | 125mm |
| 8.2 degrees | 300mm | 188mm |

■ **Super-sized subjects.** The tendency of a wide-angle lens to emphasize objects in the fore-ground, while de-emphasizing objects in the background can lead to a kind of size distortion that may be more objectionable for some types of subjects than others. Shoot a bed of flowers up close with a wide angle, and you might like the distorted effect of the larger blossoms nearer the lens. Take a photo of a family member with the same lens from the same distance, and you're likely to get some complaints about that gigantic nose in the foreground.

■ **Perspective distortion.** When you tilt the camera so the plane of the sensor is no longer per-pendicular to the vertical plane of your subject, some parts of the subject are now closer to the sensor than they were before, while other parts are farther away. So, buildings, flagpoles, or NBA players appear to be falling backwards, as you can see in Figure 10.12. While this kind of apparent distortion (it's not caused by a defect in the lens) can happen with any lens, it's most apparent when a wide angle is used.

■ **Steady cam.** You'll find that you can handhold a wide-angle lens at slower shutter speeds, without need for image stabilization, than you can with a telephoto lens. The reduced magni-fication of the wide-lens or wide-zoom setting doesn't emphasize camera shake like a telephoto lens does.

■ **Interesting angles.** Many of the factors already listed combine to produce more interesting angles when shooting with wide-angle lenses. Raising or lowering a telephoto lens a few feet probably will have little effect on the appearance of the distant subjects you're shooting. The same change in elevation can produce a dramatic effect for the much-closer subjects typically captured with a wide-angle lens or wide-zoom setting.

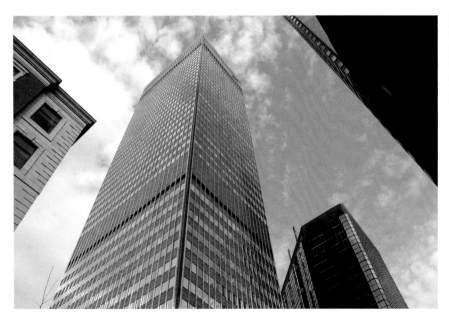

**Figure 10.12**
Tilting the camera back produces this "falling back" look in architectural photos.

The crop factor strikes again! You can see from this table that wide-angle lenses provide a broader field of view, and that, because of the T5i's 1.6 crop factor, lenses must have a shorter focal length to provide the same field of view. If you like working with a 28mm lens with your full-frame camera, you'll need an 18mm lens for your T5i to get the same field of view. (Some focal lengths have been rounded slightly for simplification.)

## DOF IN DEPTH

The depth-of-field (DOF) advantage of wide-angle lenses is diminished when you enlarge your picture; believe it or not, a wide-angle image enlarged and cropped to provide the same subject size as a telephoto shot would have the *same* depth-of-field. Try it: take a wide-angle photo of a friend from a fair distance, and then zoom in to duplicate the picture in a telephoto image. Then, enlarge the wide shot so your friend is the same size in both. The wide photo will have the same DOF (and will have much less detail, too).

# Avoiding Potential Wide-Angle Problems

Wide-angle lenses have a few quirks that you'll want to keep in mind when shooting so you can avoid falling into some common traps. Here's a checklist of tips for avoiding common problems:

- **Symptom: converging lines.** Unless you want to use wildly diverging lines as a creative effect, it's a good idea to keep horizontal and vertical lines in landscapes, architecture, and other subjects carefully aligned with the sides, top, and bottom of the frame. That will help you avoid undesired perspective distortion. Sometimes it helps to shoot from a slightly elevated position so you don't have to tilt the camera up or down.

- **Symptom: color fringes around objects.** Lenses are often plagued with fringes of color around backlit objects, produced by *chromatic aberration*, which comes in two forms: *longitudinal/axial*, in which all the colors of light don't focus in the same plane; and *lateral/transverse*, in which the colors are shifted to one side. Axial chromatic aberration can be reduced by stopping down the lens, but transverse chromatic aberration cannot. Both can be reduced by using lenses with low diffraction index glass (or UD elements, in Canon nomenclature) and by incorporating elements that cancel the chromatic aberration of other glass in the lens. For example, a strong positive lens made of low-dispersion crown glass (made of a soda-lime-silica composite) may be mated with a weaker negative lens made of high-dispersion flint glass, which contains lead.

- **Symptom: lines that bow outward.** Some wide-angle lenses cause straight lines to bow outward, with the strongest effect at the edges. In fisheye (or *curvilinear*) lenses, this defect is a feature, as you can see in Figure 10.13. When distortion is not desired, you'll need to use a lens that has corrected barrel distortion. Manufacturers like Canon do their best to minimize or eliminate it (producing a *rectilinear* lens), often using *aspherical* lens elements (which are not cross-sections of a sphere). You can also minimize less severe barrel distortion simply by framing your photo with some extra space all around, so the edges where the defect is most obvious can be cropped out of the picture.

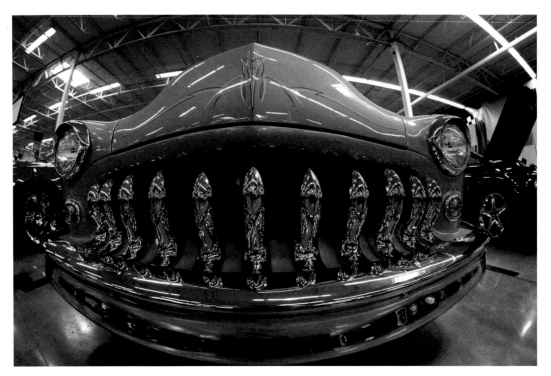

**Figure 10.13** Many wide-angle lenses cause lines to bow outward toward the edges of the image; with a fisheye lens, this tendency is especially useful for creating special effects, as in this shot.

- **Symptom: dark corners and shadows in flash photos.** The Canon EOS T5i's built-in electronic flash is designed to provide even coverage for lenses as wide as 17mm. If you use a wider lens, you can expect darkening, or *vignetting*, in the corners of the frame. At wider focal lengths, the lens hood of some lenses (my 17mm-85mm lens is a prime offender) can cast a semi-circular shadow in the lower portion of the frame when using the built-in flash. Sometimes removing the lens hood or zooming in a bit can eliminate the shadow. Mounting an external flash unit, such as the mighty Canon 580EX II or 600EX-RT, can solve both problems, as it has zoomable coverage up to 114 degrees with the included adapter, sufficient for a 15mm rectilinear lens. Its higher vantage point eliminates the problem of lens hood shadow, too.

- **Symptom: light and dark areas when using polarizing filter.** If you know that polarizers work best when the camera is pointed 90 degrees away from the sun and have the least effect when the camera is oriented 180 degrees from the sun, you know only half the story. With lenses having a focal length of 10mm to 18mm (the equivalent of 16mm-28mm), the angle of view (107 to 75 degrees diagonally, or 97 to 44 degrees horizontally) is extensive enough to cause problems. Think about it: when a 10mm lens is pointed at the proper 90-degree angle from the sun, objects at the edges of the frame will be oriented at 135 to 41 degrees, with only the center at exactly 90 degrees. Either edge will have much less of a polarized effect. The solution is to avoid using a polarizing filter with lenses having an actual focal length of less than 18mm (or 28mm equivalent).

# Using Telephoto and Tele-Zoom Lenses

Telephoto lenses also can have a dramatic effect on your photography, and Canon is especially strong in the long-lens arena, with lots of choices in many focal lengths and zoom ranges. You should be able to find an affordable telephoto or tele-zoom to enhance your photography in several different ways. Here are the most important things you need to know. In the next section, I'll concentrate on telephoto considerations that can be problematic—and how to avoid those problems.

■ **Selective focus.** Long lenses have reduced depth-of-field within the frame, allowing you to use selective focus to isolate your subject. You can open the lens up wide to create shallow depth-of-field (see Figure 10.14), or close it down a bit to allow more to be in focus. The flip side of the coin is that when you *want* to make a range of objects sharp, you'll need to use a smaller f/stop to get the depth-of-field you need. Like fire, the depth-of-field of a telephoto lens can be friend or foe.

■ **Getting closer.** Telephoto lenses bring you closer to wildlife, sports action, and candid subjects. No one wants to get a reputation as a surreptitious or "sneaky" photographer (except for paparazzi), but when applied to candids in an open and honest way, a long lens can help you capture memorable moments while retaining enough distance to stay out of the way of events as they transpire.

**Figure 10.14**
A wide f/stop helped isolate the lemur from its background.

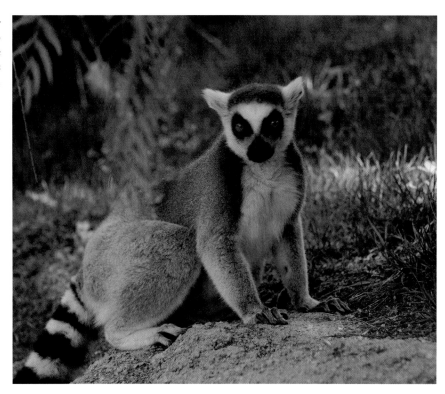

- **Reduced foreground/increased compression.** Telephoto lenses have the opposite effect of wide angles: they reduce the importance of things in the foreground by squeezing everything together. This compression even makes distant objects appear to be closer to subjects in the foreground and middle ranges. You can use this effect as a creative tool.

- **Accentuates camera shakiness.** Telephoto focal lengths hit you with a double-whammy in terms of camera/photographer shake. The lenses themselves are bulkier, more difficult to hold steady, and may even produce a barely perceptible see-saw rocking effect when you support them with one hand halfway down the lens barrel. Telephotos also magnify any camera shake. It's no wonder that image stabilization is popular in longer lenses.

- **Interesting angles require creativity.** Telephoto lenses require more imagination in selecting interesting angles, because the "angle" you do get on your subjects is so narrow. Moving from side to side or a bit higher or lower can make a dramatic difference in a wide-angle shot, but raising or lowering a telephoto lens a few feet probably will have little effect on the appearance of the distant subjects you're shooting.

# Avoiding Telephoto Lens Problems

Many of the "problems" that telephoto lenses pose are really just challenges and not that difficult to overcome. Here is a list of the seven most common picture maladies and suggested solutions.

- **Symptom: flat faces in portraits.** Head-and-shoulders portraits of humans tend to be more flattering when a focal length of 50mm to 85mm is used. Longer focal lengths compress the distance between features like noses and ears, making the face look wider and flat. A wide-angle might make noses look huge and ears tiny when you fill the frame with a face. So stick with 50mm to 85mm focal lengths, going longer only when you're forced to shoot from a greater distance, and wider only when shooting three-quarters/full-length portraits, or group shots.

- **Symptom: blur due to camera shake.** Use a higher shutter speed (boosting ISO if necessary), consider an image-stabilized lens, or mount your camera on a tripod, monopod, or brace it with some other support. Of those three solutions, only the first will reduce blur caused by *subject* motion; an IS lens or tripod won't help you freeze a race car in mid-lap.

- **Symptom: color fringes.** Chromatic aberration is the most pernicious optical problem found in telephoto lenses. There are others, including spherical aberration, astigmatism, coma, curvature of field, and similarly scary-sounding phenomena. The best solution for any of these is to use a better lens that offers the proper degree of correction, or stop down the lens to minimize the problem. But that's not always possible. Your second-best choice may be to correct the fringing in your favorite RAW conversion tool or image editor. Photoshop's Lens Correction filter offers sliders that minimize both red/cyan and blue/yellow fringing.

- **Symptom: lines that curve inward.** Pincushion distortion is found in many telephoto lenses. You might find after a bit of testing that it is worse at certain focal lengths with your particular zoom lens. Like chromatic aberration, it can be partially corrected using tools like Photoshop's Lens Correction filter and Photoshop Elements' Correct Camera Distortion filter.

■ **Symptom: low contrast from haze or fog.** When you're photographing distant objects, a long lens shoots through a lot more atmosphere, which generally is muddied up with extra haze and fog. That dirt or moisture in the atmosphere can reduce contrast and mute colors. Some feel that a skylight or UV filter can help, but this practice is mostly a holdover from the film days. Digital sensors are not sensitive enough to UV light for a UV filter to have much effect. So you should be prepared to boost contrast and color saturation in your Picture Styles menu or image editor if necessary.

■ **Symptom: low contrast from flare.** Lenses are furnished with lens hoods for a good reason: to reduce flare from bright light sources at the periphery of the picture area, or completely outside it. Because telephoto lenses often create images that are lower in contrast in the first place, you'll want to be especially careful to use a lens hood to prevent further effects on your image (or shade the front of the lens with your hand).

■ **Symptom: dark flash photos.** Edge-to-edge flash coverage isn't a problem with telephoto lenses as it is with wide angles. The shooting distance is. A long lens might make a subject that's 50 feet away look as if it's right next to you, but your camera's flash isn't fooled. You'll need extra power for distant flash shots, and probably more power than your T5i's built-in flash provides. The shoe-mount Canon 580EX II or 600EX-RT Speedlites, for example, can automatically zoom its coverage down to that of a medium telephoto lens, providing a theoretical full-power shooting aperture of about f/8 at 50 feet and ISO 400. (Try *that* with the built-in flash!)

## Telephotos and Bokeh

*Bokeh* describes the aesthetic qualities of the out-of-focus parts of an image and whether out-of-focus points of light—circles of confusion—are rendered as distracting fuzzy discs or smoothly fade into the background. *Boke* is a Japanese word for "blur," and the h was added to keep English speakers from rendering it monosyllabically to rhyme with *broke*. Although bokeh is visible in blurry portions of any image, it's of particular concern with telephoto lenses, which, thanks to the magic of reduced depth-of-field, produce more obviously out-of-focus areas.

Bokeh can vary from lens to lens, or even within a given lens depending on the f/stop in use. Bokeh becomes objectionable when the circles of confusion are evenly illuminated, making them stand out as distinct discs, or, worse, when these circles are darker in the center, producing an ugly "doughnut" effect. A lens defect called spherical aberration may produce out-of-focus discs that are brighter on the edges and darker in the center, because the lens doesn't focus light passing through the edges of the lens exactly as it does light going through the center. (Mirror or *catadioptric* lenses also produce this effect.)

Other kinds of spherical aberration generate circles of confusion that are brightest in the center and fade out at the edges, producing a smooth blending effect, as you can see at right in Figure 10.15. Ironically, when no spherical aberration is present at all, the discs are a uniform shade, which, while better than the doughnut effect, is not as pleasing as the bright center/dark edge rendition. The shape of the disc also comes into play, with round smooth circles considered the best, and nonagonal or some other polygon (determined by the shape of the lens diaphragm) considered less desirable.

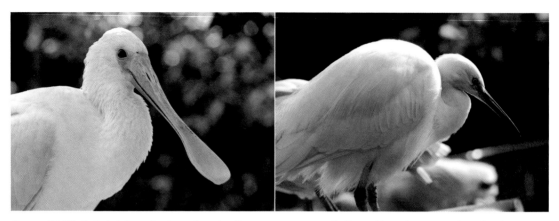

**Figure 10.15** Bokeh is less pleasing when the discs are prominent (left), and less obtrusive when they blend into the background (right).

If you plan to use selective focus a lot, you should investigate the bokeh characteristics of a particular lens before you buy. Canon user groups and forums will usually be full of comments and questions about bokeh, so the research is fairly easy.

# Add-ons and Special Features

Once you've purchased your telephoto lens, you'll want to think about some appropriate accessories for it. There are some handy add-ons available that can be valuable. Here are a couple of them to think about.

## Lens Hoods

Lens hoods are an important accessory for all lenses, but they're especially valuable with telephotos. As I mentioned earlier, lens hoods do a good job of preserving image contrast by keeping bright light sources outside the field of view from striking the lens and, potentially, bouncing around inside that long tube to generate flare that, when coupled with atmospheric haze, can rob your image of detail and snap. In addition, lens hoods serve as valuable protection for that large, vulnerable, front lens element. It's easy to forget that you've got that long tube sticking out in front of your camera and accidentally whack the front of your lens into something. It's cheaper to replace a lens hood than it is to have a lens repaired, so you might find that a good hood is valuable protection for your prized optics.

When choosing a lens hood, it's important to have the right hood for the lens, usually the one offered for that lens by Canon or the third-party manufacturer. You want a hood that blocks precisely the right amount of light: neither too much light nor too little. A hood with a front diameter that is too small can show up in your pictures as vignetting. A hood that has a front diameter that's too large isn't stopping all the light it should. Generic lens hoods may not do the job.

When your telephoto is a zoom lens, it's even more important to get the right hood, because you need one that does what it is supposed to at both the wide-angle and telephoto ends of the zoom range. Lens hoods may be cylindrical, rectangular (shaped like the image frame), or petal shaped (that is, cylindrical, but with cut-out areas at the corners which correspond to the actual image area). Lens hoods should be mounted in the correct orientation (a bayonet mount for the hood on the front of the lens usually takes care of this).

## Telephoto Extenders

Telephoto extenders (often called teleconverters outside the Canon world), multiply the actual focal length of your lens, giving you a longer telephoto for much less than the price of a lens with that actual focal length. These extenders fit between the lens and your camera and contain optical elements that magnify the image produced by the lens. Available in 1.4X and 2.0X configurations from Canon, an extender transforms, say, a 200mm lens into a 280mm or 400mm optic, respectively. Given the T5i's crop factor, your 200mm lens now has the same field of view as a 448mm or 640mm lens on a full-frame camera. At around $500 each, they're quite a bargain, aren't they?

Actually, there are some downsides. While extenders retain the closest focusing distance of your original lens, autofocus is maintained only if the lens's original maximum aperture is f/4 or larger (for the 1.4X extender) or f/2.8 or larger (for the 2X extender). The components reduce the effective aperture of any lens they are used with, by one f/stop with the 1.4X extender, and 2 f/stops with the 2X extender. So, your EF 200mm f/2.8L II USM becomes a 280mm f/4 or 400mm f/5.6 lens. Although Canon extenders are precision optical devices, they do cost you a little sharpness, but that improves when you reduce the aperture by a stop or two. Each of the extenders is compatible only with a particular set of lenses of 135mm focal length or greater, so you'll want to check Canon's compatibility chart to see if the component can be used with the lens you want to attach to it.

If your lenses are compatible and you're shooting under bright lighting conditions, the Canon Extender EF 1.4x III, and Canon Extender EF 2x III make handy accessories.

## Macro Focusing

Some telephotos and telephoto zooms available for the T5i have particularly close focusing capabilities, making them *macro* lenses. Of course, the object is not necessarily to get close (get too close and you'll find it difficult to light your subject). What you're really looking for in a macro lens is to magnify the apparent size of the subject in the final image. Camera-to-subject distance is most important when you want to back up farther from your subject (say, to avoid spooking skittish insects or small animals). In that case, you'll want a macro lens with a longer focal length to allow that distance while retaining the desired magnification.

Canon makes 50mm, 60mm, 65mm, 100mm, and 180mm lenses with official macro designations. You'll also find macro lenses, macro zooms, and other close-focusing lenses available from Sigma, Tamron, and Tokina. If you want to focus closer with a macro lens, or any other lens, you can add an accessory called an *extension tube*, shown in Figure 10.16. These add-ons move the lens farther from the focal plane, allowing it to focus more closely. Canon also sells add-on close-up lenses, which look like filters, and allow lenses to focus more closely.

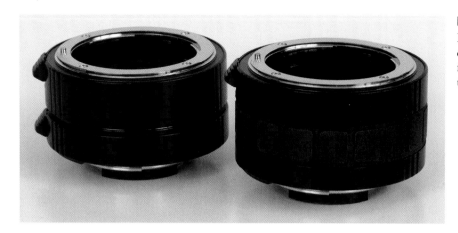

**Figure 10.16**
Extension tubes enable any lens to focus more closely to the subject.

# Image Stabilization

Canon has a burgeoning line of more than a dozen lenses with built-in image stabilization (IS) capabilities. This feature uses lens elements that are shifted internally in response to the motion of the lens during handheld photography, countering the shakiness the camera and photographer produce and which telephoto lenses magnify. However, IS is not limited to long lenses; the feature works like a champ at the 17mm zoom position of Canon's EF-S 17-85mm f/4-5.6 IS USM and EF-S 17-55mm f/2.8 IS USM lenses. Other Canon IS lenses provide stabilization with zooms that are as wide as 24-28mm.

Image stabilization provides you with camera steadiness that's the equivalent of at least two or three shutter speed increments. (Canon claims four, which I feel may be optimistic.) This extra margin can be invaluable when you're shooting under dim lighting conditions or handholding a long lens for, say, wildlife photography. Perhaps that shot of a foraging deer calls for a shutter speed of 1/1,000th second at f/5.6 with your EF 100-400mm f/4.5-5.6L IS USM lens. Relax. You can shoot at 1/250th second at f/11 and get virtually the same results, as long as the deer doesn't decide to bound off.

Or, maybe you're shooting a high school play without a tripod or monopod, and you'd really, really like to use 1/15th second at f/4. Assuming the actors aren't flitting around the stage at high speed, your 17-85mm IS lens can grab the shot for you at its wide-angle position. However, keep these facts in mind:

- **IS doesn't stop action.** Unfortunately, no IS lens is a panacea to replace the action-stopping capabilities of a higher shutter speed. Image stabilization applies only to camera shake. You still need a fast shutter speed to freeze action. IS works great in low light, when you're using long lenses, and for macro photography. It's not always the best choice for action photography (unless you're willing to let subject motion become part of your image, as in Figure 10.17). In other situations, you may need enough light to allow a sufficiently high shutter speed. But in that case, IS can make your shot even sharper.

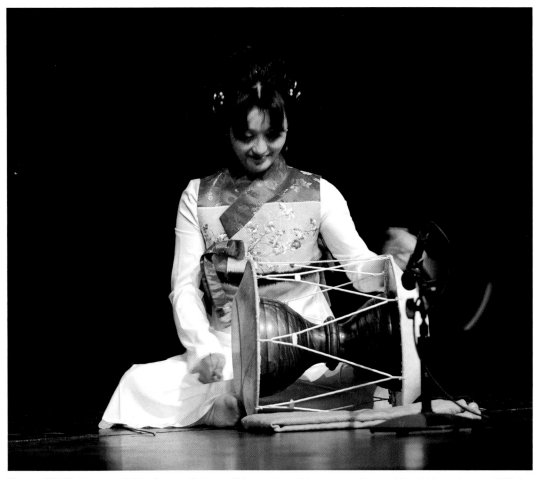

**Figure 10.17** Image stabilization made it possible to shoot this concert photo with a 200mm lens at 1/60th second. Note that the drummer's hands are still a blur, but her beautiful costume is vividly sharp.

- **IS slows you down.** The process of adjusting the lens elements takes time, just as autofocus does, so you might find that IS adds to the lag between when you press the shutter and when the picture is actually taken. That's another reason why image stabilization might not be a good choice for sports.

- **Use when appropriate.** Some IS lenses produce worse results if you use them while you're panning, although newer Canon IS lenses have a mode that works fine when the camera is deliberately moved from side to side (or up and down) during exposure. Older lenses can confuse the motion with camera shake and overcompensate. You might want to switch off IS when panning or when your camera is mounted on a tripod.

- **Do you need IS at all?** Remember that an inexpensive monopod might be able to provide the same additional steadiness as an IS lens, at a much lower cost. If you're out in the field shooting wild animals or flowers and think a tripod isn't practical, try a monopod first.

## IMAGE STABILIZATION: IN THE CAMERA OR IN THE LENS?

Sony's acquisition of Konica Minolta's dSLR assets and the introduction of an improved in-camera image-stabilization system has revived an old debate about whether IS belongs in the camera or in the lens. Perhaps it's my Canon bias showing, but I am quite happy not to have image stabilization available in the body itself. Here are some reasons:

- Should in-camera IS fail, you have to send the whole camera in for repair, and camera repairs are generally more expensive than lens repairs. I like being able to simply switch to another lens if I have an IS problem.

- IS in the camera doesn't steady your view in the viewfinder, whereas an IS lens shows you a steadied image as you shoot.

- You're stuck with the IS system built into your camera. If an improved system is incorporated into a lens and the improvements are important to you, just trade in your old lens for the new one.

- Optimized stabilization. Canon claims that it is able to produce the best possible image stabilization for each lens it introduces, something that would not be possible if a "one size fits all lenses" stabilization scheme had to be built into the camera.

## Using the Lensbaby

I'm going to depart from my Canon-only regimen to include the wonderful Lensbaby line of optics, because Canon doesn't offer anything similar, nor as delightfully affordable. The Lensbaby comes in several varieties (including Edge 80, a shift-tilt model for about $300, and the Composer Pro shown in Figure 10.18), and uses distortion-heavy glass elements mounted on a system that allows you to bend, twist, and distort the lens's alignment to produce transmogrified images unlike anything else you've ever seen. Like the legendary cheap-o Diana and Holga cameras, the pictures are prized expressly because of their plastic image quality. Jack and Meg White (formerly of the White Stripes) have, in fact, sold personalized Diana and Holga cameras on their website for wacky *lomography* (named after the Lomo, another low-quality/high-concept camera). The various Lensbaby models are for more serious photographers, if you can say that about anyone who yearns to take pictures that look like they were shot through a glob of corn syrup.

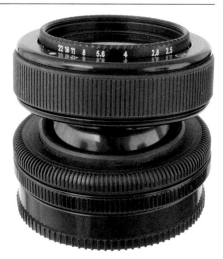

**Figure 10.18** Lensbabies are specialized lens replacements with some special soft-focus features.

Lensbabies are capable of creating all sorts of special effects. You use a Lensbaby by shifting the front mount to move the lens's sweet spot to a particular point in the scene. This is basically a selective focus lens that gets very soft outside the sweet spot. There are several different types of Lensbabies, which can be interchanged using the system's Optic Swap technology.

- **Macro.** A Lensbaby accessory makes it possible to use this tool for macro photography.

- **Wide-angle/telephoto conversion.** Add-on lenses convert the basic Lensbaby into a wide-angle or telephoto version.

- **Edge 80.** This is an 80mm f/2.8 lens with a flat field of focus—ideal for portraits. It has a 12-blade adjustable aperture, focuses as close as 17 inches, and functions as a tilt-shift lens. When canted, the Edge 80 delivers a slice of tack sharp focus through the image, bordered by a soft blur. When pointed straight ahead, Edge 80 can be used like a conventional lens. You can also use it in any of the traditional selective focus applications you'd use one of Canon's PC-E lenses for—but *not* for perspective correction. (It tilts, but does not shift from side to side.)

- **Creative aperture kit.** Various shaped cutouts can be used in place of the regular aperture inserts that control depth-of-field. These shapes can include things like hearts, stars, and other shapes.

- **Optic swap kit.** This three-lens accessory kit provides different adapters that include a pinhole lens, plastic lens, and single glass lens.

Among the interchangeable components are the Sweet 35, Fisheye, Soft Focus, Double Glass, Single Glass, and Pinhole lenses. Models include the Composer Pro, Composer, Muse, Control Freak, and Scout, each with varying amounts of adjustments. (The Scout does not bend at all, making it ideal for use with the fisheye component.)

The other Lensbaby models, like the Composer Pro, have the same tilting lens configuration as previous editions, but are designed for easier and more precise distorting movements. Hold the camera with your finger gripping the knobs as you bend the camera to move the central "sweet spot" (sharp area) to any portion of your image. With two (count 'em) multicoated optical glass lens elements, you'll get a blurry image, but the amount of distortion is under your control. F/stops from f/2 to f/22 are available to increase/decrease depth-of-field and allow you to adjust exposure. The 50mm lens focuses down to 12 inches and is strictly manual focus/manual exposure in operation. At $300 or so, these lenses are not cheap accessories, but there is really no other easy way to achieve the kind of looks you can get with a Lensbaby.

Figures 10.19 and 10.20 are examples of the type of effect you can get, in photographs crafted by Cleveland photographer Nancy Balluck. She also produced the back cover photography of yours truly, and one of her specialties is Lensbaby effects.

Nancy regularly gives demonstrations and classes on the use of these optics, and you can follow her work at www.nancyballuckphotography.com.

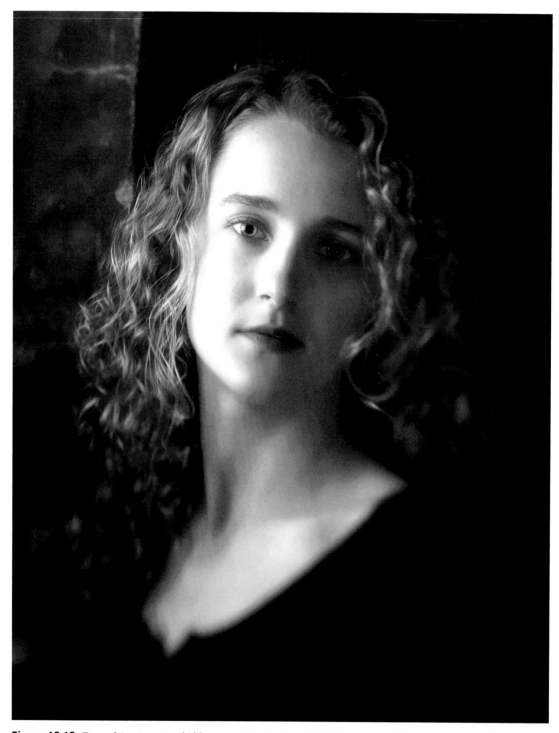

**Figure 10.19** Everything is uniquely blurry outside the Lensbaby's "sweet spot," but you can move that spot around within your frame at will.

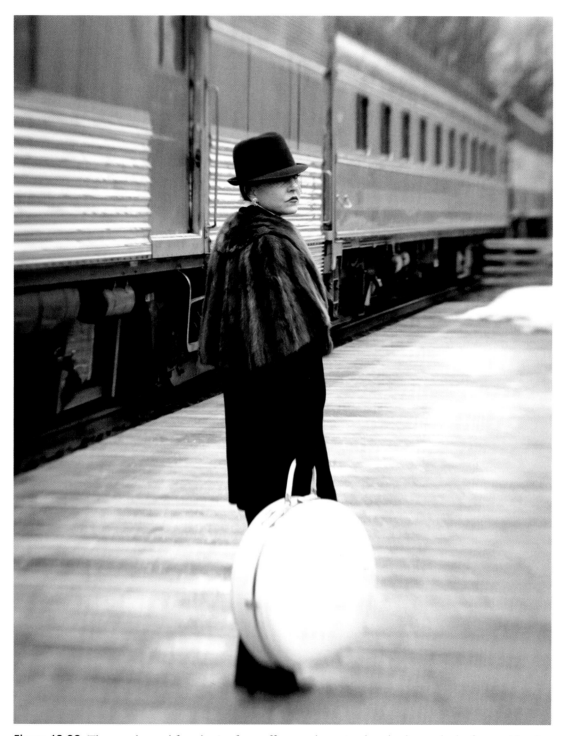

**Figure 10.20** They can be used for selective focus effects, and can simulate the dreamy look of some old-style cameras.

# 11

# Working with Light

Unless you're extraordinarily lucky, or supremely observant, great lighting, like most things of artistic value, doesn't happen by accident. It's entirely possible that you'll randomly encounter a scene or subject that's bathed in marvelous lighting, illumination that perfectly sculpts an image in highlights and shadows. But how often can you count on such luck? Ansel Adams is often quoted as saying (although he probably didn't) that "The harder I work, the luckier I get."

The great photographer *was* known for his patience in seeking out the best lighting for a composition, and he *did* actually say, "A good photograph is knowing where to stand." My own take on excellence in illumination is that you have to possess the ability to *recognize* effective lighting when it is already present, and have the skill to manipulate the light when it is not.

All successful photographers and artists have an intimate understanding of the importance of light in shaping an image. Rembrandt was a master of using light to create moods and reveal the character of his subjects. The late artist Thomas Kinkade's official tagline was "Painter of Light." Dean Collins, co-founder of Finelight Studios, revolutionized how a whole generation of photographers learned and used lighting. Photo guru Ed Pierce has a popular seminar called "Captivated by the Light." It's impossible to underestimate how the use of light adds to—and how misuse can detract from—your photographs.

All forms of visual art use light to shape the finished product. Sculptors don't have control over the light used to illuminate their finished work, so they must create shapes using planes and curved surfaces so that the form envisioned by the artist comes to life from a variety of viewing and lighting angles. Painters, in contrast, have absolute control over both shape and light in their work, as well as the viewing angle, so they can use both the contours of their two-dimensional subjects and the qualities of the "light" they use to illuminate those subjects to evoke the image they want to produce.

Photography is a third form of art. The photographer may have little or no control over the subject (other than posing human subjects) but can often adjust both viewing angle *and* the nature of the light source to create a particular compelling image. The direction and intensity of the light sources create the shapes and textures that we see. The distribution and proportions determine the contrast and tonal values: whether the image is stark or high key, or muted and low in contrast. The colors of the light (because even "white" light has a color balance that the sensor can detect), and how much of those colors the subject reflects or absorbs, paint the hues visible in the image.

As a Rebel T5i photographer, you must learn to be a painter and sculptor of light if you want to move from *taking* a picture to *making* a photograph. This chapter provides an introduction to using the two main types of illumination: *continuous* lighting (such as daylight, incandescent, or fluorescent sources) and the brief, but brilliant snippets of light we call *electronic flash.*

# Continuous Illumination versus Electronic Flash

Continuous lighting is exactly what you might think: uninterrupted illumination that is available all the time during a shooting session. Daylight, moonlight, and the artificial lighting encountered both indoors and outdoors count as continuous light sources (although all of them can be "interrupted" by passing clouds, solar eclipses, a blown fuse, or simply by switching off a lamp). Indoor continuous illumination includes both the lights that are there already (such as incandescent lamps or overhead fluorescent lights indoors) and fixtures you supply yourself, including photoflood lamps or reflectors used to bounce existing light onto your subject.

Electronic flash is notable because it can be much more intense than continuous lighting, lasts only a brief moment, and can be much more portable than supplementary incandescent sources. It's a light source you can carry with you and use anywhere. Indeed, your Rebel T5i has a flip-up electronic flash unit built in.

But you can also use an external flash, either mounted on the T5i's accessory shoe or used off-camera and linked with a cable or triggered by a slave light (which sets off a flash when it senses the firing of another unit). Studio flash units are electronic flash, too, and aren't limited to "professional" shooters, as there are economical "monolight" (one-piece flash/power supply) units available in the $200 price range. You can buy a couple to store in a closet and use to set up a home studio, or use as supplementary lighting when traveling away from home.

There are advantages and disadvantages to each type of illumination. Here's a quick checklist of pros and cons:

- **Lighting preview—Pro: continuous lighting.** With continuous lighting, you always know exactly what kind of lighting effect you're going to get and, if multiple light sources are used, how they will interact with each other, as shown in Figure 11.1, where the main light was the sun, but a bit of fill was provided by a gold reflector held up a few feet off-camera to her left. With electronic flash, the general effect you're going to see may be a mystery until you've built some experience, and you may need to review a shot on the LCD, make some adjustments, and then reshoot to get the look you want. (In this sense, a digital camera's review capabilities replace the Polaroid test shots pro photographers relied on in decades past.)

**Figure 11.1**
You always know how the lighting will look when using continuous illumination.

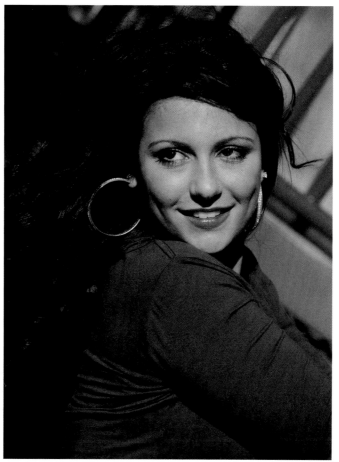

- **Exposure calculation—Pro: continuous lighting.** Your T5i has no problem calculating exposure for continuous lighting, because the illumination remains constant and can be measured through a sensor that interprets the light reaching the viewfinder. The amount of light available just before the exposure will, in almost all cases, be the same amount of light present when the shutter is released. The T5i's Spot metering mode can be used to measure and compare the proportions of light in the highlights and shadows, so you can make an adjustment (such as using more or less fill light) if necessary. You can even use a handheld light meter to measure the light yourself.

- **Exposure calculation—Con: electronic flash.** Electronic flash illumination doesn't exist until the flash fires and so can't be measured by the T5i's exposure sensor when the mirror is flipped up during the exposure. Instead, the light must be measured metering the intensity of a pre-flash triggered an instant before the main flash, as it is reflected back to the camera and through the lens. An alternative is to use a sensor built into an external flash itself and measure reflected light that has not traveled through the lens. If you have a do-it-yourself bent, there are handheld flash meters, too, including models that measure both flash and continuous light.

■ **Evenness of illumination—Pro/con: continuous lighting.** Of continuous light sources, daylight, in particular, provides illumination that tends to fill an image completely, lighting up the foreground, background, and your subject almost equally. Shadows do come into play, of course, so you might need to use reflectors or fill-in light sources to even out the illumination further, but barring objects that block large sections of your image from daylight, the light is spread fairly evenly. Indoors, however, continuous lighting is commonly less evenly distributed. The average living room, for example, has hot spots and dark corners. But on the plus side, you can *see* this uneven illumination and compensate with additional lamps.

■ **Evenness of illumination—Con: electronic flash.** Electronic flash units (like continuous light sources such as lamps that don't have the advantage of being located 93 million miles from the subject) suffer from the effects of their proximity. The *inverse square law*, first applied to both gravity and light by Sir Isaac Newton, dictates that as a light source's distance increases from the subject, the amount of light reaching the subject falls off proportionately to the square of the distance. In plain English, that means that a flash or lamp that's eight feet away from a subject provides only one-quarter as much illumination as a source that's four feet away (rather than half as much). (See Figure 11.2.) This translates into relatively shallow "depth-of-light."

■ **Action stopping—Con: continuous lighting.** Action stopping with continuous light sources is completely dependent on the shutter speed you've dialed in on the camera. And the speeds available are dependent on the amount of light available and your ISO sensitivity setting. Outdoors in daylight, there will probably be enough sunlight to let you shoot at 1/2,500th second and f/6.3 with a non-grainy sensitivity setting of ISO 400. That's a fairly useful combination of settings if you're not using a super-telephoto with a small maximum aperture. But inside, the reduced illumination quickly has you pushing your Rebel T5i to its limits. For example, if you're shooting indoor sports, there probably won't be enough available light to allow you to use a 1/2,000th second shutter speed (although I routinely shoot indoor basketball with my T5i at ISO 1600 and 1/500th second at f/4). In many indoor sports situations, you may find yourself limited to 1/500th second or slower.

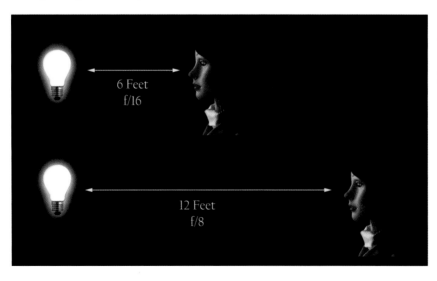

**Figure 11.2**
A light source that is twice as far away provides only one-quarter as much illumination.

■ **Action stopping—Pro: electronic flash.** When it comes to the ability to freeze moving objects in their tracks, the advantage goes to electronic flash. The brief duration of electronic flash serves as a very high "shutter speed" when the flash is the main or only source of illumination for the photo. Your Rebel T5i's shutter speed may be set for 1/200th second during a flash exposure, but if the flash illumination predominates, the *effective* exposure time will be the 1/1,000th to 1/50,000th second or less duration of the flash, as you can see in Figure 11.3, because the flash unit reduces the amount of light released by cutting short the duration of the flash. The only fly in the ointment is that, if the ambient light is strong enough, it may produce a secondary, "ghost" exposure, as I'll explain later in this chapter.

**Figure 11.3**
Electronic flash can freeze almost any action.

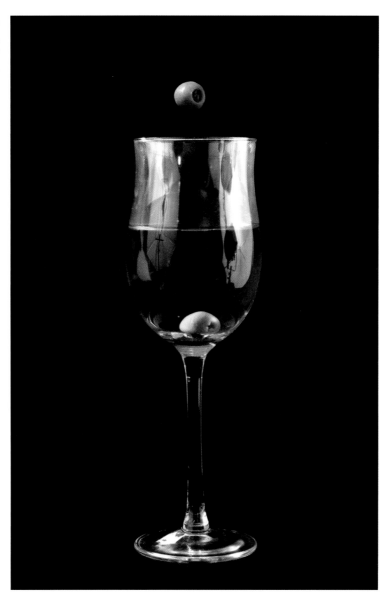

- **Cost—Pro: continuous lighting.** Incandescent or fluorescent lamps are generally much less expensive than electronic flash units, which can easily cost several hundred dollars. I've used everything from desktop high-intensity lamps to reflector flood lights for continuous illumination at very little cost. There are lamps made especially for photographic purposes, too, priced up to $50 or so. Maintenance is economical, too: many incandescent or fluorescents use bulbs that cost only a few dollars.

- **Cost—Con: electronic flash.** Electronic flash units aren't particularly cheap. The lowest-cost dedicated flash designed specifically for the Canon dSLRs is about $110. Such units are limited in features, however, and intended for those with entry-level cameras. Plan on spending some money to get the features that a sophisticated electronic flash offers.

- **Flexibility—Con: continuous lighting.** Because incandescent and fluorescent lamps are not as bright as electronic flash, the slower shutter speeds required (see Action stopping, above) mean that you may have to use a tripod more often, especially when shooting portraits. The incandescent variety of continuous lighting gets hot, especially in the studio, and the side effects range from discomfort (for your human models) to disintegration (if you happen to be shooting perishable foods like ice cream). The heat also makes it more difficult to add filtration to incandescent sources.

- **Flexibility—Pro: electronic flash.** Electronic flash's action-freezing power allows you to work without a tripod in the studio (and elsewhere), adding flexibility and speed when choosing angles and positions. Flash units can be easily filtered, and, because the filtration is placed over the light source rather than the lens, you don't need to use high-quality filter material. Roscoe or Lee lighting gels, which may be too flimsy to use in front of the lens, can be mounted or taped in front of your flash with ease.

## Continuous Lighting Basics

While continuous lighting and its effects are generally much easier to visualize and use than electronic flash, there are some factors you need to take into account, particularly the color temperature of the light. (Color temperature concerns aren't exclusive to continuous light sources, of course, but the variations tend to be more extreme and less predictable than those of electronic flash.)

## Living with Color Temperature

Canon and vendors with equipment compatible with the T5i have been valiant in their efforts to help us tame the color balance monster. One popular color balancing technology lives on in the form of ExpoDisc filter/caps (see Figure 11.4) and their ilk (www.expoimaging.com), which

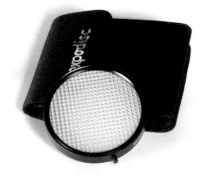

**Figure 11.4** The ExpoDisc is placed on a lens and used as a neutral subject for measuring white balance.

allow the camera's built-in custom white balance measuring feature to evaluate the illumination that passes through the disc/cap/filter/Pringle's can lid, or whatever neutral-color substitute you employ. (A white or gray card also works.)

Color temperature, in practical terms, is how "bluish" or how "reddish" the light appears to be to the digital camera's sensor. Indoor illumination is quite warm, comparatively, and appears reddish to the sensor. Daylight, in contrast, seems much bluer to the sensor. Our eyes (our brains, actually) are quite adaptable to these variations, so white objects don't appear to have an orange tinge when viewed indoors, nor do they seem excessively blue outdoors in full daylight. Yet, these color temperature variations are real and the sensor is not fooled. To capture the most accurate colors, we need to take the color temperature into account in setting the color balance (or *white balance*) of the T5i—either automatically using the camera's smarts or manually, using our own knowledge and experience.

Color temperature can be confusing, because of a seeming contradiction in how color temperatures are named: warmer (more reddish) color temperatures (measured in degrees Kelvin) are the *lower* numbers, while cooler (bluer) color temperatures are *higher* numbers. It might not make sense to say that 3,400K is warmer than 6,000K, but that's the way it is. If it helps, think of a glowing red ember contrasted with a white-hot welder's torch, rather than fire and ice.

The confusion comes from physics. Scientists calculate color temperature from the light emitted by a mythical object called a black body radiator, which absorbs all the radiant energy that strikes it, and reflects none at all. Such a black body not only *absorbs* light perfectly, but it *emits* it perfectly when heated (and since nothing in the universe is perfect, that makes it mythical).

At a particular physical temperature, this imaginary object always emits light of the same wavelength or color. That makes it possible to define color temperature in terms of actual temperature in degrees on the Kelvin scale that scientists use. Incandescent light, for example, typically has a color temperature of 3,200K to 3,400K. Daylight might range from 5,500K to 6,000K. Each type of illumination we use for photography has its own color temperature range—with some cautions. The next sections will summarize everything you need to know about the qualities of these light sources.

# Daylight

Daylight is produced by the sun, and so is moonlight (which is just reflected sunlight). Daylight is present, of course, even when you can't see the sun. When sunlight is direct, it can be bright and harsh. If daylight is diffused by clouds, softened by bouncing off objects such as walls or your photo reflectors, or filtered by shade, it can be much dimmer and less contrasty.

Daylight's color temperature can vary quite widely. It is highest (most blue) at noon when the sun is directly overhead, because the light is traveling through a minimum amount of the filtering layer we call the atmosphere. The color temperature at high noon may be 6,000K. At other times of day, the sun is lower in the sky and the particles in the air provide a filtering effect that warms the illumination to about 5,500K for most of the day. Starting an hour before dusk and for an hour after sunrise, the warm appearance of the sunlight is even visible to our eyes when the color temperature may dip below 4,500K, as shown in Figure 11.5.

Because you'll be taking so many photos in daylight, you'll want to learn how to use or compensate for the brightness and contrast of sunlight, as well as how to deal with its color temperature. I'll provide some hints later in this chapter.

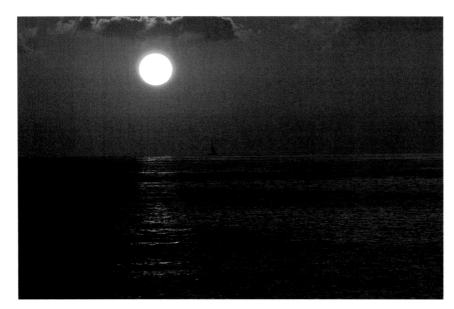

**Figure 11.5**
At dawn and dusk, the color temperature of daylight may dip below 4,500K, providing this reddish rendition.

# Incandescent/Tungsten Light

The term *incandescent* or *tungsten* illumination is usually applied to the direct descendents of Thomas Edison's original electric lamp. Such lights consist of a glass bulb that contains a vacuum, or is filled with a halogen gas, and contains a tungsten filament that is heated by an electrical current, producing photons and heat. Tungsten-halogen lamps are a variation on the basic lightbulb, using a more rugged (and longer-lasting) filament that can be heated to a higher temperature, housed in a thicker glass or quartz envelope, and filled with iodine or bromine ("halogen") gases. The higher temperature allows tungsten-halogen (or quartz-halogen/quartz-iodine, depending on their construction) lamps to burn "hotter" and whiter. Although popular for automobile headlamps today, they are also popular for photographic illumination. Although incandescent illumination isn't a perfect black body radiator, it's close enough that the color temperature of such lamps can be precisely calculated and used for photography without concerns about color variation (at least, until the very end of the lamp's life).

# Fluorescent Light/Other Light Sources

Fluorescent light has some advantages in terms of illumination, but some disadvantages from a photographic standpoint, especially when it comes to CFLs, as I outlined earlier. This type of lamp generates light through an electro-chemical reaction that emits most of its energy as visible light, rather than heat, which is why the bulbs don't get as hot. The type of light produced varies depending on the phosphor coatings and type of gas in the tube. So, the illumination fluorescent bulbs produce can vary widely in its characteristics.

That's not great news for photographers. Different types of lamps have different "color temperatures" that can't be precisely measured in degrees Kelvin, because the light isn't produced by heating. Worse, fluorescent lamps have a discontinuous spectrum of light that can have some colors missing entirely, producing that substandard Color Rendering Index. A particular type of tube can lack certain shades of red or other colors (see Figure 11.6), which is why fluorescent lamps and other alternative technologies such as sodium-vapor illumination can produce ghastly looking human skin tones. Their spectra can lack the reddish tones we associate with healthy skin and emphasize the blues and greens popular in horror movies.

**Figure 11.6**
The fluorescent lighting in this gym added a distinct greenish cast to the image.

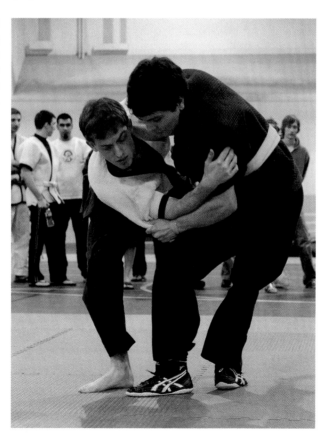

# Adjusting White Balance

I showed you how to adjust white balance bracketing in Chapter 4 (there's more on bracketing in Chapter 8, too). In most cases, however, the Rebel T5i will do a good job of calculating white balance for you, so Auto can be used as your choice most of the time. Use the preset values or set a custom white balance that matches the current shooting conditions when you need to. The only really problematic light sources are likely to be fluorescents. Vendors, such as GE and Sylvania, may actually provide a figure known as the *color rendering index* (or CRI), which is a measure of how accurately a particular light source represents standard colors, using a scale of 0 (some sodium-vapor lamps) to 100 (daylight and most incandescent lamps). Daylight fluorescents and deluxe cool white fluorescents might have a CRI of about 79 to 95, which is perfectly acceptable for most photographic applications. Warm white fluorescents might have a CRI of 55. White deluxe mercury vapor lights are less suitable with a CRI of 45, while low-pressure sodium lamps can vary from CRI 0 to 18.

Remember that if you shoot RAW, you can specify the white balance of your image when you import it into Photoshop, Photoshop Elements, or another image editor using your preferred RAW converter. While color-balancing filters that fit on the front of the lens exist, they are primarily useful for film cameras, because film's color balance can't be tweaked as extensively or as easily as that of a sensor.

# Electronic Flash Basics

Until you delve into the situation deeply enough, it might appear that serious photographers have a love/hate relationship with electronic flash. You'll often hear that flash photography is less natural looking, and that the built-in flash in most cameras should never be used as the primary source of illumination because it provides a harsh, garish look. Indeed, most "pro" cameras like the Canon EOS 1D X, Ds Mark III, and 5D Mark III don't have a built-in flash at all. Available ("continuous") lighting is praised, and built-in flash photography seems to be roundly denounced.

In truth, however, the bias is against *bad* flash photography. Indeed, flash has become the studio light source of choice for pro photographers, because it's more intense (and its intensity can be varied to order by the photographer), freezes action, frees you from using a tripod (unless you want to use one to lock down a composition), and has a snappy, consistent light quality that matches daylight. (While color balance changes as the flash duration shortens, some Canon flash units can communicate to the camera the exact white balance provided for that shot.) And even pros will cede that the built-in flash of the Rebel T5i has some important uses as an adjunct to existing light, particularly to illuminate dark shadows using a technique called *fill flash*.

But electronic flash isn't as inherently easy to use as continuous lighting. As I noted earlier, electronic flash units are more expensive, don't show you exactly what the lighting effect will be (unless you use a second source called a *modeling light* for a preview), and the exposure of electronic flash units is more difficult to calculate accurately.

# Fire When Ready!

Once the capacitor is charged, the burst of light that produces the main exposure can be initiated by a signal from the T5i that commands the internal or connected flash units to fire. External strobes can be linked to the camera in several different ways:

■ **Camera mounted/hardwired external dedicated flash.** Units offered by Canon or other vendors that are compatible with Canon's lighting system can be clipped onto the accessory "hot" shoe on top of the camera or linked through a wired system such as the Canon Off Shoe Camera Cord OC-E3.

■ **Wireless dedicated flash.** A compatible unit can be triggered by signals produced by a pre-flash (before the main flash burst begins), which offers two-way communication between the camera and flash unit. The triggering flash can be the T5i's built-in unit, an external flash unit in Master mode, or a wireless non-flashing accessory, such as the Canon Speedlite Transmitter ST-E2 and new radio-controlled wireless trigger, the Speedlite Transmitter ST-E3-RT, which each do nothing but "talk" to the external flashes. You'll find more on this mode in Chapter 12.

■ **Wired, non-intelligent mode.** If you use a third-party adapter for the hot shoe that has a PC/X connector, you can connect non-dedicated flash units, including studio strobes, through a non-intelligent camera/flash link that sends just one piece of information, one way: it tells a connected flash to fire. There is no other exchange of information between the camera and flash. The PC/X adapter connector can be used to link the T5i to studio flash units, manual flash, flash units from other vendors that can use a PC cable, or even Canon-brand Speedlites that you elect to connect to the T5i in "unintelligent" mode.

■ **Infrared/radio transmitter/receivers.** Another way to link flash units to the T5i is through third-party wireless infrared or radio *transmitters*, like a Pocket Wizard, Radio Popper, or the Paul C. Buff CyberSync trigger shown in Figure 11.7. These are generally mounted on the accessory shoe of the camera, and emit a signal when the T5i sends a command to fire through the hot shoe. The simplest of these function as a wireless PC/X connector, with no other communication between the camera and flash (other than the instruction to fire). However, sophisticated units have their own built-in controls and can send additional commands to the receivers when connected to compatible flash units. I use one to adjust the power output of my Alien Bees studio flash from the camera, without the need to walk over to the flash itself.

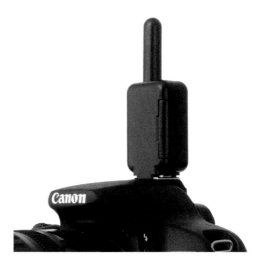

**Figure 11.7** A wireless trigger can command external flash units to fire.

■ **Simple slave connection.** In the days before intelligent wireless communication, the most common way to trigger off-camera, non-wired flash units was through a *slave* unit. These can be small external triggers connected to the remote flash (or built into the flash itself), and set off when the slave's optical sensor detects a burst initiated by the camera itself. When it "sees" the main flash (from the T5i's built-in flash, or another flash), the slave flash units are triggered quickly enough to contribute to the same exposure. The main problem with this type of connection—other than the lack of any intelligent communication between the camera and flash—is that the slave may be fooled by any pre-flashes that are emitted by the other strobes, and fire too soon. Modern slave triggers have a special "digital" mode that ignores the pre-flash and fires only from the main flash burst.

# How Electronic Flash Works

The bursts of light we call electronic flash are produced by a flash of photons generated by an electrical charge that is accumulated in a component called a *capacitor* and then directed through a glass tube containing xenon gas, which absorbs the energy and emits the brief flash. For the pop-up flash built into the Rebel T5i, the full burst of light lasts about 1/1,000th of a second and provides enough illumination to shoot a subject 10 feet away at f/4 using the ISO 100 setting. In a more typical situation, you'd use ISO 200, f/5.6 to f/8 and photograph something 8 to 10 feet away. As you can see, the built-in flash is somewhat limited in range; you'll see why external flash units are often a good idea later in this chapter.

An electronic flash (whether built in or connected to the Rebel T5i through an adapter's PC terminal or a cable plugged into a hot shoe adapter) is triggered at the instant of exposure, during a period when the sensor is fully exposed by the shutter. As I mentioned earlier in this book, the T5i has a vertically traveling shutter that consists of two curtains. The first curtain opens and moves to the opposite side of the frame, at which point the shutter is completely open. The flash can be triggered at this point (so-called *1st curtain sync*), making the flash exposure. Then, after a delay that can vary from 30 seconds to 1/200th second (with the Rebel T5i; other cameras may sync at a faster or slower speed), a second curtain begins moving across the sensor plane, covering up the sensor again. If the flash is triggered just before the second curtain starts to close, then *2nd curtain sync* is used. In both cases, though, a shutter speed of 1/200th second is the maximum that can be used to take a photo.

Figure 11.8 illustrates how this works. At upper left, you can see a fanciful illustration of a generic shutter (your Rebel T5i's shutter does *not* look like this), with both curtains tightly closed. At upper right, the first curtain begins to move downward, starting to expose a narrow slit that reveals the sensor behind the shutter. At lower left, the first curtain moves downward farther until, as you can see at lower right in the figure, the sensor is fully exposed.

## Ghost Images

The difference between triggering the flash when the shutter just opens, or just when it begins to close might not seem like much. But whether you use 1st curtain sync (the default setting) or 2nd curtain sync (an optional setting) can make a significant difference to your photograph *if the*

**Figure 11.8**
A focal plane shutter has two curtains, the upper, or front curtain, and a lower, second curtain.

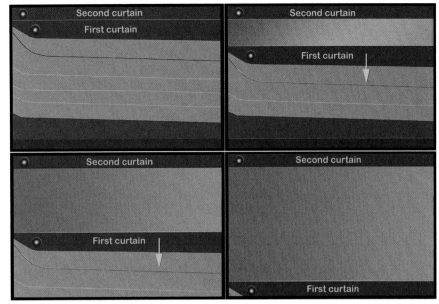

*ambient light in your scene also contributes to the image.* You can set either of these sync modes in the Shooting 1 menu, under Flash Control and the Built-in Flash Setting and External Flash Func. Setting options.

At faster shutter speeds, particularly 1/200th second, there isn't much time for the ambient light to register, unless it is very bright. It's likely that the electronic flash will provide almost all the illumination, so 1st curtain sync or 2nd curtain sync isn't very important. However, at slower shutter speeds, or with very bright ambient light levels, there is a significant difference, particularly if your subject is moving, or the camera isn't steady.

In any of those situations, the ambient light will register as a second image accompanying the flash exposure, and if there is movement (camera or subject), that additional image will not be in the same place as the flash exposure. It will show as a ghost image and, if the movement is significant enough, as a blurred ghost image trailing in front of or behind your subject in the direction of the movement.

As I noted, when you're using 1st curtain sync, the flash's main burst goes off the instant the shutter opens fully (a pre-flash used to measure exposure in auto flash modes fires *before* the shutter opens). This produces an image of the subject on the sensor. Then, the shutter remains open for an additional period (30 seconds to 1/200th second, as I said). If your subject is moving, say, toward the right side of the frame, the ghost image produced by the ambient light will produce a blur on the right side of the original subject image, making it look as if your sharp (flash-produced) image is chasing the ghost. For those of us who grew up with lightning-fast superheroes who always left a ghost trail *behind them*, that looks unnatural (see Figure 11.9).

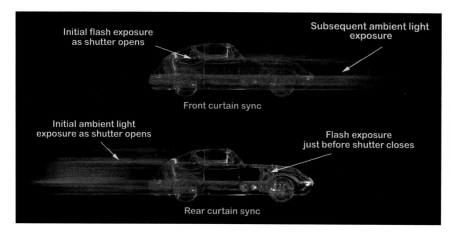

**Figure 11.9**
First curtain sync produces an image that trails in front of the flash exposure (top), whereas 2nd curtain sync creates a more "natural looking" trail behind the flash image.

So, Canon uses 2nd curtain sync to remedy the situation. In that mode, the shutter opens, as before. The shutter remains open for its designated duration, and the ghost image forms. If your subject moves from the left side of the frame to the right side, the ghost will move from left to right, too. *Then*, about 1.5 milliseconds before the second shutter curtain closes, the flash is triggered, producing a nice, sharp flash image *ahead* of the ghost image. Voilà! We have monsieur *Speed Racer* out-driving his own trailing image.

## Avoiding Sync Speed Problems

Using a shutter speed faster than 1/200th second can cause problems. Triggering the electronic flash only when the shutter is completely open makes a lot of sense if you think about what's going on. To obtain shutter speeds faster than 1/200th second, the T5i exposes only part of the sensor at one time, by starting the second curtain on its journey before the first curtain has completely opened, as shown in Figure 11.10. That effectively provides a briefer exposure as a slit, narrower than the full height of the sensor, passes over the surface of the sensor. If the flash were to fire during the time when the first and second curtains partially obscured the sensor, only the slit that was actually open would be exposed.

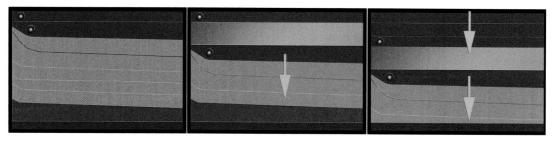

**Figure 11.10** A closed shutter (left); partially open shutter as the first curtain begins to move downward (middle); only part of the sensor is exposed as the slit moves (right).

You'd end up with only a narrow band, representing the portion of the sensor that was exposed when the picture is taken. For shutter speeds *faster* than 1/200th second, the second curtain begins moving *before* the first curtain reaches the bottom of the frame. As a result, a moving slit, the distance between the first and second curtains, exposes one portion of the sensor at a time as it moves from the top to the bottom. Figure 11.10 shows three views of our typical (but imaginary) focal plane shutter. At left is pictured the closed shutter; in the middle version you can see the first curtain has moved down about 1/4 of the distance from the top; and in the right-hand version, the second curtain has started to "chase" the first curtain across the frame toward the bottom.

If the flash is triggered while this slit is moving, only the exposed portion of the sensor will receive any illumination. You end up with a photo like the one shown in Figure 11.11. Note that a band across the bottom of the image is black. That's a shadow of the second shutter curtain, which had started to move when the flash was triggered. Sharp-eyed readers will wonder why the black band is at the *bottom* of the frame rather than at the top, where the second curtain begins its journey. The answer is simple: your lens flips the image upside down and forms it on the sensor in a reversed position. You never notice that, because the camera is smart enough to show you the pixels that make up your photo in their proper orientation. But this image flip is why, if your sensor gets dirty and you detect a spot of dust in the upper half of a test photo, if cleaning manually, you need to look for the speck in the *bottom* half of the sensor.

I generally end up with sync speed problems only when shooting in the studio, using studio flash units rather than my T5i's built-in flash or a Canon-dedicated Speedlite. That's because if you're using either type of "smart" flash, the camera knows that a strobe is attached, and remedies any unintentional goof in shutter speed settings. If you happen to set the T5i's shutter to a faster speed in Tv or M mode, the camera will automatically adjust the shutter speed down to 1/200th second. In Av, P, or any of the automatic modes, where the T5i selects the shutter speed, it will never choose a shutter speed higher than 1/200th second when using flash. In P mode, shutter speed is automatically set between 1/60th to 1/200th second when using flash.

**Figure 11.11**
If a shutter speed faster than 1/200th second is used, you can end up photographing only a portion of the image.

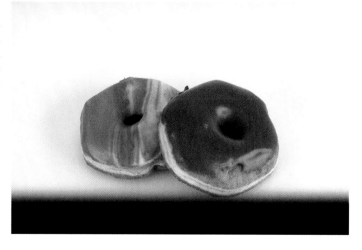

But when using a non-dedicated flash, such as a studio unit plugged into an adapter with a PC/X connector, the camera has no way of knowing that a flash is connected, so shutter speeds faster than 1/200th second can be set inadvertently. Note that the T5i can use a feature called *high-speed sync* that allows shutter speeds faster than 1/200th second with certain external dedicated Canon flash units. When using high-speed sync, the flash fires a continuous series of bursts at reduced power for the entire duration of the exposure, so that the illumination is able to expose the sensor as the slit moves. High-speed sync is set using the controls on the attached and powered-up compatible external flash.

# Determining Exposure

Calculating the proper exposure for an electronic flash photograph is a bit more complicated than determining the settings by continuous light. The right exposure isn't simply a function of how far away your subject is (which the T5i can figure out based on the autofocus distance that's locked in just prior to taking the picture). Various objects reflect more or less light at the same distance so, obviously, the camera needs to measure the amount of light reflected back and through the lens. Yet, as the flash itself isn't available for measuring until it's triggered, the T5i has nothing to measure.

The solution is to fire the flash twice. The initial shot is a pre-flash that can be analyzed, then followed by a main flash that's given exactly the calculated intensity needed to provide a correct exposure. As a result, the primary flash may be longer for distant objects and shorter for closer subjects, depending on the required intensity for exposure. This through-the-lens evaluative flash exposure system is called E-TTL II, and it operates whenever the pop-up internal flash is used, or you have attached a Canon dedicated flash unit to the T5i.

## Guide Numbers

Guide numbers, usually abbreviated GN, are a way of specifying the power of an electronic flash in a way that can be used to determine the right f/stop to use at a particular shooting distance and ISO setting. In fact, before automatic flash units became prevalent, the GN was actually used to do just that. A GN is usually given as a pair of numbers for both feet and meters that represent the range at ISO 100. For example, the Rebel T5i's built-in flash has a GN of 13/43 (meters/feet) at ISO 100. To calculate the right exposure at that ISO setting, you'd divide the guide number by the distance to arrive at the appropriate f/stop.

Using the T5i's built-in flash as an example, at ISO 100 with its GN of 43, if you wanted to shoot a subject at a distance of 10 feet, you'd use f/4.3 (43 divided by 10; round to f/4 for simplicity's sake). At 8 feet, an f/stop of f/5.3 (round up to f/5.6) would be used. Some quick mental calculations with the GN will give you any particular electronic flash's range. You can easily see that the built-in flash would begin to peter out at about 15 feet, where you'd need an aperture of roughly f/2.8 at ISO 100. Of course, in the real world you'd probably bump the sensitivity up to a setting of ISO 400 so you could use a more practical f/5.6 at that distance.

Today, guide numbers are most useful for comparing the power of various flash units. You don't need to be a math genius to see that an electronic flash with a GN of, say, 190 would be *a lot* more powerful than your built-in flash (at ISO 100, you could use f/13 instead of f/2.8 at 15 feet).

# Getting Started with the Built-in Flash

The Canon Rebel T5i's built-in flash is a handy accessory because it is available as required, without the need to carry an external flash around with you constantly. The next sections explain how to use the flip-up flash in the various Basic Zone and Creative Zone modes.

## Basic Zone Flash

When the T5i is set to one of the Basic Zone modes (except for Landscape, Sports, or Flash Off modes), the built-in flash will pop up when needed to provide extra illumination in low-light situations, or when your subject matter is backlit and could benefit from some fill flash. The flash doesn't pop up in Landscape mode because the flash doesn't have enough reach to have much effect for pictures of distant vistas in any case; nor does the flash pop up automatically in Sports mode, because you'll often want to use shutter speeds faster than 1/200th second and/or be shooting subjects that are out of flash range. Pop-up flash is disabled in Flash Off mode for obvious reasons.

If you happen to be shooting a landscape photo and do want to use flash (say, to add some illumination to a subject that's closer to the camera), or you want flash with your sports photos, or you *don't* want the flash popping up all the time when using one of the other Basic Zone modes, switch to an appropriate Creative Zone mode and use that instead.

## Creative Zone Flash

When you're using a Creative Zone mode, you'll have to judge for yourself when flash might be useful, and flip it up yourself by pressing the Flash button on the side of the pentamirror housing. The behavior of the internal flash varies, depending on which Creative Zone mode you're using.

- **P.** In this mode, the T5i fully automates the exposure process, giving you subtle fill flash effects in daylight, and fully illuminating your subject under dimmer lighting conditions. The camera selects a shutter speed from 1/60th to 1/200th second and sets an appropriate aperture.

- **Av.** In Aperture-priority mode, you set the aperture as always, and the T5i chooses a shutter speed from 30 seconds to 1/200th second. Use this mode with care, because if the camera detects a dark background, it will use the flash to expose the main subject in the foreground, and then leave the shutter open long enough to allow the background to be exposed correctly, too. If you're not using an image-stabilized lens, you can end up with blurry ghost images even of non-moving subjects at exposures longer than 1/30th second, and if your camera is not mounted on a tripod, you'll see these blurs at exposures longer than about 1/8th second even if you are using IS.

To disable use of a slow shutter speed with flash, access Flash Sync Speed in Av Mode in the Flash Control screen found in the Set-up 1 menu, and change from the default setting Auto to either 1/200-1/60sec. Auto or 1/200sec. (fixed), as described in Chapter 9.

- **Tv.** When using flash in Tv mode, you set the shutter speed from 30 seconds to 1/200th second, and the T5i will choose the correct aperture for the correct flash exposure. If you accidentally set the shutter speed higher than 1/200th second, the camera will reduce it to 1/200th second when you're using the flash.

- **M/B.** In Manual or Bulb exposure modes, you select both shutter speed (30 seconds to 1/200th second) and aperture. The camera will adjust the shutter speed to 1/200th second if you try to use a faster speed with the internal flash. The E-TTL II system will provide the correct amount of exposure for your main subject at the aperture you've chosen (if the subject is within the flash's range, of course). In Bulb mode, the shutter will remain open for as long as the release button on top of the camera is held down, or the release of your remote control is activated.

## Flash Range

The illumination of the Rebel T5i's built-in flash varies with distance, focal length, and ISO sensitivity setting.

- **Distance.** The farther away your subject is from the camera, the greater the light fall-off, thanks to the inverse square law discussed earlier. Keep in mind that a subject that's twice as far away receives only one-quarter as much light, which is two f/stops' worth.

- **Focal length.** The built-in flash "covers" only a limited angle of view, which doesn't change. So, when you're using a lens that is wider than the default focal length, the frame may not be covered fully, and you'll experience dark areas, especially in the corners. As you zoom in using longer focal lengths, some of the illumination is outside the area of view and is "wasted." (This phenomenon is why some external flash units, such as the 580EX II or 600EX-RT, "zoom" to match the zoom setting of your lens to concentrate the available flash burst onto the actual subject area.)

- **ISO setting.** The higher the ISO sensitivity, the more photons captured by the sensor. So, doubling the sensitivity from ISO 100 to 200 produces the same effect as, say, opening up your lens from f/8 to f/5.6.

## Red-Eye Reduction and Autofocus Assist

When Red-Eye Reduction is turned on in the Shooting 1 menu (as described in Chapter 8), and you are using flash with any shooting mode except for Flash Off, Landscape, Sports, or Movie, the red-eye reduction lamp on the front of the camera will illuminate for about 1.5 seconds when you press down the shutter release halfway, theoretically causing your subjects' irises to contract (if they are looking toward the camera), and thereby reducing the red-eye effect in your photograph. Red-eye effects are most frequent under low light conditions, when the pupils of your subjects' eyes open to admit more light, thus providing a larger "target" for your flash's illumination to bounce back from the retinas to the sensor.

Another phenomenon you'll encounter under low light levels may be difficulty in focusing. Canon's answer to that problem is an autofocus assist beam emitted by the T5i's built-in flash, or by any external dedicated flash unit that you may have attached to the camera (and switched on). In dim lighting conditions, the built-in flash will emit a burst of reduced-intensity flashes when you press the shutter release halfway, providing additional illumination for the autofocus system. Here are some things you need to know about the AF-assist beam:

- **Basic Zone activation.** When using a Basic Zone exposure mode other than Flash Off, Landscape, Sports, or Movie, if AF-assist is required, the T5i's built-in flash will pop up automatically.

- **Creative Zone activation.** If you're working with a Creative Zone exposure mode, you must pop up the built-in flash manually using the Flash button to enable AF-assist.

- **Focus mode.** The AF-assist beam will fire only if you are using One-Shot AF (single autofocus) or AI Focus AF (automatic autofocus). The beam is disabled if the camera is set to AI Servo AF (continuous autofocus) mode.

- **Distance.** The beam provides autofocus assistance only for subjects closer than roughly 13 feet from the camera. The illumination is too dim at great distances to improve autofocus performance. If you need more of an assist, an external flash such as the 580EX II and 600EX-RT can provide a focusing aid for subjects as far as 32.8 feet away.

- **Live View.** The AF-assist flash is disabled when using Live View's Live mode and Face Detection focusing modes, for both the built-in flash and external flash. However, if a Canon Speedlite with an LED light is used (such as the 580EX II or 600EX-RT), the beam will illuminate to provide autofocus assistance. The AF-assist beam functions normally when using Quick mode autofocus in Live View.

- **Enabling/Disabling AF-assist.** You can specify how the AF-assist beam is fired using C.Fn III-04, as described below.

## AF-Assist with Flash Disabled

You can still use the Autofocus Assist Beam function even when you don't want the flash to contribute to the exposure by disabling flash while enabling autofocus assist, using one of the Flash Control options in the Shooting 1 menu. Just follow these steps:

1. Press the MENU button and navigate to the Shooting 1 menu.

2. Use the cross keys to select the Flash Control entry.

3. Select Flash Firing, press SET, and choose Disable. That option disables both the built-in flash and any external dedicated flash you may have attached. However, the AF-assist beam will still fire as described earlier.

4. Press the MENU button twice to exit. (Or just tap the shutter release button.)

## Enabling/Disabling AF-Assist

Use C.Fn III-04 to choose whether the AF-assist beam is emitted by the built-in flash or the external Speedlite. You can disable the feature, activate it for both built-in flash and an external Speedlite, specify only external flash assist, or use only the infrared AF-assist beam included with some Canon flash units, such as the 580EX II and 600EX-RT. That option eliminates the obtrusive visible flashes, but still allows autofocus assistance using IR signals.

# Using FE Lock and Flash Exposure Compensation

If you want to lock flash exposure for a subject that is not centered in the frame, you can use the FE Lock button (*) to lock in a specific flash exposure. Just depress and hold the shutter button halfway to lock in focus, then center the viewfinder on the subject you want to correctly expose and press the * button. The pre-flash fires and calculates exposure, displaying the FEL (flash exposure lock) message in the viewfinder. Then, recompose your photo and press the shutter down the rest of the way to take the photo.

You can also manually add or subtract exposure to the flash exposure calculated by the T5i when using a Creative Zone mode. The easiest way is to use the Quick Control menu. Press the Q button and the screen shown in Figure 11.12 appears. Navigate to the flash exposure compensation box (it's highlighted in orange in the figure), and rotate the Main Dial to set flash compensation.

You can also specify flash compensation using the menus, which can be easy when working with the touch screen, even though there are a few extra steps. Just press the Choose the Flash Control entry in the Shooting 1 menu, then the Built-in Flash function setting, and choose Flash Exp. Comp. Then use the left/right cross keys or touch screen to enter flash exposure compensation plus or minus two f/stops. The exposure index scale on the LCD and in the viewfinder will indicate the change you've made, and a flash exposure compensation icon will appear to warn you that an adjustment has been made. As with non-flash exposure compensation, the compensation you make remains in effect for the pictures that follow, and even when you've turned the camera off,

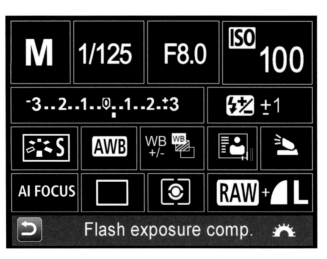

**Figure 11.12**
Set flash exposure compensation in the Quick Control screen.

remember to cancel the flash exposure compensation adjustment by reversing the steps used to set it when you're done using it.

A third way to access flash exposure compensation is to assign that feature to the SET button, using C.Fn IV-07, as described in Chapter 9. Thereafter, you can press the SET button when in Shooting mode, and rotate the Main Dial to adjust flash exposure compensation from the screen that pops up on the LCD. Flash exposure compensation can also be adjusted using the controls on your attached and active external flash unit. Those settings (any setting other than 0 dialed in with the external flash) will override any flash exposure compensation you've specified in the camera.

---

**Tip**

If you've enabled the Auto Lighting Optimizer in the Shooting 2 menu, as described in Chapter 8, it may cancel out any EV you've subtracted using flash exposure compensation. Disable the Auto Lighting Optimizer if you find your images are still too bright when using flash exposure compensation.

---

## More on Flash Control Settings

I introduced the Shooting 1 menu's Flash Control settings in Chapter 8. This next section offers additional information for using the Flash Control menu. The menu includes six options (see Figure 11.13): Flash Firing, E-TTL II Metering, Flash Sync in AV Mode, Built-in Flash Settings, External Flash Function Settings, and External Flash C.Fn Settings.

### Flash Firing

This menu entry has two options: Enable and Disable. It can be used to activate or deactivate the built-in electronic flash and any attached external electronic flash unit. When disabled, the flash

**Figure 11.13**
Six entries are available from the Flash Control menu.

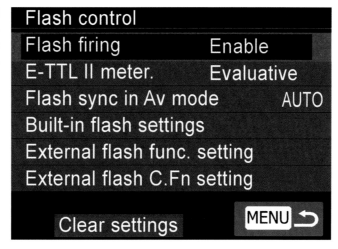

cannot fire even if you accidentally elevate it, or have an accessory flash attached and turned on. However, you should keep in mind that the AF-assist beam can still be used. If you want to disable that, too, you'll need to turn it off using C.Fn III-04. Disabling the flash here does so for all exposure modes, and so is a better choice than using the Basic Zone Flash Off setting of the Mode Dial.

Here are some applications where I always disable my flash and AF-assist beam, even though my T5i won't pop up the flash and fire without my intervention anyway. Some situations are too important to take chances. (Who knows, maybe I've accidentally set the Mode Dial to Creative Auto?)

- **Venues where flash is forbidden.** I've discovered that many No Photography signs actually mean "No Flash Photography," either because those who make the decisions feel that flash is distracting or they fear it may potentially damage works of art. Tourists may not understand the difference between flash and available light photography, or may be unable to set their camera to turn off the flash. One of the first phrases I learn in any foreign language is "Is it permitted to take photos if I do not use flash?" A polite request, while brandishing an advanced camera like the T5i (which may indicate you know what you are doing), can often result in permission to shoot away.

- **Venues where flash is ineffective anyway.** We've all seen the concert goers who stand up in the last row to shoot flash pictures from 100 yards away. I tend to not tell friends that their pictures are not going to come out, because they usually come back to me with a dismal, grainy shot (actually exposed by the dim available light) that they find satisfactory, just to prove I was wrong.

- **Venues where flash is annoying.** If I'm taking pictures in a situation where flash is permitted, but mostly supplies little more than visual pollution, I'll disable or avoid using it. Concerts or religious ceremonies may *allow* flash photography, but who needs to add to the blinding bursts when you have a camera that will take perfectly good pictures at ISO 3200? Of course, I invariably see one or two people flashing away at events where flash is not allowed, but that doesn't mean I am eager to join in the festivities.

## E-TTL II Metering

The second choice in the Flash Control menu allows you to choose the type of exposure metering the T5i uses for electronic flash. You can select the default Evaluative metering, which selectively interprets the 63 metering zones in the viewfinder to intelligently classify the scene for exposure purposes. Alternatively, you can select Average, which melds the information from all the zones together as an average exposure. You might find this mode useful for evenly lit scenes, but, in most cases, exposure won't be exactly right and you may need some flash exposure compensation adjustment.

## Flash Sync Speed in Av Mode

You can select the flash synchronization speed that will be used when working in Aperture-priority mode; choose from Auto (the T5i selects the shutter speed from 30 seconds to 1/200th second) to a range embracing only the speeds from 1/200th to 1/60th second, or fixed at 1/200th second.

Normally, in Aperture-priority mode when using flash, you specify the f/stop to be locked in. The exposure is then adjusted by varying the output of the electronic flash. Because the primary exposure comes from the flash, the main effects of the shutter speed selected is on the secondary exposure from the ambient light on the scene. Your choices include:

- **Auto.** This is your best choice under most conditions. The T5i will analyze your scene and choose a shutter speed that balances flash exposure and available light. For example, if the camera determines that a flash exposure requires an aperture of f/5.6, and then determines that the background illumination is intense enough to produce an exposure of 1/30th second at f/5.6, it might choose that slow shutter speed to provide a balanced exposure. As you might guess, the chief problem with Auto is that the T5i can choose a shutter speed that is slow enough to cause ghost images, as discussed earlier in this chapter. Don't use Auto if the ambient light is bright and your subject is far from the camera—that combination can lead to large f/stops and slow shutter speeds. (Use a tripod in such situations.) On the other hand, if your subject is fairly close to the camera—10 feet or closer—Auto will rarely get you into trouble. (See Figure 11.14.)

- **1/200-1/60 sec auto.** If you want to ensure that a slow shutter speed won't be used, activate this option, to lock out shutter speeds slower than 1/60th second.

- **1/200 sec (fixed).** This setting ensures that the T5i will always select 1/200th second. You'll end up with pitch-black backgrounds much of the time, but won't have to worry about ghost images.

**Figure 11.14**
At left, a shutter speed of 1/60th second was used, allowing ambient illumination to brighten the background. At right, a 1/200th second shutter speed produced a black background.

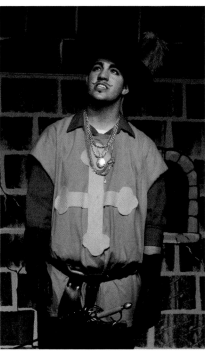
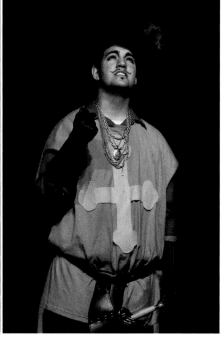

# Built-in Flash Settings

There are four main choices for this menu choice, which normally appears as shown in Figure 11.15. You cannot select Built-in Flash Settings if an external flash is attached to the accessory shoe. A message will pop up explaining that this menu option has been disabled.

However, that does not mean that you can't use an external flash; your add-on flash unit must be used off-camera and not attached to the T5i's accessory shoe. Indeed, this menu entry has additional settings that apply when using an off-camera wireless external flash, such as Channel (see Figure 11.16), which I'll address in the sections on external flash. Here's a quick summary of the main built-in flash selections, plus additional options that appear when you change the Built-in Flash setting to one of the two wireless flash modes. I'll explain each in more detail in the sections that follow this one, and in Chapter 12.

- **Built-in flash.** Your choices here are Normal Firing, Easy Wireless, and Custom Wireless. The first choice is used when you're working with the built-in flash only. Easy Wireless is a long-needed basic wireless flash shooting mode that allows you to quickly set up your T5i to trigger an external flash that is not physically wired to the camera. Custom Wireless is a more fully featured (and potentially fully confusing) wireless option that requires you to make key settings yourself. I'll explain wireless flash in more detail in Chapter 12.

- **Flash mode.** This entry is available only if you've selected Custom Wireless (above), and allows you to choose automatic exposure calculation (E-TTL II).

- **Shutter sync.** Available only in Normal Firing mode, you can choose 1st curtain sync, which fires the pre-flash used to calculate the exposure before the shutter opens, followed by the main flash as soon as the shutter is completely open. This is the default mode, and you'll generally perceive the pre-flash and main flash as a single burst. Alternatively, you can select 2nd curtain sync, which fires the pre-flash as soon as the shutter opens, and then triggers the main flash in a second burst at the end of the exposure, just before the shutter starts to close. (If the shutter

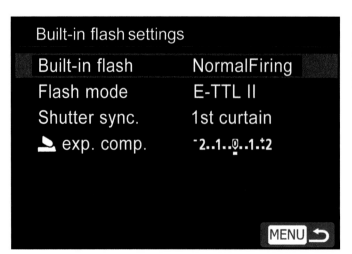

**Figure 11.15**

Four entries are available from the Built-in Flash Settings menu.

**Figure 11.16**
Choose Wireless Flash settings and additional options appear.

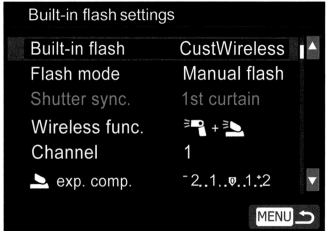

speed is slow enough, you may clearly see both the pre-flash and main flash as separate bursts of light.) This action allows photographing a blurred trail of light of moving objects with sharp flash exposures at the beginning and the end of the exposure. This type of flash exposure is slightly different from what some other cameras produce using 2nd curtain sync.

If you have an external compatible Speedlite attached, you can also choose High-speed sync, which allows you to use shutter speeds faster than 1/200th second, using the External Flash Function Setting menu.

- **Flash exposure compensation.** You can use the Quick Control screen (press the Q button) and enter flash exposure compensation. If you'd rather adjust flash exposure using a menu, you can do that here. Select this option with the SET button, then dial in the amount of flash EV compensation you want using the cross keys. The EV that was in place before you started to make your adjustment is shown as a blue indicator, so you can return to that value quickly. Press SET again to confirm your change, then press the MENU button twice to exit.

- **Wireless functions.** These choices appear when you've selected Custom Wireless, and include Mode, Channel, Firing Group, and other options used only when you're working in wireless mode to control an external flash. If you've disabled wireless functions, the other options don't appear on the menu. I'm going to leave the explanation of these options for Chapter 12, which is an entire chapter dedicated to using the Rebel T5i's wireless shooting capabilities, first introduced in the EOS 7D.

## Using Flash Mode

As I noted, Flash Mode is grayed out and unavailable when the T5i is set to Normal Firing or Easy Wireless. If you select Custom Wireless, you can select Flash Mode and choose one of two options: E-TTL II and Manual Flash.

## E-TTL II

You'll leave Flash Mode at this setting most of the time. In this mode, the camera fires a pre-flash prior to the exposure, and measures the amount of light reflected to calculate the proper settings. As noted earlier, when you've selected the E-TTL II Flash mode, you can also choose either Evaluative or Average metering methods. If you select Manual Flash or MULTI Flash (which are only available when using an external flash), that option is removed from the Built-in Flash Setting menu.

## Manual Flash

Use this setting when you want to specify exactly how much light is emitted by the flash units, and don't want the T5i's E-TTL II exposure system to calculate the f/stop for you. When you activate this option, the two flash exposure compensation entries are replaced by internal and external flash output scales (the built-in and external flash units are represented by icons). You can select from 1/4 to 1/128th power for the built-in flash, and 1/1 to 1/128th power for the external flash. A blue indicator appears under the previous setting, and a white indicator under your new setting, a reminder that you've chosen reduced power. Click on External flash func. setting, then click ETTL and select M or Multi with the cross keys.

Here are some situations where you might want to use manual flash settings:

- **Close-ups.** You're shooting macro photos and the E-TTL II exposure is not precisely what you'd like. You can dial in exposure compensation, or set the output manually. Close-up photos are problematic, because the power of the built-in flash may be too much (choose 1/128 power to minimize the output), or the reflected light may not be interpreted accurately by the through-the-lens metering system. Manual flash gives you greater control.

- **Fill flash.** Although E-TTL II can be used in full daylight to provide fill flash to brighten shadows, using manual flash allows you to tweak the amount of light being emitted in precise steps. Perhaps you want just a little more illumination in the shadows to retain a dramatic lighting effect without the dark portions losing all detail. Again, you can try using exposure compensation to make this adjustment, but I prefer to use manual flash settings. (See Figure 11.17.)

- **Action stopping.** The lower the power of the flash, the shorter the effective exposure. Use 1/128th power in a darkened room (so that there is no ambient light to contribute to the exposure and cause a "ghost" image, like that seen in Figure 11.18) and you can end up with a "shutter speed" that's the equivalent of 1/50,000th second! Of course, with such a minimal amount of flash power, you need to be very close to your subject.

# External Flash Function Setting

You can access this menu only when you have a compatible electronic flash attached and switched on. The settings available are shown in Figure 11.19.

- **Flash mode.** This entry allows you to set the flash mode for the external flash, from E-TTL II, Manual flash, and MULTI flash.

**Figure 11.17**
You can fine-tune fill illumination by adjusting the output of your camera's built-in flash manually.

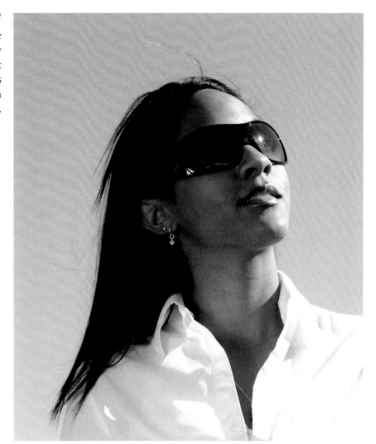

**Figure 11.18**
At 1/128th power, the duration of the flash is very brief, producing the same effect as a fast shutter speed.

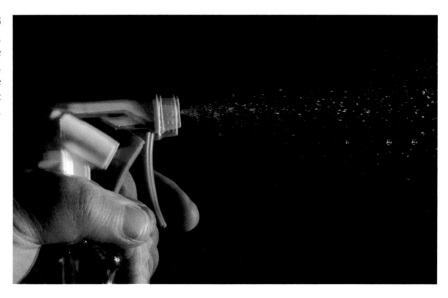

- **Wireless functions.** These functions are available when using wireless flash, and will be explained in Chapter 12. This setting allows you to enable or disable wireless functions. You can choose Wireless: Off, Wireless: On (Optical Transmission), or Wireless: On (Radio Transmission). The last choice is shown and available only when using a radio-capable triggering device or flash, such as the 600EX-RT.

- **Flash Zoom.** Some flash units can vary their coverage to better match the field of view of your lens at a particular focal length. You can allow the external flash to zoom automatically, based on information provided, or manually, using a zoom button on the flash itself. This setting is disabled when using a flash like the Canon 270EX II, which does not have zooming capability. You can select Auto, in which case the camera will tell the flash unit the focal length of the lens, or choose individual focal lengths including 24mm, 28mm, 35mm, 50mm, 70mm, 80mm, and 105mm. The 600EX-RT offers an additional setting of 200mm.

- **Shutter synchronization.** As with the T5i's internal flash, you can choose 1st curtain sync, which fires the flash as soon as the shutter is completely open (this is the default mode). Alternatively, you can select 2nd curtain sync, which fires the flash as soon as the shutter opens, and then triggers a second flash at the end of the exposure, just before the shutter starts to close. If a compatible Canon flash, such as the Speedlite 580EX II or 600EX-RT is attached and turned on, you can also select High-speed sync. and shoot using shutter speeds faster than 1/200th second. HSS does not work in wireless mode, as I'll explain in Chapter 12.

- **Flash exposure compensation.** You can add/subtract exposure compensation for the external flash unit, in a range of –2 to +2 EV. Dial in the amount of flash EV compensation you want using the cross keys. The EV that was in place before you started to make your adjustment is shown as a blue indicator, so you can return to that value quickly.

- **Flash exposure bracketing.** Flash Exposure Bracketing (FEB) operates similarly to ordinary exposure bracketing, providing a series of different exposures to improve your chances of getting the exact right exposure, or to provide alternative renditions for creative purposes.

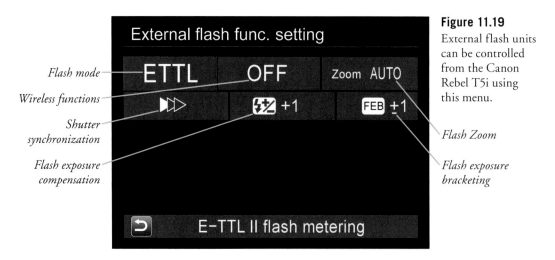

**Figure 11.19**
External flash units can be controlled from the Canon Rebel T5i using this menu.

If you enable wireless flash, additional options appear in this menu. I'll cover these in more detail in Chapter 12:

- **Channel.** All flashes used wirelessly can communicate on one of four channels. This setting allows you to choose which channel is used. Channels are especially helpful when you're working around other Canon photographers; each can select a different channel so one photographer's flash units don't trigger those of another photographer.

- **Master flash.** You can enable or disable use of the external flash as the master controller for the other wireless flashes. When set to enable, the attached external flash is used as the master; when disabled, the external flash becomes a slave unit triggered by the T5i's built-in flash.

- **Flash Firing Group.** Multiple flash units can be assigned to a group. This choice allows specifying which groups are triggered, A/B, A/B plus C, or All. The 600EX-RT offers additional groups when using radio control mode, Groups D and E.

- **A:B fire ratio.** If you select A/B or A/B plus C, this option appears, and allows you to set the proportionate outputs of Groups A and B, in ratios from 8:1 to 1:8 as explained in Chapter 12.

- **Group C exposure compensation.** If you select A/B plus C, this option appears, too, allowing you to set flash exposure compensation separately for Group C flashes.

## Learning about MULTI Flash

The MULTI flash setting makes it possible to shoot cool stroboscopic effects, with the flash firing several times in quick succession. You can use the capability to produce multiple images of moving objects, to trace movement (say, your golf swing). When you've activated MULTI flash, three parameters appear on the External Flash Function Setting menu, as shown in Figure 11.20.

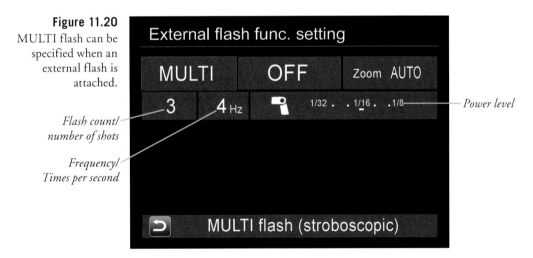

**Figure 11.20**
MULTI flash can be specified when an external flash is attached.

*Flash count/ number of shots*

*Frequency/ Times per second*

*Power level*

They include:

- **Frequency/Times per second.** This figure specifies the number of bursts per second. With the built-in flash, you can choose (theoretically) 1 to 199 bursts per second. The actual number of flashes produced will be determined by your flash count (which turns off the flash after the specified number of flashes), flash output (higher output levels will deplete the available energy in your flash unit), and your shutter speed.
- **Flash count/number of shots.** This setting determines the number of flashes in a given burst, and can be set from 1 to 50 flashes.
- **Power level.** Adjust the output of the flash for each burst, from 1/4 to 1/128th power.

These factors work together to determine the maximum number of flashes you can string together in a single shot. The exact number will vary, depending on your settings.

## High-Speed Sync

High-speed sync is a special mode that allows you to synchronize an *external* flash (but not the built-in flash) at all shutter speeds, rather than just 1/200th second and slower. The entire frame is illuminated by a series of continuous bursts as the shutter opening moves across the sensor plane, so you do *not* end up with a horizontal black band, as shown earlier in Figure 11.11.

HSS is especially useful in three situations, all related to problems associated with high ambient light levels:

- **Eliminate "ghosts" with moving images.** When shooting with flash, the primary source of illumination may be the flash itself. However, if there is enough available light, a secondary image may be recorded by that light (as described under "Ghost Images" earlier in this chapter). If your main subject is not moving, the secondary image may be acceptable or even desirable. Indeed, the T5i has a provision for slow sync in its Basic Mode Night Portrait setting that allows using a slow shutter speed to record the ambient light and help illuminate dark backgrounds. But if your subject is moving, the secondary image creates a ghost image.

  High-speed sync gives you the ability to use a higher shutter speed. If ambient light produces a ghost image at 1/200th second, upping the shutter speed to 1/500th or 1/1,000th second may eliminate it.

  Of course, HSS *reduces* the amount of light the flash produces. If your subject is not close to the camera, the waning illumination of the flash may force you to use a larger f/stop to capture the flash exposure. So, while shifting from 1/200th second at f/8 to 1/500th second at f/8 *will* reduce ghost images, if you switch to 1/500th second at f/5.6 (because the flash is effectively less intense), you'll end up with the same ambient light exposure. Still, it's worth a try.

- **Improved fill flash in daylight.** The T5i can use the built-in flash or an attached unit to fill in inky shadows—both automatically and using manually specified power ratios, as described earlier in this chapter. However, both methods force you to use a 1/200th second (or slower) shutter speed. That limitation can cause three complications.

First, in very bright surroundings, such as beach or snow scenes, it may be difficult to get the correct exposure at 1/200th second. You might have to use f/16 or a smaller f/stop to expose a given image, even at ISO 100. If you want to use a larger f/stop for selective focus, then you encounter the second problem—1/200th second won't allow apertures wider than f/8 or f/5.6 under many daylight conditions at ISO 100. (See the discussion of fill flash with Aperture-priority in the next bullet.)

Finally, if you're shooting action, you'll probably want a shutter speed faster than 1/200th second, if at all possible under the current lighting. That's because, in fill flash situations, the ambient light (often daylight) provides the primary source of illumination. For many sports and fast-moving subjects, 1/500th second, or faster, is desirable. HSS allows you to increase your shutter speed and still avail yourself of fill flash. This assumes that your subject is close enough to your camera that the fill flash has some effect; forget about using fill and HSS with subjects a dozen feet away or farther. The flash won't be powerful enough to have much effect on the shadows.

■ **When using fill flash with Aperture-priority.** The difficulties of using selective focus with fill flash, mentioned earlier, become particularly acute when you switch to Av exposure mode. Selecting f/5.6, f/4, or a wider aperture when using flash is guaranteed to create problems when photographing close-up subjects, particularly at ISO settings higher than ISO 100. If you own an external flash unit, HSS may be the solution you are looking for.

## ALL HSS, ALL THE TIME

If you are using a compatible flash unit, it's safe to enable high-speed sync *all the time.* That's because if you set the camera for 1/200th second or slower, the flash will fire normally at its set power output, just as if HSS were not enabled. But once you venture past 1/200th second to a faster shutter speed, the camera/flash combination is smart enough to use HSS. However, it's your responsibility to remember that you've enabled high-speed sync, and realize that as you increase the shutter speed, the effective range of the flash is reduced. At 1/1000th second, the 600EX-RT is "good" out to about two feet from the camera. (Remember, HSS does not work in wireless mode, so the flash must be attached to the camera's hot shoe.) At 1/8000th second, the flash will illuminate subjects no more than about one foot from the flash/camera.

To activate HSS using the 580EX II or 600EX-RT, just follow these steps:

1. **Attach the flash.** Mount/connect the external flash on the T5i, using the hot shoe or a cable. (HSS cannot be used in wireless mode, nor with a flash linked through an adapter that provides a PC/X terminal.)
2. **Power up.** Turn the flash and camera on.

3. **Select HSS in the camera.** Set the External Flash Function Setting in the camera to HSS as the T5i's sync mode.

    a.  Choose Flash Control in the Shooting 1 menu.

    b.  Select External Flash Func. Setting.

    c.  Navigate to the Shutter Sync. Entry, press SET, and choose High-Speed (at the far right of the list). Press SET again to confirm.

4. **Choose HSS on the flash.** Activate HSS (FP flash) on your attached external flash. With the 580EX II, press the High-speed sync button on the back of the flash unit (it's the second from the right under the LCD). (See Figure 11.21.) With the 600EX-RT, press Function Button 4 (Sync), located at the far right of the row of four buttons just under the LCD.

5. **Confirm HSS is active.** The HSS icon will be displayed on the flash unit's LCD (at the upper-left side with the 580EX II), and at bottom left in the T5i's viewfinder. If you choose a shutter speed of 1/200th second or slower, the indicator will not appear in the viewfinder, as HSS will not be used at slower speeds.

6. **View minimum/maximum shooting distance.** Choose a distance based on the maximum shown in the line at the bottom of the flash's LCD display (from 0.5 to 18 meters).

7. **Shoot.** Take the picture. To turn off HSS, press the button on the flash again. Remember that you can't use MULTI flash or Wireless flash when working with High-speed sync.

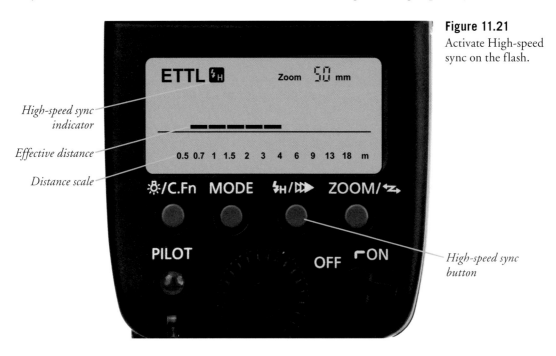

**Figure 11.21**
Activate High-speed sync on the flash.

*High-speed sync indicator*

*Effective distance*

*Distance scale*

*High-speed sync button*

## External Flash Custom Function Setting

Some external Speedlites from Canon include their own list of Custom Functions, which can be used to specify things like flash metering mode and flash bracketing sequences, as well as more sophisticated features, such as modeling light/flash (if available), use of external power sources (if attached), and functions of any slave unit attached to the external flash. This menu entry allows you to set an external flash unit's Custom Functions from your T5i's menu. The settings available in the T5i for the Speedlite 580EX II are shown later in the section that describes that flash.

## Clear External Flash Custom Function Setting

This entry allows you to zero-out any changes you've made to your external flash's Custom Functions, and return them to their factory default settings.

# Using External Electronic Flash

Canon offers a broad range of accessory electronic flash units for the Rebel T5i. They can be mounted to the flash accessory shoe, or used off-camera with a dedicated cord that plugs into the flash shoe to maintain full communications with the camera for all special features. (Non-dedicated flash units, such as studio flash, can be connected using a PC terminal adapter mounted in the accessory shoe.) They range from the Speedlite 600EX-RT and Speedlite 580EX II, which can correctly expose subjects up to 24 feet away at f/11 and ISO 200, to the 270EX, which is good out to 9 feet at f/11 and ISO 200. (You'll get greater ranges at even higher ISO settings, of course.) There are also two electronic flash units specifically for specialized close-up flash photography.

I power my Speedlites with Sanyo Eneloop AA nickel metal hydride batteries, seen in Figure 11.22. These are a special type of rechargeable battery with a feature that's ideal for electronic flash use.

**Figure 11.22**
Sanyo's Eneloop AA batteries are a perfect power source for Canon Speedlites.

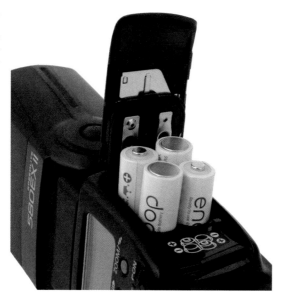

The Eneloop cells, unlike conventional batteries, don't self-discharge over relative short periods of time. Once charged, they can hold onto their juice for a year or more. That means you can stuff some of these into your Speedlite, along with a few spares in your camera bag, and not worry about whether the batteries have retained their power between uses. There's nothing worse than firing up your strobe after not using it for a month, and discovering that the batteries are dead.

## Speedlite 600EX-RT

This flagship of the Canon accessory flash line (and most expensive at about $550) is the most powerful unit the company offers, with a GN of 197, and a manual/automatic zoom flash head that covers the full frame of lenses from 24mm wide angle to 200mm telephoto. (There's a flip-down, wide-angle diffuser that spreads the flash to cover a 14mm lens's field of view, too.) All angle specifications given by Canon refer to full-frame sensors, but this flash unit automatically converts its field of view coverage to accommodate the crop factor of the Rebel T5i and the other 1.6X crop Canon dSLRs. The 600EX-RT shares its basic features with the 580EX II, described next, so I won't repeat them here, because the typical Rebel T5i owner is more likely to own one of the less expensive Speedlites.

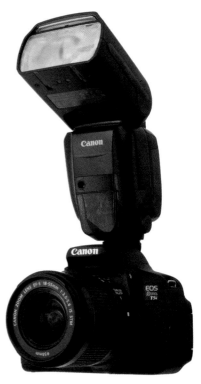

The killer feature of this unit (see Figure 11.23) is the new wireless two-way radio communication between the camera and this flash (or ST-E3-RT wireless controller and the flash) at distances of up to 98 feet. You can link up to 15 different flash units with radio control, using *five* groups (A, B, C, D, and E), and no line-of-sight connection is needed. (You can hide the flash under a desk or in a potted plant.) With the latest Canon cameras having a revised "intelligent" hot shoe (which includes the T5i), a second 600EX-RT can be used to trigger a *camera* that also has a 600EX-RT mounted, from a remote location. That means you can set up multiple cameras equipped with multiple flash units to all fire simultaneously! For example, if you were shooting a wedding, you could photograph the bridal couple from two different angles, with the second camera set up on a tripod, say, behind the altar. A pro

**Figure 11.23** The Canon Speedlite 580EX II is the second-most powerful shoe-mount flash Canon offers.

---

### 600EX (NON-RADIO)

If you see references to a 600EX model (non-RT), you'll find that a version with the radio control crippled is sold only outside the USA in countries where obtaining permission to use the relevant radio spectrum is problematic.

shooter might find the T5i to be an excellent, affordable second (or third) camera to use in such situations.

The 600EX-RT maintains backward compatibility with optical transmission used by earlier cameras. However, it's a bit pricey for the average EOS T5i owner, who is unlikely to be able to take advantage of all its features. If you're looking for a high-end flash unit and don't need radio control, I still recommend the Speedlite 580EX II (described next), which remains in the line.

Remember that with the 600EX-RT, you can't use radio control and some other features unless you own at least *two* of these Speedlites, or one 600EX-RT plus the ST-E3-RT, which costs half as much. Radio control is possible only between a camera that has a 600EX-RT or ST-E3-RT in the hot shoe, and an additional 600EX-RT flash or ST-E3-RT.

Some 18 Custom Functions of the 600EX-RT can be set using the T5i's External Flash C.Fn Setting menu. Additional Personal Functions can be specified on the flash itself. The T5i-friendly functions include:

**C.Fn-00**  Distance indicator display (Meters/Feet)

**C.Fn-01**  Auto power off (Enabled/Disabled)

**C.Fn-02**  Modeling flash (Enabled-DOF preview button/Enabled-test firing button/Enabled-both buttons/Disabled)

**C.Fn-03**  FEB Flash exposure bracketing auto cancel (Enabled/Disabled)

**C.Fn-04**  FEB Flash exposure bracketing Sequence (Metered > Decreased > Increased Exposure/Decreased > Metered > Increased Exposure)

**C.Fn-05**  Flash metering mode (E-TTL II-E-TTL/TTL/External metering: Auto/External metering: Manual

**C.Fn-06**  Quickflash with continuous shot (Disabled/Enabled)

**C.Fn-07**  Test firing with autoflash (1/32/Full power)

**C.Fn-08**  AF-assist beam firing (Enabled/Disabled)

**C.Fn-09**  Auto zoom adjusted for image/sensor size (Enabled/Disabled)

**C.Fn-10**  Slave auto power off timer (60 minutes/10 minutes)

**C.Fn-11**  Cancellation of slave unit auto power off by master unit (Within 8 Hours/Within 1 Hour)

**C.Fn-12**  Flash recycling on external power (Use internal and external power/Use only external power)

**C.Fn-13**  Flash exposure metering setting button (Speedlite button and dial/Speedlite dial only)

**C.Fn-20**  Beep (Enable/Disable)

**C.Fn-21**  Light Distribution (Standard, Guide Number Priority, Even Coverage)

**C.Fn-22**  LCD panel illumination (On for 12 seconds, Disable, Always On)

**C.Fn-23**  Slave Flash Battery Check (AF-assist beam/Flash Lamp, Flash Lamp only)

The Personal Functions available include the following. Note that you can set the LCD panel color to differentiate at a glance whether a given flash is functioning in Master or Slave mode.

**P.Fn-01**    LCD panel display contrast (Five levels of contrast)

**P.Fn-02**    LCD panel illumination color: Normal (Green, Orange)

**P.Fn-03**    LCD panel illumination color: Master (Green, Orange)

**P.Fn-04**    LCD panel illumination color: Slave (Green, Orange)

**P.Fn-05**    Color filter auto detection (Auto, Disable)

**P.Fn-06**    Wireless button toggle sequence (Normal>Radio>Optical, Normal< >Radio, Normal< >Optical)

**P.Fn-07**    Flash firing during linked shooting (Disabled, Enabled)

# Speedlite 580EX II

This deposed flagship of the Canon accessory flash line (and still reasonably priced compared to the 600EX-RT) is the second-most powerful unit the company offers, with a GN of 190, and a manual/automatic zoom flash head that covers the full frame of lenses from 24mm wide angle to 105mm telephoto, as well as 14mm optics with a flip-down diffuser

Like the 600EX-RT, this unit offers full-swivel, 180 degrees in either direction, and has its own built-in AF-assist beam and an exposure system that's compatible with the nine focus points of the T5i. Powered by economical AA-size batteries, the unit recycles in 0.1 to 6 seconds, and can squeeze 100 to 700 flashes from a set of alkaline batteries.

The 580EX II automatically communicates white balance information to your camera, allowing it to adjust WB to match the flash output. You can even simulate a modeling light effect: When you press the depth-of-field preview button on the T5i, the 580EX II emits a one-second burst of light that allows you to judge the flash effect. If you're using multiple flash units with Canon's wireless E-TTL system, this model can serve as a master flash that controls the slave units you've set up (more about this later) or function as a slave itself.

It's easy to access all the features of this unit, because it has a large backlit LCD panel on the back that provides information about all flash settings. There are 14 Custom Functions that can be controlled from the flash, numbered from 00 to 13. These functions are (the first setting is the default value):

**C.Fn-00**    Distance indicator display (Meters/Feet)

**C.Fn-01**    Auto power off (Enabled/Disabled)

**C.Fn-02**    Modeling flash (Enabled, -DOF preview button/Enabled, -test firing button/ Enabled, -both buttons/Disabled)

**C.Fn-03**    FEB Flash exposure bracketing auto cancel (Enabled/Disabled)

**C.Fn-04**  FEB Flash exposure bracketing sequence (Metered > Decreased > Increased Exposure/Decreased > Metered > Increased Exposure)

**C.Fn-05**  Flash metering mode (E-TTL II-E-TTL/TTL/External metering: Auto/External metering: Manual)

**C.Fn-06**  Quickflash with continuous shot (Disabled/Enabled)

**C.Fn-07**  Test firing with autoflash (1/32/Full power)

**C.Fn-08**  AF-assist beam firing (Enabled/Disabled)

**C.Fn-09**  Auto zoom adjusted for image/sensor size (Enabled/Disabled)

**C.Fn-10**  Slave auto power off timer (60 minutes/10 minutes)

**C.Fn-11**  Cancellation of slave unit auto power off by master unit (Within 8 Hours/Within 1 Hour)

**C.Fn-12**  Flash recycling on external power (Use internal and external power/Use only external power)

**C.Fn-13**  Flash exposure metering setting button (Speedlite button and dial/Speedlite dial only)

# Speedlite 430EX II

This less pricey electronic flash (available for less than $300) has automatic and manual zoom coverage from 24mm to 105mm, and the same wide-angle pullout panel found on the 580EX II that covers the area of a 14mm lens on a full-frame camera, and automatic conversion to the cropped frame area of the 5D Mark III and other 1.6X crop Canon dSLRs. The 430EX II also communicates white balance information with the camera, and has its own AF-assist beam. Compatible with Canon's wireless E-TTL system, it makes a good slave unit, but cannot serve as a master flash. It, too, uses AA batteries, and offers recycle times of 0.1 to 3.7 seconds for 200 to 1,400 flashes, depending on subject distance.

The Canon Speedlite 430EX II offers a sophisticated set of features, including an LCD panel that allows you to navigate the unit's menu and view its status. These features, along with powerful output and automatic zoom means this unit has more in common with Canon's high-end Speedlites than it does with the 320EX or the 270EX II. The Speedlite 430EX II is compatible with E-TTL II and earlier flash technologies. It can serve as a slave unit in an optical wireless configuration. The Speedlite 430EX II has a Guide Number of 43/141 (meters/feet) at ISO 100, at 105mm focal length.

This is another aging unit, dating from mid-2008, and possibly due for replacement. It's a bit more powerful than the just-introduced Speedlite 320EX (described next), which is roughly in the same price range. So, I'm guessing that there will be a slightly more powerful 400-series Speedlite unveiled in the near future with a roughly $325 price point.

# Speedlite 320EX

One of two new flash units (with the Speedlite 270EX II, described next) introduced early in 2011, this $249 flash has a GN of 105. Lightweight and more pocket-sized than the 430EX II or 580EX II, this bounceable (both horizontally and vertically) flash has some interesting features, including a built-in LED video light that can be used for shooting movies with the T5i, or as a modeling light or even AF-assist beam when shooting with live view. Canon says that this efficient LED light can provide up to four hours of illumination with a set of AA batteries. It can be used as a wireless slave unit, and has a new flash release function that allows the shutter to be triggered remotely with a two-second delay.

# Speedlite 270EX II

The Canon Speedlite 270EX II is designed to work with compatible EOS cameras utilizing E-TTL II and E-TTL automatic flash technologies. This flash unit is entirely controlled from the camera, making it as simple to use as a built-in flash. Its options can be selected and set via the camera's menu system. The 270EX II can also be used as an off-camera slave unit when controlled by a master Speedlite, transmitter unit, or a camera with an integrated Speedlite transmitter. One interesting feature of this unit is that it is also a remote control transmitter, allowing you to wirelessly release the shutter on cameras compatible with certain remote controller units. The Speedlite 270EX II has a Guide Number of 27/89 (meters/feet) at ISO 100, with the flash head pulled forward.

This $170 ultra-compact unit is Canon's entry-level Speedlite, and suitable for 5D Mark III owners who want a simple strobe for occasional use, without sacrificing the ability to operate it as a wireless slave unit. With its modest guide number, it provides a little extra pop for fill flash applications. It has vertical bounce capabilities of up to 90 degrees, and can be switched between Tele modes to Normal (28mm full-frame coverage) at a reduced guide number of 72.

The 270EX II functions as a wireless slave unit triggered by any Canon EOS unit or flash (such as the 580EX II) with a Master function. It also has the new flash release function with a two-second delay that lets you reposition the flash. There's a built-in AF-assist beam, and this 5.5-ounce, 2.6 × 2.6 × 3–inch unit is powered by just two AA-size batteries.

# Ring Lites

Canon has offered two ring lites, the Macro Ring Lite MR-14EX, and Macro Twin Lite Ring Lite flash MT-24EX. As you might guess from their names, ring lites are especially suitable for close-up, or macro photography, because they provide a relatively shadowless illumination. It's always tricky photographing small subjects up close, because there often isn't room enough between the camera lens and the subject to position lights effectively. Ring lites, especially those with their own modeling lamps to help you visualize the illumination you're going to get, mount around the lens at the camera position, and help solve many close-up lighting problems.

But, in recent years, the ring lite has gone far beyond the macro realm and is now probably even more popular as a light source for fashion and glamour photography. The right ring lite, properly used, can provide killer illumination for glamour shots, while eliminating the need to move and reset lights for those shots that lend themselves to ring lite illumination. As you, the photographer, move around your subject, the ring lite moves with you.

One of the key drawbacks to ring lites (whether used for macro or glamour photography) is that they are somewhat bulky and clumsy to use (they must be fastened around the camera lens itself, or the photographer must position the ring lite, and then shoot "through" the opening or ring). That means that you might not be moving round your subject as much as you thought and will, instead, mount the ring lite and camera on a tripod, studio stand, or other support.

Another drawback is the cost. The MR-14EX and MR-24EX are priced in the $550 and $800 range, respectively. You have to be planning a *lot* of macro or fashion work to pay for one of those. Specialists take note. I tend to favor a third-party substitute, the Alien Bees ABR800 Ringflash, shown in Figure 11.24. It's priced at about $400, and, besides, it integrates very well with my other Alien Bees studio flash units.

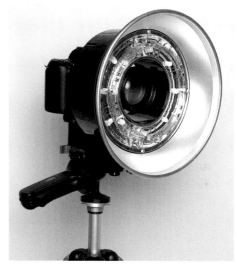

**Figure 11.24** This Alien Bees ringflash is a more economical alternative to Canon's own units.

## More Advanced Lighting Techniques

As you advance in your Canon Rebel T5i photography, you'll want to learn more sophisticated lighting techniques, using more than just straight-on flash, or using just a single flash unit. Check out *David Busch's Guide to Canon Flash Photography* if you want to delve further. I'm going to provide a quick introduction to some of the techniques you should be considering.

## Diffusing and Softening the Light

Direct light can be harsh and glaring, especially if you're using the flash built into your camera, or an auxiliary flash mounted in the hot shoe and pointed directly at your subject. The first thing you should do is stop using direct light (unless you're looking for a stark, contrasty appearance as a creative effect). There are a number of simple things you can do with both continuous and flash illumination.

- **Use window light.** Light coming in a window can be soft and flattering, and a good choice for human subjects. Move your subject close enough to the window that its light provides the primary source of illumination. You might want to turn off other lights in the room, particularly to avoid mixing daylight and incandescent light (see Figure 11.25).

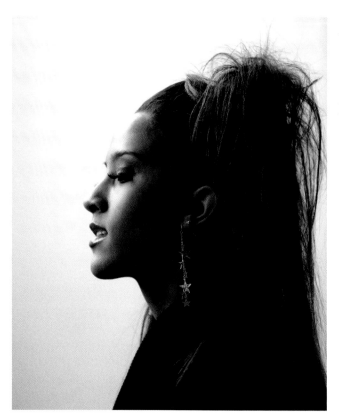

**Figure 11.25**
Window light makes
the perfect diffuse
illumination for
informal soft-focus
portraits like this
one.

- **Use fill light.** Your T5i's built-in flash makes a perfect fill-in light for the shadows, brightening inky depths with a kicker of illumination (see Figure 11.17, earlier in the chapter).

- **Bounce the light.** External electronic flash units mounted on the T5i usually have a swivel that allows them to be pointed up at a ceiling for a bounce light effect. You can also bounce the light off a wall. You'll want the surface to be white or have a neutral gray color to avoid a color cast.

- **Use reflectors.** Another way to bounce the light is to use reflectors or photo umbrellas that you can position yourself to provide a greater degree of control over the quantity and direction of the bounced light. Good reflectors can be pieces of foamboard, Mylar, or a reflective disk held in place by a clamp and stand. Although some expensive photo umbrellas and reflectors are available, spending a lot isn't necessary. A simple piece of white foamboard does the job beautifully. Umbrellas have the advantage of being compact and foldable, while providing a soft, even kind of light. They're relatively cheap, too, with a good 40-inch umbrella designed specifically for photographic applications available for as little as $20.

- **Use diffusers.** Sto-Fen and some other vendors offer clip-on diffusers like the one shown in Figures 11.26 (furnished with the 580EX II) and 11.27 (an aftermarket unit), that fit over your electronic flash head and provide a soft, flattering light. These add-ons are more portable than umbrellas and other reflectors, yet provide a nice diffuse lighting effect.

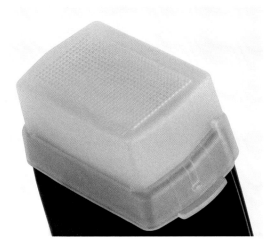

**Figure 11.26** The Sto-Fen OmniBounce is a clip-on diffuser that softens the light of an external flash unit.

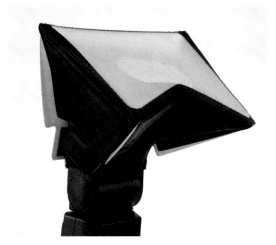

**Figure 11.27** Soft boxes use Velcro strips to attach them to third-party flash units (like the one shown) or any Canon external flash.

# Using Multiple Light Sources

Once you gain control over the qualities and effects you get with a single light source, you'll want to graduate to using multiple light sources. Using several lights allows you to shape and mold the illumination of your subjects to provide a variety of effects, from backlighting to side lighting to more formal portrait lighting. You can start simply with several incandescent light sources, bounced off umbrellas or reflectors that you construct. Or you can use more flexible multiple electronic flash setups.

Effective lighting is the one element that differentiates great photography from candid or snapshot shooting. Lighting can make a mundane subject look a little more glamorous. Make subjects appear to be soft when you want a soft look, or bright and sparkly when you want a vivid look, or strong and dramatic if that's what you desire. As you might guess, having control over your lighting means that you probably can't use the lights that are already in the room. You'll need separate, discrete lighting fixtures that can be moved, aimed, brightened, and dimmed on command.

Selecting your lighting gear will depend on the type of photography you do, and the budget you have to support it. It's entirely possible for a beginning T5i photographer to create a basic, inexpensive lighting system capable of delivering high-quality results for a few hundred dollars, just as you can spend megabucks ($1,000 and up) for a sophisticated lighting system.

## Basic Flash Setups

If you want to use multiple electronic flash units, the Canon Speedlites described earlier will serve admirably. The two higher-end models can be used with Canon's wireless E-TTL feature, which allows you to set up to three separate groups of flash units (several flashes can be included in each group) and trigger them using a master flash (such as the 580EX II) and the camera. Just set up one master unit (there's a switch on the unit's foot that sets it for master mode) and arrange the compatible slave units around your subject. You can set the relative power of each unit separately, thereby controlling how much of the scene's illumination comes from the main flash, and how much from the auxiliary flash units, which can be used as fill flash, background lights, or, if you're careful, to illuminate the hair of portrait subjects. You'll find more about wireless flash in Chapter 12.

## Studio Flash

If you're serious about using multiple flash units, a studio flash setup might be more practical. The traditional studio flash is a multi-part unit, consisting of a flash head that mounts on your light stand, and is tethered to an AC (or sometimes battery) power supply. A single power supply can feed two or more flash heads at a time, with separate control over the output of each head.

When they are operating off AC power, studio flash don't have to be frugal with the juice, and are often powerful enough to illuminate very large subjects or to supply lots and lots of light to smaller subjects. The output of such units is measured in watt seconds (ws), so you could purchase a 200ws, 400ws, or 800ws unit, and a power pack to match.

Their advantages include greater power output, much faster recycling, built-in modeling lamps, multiple power levels, and ruggedness that can stand up to transport, because many photographers pack up these kits and tote them around as location lighting rigs. Studio lighting kits can range in price from a few hundred dollars for a set of lights, stands, and reflectors, to thousands for a high-end lighting system complete with all the necessary accessories.

A more practical choice these days are *monolights* (see Figure 11.28), which are "all-in-one" studio lights that sell for about $200–$400. They have the flash tube, modeling light, and power supply

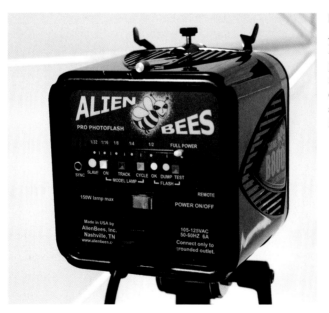

**Figure 11.28**

All-in-one "monolights" contain flash, power supply, and a modeling light in one compact package (umbrella not included).

built into a single unit that can be mounted on a light stand. Monolights are available in AC-only and battery-pack versions, although an external battery eliminates some of the advantages of having a flash with everything in one unit. They are very portable, because all you need is a case for the monolight itself, plus the stands and other accessories you want to carry along. Because these units are so popular with photographers who are not full-time professionals, the lower-cost monolights are often designed more for lighter duty than professional studio flash. That doesn't mean they aren't rugged; you'll just need to handle them with a little more care, and, perhaps, not expect them to be used eight hours a day for weeks on end. In most other respects, however, monolights are the equal of traditional studio flash units in terms of fast recycling, built-in modeling lamps, adjustable power, and so forth.

## Other Lighting Accessories

Once you start working with light, you'll find there are plenty of useful accessories that can help you. Here are some of the most popular that you might want to consider.

### Soft Boxes

Soft boxes are large square or rectangular devices that may resemble a square umbrella with a front cover, and produce a similar lighting effect. They can extend from a few feet square to massive boxes that stand five or six feet tall—virtually a wall of light. With a flash unit or two inside a soft box, you have a very large, semi-directional light source that's very diffuse and very flattering for portraiture and other people photography.

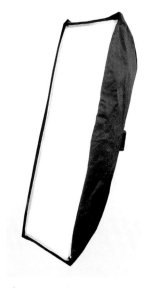

Soft boxes are also handy for photographing shiny objects. They not only provide a soft light, but if the box itself happens to reflect in the subject (say you're photographing a chromium toaster), the box will provide an interesting highlight that's indistinct and not distracting.

You can buy soft boxes (like the one shown in Figure 11.29) or make your own. Some lengths of friction-fit plastic pipe and a lot of muslin cut and sewed just so may be all that you need.

**Figure 11.29** Soft boxes provide an even, diffuse light source.

### Light Stands

Both electronic flash and incandescent lamps can benefit from light stands. These are lightweight, tripod-like devices (but without a swiveling or tilting head) that can be set on the floor, tabletops, or other elevated surfaces and positioned as needed. Light stands should be strong enough to support an external lighting unit, up to and including a relatively heavy flash with soft box or umbrella reflectors. You want the supports to be capable of raising the lights high enough to be effective. Look for light stands capable of extending six to seven feet high. The nine-foot units usually have larger, steadier bases, and extend high enough that you can use them as background supports. You'll be using these stands for a lifetime, so invest in good ones. I bought the light stand shown in Figure 11.30 when I was in college, and I have been using it for decades.

## Backgrounds

Backgrounds can be backdrops of cloth, sheets of muslin you've painted yourself using a sponge dipped in paint, rolls of seamless paper, or any other suitable surface your mind can dream up. Backgrounds provide a complementary and non-distracting area behind subjects (especially portraits) and can be lit separately to provide contrast and separation that outlines the subject, or which helps set a mood.

I like to use plain-colored backgrounds for portraits, and white seamless backgrounds for product photography. You can usually construct these yourself from cheap materials and tape them up on the wall behind your subject, or mount them on a pole stretched between a pair of light stands.

## Snoots and Barn Doors

These fit over the flash unit and direct the light at your subject. Snoots are excellent for converting a flash unit into a hair light, while barn doors give you enough control over the illumination by opening and closing their flaps that you can use another flash as a background light, with the capability of feathering the light exactly where you want it on the background. A barn door unit is shown in Figure 11.31.

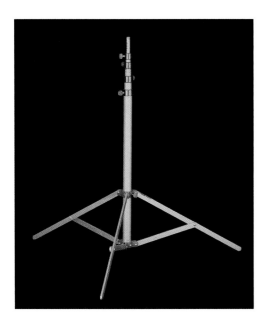

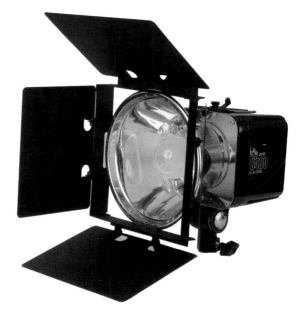

**Figure 11.30** Light stands can hold lights, umbrellas, backdrops, and other equipment.

**Figure 11.31** Barn doors allow you to modulate the light from a flash or lamp, and they are especially useful for hair lights and background lights.

# 12

# Working with Wireless Flash

As I mentioned in the last chapter, one of the chief objections to the use of electronic flash is the stark, flat look of direct/on-camera flash. But as flash wizard Joe McNally, author of *The Hotshoe Diaries*, has proven, small flash units can produce amazingly creative images when used properly.

The key to effective flash photography is to get the flash off the camera, so its illumination can be used to paint your subject in interesting and subtle ways from a variety of angles. But, sometimes, using a cable to liberate your flash from the accessory shoe isn't enough. Nor is the use of just a single electronic flash always the best solution. What we really have needed is a way to trigger one—or more—flash units wirelessly, giving us the freedom to place the electronic flash anywhere in the scene and, if our budgets and time allow, to work in this mode with multiple flashes.

## Wireless Evolution

For all Canon cameras prior to the introduction of the Canon EOS 7D (and that includes the Rebel T2i, the "grandparent" of the current T5i), wireless operation was an add-on option. The built-in flash of those earlier cameras was not capable of triggering any off-camera Canon Speedlite with full E-TTL exposure automation. (And, of course, cameras like EOS 5D Mark III, which do not have any built-in flash at all, were in the same boat.)

Because wireless triggering was not built into the camera itself, to control other flash units it was necessary to use either a Canon Speedlite Transmitter ST-E2 (a $250 accessory that uses hard-to-find and expensive 2CR5 batteries) or mount a "master" flash on the camera. Dedicating a flash meant sinking another $400 or more into a unit like the Speedlite 580EX II, or, more recently, a 600EX-RT (at a cost north of $500) to your camera just to trigger your wireless strobes. It was especially frustrating when you did not want to use the on-camera flash to contribute to the exposure. Your "triggering" device was invariably an expensive accessory. This, of course, led to the popularity of third-party triggers, like the Pocket Wizard and Radio Popper product lines.

The situation changed dramatically when the Canon EOS 7D was introduced as the first camera to offer built-in wireless triggering capabilities using the built-in flash. This feature was subsequently matched by the EOS 60D, T3i, T4i, the T5i, and other mid-level cameras that followed. Of course, while Canon shooters who owned cameras introduced *before* the 7D have long had access to wireless flash capabilities using add-ons, I was very pleased when Canon introduced the built-in wireless flash control through the pop-up flash. It's an improvement many photographers have welcomed. Any time a new feature eliminates the need to carry a costly accessory and its unusual batteries, the manufacturer has made life simpler and easier for the photographer.

It's not possible to cover every aspect of wireless flash in one chapter. There are too many permutations involved. For example, you can use the T5i's built-in flash, an external flash, or the ST-E2 optical transmitter (or ST-E3-RT radio transmitter) as the master. You may have one external "slave" flash, or use several. It's possible to control all your wireless flash units as if they were one multi-headed flash, or you can allocate them into "groups" that can be managed individually. You may select one of several "channels" to communicate with your strobes (or any of multiple wireless IDs when using radio controlled units like the 600EX-RT). These are all aspects that you'll want to explore as you become used to working with the T5i's amazing wireless capabilities.

What I hope to do in this chapter is provide the introduction to the basics that you won't find in the other guidebooks, so you can learn how to operate the T5i's wireless capabilities quickly, and then embark on your own exploration of the possibilities. Canon has taken a giant step forward by introducing the Easy Wireless feature in the T5i, making this "pro" feature more accessible to owners of a mid-entry-level camera like yours. You'll find more complete information in *David Busch's Guide to Canon Flash Photography*.

This chapter builds on the information in Chapter 11 and shows how to take advantage of the T5i's built-in wireless controller. While it may seem complicated at first, it really isn't. Learning the T5i's controls doesn't take a lot of effort, and once you get the hang of it, you'll be able to make changes quickly.

## YOUR STEPS MAY VARY

This chapter is intended to teach you the basics of wireless flash: why to use it, how the T5i or another dedicated flash can be used to trigger and control additional units, and what lighting ratios, channels, and groups are. I'm going to provide instructions on getting set up with wireless flash, but, depending on what flash unit you're working with (and how many you have), your specific steps may vary. The final authority on working with wireless flash has to be the manual furnished with your flash unit.

# Elements of Wireless Flash

Here are some of the key concepts to electronic flash and wireless flash that I'll be describing in this chapter. Learn what these are, and you'll have gone a long way toward understanding how to use wireless flash. You need to understand the various combinations of flashes that can be used, how they can be controlled individually and together, and why you might want to use multiple and off-camera flash units. I'm going to address all these points in this section.

## Flash Combinations

Your T5i has a built-in flash unit, which can be used alone, or in combination with other, external flash units. Here's a quick summary of the permutations available to you:

- **Built-in flash used alone.** Your built-in flash can function as the only flash illumination used to take a picture. In that mode, the flash can provide the primary illumination source (the traditional "flash photo") with the ambient light in the scene contributing little to the overall exposure. (See Figure 12.1, left.) Or, the built-in flash can be used in conjunction with the scene's natural illumination to provide a balanced lighting effect. (See Figure 12.1, center.) In this mode, the flash doesn't overpower the ambient light, but, instead, serves to supplement it. Finally, the built-in flash can be used as a "fill" light in scenes that are illuminated predominantly by a natural main light source, such as daylight. In this mode, the flash serves to brighten dark shadows created by the primary illumination, such as the glaring daylight in Figure 12.1, right. I covered the use of the pop-up flash alone in Chapter 11.

- **Built-in flash used simultaneously with off-camera flash.** You can use the off-camera flash as a *main light* and supply *fill light* from the built-in flash to produce interesting effects and pleasing portraits.

- **Built-in flash used as a trigger only for off-camera flash.** Use the T5i's built-in wireless flash controller to command single or multiple Speedlites for studio-like lighting effects, without having the pop-up flash contribute to the exposure itself.

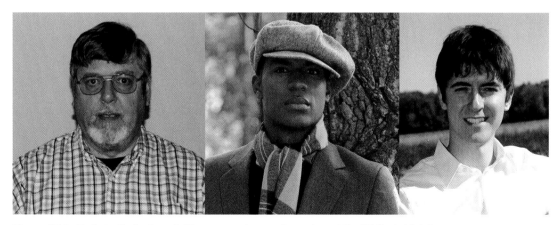

**Figure 12.1** Built-in flash alone (left), as a supplement (center), and for fill flash (right).

# Controlling Flash Units

There are multiple ways of controlling flash units, both through direct or wired connections and wirelessly. Here are the primary methods used:

- **Direct connection.** The built-in flash, of course, is directly connected to the T5i, and triggered electronically when a picture is taken. External flash units can also be controlled directly, either by plugging them into the accessory shoe on top of the camera, or by linking them to a camera with a dedicated flash cord that in turn attaches to the accessory hot shoe. When used in these modes, the camera has full communication with the flash, which can receive information about zoom lens position, correct exposure required, and the signals required to fire the flash. There also exist accessory shoe adapters that provide a PC/X connection, allowing non-dedicated strobes, such as studio flash units, to be fired by the camera. These connections are "dumb" and convey no information other than the signal to fire.

- **Dedicated wireless signals.** In this mode, external flash units communicate with the camera through a pre-flash, which is used to measure exposure prior to the "real" flash burst an instant later. The pre-flash can also wirelessly send information from the camera to the flash unit, used to adjust zoom head position (if the flash has that), and required flash duration to produce the desired exposure. In the case of Canon flash units, the pre-flash information is sent and received as pulses of illumination—much like the remote control of your television. (And, also like your TV remote, the optical signal can bounce around the room somewhat, but you more or less need a line-of-sight connection for the communication to work properly.)

- **Dedicated wireless infrared signals.** Some devices, such as the Canon ST-E2 Speedlite Transmitter, can communicate with dedicated flash units through their own infrared signals. The transmitter attaches to the accessory shoe or is connected to the accessory shoe through a dedicated cable. It was an option for wireless flash for Canon cameras prior to the EOS 7D (and later models with a built-in wireless controller), as well as for Canon cameras that have no flash unit at all (such as the EOS 1D, 1Ds, and 5D series). Although the ST-E2 costs about $350, it's still less expensive than using a unit like the 580EX II or 600EX-RT as a master controller, particularly when on-camera flash is not desired.

- **Canon and third-party IR and radio transmitters.** The 600EX-RT and ST-E3-RT units from Canon can communicate using radio signals as well as infrared. In addition, some excellent wireless flash controllers that use IR or radio signals to operate external flash units are available from sources like PocketWizard and RadioPopper. One advantage some of these third-party units have is the ability to dial in exposure/output adjustments from the transmitter mounted on the accessory shoe of the camera.

- **Optical slave units.** A relatively low-tech/low-versatility option is to use optical slave units that trigger the off-camera flash units when they detect the firing of the main flash. Slave triggers are inexpensive, but dumb: they don't allow making any adjustments to the external flash units, and are not compatible with the T5i's E-TTL II exposure system. Moreover, you should make sure that the slave trigger responds to the *main* flash burst only, rather than a pre-flash, using a so-called *digital* mode. Otherwise, your slave units will fire before the main flash, and not contribute to the exposure.

# Why Use Wireless Flash?

Canon's wireless flash system gives you a number of advantages that include the ability to use directional lighting, which can help bring out detail or emphasize certain aspects of the picture area. It also lets you operate multiple strobes; with the 580EX II that's as many as four flash units in each of three groups, or twelve in all (although most of us won't own 12 Canon Speedlites). With the 600EX-RT, which also has radio control in addition to optical transmission, you can control many more flash units optically, but only 15 radio-controlled Speedlites, in five different groups.

You can set up complicated portrait or location lighting configurations. Since the two top Canon Speedlites pump out a lot of light for a shoe mount flash, a set of these units can give you near studio-quality lighting. Of course, the cost of these high-end Speedlites approaches or exceeds that of some studio monolights—but the Canon battery-powered units are more portable and don't require an external AC or DC power source.

# Key Wireless Concepts

There are three key concepts you must understand before jumping into wireless flash photography: channels, groups, and flash ratios. Here is an explanation of each:

- **Channel controls.** Canon's wireless flash system offers users the ability to determine on which of four possible channels the flash units can communicate. (The pilots, ham radio operators, or scanner listeners among you can think of the channels as individual communications frequencies.) When using optical transmission, the channels are numbered 1, 2, 3, and 4, and each flash must be assigned to one of them. Moreover, in general, each of the flash units you are working with should be assigned to the *same* channel, because the slave Speedlites will respond *only* to a master flash that is on the same channel.

  When using the 600EX-RT in radio control mode, there are 15 different channels, plus an Auto setting that allows the flash to select a channel. In addition, you can assign a four-digit Wireless Radio ID that further differentiates the communications channel your flashes use.

  The channel ability is important when you're working around other photographers who are also using the same system. Photojournalists, including sports photographers, encounter this situation frequently. At any event populated by a sea of "white" lenses you'll often find photographers who are using Canon flash units triggered by Canon's own optical or (now) radio control. Third-party triggers from PocketWizard or RadioPopper are also popular, but Canon's technology remains a mainstay for many shooters.

  Each photographer sets flash units to a different channel so as to not accidentally trigger other users' strobes. (At big events with more than four photographers using Canon flash and optical transmission, you may need to negotiate.) I use this capability at workshops I conduct where we have two different setups. Photographers working with one setup use a different channel than those using the other setup, and can work independently even though we're at opposite ends of the same large room.

There is less chance of a channel conflict when working with radio control and all 600EX-RT flash units. With 15 channels to select from, and almost 10,000 wireless radio IDs to choose from, any overlap is unlikely. (It's smart not to use a radio ID like 0000, 1111, 2222, etc., to avoid increasing the chances of conflicts. I use the last four digits of my mother-in-law's Social Security Number.) Remember that you must use either all optical or all radio transmission for all your flash units; you can't mix and match.

- **Groups.** Canon's wireless flash system lets you designate multiple flash units in separate groups. There can be as many as three groups with the T5i's built-in controller and speedlites like the 580EX II, labeled A, B, and C.

  With the 600EX-RT and ST-E3-RT, up to five groups (A, B, C, D, and E) can be used with as many as 15 different flash units. All the flashes in all the groups use the exact same *channel* and all respond to the same master controller, but you can set the output levels of each group separately. So, Speedlites in Group A might serve as the main light, while Speedlites in Group B might be adjusted to produce less illumination and serve as a fill light. It's convenient to be able to adjust the output of all the units within a given group simultaneously. This lets you create different styles of lighting for portraits and other shots.

---

**TIP**

It's often smart to assign flash units that will reside to the left of the camera to the A group, and flashes that will be placed to the right of the camera to the B group. It's easier to adjust the compara-tive power ratios because you won't have to stop and think where your groups are located. That's because the adjustment controls in the *menus* are always arranged in the same A-B-C left-to-right alignment.

For example, if your A group is used as a main light on the left, and the B group as fill on the right, you intuitively know to specify more power to the A group, and less output to the B group. Reserve the C group (if used) to some other purpose, such as background or hair lights.

---

- **Flash ratios.** This ability to control the output of one flash (or set of flashes) compared to another flash or set allows you to produce lighting *ratios*. You can control the power of multiple off-camera Speedlites to adjust each unit's relative contribution to the image, for more dramatic portraits and other effects.

# Which Flashes Can Be Operated Wirelessly?

A particular Speedlite can have one of two functions. It can serve as a *master* flash that's capable of triggering other compatible Canon units that are on the same channel. Or, a Speedlite can be trig-gered wirelessly as a *slave unit* that's activated by a *master*, with full control over exposure through the T5i's eTTL flash system. The second function is easy: all current Canon shoe-mount flash, including the 600EX-RT, 580EX II, 430EX II, 320EX, and 270EX II can be triggered wirelessly. In addition, some Speedlites and the T5i's built-in flash have the ability to serve as a master flash.

I'm not going to discuss older, discontinued flash units in this chapter; if you own one, particularly a non-Canon unit, it may or may not function as a slave. For example, the early Speedlite 380EX lacked the wireless capabilities added with later models, such as the 420EX, 430EX, and 430EX II.

Here's a quick run-down of current flash capabilities:

- **Built-in flash.** The flash built into the Canon EOS T5i can serve as a master, triggering any of the other current flash units wirelessly. It shares that capability with the EOS 7D (which introduced wireless in-camera triggering to the Canon line), the T3i, T4i, and the Canon EOS 60D. At this writing, all other Canon cameras with a built-in flash, introduced *prior* to the T5i, can activate external flash units wirelessly *only* when physically connected to an external flash that has master capabilities, the Canon ST-E2/ST-E3-RT transmitter, or third-party transmitters. The Canon EOS Rebel SL1/100D is a newer camera that cannot function as a master flash. T5i's built-in flash (of course) cannot itself function as a slave unit. (It has no facility for receiving signals from a master flash.)

- **Canon Speedlite 600EX-RT.** This top of the line flash can function as a master flash when physically attached to any Canon EOS model, using either optical or radio transmission, and can be triggered wirelessly by another master flash (a 7D/60D/T3i/T4i/T5i camera, another 600EX-RT or 580EX II, or the ST-E2/ST-E3-RT transmitters).

- **Canon Speedlite 580EX II.** This flash can function as a master flash when physically attached to any Canon EOS model, and can be triggered wirelessly by an optical (not radio) transmission from another master flash (a 7D/60D/T3i/T4i/T5i camera, another 580EX II, a 600EX-RT, the ST-E2 transmitter, or ST-E3-RT transmitter in optical mode).

- **Canon Speedlite 430EX II.** This flash cannot function as a master, but can be triggered wirelessly by a master flash (a 7D/60D/T3i/T4i/T5i camera, a Speedlite 600EX-RT/580EX II, or the ST-E-2 and ST-E3-RT transmitters in optical mode).

- **Canon Speedlite 320EX.** This flash can be triggered wirelessly by a master flash (a 7D/60D/T3i/T4i/T5i camera, a 600EX-RT/580EX II, or the ST-E-2 and ST-E3-RT transmitters in optical mode).

- **Canon Speedlite 270EX II.** This flash can be triggered wirelessly by a master flash (a 7D/60D/T3i/T4i/T5i camera, a 600EX-RT/580EX II, or the ST-E-2 and ST-E3-RT transmitters in optical mode).

You can use any combination of compatible flash units in your wireless setup. The T5i can serve as the master, or you can use an attached 600EX-RT, 580EX II, or ST-E2/ST-E3-RT as a master, with any number of 600EX-RT, 580EX II, 430EX II, 320EX, or 270EX II units (or older compatible Speedlites not discussed in this chapter) as wireless slaves. I'll get you started assigning these flash to groups and channels later on.

# Getting Started

The EOS T5i has two wireless flash modes, Easy Wireless Flash Shooting and Custom Wireless Flash Shooting. Since it's necessary to set up both the camera and the strobes for wireless operation, this guide will help you with both, starting with prepping the camera and flash. To configure your equipment for wireless flash, just follow these steps. (I'm going to condense them a bit, because many of these settings have been introduced in previous chapters.)

We're going to begin by assuming that you want to use the T5i's built-in flash as the master controller flash. If that's the case, you need to follow these steps with your external flash units first:

1. **Set the wireless off-camera Speedlite to slave mode.** Any of the flash units listed earlier can be used as a slave flash. The first step is to set the off-camera flash to slave mode. The procedure differs for each individual flash model. Check your manual for exact instructions. I'll use the 580EX II as a typical example: Press the ZOOM button for two seconds until the display flashes, then rotate the control dial on the flash until the Slave indicator blinks on the LCD. Press the control dial's center button to confirm your choice.

2. **Assign a channel.** All units must use the same channel. The default channel is 1. If you need to change to a different communications channel, do so using the instructions for your particular flash unit. With the 580EX II, press the ZOOM button several times until the CH indicator flashes. Then rotate the control dial on the flash until the channel you want appears on the LCD. Press the control dial center button to confirm your choice.

3. **Assign slave to a group.** If you want to use a flash ratio to adjust the output of some slave units separately, you'll want to assign the slave flash to a group, either Group A (the default) or Group B. All units within a particular group fire at the same proportionate level. If you've set Group B to fire at half power, *all* the Speedlites that have been assigned to Group B will fire at half power.

   And remember that all flash units on a particular channel are controlled by the same master flash, regardless of the group they belong to. Set the group according to the instructions for your particular flash. For the 580EX II, press the ZOOM button until the A flashes on the LCD. Then rotate the control dial on the flash to choose B. Press the control dial center button to confirm your choice.

4. **Position the off-camera flash units, with the Speedlite's wireless sensor facing the camera/master flash.** Indoors, you can position the external flash up to 33 feet from the master unit; outdoors, keep the distance to 23 feet or less. Your ability to use a flash wirelessly can depend on whether the Speedlite's sensor can receive communication from the master flash. Factors can include the direction the slave flash is pointed, and whether light can bounce off walls or other surfaces to reach the sensor. When working with the 600EX-RT's radio controls, Canon guarantees "reception" up to 98 feet from the master flash/trigger, but many shooters report no problems at distances of 150 to 200 feet (and no line-of-sight required!)

# Easy Wireless Flash Shooting

Wireless flash is a breeze if you're using your camera's built-in flash as the master, and one external flash as the slave. Just follow these steps:

1. **Using the built-in flash as a wireless flash controller.** Start by using a Creative Zone mode and popping up the camera's built-in flash. You can use this flash in conjunction with your remote, off-camera strobes (adding some illumination to your photos), or just to control them (with no illumination from your pop-up flash contributing to the exposure). The built-in flash needs to be in the up position to use the T5i's wireless flash controller either way.

2. **Enable internal flash.** Press the MENU button and navigate to the Shooting 1 menu. Choose the Flash Control entry, as described in Chapter 11, and press the SET button. This brings up the Flash Control menu (which is at the bottom of the menu). Press the SET button to enter the Flash Control menu. Next, select the Flash Firing setting and set the camera to Enable. This activates the built-in flash, which makes wireless flash control with the T5i possible. (See Figure 12.2.)

3. **Confirm/Enable E-TTL II exposure.** Although you can use wireless flash techniques and manual flash exposure, you're better off learning to use wireless features with the EOS T5i set to automatic exposure. So, from the Flash Control menu, choose E-TTL II metering and select Evaluative exposure.

4. **Enable wireless functions.** Next, choose Built-in Flash Settings and select EasyWireless from the Built-in Flash entry. Press MENU to exit.

5. **Choose a channel.** Scroll down to Channel, press SET, and select the channel you want to use (generally that will be Channel 1). Press MENU to exit. The flash will emit a blinking red signal when it is set and waiting for the camera to trigger it.

6. **Take photos.** You're all set! You can now take photos wirelessly.

7. **Exit wireless mode.** When you're finished using wireless flash, navigate to the Built-in Flash setting in the Flash Control menu and select NormalFiring. Wireless flash is deactivated.

**Figure 12.2**
Enable the built-in flash.

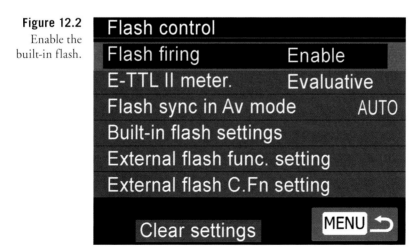

If you want to use more than one slave unit, follow these instructions. All additional units using the same communications channel will fire at once, regardless of the slave ID (Group) assignment.

## Custom Wireless Flash Shooting

The procedures for using this mode are basically the same as for Easy Wireless Flash shooting, except that you have more options for adjusting things like flash ratios. Just follow these steps:

1. **Using the built-in flash as a wireless flash controller.** Start by using a Creative Zone mode and popping up the camera's built-in flash. You can use this flash in conjunction with your remote, off-camera strobes (adding some illumination to your photos), or just to control them (with no illumination from your pop-up flash contributing to the exposure). The built-in flash needs to be in the up position to use the T5i's wireless flash controller either way.

2. **Enable internal flash.** Press the MENU button and navigate to the Shooting 1 menu. Choose the Flash Control entry, as described in Chapter 11, and press the SET button. This brings up the Flash Control menu (which is at the bottom of the menu). Press the SET button to enter the Flash Control menu. Next, select the Flash Firing setting and set the camera to Enable. This activates the built-in flash, which makes wireless flash control with the T5i possible.

3. **Confirm/Enable E-TTL II exposure.** As with EasyWireless, while you can use wireless flash techniques and manual flash exposure, you're better off learning to use wireless features with the EOS T5i set to automatic exposure. So, from the Flash Control menu, choose E-TTL II metering and select Evaluative exposure.

4. **Enable wireless functions.** Next, choose Built-in Flash Settings and select CustWireless from the Built-in Flash entry. Press SET to confirm and return to the Built-in Flash Settings menu.

5. **Access wireless configuration.** In the Built-in Flash Setting menu, scroll down to Wireless Func. (see Figure 12.3) and press SET.

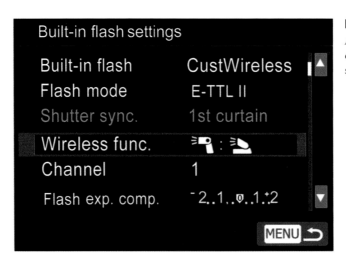

**Figure 12.3**
Access the wireless configuration screen.

6. **Select wireless configuration.** Choose the External Flash:Built-in Flash icon at the top of the list of choices (see Figure 12.4). Press SET to confirm. The colon between the two flash icons indicates that in this mode you can set a flash *ratio* between the units.

7. **Choose a channel.** Scroll down to Channel, press SET, and select the channel you want to use (generally that will be Channel 1).

8. **Set flash ratio.** Scroll down to the Ratio Setting entry (it's directly under the Flash Exp. Comp entry) and set a flash ratio between 1:1 (equal output) and 8:1 (external flash 8X the output of the internal flash, or, three stops). Ratios where the internal flash is *more* powerful than the external flash (i.e., 1:2, 1:4, etc.) are not possible.

9. **Take photos.** You're all set! You can now take photos wirelessly.

10. **Exit wireless mode.** When you're finished using wireless flash, navigate to the Built-in Flash Settings in the Flash Control menu and select NormalFiring. Wireless flash is deactivated.

**Figure 12.4**
Choose the Ratio (External Flash:Internal Flash) configuration.

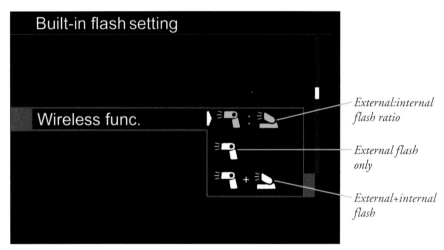

Once you've completed the steps above, your T5i is set up to begin using wireless flash using your camera's built-in flash and one external off-camera flash. Additional options are available for the brave. I'll show you each of these one at a time.

## WIRELESS SETTING FOR EXTERNAL FLASH

As noted, you must switch your external flash from normal to wireless modes. The procedure will vary, depending on your flash unit. With the 580EX II, press and hold the ZOOM button for two seconds or longer until the display blinks. Then rotate the flash's control dial until either Master or Slave appears on the flash's LCD. Press the dial's center button to confirm your choice of Master or Slave wireless operation.

**REMINDER**

Keep in mind that when the Canon Speedlite 580EX II and most other Canon units are ready to fire as a slave, the AF-assist beam will blink at one-second intervals. The unit will *not* go into a sleep mode while it is waiting to be used as a slave, but the camera will shut off at the interval you've specified in the menus.

# Setting Up an External Master Flash or Controller

The first step in using an external flash or controller as the master (instead of the built-in flash) is to set up one unit (either a flash or controller) as the external *master*. You can mount a Speedlite 580EX, 580EX II, or 600EX-RT to your camera, which can serve as the master unit, transmitting E-TTL II optical signals to one or more off-camera Speedlite *slave* units. The master unit can have its flash output set to "off" so that it controls the remote units without contributing any flash output of its own to the exposure. This is useful for images where you don't want noticeable flash illumination coming in from the camera position. The next sections explain your options for setting up a master unit for fully automatic, E-TTL II exposure.

**WIRELESS MANUAL EXPOSURE**

You can also use manual exposure instead of E-TTL II automatic exposure in wireless mode. Setting up your master flash for manual operation is beyond the scope of this book, but you'll find instructions in my Canon flash book, described earlier.

## Using a Speedlite as the Master

Here are the steps to follow to set up and use a compatible Speedlite as a camera-mounted master unit for automatic exposure.

### 600EX-RT

1. Press the Wireless button repeatedly until the LCD panel indicates you are in optical wireless master mode.
2. Press MODE to cycle through the ETTL, M, and Multi modes.
3. Use the menu system to control and make changes to RATIO, output, and other options on the master and slave units.

## 580EX II

1. Press and hold the ZOOM button to bring up the wireless options. Use the Select dial to cycle through the OFF, MASTER on, and SLAVE on options. Select and confirm MASTER on.

2. Press MODE to cycle through the ETTL, M, and Multi modes.

3. Press the ZOOM button repeatedly to cycle through the following options: Flash zoom, RATIO, CH., flash emitter ON/OFF. Use the Select dial and Select/SET button to make any changes to these options.

4. Use the Select/SET button to select and confirm the output power settings when using Manual and Multi modes, or to use FEC or FEB when in ETTL mode.

## 580EX

1. Slide the OFF/MASTER/SLAVE wireless switch near the base of the unit to MASTER.

2. Press MODE to cycle through the ETTL, M, and Multi modes.

3. Press the ZOOM button repeatedly to cycle through the following options: Flash zoom, RATIO, CH., flash emitter ON/OFF. Use the Select dial and Select/SET button to make any changes to these options.

4. Use the Select/SET button to select and confirm the output power settings when using Manual and Multi modes, or to use FEC or FEB when in ETTL mode.

# Using the ST-E2 Transmitter as Master

Canon's Speedlite Transmitter (ST-E2) is mounted on the camera's hot shoe and provides a way to control one or more Speedlites and/or units assigned to Groups A and B. The ST-E2 does not provide any flash output of its own and will not trigger units assigned to Group C. It has the following features and controls:

- **Transmitter.** Located on the top front of the unit, the transmitter emits E-TTL II pulses through an infrared filter.

- **AF-assist beam emitter.** Just below the transmitter, the AF-assist beam emitter works similarly to the Speedlite 430EX II and higher models.

- **Battery compartment.** The ST-E2 uses a 6.0V 2CR5 lithium battery. The battery compartment is accessed from the top of the unit.

- **Lock slider and mounting foot.** The lock slider is located on the right side of the unit when facing the front. Sliding it to the left lowers the lock pin in the mounting foot (located on the bottom of the unit) to secure it to the camera's hot shoe.

- **Back panel.** The rear of the unit features several indicators and controls:
  - **Ratio indicator.** A series of red LED lights indicating the current A:B ratio setting.
  - **Flash ratio control lamp.** A red LED that lights up when flash ratio is in use.
  - **Flash ratio setting button.** Next to the flash ratio control lamp. Press this button to activate flash ratio control.
  - **Flash ratio adjustment buttons.** Two buttons with raised arrows (same color as buttons) pointing left and right. Use these to change the A:B ratio setting.
  - **Channel indicator.** The channel number in use (1–4) glows red.
  - **Channel selector button.** Next to the channel indicator. Press this button to select the communication channel.
  - **High-speed sync (FP flash) indicator.** A red LED that glows when high-speed sync is in use.
  - **High-speed sync button.** Press this button to activate/deactivate high-speed sync.
  - **ETTL indicator.** A red LED that glows when E-TTL II is in use.
  - **Off/On/HOLD switch.** Slide this switch to turn the unit off, on, or on with adjustments disabled (HOLD). The ST-E2 will power off after approximately 90 seconds of idle time. It will turn back on when the shutter button or test transmission button is pressed.
  - **Pilot lamp/Test transmission button.** This lamp works similarly to the Speedlite pilot lamp/test buttons. The lamp glows red when ready to transmit. Press the lamp button to send a test transmission to the slave units.
  - **Flash confirmation lamp.** This lamp glows green for about three seconds when the ST-E2 detects a good flash exposure.

Here are the steps to follow to set up and use the ST-E2 transmitter as a camera-mounted master unit:

1. Mount the ST-E2 unit on your T5i.
2. Make sure both the ST-E2 unit and your camera are powered on.
3. Make sure the slave units are set to E-TTL II, assigned to the appropriate group(s), and that all units are operating on the same channel.
4. If you'd like to set a flash ratio between Groups A and B, press the flash ratio setting button and flash ratio adjustment buttons to select the desired ratio. Press the high-speed sync button to use high-speed sync (often helpful with outdoor shooting).

# Using the Speedlite 600EX-RT as Radio Master

The Speedlite 600EX-RT can serve as the master unit when mounted to your camera, transmitting radio signals to one or more off-camera Speedlite 600EX-RT slave units. The master unit can have its flash output set to "off" so that it controls the remote units without contributing any flash output of its own to the exposure. This is useful for images where you don't want noticeable flash illumination coming in from the camera position.

Here are the steps to follow to set up and use a Speedlite 600EX-RT as a camera-mounted master unit for radio wireless E-TTL II operation.

1. Mount the Speedlite 600EX-RT to your T5i.
2. Make sure the 600EX-RT master units, slave units, and the camera are powered on.
3. Set the camera-mounted 600EX-RT to radio wireless MASTER mode. Press the Wireless button until the LCD panel indicates you are on radio wireless master mode.
4. Set the slave 600EX-RT units to radio wireless SLAVE mode. For each unit, press the Wireless button until the LCD panel indicates you are on radio wireless slave mode.
5. Confirm that all units are set to E-TTL II, assigned to the appropriate group(s), and that all units are operating on the same channel and ID number. The LINK lamps on all units should glow green.

# Using the ST-E3-RT as Radio Master

The ST-E3-RT transmitter can be mounted to the camera's hot shoe and used as a master controller to one or more slave Speedlite 600EX-RT units. The ST-E3-RT and the 600EX-RT share essentially the same radio control capabilities except that the ST-E3-RT does not produce flash, provide AF-assist, or otherwise emit light and is therefore incapable of optical wireless transmission.

The layout of the ST-E3-RT's control panel is virtually identical to the 600EX-RT. So is the menu system and operation, except that, as stated earlier, it will only operate as a radio wireless transmitter. Here are the steps to follow to set up and use the ST-E3-RT transmitter as a camera-mounted master unit for radio wireless E-TTL II operation:

1. Mount the ST-E3-RT unit on your T5i.
2. Make sure both the ST-E3-RT unit and your camera are powered on.
3. Set the slave 600EX-RT units to radio wireless SLAVE mode. For each unit, press the Wireless button until the LCD panel indicates you are on radio wireless slave mode.
4. Confirm that all units are set to E-TTL II, assigned to the appropriate group(s), and that all units are operating on the same channel and ID number. The LINK lamps on all units should glow green.

The ST-E3-RT controls slave units as described earlier in the section, "Speedlite 600EX-RT as Radio Wireless Master Using E-TTL II."

# Setting Up a Slave Flash

The whole point of working wirelessly is to have a master flash/controller trigger and adjust one or more slave flash units. So, once you've defined your master flash, the next step is to switch your remaining Speedlites into slave mode. That's done differently with each particular Canon Speedlite.

- **Speedlite 600EX-RT.** Press the Wireless button repeatedly until the LCD panel indicates that the unit is in optical wireless slave mode or radio wireless slave mode. In this mode, the 600EX-RT is assigned a flash mode by the master transmitter, either a flash or ST-E2 or ST-E3-RT.

- **Speedlite 580EX II.** Press and hold the ZOOM button until the wireless setting options appear. Use the Select dial and Select/SET button to select and confirm that wireless is on and in slave mode.

- **Speedlite 430EX II.** Press and hold the ZOOM button until the wireless setting options appear. Use the Select dial and Select/SET button to select and confirm that wireless is on and in slave mode.

- **Speedlite 320EX.** This flash has an On/Off/Slave switch at the lower left of the back panel. In Slave mode, you can use the flash's C.Fn 10 to tell the unit to power down after either 10 or 60 minutes of idle time. That can help preserve the 320EX's batteries. The unit's C.Fn 11 can be set to allow the master transmitter to "wake" a sleeping 320EX after your choice of within 1 hour or within 8 hours. Note that the C.Fn settings of the 320EX and 270EX II (described next) can be set only while the Speedlites are connected to the camera with the hot shoe.

- **Speedlite 270EX II.** This flash has an Off/Slave/On switch. If left on and idle, the 270EX II will power itself off after approximately 90 seconds. C. Fn. 01 can be used to disable auto power off. As with the 320EX, in Slave mode, you can use the flash's C.Fn 10 to tell the unit to power down after either 10 or 60 minutes of idle time. The unit's C.Fn 11 can be set to allow the master transmitter to "wake" a sleeping unit after your choice of within 1 hour or within 8 hours.

# More Wireless Options and Capabilities

If you're ready to immerse yourself even more deeply in wireless flash photography, the next sections will provide a little more detail on using some of the settings for ratios, channels, and groups.

## Internal/External Flash Ratio Setting

Your built-in flash and your wireless flash units have their own individual *oomph*—how much illumination they put out. This option lets you choose the relationship between these units, a *power ratio* between your built-in flash and your wireless flash units—the relative strength of each—as we did in Step 8 in the last section. That ability can be especially useful if you want to use the built-in flash for just a little fill light (it's not very powerful, anyway), while letting your off-camera units do the heavy work. This setting is the top choice in the Wireless Function menu, designated with icons that show an external flash and a raised camera flash.

Having the ability to vary the power of each flash unit or group of flash units wirelessly gives you greater flexibility and control. Varying the light output of each flash unit makes it possible to create specific types of lighting (such as traditional portrait lighting which frequently calls for a 3:1 lighting ratio between main light and fill light) or to use illumination to highlight one part of the photo while reducing contrast in another.

Lighting ratios determine the contrast between the main (sometimes called a "key" light) and fill light. For portraiture, usually the main light is typically placed at a 45-degree angle to the subject (although there are some variations), with the fill-in light on the opposite side or closer to the camera position. Choosing the right lighting ratio can do a lot to create a particular look or mood. For instance, a 1:1 ratio produces what's known as "flat" lighting. While this is good for copying or documentation, it's not usually as interesting for portraiture. Instead, making the main light more powerful than the fill light creates interesting shadows for more dramatic images. (See Figure 12.5.)

By selecting the power ratio between the flash units, you can change the relative illumination between them. Figure 12.6 shows a series of four images with a single main flash located at a 45-degree angle off to the right and slightly behind the model. The built-in flash at the camera provided illumination to fill in the shadows on the side of the face closest to the camera. The ratio between the external and internal flash were varied using 2:1 (upper left), 3:1 (upper right), 4:1 (lower left), and 5:1 (lower right) ratios.

Here's how to set the lighting ratio between the internal flash and one external wireless flash unit:

1. **Enable wireless functions.** Choose Built-in Flash Settings and select CustWireless from the Built-in Flash entry. Press SET.

2. **Choose Ratio Setting in Wireless Func. menu.** In the Built-in Flash Setting menu, highlight Wireless Func., press SET, and choose Ratio Setting (it's the top entry, as shown earlier in Figure 12.4). Press SET again to confirm and return to the previous menu.

**Figure 12.5**
More dramatic lighting ratios produce more dramatic-looking illumination.

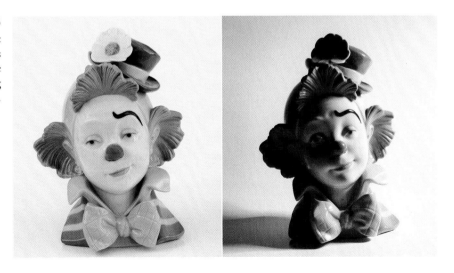

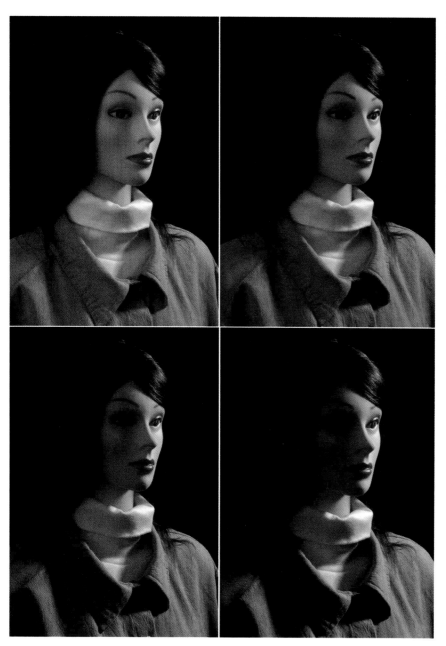

**Figure 12.6**
The main light (to the right and behind the model) and fill light (at the camera position) were varied using 2:1 and 3:1 (top row, left to right) as well as 4:1 and 5:1 (bottom row, left to right) ratios.

3. **Access the Power Ratio entry.** Now you can set the power ratio by scrolling down just below Flash Exp. Comp., represented by a pair of icons corresponding to an external and internal flash unit.

4. **Set the control.** Press the SET button.

5. **Choose the desired ratio.** Then use the cross keys to choose the setting you want. (See Figure 12.7.) Your choices range from 1:1 (the off-camera and built-in flash have equal output) to 8:1 (the off-camera flash supplies 8X output compared to the internal flash). Set the ratio to 4:1, for example, and the external flash will produce four times as much light as the on-camera flash, which is then used as fill illumination. For most subjects, ratios of 2:1 to 5:1 will produce the best results, as shown earlier in Figure 12.6.

6. **Confirm.** Press SET to confirm your ratio.

**Figure 12.7**
Select a ratio from
8:1 to 1:1.

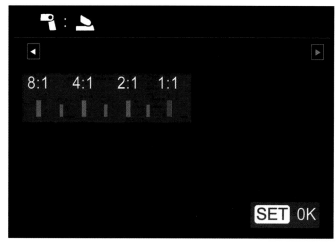

# Wireless Flash Only

This setting, represented earlier in Figure 12.4 by an icon of a flash unit alone, allows you to turn off the flash output of your T5i's built-in flash, while allowing it to emit a wireless controller flash that signals the external flash units you're working with. You'll still see a burst from your camera's built-in flash, but that burst will not contribute to the exposure. It will only be used to tell the remote/slave flash units to fire.

This is the setting to choose if you only want to use the flash controller to operate your remote flashes. It's probably the most commonly used choice when you don't want to use the internal flash for fill light, since firing the built-in flash increases the risk of red-eye effects.

Photographers prefer this mode in part because Canon's portable shoe mount flash units are much more powerful than a camera's built-in flash. They want to avoid using a light source that is directly above the lens and close to the lens, since red-eye is caused by light from the flash unit reflecting off the subject's retinas and bouncing back into the lens.

Using off-camera flash lets the photographer precisely control light direction and effect. It also makes it possible for the photographer to move around within the constraints of the flash units' ability to illuminate a scene, without worrying about getting too far from the subject for the flash unit(s) to be effective. Only the camera to subject position changes and not the light to subject position and ratio. Once you've set up the flash units relative to your subject, you can move around freely.

Being able to control lighting direction is a very useful capability since it can lead to more dramatic images. In Figure 12.8 a single flash unit was used to light the model. A grid (a small light "concentrator") was placed on the flash head to restrict the light from the unit. In this case, the lighting effect is dramatic.

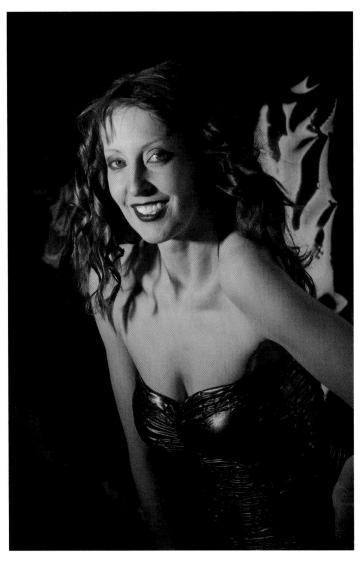

**Figure 12.8**
The subject was lit by a Canon 600EX-RT flash unit with a Honl Speed Grid. The flash unit was placed on a light stand positioned to the left of the model and angled slightly downward.

Here are the steps to follow when using wireless flash only (whether you're working with a single external flash, or multiple units).

1. **Choose wireless flash only.** Navigate to the Wireless Func. menu as you did earlier, but choose Wireless Flash Only (the single-flash icon in the middle of the list).

2. **Confirm.** Press the SET button to confirm the Wireless Flash Only setting.

3. **Set the Power Ratio (optional).** If you are using more than one external flash, and have assigned flash units to different groups, you can then set the power ratios between groups. (I'll explain groups later in this chapter.) If you are using only one flash, or all the flash units are assigned to the same group, you don't need to do this; setting a power ratio won't make any difference. The Firing Group entry will read "All" and the fire ratio entry will not be visible. You can only select a power ratio if you've chosen A:B in the Firing Group entry. (Remember to change the power ratio back to normal when you are finished with a session; Canon's Speedlites retain the settings you make, even after a quick battery change.)

## Using Wireless and Built-in Flash

This option in the Wireless Func. screen, represented by an icon of an external unit *plus* an icon of a raised camera flash, adds the built-in flash to whatever wireless groups you're using. You can then use the built-in flash in conjunction with whatever firing groups you've set up. In this case you're still using the external flash units as the main sources of light, but the built-in flash can either serve to provide some extra fill (such as to illuminate the face under the brim of a hat) or to provide a second light when you only have one off-camera flash available.

It is also possible to set up a two-light portrait using an off-camera flash as a main light (about 45 degrees to the model) and the built-in flash as the fill light, as discussed earlier. Use the External/Internal Flash Ratio Setting to adjust their relative contribution to the image.

Some photographers do like to position their fill light directly above the camera and straight toward the model. The lighting ratio for such a setup would have the built-in and external strobes set to 1:1 or 2:1. Keep in mind that if using such a configuration, the light from the built-in flash is striking the subject head on and needs to be added to your calculations for the main light. In other words, setting your lighting ratio to 1:1 would actually provide a 2:1 effective lighting ratio since you would have 1 part light from the main light and 1 part light from the built-in flash illuminating one side of the subject and just 1 part light from the built-in flash illuminating the other side. Setting your lighting ratio to 2:1 would effectively provide a 3:1 lighting ratio this way. If you have set the camera to E-TTL II exposure as recommended, the lighting you choose will be automatically accounted for in the exposure selected by the camera, so no calculations are necessary by the photographer.

## Working with Groups

With what you've already learned, you can shoot wirelessly using your camera's built-in flash and one or more external flash units. All these strobes will work together with the T5i for automatic exposure using E-TTL II exposure mode. You can vary the power ratio between your built-in flash and the external units. As you become more comfortable with wireless flash photography, you can even switch the individual external flash units into manual mode, and adjust their lighting ratios manually.

But there's a lot more you can do if you've splurged and own two or more compatible external flash units (some photographers I know own five or six Speedlite 580EX II or 600EX-RT units). Canon wireless photography lets you collect individual strobes into *groups*, and control all the Speedlites within a given group together. You can operate as few as two strobes in two groups or three strobes in three groups, while controlling more units if desired. You can also have them fire at equal output settings (A+B+C mode) versus using them at different power ratios (A:B or A:B C modes). Setting each group's strobes to different power ratios gives you more control over lighting for portraiture and other uses.

This is one of the more powerful options of the EOS wireless flash system. I prefer to keep my Speedlites set to different groups normally. I can always set the power ratio to 1:1 if I want to operate the flash units all at the same power. If I change my mind and need to make adjustments, I can just change the wireless flash controller and then manipulate the different groups' output as desired.

Canon's wireless flash system works with a number of Canon flashes and even some third-party units. I routinely mix a 600EX-RT, 580EX II, 550EX, and 420EX plus sometimes add a Sigma EF-500 Super. I control these flash units either with the EOS T5i's built-in wireless capabilities or using a Canon ST-E2 Speedlite Transmitter.

The ST-E2 is a hot shoe mount device that offers wireless flash control for a wide variety of Canon wireless flash capable strobes and can even control flash units wirelessly for High-speed sync (HSS) photography. (HSS is described in Chapter 11.) The ST-E2 can only control three flash groups though and also can support flash exposure bracketing. Its range isn't as great as the T5i's though.

Canon flash units that can be operated wirelessly include: 580EX II, 580EX, 550EX, 430EX, 420EX, 320EX, MR-14EX, MT-24EX. The 270EX, 220EX, 380EX, and earlier Canon flash units cannot be operated wirelessly via Canon's wireless flash system. There are third-party flash units that can (such as the Sigma I use), but you must use one designed to work with Canon's wireless flash system only.

Here's how you set up groups:

1. **Determine lighting setup.** Decide whether you're using the built-in flash as part of your lighting scheme or just using the external flash units. If you do want the internal flash to contribute to the exposure, then you can scroll down in the Built-in Flash Setting entry to the External Flash/Built-in Flash Lighting Ratio Control (if you're using lighting ratios) and set that control (from 8:1 to 2:1, as noted earlier).

2. **Access lighting groups.** If you're not using the built-in flash (Wireless Func. is set to the external flash only icon), scroll down to the Firing Group entry that appears and press SET.

3. **Select the group configuration you want.** From top to bottom, the choices are as follows:

   ■ **All external.** Multiple external flash units functioning as one big flash.

   ■ **A:B.** Multiple external units in two groups.

   I'll explain exactly what these two configurations do next.

4. **Allocate flash units into groups.** You must do this at the flash unit itself. You'll need to tell each flash which group it "belongs" to, so it will respond, along with any other strobes (if any) in its group, to wireless commands directed at that particular group. The procedure for setting each flash unit's slave ID/group varies depending on what flash you are using, so consult your Speedlite's manual.

---

### SETTING SLAVE/GROUP ID WITH THE 580EX II

1. Press the ZOOM button for two seconds or longer until the display blinks.

2. Rotate the control dial until the Slave indicator blinks.

3. Press the control dial button to confirm Slave operation.

4. To change from Group A to another group, press the ZOOM button until the Group A indicator blinks.

5. Rotate the control dial until the A indicator is replaced by the B or C indicators.

6. Press the control dial button to confirm the group ID.

---

# Ratio Control

By default, all the flashes in each group will fire at full power. However, for more advanced lighting setups, you can select lighting ratios.

Here's how to set the lighting ratio between the internal flash and one external wireless flash unit:

1. **Navigate to the T5i's Flash Group selection option.** With wireless flash already activated, visit the External Speedlite Control entry in the Shooting 1 menu, navigate to the Flash Function Settings choice, Flash Functions. Navigate to the Flash Group choice at the lower left of the screen and choose SET.

2. **Choose Group Configuration.** You can select ALL, A:B, or A:B C. If you're using the 600EX-RT in radio transmission mode, you can also select Groups D and E. Press SET to confirm.

3. **Select Ratio.** If you've chosen A:B C, navigate to the A:B Ratio Control option, and select a ratio from 8:1 to 1:8. At 8:1, Group A supplies 8X output of Group B. At 1:8, the ratio is reversed.

4. **Confirm.** Press SET to confirm your ratio.

Here's how the various basic Group Configurations work:

- **ALL.** All groups will fire at the power level set at the flash unit itself. That may be full power, or you may have set individual flashes to fire at some other power level. It's usually simpler to set your flashes at full power and allow the master to control their output.

- **A:B.** In this configuration, you can specify the ratio of the power levels of Groups A and B, as described in Step 3 above.

- **A:B C.** In this Group configuration, you can specify the power ratio between Groups A and B, but *not* the output of Group C flashes. Those can be controlled only using Flash Exposure Compensation, the option immediately below the A:B Power Ratio setting in Figure 10.6.

## Choosing a Channel

Canon's wireless flash system can work on any of four channels, so if more than one photographer is using the Canon system, each can set his gear to a different channel so they don't accidentally trigger each other's strobes. You need to be sure all of your gear is set to the same channel. Selecting a channel is done differently with each particular flash model.

The ability to operate flash units on one of four channels isn't really important unless you're shooting in an environment where other photographers are also using the Canon wireless flash system. If the system only offered one channel, then each photographer's wireless flash controller would be firing every Canon flash set for wireless operation. By having four channels available, the photographers can coordinate their use to avoid that problem. Such situations are common at sporting events and other activities that draw a lot of shooters.

It's always a good idea to double-check your flash units before you set them up to make sure they're all set to the same channel, and this should also be one of your first troubleshooting questions if a flash doesn't fire the first time you try to use it wirelessly.

You do this as follows:

1. **Set flash units to the channel you want to use for all your groups.** Each flash unit may use its own procedure for setting that strobe's channel. Consult your Speedlite's manual for instructions. With the 580EX II, press the ZOOM button repeatedly until the CH. Indicator blinks, then rotate the control dial to select Channel 1, 2, 3, or 4. Press the control dial center button to confirm.

2. **Navigate to the T5i's channel selection option.** In the Built-in Flash Func. Settings screen, use the cross keys to scroll down to the Channel Setting and push the SET button.

3. **Select the channel your flashes are set to.** You can then use the up/down cross keys to advance the channel number from 1 to 4 or back down again (you have to reverse the cross keys direction to get back to one; you can't just keep advancing it to get there—it doesn't "wrap around).

4. **Double-check to make sure your flash units are set to the appropriate channel.** Your wireless flash units must be set to the same channel as the T5i's wireless flash controller; otherwise, the Speedlites won't fire.

# Flash Release Function

The Canon Speedlite 320EX and Speedlite 270EX II have a nifty feature called the Remote Release Function, which, as I write this, is completely novel in the Canon accessory flash line-up. The feature allows you to detach the Speedlite from certain EOS cameras (right now the 5D Mark II and Mark III, 6D, 7D, 60D, T5i, T4i, T3i, T2i, T1i, Xsi, Xti, XT, and 2003-era original Digital Rebel), and then use a button on the flash unit as a remote control to trigger the camera from up to 16 feet away. That's right, your 320EX and 270EX II can function as a wireless remote control, just like the Canon RC-6, RC-5, and RC-1 infrared controls!

As you can see from the list of cameras, it works with any EOS camera that can be triggered by an IR remote. There's a (mandatory) two-second delay after you press the flash's remote release, and the flash itself does not have to fire and contribute to the exposure. An invisible infrared signal emitted by the flash triggers the camera.

To use the feature with the T5i, use the Drive function, described earlier, and select the self-timer/ infrared remote option. If you don't want the T5i's flash to fire, make sure it's set to P or a Creative Zone mode where the flash doesn't pop up automatically. With the 320EX or 270EX II turned on and detached from the camera, position the flash so it "sees" the remote control sensor on the front of the camera. Press the remote release button on the side of the flash, and the camera will fire two seconds later. If you're taking a picture of yourself, this delay allows you to stash the flash out of sight and grin. The flash will not fire.

If you prefer to have the flash fire and contribute to the exposure, move the On/Off switch on the back to the middle "slave" position. In this mode, the camera itself must serve as the master, or you must have another master unit physically attached to the camera. To use the camera in master mode, use the Built-in Flash Control menu entry to activate the T5i's master mode, as described previously. Or, you can connect a 580EX II, set to master mode, either by putting it in the accessory shoe or linked with a cable, such as the Off Camera Cord OC-E3. Alternatively, you can connect the Speedlite Transmitter ST-E2.

When you're ready, point the 320EX or 270EX II at the front of the camera/master flash within 16 feet of the camera, and press the remote control button on the side of the flash. During the two-second delay, you can then point the 320EX or 270EX II in a different direction (as is likely, because you're probably using this feature to illuminate the scene, not the camera). That's the real reason for the two-second delay, by the way: giving you the ability to reposition the "remote" release flash.

The 600EX-RT has its own remote release function, which allows you to use a slave unit to trigger your camera by remote control when using radio transmission mode. EOS cameras released since 2012 (including the T5i) can be triggered in this way through the intelligent hot shoe, using one 600EX-RT mounted on the camera as a receiver, and the slave 600EX-RT off camera as the remote trigger. Older cameras can still be used in this mode, but you'll need to connect the on-camera 600EX-RT to the camera's N3 remote control terminal using an optional Release Cable SR-N3. (If your camera uses a different type of remote release, you're out of luck.)

# Using Wireless Flash Creatively

Getting the flash off the camera is fundamental to improving the quality of your lighting. Wireless flash lets you control the light's direction and allows you to use a number of light sources to create more interesting and attractive images.

These next sections look at some ways of using wireless flash to improve your photography. They break down into tips and tricks based on the number of flash units used to create an image. Keep in mind, even just one small flash unit, used creatively, can lead to a significant improvement in your photos, especially when you can use your external flash off camera and you're not tied down to the accessory shoe.

# Single-Flash Unit Ideas

As you've seen, using a Canon Speedlite wirelessly is simple with the T5i. Many Canon flash units come with a handy table stand accessory that allows you to set up the flash as a freestanding light. Just configure the strobe for wireless connectivity to the camera, as described previously in this chapter, and then position it wherever you want. So long as the strobe and the camera can see each other (the wireless signal from the T5i can even be bounced off of walls to connect with the flash), they will communicate with each other.

Some handy uses for a single off-camera flash include moving it closer to the subject to increase its effectiveness (remember the inverse square law), placing it off to the side of the subject to show detail (or positioned alongside a reflective surface such as a white wall or reflector to provide main light and fill), or raised up high and angled to one side to get rid of harsh shadows.

While the number of possibilities is endless, here are some examples of things that can be done with a single off-camera flash. Some of these are done with just a basic flash unit, while others rely on light modifiers to create unusual effects.

## Single-Flash Unit and Sunlight

When shooting outdoors you can often combine sunlight and an off-camera flash to create a more pleasing looking portrait. Position your subject so the sun is at a 45-degree angle to her and your off-camera flash is lighting her from the parallel 45-degree angle. You can either go with equal exposures (for flat portrait lighting) or expose the flashlit side brighter or darker than the sun's exposure for a more stylistic type of lighting.

You can improve the quality of the light by firing the flash unit into a soft box or umbrella, as in this photograph of a young model (shown in Figure 12.9). Placing the soft box and flash closer to the subject would soften the light even more (the larger the light source in relation to the subject, the softer the light) and make the flash unit's effective output even greater.

**Figure 12.9**

A Canon 600EX-RT Speedlite was mounted on a light stand and fired through a soft box to one side, while the sun illuminated the young lady from the other.

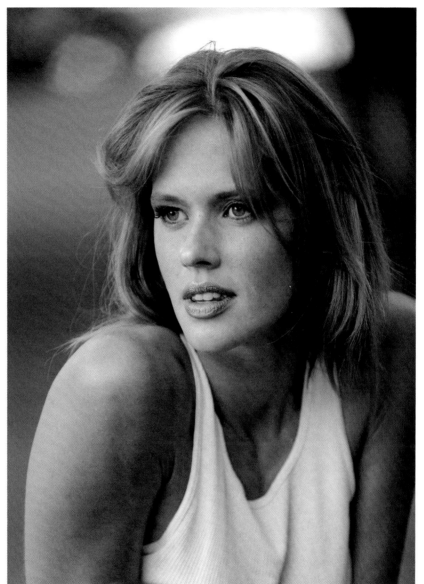

# Single-Flash Unit with a Reflector

This is similar to the sun and flash combo shot, but this approach relies on the off-camera flash as the main light and uses reflected ("bounced") light from either a white wall or a reflector of some kind. Here the flash will be the stronger light source, and the distance the reflector is positioned from the light will determine the lighting ratio between the two light sources (flash and reflector). Generally, you want to have the reflector pretty close to the subject to keep the lighting ratio manageable. If it's too far away, one side of the face will end up in deep shadow.

# Side Lighting for Effect

Lighting from the side is useful for showing texture and detail as the light fills in shadows on one side and emphasizes them on the other. It's also a more dramatic style of light, particularly if the light is restricted as this photo shows (see Figure 12.10).

This is a very moody and dramatic style of lighting. Depending on how you modify the light it can produce a very dramatic effect (by restricting the light with a snoot, barn doors, or grids or by allowing the light to spread a bit by firing the flash directly from the side). You can even try bouncing it off a wall from the side to spread the light a bit more. Each technique can produce a compelling image.

**Figure 12.10**
A Canon 600EX-RT mounted on a light stand set to the right and slightly behind the subject provided all the illumination in this portrait.

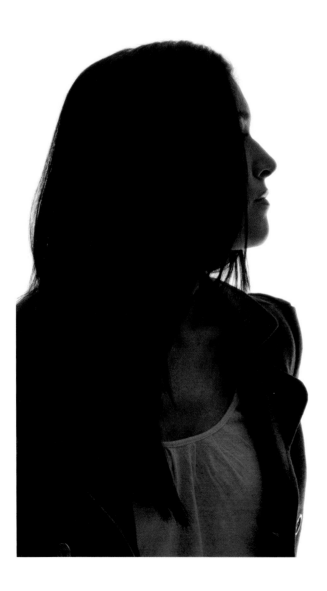

# Shooting Through Blinds

You can fire a flash unit through a set of window blinds to mimic the effect of sunlight streaming through a window. I even keep a set of blinds in my studio for this effect. Position the blinds and a flash unit on a light stand both angled to the side of your subject and fire the flash unit through the blinds.

There are even some interesting variations you can try with this idea. One is to attach a 1/4 or 1/2 yellow or orange gel to the flash head to add some color to the light. This will mimic the effect of early or late daylight streaming through the blinds. Another option is to add a second light or reflector to fill in some of the shadows.

# Adding a Gel for a Special Effect

Gels are colored filters for your flash. Some units, such as the 580EX II and 600EX-RT are furnished with gel holders that fit over the flash head. You can also tape gels over the head using gaffer's tape. Gels are a convenient way to color the light from the flash. You can use a red, yellow, or orange gel to create a late day type of light. Or, you can use funkier colors to go for something on the wild side. I use the orange gel furnished with my 600EX-RT to balance the Speedlite with incandescent light indoors when I want to use both sources of illumination.

You can also put a gel on a background flash and use it to turn a white or gray background into a background of a different color. I know photographers who routinely use neutral backgrounds and then color them with flash as required.

# Raising Your Flash up High via Monopod or Light Stand

Mounting your flash on a monopod, using one of the many available flash shoe/tripod adapters, gives you the option of positioning your light farther from your camera and allows you to direct its light where you need it (you may have to hold the camera with just one hand or talk someone else into holding the monopod flash combo for you). While it's common to raise it up to get rid of shadows, you can also position it to light from the side. If you're using a monopod with built-in legs (such as the Trek Tech Go! Pro, http://www.trek-tech.com/), you now have a freestanding light stand too. Or, if you have a portable light stand, you can do the same thing.

# 13

# Downloading, Editing, and Printing Your Images

Taking the picture is only half the work and, in some cases, only half the fun. After you've captured some great images and have them safely stored on your Canon EOS T5i's memory card, you'll need to transfer them from your camera and memory card to your computer, where they can be organized, fine-tuned in an image editor, and prepared for web display, printing, or some other final destination.

Fortunately, there are lots of software utilities and applications to help you do all these things. This chapter will introduce you to a few of them.

## Printing

You can print your images directly from some of the software applications and utilities described later in this chapter, but your EOS T5i can also be used to print from the camera, and to set up print "orders." These next sections will explain your options.

### Direct Printing from the Camera

You can print photos stored on your camera's memory card directly to a PictBridge-compatible printer using the cable supplied with the T5i. Just follow these steps to get started:

1. **Set up your printer.** Follow the instructions for your PictBridge-compatible printer to load it with paper, and prepare it for printing.

2. **Connect the camera to the printer.** With the T5i and printer both powered down, open the port cover on the left side of the camera (the one closest to the back of the camera when it's held

in shooting position), and plug the Interface Cable IFC-200U into the A/V Out/Digital port. Connect the other end to the PictBridge USB input port of your printer.

3. **Turn printer and camera on.** Flip the switch on the T5i, and power up your printer using its power switch.

4. **Press the Playback button on the camera.** Navigate to the image on your memory card that you want to print using the cross keys. Press SET to select the image.

5. **Select options.** The image, overlaid with the current status for options like those shown in Figure 13.1, will appear when the camera and printer are connected with a cable. (The options will vary, depending on what printer you have.) I'll describe the options next.

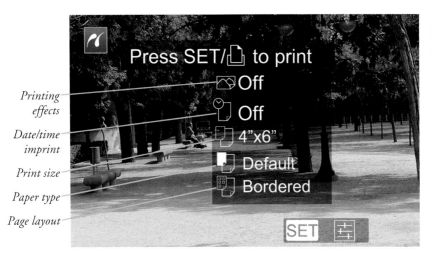

*Printing effects*
*Date/time imprint*
*Print size*
*Paper type*
*Page layout*

**Figure 13.1**
You can print directly from the EOS T5i.

The EOS T5i offers a surprising number of options when direct printing from your camera. You can choose effects, print date and time on your hardcopies, select the number of copies to be output, trim the image, and select paper settings—from your camera! While you can print using the current values as shown in the status screen, to adjust the settings, follow these steps, briefly summarized here with the camera connected to the printer:

■ **Access the print options screen.** Press SET when the screen shown in Figure 13.1 is shown on your LCD. The PictBridge icon shows that the camera has successfully linked to the printer.

■ **Use the cross keys.** Highlight the options shown at right in Figure 13.2 in any order, and press SET to adjust that option. Within each option, use the SET button to confirm your entry, or the MENU button to back out of the option's screen.

■ **Printing effects.** Use the cross keys to choose Off (no effects), On (the printer's automatic corrections will be applied), Default (values stored in your printer, and which will vary depending on your printer), Vivid (higher saturation in blues and greens), or NR (noise reduction is applied). Three B/W choices are also available, for B/W (true blacks), B/W Cool tone (bluish blacks), and B/W Warm tone (yellowish blacks). Natural and Natural M choices are also available to provide true colors. If the INFO. icon appears, you can press it to make some adjustments to the printing effect, including image brightening, levels, and red-eye correction.

**Figure 13.2**
Choose the number of copies, crop the image, and apply other settings and preferences.

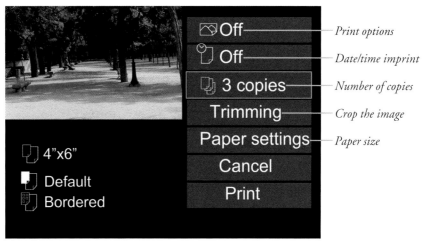

Print options

Date/time imprint

Number of copies

Crop the image

Paper size

- **Date/time imprint.** You can set this On or Off.

- **Copies.** Select 1 to 99 copies of the selected image.

- **Trimming.** Use this to crop your image. Your image appears on a trimming screen. Press the Zoom In and Zoom Out buttons to magnify or reduce the size of the cropping frame. Use the cross keys to move the cropping frame around within the image. Press the INFO. button to toggle the cropping frame between horizontal and vertical orientations. When you've defined the crop for the image, press the SET button to apply your trimming to the image.

- **Paper settings.** Choose the paper size, type, and layout. Use the cross keys to select your paper size, with choices from credit card size through 8.5 × 11 inches. Press SET to confirm, and the screen changes to a Paper Type selection. After choosing Paper Type, press SET once more and choose a layout, from Borderless, Bordered, 2-up, 4-up, 9-up, 16-up, and 20-up (multiple copies of the image on a single sheet). When using Letter size (8.5 × 11–inch) paper, you can also elect to print 20-up and 35-up thumbnails of images you've chosen using the DPOF options described later in this chapter. The 20-up version will also include shooting information, such as camera and lens used, shooting mode, shutter speed, aperture, and other data. Another press of the SET button confirms Paper Type and returns to the settings screen.

- **Cancel.** Returns to the status screen (seen in Figure 13.1).

- **Print.** Starts the printing process with the selected options. The camera warns you not to disconnect the cable during printing. To print another photo using the same settings, just select it, highlight Print, and press the SET button.

# Direct Print Order Format (DPOF) Printing

If you don't want to print directly from the camera, you can set some of the same options from the Playback 1 menu's Print Order entry, and designate single or multiple images on your memory card for printing. Once marked for DPOF printing, you can print the selected images, or take your memory card to a digital lab or kiosk, which is equipped to read the print order and make the copies you've specified. (You can't "order" prints of RAW images or movies.)

To create a DPOF print order, just follow these steps:

1. **Access Print Order screen.** In the Playback 1 menu, navigate to Print Order. (See Figure 13.3.) Press SET.
2. **Access Set up.** The Print Order screen will appear. (See Figure 13.4.) Use the cross keys to highlight Set Up. Press SET.
3. **Select Print type.** Choose Print Type (Standard, Index/Thumbnails print, or Both), and specify whether Date or File Number imprinting should be turned on or off. (You can turn one or the other on, but not both Date and File Number imprinting.) Press MENU to return to the Print Order screen.

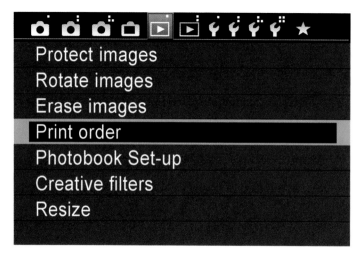

**Figure 13.3**
Print orders can be assembled from the Playback 1 menu.

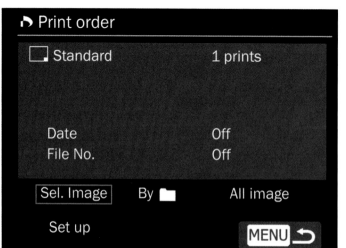

**Figure 13.4**
Select the images to be printed individually, by folder, or all the images on your memory card.

4. **Choose selection method.** Highlight Sel. Image (choose individual images), By Folder (to select/deselect all images in a folder), or All Image (to mark/unmark all the images on your memory card). Press SET.

5. **Select individual images.** With Sel. Image, use the cross keys to view the images, and press SET to mark or unmark an image for printing. If you'd rather view thumbnails of images, press the Thumbnail/Zoom In button. Press the Magnify/Zoom Out button to return to single-image view.

6. **Choose number of prints.** Once an image is selected, rotate the cross keys to specify 1 to 99 prints for that image. (For Index prints, you can only specify whether the selected image is included in the index print, not the number of copies.) Press SET to confirm. You can then use the cross keys to select additional images. Press MENU when finished selecting to return to the Print Order screen.

7. **Output your hardcopies.** If the camera is linked to a PictBridge-compatible printer, an additional option appears on the Print Order screen—Print. You can select that; optionally, adjust Paper Settings as described in the previous section, and start the printing process. Alternately, you can exit the Print Order screen by tapping the shutter release button. Then turn off the camera and printer, remove the memory card, and insert it in the memory card slot of a compatible printer, retailer kiosk, or digital minilab.

# Using the Supplied Software

Your Canon EOS T5i came with software programs on CD for both Windows PCs and Macs. Pop the CD into your computer and it will self-install a selection of these useful applications and utilities. Manuals for all these programs are included on a separate CD, but here's a summary of what you get on the EOS Digital Solutions disc:

## EOS Utility

Both Windows and Mac versions are provided for this useful program. It serves as a command center for several useful functions, all available from the main control panel. Using the Control Camera panel, you can jump to modules that download images to either Digital Photo Professional or ZoomBrowser EX, change camera settings when your T5i is linked to your computer with the USB cable, shoot remotely with a live view image previewed on your computer screen, and monitor folders for new images.

The most-used of these options will probably be the download utility. But many will appreciate the Camera Settings/Remote Shooting module that allows you to link your computer with the T5i and use a dialog box to change camera settings and to control the camera for remote shooting. You can have access to many of the T5i's menus right from the software. The Settings feature is especially useful for changing Picture Styles quickly, while you'll find the remote shooting capabilities useful when you want to program a delay before the camera takes a picture, or do some interval (time-lapse) shooting. The updated version of the utility supports the T5i's Live View and Dust Delete Data functions. It includes many preferences you can use to tailor its operation.

The Accessories panel includes modules for working with the optional WFT-E3/E3A/B/C/D wireless communications link (for saving your pictures directly to external media over a Wi-Fi network). If you're using the OSK-E3 Data Security Kit, you can access the Original Data Security (ODS) Administrator tool and Utility, which are used to register and manage OS card verification information for image encryption and decryption, management of authorized users and cameras, verified card duplication, and other functions. There is also a link to the Picture Style Editor.

## Digital Photo Professional

While far from a Photoshop replacement, Digital Photo Professional is a useful image-editing program that helps you organize, trim, correct, and print images. You can make RAW adjustments, and correct tonal curves, color tone, color saturation, sharpness, as well as brightness and contrast. Especially handy are the "recipes" that can be developed and saved so that a given set of corrections can be kept separate from the file itself, and, if desired, applied to other images.

## Picture Style Editor

The Picture Style Editor allows you to create your own custom Picture Styles, or edit existing styles, including the Standard, Landscape, Faithful, and other predefined settings already present in your T5i. You can change sharpness, contrast, color saturation, and color tone—and a lot more—and then save the modifications as a PF2 file that can be uploaded to the camera, or used by Digital Photo Professional (described later in this chapter) to modify a RAW image as it is imported.

You can define your own color response using a color picker in a sample RAW photograph to choose a specific hue, which you can then modify using hue/saturation/luminance adjustments. The range of adjacent colors affected by your new settings can also be specified. Before/after views let you compare the Picture Style settings you've entered with standard settings using a sample image you upload.

## ZoomBrowser/ImageBrowser

This is an image viewing and editing application for Windows PCs (the equivalent program for Macs is called ImageBrowser and performs the same functions). You can organize, sort, classify, and rename files, and convert JPEG files in batches. This utility is especially useful for printing index sheets of groups of images. It can also prepare images for e-mailing. It works with RAW Image Task for converting CR2 files to some other format for editing.

The simple image-editing facilities of ZoomBrowser/ImageBrowser allow red-eye correction, brightness/contrast and color correction, manipulating sharpness, trimming photos, and a few other functions. For more complex editing, you can transfer images directly from this application to Photoshop or another image editor. The software also includes applications for planning and editing movies, and for extracting still photos from video clips.

# PhotoStitch

This Windows/Mac utility, available free from Canon, allows you to take several JPEG images and combine them to create a panorama in a single new file. You can choose the images to be merged in ZoomBrowser and then transfer them to PhotoStitch, or operate the utility as a stand-alone module and select the images using the standard File > Open commands.

# Transferring Your Photos

While it's rewarding to capture some great images and have them ensconced in your camera, eventually you'll be transferring them to your laptop or PC, whether you're using a Windows or Macintosh machine. You have three options for image transfer: direct transfer over a USB cable, automated transfer using a card reader and transfer software such as the EOS Utility or Adobe Photoshop Elements Photo Downloader, or manual transfer using drag and drop from a memory card inserted in a card reader.

## Using a Card Reader and Software

You can also use a memory card reader and software to transfer photos and automate the process using the EOS Utility, Photoshop Elements' Photo Downloader, or the downloading program supplied with some other third-party applications. This method is more frugal in its use of your T5i's battery and can be faster if you have a speedy USB 2.0/3.0 or FireWire card reader attached to an appropriate port.

The installed software automatically remains in memory as you work, and it recognizes when a memory card is inserted in your card reader; you don't have to launch it yourself. With Photoshop Elements's Photo Downloader, you can click Get Photos to begin the transfer of all images immediately or choose Advanced Dialog to produce a dialog box that allows you to select which images to download from the memory card by marking their thumbnails with a check. You can select the photos you want to transfer, plus options such as Automatically Fix Red Eyes. Start the download, and a confirmation dialog box shows the progress.

## Dragging and Dropping

The final way to move photos from your memory card to your computer is the old-fashioned way: manually dragging and dropping the files from one window on your computer to another. The procedure works pretty much the same whether you're using a Mac or a PC.

1. Remove the memory card from the T5i and insert it in your memory card reader.
2. Using Windows Explorer, My Computer, or your Mac desktop, open the icon representing the memory card, which appears on your desktop as just another disk drive. (You can also link your camera directly to your computer with a USB cable, and it will appear as a disk drive, too.)

3. Open a second window representing the folder on your computer that you want to use as the destination for the files you are copying or moving.

4. Drag and drop the files from the memory card window to the folder on your computer. You can select individual files, press Ctrl/Command+A to select all the files, or Ctrl/Command+click to select multiple files.

# Editing Your Photos

Image manipulation tasks fall into several categories. You might want to fine-tune your images, retouch them, change color balance, composite several images together, and perform other tasks we know as image editing, with a program like Adobe Photoshop, Photoshop Elements, or Corel Photo Paint.

You might want to play with the settings in RAW files, too, as you import them from their CR2 state into an image editor. There are specialized tools expressly for tweaking RAW files, ranging from Canon's own Digital Photo Professional to Adobe Camera Raw, and PhaseOne's Capture One Pro (C1 Pro). A third type of manipulation is the specialized task of noise reduction, which can be performed within Photoshop, Adobe Camera Raw, or tools like Bibble Professional. There are also specialized tools just for noise reduction, such as Noise Ninja (also included with Bibble) and Neat Image.

Each of these utilities and applications deserves a chapter of its own, so I'm simply going to enumerate some of the most popular image-editing and RAW conversion programs here and tell you a little about what they do.

## Image Editors

Image editors are general-purpose photo-editing applications that can do color correction, tonal modifications, retouching, combining of several images into one, and usually include tools for working with RAW files and reducing noise. So, you'll find programs like those listed here good for all-around image manipulation. The leading programs are as follows:

**Adobe Photoshop/Photoshop Elements/Photoshop Elements Premiere.** Photoshop is the serious photographer's number one choice for image editing, and Elements is an excellent option for those who need most of Photoshop's power, but not all of its professional-level features. Both editors use the latest version of Adobe's Camera Raw plug-in, which makes it easy to adjust things like color space profiles, color depth (either 8 bits or 16 bits per color channel), image resolution, white balance, exposure, shadows, brightness, sharpness, luminance, and noise reduction. One plus with the Adobe products is that they are available in identical versions for both Windows and Macs. Elements Premiere adds video editing features that T5i owners who shoot a lot of video will find useful.

**Corel Photo Paint.** This is the image-editing program that is included in the popular CorelDRAW Graphics suite. Although a Mac version was available in the past, this is primarily a Windows application today. It's a full-featured photo retouching and image-editing program with selection, retouching, and painting tools for manual image manipulations, and it also includes convenient automated commands for a few common tasks, such as red-eye removal. Photo Paint accepts Photoshop plug-ins to expand its assortment of filters and special effects.

**Corel Paint Shop Pro.** This is a general-purpose Windows-only image editor that has gained a reputation as the "poor man's Photoshop" for providing a substantial portion of Photoshop's capabilities at a fraction of the cost. It includes a nifty set of wizard-like commands that automate common tasks, such as removing red-eye and scratches, as well as filters and effects, which can be expanded with other Photoshop plug-ins.

**Corel Painter.** Here's another image-editing program from Corel for both Mac and Windows. This one's strength is in mimicking natural media, such as charcoal, pastels, and various kinds of paint. Painter includes a basic assortment of tools that you can use to edit existing images, but the program is really designed for artists to use in creating original illustrations. As a photographer, you might prefer another image editor, but if you like to paint on top of your photographic images, nothing else really does the job of Painter.

**Corel PhotoImpact.** Corel finally brought one of the last remaining non-Adobe image editors into its fold when it acquired Ulead PhotoImpact. This is a general-purpose photo-editing program for Windows with a huge assortment of brushes for painting, retouching, and cloning, in addition to the usual selection, cropping, and fill tools. If you frequently find yourself performing the same image manipulations on a number of files, you'll appreciate PhotoImpact's batch operations. Using this feature, you can select multiple image files and then apply any one of a long list of filters, enhancements, or auto-process commands to all the selected files.

# RAW Utilities

Your software choices for manipulating RAW files are broader than you might think. Camera vendors always supply a utility to read their cameras' own RAW files, but sometimes, particularly with those point-and-shoot cameras that can produce RAW files, the options are fairly limited. Other vendors, such as Nikon (with its Nikon Capture), offer RAW file handling that is much more flexible and powerful.

Because in the past digital camera vendors offered RAW converters that weren't very good (Canon's File View Utility comes to mind), there is a lively market for third-party RAW utilities available at extra cost. However, the EOS Utility and Digital Photo Professional do a good job and may be all that you need.

The third-party solutions are usually available as stand-alone applications (often for both Windows and Macintosh platforms), as Photoshop-compatible plug-ins, or both. Because the RAW plug-ins displace Photoshop's own RAW converter, I tend to prefer to use most RAW utilities in stand-alone mode. That way, if I choose to open a file directly in Photoshop, it automatically opens using Photoshop's fast and easy-to-use Adobe Camera Raw (ACR) plug-in. If I have more time or need the capabilities of another converter, I can load that, open the file, and make my corrections there. Most are able to transfer the processed file directly to Photoshop even if you aren't using plug-in mode.

This section provides a quick overview of the range of RAW file handlers, so you can get a better idea of the kinds of information available with particular applications. I'm going to include both high-end and low-end RAW browsers so you can see just what is available.

## Digital Photo Professional

Digital Photo Professional, introduced earlier in this chapter, is preferred by many for Canon dSLR cameras like the T5i. DPP offers much higher-speed processing of RAW images than was available with the late, not lamented, sluggardly File Viewer Utility (as much as six times faster). Canon says this utility rivals third-party stand-alone and plug-in RAW converters in speed and features. It supports both Canon's original CRW format and the newer CR2 RAW format used by the T5i, along with TIFF, Exif TIFF, and JPEG.

You can save settings that include multiple adjustments and apply them to other images, and use the clever comparison mode to compare your original and edited versions of an image either side by side or within a single split image. The utility allows easy adjustment of color channels, tone curves, exposure compensation, white balance, dynamic range, brightness, contrast, color saturation, ICC Profile embedding, and assignment of monitor profiles. A new feature is the ability to continue editing images while batches of previously adjusted RAW files are rendered and saved in the background.

## IrfanView

At the low (free) end of the price scale is IrfanView, a Windows freeware program you can download at www.irfanview.com. It can read many common RAW photo formats. It's a quick way to view RAW files (just drag and drop to the IrfanView window) and make fast changes to the unprocessed file. You can crop, rotate, or correct your image, and do some cool things like swap the colors around (red for blue, blue for green, and so forth) to create false color pictures.

The price is right, and IrfanView has some valuable capabilities. Check out www.irfanview.com.

## Phase One Capture One Pro (C1 Pro)

If there is a Cadillac of RAW converters for Nikon and Canon digital SLR cameras, C1 Pro has to be it. This premium-priced program does everything, does it well, and does it quickly. If you can't justify the price tag of this professional-level software, there are "lite" versions for serious amateurs and cash-challenged professionals called Capture and Capture One Pro 6 at $299 and Capture One Express 6, which costs as little as $99.

Aimed at photographers with high-volume needs (that would include school and portrait photographers, as well as busy commercial photographers), C1 Pro is available for both Windows and Mac OS X, and supports a broad range of Canon digital cameras. Phase One is a leading supplier of megabucks digital camera backs for medium and larger format cameras, so they really understand the needs of photographers.

The latest features include individual noise reduction controls for each image, automatic levels adjustment, a "quick develop" option that allows speedy conversion from RAW to TIFF or JPEG formats, dual-image side-by-side views for comparison purposes, and helpful grids and guides that can be superimposed over an image. Photographers concerned about copyright protection will appreciate the ability to add watermarks to the output images. See www.phaseone.com.

### BreezeBrowser

BreezeBrowser was long the RAW converter of choice for Canon dSLR owners who run Windows and who were dissatisfied with Canon's lame antique File Viewer Utility. It works quickly and has lots of options for converting CRW and CR2 files to other formats. You can choose to show highlights that will be blown out in your finished photo as flashing areas (so they can be more easily identified and corrected), use histograms to correct tones, add color profiles, auto rotate images, and adjust all those raw image parameters, such as white balance, color space, saturation, contrast, sharpening, color tone, EV compensation, and other settings.

You can also control noise reduction (choosing from low, normal, or high reduction), evaluate your changes in the live preview, and then save the file as a compressed JPEG or as either an 8-bit or 16-bit TIFF file. BreezeBrowser can also create HTML web galleries directly from your selection of images. See www.breezesys.com.

# Photoshop, Lightroom, or Both?

I've been using Photoshop since Version 2.0, and as far back in the 1980s struggled with a variety of other programs with names like Digital Darkroom, Image Studio, Picture Publisher, SuperPaint, UltraPaint, Dr. Halo, and Gray F/X (believe it or not, many early image editors could not handle *color* photos). Over the years, Photoshop has grown from being a simple image-editing program that was difficult to learn to a complete suite with basic and "extended" versions, and the capability to satisfy everyone from photographers to graphic designers to 3D artists working on motion picture production. It's gone from being difficult to learn to something akin to quantum mechanics: nobody seems to know everything about it, and most of us could spend a lifetime adding little pieces of expertise in it to our repertoires.

Today Photoshop folds the capabilities of many other applications into its bulk. It does a decent job of assembling multiple RAW images into an HDR photograph. It retouches, it color corrects, it does an amazing job of compositing, and it can tame noise and create animations. My biggest relief when I upgraded to Photoshop CS6 was that, unlike some previous versions, the new edition was enough like the old one that I was able to use it comfortably from day one. Drastic paradigm shifts are not as bad as they appear to be—but not when I'm trying to get work done. I'll probably be sticking with CS6 for a while, as Adobe has announced that it will be the last stand-alone version; all future upgrades will come as part of the Adobe Creative Cloud subscription program, which will be the only way you will be able to license future versions of this software.

Lightroom, on the other hand, will, according to Adobe, remain as a stand-alone program as well as part of the Creative Cloud subscription program. It is a newer tool that has some limited image-editing features similar to some of the pixel manipulation tools in Photoshop. However, the intent of Lightroom is to function as a workflow management application. Photoshop can do just about anything, except help you manage 100,000 different images effectively (even using its Bridge and Mini-Bridge organizing tools). Lightroom *can't* do everything, but it excels at giving you a way to manage tens or hundreds of thousands of images easily. In these days of inexpensive, huge hard drives, bracketing, and ridiculously fast continuous shooting rates, it's easy to amass that many photos. Two 3TB internal hard drives in my computer are dedicated to storing the images I shoot. (Don't worry, all those photos are safely backed up to a pair of 6TB RAID-like arrays, plus multiple duplicate hard drives stored off-site.) It would be impossible to manage all those images without something like Lightroom.

The secret behind Lightroom's image management prowess is a database it builds automatically from the EXIF data embedded in each image, with information that includes the camera model, date and time the image was captured, shutter speed, aperture, ISO, white balance, and other information. You can add more information to its catalog, including keywords that will help you retrieve a specific image later and star ratings.

Lightroom's Develop module includes correction using histograms, cropping/straightening, the ability to remove spots and correct red-eye problems, along with white balance. The exposure tools include recovery, fill light, blacks, brightness/contrast, clarity, vibrance, and saturation modules, similar to those found in Adobe Camera Raw. You can also adjust curves, perform sharpening and noise reduction, correct lens distortion, chromatic aberration, and vignetting from profiles specific for each lens. When you're done with your images, you can assemble them into slide shows or web galleries quickly.

Photoshop has all those image manipulation tools—many of them embedded in Adobe Camera Raw. Indeed, when a new release of ACR becomes available, the update fine-tunes both Lightroom and Camera Raw to offer the same functionality. But while Photoshop has more extensive image-editing features, including sophisticated selection (including Skin-Tone Selection), layering, and masking tools, its changes to your files are usually "destructive." You'll need to save snapshots as you work, or use a limited history of Undo steps to reverse your changes. Lightroom, in contrast, never applies permanent changes to the original file.

Which to choose? If you have large numbers of images to catalog and don't need the most advanced Photoshop editing tools, Lightroom may be your best bet for organizing your workflow. While Photoshop includes image management in its Bridge module, there is no database catalog system comparable to Lightroom available in Photoshop. Lightroom is also best for batch processing many files quickly. You'll probably find it easier to learn.

If you need to manipulate your images in complex ways, including compositing to combine objects from one image to another (or to move objects around within the same image), or to creatively *remove* unwanted image areas, dig in and learn Photoshop in more depth. My favorite capabilities are probably Photoshop's Content Aware editing tools, including the new Content Aware Move tool in CS6 that lets you seamlessly replace part of an image with a pattern that resembles the surrounding area. Should you be shooting a lot of movies with your T5i, Photoshop CS6 is a great deal more video-friendly than the last edition of the program.

Now, should you need *both* the most sophisticated editing tools available *and* comprehensive workflow/image management capabilities, you probably will want both Photoshop and Lightroom. Buying both—even if you qualify for upgrades for one or the other—isn't cheap. The full version of the basic Photoshop CS6 may be difficult to purchase as Adobe phases it out, but at this writing the program costs $700, or $199 for the Photoshop CS6 upgrade. Creative Cloud subscriptions vary from $20 to $49 per month, depending on how many of the CC applications you want to use. Lightroom 4 is $149 or around $80 for the Lightroom 4 update.

# 14

# Troubleshooting and Prevention

One of the nice things about modern electronic cameras like the Canon EOS T5i is that they have fewer mechanical moving parts to fail, so they are less likely to "wear out." No film transport mechanism, no wind lever or motor drive, and no complicated mechanical linkages from camera to lens to physically stop down the lens aperture. Instead, tiny, reliable motors are built into each lens (and you lose the use of only that lens should something fail), and one of the few major moving parts in the camera itself is a lightweight mirror (its small size one of the results of the T5i's 1.6X crop factor) that flips up and down with each shot.

Of course, the camera also has a moving shutter that can fail, but the shutter is built rugged enough that you can expect it to last 100,000 shutter cycles or more. Unless you're shooting sports in continuous mode day in and day out, the shutter on your T5i is likely to last as long as you expect to use the camera.

The only other things on the camera that move are switches, dials, buttons, the flip-up electronic flash, and the door that slides open to allow you to remove and insert the memory card. Unless you're extraordinarily clumsy or unlucky or give your built-in flash a good whack while it is in use, there's not a lot that can go wrong mechanically with your EOS T5i.

On the other hand, one of the chief drawbacks of modern electronic cameras is that they are modern *electronic* cameras. Your T5i is fully dependent on two different batteries. Without them, the camera can't be used. There are numerous other electrical and electronic connections in the camera (many connected to those mechanical switches and dials), and components like the color LCD that can potentially fail or suffer damage. The camera also relies on its "operating system," or *firmware*, which can be plagued by bugs that cause unexpected behavior. Luckily, electronic components are generally more reliable and trouble-free, especially when compared to their mechanical counterparts from the pre-electronic film camera days. (Film cameras of the last 10 to 20 years have had almost as many electronic features as digital cameras, but, believe it or not, there were whole generations of film cameras that had *no* electronics or batteries.)

Digital cameras have problems unique to their breed, too; the most troublesome being the need to clean the sensor of dust and grime periodically. This chapter will show you how to diagnose problems, fix some common ills, and, importantly, learn how to avoid them in the future.

# Updating Your Firmware

As I said, the firmware in your EOS T5i is the camera's operating system, which handles everything from menu display (including fonts, colors, and the actual entries themselves), what languages are available, and even support for specific devices and features. Upgrading the firmware to a new version makes it possible to add new features while fixing some of the bugs that sneak in.

## Official Firmware

Official firmware for your T5i is given a version number that you can view by turning the power on, pressing the MENU button, and navigating to Firmware Ver. x.x.x in the Set-up 4 menu. As I write this, the current version is 1.1.1. The first number in the string represents the major release number, while the second and third represent less significant upgrades and minor tweaks, respectively. Theoretically, a camera should have a firmware version number of 1.0.0 when it is introduced, but vendors have been known to do some minor fixes during testing and unveil a camera with a 1.0.5 firmware designation. If a given model is available long enough, it can evolve into significant upgrades, such as 2.0.3.

Firmware upgrades are used for both cameras and certain lenses, most frequently to fix bugs in the software, and much less frequently to add or enhance features. For example, previous firmware upgrades for Canon cameras have mended things like incorrect color temperature reporting when using specific Canon Speedlites, or problems communicating with memory cards under certain conditions. The exact changes made to the firmware are generally spelled out in the firmware release announcement. You can examine the remedies provided and decide if a given firmware patch is important to you. If not, you can usually safely wait a while before going through the bother of upgrading your firmware—at least long enough for the early adopters to report whether the bug fixes have introduced new bugs of their own. Each new firmware release incorporates the changes from previous releases, so if you skip a minor upgrade you should have no problems.

## Upgrading Your Firmware

If you're computer savvy, you might wonder how your EOS T5i is able to overwrite its own operating system—that is, how can the existing firmware be used to load the new version on top of itself? It's a little like lifting yourself by reaching down and pulling up on your bootstraps. Not ironically, that's almost exactly what happens: At your command (when you start the upgrade process), the T5i shifts into a special mode in which it is no longer operating from its firmware but, rather, from a small piece of software called a *bootstrap loader*, a separate, protected software program that functions only at startup or when upgrading firmware. The loader's function is to look for firmware to launch or, when directed, to copy new firmware from a memory card or your computer to the internal memory space where the old firmware is located. Once the new firmware has replaced the old, you can turn your camera off and then on again, and the updated operating system will be loaded.

Because the loader software is small in size and limited in function, there are some restrictions on what it can do. For example, the loader software isn't set up to go hunting through your memory card for the firmware file. It looks only in the top or root directory of your card, so that's where you must copy the firmware you download. Once you've determined that a new firmware update is available for your camera and that you want to install it, just follow these steps. (If you chicken out, any Canon service center can install the firmware upgrade for you.)

---

**WARNING**

Use a fully charged battery or Canon's optional ACK-E8 AC adapter kit to ensure that you'll have enough power to operate the camera for the entire upgrade. Moreover, you should not turn off the camera while your old firmware is being overwritten. Don't open the memory card door or do anything else that might disrupt operation of the T5i while the firmware is being installed.

---

1. Download the firmware from Canon (you'll find it in the Downloads section of the Support portion of Canon's website) and place it on your computer's hard drive. The firmware is contained in a self-extracting file for either Windows or Mac OS. It will have a name such as T5i000102.fir.

2. In your camera, format a memory card. Choose Format from the Set-up menu, and initialize the card (make sure you don't have images you want to keep before you do this!).

3. You can copy the upgrade software to the card either using a memory card reader or by connecting the camera to your computer with a USB cable and using the EOS Utility application furnished with your camera (and described in the next section). The Firmware Version entry in the Set-up 4 menu will remind you that a memory card containing the firmware is required before you can proceed.

4. Insert the memory card in the camera and then turn the camera on. With the T5i set to any mode other than Creative Auto or Full Auto, press MENU and scroll to Firmware Ver. x.x.x in the Set-up 4 menu (see Figure 14.1) and press SET.

5. You'll see the current firmware version, and an option to update, as shown in Figure 14.2. (This is a "fictional" update, as no new firmware has been released for the T5i as I write this. As a result, the screens you see when you update your camera may be slightly different.) Choose OK and press the SET button to begin loading the update program.

6. A confirmation screen will appear (see Figure 14.3). Select OK and press SET to continue. As the Firmware Update Program loads, you'll see the screen shown in Figure 14.4.

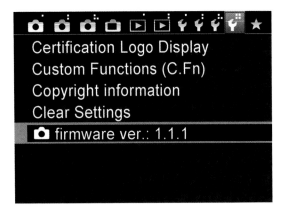

**Figure 14.1** Determine the current version number.

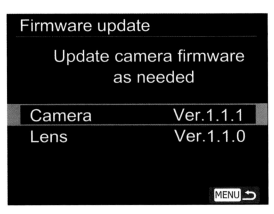

**Figure 14.2**

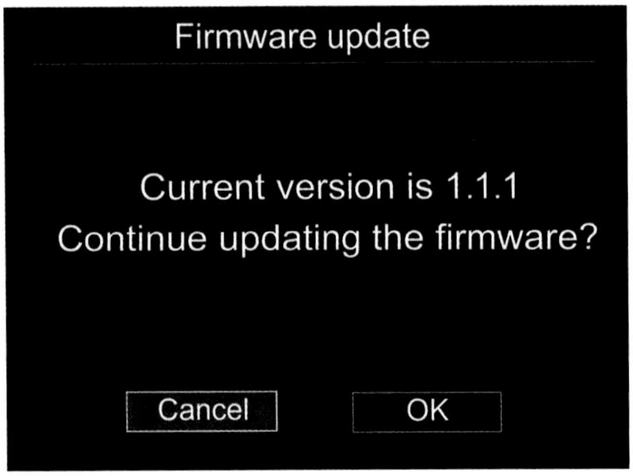

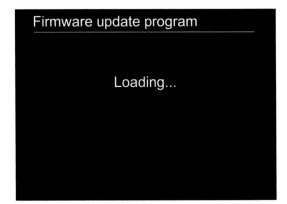

**Figure 14.3**

**Figure 14.4**

7. Next, you'll get the opportunity to confirm that the version you're upgrading to is the one you want, as you can see in Figure 14.5. You can press the MENU button to cancel. (Yes, I know there are a lot of confirmation screens; Canon wants to make sure you don't upgrade your firmware by accident, or, possibly, intentionally.)

8. Finally, the very last confirmation screen is shown in Figure 14.6. Select OK, and press SET, and, I promise, the actual firmware update will really begin.

9. While the firmware updates, you'll be warned not to turn off the power switch or touch any of the T5i's buttons. (See Figure 14.7.)

10. When the update complete screen appears (Figure 14.8), you can turn off the EOS T5i, remove the AC adapter, if used, and replace or recharge the battery. Then turn the camera on to boot up your camera with the new firmware update.

11. Be sure to reformat the card before returning it to regular use to remove the firmware software.

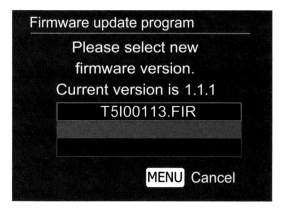

Figure 14.5

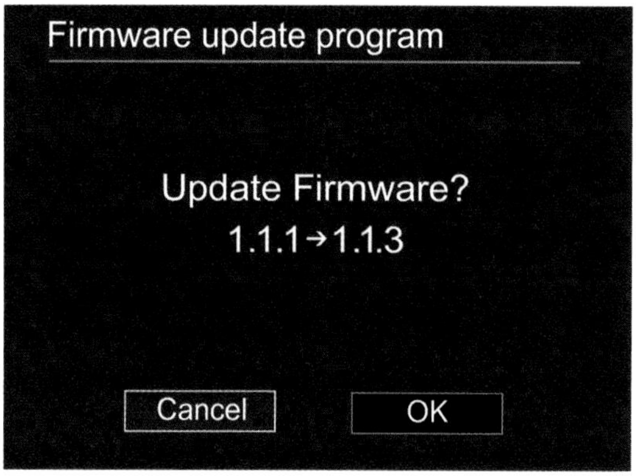

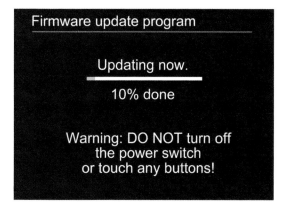

Figure 14.7

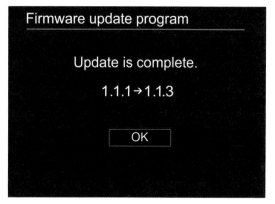

Figure 14.6

Figure 14.8

## Using Direct Camera USB Link to Copy the Software

The procedure is slightly different (and a little more automated) if you choose to transfer the firmware software to the camera through a USB linkup. Follow these instructions to get started:

1. Connect the camera (with a freshly charged battery or attached to the AC Adapter) to the computer using the USB cable and turn it on.

2. Load the EOS Utility.

3. Click the Camera/Settings/Remote Shooting button.

4. Select the Firmware Update option. When the Update Firmware window appears at the bottom of the EOS Utility, choose OK.

5. Click Yes in the confirmation screen.

6. Follow the instructions in the dialog boxes that pop up next by pressing the SET button on the camera.

# Protecting Your LCD

The color LCD on the back of your EOS T5i almost seems like a target for banging, scratching, and other abuse. Fortunately, it's quite rugged, and a few errant knocks are unlikely to shatter the protective cover over the LCD, and scratches won't easily mar its surface. However, if you want to be on the safe side, there are a number of protective products you can purchase to keep your LCD safe—and, in some cases, make it a little easier to view. I've found that the capacitive touch screen does continue to be responsive to touches and gestures with the protectors I've tried, but I haven't tried them all. Here's a quick overview of your options:

- **Plastic overlays.** The simplest solution (although not always the cheapest) is to apply a plastic overlay sheet or "skin" cut to fit your LCD. These adhere either by static electricity or through a light adhesive coating that's even less clingy than stick-it notes. You can cut down overlays made for PDAs (although these can be pricey at up to $19.95 for a set of several sheets), or purchase overlays sold specifically for digital cameras. Vendors such as Hoodman (www.hood-manusa.com) offer overlays of this type. These products will do a good job of shielding your T5i's LCD screen from scratches and minor impacts, but will not offer much protection from a good whack. These are your best choice if you plan to reverse the LCD so it faces the camera; thicker shields may not allow the LCD panel to close completely in the reversed position.

- **Flip-up hoods.** These protectors slip on using the flanges around your T5i's eyepiece, and provide a cover that completely shields the LCD, but unfolds to provide a three-sided hood that allows viewing the LCD while minimizing the extraneous light falling on it and reducing contrast. They're sold for about $40 by Hoodman and Delkin (www.delkin.com). If you want to completely protect your LCD from hard knocks and need to view the screen outdoors in bright sunlight, there is nothing better. However, I have a couple problems with these devices. First, with the cover closed, you can't peek down after taking a shot to see what your image looks like during picture review. You must open the cap each time you want to look at the LCD. Moreover, with the hood unfolded, it's difficult to look through the viewfinder: Don't count on being able to use the viewfinder *and* the LCD at the same time with one of these hoods in place.

- **Magnifiers.** If you look hard enough, you should be able to find an LCD magnifier that fits over the monitor panel and provides a 2X magnification. These often strap on clumsily, and serve better as a way to get an enlarged view of the LCD than as protection. Hoodman and other suppliers offer these specialized devices.

# Troubleshooting Memory Cards

Sometimes good memory cards go bad. Sometimes good photographers can treat their memory cards badly. It's possible that a memory card that works fine in one camera won't be recognized when inserted into another. In the worst case, you can have a card full of important photos and find that the card seems to be corrupted and you can't access any of them. Don't panic! If these scenarios sound horrific to you, there are lots of things you can do to prevent them from happening, and a variety of remedies available if they do occur. You'll want to take some time—before disaster strikes—to consider your options.

## All Your Eggs in One Basket?

The debate about whether it's better to use one large memory card or several smaller ones has been going on since even before there were memory cards. I can remember when computer users wondered whether it was smarter to install a pair of 200MB (not *gigabyte*) hard drives in their computer, or if they should go for one of those new-fangled 500MB models. By the same token, a few years ago the user groups were full of proponents who insisted that you ought to use 128MB memory cards rather than the huge 512MB versions. Today, most of the arguments involve 8GB cards versus 16GB or 32GB cards, and I expect that as prices for 64GB memory cards continue to drop, they'll find their way into the debate as well. Size is especially important when you're using a camera like the T5i that captures 18-megapixel images.

Why all the fuss? Are 16GB memory cards more likely to fail than 8GB cards? Are you risking all your photos if you trust your images to a larger card? Isn't it better to use several smaller cards, so that if one fails you lose only half as many photos? Or, isn't it wiser to put all your photos onto one larger card, because the more cards you use, the better your odds of misplacing or damaging one and losing at least some pictures?

In the end, the "eggs in one basket" argument boils down to statistics, and how you happen to use your T5i. The rationales can go both ways. If you have multiple smaller cards, you do increase your chances of something happening to one of them, so, arguably, you might be boosting the odds of losing some pictures. If all your images are important, the fact that you've lost 100 rather than 200 pictures isn't very comforting.

Also consider that the eggs/basket scenario assumes that the cards that are lost or damaged are always full. It's actually likely that your 16GB card might suffer a mishap when it's less than half-full (indeed, it's more likely that a large card won't be completely filled before it's offloaded to a computer), so you really might not lose any more shots with a single 16GB card than with multiple 8GB cards.

If you shoot photojournalist-type pictures, you probably change memory cards when they're less than completely full in order to avoid the need to do so at a crucial moment. (When I shoot sports, my cards rarely reach 80 to 90 percent of capacity before I change them.) Using multiple smaller cards means you have to change them that more often, which can be a real pain when you're taking a lot of photos. As an example, if you use tiny 2GB memory cards with an EOS T5i and shoot RAW+JPEG FINE, you may get only 68 pictures on the card. That's not even twice the capacity of a 36-exposure roll of film (remember those?). In my book, I prefer keeping all my eggs in one basket, and then making very sure that nothing happens to that basket.

There are only two really good reasons to justify limiting yourself to smaller memory cards when larger ones can be purchased at the same cost per-gigabyte. One of them is when every single picture is precious to you and the loss of any of them would be a disaster. If you're a wedding photographer, for example, and unlikely to be able to restage the nuptials if a memory card goes bad, you'll probably want to shoot no more pictures than you can afford to lose on a single card, and have an assistant ready to copy each card removed from the camera onto a backup hard drive or DVD onsite.

To be even safer, you'd want to alternate cameras or have a second photographer at least partially duplicating your coverage so your shots are distributed over several memory cards simultaneously. (Strictly speaking, the safest route of all is to spend some significant bucks on Canon's Wireless File Transmitter WFT-E5/WFT-E5A/B/C/D, and beam the images to a computer as you shoot them.)

If none of these options are available to you, consider *interleaving* your shots. Say you don't shoot weddings, but you do go on vacation from time to time. Take 50 or so pictures on one card, or whatever number of images might fill about 25 percent of its capacity. Then, replace it with a different card and shoot about 25 percent of that card's available space. Repeat these steps with diligence (you'd have to be determined to go through this inconvenience), and, if you use four or more memory cards, you'll find your pictures from each location scattered among the different memory cards. If you lose or damage one, you'll still have *some* pictures from all the various stops on your trip on the other cards. That's more work than I like to do (I usually tote around a portable hard disk and copy the files to the drive as I go), but it's an option.

# What Can Go Wrong?

There are lots of things that can go wrong with your memory card, but the ones that aren't caused by human stupidity are statistically very rare. Yes, a memory card's internal bit bin or controller can suddenly fail due to a manufacturing error or some inexplicable event caused by old age. However, if your memory card works for the first week or two that you own it, it should work forever. There's really not a lot that can wear out.

The typical memory card is rated for a Mean Time Between Failures of 1,000,000 hours of use. That's constant use 24/7 for more than 100 years! According to the manufacturers, they are good for 10,000 insertions in your camera, and should be able to retain their data (and that's without an external power source) for something on the order of 11 years. Of course, with the millions of memory cards in use, there are bound to be a few lemons here or there.

Given the reliability of solid-state memory, compared to magnetic memory, though, it's more likely that your memory problems will stem from something that you do. Memory cards are small and easy to misplace if you're not careful. For that reason, it's a good idea to keep them in their original cases or a "card safe" offered by Gepe (www.gepecardsafe.com), Pelican (www.pelican.com), and others. Always placing your memory card in a case can provide protection from the second-most common mishap that befalls memory cards: the common household laundry. If you slip a memory card in a pocket, rather than a case or your camera bag, often enough, sooner or later it's going to end up in the washing machine and probably the clothes dryer, too. There are plenty of reports of relieved digital camera owners who've laundered their memory cards and found they still worked fine, but it's not uncommon for such mistreatment to do some damage.

Memory cards can also be stomped on, accidentally bent, dropped into the ocean, chewed by pets, and otherwise rendered unusable in myriad ways. It's also possible to force a card into your T5i's memory card slot incorrectly if you're diligent enough, doing little damage to the card itself, but bending the connector pins in the camera, eliminating its ability to read or write to any memory card. Or, if the card is formatted in your computer with a memory card reader, your T5i may fail to recognize it. Occasionally, I've found that a memory card used in one camera would fail if used in a different camera (until I reformatted it in Windows, and then again in the camera). Every once in awhile, a card goes completely bad and—seemingly—can't be salvaged.

Another way to lose images is to do commonplace things with your memory card at an inopportune time. If you remove the card from the T5i while the camera is writing images to the card, you'll lose any photos in the buffer and may damage the file structure of the card, making it difficult or impossible to retrieve the other pictures you've taken. The same thing can happen if you remove the memory card from your computer's card reader while the computer is writing to the card (say, to erase files you've already moved to your computer). You can avoid this by *not* using your computer to erase files on a memory card but, instead, always reformatting the card in your T5i before you use it again.

## What Can You Do?

Pay attention: If you're having problems, the *first* thing you should do is *stop* using that memory card. Don't take any more pictures. Don't do anything with the card until you've figured out what's wrong. Your second line of defense (your first line is to be sufficiently careful with your cards that you avoid problems in the first place) is to *do no harm* that hasn't already been done. Read the rest of this section and then, if necessary, decide on a course of action (such as using a data recovery service or software described later) before you risk damaging the data on your card further.

Now that you've calmed down, the first thing to check is whether you've actually inserted a card in the camera. If you've set the camera in the Shooting menu so that Shoot w/o Card has been turned on, it's entirely possible (although not particularly plausible) that you've been snapping away with no memory card to store the pictures to, which can lead to massive disappointment later on. Of course, the No Memory Card message appears on the LCD when the camera is powered up, and it is superimposed on the review image after every shot, but maybe you're inattentive, aren't using picture review, or have purchased one of those LCD fold-up hoods mentioned earlier in this chapter. You can avoid all this by turning the Shoot w/o Card feature off and leaving it off.

Things get more exciting when the card itself is put in jeopardy. If you lose a card, there's not a lot you can do other than take a picture of a similar card and print up some Have You Seen This Lost Flash Memory? flyers to post on utility poles all around town.

If all you care about is reusing the card, and have resigned yourself to losing the pictures, try reformatting the card in your camera. You may find that reformatting removes the corrupted data and restores your card to health. Sometimes I've had success reformatting a card in my computer using a memory card reader (this is normally a no-no because your operating system doesn't understand the needs of your T5i), and *then* reformatting again in the camera.

If your memory card is not behaving properly, and you *do* want to recover your images, things get a little more complicated. If your pictures are very valuable, either to you or to others (for example, a wedding), you can always turn to professional data recovery firms. Be prepared to pay hundreds of dollars to get your pictures back, but these pros often do an amazing job. You wouldn't want them working on your memory card on behalf of the police if you'd tried to erase some incriminating pictures. There are many firms of this type, and I've never used them myself, so I can't offer a recommendation. Use a Google search to turn up a ton of them. I use a software program called RescuePro, which came free with one of my SanDisk memory cards.

## THE ULTIMATE IRONY

I recently purchased an 8GB Kingston memory card that was furnished with some nifty OnTrack data recovery software. The first thing I did was format the card to make sure it was okay. Then I hunted around for the free software, only to discover it was preloaded onto the memory card. I was supposed to copy the software to my computer before using the memory card for the first time.

Fortunately, I had the OnTrack software that would reverse my dumb move, so I could retrieve the software. No, wait. I *didn't* have the software I needed to recover the software I erased. I'd reformatted it to oblivion. Chalk this one up as either the ultimate irony or Stupid Photographer Trick #523.

A more reasonable approach is to try special data recovery software you can install on your computer and use to attempt to resurrect your "lost" images yourself. They may not actually be gone completely. Perhaps your memory card's "table of contents" is jumbled, or only a few pictures are damaged in such a way that your camera and computer can't read some or any of the pictures on the card. Some of the available software was written specifically to reconstruct lost pictures, while other utilities are more general-purpose applications that can be used with any media, including floppy disks and hard disk drives. They have names like OnTrack, Photo Rescue 2, Digital Image Recovery, MediaRecover, Image Recall, and the aptly named Recover My Photos. You'll find a comprehensive list and links, as well as some picture-recovery tips at www.ultimateslr.com/memory-card-recovery.php.

## DIMINISHING RETURNS

Usually, once you've recovered any images on a memory card, reformatted it, and returned it to service, it will function reliably for the rest of its useful life. However, if you find a particular card going bad more than once, you'll almost certainly want to stop using it forever. See if you can get it replaced by the manufacturer, if you can, but, in the case of memory card failures, the third time is never the charm.

# Cleaning Your Sensor

There's no avoiding dust. No matter how careful you are, some of it is going to settle on your camera and on the mounts of your lenses, eventually making its way inside your camera to settle in the mirror chamber. As you take photos, the mirror flipping up and down causes the dust to become airborne and eventually make its way past the shutter curtain to come to rest on the anti-aliasing filter atop your sensor. There, dust and particles can show up in every single picture you take at a small enough aperture to bring the foreign matter into sharp focus. No matter how careful you are and how cleanly you work, eventually you will get some of this dust on your camera's sensor. Some say that CMOS sensors, like the one found in the EOS T5i, "attract" less dust than CCD sensors found in cameras from other vendors. But even the cleanest-working photographers using Canon cameras are far from immune.

Fortunately, one of the EOS T5i's most useful features is the automatic sensor cleaning system that reduces or eliminates the need to clean your camera's sensor manually. Canon has applied anti-static coatings to the sensor and other portions of the camera body interior to counter charge build-ups that attract dust. A separate filter over the sensor vibrates ultrasonically each time the T5i is powered on or off, shaking loose any dust.

Although the automatic sensor cleaning feature operates when you power the camera up or turn it off, you can activate it at any time. Choose Sensor Cleaning from the Set-up 3 menu, and select Clean Now. If you'd rather turn the feature on or off, choose Auto Cleaning instead, and then choose either Enable or Disable with the cross keys. Press SET, then press the MENU button to return to the Set-up 3 menu (see Figure 14.9).

If some dust does collect on your sensor, you can often map it out of your images (making it invisible) using software techniques with the Dust Delete Data feature in the Shooting 3 menu. Operation of this feature is described in Chapter 8. Of course, even with the EOS T5i's automatic

**Figure 14.9**
You can activate automatic sensor cleaning immediately or enable/disable the feature.

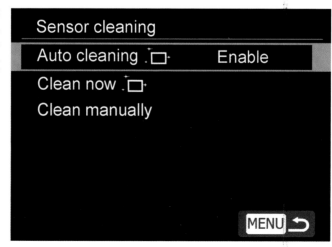

sensor cleaning/dust resistance features, you may still be required to manually clean your sensor from time to time. This section explains the phenomenon and provides some tips on minimizing dust and eliminating it when it begins to affect your shots. I also cover this subject in my book, *Digital SLR Pro Secrets*, with complete instructions for constructing your own sensor cleaning tools. However, I'll provide a condensed version here of some of the information in that book, because sensor dust and sensor cleaning are two of the most contentious subjects Canon EOS T5i owners have to deal with.

## Dust the FAQs, Ma'am

Here are some of the most frequently asked questions about sensor dust issues:

**Q. I see tiny specks in my viewfinder. Do I have dust on my sensor?**

**A.** If you see sharp, well-defined specks, they are clinging to the underside of your focus screen and not on your sensor. They have absolutely no effect on your photographs, and are merely annoying or distracting.

**Q. I can see dust on my mirror. How can I remove it?**

**A.** Like focus screen dust, any artifacts that have settled on your mirror won't affect your photos. You can often remove dust on the mirror or focus screen with a bulb air blower, which will loosen it and whisk it away. Stubborn dust on the focus screen can sometimes be gently flicked away with a soft brush designed for cleaning lenses. I don't recommend brushing the mirror or touching it in any way. The mirror is a special front-surface-silvered optical device (unlike conventional mirrors, which are silvered on the back side of a piece of glass or plastic) and can be easily scratched. If you can't blow mirror dust off, it's best to just forget about it. You can't see it in the viewfinder, anyway.

**Q. I see a bright spot in the same place in all of my photos. Is that sensor dust?**

**A.** You've probably got either a "hot" pixel or one that is permanently "stuck" due to a defect in the sensor. A hot pixel is one that shows up as a bright spot only during long exposures as the sensor warms. A pixel stuck in the "on" position always appears in the image. Both show up as bright red, green, or blue pixels, usually surrounded by a small cluster of other improperly illuminated pixels, caused by the camera's interpolating the hot or stuck pixel into its surroundings, as shown in Figure 14.10. A stuck pixel can also be permanently dark. Either kind is likely to show up when they contrast with plain, evenly colored areas of your image.

**Figure 14.10** A stuck pixel is surrounded by improperly interpolated pixels created by the T5i's demosaicing algorithm.

Finding one or two hot or stuck pixels in your sensor is unfortunately fairly common. They can be "removed" by telling the T5i to ignore them through a simple process called *pixel mapping*. If the bad pixels become bothersome, Canon can remap your sensor's pixels with a quick trip to a service center.

Bad pixels can also show up on your camera's color LCD panel, but, unless they are abundant, the wisest course is to just ignore them.

**Q. I see an irregular out-of-focus blob in the same place in my photos. Is that sensor dust?**

**A.** Yes. Sensor contaminants can take the form of tiny spots, larger blobs, or even curvy lines if they are caused by minuscule fibers that have settled on the sensor. They'll appear out of focus because they aren't actually on the sensor surface but, rather, a fraction of a millimeter above it on the filter that covers the sensor. The smaller the f/stop used, the more in-focus the dust becomes. At large apertures, it may not be visible at all.

**Q. I never see any dust on my sensor. What's all the fuss about?**

**A.** Those who never have dust problems with their EOS T5i fall into one of four categories: those for whom the camera's automatic dust removal features are working well; those who seldom change their lenses and have clean working habits that minimize the amount of dust that invades their cameras in the first place; those who simply don't notice the dust (often because they don't shoot many macro photos or other pictures using the small f/stops that makes dust evident in their images); and those who are very, very lucky.

## Identifying and Dealing with Dust

Sensor dust is less of a problem than it might be because it shows up only under certain circumstances. Indeed, you might have dust on your sensor right now and not be aware if it. The dust doesn't actually settle on the sensor itself, but, rather, on a protective filter a very tiny distance above the sensor, subjecting it to the phenomenon of *depth-of-focus*. Depth-of-focus is the distance the focal plane can be moved and still render an object in sharp focus. At f/2.8 to f/5.6 or even smaller, sensor dust, particularly if small, is likely to be outside the range of depth-of-focus and blur into an unnoticeable dot.

However, if you're shooting at f/16 to f/22 or smaller, those dust motes suddenly pop into focus. Forget about trying to spot them by peering directly at your sensor with the shutter open and the lens removed. The period at the end of this sentence, about .33mm in diameter, could block a group of pixels measuring 40 × 40 pixels (160 pixels in all!). Dust spots that are even smaller than that can easily show up in your images if you're shooting large, empty areas that are light colored. Dust motes are most likely to show up in the sky, as in Figure 14.11, or in white backgrounds of your seamless product shots and are less likely to be a problem in images that contain lots of dark areas and detail.

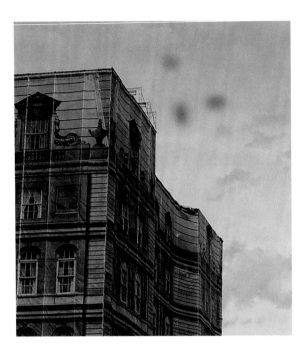

**Figure 14.11**
Only the dust spots in the sky are apparent in this shot.

To see if you have dust on your sensor, take a few test shots of a plain, blank surface (such as a piece of paper or a cloudless sky) at small f/stops, such as f/22, and a few wide open. Open Photoshop, copy several shots into a single document in separate layers, then flip back and forth between layers to see if any spots you see are present in all layers. You may have to boost contrast and sharpness to make the dust easier to spot.

## Avoiding Dust

Of course, the easiest way to protect your sensor from dust is to prevent it from settling on the sensor in the first place. Some Canon lenses come with rubberized seals around the lens mounts that help keep dust from infiltrating, but you'll find that dust will still find a way to get inside. Here are my tips for eliminating the problem before it begins:

- **Clean environment.** Avoid working in dusty areas if you can do so. Hah! Serious photographers will take this one with a grain of salt, because it usually makes sense to go where the pictures are. Only a few of us are so paranoid about sensor dust (considering that it is so easily removed) that we'll avoid moderately grimy locations just to protect something that is, when you get down to it, just a tool. If you find a great picture opportunity at a raging fire, during a sandstorm, or while surrounded by dust clouds, you might hesitate to take the picture, but, with a little caution (don't remove your lens in these situations, and clean the camera afterward!) you can still shoot. However, it still makes sense to store your camera in a clean environment. One place cameras and lenses pick up a lot of dust is inside a camera bag. Clean your bag from time to time, and you can avoid problems.

- **Clean lenses.** There are a few paranoid types that avoid swapping lenses in order to minimize the chance of dust getting inside their cameras. It makes more sense just to use a blower or brush to dust off the rear lens mount of the replacement lens first, so you won't be introducing dust into your camera simply by attaching a new, dusty lens. Do this before you remove the lens from your camera, and then avoid stirring up dust before making the exchange.

- **Work fast.** Minimize the time your camera is lens-less and exposed to dust. That means having your replacement lens ready and dusted off, and a place to set down the old lens as soon as it is removed, so you can quickly attach the new lens.

- **Let gravity help you.** Face the camera downward when the lens is detached so any dust in the mirror box will tend to fall away from the sensor. Turn your back to any breezes, indoor forced air vents, fans, or other sources of dust to minimize infiltration.

- **Protect the lens you just removed.** Once you've attached the new lens, quickly put the end cap on the one you just removed to reduce the dust that might fall on it.

- **Clean out the vestibule.** From time to time, remove the lens while in a relatively dust-free environment and use a blower bulb like the one shown in Figure 14.12 (*not* compressed air or a vacuum hose) to clean out the mirror box area. A blower bulb is generally safer than a can of compressed air, or a strong positive/negative airflow, which can tend to drive dust further into nooks and crannies.

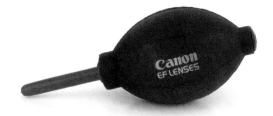

**Figure 14.12**  Use a robust air bulb for cleaning your sensor.

- **Be prepared.** If you're embarking on an important shooting session, it's a good idea to clean your sensor *now*, rather than come home with hundreds or thousands of images with dust spots caused by flecks that were sitting on your sensor before you even started. Before I left on my recent trip to Spain, I put both cameras I was taking through a rigid cleaning regimen, figuring they could remain dust-free for a measly 10 days. I even left my bulky blower bulb at home. It was a big mistake, but my intentions were good.

- **Clone out existing spots in your image editor.** Photoshop and other editors have a clone tool or healing brush you can use to copy pixels from surrounding areas over the dust spot or dead pixel. This process can be tedious, especially if you have lots of dust spots and/or lots of images to be corrected. The advantage is that this sort of manual fix-it probably will do the least damage to the rest of your photo. Only the cloned pixels will be affected.

- **Use filtration in your image editor.** A semi-smart filter like Photoshop's Dust & Scratches filter can remove dust and other artifacts by selectively blurring areas that the plug-in decides represent dust spots. This method can work well if you have many dust spots, because you won't need to patch them manually. However, any automated method like this has the possibility of blurring areas of your image that you didn't intend to soften.

# Sensor Cleaning

Those new to the concept of sensor dust actually hesitate before deciding to clean their camera themselves. Isn't it a better idea to pack up your T5i and send it to a Canon service center so their crack technical staff can do the job for you? Or, at the very least, shouldn't you let the friendly folks at your local camera store do it?

Of course, if you choose to let someone else clean your sensor, they will be using methods that are more or less identical to the techniques you would use yourself. None of these techniques are difficult, and the only difference between their cleaning and your cleaning is that they might have done it dozens or hundreds of times. If you're careful, you can do just as good a job.

Of course vendors like Canon won't tell you this, but it's not because they don't trust you. It's not that difficult for a real goofball to mess up his camera by hurrying or taking a shortcut. Perhaps the person uses the "Bulb" method of holding the shutter open and a finger slips, allowing the shutter curtain to close on top of a sensor cleaning brush. Or, someone tries to clean the sensor using masking tape, and ends up with goo all over its surface. If Canon recommended *any* method that's mildly risky, someone would do it wrong, and then the company would face lawsuits from those who'd contend they did it exactly in the way the vendor suggested, so the ruined camera is not their fault. If you visit Canon's website, you'll find this recommendation: "If the image sensor needs cleaning, we recommend having it cleaned at a Canon service center, as it is a very delicate component."

You can see that vendors like Canon tend to be conservative in their recommendations, and, in doing so, make it seem as if sensor cleaning is more daunting and dangerous than it really is. Some vendors recommend only dust-off cleaning, through the use of reasonably gentle blasts of air, while condemning more serious scrubbing with swabs and cleaning fluids. However, these cleaning kits for the exact types of cleaning they recommended against are for sale in Japan only, where, apparently, your average photographer is more dexterous than those of us in the rest of the world. These kits are similar to those used by official repair staff to clean your sensor if you decide to send your camera in for a dust-up.

As I noted, sensors can be affected by dust particles that are much smaller than you might be able to spot visually on the surface of your lens. The filters that cover sensors tend to be fairly hard compared to optical glass. Cleaning the 22.3mm × 14.9mm sensor in your Canon T5i within the tight confines of the mirror box can call for a steady hand and careful touch. If your sensor's filter becomes scratched through inept cleaning, you can't simply remove it yourself and replace it with a new one.

There are four basic kinds of cleaning processes that can be used to remove dusty and sticky stuff that settles on your dSLR's sensor. All of these must be performed with the shutter locked open. I'll describe these methods and provide instructions for locking the shutter later in this section.

- **Air cleaning.** This process involves squirting blasts of air inside your camera with the shutter locked open. This works well for dust that's not clinging stubbornly to your sensor.
- **Brushing.** A soft, very fine brush is passed across the surface of the sensor's filter, dislodging mildly persistent dust particles and sweeping them off the imager.

- **Liquid cleaning.** A soft swab dipped in a cleaning solution such as ethanol is used to wipe the sensor filter, removing more obstinate particles.

- **Tape cleaning.** There are some who get good results by applying a special form of tape to the surface of their sensor. When the tape is peeled off, all the dust goes with it. Supposedly. I'd be remiss if I didn't point out right now that this form of cleaning is somewhat controversial; the other three methods are much more widely accepted. Now that Canon has equipped the front-sensor filter with a special anti-dust coating, I wouldn't chance damaging that coating by using any kind of adhesive tape.

### Placing the Shutter in the Locked and Fully Upright Position for Cleaning

Make sure you're using a fully charged battery or the optional AC Adapter Kit ACK-E6.

1. Remove the lens from the camera and then turn the camera on.

2. Set the EOS T5i to any one of the non-fully automatic modes.

3. You'll find the Clean Manually menu choice in the Set-up 2 menu under Sensor Cleaning (see Figure 14.9, shown earlier). Press the SET button.

4. Select OK and press SET again. The mirror will flip up and the shutter will open.

5. Use one of the methods described below to remove dust and grime from your sensor. Be careful not to accidentally switch the power off or open the memory card or battery compartment doors as you work. If that happens, the shutter may be damaged if it closes onto your cleaning tool.

6. When you're finished, turn the power off, replace your lens, and switch your camera back on.

### Air Cleaning

Your first attempts at cleaning your sensor should always involve gentle blasts of air. Many times, you'll be able to dislodge dust spots, which will fall off the sensor and, with luck, out of the mirror box. Attempt one of the other methods only when you've already tried air cleaning and it didn't remove all the dust.

Here are some tips for doing air cleaning:

- **Use a clean, powerful air bulb.** Your best bet is bulb cleaners designed for the job, like the Giottos Rocket. Smaller bulbs, like those air bulbs with a brush attached sometimes sold for lens cleaning or weak nasal aspirators, may not provide sufficient air or a strong enough blast to do much good.

- **Hold the EOS T5i upside down.** Then look up into the mirror box as you squirt your air blasts, increasing the odds that gravity will help pull the expelled dust downward, away from the sensor. You may have to use some imagination in positioning yourself. (See Figure 14.13.)

- **Never use air canisters.** The propellant inside these cans can permanently coat your sensor if you tilt the can while spraying. It's not worth taking a chance.

- **Avoid air compressors.** Super-strong blasts of air are likely to force dust under the sensor filter.

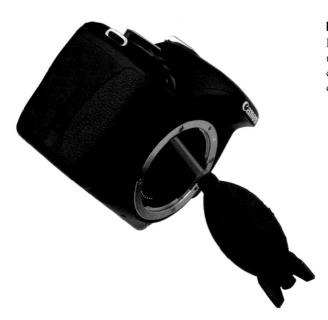

**Figure 14.13**
Hold the camera upside down when cleaning to allow dust to fall out.

## Brush Cleaning

If your dust is a little more stubborn and can't be dislodged by air alone, you may want to try a brush, charged with static electricity, that can pick off dust spots by electrical attraction. One good, but expensive, option is the Sensor Brush sold at www.visibledust.com. A cheaper version can be purchased at www.copperhillimages.com. You need a 16mm version, like the one shown in Figure 14.14, that can be stroked across the short dimension of your T5i's sensor.

Ordinary artist's brushes are much too coarse and stiff and have fibers that are tangled or can come loose and settle on your sensor. A good sensor brush's fibers are resilient and described as "thinner than a human hair." Moreover, the brush has a wooden handle that reduces the risk of static sparks.

Brush cleaning is done with a dry brush by gently swiping the surface of the sensor filter with the tip. The dust particles are attracted to the brush particles and cling to them. You should clean the brush with compressed air before and after each use, and store it in an appropriate air-tight container between applications to keep it clean and dust-free. Although these special brushes are expensive, one should last you a long time.

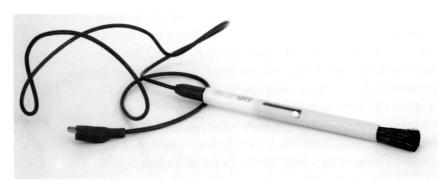

**Figure 14.14**
A proper brush, preferably with a grounding strap to eliminate static electricity, is required for dusting off your sensor.

## Liquid Cleaning

Unfortunately, you'll often encounter really stubborn dust spots that can't be removed with a blast of air or flick of a brush. These spots may be combined with some grease or a liquid that causes them to stick to the sensor filter's surface. In such cases, liquid cleaning with a swab may be necessary. During my first clumsy attempts to clean my own sensor, I accidentally got my blower bulb tip too close to the sensor, and some sort of deposit from the tip of the bulb ended up on the sensor. I panicked until I discovered that liquid cleaning did a good job of removing whatever it was that took up residence on my sensor.

You can make your own swabs out of pieces of plastic (some use fast food restaurant knives, with the tip cut at an angle to the proper size) covered with a soft cloth or Pec-Pad, as shown in Figures 14.15 and 14.16. However, if you've got the bucks to spend, you can't go wrong with good-quality commercial sensor cleaning swabs, such as those sold by Photographic Solutions, Inc. (www.photosol.com).

You want a sturdy swab that won't bend or break so you can apply gentle pressure to the swab as you wipe the sensor surface. Use the swab with methanol (as pure as you can get it, particularly medical grade; other ingredients can leave a residue), or the Eclipse solution also sold by Photographic Solutions. Eclipse is actually quite a bit purer than even medical-grade methanol. A couple drops of solution should be enough, unless you have a spot that's extremely difficult to remove. In that case, you may need to use extra solution on the swab to help "soak" the dirt off.

Once you overcome your nervousness at touching your T5i's sensor, the process is easy. You'll wipe continuously with the swab in one direction, then flip it over and wipe in the other direction. You need to completely wipe the entire surface; otherwise, you may end up depositing the dust you collect at the far end of your stroke. Wipe; don't rub.

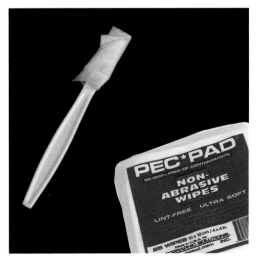

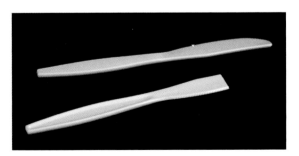

**Figure 14.15** You can make your own sensor swab from a plastic knife that's been truncated.

**Figure 14.16** Carefully wrap a Pec-Pad around the swab.

If you want a close-up look at your sensor to make sure the dust has been removed, you can pay $50–$100 for a special sensor "microscope" with an illuminator. (See Figure 14.17.) Or, you can do like I do and work with a plain old Carson MiniBrite PO-55 illuminated 5X magnifier, as seen in Figure 14.18. It has a built-in LED and, held a few inches from the lens mount with the lens removed from your T5i, provides a sharp, close-up view of the sensor, with enough contrast to reveal any dust that remains. You can read more about this great device at http://dslrguides.com/carson.

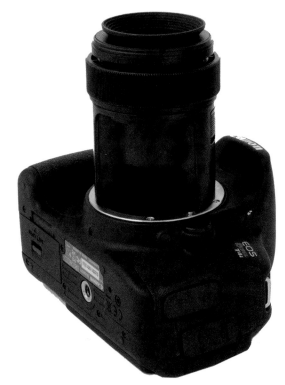

**Figure 14.17**
This SensorKlear magnifier provides a view of your sensor as you work.

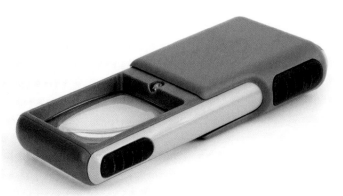

**Figure 14.18**
An illuminated magnifier like this Carson MiniBrite PO-55 can be used as a 'scope to view your sensor.

# Index

# Get the eBooks FREE!

## (PDF, ePub, and Kindle all included)

We believe that once you buy a book from us,
you should be able to read it in any format
we have available. To get electronic versions
of this book at no additional cost to you,
purchase and then register this book at the
Manning website following the instructions
inside this insert.

# That's it!

# Thanks from Manning!

D1604866

# Unity in Action

*Multiplatform Game Development in C#*

JOSEPH HOCKING

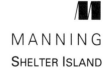

MANNING

SHELTER ISLAND

For online information and ordering of this and other Manning books, please visit
www.manning.com. The publisher offers discounts on this book when ordered in quantity.
For more information, please contact

Special Sales Department
Manning Publications Co.
20 Baldwin Road
PO Box 761
Shelter Island, NY 11964
Email: orders@manning.com

Manning Publications Co.
20 Baldwin Road
PO Box 761
Shelter Island, NY 11964

Development editor: Dan Maharry
Technical development editor: Scott Chaussee
Copyeditor: Elizabeth Welch
Proofreader: Melody Dolab
Technical proofreader: Christopher Haupt
Typesetter: Marija Tudor
Cover designer: Marija Tudor

ISBN: 9781617292323
Printed in the United States of America
7 8 9 10 – EBM – 20 19 18 17

Corrected printing March 2017

# brief contents

# contents

# foreword

I started programming games in 1982. It wasn't easy. We had no internet. Resources were limited to a handful of mostly terrible books and magazines that offered fascinating but confusing code fragments, and as for game engines—well, there weren't any! Coding games was a massive uphill battle.

How I envy you, reader, holding the power of this book in your hands. The Unity engine has done so much to open game programming to so many people. Unity has managed to strike an excellent balance by being a powerful, professional game engine that's still affordable and approachable for someone just getting started.

Approachable, that is, with the right guidance. I once spent time in a circus troupe run by a magician. He was kind enough to take me in and help guide me toward becoming a good performer. "When you stand on a stage," he pronounced, "you make a promise. And that promise is 'I will not waste your time.'"

What I love most about *Unity in Action* is the "action" part. Joe Hocking wastes none of your time and gets you coding fast—and not just nonsense code, but interesting code that you can understand and build from, because he knows you don't just want to read his book, and you don't just want to program his examples—you want to be coding *your own game*.

And with his guidance, you'll be able to do that sooner than you might expect. Follow Joe's steps, but when you feel ready, don't be shy about diverging from his path and breaking out on your own. Skip around to what interests you most—try experiments, be bold and brave! You can always return to the text if you get too lost.

But let's not dally in this foreword—the entire future of game development is impatiently waiting for you to begin! Mark this day on your calendar, for today is the day that everything changed. It will be forever remembered as the day you started making games.

JESSE SCHELL
CEO OF SCHELL GAMES
AUTHOR OF *THE ART OF GAME DESIGN*

I've been programming games for quite some time, but only started using Unity relatively recently. Unity didn't exist when I first started developing games; the first version was released in 2005. Right from the start, it had a lot of promise as a game development tool, but it didn't come into its own until several versions later. In particular, platforms like iOS and Android (collectively referred to as "mobile") didn't emerge until later, and those platforms factor heavily into Unity's growing prominence.

Initially, I viewed Unity as a curiosity, an interesting development tool to keep an eye on but not actually use. During this time, I was programming games for both desktop computers and websites and doing projects for a range of clients. I was using tools like Blitz3D and Flash, which were great to program in but were limiting in a lot of ways. As those tools started to show their age, I kept looking for better ways to develop games.

I started experimenting with Unity around version 3, and then completely switched to it when Synapse Games (the company I work for now) started developing mobile games. At first, I worked for Synapse on web games, but we eventually moved over to mobile games. And then we came full circle because Unity enabled us to deploy to the web in addition to mobile, all from one codebase!

I've always seen sharing knowledge as important, and I've taught game development for the last several years. In large part I do this because of the example set for me by the many mentors and teachers I've had. (Incidentally, you may even have heard of one of my teachers because he was such an inspiring person: Randy Pausch delivered the Last Lecture shortly before he passed away in 2008.) I've taught classes at several schools, and I've always wanted to write a book about game development.

In many ways, what I've written here is the book I wish had existed back when I was first learning Unity. Among Unity's many virtues is the availability of a huge treasure trove of learning resources, but those resources tend to take the form of unfocused fragments (like the script reference or isolated tutorials) and require a great deal of digging to find what you need. Ideally, I'd have a book that wrapped up everything I needed to know in one place and presented it in a clear and logically constructed manner, so now I'm writing such a book for you. I'm targeting people who already know how to program, but who are newcomers to Unity, and possibly new to game development in general. The choice of projects reflects my experience of gaining skills and confidence by doing a variety of freelance projects in rapid succession.

In learning to develop games using Unity, you're setting out on an exciting adventure. For me, learning how to develop games meant putting up with a lot of hassles. You, on the other hand, have the advantage of a single coherent resource to learn from: this book!

# acknowledgments

I would like to thank Manning Publications for giving me the opportunity to write this book. The editors I worked with, including Robin de Jongh and especially Dan Maharry, helped me throughout this undertaking, and the book is much stronger for their feedback. Meanwhile, Mary Piergies expertly managed the production process and patiently guided me through the book's release. My sincere thanks also to the many others who worked with me during the development and production of the book.

My writing benefited from the scrutiny of reviewers every step of the way. Thanks to Alex Lucas, Craig Hoffman, Dan Kacenjar, Joshua Frederick, Luca Campobasso, Mark Elston, Philip Taffet, René van den Berg, Sergio Arbeo Rodríguez, Shiloh Morris, and Victor M. Perez. Special thanks to the notable review work by technical development editor Scott Chaussee and by technical proofreader Christopher Haupt. And I also want to thank Jesse Schell for writing the foreword to my book.

Next, I'd like to recognize the people who've made my experience with Unity a fruitful one. That, of course, starts with Unity Technologies, the company that makes Unity (the game engine). I owe a debt to the community at gamedev.stackexchange.com. I visit that QA site almost daily to learn from others and to answer questions. And the biggest push for me to use Unity came from Alex Reeve, my boss at Synapse Games. Similarly, I've picked up tricks and techniques from my coworkers, and they all show up in the code I write.

Finally, I want to thank my wife Virginia for her support during the time I was writing the book. Until I started working on it, I never really understood how much a book project takes over your life and affects everyone around you. Thank you so much for your love and encouragement.

# *about this book*

This is a book about programming games in Unity. Think of it as an intro to Unity for experienced programmers. The goal of this book is straightforward: to take people who have some programming experience but no experience with Unity and teach them how to develop a game using Unity.

The best way of teaching development is through example projects, with students learning by doing, and that's the approach this book takes. I'll present topics as steps toward building sample games, and you'll be encouraged to build these games in Unity while exploring the book. We'll go through a selection of different projects every few chapters, rather than one monolithic project developed over the entire book; sometimes other books take the "one monolithic project" approach, but that can make it hard to jump into the middle if the early chapters aren't relevant to you.

This book will have more rigorous programming content than most Unity books (especially beginners' books). Unity is often portrayed as a list of features with no programming required, which is a misleading view that won't teach people what they need to know in order to produce commercial titles. If you don't already know how to program a computer, I suggest going to a resource like Codecademy first (the computer programming lessons at Khan Academy work well, too) and then come back to this book after learning how to program.

Don't worry about the exact programming language; C# is used throughout this book, but skills from other languages will transfer quite well. Although the first half of the book will take its time introducing new concepts and will carefully and deliberately step you through developing your first game in Unity, the remaining chapters will move a lot faster in order to take readers through projects in multiple game genres. The book will end with a chapter describing deployment to various platforms like the web and mobile, but the main thrust of the book won't make any reference to the ultimate deployment target because Unity is wonderfully platform-agnostic.

As for other aspects of game development, extensive coverage of art disciplines would water down how much the book can cover and would be largely about software external to Unity (for example, the animation software used). Discussion of art tasks will be limited to aspects specific to Unity or that all game developers should know. (Note, though, that there is an appendix about modeling custom objects.)

## *Roadmap*

Chapter 1 introduces you to Unity, the cross-platform game development environment. You'll learn about the fundamental component system underlying everything in Unity, as well as how to write and execute basic scripts.

Chapter 2 progresses to writing a demo of movement in 3D, covering topics like mouse and keyboard input. Defining and manipulating both 3D positions and rotations are thoroughly explained.

Chapter 3 turns the movement demo into a first-person shooter, teaching you raycasting and basic AI. Raycasting (shooting a line into the scene and seeing what intersects) is a useful operation for all sorts of games.

Chapter 4 covers art asset importing and creation. This is the one chapter of the book that does not focus on code, because every project needs (basic) models and textures.

Chapter 5 teaches you how to create a 2D game in Unity. Although Unity started exclusively for 3D graphics, there's now excellent support for 2D graphics.

Chapter 6 introduces you to the latest GUI functionality in Unity. Every game needs a UI, and the latest versions of Unity feature an improved system for creating user interfaces.

Chapter 7 shows how to create another movement demo in 3D, only seen from the third person this time. Implementing third-person controls will demonstrate a number of key 3D math operations, and you'll learn how to work with an animated character.

Chapter 8 goes over how to implement interactive devices and items within your game. The player will have a number of ways of operating these devices, including touching them directly, touching triggers within the game, or pressing a button on the controller.

Chapter 9 covers how to communicate with the internet. You'll learn how to send and receive data using standard internet technologies, like HTTP requests to get XML data from a server.

Chapter 10 teaches how to program audio functionality. Unity has great support for both short sound effects and long music tracks; both sorts of audio are crucial for almost all video games.

Chapter 11 walks you through bringing together pieces from different chapters into a single game. In addition, you'll learn how to program point-and-click controls and how to save the player's game.

Chapter 12 goes over building the final app, with deployment to multiple platforms like desktop, web, and mobile. Unity is wonderfully platform-agnostic, enabling you to create games for every major gaming platform!

There are also four appendixes with additional information about scene navigation, external tools, Blender, and learning resources.

### Code conventions, requirements, and downloads

All the source code in the book, whether in code listings or snippets, is in a `fixed-width font like this`, which sets it off from the surrounding text. In most listings, the code is annotated to point out key concepts, and numbered bullets are sometimes used in the text to provide additional information about the code. The code is formatted so that it fits within the available page space in the book by adding line breaks and using indentation carefully.

The only software required is Unity; this book uses Unity 5.0, which is the latest version as I write this. Certain chapters do occasionally discuss other pieces of software, but those are treated as optional extras and not core to what you're learning.

> **WARNING** Unity projects remember which version of Unity they were created in and will issue a warning if you attempt to open them in a different version. If you see that warning while opening this book's sample downloads, click Continue and ignore it.

The code listings sprinkled throughout the book generally show what to add or change in existing code files; unless it's the first appearance of a given code file, don't replace the entire file with subsequent listings. Although you can download complete working sample projects to refer to, you'll learn best by typing out the code listings and only looking at the working samples for reference. Those downloads are available from the publisher's website at www.manning.com/UnityinAction.

### Author Online

The purchase of *Unity in Action* includes free access to a private web forum run by Manning Publications, where you can make comments about the book, ask technical questions, and receive help from the author and from other users. To access the forum and subscribe to it, point your web browser to www.manning.com/Unityin Action. This page provides information on how to get on the forum once you are registered, what kind of help is available, and the rules of conduct on the forum.

Manning's commitment to our readers is to provide a venue where a meaningful dialogue between individual readers and between readers and the author can take place. It is not a commitment to any specific amount of participation on the part of the author whose contribution to the forum remains voluntary (and unpaid). We suggest you try asking the author some challenging questions lest his interest stray!

The Author Online forum and the archives of previous discussions will be accessible from the publisher's website as long as the book is in print.

## About the author

Joseph Hocking is a software engineer living in Chicago, specializing in interactive media development. He works for Synapse Games as a developer of web and mobile games, such as the recently released *Tyrant Unleashed*. He also teaches classes in game development at Columbia College Chicago, and his website is www.newarteest.com.

## About the cover illustration

The figure on the cover of *Unity in Action* is captioned "Habit of the Master of Ceremonies of the Grand Signior." The Grand Signior was another name for a sultan of the Ottoman Empire. The illustration is taken from Thomas Jefferys' *A Collection of the Dresses of Different Nations, Ancient and Modern* (4 volumes), London, published between 1757 and 1772. The title page states that these are hand-colored copperplate engravings, heightened with gum arabic. Thomas Jefferys (1719–1771), was called "Geographer to King George III." An English cartographer who was the leading map supplier of his day, Jeffreys engraved and printed maps for government and other official bodies and produced a wide range of commercial maps and atlases, especially of North America. His work as a mapmaker sparked an interest in local dress customs of the lands he surveyed, which are brilliantly displayed in this four-volume collection.

Fascination with faraway lands and travel for pleasure were relatively new phenomena in the late eighteenth century and collections such as this one were popular, introducing both the tourist as well as the armchair traveler to the inhabitants of other countries. The diversity of the drawings in Jeffreys' volumes speaks vividly of the uniqueness and individuality of the world's nations some 200 years ago. Dress codes have changed since then and the diversity by region and country, so rich at the time, has faded away. It is now hard to tell the inhabitant of one continent apart from another. Perhaps, trying to view it optimistically, we have traded a cultural and visual diversity for a more varied personal life, or a more varied and interesting intellectual and technical life.

At a time when it is hard to tell one computer book from another, Manning celebrates the inventiveness and initiative of the computer business with book covers based on the rich diversity of regional life of two centuries ago, brought back to life by Jeffreys' pictures.

# Part 1

## First steps

I t's time to take your first steps in using Unity. If you don't know anything about Unity, that's okay! I'm going to start by explaining what Unity *is*, including fundamentals of how to program games in it. Then we'll walk through a tutorial about developing a simple game in Unity. This first project will teach you a number of specific game development techniques as well as give you a good overview of how the process works.

Onward to chapter 1!

# Getting to know Unity

**This chapter covers**

- What makes Unity a great choice
- Operating the Unity editor
- Programming in Unity
- Comparing C# and JavaScript

If you're anything like me, you've had developing a video game on your mind for a long time. But it's a big jump from simply playing games to actually making them. Numerous game development tools have appeared over the years, and we're going to discuss one of the most recent and most powerful of these tools. Unity is a professional-quality game engine used to create video games targeting a variety of platforms. Not only is it a professional development tool used daily by thousands of seasoned game developers, it's also one of the most accessible modern tools for novice game developers. Until recently, a newcomer to game development (especially 3D games) would face lots of imposing barriers right from the start, but Unity makes it easy to start learning these skills.

Because you're reading this book, chances are you're curious about computer technology and you've either developed games with other tools or built other kinds of software, like desktop applications or websites. Creating a video game isn't fundamentally different from writing any other kind of software; it's mostly a difference of degree. For example, a video game is a lot more interactive than most websites and thus involves very different sorts of code, but the skills and processes involved in creating both are similar. If you've already cleared the first hurdle on your path to learning game development, having learned the fundamentals of programming software, then your next step is to pick up some game development tools and translate that programming knowledge into the realm of gaming. Unity is a great choice of game development environment to work with.

---

**A warning about terminology**

This book is about programming in Unity and is therefore primarily of interest to coders. Although many other resources discuss other aspects of game development and Unity, this is a book where programming takes front and center.

Incidentally, note that the word *developer* has a possibly unfamiliar meaning in the context of game development: *developer* is a synonym for *programmer* in disciplines like web development, but in game development the word *developer* refers to anyone who works on a game, with *programmer* being a specific role within that. Other kinds of game developers are artists and designers, but this book will focus on programming.

---

To start, go to the website www.unity3d.com to download the software. This book uses Unity 5.0, which is the latest version as of this writing. The URL is a leftover from Unity's original focus on 3D games; support for 3D games remains strong, but Unity works great for 2D games as well. Meanwhile, although advanced features are available in paid versions, the base version is completely free. Everything in this book works in the free version and doesn't require Unity Pro; the differences between those versions are in advanced features (that are beyond the scope of this book) and commercial licensing terms.

## 1.1 Why is Unity so great?

Let's take a closer look at that description from the beginning of the chapter: Unity is a professional-quality game engine used to create video games targeting a variety of platforms. That is a fairly straightforward answer to the straightforward question "What is Unity?" However, what exactly does that answer mean, and why is Unity so great?

### 1.1.1 Unity's strengths and advantages

A game engine provides a plethora of features that are useful across many different games, so a game implemented using that engine gets all those features while adding custom art assets and gameplay code specific to that game. Unity has physics simulation, normal maps, screen space ambient occlusion (SSAO), dynamic shadows…and the list goes on. Many game engines boast such features, but Unity has two main advantages over other similarly cutting-edge game development tools: an extremely productive visual workflow, and a high degree of cross-platform support.

The visual workflow is a fairly unique design, different from most other game development environments. Whereas other game development tools are often a complicated mishmash of disparate parts that must be wrangled, or perhaps a programming library that requires you to set up your own integrated development environment (IDE), build-chain and whatnot, the development workflow in Unity is anchored by a sophisticated visual editor. The editor is used to lay out the scenes in your game and to tie together art assets and code into interactive objects. The beauty of this editor is that it enables professional-quality games to be built quickly and efficiently, giving developers tools to be incredibly productive while still using an extensive list of the latest technologies in video gaming.

> **NOTE** Most other game development tools that have a central visual editor are also saddled with limited and inflexible scripting support, but Unity doesn't suffer from that disadvantage. Although everything created for Unity ultimately goes through the visual editor, this core interface involves a lot of linking projects to custom code that runs in Unity's game engine. That's not unlike linking in classes in the project settings for an IDE like Visual Studio or Eclipse. Experienced programmers shouldn't dismiss this development environment, mistaking it for some click-together game creator with limited programming capability!

The editor is especially helpful for doing rapid iteration, honing the game through cycles of prototyping and testing. You can adjust objects in the editor and move things around even while the game is running. Plus, Unity allows you to customize the editor itself by writing scripts that add new features and menus to the interface.

Besides the editor's significant productivity advantages, the other main strength of Unity's toolset is a high degree of cross-platform support. Not only is Unity multiplatform in terms of the deployment targets (you can deploy to the PC, web, mobile, or consoles), but it's multiplatform in terms of the development tools (you can develop the game on Windows or Mac OS). This platform-agnostic nature is largely because Unity started as Mac-only software and was later ported to Windows. The first version launched in 2005, but now Unity is up to its fifth major version (with lots of minor updates released frequently). Initially, Unity supported only Mac for both developing and deployment, but within a few months Unity had been updated to work on Windows as well. Successive versions gradually added more deployment platforms, such as a cross-platform web player in 2006, iPhone in 2008, Android in 2010, and even game consoles like Xbox and PlayStation. Most recently they've added deployment to WebGL, the new framework for 3D graphics in web browsers. Few game engines support as many deployment targets as Unity, and none make deploying to multiple platforms so simple.

Meanwhile, in addition to these main strengths, a third and subtler benefit comes from the modular component system used to construct game objects. In a component

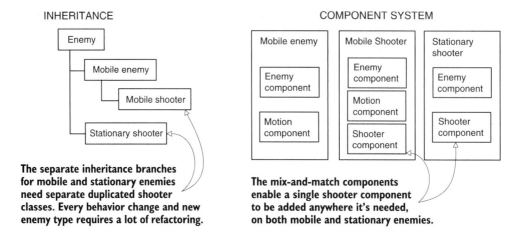

Figure 1.1   Inheritance vs. components

system, "components" are mix-and-match packets of functionality, and objects are built up as a collection of components, rather than as a strict hierarchy of classes. In other words, a component system is a different (and usually more flexible) approach to doing object-oriented programming, where game objects are constructed through composition rather than inheritance. Figure 1.1 diagrams an example comparison.

In a component system, objects exist on a flat hierarchy and different objects have different collections of components, rather than an inheritance structure where different objects are on completely different branches of the tree. This arrangement facilitates rapid prototyping, because you can quickly mix-and-match different components rather than having to refactor the inheritance chain when the objects change.

Although you could write code to implement a custom component system if one didn't exist, Unity already has a robust component system, and this system is even integrated seamlessly with the visual editor. Rather than only being able to manipulate components in code, you can attach and detach components within the visual editor. Meanwhile, you aren't limited to only building objects through composition; you still have the option of using inheritance in your code, including all the best-practice design patterns that have emerged based on inheritance.

### 1.1.2   Downsides to be aware of

Unity has many advantages that make it a great choice for developing games and I highly recommend it, but I'd be remiss if I didn't mention its weaknesses. In particular, the combination of the visual editor and sophisticated coding, though very effective with Unity's component system, is unusual and can create difficulties. In complex scenes, you can lose track of which objects in the scene have specific components attached. Unity does provide search functionality for finding attached scripts, but that search could be more robust; sometimes you still encounter situations where you need to manually inspect everything in the scene in order to find script linkages. This doesn't happen often, but when it does happen it can be tedious.

Another disadvantage that can be surprising and frustrating for experienced programmers is that Unity doesn't support linking in external code libraries. The many libraries available must be manually copied into every project where they'll be used, as opposed to referencing one central shared location. The lack of a central location for libraries can make it awkward to share functionality between multiple projects. This disadvantage can be worked around through clever use of version control systems, but Unity doesn't support this functionality out of the box.

> **NOTE** Difficulty working with version control systems (such as Subversion, Git, and Mercurial) used to be a significant weakness, but more recent versions of Unity work just fine. You may find out-of-date resources telling you that Unity doesn't work with version control, but newer resources will describe.meta files (the mechanism Unity introduced for working with version-control systems) and which folders in the project do or don't need to be put in the repository. To start out with, read this page in the documentation: http://docs.unity3d.com/Manual/ExternalVersionControlSystemSupport.html

A third weakness has to do with working with prefabs. Prefabs are a concept specific to Unity and are explained in chapter 3; for now, all you need to know is that prefabs are a flexible approach to visually defining interactive objects. The concept of prefabs is both powerful and unique to Unity (and yes, it's tied into Unity's component system), but it can be surprisingly awkward to edit prefabs. Considering prefabs are such a useful and central part of working with Unity, I hope that future versions improve the workflow for editing prefabs.

### 1.1.3 *Example games built with Unity*

You've heard about the pros and cons of Unity, but you might still need convincing that the development tools in Unity can give first-rate results. Visit the Unity gallery at http://unity3d.com/showcase/gallery to see a constantly updated list of hundreds of games and simulations developed using Unity. This section explores just a handful of games showcasing a number of genres and deployment platforms.

#### DESKTOP (WINDOWS, MAC, LINUX)

Because the editor runs on the same platform, deployment to Windows or Mac is often the most straightforward target platform. Here are a couple of examples of desktop games in different genres:

- Guns of Icarus Online (figure 1.2), a first-person shooter developed by Muse Games

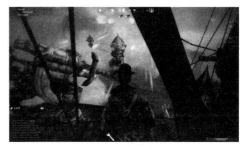

**Figure 1.2  Guns of Icarus Online**

- Gone Home (figure 1.3), an exploration adventure developed by The Fullbright Company

**MOBILE (IOS, ANDROID)**

Unity can also deploy games to mobile platforms like iOS (iPhones and iPads) and Android (phones and tablets). Here are a few examples of mobile games in different genres:

- Dead Trigger (figure 1.4), a first-person shooter developed by Madfinger Games
- Bad Piggies (figure 1.5), a physics puzzle game developed by Rovio
- Tyrant Unleashed (figure 1.6), a collectible card game developed by Synapse Games

**CONSOLE (PLAYSTATION, XBOX, WII)**

Unity can even deploy to game consoles, although the developer must obtain licensing from Sony, Microsoft, or Nintendo. Because of this requirement and Unity's easy cross-platform deployment, console games are often available on desktop computers as well. Here are a couple examples of console games in different genres:

- Assault Android Cactus (figure 1.7), an arcade shooter developed by Witch Beam
- The Golf Club (figure 1.8), a sports simulation developed by HB Studios

As you can see from these examples, Unity's strengths definitely can translate into commercial-quality games. But even with Unity's significant advantages over other game development tools, newcomers may have a misunderstanding about the involvement of programming in the development process. Unity

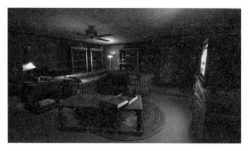

Figure 1.3    Gone Home

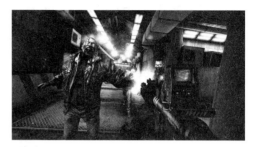

Figure 1.4    Dead Trigger

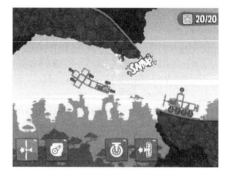

Figure 1.5    Bad Piggies

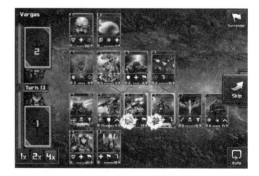

Figure 1.6    Tyrant Unleashed

is often portrayed as simply a list of features with no programming required, which is a misleading view that won't teach people what they need to know in order to produce commercial titles. Though it's true that you can click together a fairly elaborate prototype using preexisting components even without a programmer involved (which is itself a pretty big feat), rigorous programming is required to move beyond an interesting prototype to a polished game for release.

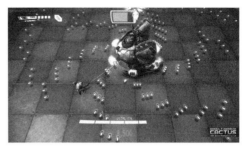

**Figure 1.7   Assault Android Cactus**

## 1.2   *How to use Unity*

The previous section talked a lot about the productivity benefits from Unity's visual editor, so let's go over what the interface looks like and how it operates. If you haven't done so already, download the program from www.unity3d

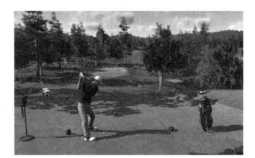

**Figure 1.8   The Golf Club**

.com and install it on your computer (be sure to include "Example Project" if that's unchecked in the installer). After you install it, launch Unity to start exploring the interface.

You probably want an example to look at, so open the included example project; a new installation should open the example project automatically, but you can also select File > Open Project to open it manually. The example project is installed in the shared user directory, which is something like C:\Users\Public\Documents\Unity Projects\ on Windows, or Users/Shared/Unity/ on Mac OS. You may also need to open the example scene, so double-click the Car scene file (highlighted in figure 1.9; scene files have the Unity cube icon) that's found by going to SampleScenes/Scenes/ in the file browser at the bottom of the editor. You should be looking at a screen similar to figure 1.9.

The interface in Unity is split up into different sections: the Scene tab, the Game tab, the Toolbar, the Hierarchy tab, the Inspector, the Project tab, and the Console tab. Each section has a different purpose but all are crucial for the game-building lifecycle:

- You can browse through all the files in the Project tab.
- You can place objects in the 3D scene being viewed using the Scene tab.
- The Toolbar has controls for working with the scene.
- You can drag and drop object relationships in the Hierarchy tab.
- The Inspector lists information about selected objects, including linked code.
- You can test playing in Game view while watching error output in the Console tab.

Scene and Game are
tabs for viewing the
3D scene and playing
the game, respectively.

The whole top area is the Toolbar.
To the left are buttons for looking
around and moving objects, and in
the middle is the Play button.

The inspector fills the right side.
This displays information about
the currently selected object
(a list of components mostly).

Hierarchy shows a
text list of all objects
in the scene, nested
according to how
they're linked together.
Drag objects in the
hierarchy to link them.

Project and Console
are tabs for viewing
all files in the project
and messages from
the code, respectively.

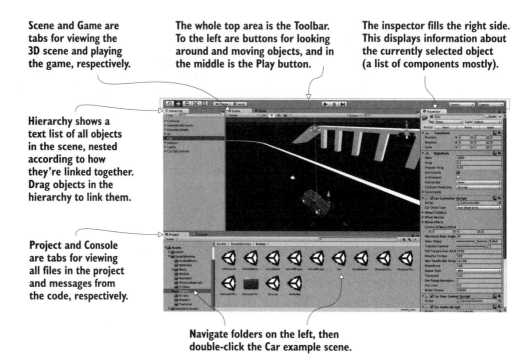

Navigate folders on the left, then
double-click the Car example scene.

**Figure 1.9   Parts of the interface in Unity**

This is just the default layout in Unity; all of the various views are in tabs and can be moved around or resized, docking in different places on the screen. Later you can play around with customizing the layout, but for now the default layout is the best way to understand what all the views do.

### 1.2.1   Scene view, Game view, and the Toolbar

The most prominent part of the interface is the Scene view in the middle. This is where you can see what the game world looks like and move objects around. Mesh objects in the scene appear as, well, the mesh object (defined in a moment). You can also see a number of other objects in the scene, represented by various icons and colored lines: cameras, lights, audio sources, collision regions, and so forth. Note that the view you're seeing here isn't the same as the view in the running game—you're able to look around the scene at will without being constrained to the game's view.

> **DEFINITION**   A *mesh object* is a visual object in 3D space. Visuals in 3D are constructed out of lots of connected lines and shapes; hence the word *mesh*.

The Game view isn't a separate part of the screen but rather another tab located right next to Scene (look for tabs at the top left of views). A couple of places in the interface have multiple tabs like this; if you click a different tab, the view is replaced by the new

Options for aspects of the scene to display
(e.g., toggle button to show lighting)     Play     Toolbar

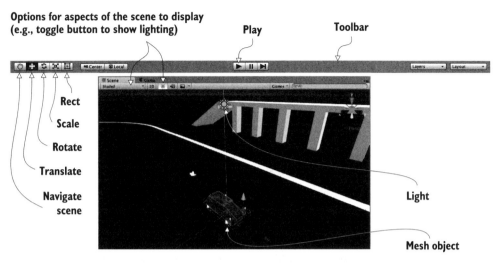

Rect

Scale

Rotate

Translate

Navigate
scene

Light

Mesh object

**Figure 1.10   Editor screenshot cropped to show Toolbar, Scene, and Game**

active tab. When the game is running, what you see in this view is the game. It isn't necessary to manually switch tabs every time you run the game, because the view automatically switches to Game when the game starts.

> **TIP**   While the game is running, you can switch back to the Scene view, allowing you to inspect objects in the running scene. This capability is hugely useful for seeing what's going on while the game is running and is a helpful debugging tool that isn't available in most game engines.

Speaking of running the game, that's as simple as hitting the Play button just above the Scene view. That whole top section of the interface is referred to as the Toolbar, and Play is located right in the middle. Figure 1.10 breaks apart the full editor interface to show only the Toolbar at the top, as well as the Scene/Game tabs right underneath.

At the left side of the Toolbar are buttons for scene navigation and transforming objects—how to look around the scene and how to move objects. I suggest you spend some time practicing looking around the scene and moving objects, because these are two of the most important activities you'll do in Unity's visual editor (they're so important that they get their own section following this one). The right side of the Toolbar is where you'll find drop-down menus for layouts and layers. As mentioned earlier, the layout of Unity's interface is flexible, so the Layouts menu allows you to switch between layouts. As for the Layers menu, that's advanced functionality that you can ignore for now (layers will be mentioned in future chapters).

### 1.2.2   *Using the mouse and keyboard*

Scene navigation is primarily done using the mouse, along with a few modifier keys used to modify what the mouse is doing. The three main navigation maneuvers are

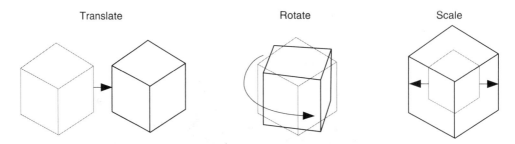

**Figure 1.11  Applying the three transforms: Translate, Rotate, and Scale. (The lighter lines are the previous state of the object before it was transformed.)**

Move, Orbit, and Zoom. The specific mouse movements for each are described in appendix A at the end of this book, because they vary depending on what mouse you're using. Basically, the three different movements involve clicking-and-dragging while holding down some combination of Alt (or Option on Mac) and Ctrl. Spend a few minutes moving around in the scene to understand what Move, Orbit, and Zoom do.

> **TIP**   Although Unity can be used with one- or two-button mice, I highly recommend getting a three-button mouse (and yes, a three-button mouse works fine on Mac OS X).

Transforming objects is also done through three main maneuvers, and the three scene navigation moves are analogous to the three transforms: Translate, Rotate, and Scale (figure 1.11 demonstrates the transforms on a cube).

   When you select an object in the scene, you can then move it around (the mathematically accurate technical term is *translate*), rotate the object, or scale how big it is. Relating back to scene navigation, Move is when you Translate the camera, Orbit is when you Rotate the camera, and Zoom is when you Scale the camera. Besides the buttons on the Toolbar, you can switch between these functions by pressing W, E, or R on the keyboard. When you activate a transform, you'll notice a set of color-coded arrows or circles appears over the object in the scene; this is the Transform gizmo, and you can click-and-drag this gizmo to apply the transformation.

   There's also a fourth tool next to the transform buttons. Called the Rect tool, it's designed for use with 2D graphics. This one tool combines movement, rotation, and scaling. These operations have to be separate tools in 3D but are combined in 2D because there's one less dimension to worry about. Unity has a host of other keyboard shortcuts for speeding up a variety of tasks. Refer to appendix A to learn about them. And with that, on to the remaining sections of the interface!

### 1.2.3   *The Hierarchy tab and the Inspector*

Looking at the sides of the screen, you'll see the Hierarchy tab on the left and the Inspector on the right (see figure 1.12). Hierarchy is a list view with the name of every

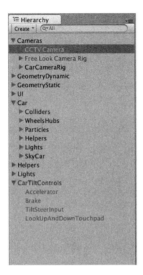
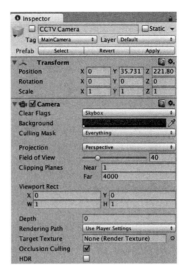

**Figure 1.12   Editor screenshot cropped to show the Hierarchy and Inspector tabs**

object in the scene listed, with the names nested together according to their hierarchy linkages in the scene. Basically, it's a way of selecting objects by name instead of hunting them down and clicking them within Scene. The Hierarchy linkages group objects together, visually grouping them like folders and allowing you to move the entire group together.

The Inspector shows you information about the currently selected object. Select an object and the Inspector is then filled with information about that object. The information shown is pretty much a list of components, and you can even attach or remove components from objects. All game objects have at least one component, Transform, so you'll always at least see information about positioning and rotation in the Inspector. Many times objects will have several components listed here, including scripts attached to that object.

## 1.2.4   *The Project and Console tabs*

At the bottom of the screen you'll see Project and Console (see figure 1.13). As with Scene and View, these aren't two separate portions of the screen but rather tabs that you can switch between. Project shows all the assets (art, code, and so on) in the

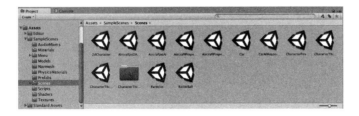

**Figure 1.13   Editor screenshot cropped to show the Project and Console tabs**

project. Specifically, on the left side of the view is a listing of the directories in the project; when you select a directory, the right side of the view shows the individual files in that directory. The directory listing in Project is similar to the list view in Hierarchy, but whereas Hierarchy shows objects in the scene, Project shows files that aren't contained within any specific scene (including scene files—when you save a scene, it shows up in Project!).

> **TIP** Project view mirrors the Assets directory on disk, but you generally shouldn't move or delete files directly by going to the Assets folder. If you do those things within the Project view, Unity will keep in sync with that folder.

The Console is the place where messages from the code show up. Some of these messages will be debug output that you placed deliberately, but Unity also emits error messages if it encounters problems in the script you wrote.

## 1.3 Getting up and running with Unity programming

Now let's look at how the process of programming works in Unity. Although art assets can be laid out in the visual editor, you need to write code to control them and make the game interactive. Unity supports a few programming languages, in particular JavaScript and C#. There are pros and cons to both choices, but you'll be using C# throughout this book.

---

### Why choose C# over JavaScript?

All of the code listings in this book use C# because it has a number of advantages over JavaScript and fewer disadvantages, especially for professional developers (it's certainly the language I use at work).

One benefit is that C# is strongly typed, whereas JavaScript is not. Now, there are lots of arguments among experienced programmers about whether or not dynamic typing is a better approach for, say, web development, but programming for certain gaming platforms (such as iOS) often benefits from or even requires static typing. Unity has even added the directive `#pragma strict` to force static typing within JavaScript. Although technically this works, it breaks one of the bedrock principles of how JavaScript operates, and if you're going to do that, then you're better off using a language that's intrinsically strongly typed.

This is just one example of how JavaScript within Unity isn't quite the same as JavaScript elsewhere. JavaScript in Unity is certainly similar to JavaScript in web browsers, but there are lots of differences in how the language works in each context. Many developers refer to the language in Unity as UnityScript, a name that indicates similarity to but separateness from JavaScript. This "similar but different" state can create issues for programmers, both in terms of bringing in knowledge about JavaScript from outside Unity, and in terms of applying programming knowledge gained by working in Unity.

Let's walk through an example of writing and running some code. Launch Unity and create a new project; choose File > New Project to open the New Project window. Type a name for the project, and then choose where you want to save it. Realize that a Unity project is simply a directory full of various asset and settings files, so save the project anywhere on your computer. Click Create Project and then Unity will briefly disappear while it sets up the project directory.

> **WARNING** Unity projects remember which version of Unity they were created in and will issue a warning if you attempt to open them in a different version. Sometimes it doesn't matter (for example, just ignore the warning if it appears while opening this book's sample downloads), but sometimes you will want to back up your project before opening it.

When Unity reappears you'll be looking at a blank project. Next, let's discuss how your programs get executed in Unity.

### 1.3.1 *How code runs in Unity: script components*

All code execution in Unity starts from code files linked to an object in the scene. Ultimately it's all part of the component system described earlier; game objects are built up as a collection of components, and that collection can include scripts to execute.

> **NOTE** Unity refers to the code files as scripts, using a definition of "script" that's most commonly encountered with JavaScript running in a browser: the code is executed within the Unity game engine, versus compiled code that runs as its own executable. But don't get confused because many people define the word differently; for example, "scripts" often refer to short, self-contained utility programs. Scripts in Unity are more akin to individual OOP classes, and scripts attached to objects in the scene are the object instances.

As you've probably surmised from this description, in Unity, scripts *are* components—not all scripts, mind you, only scripts that inherit from `MonoBehaviour`, the base class for script components. `MonoBehaviour` defines the invisible groundwork for how components attach to game objects, and (as shown in listing 1.1) inheriting from it provides a couple of automatically run methods that you can override. Those methods include `Start()`, which is called once when the object becomes active (which is generally as soon as the level with that object has loaded), and `Update()`, which is called every frame. Thus your code is run when you put it inside these predefined methods.

> **DEFINITION** A *frame* is a single cycle of the looping game code. Nearly all video games (not just in Unity, but video games in general) are built around a core game loop, where the code executes in a cycle while the game is running. Each cycle includes drawing the screen; hence the name *frame* (just like the series of still frames of a movie).

> **Listing 1.1   Code template for a basic script component**

```
using UnityEngine;
using System.Collections;

public class HelloWorld : MonoBehaviour {

    void Start() {
        // do something once
    }

    void Update() {
        // do something every frame
    }
}
```

◁ **Include namespaces for Unity and Mono classes.**

◁ **The syntax for inheritance**

◁ **Put code in here that runs once.**

◁ **Put code in here that runs every frame.**

This is what the file contains when you create a new C# script: the minimal boilerplate code that defines a valid Unity component. Unity has a script template tucked away in the bowels of the application, and when you create a new script it copies that template and renames the class to match the name of the file (which is HelloWorld.cs in my case). There are also empty shells for `Start()` and `Update()` because those are the two most common places to call your custom code from (although I tend to adjust the whitespace around those functions a tad, because the template isn't quite how I like the whitespace and I'm finicky about that).

To create a script, select C# Script from the Create menu that you access either under the Assets menu (note that Assets and GameObjects both have listings for Create but they're different menus) or by right-clicking in the Project view. Type in a name for the new script, such as HelloWorld. As explained later in the chapter (see figure 1.15), you'll click-and-drag this script file onto an object in the scene. Double-click the script and it'll automatically be opened in another program called Mono-Develop, discussed next.

### 1.3.2   Using MonoDevelop, the cross-platform IDE

Programming isn't done within Unity exactly, but rather code exists as separate files that you point Unity to. Script files can be created within Unity, but you still need to use some text editor or IDE to write all the code within those initially empty files. Unity comes bundled with MonoDevelop, an open source, cross-platform IDE for C# (figure 1.14 shows what it looks like). You can visit www.monodevelop.com to learn more about this software, but the version to use is the version bundled along with Unity, rather than a version downloaded from their website, because some modifications were made to the base software in order to better integrate it with Unity.

> **NOTE**   MonoDevelop organizes files into groupings called a *solution*. Unity automatically generates a solution that has all the script files, so you usually don't need to worry about that.

Because C# originated as a Microsoft product, you may be wondering if you can use Visual Studio to do programming for Unity. The short answer is yes, you can. Support

**Don't hit the Run button within MonoDevelop; hit Play in Unity to run the code.**

**Script files open as tabs in the main viewing area. Multiple script files can be open at once.**

**Solution view shows all script files in the project.**

**Document Outline may not be showing by default. Select it under View > Pads and then drag the tab to where you want it.**

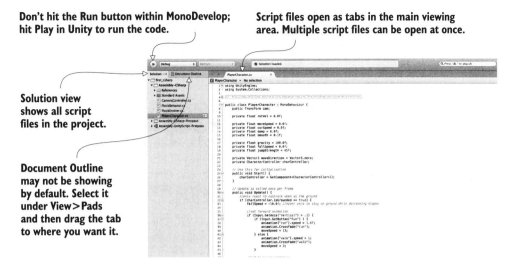

**Figure 1.14   Parts of the interface in MonoDevelop**

tools are available from www.unityvs.com but I generally prefer MonoDevelop, mostly because Visual Studio only runs on Windows and using that IDE would tie your workflow to Windows. That's not necessarily a bad thing, and if you're already using Visual Studio to do programming then you could keep using it and not have any problems following along with this book (beyond this introductory chapter, I'm not going to talk about the IDE). Tying your workflow to Windows, though, would run counter to one of the biggest advantages of using Unity, and doing so could prove problematic if you need to work with Mac-based developers on your team and/or if you want to deploy your game to iOS. Although C# originated as a Microsoft product and thus only worked on Windows with the .NET Framework, C# has now become an open language standard and there's a significant cross-platform framework: Mono. Unity uses Mono for its programming backbone, and using MonoDevelop allows you to keep the entire development workflow cross-platform.

Always keep in mind that although the code is written in MonoDevelop, the code isn't actually run there. The IDE is pretty much a fancy text editor, and the code is run when you hit Play within Unity.

### 1.3.3   *Printing to the console: Hello World!*

All right, you already have an empty script in the project, but you also need an object in the scene to attach the script to. Recall figure 1.1 depicting how a component system works; a script is a component, so it needs to be set as one of the components on an object.

Select GameObject > Create Empty, and a blank GameObject will appear in the Hierarchy list. Now drag the script from the Project view over to the Hierarchy view and drop it on the empty GameObject. As shown in figure 1.15, Unity will highlight

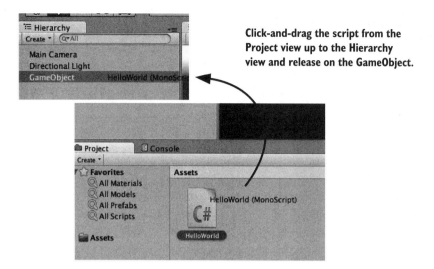

**Click-and-drag the script from the Project view up to the Hierarchy view and release on the GameObject.**

**Figure 1.15   How to link a script to a GameObject**

valid places to drop the script, and dropping it on the GameObject will attach the script to that object. To verify that the script is attached to the object, select the object and look at the Inspector view. You should see two components listed: the Transform component that's the basic position/rotation/scale component all objects have and that can't be removed, and below that, your script.

> **NOTE**   Eventually this action of dragging objects from one place and dropping them on other objects will feel routine. A lot of different linkages in Unity are created by dragging things on top of each other, not just attaching scripts to objects.

When a script is linked to an object, you'll see something like figure 1.16, with the script showing up as a component in the Inspector. Now the script will execute when you play the scene, although nothing is going to happen yet because you haven't written any code. Let's do that next!

Open the script in MonoDevelop to get back to listing 1.1. The classic place to start when learning a new programming environment is having it print the

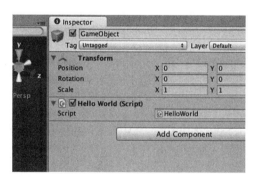

**Figure 1.16   Linked script being displayed in the Inspector**

text "Hello World!" so add this line inside the `Start()` method, as shown in the following listing.

**Listing 1.2  Adding a console message**

```
void Start() {
    Debug.Log("Hello World!");          Add the logging command here.
}
```

What the `Debug.Log()` command does is print a message to the Console view in Unity. Meanwhile that line goes in the `Start()` method because, as was explained earlier, that method is called as soon as the object becomes active. In other words, `Start()` will be called once as soon as you hit Play in the editor. Once you've added the log command to your script (be sure to save the script), hit Play in Unity and switch to the Console view. You'll see the message "Hello World!" appear. Congratulations, you've written your first Unity script! In later chapters the code will be more elaborate, of course, but this is an important first step.

---

**"Hello World!" steps in brief**

Let's reiterate and summarize the steps from the last several pages:

1. Create a new project.
2. Create a new C# script.
3. Create an empty GameObject.
4. Drag the script onto the object.
5. Add the log command to the script.
6. Press Play!

---

You could now save the scene; that would create a .unity file with the Unity icon. The scene file is a snapshot of everything currently loaded in the game so that you can reload this scene later. It's hardly worth saving this scene because it's so simple (just a single empty GameObject), but if you don't save the scene then you'll find it empty again when you come back to the project after quitting Unity.

---

**Errors in the script**

To see how Unity indicates errors, purposely put a typo in the HelloWorld script. For example, if you type an extra parenthesis symbol, this error message will appear in the Console with a red error icon:

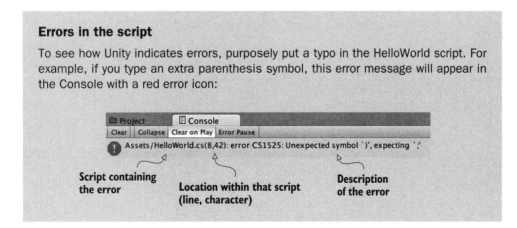

## *1.4   Summary*

In this chapter you've learned that

- Unity is a multiplatform development tool.
- Unity's visual editor has several sections that work in concert.
- Scripts are attached to objects as components.
- Code is written inside scripts using MonoDevelop.

# Building a demo that
# puts you in 3D space

**This chapter covers**

- Understanding 3D coordinate space
- Putting a player in a scene
- Writing a script that moves objects
- Implementing FPS controls

Chapter 1 concluded with the traditional "Hello World!" introduction to a new programming tool; now it's time to dive into a nontrivial Unity project, a project with interactivity and graphics. You'll put some objects into a scene and write code to enable a player to walk around that scene. Basically, it'll be Doom without the monsters (something like what figure 2.1

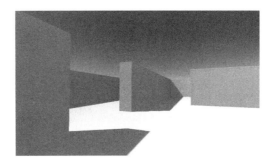

**Figure 2.1  Screenshot of the 3D demo (basically, Doom without the monsters)**

depicts). The visual editor in Unity enables new users to start assembling a 3D proto-type right away, without needing to write a lot of boilerplate code first (for things like initializing a 3D view or establishing a rendering loop).

It's tempting to immediately start building the scene in Unity, especially with such a simple (in concept!) project. But it's always a good idea to pause at the beginning and plan out what you're going to do, and this is especially important right now because you're new to the process.

## 2.1   *Before you start...*

Unity makes it easy for a newcomer to get started, but let's go over a couple of points before you build the complete scene. Even when working with a tool as flexible as Unity, you do need to have some sense of the goal you're working toward. You also need a grasp of how 3D coordinates operate or you could get lost as soon as you try to position an object in the scene.

### 2.1.1   *Planning the project*

Before you start programming anything, you always want to pause and ask yourself, "So what am I building here?" Game design is a huge topic unto itself, with many impressively large books focused on how to design a game. Fortunately for our pur-poses, you only need a brief outline of this simple demo in mind in order to develop a basic learning project. These initial projects won't be terribly complex designs anyway, in order to avoid distracting you from learning programming concepts; you can (and should!) worry about higher-level design issues after you've mastered the fundamen-tals of game development.

For this first project you'll build a basic FPS (first-person shooter) scene. There will be a room to navigate around, players will see the world from their character's point of view, and the player can control the character using the mouse and keyboard. All the interesting complexity of a complete game can be stripped away for now in order

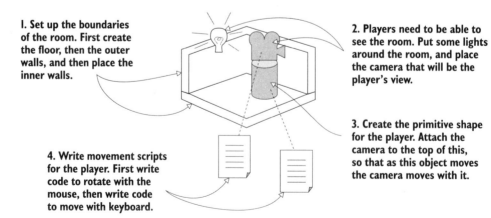

**I. Set up the boundaries of the room.** First create the floor, then the outer walls, and then place the inner walls.

**2. Players need to be able to see the room.** Put some lights around the room, and place the camera that will be the player's view.

**3. Create the primitive shape for the player.** Attach the camera to the top of this, so that as this object moves the camera moves with it.

**4. Write movement scripts for the player.** First write code to rotate with the mouse, then write code to move with keyboard.

Figure 2.2   Roadmap for the 3D demo

to concentrate on the core mechanic: moving around in a 3D space. Figure 2.2 depicts the roadmap for this project, basically laying out the mental checklist I built in my head:

1  Set up the room: create the floor, outer walls, and inner walls.
2  Place the lights and camera.
3  Create the player object (including attaching the camera on top).
4  Write movement scripts: rotate with the mouse and move with the keyboard.

Don't be scared off by everything in this roadmap! It sounds like there's a lot in this chapter, but Unity makes it easy. The upcoming sections about movement scripts are so extensive only because we'll be going through every line to understand all the concepts in detail. This project is a first-person demo in order to keep the art requirements simple; because you can't see yourself, it's fine for "you" to be a cylindrical shape with a camera on top! Now you just need to understand how 3D coordinates work, and it will be easy to place everything in the visual editor.

### 2.1.2  Understanding 3D coordinate space

If you think about the simple plan we're starting with, there are three aspects to it: a room, a view, and controls. All of those items rely on you understanding how positions and movements are represented in 3D computer simulations, and if you're new to working with 3D graphics you might not already know that stuff.

It all boils down to numbers that indicate points in space, and the way those numbers correlate to the space is through coordinate axes. If you think back to math class, you've probably seen and used X- and Y-axes (see figure 2.3) for assigning coordinates to points on the page, which is referred to as a Cartesian coordinate system.

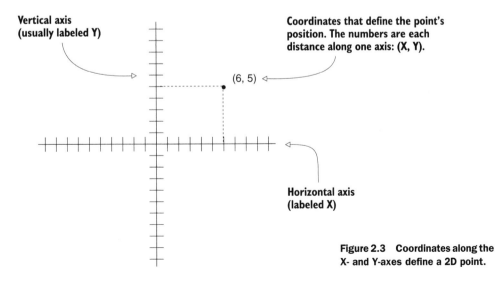

Figure 2.3  Coordinates along the X- and Y-axes define a 2D point.

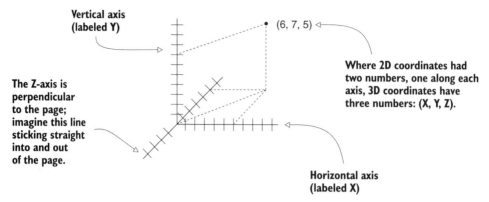

**Vertical axis (labeled Y)**

**(6, 7, 5)**

**The Z-axis is perpendicular to the page; imagine this line sticking straight into and out of the page.**

**Where 2D coordinates had two numbers, one along each axis, 3D coordinates have three numbers: (X, Y, Z).**

**Horizontal axis (labeled X)**

**Figure 2.4　Coordinates along the X-, Y-, and Z-axes define a 3D point.**

Two axes give you 2D coordinates, with all points in the same plane. Three axes are used to define 3D space. Because the X-axis goes along the page horizontally and the Y-axis goes along the page vertically, we now imagine a third axis that sticks straight into and out of the page, perpendicular to both the X and Y axes. Figure 2.4 depicts the X-, Y-, and Z-axes for 3D coordinate space. Everything that has a specific position in the scene will have XYZ coordinates: position of the player, placement of a wall, and so forth.

In Unity's Scene view you can see these three axes displayed, and in the Inspector you can type in the three numbers to position an object. Not only will you write code to position objects using these three-number coordinates, but you can also define movements as a distance to move along each axis.

## Left-handed vs. right-handed coordinates

The positive and negative direction of each axis is arbitrary, and the coordinates still work no matter which direction the axes point. You simply need to stay consistent within a given 3D graphics tool (animation tool, game development tool, and so forth).

But in almost all cases X goes to the right and Y goes up; what differs between different tools is whether Z goes into or comes out of the page. These two directions are referred to as "left-handed" or "right-handed"; as this figure shows, if you point your thumb along the X-axis and your index finger along the Y-axis, then your middle finger points along the Z-axis.

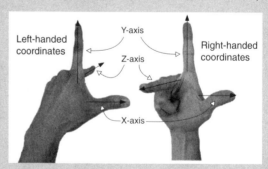

Left-handed coordinates

Y-axis

Z-axis

Right-handed coordinates

X-axis

**The Z-axis points in a different direction on the left hand versus the right hand.**

Unity uses a left-handed coordinate system, as do many 3D art applications. Many other tools use right-handed coordinate systems (OpenGL, for example), so don't get confused if you ever see different coordinate directions.

Now that you have a plan in mind for this project and you know how coordinates are used to position objects in 3D space, it's time to start building the scene.

## 2.2 Begin the project: place objects in the scene

All right, let's create and place objects in the scene. First you'll set up all the static scenery—the floor and walls. Then you'll place lights around the scene and position the camera. Last you'll create the object that will be the player, the object to which you'll attach scripts to walk around the scene. Figure 2.5 shows what the editor will look like with everything in place.

Chapter 1 showed how to create a new project in Unity, so you'll do that now. Remember: Choose File > New Project and then name your new project in the window that pops up. After creating the new project, immediately save the current empty default scene, because the project doesn't have any Scene file initially. The scene starts out empty, and the first objects to create are the most obvious ones.

### 2.2.1 The scenery: floor, outer walls, inner walls

Select the GameObject menu at the top of the screen, and then hover over 3D Object to see that drop-down menu. Select Cube to create a new cube object in the scene

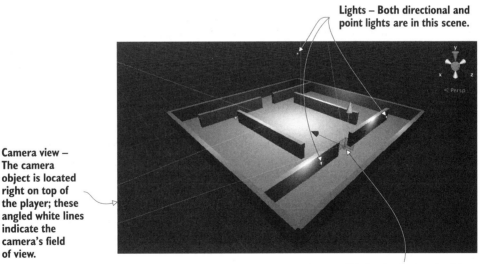

Lights – Both directional and point lights are in this scene.

Camera view – The camera object is located right on top of the player; these angled white lines indicate the camera's field of view.

Player – This is a basic capsule object.

**Figure 2.5  Scene in the Editor with floor, walls, lights, a camera, and the player**

**2. Position and scale the cube in order to create a floor for the room. Or rather "cube," since it won't look like a cube anymore after being stretched out with differing scale values on different axes.**

**Meanwhile the position is lowered very slightly to compensate for the height; we set the Y scale to 1, and the object is positioned around its center.**

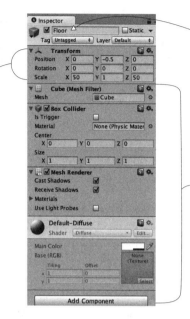

**1. At the top you can type in a name for the object. For example, call the floor object "Floor."**

**The remaining components filling the view come with a new Cube object but don't need to be adjusted right now. These components include a Mesh Filter (to define the geometry of the object), a Mesh Renderer (to define the material on the object), and a Box Collider (so that the object can be collided with during movement).**

Figure 2.6   Inspector view for the floor

(later we'll use other shapes like Sphere and Capsule). Adjust the position and scale of this object, as well as its name, in order to make the floor; figure 2.6 shows what values the floor should be set to in the Inspector (it's only a cube initially, before you stretch it out).

> **NOTE**   The numbers for position can be any units you want, as long as you're consistent throughout the scene. The most common choice for units is meters and that's what I generally choose, but I also use feet sometimes and I've even seen other people decide that the numbers are inches!

Repeat the same steps in order to create outer walls for the room. You can create new cubes each time, or you can copy and paste existing objects using the standard shortcuts. Move, rotate, and scale the walls to form a perimeter around the floor, as shown in figure 2.5. Experiment with different numbers (for example, 1, 4, 50 for scale) or use the transform tools first seen in section 1.2.2 (remember that the mathematical term for moving and rotating in 3D space is "transform").

> **TIP**   Also recall the navigation controls so that you can view the scene from different angles or zoom out for a bird's-eye view. If you ever get lost in the scene, press F to reset the view on the currently selected object.

The exact transform values the walls end up with will vary depending on how you rotate and scale the cubes in order to fit, and on how the objects are linked together in the Hierarchy view. For example, in figure 2.7 the walls are all children of an empty root object, so that the Hierarchy list will look organized. If you need an example to copy working values from, download the sample project and refer to the walls there.

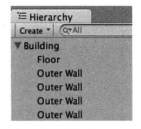

Figure 2.7 The Hierarchy view showing the walls and floor organized under an empty object

> **TIP** Drag objects on top of each other in the Hierarchy view to establish linkages. Objects that have other objects attached are referred to as *parent*; objects attached to other objects are referred to as *children*. When the parent object is moved (or rotated or scaled), the child objects are transformed along with it.

> **TIP** Empty game objects can be used to organize the scene in this way. By linking visible objects to a root object, their Hierarchy list can be collapsed. Be warned: before linking any child objects to it, you want to position the empty root object at 0, 0, 0 to avoid any positioning oddities later.

---

**What is `GameObject`?**

All scene objects are instances of the class `GameObject`, similar to how all script components inherit from the class `MonoBehaviour`. This fact was more explicit with the empty object actually named `GameObject` but is still true regardless of whether the object is named `Floor`, `Camera`, or `Player`.

`GameObject` is really just a container for a bunch of components. The main purpose of `GameObject` is so that `MonoBehaviour` has something to attach to. What exactly the object is in the scene depends on what components have been added to that `GameObject`. `Cube` objects have a Cube component, `Sphere` objects have a Sphere component, and so on.

---

Once the outer walls are in place, create some inner walls to navigate around. Position the inner walls however you like; the idea is to create some hallways and obstacles to walk around once you write code for movement.

Now the scene has a room in it, but without any lights the player won't be able to see any of it. Let's take care of that next.

### 2.2.2 *Lights and cameras*

Typically you light a 3D scene with a directional light and then a series of point lights. First start with a directional light; the scene probably already has one by default, but if not then create one by choosing GameObject > Light and selecting Directional Light.

---

**Types of lights**

You can create several types of light sources, defined by how and where they project light rays. The three main types are point, spot, and directional.

*(continued)*

*Point lights* are a kind of light source where all the light rays originate from a single point and project out in all directions, like a lightbulb in the real world. The light is brighter up close because the light rays are bunched up.

*Spot lights* are a kind of light source where all the light rays originate from a single point but only project out in a limited cone. No spot lights are used in the current project, but these lights are commonly used to highlight parts of a level.

*Directional lights* are a kind of light source where all the light rays are parallel and project evenly, lighting everything in the scene the same way. This is like the sun in the real world.

The position of a directional light doesn't affect the light cast from it, only the rotation the light source is facing, so technically you could place that light anywhere in the scene. I recommend placing it high above the room so that it intuitively feels like the sun and so that it's out of the way when you're manipulating the rest of the scene. Rotate this light and watch the effect on the room; I recommend rotating it slightly on both the X- and Y-axes to get a good effect. You can see an Intensity setting when you look in the Inspector (see figure 2.8). As the name implies, that setting controls the brightness of the light. If this were the only light, it'd have to be more intense, but because you'll add a bunch of point lights as well, this directional light can be pretty dim, like 0.6 Intensity.

As for point lights, create several using the same menu and place them around the room in dark spots in order to make sure all the walls are lit. You don't want too many (performance will degrade if the game has lots of lights), but one near each corner should be fine (I suggest raising them to the tops of the walls), plus one placed high above the scene (like a Y of 18) to give some variety to the light in the room. Note that point lights have a setting for Range added to the Inspector (see figure 2.9). This controls how far away the light reaches; whereas directional lights cast light evenly throughout the entire scene, point lights are brighter when an object is closer. The point lights lower to the floor should have a range around 18, but the light placed high up should have a range of around 40 in order to reach the entire room.

The other kind of object needed in order for the player to see the scene is a camera, but the "empty" scene already came with a main camera, so you'll use that. If you

The remaining settings don't need to be adjusted right now. These settings include the color of the light, shadows cast by the light, and even a silhouette projection (think of the Bat signal).

Here is where you control the light's brightness, from 0 for completely dark.

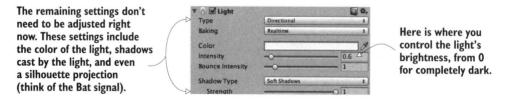

**Figure 2.8   Directional light settings in the Inspector**

Other than Range, the settings for point lights are the same as for directional lights.

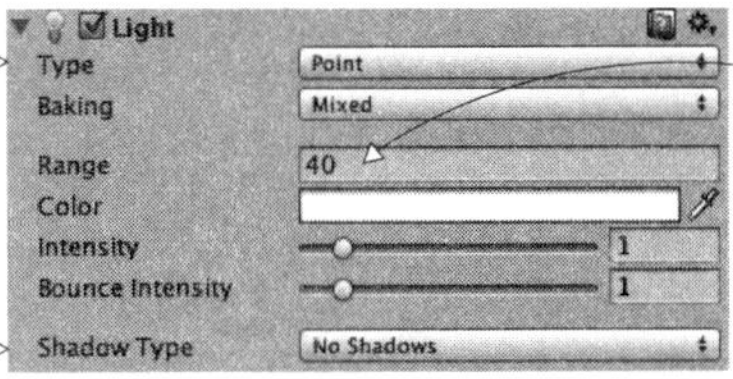

Here is where you control light range, with the same units as position and scale.

(If you see an error about "realtime not supported," just ignore it or switch Baking to "Mixed.")

**Figure 2.9   Point light settings in the Inspector**

ever need to create new cameras (such as for split-screen views in multiplayer games), Camera is another choice in the same GameObject menu as Cube and Lights. The camera will be positioned around the top of the player so that the view appears to be the player's eyes.

### 2.2.3   *The player's collider and viewpoint*

For this project, a simple primitive shape will do to represent the player. In the GameObject menu (remember, hover over 3D Object to expand the menu) click Capsule. Unity creates a cylindrical shape with rounded ends; this primitive shape will represent the player. Position this object at 1.1 on the Y-axis (half the height of the object, plus a bit to avoid overlapping the floor). You can move the object on X and Z wherever you like, as long as it's inside the room and not touching any walls. Name the object Player.

In the Inspector you'll notice that this object has a capsule collider assigned to it. That's a logical default choice for a capsule object, just like cube objects had a box collider by default. But this particular object will be the player and thus needs a slightly different sort of component than most objects. Remove the capsule collider by clicking the gear icon toward the top-right of that component, shown in figure 2.10; that will display a menu that includes the option Remove Component. The collider is a green mesh surrounding the object, so you'll see the green mesh disappear after deleting the capsule collider.

Instead of a capsule collider we're going to assign a character controller to this object. At the bottom of the Inspector there's a button labeled Add Component; click that button to open a menu of components that you can add. In the Physics section of

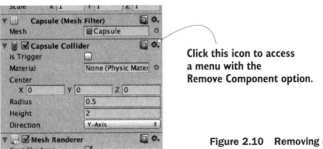

Click this icon to access a menu with the Remove Component option.

**Figure 2.10   Removing a component in the Inspector**

this menu you'll find Character Controller; select that option. As the name implies, this component will allow the object to behave like a character.

You need to complete one last step to set up the player object: attaching the camera. As mentioned in the earlier section on floors and walls, objects can be dragged onto each other in the Hierarchy view. Drag the camera object onto the player capsule to attach the camera to the player. Now position the camera so that it'll look like the player's eyes (I suggest a position of 0, 0.5, 0). If necessary, reset the camera's rotation to 0, 0, 0 (this will be off if you rotated the capsule).

You've created all the objects needed for this scene. What remains is writing code to move the player object.

## 2.3    *Making things move: a script that applies transforms*

To have the player walk around the scene, you'll write movement scripts attached to the player. Remember, components are modular bits of functionality that you add to objects, and scripts are a kind of component. Eventually those scripts will respond to keyboard and mouse input, but first just make the player spin in place. This beginning will teach you how to apply transforms in code. Remember that the three transforms are Translate, Rotate, and Scale; spinning an object means changing the rotation. But there's more to know about this task than just "this involves rotation."

### 2.3.1    *Diagramming how movement is programmed*

Animating an object (such as making it spin) boils down to moving it a small amount every frame, with the frames playing over and over. By themselves transforms apply instantly, as opposed to visibly moving over time. But applying the transforms over and over causes the object to visibly move, just like a series of still drawings in a flipbook. Figure 2.11 diagrams how this works.

Recall that script components have an `Update()` method that runs every frame. To spin the cube, add code inside `Update()` that rotates the cube a small amount. This code will run over and over every frame. Sounds pretty simple, right?

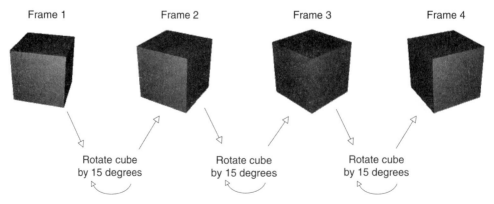

**Figure 2.11    The appearance of movement: cyclical process of transforming between still pictures**

### 2.3.2 *Writing code to implement the diagram*

Now let's put in action the concepts just discussed. Create a new C# script (remember it's in the Create submenu of the Assets menu), name it Spin, and write in the code from the following listing (don't forget to save the file after typing in it!).

---
**Listing 2.1   Making the object spin**

```
using UnityEngine;
using System.Collections;

public class Spin : MonoBehaviour {
    public float speed = 3.0f;

    void Update() {
        transform.Rotate(0, speed, 0);
    }
}
```

> Declare a public variable
> for the speed of rotation.

> Put the Rotate command here
> so that it runs every frame.

To add the script component to the player object, drag the script up from the Project view and drop it onto Player in the Hierarchy view. Now hit Play and you'll see the view spin around; you've written code to make an object move! This code is pretty much the default template for a new script plus two new added lines, so let's examine what those two lines do.

First there's the variable for speed added toward the top of the class definition (the f after the number tells the computer to treat this as a float value; otherwise C# treats decimal numbers as a double). The rotation speed is defined as a variable rather than a constant because Unity does something handy with public variables in script components, as described in the following tip.

> **TIP** Public variables are exposed in the Inspector so that you can adjust the component's values after adding a component to a game object. This is referred to as "serializing" the value, because Unity saves the modified state of the variable.

Figure 2.12 shows what the script component looks like in the Inspector. You can type in a new number, and then the script will use that value instead of the default value defined in the code. This is a handy way to adjust settings for the component on different objects, working within the visual editor instead of hardcoding every value.

The second line to examine from listing 2.1 is the Rotate() method. That's inside Update() so that the command runs every frame. Rotate() is a method of the Transform class, so it's called with dot notation through the transform component of this object (as in most object-oriented languages, this.transform is implied if you type

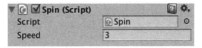

**Figure 2.12   The Inspector displaying a public variable declared in the script**

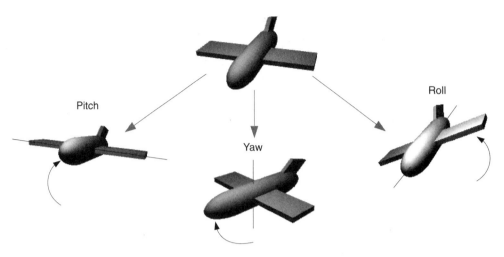

**Figure 2.13   Illustration of pitch, yaw, and roll rotation of an aircraft**

transform). The transform is rotated by speed degrees every frame, resulting in a smooth spinning movement. But why are the parameters to Rotate() listed as (0, speed, 0) as opposed to, say, (speed, 0, 0)?

Recall that there are three axes in 3D space, labeled X, Y, and Z. It's fairly intuitive to understand how these axes relate to positions and movements, but these axes can also be used to describe rotations. Aeronautics describes rotations in a similar way, so programmers working with 3D graphics often use a set of terms borrowed from aeronautics: pitch, yaw, and roll. Figure 2.13 illustrates what these terms mean; pitch is rotation around the X-axis, yaw is rotation around the Y-axis, and roll is rotation around the Z-axis.

Given that we can describe rotations around the X-, Y-, and Z-axes, that means the three parameters for Rotate() are X, Y, and Z rotation. Because we only want the player to spin around sideways, as opposed to tilting up and down, there should only be a number given for the Y rotation, and just 0 for X and Z rotation. Hopefully you can guess what will happen if you change the parameters to (speed, 0, 0) and then play it; try that now!

There's one other subtle point to understand about rotations and 3D coordinate axes, embodied in an optional fourth parameter to the Rotate() method.

### 2.3.3   *Local vs. global coordinate space*

By default, the Rotate() method operates on what are called local coordinates. The other kind of coordinates you could use are global. You tell the method whether to use local or global coordinates using an optional fourth parameter by writing either Space.Self or Space.World like so:

```
Rotate(0, speed, 0, Space.World)
```

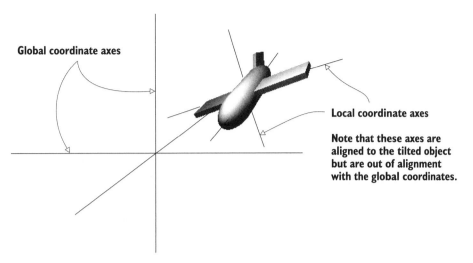

**Global coordinate axes**

**Local coordinate axes**

**Note that these axes are aligned to the tilted object but are out of alignment with the global coordinates.**

**Figure 2.14   Local vs. global coordinate axes**

Refer back to the explanation about 3D coordinate space, and ponder these questions: Where is (0, 0, 0) located? What direction is the X-axis pointed in? Can the coordinate system itself move around?

It turns out that every single object has its own origin point, as well as its own direction for the three axes, and this coordinate system moves around with the object. This is referred to as local coordinates. The overall 3D scene also has its own origin point and its own direction for the three axes, and this coordinate system never moves. This is referred to as global coordinates. Thus, when you specify local or global for the `Rotate()` method, you're telling it whose X-, Y-, and Z-axes to rotate around (see figure 2.14).

If you're new to 3D graphics, this is somewhat of a mind-bending concept. The different axes are depicted in figure 2.14 (notice how "left" to the plane is a different direction than "left" to the world) but the easiest way to understand local and global is through an example.

First, select the player object and then tilt it a bit (something like 30 for X rotation). This will throw off the local coordinates, so that local and global rotations will look different. Now try running the Spin script both with and without `Space.World` added to the parameters; if it's too hard for you to visualize what's happening, try removing the spin component from the player object and instead spin a tilted cube placed in front of the player. You'll see the object rotating around different axes when you set the command to local or global coordinates.

## 2.4    *Script component for looking around: MouseLook*

Now you'll make rotation respond to input from the mouse (that is, rotation of the object this script is attached to, which in this case will be the player). You'll do this in several steps, progressively adding new movement abilities to the character. First the player will only rotate side to side, and then the player will only rotate up and down. Eventually the player will be able to look around in all directions (rotating horizontally and vertically at the same time), a behavior referred to as *mouse-look*.

Given that there will be three different types of rotation behavior (horizontal, vertical, and both), you'll start by writing the framework for supporting all three. Create a new C# script, name it MouseLook, and write in the code from the next listing.

**Listing 2.2  MouseLook framework with enum for the Rotation setting**

```csharp
using UnityEngine;
using System.Collections;

public class MouseLook : MonoBehaviour {          // Define an enum data
  public enum RotationAxes {                       // structure to associate
    MouseXAndY = 0,                                // names with settings.
    MouseX = 1,
    MouseY = 2
  }
  public RotationAxes axes = RotationAxes.MouseXAndY;   // Declare a public
                                                        // variable to set in
                                                        // Unity's editor.

  void Update() {
    if (axes == RotationAxes.MouseX) {              // Put code here for
      // horizontal rotation here                   // horizontal rotation only.
    }
    else if (axes == RotationAxes.MouseY) {         // Put code here for
      // vertical rotation here                     // vertical rotation only.
    }
    else {
      // both horizontal and vertical rotation here  // Put code here for
    }                                                // both horizontal and
  }                                                  // vertical rotation.
}
```

Notice that an enum is used to choose horizontal or vertical rotation for the Mouse-Look script. Defining an enum data structure allows you to set values by name, rather than typing in numbers and trying to remember what each number means (is 0 horizontal rotation? Is it 1?). If you then declare a public variable typed to that enum, that will display in the Inspector as a drop-down menu (see figure 2.15), which is useful for selecting settings.

Remove the Spin component (the same way you removed the capsule collider earlier) and attach this new script to the player object instead. Use the Axes drop-down menu in the Inspector to switch the direction of rotation. With the horizontal/vertical rotation setting in place, you can fill in code for each branch of the conditional.

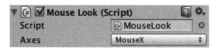

**Figure 2.15  The Inspector displays public enum variables as a drop-down menu.**

### 2.4.1 Horizontal rotation that tracks mouse movement

The first and simplest branch is horizontal rotation. Start by writing the same rotation command you used in listing 2.1 to make the object spin. Don't forget to declare a public variable for the rotation speed; declare the new variable after `axes` but before `Update()`, and call the variable `sensitivityHor` because speed is too generic a name once you have multiple rotations involved. Increase the value of the variable to 9 this time because that value needs to be bigger once the code starts scaling it (which will be soon). The adjusted code should look like the following listing.

**Listing 2.3    Horizontal rotation, not yet responding to the mouse**

```
...
public RotationAxes axes = RotationAxes.MouseXAndY;          Italicized code was
                                                            already in script; it's
public float sensitivityHor = 9.0f;                         shown here for reference.
                                     Declare a variable for
void Update() {                      the speed of rotation.
  if (axes == RotationAxes.MouseX) {
    transform.Rotate(0, sensitivityHor, 0);
  }                                        Put the Rotate command here
...                                        so that it runs every frame.
```

Set the Axes menu of the MouseLook component to horizontal rotation and play the script; the view will spin as before. The next step is to make the rotation react to mouse movement, so let's introduce a new method: `Input.GetAxis()`. The `Input` class has a bunch of methods for handling input devices (such as the mouse) and the method `GetAxis()` returns numbers correlated to the movement of the mouse (positive or negative, depending on the direction of movement). `GetAxis()` takes the name of the axis desired as a parameter, and the horizontal axis is called Mouse X.

If you multiply the rotation speed by the axis value, the rotation will respond to mouse movement. The speed will scale according to mouse movement, scaling down to zero or even reversing direction. The `Rotate` command now looks like the next listing.

**Listing 2.4    `Rotate` command adjusted to respond to the mouse**

```
...
transform.Rotate(0, Input.GetAxis("Mouse X") * sensitivityHor, 0);
...
                                          Note the use of GetAxis()
                                          to get mouse input.
```

Hit Play and then move the mouse around. As you move the mouse from side to side, the view will rotate from side to side. That's pretty cool! The next step is to rotate vertically instead of horizontally.

### 2.4.2 Vertical rotation with limits

For horizontal rotation we've been using the `Rotate()` method, but we'll take a different approach with vertical rotation. Although that method is convenient for applying transforms, it's also kind of inflexible. It's only useful for incrementing the rotation without limit, which was fine for horizontal rotation, but vertical rotation needs limits on how much the view can tilt up or down. The following listing shows the vertical rotation code for MouseLook; a detailed explanation of the code will come right after.

> **Listing 2.5   Vertical rotation for MouseLook**

```
. . .
public float sensitivityHor = 9.0f;            Declare variables used
public float sensitivityVert = 9.0f;           for vertical rotation.

public float minimumVert = -45.0f;
public float maximumVert = 45.0f;
                                               Declare a private variable
private float _rotationX = 0;                  for the vertical angle.
                                                                    Increment the
                                                                    vertical angle based
void Update() {                                                     on the mouse.
  if (axes == RotationAxes.MouseX) {
    transform.Rotate(0, Input.GetAxis("Mouse X") * sensitivityHor, 0);
  }
  else if (axes == RotationAxes.MouseY) {
    _rotationX -= Input.GetAxis("Mouse Y") * sensitivityVert;
    _rotationX = Mathf.Clamp(_rotationX, minimumVert, maximumVert);

    float rotationY = transform.localEulerAngles.y;

    transform.localEulerAngles = new Vector3(_rotationX, rotationY, 0);
  }
. . .
```

**Clamp the vertical angle between minimum and maximum limits.**

**Keep the same Y angle (i.e., no horizontal rotation).**

**Create a new vector from the stored rotation values.**

Set the Axes menu of the MouseLook component to vertical rotation and play the new script. Now the view won't rotate sideways, but it'll tilt up and down when you move the mouse up and down. The tilt stops at upper and lower limits.

There are several new concepts in this code that need to be explained. First off, we're not using Rotate() this time, so we need a variable (called _rotationX here, because vertical rotation goes around the X-axis) in which to store the rotation angle. The Rotate() method increments the current rotation, whereas this code sets the rotation angle directly. In other words, it's the difference between saying "add 5 to the angle" and "set the angle to 30." We do still need to increment the rotation angle, but that's why the code has the -= operator: to subtract a value from the rotation angle, rather than set the angle to that value. By not using Rotate() we can manipulate the rotation angle in various ways aside from only incrementing it. The rotation value is multiplied by Input.GetAxis() just like in the code for horizontal rotation, except now we ask for Mouse Y because that's the vertical axis of the mouse.

The rotation angle is manipulated further on the very next line. We use Mathf.Clamp() to keep the rotation angle between minimum and maximum limits.

Those limits are public variables declared earlier in the code, and they ensure that the view can only tilt 45 degrees up or down. The `Clamp()` method isn't specific to rotation, but is generally useful for keeping a number variable between limits. Just to see what happens, try commenting out the `Clamp()` line; now the tilt doesn't stop at upper and lower limits, allowing you to even rotate completely upside down! Clearly, viewing the world upside down is undesirable; hence the limits.

Because the angles property of `transform` is a Vector3, we need to create a new Vector3 with the rotation angle passed in to the constructor. The `Rotate()` method was automating this process for us, incrementing the rotation angle and then creating a new vector.

> **DEFINITION** A *vector* is multiple numbers stored together as a unit. For example, a Vector3 is 3 numbers (labeled x, y, z).

> **WARNING** The reason why we need to create a new Vector3 instead of changing values in the existing vector in the transform is because those values are read-only for transforms. This is a common mistake that can trip you up.

---

### Euler angles vs. quaternion

You're probably wondering why the property is called `localEulerAngles` and not `localRotation`. First you need to know about a concept called *quaternions*.

Quaternions are a different mathematical construct for representing rotations. They're distinct from Euler angles, which is the name for the X-, Y-, Z-axes approach we've been taking. Remember the whole discussion of pitch, yaw, and roll? Well, that method of representing rotations is Euler angles. Quaternions are...different. It's hard to explain what quaternions are, because they're an obscure aspect of higher math, involving movement through four dimensions. If you want a detailed explanation, try reading the document found here:

www.flipcode.com/documents/matrfaq.html#Q47

It's a bit easier to explain why quaternions are used to represent rotations: interpolating between rotation values (that is, going through a bunch of in-between values to gradually change from one value to another) looks smoother and more natural when using quaternions.

To return to the initial question, it's because `localRotation` is a quaternion, not Euler angles. Unity also provides the Euler angles property to make manipulating rotations easier to understand; the Euler angles property is converted to and from quaternion values automatically. Unity handles the harder math for you behind the scenes, so you don't have to worry about handling it yourself.

---

There's one more rotation setting for MouseLook that needs code: horizontal and vertical rotation at the same time.

### 2.4.3 *Horizontal and vertical rotation at the same time*

This last chunk of code won't use `Rotate()` either, for the same reason: the vertical rotation angle is clamped between limits after being incremented. That means the horizontal rotation needs to be calculated directly now. Remember, `Rotate()` was automating the process of incrementing the rotation angle (see the next listing).

---

**Listing 2.6    Horizontal and vertical MouseLook**

```
...
else {
  _rotationX -= Input.GetAxis("Mouse Y") * sensitivityVert;
  _rotationX = Mathf.Clamp(_rotationX, minimumVert, maximumVert);

  float delta = Input.GetAxis("Mouse X") * sensitivityHor;
  float rotationY = transform.localEulerAngles.y + delta;

  transform.localEulerAngles = new Vector3(_rotationX, rotationY, 0);
}
...
```

*delta is the amount to change the rotation by.*

*Increment the rotation angle by delta.*

The first couple of lines, dealing with `_rotationX`, are exactly the same as in the last section. Just remember that rotating around the object's X-axis is vertical rotation. Because horizontal rotation is no longer being handled using the `Rotate()` method, that's what the `delta` and `rotationY` lines are doing. *Delta* is a common mathematical term for "the amount of change," so our calculation of delta is the amount that rotation should change. That amount of change is then added to the current rotation angle to get the desired new rotation angle.

Finally, both angles, vertical and horizontal, are used to create a new vector that's assigned to the transform component's angle property.

---

#### Disallow physics rotation on the player

Although this doesn't matter quite yet for this project, in most modern FPS games there's a complex physics simulation affecting everything in the scene. This will cause objects to bounce and tumble around; this behavior looks and works great for most objects, but the player's rotation needs to be solely controlled by the mouse and not affected by the physics simulation.

For that reason, mouse input scripts usually set the `freezeRotation` property on the player's Rigidbody. Add this `Start()` method to the MouseLook script:

```
...
void Start() {
    Rigidbody body = GetComponent<Rigidbody>();
    if (body != null)
        body.freezeRotation = true;
}
...
```

*Check if this component exists.*

(A Rigidbody is an additional component an object can have. The physics simulation acts on Rigidbodies and manipulates objects they're attached to.)

In case you've gotten lost on where to make the various changes and additions we've gone over, the next listing has the full finished script. Alternatively, download the example project.

**Listing 2.7  The finished MouseLook script**

```
using UnityEngine;
using System.Collections;

public class MouseLook : MonoBehaviour {
  public enum RotationAxes {
    MouseXAndY = 0,
    MouseX = 1,
    MouseY = 2
  }
  public RotationAxes axes = RotationAxes.MouseXAndY;

  public float sensitivityHor = 9.0f;
  public float sensitivityVert = 9.0f;

  public float minimumVert = -45.0f;
  public float maximumVert = 45.0f;

  private float _rotationX = 0;

  void Start() {
    Rigidbody body = GetComponent<Rigidbody>();
    if (body != null)
        body.freezeRotation = true;
  }

  void Update() {
    if (axes == RotationAxes.MouseX) {
      transform.Rotate(0, Input.GetAxis("Mouse X") * sensitivityHor, 0);
    }
    else if (axes == RotationAxes.MouseY) {
      _rotationX -= Input.GetAxis("Mouse Y") * sensitivityVert;
      _rotationX = Mathf.Clamp(_rotationX, minimumVert, maximumVert);

      float rotationY = transform.localEulerAngles.y;

      transform.localEulerAngles = new Vector3(_rotationX, rotationY, 0);
    }
    else {
      _rotationX -= Input.GetAxis("Mouse Y") * sensitivityVert;
      _rotationX = Mathf.Clamp(_rotationX, minimumVert, maximumVert);

      float delta = Input.GetAxis("Mouse X") * sensitivityHor;
      float rotationY = transform.localEulerAngles.y + delta;

      transform.localEulerAngles = new Vector3(_rotationX, rotationY, 0);
    }
  }
}
```

When you set the Axes menu and run the new code, you're able to look around in all directions while moving the mouse. Great! But you're still stuck in one place, looking around as if mounted on a turret. The next step is moving around the scene.

## 2.5   *Keyboard input component: first-person controls*

Looking around in response to mouse input is an important part of first-person controls, but you're only halfway there. The player also needs to move in response to keyboard input. Let's write a keyboard controls component to complement the mouse controls component; create a new C# script called FPSInput and attach that to the player (alongside the MouseLook script). For the moment set the MouseLook component to horizontal rotation only.

> **TIP**   The keyboard and mouse controls explained here are split up into separate scripts. You don't have to structure the code this way, and you could have everything bundled into a single "player controls" script, but a component system (such as the one in Unity) tends to be most flexible and thus most useful when you have functionality split into several smaller components.

The code you wrote in the previous section affected rotation only, but now we'll change the object's position instead. As shown in listing 2.8, refer back to the rotation code from before we added mouse input; type that into FPSInput, but change `Rotate()` to `Translate()`. When you hit Play, the view slides up instead of spinning around. Try changing the parameter values to see how the movement changes (in particular, try swapping the first and second numbers); after experimenting with that for a bit, you can move on to adding keyboard input.

---

**Listing 2.8   Spin code from the first listing, with a couple of minor changes**

```
using UnityEngine;
using System.Collections;

public class FPSInput : MonoBehaviour {          Not required, but you probably
  public float speed = 6.0f;                     want to increase the speed

  void Update() {
    transform.Translate(0, speed, 0);            Changing Rotate() to Translate()
  }
}
```

### 2.5.1   *Responding to key presses*

The code for moving according to key presses (shown in the following listing) is similar to the code for rotating according to the mouse. The `GetAxis()` method is used here as well, and in a very similar way. The following listing demonstrates how to use that command.

**Listing 2.9  Positional movement responding to key presses**

```
. . .
void Update() {
  float deltaX = Input.GetAxis("Horizontal") * speed;        ◁     "Horizontal" and "Vertical"
  float deltaZ = Input.GetAxis("Vertical") * speed;                are indirect names for
  transform.Translate(deltaX, 0, deltaZ);                          keyboard mappings.
}
. . .
```

As before, the GetAxis() values are multiplied by speed in order to determine the amount of movement. Whereas before the requested axis was always "Mouse something," now we pass in either Horizontal or Vertical. These names are abstractions for input settings in Unity; if you look in the Edit menu under Project Settings and then look under Input, you'll find a list of abstract input names and the exact controls mapped to those names. Both the left/right arrow keys and the letters A/D are mapped to Horizontal, whereas both the up/down arrow keys and the letters W/S are mapped to Vertical.

Note that the movement values are applied to the X and Z coordinates. As you probably noticed while experimenting with the Translate() method, the X coordinate moves from side to side and the Z coordinate moves forward and backward.

Put in this new movement code and you should be able to move around by pressing either the arrow keys or WASD letter keys, the standard in most FPS games. The movement script is nearly complete, but we have a few more adjustments to go over.

### 2.5.2  Setting a rate of movement independent of the computer's speed

It's not obvious right now because you've only been running the code on one computer (yours), but if you ran it on different machines it'd run at different speeds. That's because some computers can process code and graphics faster than others. Right now the player would move at different speeds on different computers because the movement code is tied to the computer's speed. That is referred to as *frame rate dependent*, because the movement code is dependent on the frame rate of the game.

For example, imagine you run this demo on two different computers, one that gets 30 fps (frames per second) and one that gets 60 fps. That means Update() would be called twice as often on the second computer, and the same speed value of 6 would be applied every time. At 30 fps the rate of movement would be 180 units/second, and the movement at 60 fps would be 360 units/second. For most games, movement speed that varies like this would be bad news.

The solution is to adjust the movement code to make it *frame rate independent*. That means the speed of movement is not dependent on the frame rate of the game. The way to achieve this is by not applying the same speed value at every frame rate. Instead, scale the speed value higher or lower depending on how quickly the computer runs. This is achieved by multiplying the speed value by another value called deltaTime, as shown in the next listing.

**Listing 2.10    Frame rate independent movement using `deltaTime`**

```
...
void Update() {
  float deltaX = Input.GetAxis("Horizontal") * speed;
  float deltaZ = Input.GetAxis("Vertical") * speed;
  transform.Translate(deltaX * Time.deltaTime, 0, deltaZ * Time.deltaTime);
}
...
```

That was a simple change. The `Time` class has a number of properties and methods useful for timing, and one of those properties is `deltaTime`. Because we know that delta means the amount of change, that means `deltaTime` is the amount of change in time. Specifically, `deltaTime` is the amount of time between frames. The time between frames varies at different frame rates (for example, 30 fps is a `deltaTime` of 1/30th of a second), so multiplying the speed value by `deltaTime` will scale the speed value on different computers.

Now the movement speed will be the same on all computers. But the movement script is still not quite done; when you move around the room you can pass through walls, so we need to adjust the code further to prevent that.

### 2.5.3    *Moving the CharacterController for collision detection*

Directly changing the object's transform doesn't apply collision detection, so the character will pass through walls. To apply collision detection, what we want to do instead is use CharacterController. CharacterController is a component that makes the object move more like a character in a game, including colliding with walls. Recall that back when we set up the player, we attached a CharacterController, so now we'll use that component with the movement code in FPSInput (see the following listing).

**Listing 2.11    Moving CharacterController instead of Transform**

```
...
private CharacterController _charController;          ◁  Variable for referencing
                                                        the CharacterController
void Start() {
  _charController = GetComponent<CharacterController>();  ◁  Access other
}                                                            components attached
                                                             to the same object.
void Update() {
  float deltaX = Input.GetAxis("Horizontal") * speed;
  float deltaZ = Input.GetAxis("Vertical") * speed;
  Vector3 movement = new Vector3(deltaX, 0, deltaZ);        Limit diagonal movement
  movement = Vector3.ClampMagnitude(movement, speed);  ◁  to the same speed as
                                                           movement along an axis.
  movement *= Time.deltaTime;
  movement = transform.TransformDirection(movement);
  _charController.Move(movement);
}                                                    ◁  Tell the CharacterController
...                                                     to move by that vector.
```

Transform the movement vector from local to global coordinates.

This code excerpt introduces several new concepts. The first concept to point out is the variable for referencing the CharacterController. This variable simply creates a local reference to the object (code object, that is—not to be confused with scene objects); multiple scripts can have references to this one CharacterController instance.

That variable starts out empty, so before you can use the reference you need to assign an object to it for it to refer to. This is where `GetComponent()` comes into play; that method returns other components attached to the same `GameObject`. Rather than pass a parameter inside the parentheses, you use the C# syntax of defining the type inside angle brackets, <>.

Once you have a reference to the CharacterController, you can call `Move()` on the controller. Pass in a vector to that method, similar to how the mouse rotation code used a vector for rotation values. Also similar to how rotation values were limited, use `Vector3.ClampMagnitude()` to limit the vector's magnitude to the movement speed; the clamp is used because otherwise diagonal movement would have a greater magnitude than movement directly along an axis (picture the sides and hypotenuse of a right triangle).

But there's one tricky aspect to the movement vector here, and it has to do with local versus global, as we discussed earlier for rotations. We'll create the vector with a value to move, say, to the left. That's the *player's* left, though, which may be a completely different direction from the *world's* left. That is, we're talking about left in local space, not global space. We need to pass a movement vector defined in global space to the `Move()` method, so we're going to need to convert the local space vector into global space. Doing that conversion is extremely complex math, but fortunately for us Unity takes care of that math for us, and we simply need to call the method `TransformDirection()` in order to, well, transform the direction.

> **DEFINITION** *Transform* used as a verb means to convert from one coordinate space to another (refer back to section 2.3.3 if you don't remember what a coordinate space is). Don't get confused with the other definitions of transform, including both the Transform component and the action of moving the object around the scene. It's sort of an overloaded term, because all these meanings refer to the same underlying concept.

Test playing the movement code now. If you haven't done so already, set the Mouse-Look component to both horizontal and vertical rotation. You can look around the scene fully and fly around the scene using keyboard controls. This is pretty great if you want the player to fly around the scene, but what if you want the player walking around on the ground?

### 2.5.4 Adjusting components for walking instead of flying

Now that collision detection is working, the script can have gravity and the player will stay down against the floor. Declare a gravity variable and then use that gravity value for the Y-axis, as shown in the next listing.

**Listing 2.12   Adding gravity to the movement code**

```
...
public float gravity = -9.8f;
...
void Update() {
  ...
  movement = Vector3.ClampMagnitude(movement, speed);     Use the gravity value
  movement.y = gravity;                                    instead of just 0.
  ...
```

Now there's a constant downward force on the player, but it's not always pointed straight down, because the player object can tilt up and down with the mouse. Fortunately everything we need to fix that is already in place, so we just need to make some minor adjustments to how components are set up on the player. First set the Mouse-Look component on the player object to horizontal rotation only. Next add the MouseLook component to the camera object, and set that one to vertical rotation only. That's right; you're going to have two different objects responding to the mouse!

Because the player object now only rotates horizontally, there's no longer any problem with the downward force of gravity being tilted. The camera object is parented to the player object (remember when we did that in the Hierarchy view?), so even though it rotates vertically independently from the player, the camera rotates horizontally along with the player.

---

**Polishing the finished script**

Use the `RequireComponent()` method to ensure that other components needed by the script are also attached. Sometimes other components are optional (that is, code that says "If this other component is also attached, then…"), but sometimes you want to make the other components mandatory. Add the method to the top of the script in order to enforce that dependency and give the required component as a parameter.

Similarly, if you add the method `AddComponentMenu()` to the top of your scripts, that script will be added to the component menu in Unity's editor. Tell the command the name of the menu item you want to add, and then the script can be selected when you click Add Component at the bottom of the Inspector. Handy!

A script with both methods added to the top would look something like this:

```
using UnityEngine;
using System.Collections;

[RequireComponent(typeof(CharacterController))]
[AddComponentMenu("Control Script/FPS Input")]
public class FPSInput : MonoBehaviour {
    ...
```

---

Listing 2.13 shows the full finished script. Along with the small adjustments to how components are set up on the player, the player can walk around the room. Even with the gravity variable being applied, you can still use this script for flying movement by setting Gravity to 0 in the Inspector.

**Listing 2.13   The finished FPSInput script**

```
using UnityEngine;
using System.Collections;

[RequireComponent(typeof(CharacterController))]
[AddComponentMenu("Control Script/FPS Input")]
public class FPSInput : MonoBehaviour {
  public float speed = 6.0f;
  public float gravity = -9.8f;

  private CharacterController _charController;

  void Start() {
    _charController = GetComponent<CharacterController>();
  }

  void Update() {
    float deltaX = Input.GetAxis("Horizontal") * speed;
    float deltaZ = Input.GetAxis("Vertical") * speed;
    Vector3 movement = new Vector3(deltaX, 0, deltaZ);
    movement = Vector3.ClampMagnitude(movement, speed);

    movement.y = gravity;

    movement *= Time.deltaTime;
    movement = transform.TransformDirection(movement);
    _charController.Move(movement);
  }
}
```

Congratulations on building this 3D project! We covered a lot of ground in this chapter, and now you're well-versed in how to code movement in Unity. As exciting as this first demo is, it's still a long way from being a complete game. After all, the project plan described this as a basic FPS scene, and what's a shooter if you can't shoot? So give yourself a well-deserved pat on the back for this chapter's project, and then get ready for the next step.

## 2.6   *Summary*

In this chapter you learned that

- 3D coordinate space is defined by X-, Y-, and Z-axes.
- Objects and lights in a room set the scene.
- The player in a first-person scene is essentially a camera.
- Movement code applies small transforms repeatedly in every frame.
- FPS controls consist of mouse rotation and keyboard movement.

# 3

# Adding enemies and projectiles to the 3D game

## This chapter covers

- Taking aim and firing, both for the player and for enemies
- Detecting and responding to hits
- Making enemies that wander around
- Spawning new objects in the scene

The movement demo from the previous chapter was pretty cool but still not really a game. Let's turn that movement demo into a first-person shooter. If you think about what else we need now, it boils down to the ability to shoot, and things to shoot at. First we're going to write scripts that enable the player to shoot objects in the scene. Then we're going to build enemies to populate the scene, including code to both wander around aimlessly and react to being hit. Finally we're going to enable the enemies to fight back, emitting fireballs at the player. None of the scripts from chapter 2 need to change; instead, we'll add scripts to the project—scripts that handle the additional features.

I've chosen a first-person shooter for this project for a couple of reasons. One is simply that FPS games are popular; people like shooting games, so let's make a shooting game. A subtler reason has to do with the techniques you'll learn; this project is a great way to learn about several fundamental concepts in 3D simulations. For example, shooting games are a great way to teach raycasting. In a bit we'll get into the specifics of what *raycasting* is, but for now you just need to know that it's a tool that's useful for many different tasks in 3D simulations. Although raycasting is useful in a wide variety of situations, it happens that using raycasting makes the most intuitive sense for shooting.

Creating wandering targets to shoot at gives us a great excuse to explore code for computer-controlled characters, as well as use techniques for sending messages and spawning objects. In fact, this wandering behavior is another place that raycasting is valuable, so we're already going to be looking at a different application of the technique after having first learned it with shooting. Similarly, the approach to sending messages that's demonstrated in this project is also useful elsewhere. In future chapters you'll see other applications for these techniques, and even within this one project we'll go over alternative situations.

Ultimately we'll approach this project one new feature at a time, with the game always playable at every step but also always feeling like there's a missing part to work on next. This roadmap breaks down the steps into small, understandable changes, with only one new feature added in each step:

1 Write code enabling the player to shoot into the scene.
2 Create static targets that react to being hit.
3 Make the targets wander around.
4 Spawn the wandering targets automatically.
5 Enable the targets/enemies to shoot fireballs at the player.

**NOTE** This chapter's project assumes you already have a first-person movement demo to build on. We created a movement demo in chapter 2, but if you skipped to this chapter then you will need to download the sample files for chapter 2.

## 3.1 Shooting via raycasts

The first new feature to introduce into the 3D demo is shooting. Looking around and moving are certainly crucial features for a first-person shooter, but it's not a game until players can affect the simulation and apply their skills. Shooting in 3D games can be implemented with a few different approaches, and one of the most important approaches is raycasting.

### 3.1.1 What is raycasting?

As the name indicates, raycasting is when you cast a ray into the scene. Clear, right? Well, okay, so what exactly is a *ray*?

**DEFINITION** A *ray* is an imaginary or invisible line in the scene that starts at some origin point and extends out in a specific direction.

Raycasting is when you create a ray and then determine what intersects that ray; figure 3.1 illustrates the concept. Consider what happens when you fire a bullet from a gun: the bullet starts at the position of the gun and then flies forward in a straight line until it hits something. A ray is analogous to the path of the bullet, and raycasting is analogous to firing the bullet and seeing where it hits.

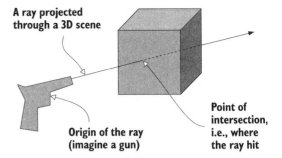

**Figure 3.1  A ray is an imaginary line, and raycasting is finding where that line intersects.**

As you can imagine, the math behind raycasting often gets complicated. Not only is it tricky to calculate the intersection of a line with a 3D plane, but you need to do that for all polygons of all mesh objects in the scene (remember, a mesh object is a 3D visual constructed from lots of connected lines and shapes). Fortunately, Unity handles the difficult math behind raycasting, but you still have to worry about higher-level concerns like where the ray is being cast from and why.

In this project the answer to the latter question (why) is to simulate a bullet being fired into the scene. For a first-person shooter, the ray generally starts at the camera position and then extends out through the center of the camera view. In other words, you're checking for objects straight in front of the camera; Unity provides commands to make that task simple. Let's take a look at these commands.

### 3.1.2  Using the command ScreenPointToRay for shooting

You'll implement shooting by projecting a ray that starts at the camera and extends forward through the center of the view. Projecting a ray through the center of the camera view is a special case of an action referred to as *mouse picking*.

> **DEFINITION**  *Mouse picking* is the action of picking out the spot in the 3D scene directly under the mouse cursor.

Unity provides the method `ScreenPointToRay()` to perform this action. Figure 3.2 illustrates what happens. The method creates a ray that starts at the camera and projects

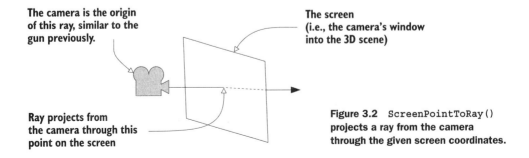

**Figure 3.2  `ScreenPointToRay()` projects a ray from the camera through the given screen coordinates.**

at an angle passing through the given screen coordinates. Usually the coordinates of the mouse position are used for mouse picking, but for first-person shooting the center of the screen is used. Once you have a ray, it can be passed to the method `Physics.Raycast()` to perform raycasting using that ray.

Let's write some code that uses the methods we just discussed. In Unity create a new C# script, attach that script to the camera (not the player object), and then write the code from the next listing in it.

**Listing 3.1 RayShooter script to attach to the camera**

```
using UnityEngine;
using System.Collections;

public class RayShooter : MonoBehaviour {
  private Camera _camera;

  void Start() {                                    ← Access other components
    _camera = GetComponent<Camera>();                 attached to the same object.
  }

  void Update() {                                   ← Respond to the mouse button.
    if (Input.GetMouseButtonDown(0)) {
      Vector3 point = new Vector3(_camera.pixelWidth/2, _camera.pixelHeight/2, 0);
      Ray ray = _camera.ScreenPointToRay(point);
      RaycastHit hit;
      if (Physics.Raycast(ray, out hit)) {
        Debug.Log("Hit " + hit.point);            ← The raycast fills a referenced
      }                                               variable with information.
    }
  }
}
```

*The middle of the screen is half its width and height.* → *Create the ray at that position using ScreenPointToRay().* → *Retrieve coordinates where the ray hit.*

You should note a number of things in this code listing. First, the camera component is retrieved in `Start()`, just like the CharacterController in the previous chapter. Then the rest of the code is put in `Update()` because it needs to check the mouse over and over repeatedly, as opposed to just one time. The method `Input.GetMouseButtonDown()` returns `true` or `false` depending on whether the mouse has been clicked, so putting that command in a conditional means the enclosed code runs only when the mouse has been clicked. You want to shoot when the player clicks the mouse; hence the conditional check of the mouse button.

A vector is created to define the screen coordinates for the ray (remember that a vector is several related numbers stored together). The camera's `pixelWidth` and `pixelHeight` values give you the size of the screen, so dividing those values in half gives you the center of the screen. Although screen coordinates are 2D, with only horizontal and vertical components and no depth, a Vector3 was created because `ScreenPointToRay()` requires that data type (presumably because calculating the ray involves arithmetic on 3D vectors). `ScreenPointToRay()` was called with this set of coordinates, resulting in a Ray object (code object, that is, not a game object; the two can be confusing sometimes).

The ray is then passed to the `Raycast()` method, but it's not the only object passed in. There's also a `RaycastHit` data structure; `RaycastHit` is a bundle of information about the intersection of the ray, including where the intersection happened and what object was intersected. The C# syntax `out` ensures that the data structure manipulated within the command is the same object that exists outside the command, as opposed to the objects being separate copies in the different function scopes.

Finally the code calls the `Physics.Raycast()` method. This method checks for intersections with the given ray, fills in data about the intersection, and returns `true` if the ray hit anything. Because a Boolean value is returned, this method can be put in a conditional check, just as you used `Input.GetMouseButtonDown()` earlier.

For now the code emits a console message to indicate when an intersection occurred. This console message displays the 3D coordinates of the point where the ray hit (the XYZ values we discussed in chapter 2). But it can be hard to visualize where exactly the ray hit; similarly, it can be hard to tell where the center of the screen is (that is, where the ray shoots through). Let's add visual indicators to address both problems.

### 3.1.3  *Adding visual indicators for aiming and hits*

Our next step is to add two kinds of visual indicators: an aiming spot on the center of the screen, and a mark in the scene where the ray hit. For a first-person shooter the latter is usually bullet holes, but for now you're going to put a blank sphere on the spot (and use a coroutine to remove the sphere after one second). Figure 3.3 shows what you'll see.

> **DEFINITION**  *Coroutines* are a Unity-specific way of handling tasks that execute incrementally over time, as opposed to how most functions make the program wait until they finish.

First let's add indicators to mark where the ray hits. Listing 3.2 shows the script after making this addition. Run around the scene shooting; it's pretty fun seeing the sphere indicators!

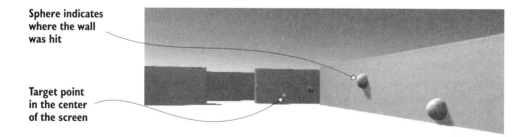

**Sphere indicates where the wall was hit**

**Target point in the center of the screen**

**Figure 3.3  Shooting repeatedly after adding visual indicators for aiming and hits**

**Listing 3.2   RayShooter script with sphere indicators added**

```
using UnityEngine;
using System.Collections;

public class RayShooter : MonoBehaviour {
  private Camera _camera;

  void Start() {
    _camera = GetComponent<Camera>();
  }

  void Update() {
    if (Input.GetMouseButtonDown(0)) {
      Vector3 point = new Vector3(_camera.pixelWidth/2, _camera.pixelHeight/2, 0);
      Ray ray = _camera.ScreenPointToRay(point);
      RaycastHit hit;
      if (Physics.Raycast(ray, out hit)) {
        StartCoroutine(SphereIndicator(hit.point));
      }
    }
  }

  private IEnumerator SphereIndicator(Vector3 pos) {
    GameObject sphere = GameObject.CreatePrimitive(PrimitiveType.Sphere);
    sphere.transform.position = pos;

    yield return new WaitForSeconds(1);

    Destroy(sphere);
  }
}
```

This function is mostly the same raycasting code from listing 3.1.

Launch a coroutine in response to a hit.

Coroutines use IEnumerator functions.

The yield keyword tells coroutines where to pause.

Remove this GameObject and clear its memory.

The new method is `SphereIndicator()`, plus a one-line modification in the existing `Update()` method. This method creates a sphere at a point in the scene and then removes that sphere a second later. Calling `SphereIndicator()` from the raycasting code ensures that there will be visual indicators showing exactly where the ray hit. This function is defined with `IEnumerator`, and that type is tied in with the concept of coroutines.

Technically, coroutines aren't asynchronous (asynchronous operations don't stop the rest of the code from running; think of downloading an image in the script of a website), but through clever use of enumerators, Unity makes coroutines behave similarly to asynchronous functions. The secret sauce in coroutines is the `yield` keyword; that keyword causes the coroutine to temporarily pause, handing back the program flow and picking up again from that point in the next frame. In this way, coroutines seemingly run in the background of a program, through a repeated cycle of running partway and then returning to the rest of the program.

As the name implies, `StartCoroutine()` sets a coroutine in motion. Once a coroutine is started, it keeps running until the function is finished; it just pauses along the way. Note the subtle but significant point that the method passed to `StartCoroutine()`

has a set of parentheses following the name: this syntax means you're calling that function, as opposed to passing its name. The called function runs until it hits a `yield` command, at which point the function pauses.

`SphereIndicator()` creates a sphere at a specific point, pauses for the `yield` statement, and then destroys the sphere after the coroutine resumes. The length of the pause is controlled by the value returned at `yield`. A few different types of return values work in coroutines, but the most straightforward is to return a specific length of time to wait. Returning `WaitForSeconds(1)` causes the coroutine to pause for one second. Create a sphere, pause for one second, and then destroy the sphere: that sequence sets up a temporary visual indicator.

Listing 3.2 gave you indicators to mark where the ray hits. But you also want an aiming spot in the center of the screen, so that's done in the next listing.

**Listing 3.3   Visual indicator for aiming**

```
...
void Start() {
  _camera = GetComponent<Camera>();

  Cursor.lockState = CursorLockMode.Locked;     Hide the mouse cursor at
  Cursor.visible = false;                        the center of the screen.
}

void OnGUI() {
  int size = 12;
  float posX = _camera.pixelWidth/2 - size/4;
  float posY = _camera.pixelHeight/2 - size/2;     The command GUI.Label()
  GUI.Label(new Rect(posX, posY, size, size), "*");   displays text on screen.
}
...
```

Another new method has been added to the `RayShooter` class, called `OnGUI()`. Unity comes with both a basic and more advanced user interface (UI) system; because the basic system has a lot of limitations, we'll build a more flexible advanced UI in future chapters, but for now it's much easier to display a point in the center of the screen using the basic UI. Much like `Start()` and `Update()`, every `MonoBehaviour` automatically responds to an `OnGUI()` method. That function runs every frame right after the 3D scene is rendered, resulting in everything drawn during `OnGUI()` appearing on top of the 3D scene (imagine stickers applied to a painting of a landscape).

> **DEFINITION**   *Render* is the action of the computer drawing the pixels of the 3D scene. Although the scene is defined using XYZ coordinates, the actual display on your monitor is a 2D grid of colored pixels. Thus in order to display the 3D scene, the computer needs to calculate the color of all the pixels in the 2D grid; running that algorithm is referred to as *rendering*.

Inside `OnGUI()` the code defines 2D coordinates for the display (shifted slightly to account for the size of the label) and then calls `GUI.Label()`. That method displays a text label; because the string passed to the label is an asterisk (*), you end up with that character displayed in the center of the screen. Now it's much easier to aim in our nascent FPS game!

Listing 3.3 also added some cursor settings to the `Start()` method. All that's happening is that the values are being set for cursor visibility and locking. The script will work perfectly fine if you omit the cursor values, but these settings make first-person controls work a bit more smoothly. The mouse cursor will stay in the center of the screen, and to avoid cluttering the view it will turn invisible and will only reappear when you hit Esc.

> **WARNING** Always remember that you can hit Esc to unlock the mouse cursor. While the mouse cursor is locked, it's impossible to click the Play button and stop the game.

That wraps up the first-person shooting code…well, that wraps up the player's end of the interaction, anyway, but we still need to take care of targets.

## 3.2 Scripting reactive targets

Being able to shoot is all well and good, but at the moment players don't have anything to shoot at. We're going to create a target object and give it a script that will respond to being hit. Or rather, we'll slightly modify the shooting code to notify the target when hit, and then the script on the target will react when notified.

### 3.2.1 Determining what was hit

First you need to create a new object to shoot at. Create a new cube object (GameObject > 3D Object > Cube) and then scale it up vertically by setting the Y scale to 2 and leaving X and Z at 1. Position the new object at 0, 1, 0 to put it on the floor in the middle of the room, and name the object Enemy. Create a new script called ReactiveTarget and attach that to the newly created box. Soon you'll write code for this script, but leave it at the default for now; you're only creating the script file because the next code listing requires it to exist in order to compile. Go back to RayShooter.cs and modify the raycasting code according to the following listing. Run the new code and shoot the new target; debug messages appear in the console instead of sphere indicators in the scene.

**Listing 3.4  Detecting whether the target object was hit**

```
...
if (Physics.Raycast(ray, out hit)) {
  GameObject hitObject = hit.transform.gameObject;          Retrieve the object
  ReactiveTarget target = hitObject.GetComponent<ReactiveTarget>();   the ray hit.
  if (target != null) {
    Debug.Log("Target hit");                                Check for the ReactiveTarget
  } else {                                                  component on the object.
    StartCoroutine(SphereIndicator(hit.point));
  }
}
...
```

Notice that you retrieve the object from `RaycastHit`, just like the coordinates were retrieved for the sphere indicators. Technically, the hit information doesn't return the game object hit; it indicates the Transform component hit. You can then access `gameObject` as a property of `transform`.

Then, you use the method `GetComponent()` on the object to check whether it's a reactive target (that is, if it has the ReactiveTarget script attached). As you saw previously, that method returns components of a specific type that are attached to the `GameObject`. If no component of that type is attached to the object, then `GetComponent()` won't return anything. You check whether `null` was returned and run different code in each case.

If the hit object is a reactive target, the code emits a debug message instead of starting the coroutine for sphere indicators. Now let's inform the target object about the hit so that it can react.

## 3.2.2   *Alert the target that it was hit*

All that's needed in the code is a one-line change, as shown in the following listing.

**Listing 3.5   Sending a message to the target object**

```
...
if (target != null) {                              Call a method of the target instead
  target.ReactToHit();                             of just emitting the debug message.
} else {
  StartCoroutine(SphereIndicator(hit.point));
}
...
```

Now the shooting code calls a method of the target, so let's write that target method. In the ReactiveTarget script, write in the code from the next listing. The target object will fall over and disappear when you shoot it; refer to figure 3.4.

**Listing 3.6   ReactiveTarget script that dies when hit**

```
using UnityEngine;
using System.Collections;

public class ReactiveTarget : MonoBehaviour {

  public void ReactToHit() {                        Method called by the
    StartCoroutine(Die());                          shooting script
  }

  private IEnumerator Die() {                        Topple the enemy, wait 1.5 seconds,
    this.transform.Rotate(-75, 0, 0);               then destroy the enemy.

    yield return new WaitForSeconds(1.5f);

    Destroy(this.gameObject);                        Object can destroy itself
  }                                                  just like a separate object.
}
```

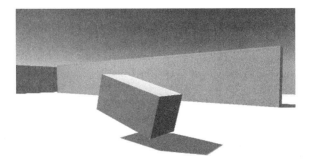

**Figure 3.4   The target object falling over when hit**

Most of this code should already be familiar to you from previous scripts, so we'll only go over it briefly. First, you define the method `ReactToHit()`, because that's the method name called in the shooting script. This method starts a coroutine that's similar to the sphere indicator code from earlier; the main difference is that it operates on the object of this script rather than creating a separate object. Expressions like `this.gameObject` refer to the `GameObject` that this script is attached to (and the `this` keyword is optional, so code could refer to `gameObject` without anything in front of it).

The first line of the coroutine function makes the object tip over. As discussed in chapter 2, rotations can be defined as an angle around each of the three coordinate axes, X Y, and Z. Because we don't want the object to rotate side to side at all, leave Y and Z as 0 and assign an angle to the X rotation.

> **NOTE** The transform is applied instantly, but you may prefer seeing the movement when objects topple over. Once you start looking beyond this book for more advanced topics, you might want to look up *tweens*, systems used to make objects move smoothly over time.

The second line of the method uses the `yield` keyword that's so significant to coroutines, pausing the function there and returning the number of seconds to wait before resuming. Finally, the game object destroys itself in the last line of the function. `Destroy(this.gameObject)` is called after the wait time, just like the code called `Destroy(sphere)` before.

> **WARNING** Be sure to call `Destroy()` on `this.gameObject` and not simply `this`! Don't get confused between the two; `this` only refers to this script component, whereas `this.gameObject` refers to the object the script is attached to.

The target now reacts to being shot; great! But it doesn't do anything else on its own, so let's add more behavior to make this target a proper enemy character.

## 3.3   *Basic wandering AI*

A static target isn't terribly interesting, so let's write code that'll make the enemy wander around. Code for wandering around is pretty much the simplest example of AI;

artificial intelligence (AI) refers to computer-controlled entities. In this case the entity is an enemy in a game, but it could also be a robot in the real world, or a voice that plays chess, for example.

### 3.3.1 Diagramming how basic AI works

There are a number of different approaches to AI (seriously, artificial intelligence is a major area of research for computer scientists), but for our purposes we'll stick with a simple approach. As you become more experienced and your games get more sophisticated, you'll probably want to explore various approaches to AI.

Figure 3.5 depicts the basic process. Every frame, the AI code will scan around its environment to determine whether it needs to react. If an obstacle appears in its way, the enemy turns to face a different direction. Regardless of whether the enemy needs to turn, it will always move forward steadily. Thus the enemy will ping-pong around the room, always moving forward and turning to avoid walls.

The actual code will look pretty familiar, because it moves enemies forward using the same commands as moving the player forward. The AI code will also use raycasting, similar to but in a different context from shooting.

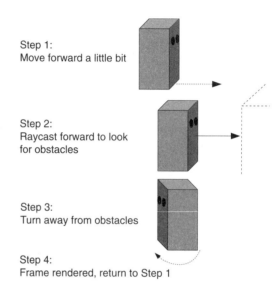

Step 1:
Move forward a little bit

Step 2:
Raycast forward to look for obstacles

Step 3:
Turn away from obstacles

Step 4:
Frame rendered, return to Step 1

**Figure 3.5   Basic AI: cyclical process of moving forward and avoiding obstacles**

### 3.3.2 "Seeing" obstacles with a raycast

As you saw in the introduction to this chapter, raycasting is a technique that's useful for a number of tasks within 3D simulations. One easily grasped task was shooting, but another place raycasting can be useful is for scanning around the scene. Given that scanning around the scene is a step in AI code, that means raycasting is used in AI code.

Earlier you created a ray that originated at the camera, because that's where the player was looking from; this time you'll create a ray that originates at the enemy. The first ray shot out through the center of the screen, but this time the ray will shoot forward in front of the character; figure 3.6 illustrates this. Then just like the shooting code used `RaycastHit` information to determine whether anything was hit and where, the AI code will use `RaycastHit` information to determine whether anything is in front of the enemy and, if so, how far away.

One difference between raycasting for shooting and raycasting for AI is the radius of the ray detected against. For shooting the ray was treated as infinitely thin, but for AI the ray will be treated as having a large cross-section; in terms of the code, this means using the method SphereCast() instead of Raycast(). The reason for this difference is that bullets are tiny, whereas to check for obstacles in front of the character we need to account for the width of the character.

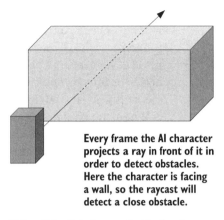

**Every frame the AI character projects a ray in front of it in order to detect obstacles. Here the character is facing a wall, so the raycast will detect a close obstacle.**

Create a new script called WanderingAI, attach that to the target object (alongside the ReactiveTarget script), and write the

**Figure 3.6  Using raycasting to "see" obstacles**

code from the next listing. Play the scene now and you should see the enemy wandering around the room; you can still shoot the target and it reacts the same way as before.

**Listing 3.7  Basic WanderingAI script**

```
using UnityEngine;
using System.Collections;

public class WanderingAI : MonoBehaviour {          Values for the speed of movement and
   public float speed = 3.0f;                        how far away to react to obstacles
   public float obstacleRange = 5.0f;

   void Update() {                                    Move forward
      transform.Translate(0, 0, speed * Time.deltaTime);   continuously every frame,
                                                            regardless of turning.
      Ray ray = new Ray(transform.position, transform.forward);
      RaycastHit hit;
      if (Physics.SphereCast(ray, 0.75f, out hit)) {       A ray at the same position
         if (hit.distance < obstacleRange) {               and pointing the same
            float angle = Random.Range(-110, 110);         direction as the character
            transform.Rotate(0, angle, 0);
         }
      }
   }
}
```

**Do raycasting with a circumference around the ray.**

**Turn toward a semirandom new direction.**

The listing added a couple of variables to represent the speed of movement and from how far away to react to obstacles. Then a Translate() method was added in the Update() method in order to move forward continuously (including the use of deltaTime for frame rate–independent movement). In Update() you'll also see raycasting code that looks a lot like the shooting script from earlier; again, the same technique of raycasting is being used here to see instead of shoot. The ray is created using the enemy's position and direction, instead of using the camera.

As explained earlier, the raycasting calculation was done using the method `Physics.SphereCast()`. This method takes a radius parameter to determine how far around the ray to detect intersections, but in every other respect it's exactly the same as `Physics.Raycast()`. This similarity includes how the command fills in hit information, checks for intersections just like before, and uses the `distance` property to be sure to react only when the enemy gets near an obstacle (as opposed to a wall across the room).

When the enemy has a nearby obstacle right in front of it, the code rotates the character a semi-random amount toward a new direction. I say "semi-random" because the values are constrained to minimum and maximum values that make sense for this situation. Specifically, we use the method `Random.Range()` that Unity provides for obtaining a random value between constraints. In this case the constraints were just slightly beyond an exact left or right turn, allowing the character to turn sufficiently to avoid obstacles.

### 3.3.3   *Tracking the character's state*

One oddity of the current behavior is that the enemy keeps moving forward after falling over from being hit. That's because right now the `Translate()` method runs every frame no matter what. Let's make small adjustments to the code in order to keep track of whether or not the character is alive—or to put it in another (more technical) way, we want to track the "alive" state of the character. Having the code keep track of and respond differently to the current state of the object is a common code pattern in many areas of programming, not just AI. More sophisticated implementations of this approach are referred to as *state machines*, or possibly even *finite state machines*.

> **DEFINITION**   *Finite state machine (FSM)* is a code structure in which the current state of the object is tracked, well-defined transitions exist between states, and the code behaves differently based on the state.

We're not going to implement a full FSM, but it's no coincidence that a common place to see the initials FSM is in discussions of AI. A full FSM would have many states for all the different behaviors of a sophisticated AI, but in this basic AI we just need to track whether or not the character is alive. The next listing adds a Boolean value, `_alive`, toward the top of the script, and the code needs occasional conditional checks of that value. With those checks in place, the movement code only runs while the enemy is alive.

---

**Listing 3.8   WanderingAI script with "alive" state added**

```
...
private bool _alive;                          Boolean value to track
                                              whether the enemy is alive
void Start() {
  _alive = true;                              Initialize that value.
}
```

```
void Update() {
  if (_alive) {
    transform.Translate(0, 0, speed * Time.deltaTime);
    ...
  }
}

public void SetAlive(bool alive) {
  _alive = alive;
}
...
```

**Only move if the character is alive.**

**Public method allowing outside code to affect the "alive" state**

The ReactiveTarget script can now tell the WanderingAI script when the enemy is or isn't alive (see the following listing).

**Listing 3.9  ReactiveTarget tells WanderingAI when it dies**

```
...
public void ReactToHit() {
    WanderingAI behavior = GetComponent<WanderingAI>();
    if (behavior != null) {
        behavior.SetAlive(false);
    }
    StartCoroutine(Die());
}
...
```

**Check if this character has a WanderingAI script; it might not.**

## AI code structure

The AI code in this chapter is contained within a single class so that learning and understanding it is straightforward. This code structure is perfectly fine for simple AI needs, so don't be afraid that you've done something "wrong" and that a more complex code structure is an absolute requirement. For more complex AI needs (such as a game with a wide variety of highly intelligent characters), a more robust code structure can help facilitate developing the AI.

As alluded to in chapter 1's example for composition versus inheritance, sometimes you'll want to split chunks of the AI into separate scripts. Doing so will enable you to mix and match components, generating unique behavior for each character. Think about the similarities and differences between your characters, and those differences will guide you as you design your code architecture. For example, if your game has some enemies that move by charging headlong at the player and some that slink around in the shadows, you may want to make Locomotion a separate component. Then you can create scripts for both LocomotionCharge and LocomotionSlink, and use different Locomotion components on different enemies.

The exact AI code structure you want depends on the design of your specific game; there's no one "right" way to do it. Unity makes it easy to design flexible code architectures like this.

## 3.4    Spawning enemy prefabs

At the moment there's just one enemy in the scene, and when it dies, the scene is empty. Let's make the game spawn enemies so that whenever the enemy dies, a new one appears. This is easily done in Unity using a concept called *prefabs.*

### 3.4.1    What is a prefab?

Prefabs are a flexible approach to visually defining interactive objects. In a nutshell, a prefab is a fully fleshed-out game object (with components already attached and set up) that doesn't exist in any specific scene but rather exists as an asset that can be copied into any scene. This copying can be done manually, to ensure that the enemy object (or other prefab) is the same in every scene. More important, though, prefabs can also be spawned from code; you can place copies of the object into the scene using commands in scripts and not only by doing it manually in the visual editor.

> **DEFINITON**    An *asset* is any file that shows up in the Project view; these could be 2D images, 3D models, code files, scenes, and so on. I mentioned the term *asset* briefly in chapter 1, but I didn't emphasize it until now.

The term for one of these copies of a prefab is an *instance*, analogous to how the word instance refers to a specific code object created from a class. Try to keep the terminology straight; *prefab* refers to the game object existing outside of any scene, whereas *instance* refers to a copy of the object that's placed in a scene.

> **DEFINITION**    Also analogous to object-oriented terminology, *instantiate* is the action of creating an instance.

### 3.4.2    Creating the enemy prefab

To create a prefab, first create an object in the scene that will become the prefab. Because our enemy object will become a prefab, we've already done this first step. Now all we do is drag the object down from the Hierarchy view and drop it in the Project view; this will automatically save the object as a prefab (see figure 3.7). Back in the Hierarchy view the original object's name will turn blue to signify that it's now linked to a prefab. If you wanted to edit the prefab further (such as by adding new components), you'd make those changes on the object in the scene and then select GameObject > Apply Changes To Prefab. But we don't want the object in the scene anymore (we're going to spawn the prefab, not use the instance already in the scene), so delete the enemy object now.

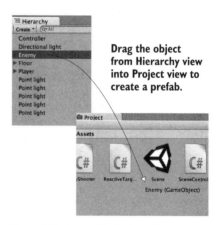

**Figure 3.7    Drag objects from Hierarchy to Project in order to create prefabs.**

> **WARNING** The interface for working with prefabs is somewhat awkward, and the relationship between prefabs and their instances in scenes can be brittle. For example, you often have to drag a prefab into a scene to edit it, and then delete the object once you're done editing. In the first chapter I mentioned this as a downside to Unity, and I hope the workflow with prefabs improves in future versions of Unity.

Now we have the actual prefab object to spawn in the scene, so let's write code to create instances of the prefab.

### 3.4.3 Instantiating from an invisible SceneController

Although the prefab itself doesn't exist in the scene, there has to be some object in the scene for the enemy spawning code to attach to. What we'll do is create an empty game object; we can attach the script to that, but the object won't be visible in the scene.

> **TIP** The use of empty `GameObjects` for attaching script components is a common pattern in Unity development. This trick is used for abstract tasks that don't apply to any specific object in the scene. Unity scripts are intended to be attached to visible objects, but not every task makes sense that way.

Choose GameObject > Create Empty, rename the new object to `Controller`, and then set its position to 0, 0, 0 (technically the position doesn't matter because the object isn't visible, but putting it at the origin will make life simpler if you ever parent anything to it). Create a script called SceneController, as shown in the following listing.

---

**Listing 3.10  SceneController that spawns the enemy prefab**

```
using UnityEngine;
using System.Collections;

public class SceneController : MonoBehaviour {
    [SerializeField] private GameObject enemyPrefab;
    private GameObject _enemy;

    void Update() {
        if (_enemy == null) {
            _enemy = Instantiate(enemyPrefab) as GameObject;
            _enemy.transform.position = new Vector3(0, 1, 0);
            float angle = Random.Range(0, 360);
            _enemy.transform.Rotate(0, angle, 0);
        }
    }
}
```

*Serialized variable for linking to the prefab object*

*A private variable to keep track of the enemy instance in the scene*

*Only spawn a new enemy if there isn't already one in the scene.*

*The method that copies the prefab object*

Attach this script to the controller object, and in the Inspector you'll see a variable slot for the enemy prefab. This works similarly to public variables, but there's an important difference (see the following warning).

> **WARNING** I recommend private variables with `SerializeField` to reference objects in Unity's editor because you want to expose that variable in the

Inspector but don't want the value to be changed by other scripts. As explained in chapter 2, public variables show up in the Inspector by default (in other words, they're serialized by Unity), so most tutorials and sample code you'll see use public variables for all serialized values. But these variables can also be modified by other scripts (these are public variables, after all); in many cases, you don't want the value to be modified in code but only set in the Inspector.

Drag up the prefab asset from Project to the empty variable slot; when the mouse gets near, you should see the slot highlight to indicate that the object can be linked there (see figure 3.8). Once the enemy prefab is linked to the SceneController script, play the scene in order to see the code in action. An enemy will appear in the middle of the room just like before, but now if you shoot the enemy it will be replaced by a new enemy. Much better than just one enemy that's gone forever!

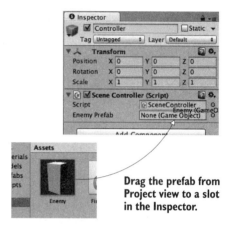

Drag the prefab from Project view to a slot in the Inspector.

**Figure 3.8   Drag the enemy prefab from Project up to the Enemy Prefab slot in the Inspector.**

**TIP** This approach of dragging objects onto the Inspector's variable slots is a handy technique that comes up in a lot of different scripts. Here we linked a prefab to the script, but you can also link to objects in the scene, or even specific components (because the code needs to call public methods in that specific component). In future chapters we'll use this technique again.

The core of this script is the Instantiate() method, so take note of that line. When we instantiate the prefab, that creates a copy in the scene. By default, Instantiate() returns the new object as a generic Object type, but Object is pretty useless directly and we need to handle it as a GameObject. In C#, use the as keyword for typecasting to convert from one type of code object into another type (written with the syntax original-object as new-type).

The instantiated object is stored in _enemy, a private variable of type GameObject (and again, keep straight the distinction between a prefab and an instance of the prefab; enemyPrefab stores the prefab whereas _enemy stores the instance). The if statement that checks the stored object ensures that Instantiate() is called only when _enemy is empty (or null, in coder-speak). The variable starts out empty, so the instantiating code runs once right from the beginning of the session. The object returned by Instantiate() is then stored in _enemy so that the instantiating code won't run again.

Because the enemy destroys itself when shot, that empties the _enemy variable and causes Instantiate() to be run again. In this way, there's always an enemy in the scene.

> ## Destroying `GameObjects` and memory management
>
> It's somewhat unexpected that existing references become `null` when an object destroys itself. In a memory-managed programming language like C#, normally you aren't able to directly destroy objects; you can only dereference them so that they can be destroyed automatically. This is still true within Unity, but the way `GameObjects` are handled behind the scenes makes it look like they were destroyed directly.
>
> To display objects in the scene, Unity has to have a reference to all objects in its scene graph. Thus even if you removed all references to the `GameObject` in your code, there would still be this scene graph reference preventing the object from being destroyed automatically. Because of this, Unity provided the method `Destroy()` to tell the game engine "Remove this object from the scene graph." As part of that behind-the-scenes functionality, Unity also overloaded the `==` operator to return `true` when checking for `null`. Technically that object still exists in memory, but it may as well not exist anymore, so Unity has it appearing to be `null`. You could confirm this by calling `GetInstanceID()` on the destroyed object.
>
> Note, though, that the developers of Unity are considering changing this behavior to more standard memory management. If they do, then the spawning code will need to change as well, probably by swapping the (`_enemy==null`) check with a new parameter like (`_enemy.isDestroyed`). Refer to their blog/Facebook page:
>
> https://www.facebook.com/unity3d/posts/10152271098591773
>
> (If most of this discussion was Greek to you, then don't worry about it; this was a tangential technical discussion for people interested in these obscure details.)

## 3.5 Shooting via instantiating objects

All right, let's add another bit of functionality to the enemies. Much as we did with the player, first we made them move—now let's make them shoot! As I mentioned back when introducing raycasting, that was just one of the approaches to implementing shooting. Another approach involves instantiating prefabs, so let's take that approach to making the enemies shoot back. The goal of this section is to see figure 3.9 when playing.

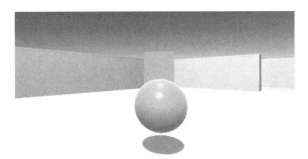

Figure 3.9   Enemy shooting a "fireball" at the player

### 3.5.1  *Creating the projectile prefab*

Whereas the shooting before didn't involve any actual projectile in the scene, this time shooting will involve a projectile in the scene. Shooting with raycasting was basically instantaneous, registering a hit the moment the mouse was clicked, but this time enemies are going to emit fireballs that fly through the air. Admittedly, they'll be moving pretty fast, but it won't be instantaneous, giving the player a chance to dodge out of the way. Instead of using raycasting to detect hits, we'll use collision detection (the same collision system that keeps the moving player from passing through walls).

The code will spawn fireballs in the same way that enemies spawn: by instantiating a prefab. As explained in the previous section, the first step when creating a prefab is to create an object in the scene that will become the prefab, so let's create a fireball. To start, choose GameObject > 3D Object > Sphere. Rename the new object `Fireball`. Now create a new script, also called Fireball, and attach that script to this object. Eventually we'll write code in this script, but leave it at default for now while we work on a few other parts of the fireball object. So that it appears like a fireball and not just a gray sphere, we're going to give the object a bright orange color. Surface properties such as color are controlled using materials.

> **DEFINITION**  A *material* is a packet of information that defines the surface properties of any 3D object that the material is attached to. These surface properties can include color, shininess, and even subtle roughness.

Choose Assets > Create > Material. Name the new material something like Flame, and drag it onto the object in the scene. Select the material in the Project view in order to see the material's properties in the Inspector. As figure 3.10 shows, click the color swatch labeled Albedo (that's a technical term that refers to the main color of a surface). Clicking that will bring up a color picker in its own window; slide both the rainbow-colored bar on the right side and main picking area to set the color to orange.

We're also going to brighten up the material to make it look more like fire. Adjust the Emission value (one of the other attributes in the Inspector). It defaults to 0, so type in `.3` to brighten up the material.

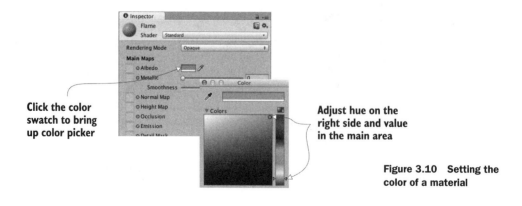

**Click the color swatch to bring up color picker**

**Adjust hue on the right side and value in the main area**

**Figure 3.10  Setting the color of a material**

Now you can turn the fireball object into a prefab by dragging the object down from Hierarchy into Project, just as you did with the enemy prefab. Great, we have a new prefab to use as a projectile! Next up is writing code to shoot using that projectile.

### 3.5.2 Shooting the projectile and colliding with a target

Let's make some adjustments to the enemy in order to emit fireballs. Because code to recognize the player will require a new script (just like ReactiveTarget was required by the code to recognize the target), first create a new script and name that script Player-Character. Attach this script to the player object in the scene.

Now open up WanderingAI and add to the code from the following listing.

**Listing 3.11   WanderingAI additions for emitting fireballs**

```
...
[SerializeField] private GameObject fireballPrefab;        ◁   Add these two fields before
private GameObject _fireball;                                   any methods, just like in
...                                                             SceneController.
if (Physics.SphereCast(ray, 0.75f, out hit)) {
  GameObject hitObject = hit.transform.gameObject;
  if (hitObject.GetComponent<PlayerCharacter>()) {         ◁   The player is
    if (_fireball == null) {                                    detected in the same
      _fireball = Instantiate(fireballPrefab) as GameObject;    way as the target
      _fireball.transform.position =                       ◁   object in RayShooter.
      transform.TransformPoint(Vector3.forward * 1.5f);
      _fireball.transform.rotation = transform.rotation;
    }
  }
  else if (hit.distance < obstacleRange) {
    float angle = Random.Range(-110, 110);
    transform.Rotate(0, angle, 0);
  }
}
...
```

**The same null GameObject logic as SceneController**

**The Instantiate() method here is just like it was in SceneController.**

**Place the fireball in front of the enemy and point in the same direction.**

You'll notice that all the annotations in this listing refer to similar (or the same) bits in previous scripts. Previous code listings already showed everything needed for emitting fireballs; now we're mashing together and remixing bits of code to fit in the new context. Just like in SceneController, you need to add two GameObject fields toward the top of the script: a serialized variable for linking the prefab to, and a private variable for keeping track of the instance copied by the code. After doing a raycast, the code checks for the PlayerCharacter on the object hit; this works just like when the shooting code checked for ReactiveTarget on the object hit. The code that instantiates a fireball when there isn't already one in the scene works like the code that instantiates an enemy. The positioning and rotation are different, though; this time, you place the instance just in front of the enemy and point it in the same direction.

Once all the new code is in place, a new Fireball Prefab slot will appear when you view the component in the Inspector, like the Enemy Prefab slot in the Scene-Controller component. Click the enemy prefab in the Project view and the Inspector will show that object's components, as if you'd selected an object in the scene. Although the earlier warning about interface awkwardness often applies when editing prefabs, the interface makes it easy to adjust components on the object, and that's all we're doing. As shown in figure 3.11, drag up the fireball prefab from Project onto the Fireball Prefab slot in the Inspector (again, just as you did with SceneController).

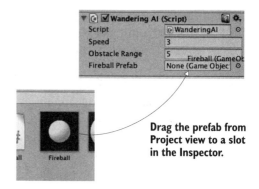

Drag the prefab from Project view to a slot in the Inspector.

**Figure 3.11    Drag the fireball prefab from Project up to the Fireball Prefab slot in the Inspector.**

Now the enemy will fire at the player when the player is directly ahead of it...well, try to fire; the bright orange sphere appears in front of the enemy, but it just sits there because we haven't written its script yet. Let's do that now. The next listing shows the code for the Fireball script.

**Listing 3.12    Fireball script that reacts to collisions**

```
using UnityEngine;
using System.Collections;

public class Fireball : MonoBehaviour {
  public float speed = 10.0f;
  public int damage = 1;

  void Update() {
    transform.Translate(0, 0, speed * Time.deltaTime);
  }

  void OnTriggerEnter(Collider other) {
    PlayerCharacter player = other.GetComponent<PlayerCharacter>();
    if (player != null) {
      Debug.Log("Player hit");
    }
    Destroy(this.gameObject);
  }
}
```

This function is called when another object collides with this trigger.

Check if the other object is a PlayerCharacter.

The crucial new bit to this code is the `OnTriggerEnter()` method. That method is called automatically when the object has a collision, such as colliding with the walls or with the player. At the moment this code won't work entirely; if you run it, the fireball will fly forward thanks to the `Translate()` line, but the trigger won't run, queuing up a new fireball by destroying the current one. There need to be a couple of other adjustments made to components on the fireball object. The first change is making the collider a trigger. To adjust that, click the Is Trigger check box in the Sphere Collider component.

**TIP** A Collider component set as a trigger will still react to touching/overlapping other objects, but it will no longer stop other objects from physically passing through.

The fireball also needs a Rigidbody, a component used by the physics system in Unity. By giving the fireball a Rigidbody component, you ensure that the physics system is able to register collision triggers for that object. In the Inspector, click Add Component and choose Physics > Rigidbody. In the component that's added, deselect Use Gravity (see figure 3.12) so that the fireball won't be pulled down due to gravity.

Play now, and fireballs are destroyed when they hit something. Because the fireball-emitting code runs whenever there isn't already a fireball in the scene, the enemy will shoot more fireballs at the player. Now there's just one more bit remaining for shooting at the player: making the player react to being hit.

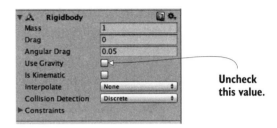

**Uncheck this value.**

**Figure 3.12** Turn off gravity in the Rigidbody component.

### 3.5.3 Damaging the player

Earlier you created a PlayerCharacter script but left it empty. Now you'll write code to have it react to being hit, as the following listing shows.

**Listing 3.13  Player that can take damage**

```
using UnityEngine;
using System.Collections;

public class PlayerCharacter : MonoBehaviour {
  private int _health;

  void Start() {                      Initialize the health value.
    _health = 5;
  }

  public void Hurt(int damage) {      Decrement the player's health.
    _health -= damage;
    Debug.Log("Health: " + _health);
  }
}
```

The listing defines a field for the player's health and reduces the health on command. In later chapters we'll go over text displays to show information on the screen, but for now we can just display information about the player's health using debug messages.

Now we need to go back to the Fireball script to call the player's Hurt() method. Replace the debug line in the Fireball script with `player.Hurt(damage)` to tell the player they've been hit. And that's the final bit of code we needed!

Whew, that was a pretty intense chapter, with lots of code being introduced. Between the previous chapter and this one, you now have most of the functionality in place for a first-person shooter.

## 3.6    *Summary*

In this chapter you've learned that

- A ray is an imaginary line projected into the scene.
- For both shooting and sensing obstacles, do a raycast with that line.
- Making a character wander around involves basic AI.
- New objects are spawned by instantiating prefabs.
- Coroutines are used to spread out functions over time.

# Developing graphics for your game

**This chapter covers**

- Understanding art assets
- Understanding whiteboxing
- Using 2D images in Unity
- Importing custom 3D models
- Building particle effects

We've been focusing mostly on how the game functions and not as much on how the game looks. That was no accident—this book is mostly about programming games in Unity. Still, it's important to understand how to work on and improve the visuals. Before we get back to the book's main focus on coding different parts of the game, let's spend a chapter learning about game art so that your projects won't always end with just blank boxes sliding around.

All of the visual content in a game is made up of what are called *art assets*. But what exactly does that mean?

## 4.1 Understanding art assets

An art asset is an individual unit of visual information (usually a file) used by the game. It's an overarching umbrella term for all visual content; image files are art

69

assets, 3D models are art assets, and so on. Indeed, the term *art asset* is simply a specific case of an asset, which you've learned is any file used by the game (such as a script)—hence the main Assets folder in Unity. Table 4.1 lists and describes the five main kinds of art assets used in building a game.

Table 4.1   **Types of art assets**

| Type of art asset | Definition of this type |
| --- | --- |
| 2D image | Flat pictures. To make a real-world analogy, 2D images are like paintings and photographs. |
| 3D model | 3D virtual objects (almost a synonym for "mesh objects"). To make a real-world analogy, 3D models are like sculptures. |
| Material | A packet of information that defines the surface properties of any object that the material is attached to. These surface properties can include color, shininess, and even subtle roughness. |
| Animation | A packet of information that defines movement of the associated object. These are detailed movement sequences created ahead of time, as opposed to code that calculates positions on the fly. |
| Particle system | An orderly mechanism for creating and controlling large numbers of small moving objects. Many visual effects are done this way, such as fire, smoke, or spraying water. |

Creating art for a new game generally starts with either 2D images or 3D models because those assets form a base on which everything else relies. As the names imply, 2D images are the foundation of 2D graphics, whereas 3D models are the foundation of 3D graphics. Specifically, 2D images are flat pictures; even if you have no previous familiarity with game art, you're probably already familiar with 2D images from the graphics used on websites. Three-dimensional models, on the other hand, may be unfamiliar to a newcomer, so I'm providing the following definition.

> **DEFINITION**   A *model* is a 3D virtual object. In chapter 1 you were introduced to the term mesh object; *3D model* is practically a synonym. The terms are frequently used interchangeably, but *mesh object* strictly refers to the geometry of the 3D object (the connected lines and shapes) whereas *model* is a bit more ambiguous and often includes other attributes of the object.

The next two types of assets on the list are materials and animations. Unlike 2D images and 3D models, materials and animations don't do anything in isolation and are much harder for newcomers to understand. Two-dimensional images and 3D models are easily understood through real-world analogs: paintings for the former, sculptures for the latter. Materials and animations aren't as directly relatable to the real world. Instead, both are abstract packets of information that layer onto 3D models. For example, materials were already introduced in a basic sense in chapter 3.

**DEFINITION** A *material* is a packet of information that defines the surface properties of any 3D object that the material is attached to. These surface properties can include color, shininess, and even subtle roughness.

Continuing the art analogy, you can think of a material as the media (clay, brass, marble, and so on) that the sculpture is made of. Similarly, an animation is also an abstract layer of information that's attached to a visible object.

**DEFINITION** An *animation* is a packet of information that defines movement of the associated object. Because these movements can be defined independently from the object itself, they can be used in a mix-and-match way with multiple objects.

For a concrete example, think about a character walking around. The overall position of the character is handled by the game's code (for example, the movement scripts you wrote in chapter 2). But the detailed movements of feet hitting the ground, arms swinging, and hips rotating are an animation sequence that's being played back; that animation sequence is an art asset.

To help you understand how animations and 3D models relate to each other, let's make an analogy to puppeteering: the 3D model is the puppet, the animator is the puppeteer who makes the puppet move, and the animation is a recording of the puppet's movements. The movements defined this way are created ahead of time and are usually small-scale movements that don't change the overall positioning of the object. This is in contrast to the sort of large-scale movements that were done in code in previous chapters.

The final kind of art asset from table 4.1 is a particle system (see the following definition).

**DEFINITION** A *particle system* is an orderly mechanism for creating and controlling large numbers of moving objects. These moving objects are usually small—hence the name *particle*—but they don't have to be.

Particle systems are useful for creating visual effects, such as fire, smoke, or spraying water. The particles (that is, the individual objects under the control of a particle system) can be any mesh object that you choose, but for most effects the particles will be a square displaying a picture (a flame spark or a smoke puff, for example).

Much of the work of creating game art is done in external software, not within Unity itself. Materials and particle systems are created within Unity, but the other art assets are created using external software. Refer to appendix B to learn more about external tools; a variety of art applications are used for creating 3D models and animation. Three-dimensional models created in an external tool are then saved as an art asset that's imported by Unity. I use Blender in appendix C when explaining how to model (download it from www.blender.org), but that's just because Blender is open source and thus available to all readers.

> **NOTE** The project download for this chapter includes a folder named "scratch." Although that folder is in the same place as the Unity project, it's not part of the Unity project; that's where I put extra external files.

As you work through the project for this chapter, you'll see examples of most of these types of art assets (animations are a bit too complex for now and will be addressed later in the book). You're going to build a scene that uses 2D images, 3D models, materials, and a particle system. In some cases you'll bring in already existing art assets and learn how to import them into Unity, but at other times (especially with the particle system) you'll create the art asset from scratch within Unity.

This chapter only scratches the surface of game art creation. Because this book focuses on how to do programming in Unity, extensive coverage of art disciplines would reduce how much the book could cover. Creating game art is a giant topic in and of itself, easily able to fill several books. In most cases a game programmer would need to partner with a game artist who specializes in that discipline. That said, it's extremely useful for game programmers to understand how Unity works with art assets and possibly even create their own rough stand-ins to be replaced later (commonly known as *programmer art*).

> **NOTE** Nothing in this chapter directly requires projects from the previous chapters. But you'll want to have movement scripts like the ones from chapter 2 so that you can walk around the scene you'll build; if necessary, you can grab the player object and scripts from the project download. Similarly, this chapter ends with moving objects that are similar to the ones created in previous chapters.

## 4.2 Building basic 3D scenery: whiteboxing

The first content creation topic we'll go over is whiteboxing. This process is usually the first step in building a level on the computer (following designing the level on paper). As the name implies, you block out the walls of the scene with blank geometry (that is, white boxes). Looking at the list of different art assets, this blank scenery is the most basic sort of 3D model, and it provides a base on which to display 2D images. If you think back to the primitive scene you created in chapter 2, that was basically whiteboxing (you just hadn't learned the term yet). Some of this section will be a rehash of work done in the beginning of chapter 2, but we'll cover the process a lot faster this time as well as discuss more new terminology.

> **NOTE** Another term that is frequently used is *grayboxing*. It means the same thing. I tend to use whiteboxing because that was the term I first learned, but others use grayboxing and that term is just as accepted. The actual color used varies, anyway, similar to how blueprints aren't necessarily blue.

### 4.2.1 Whiteboxing explained

Blocking out the scene with blank geometry serves a couple of purposes. First, this process enables you to quickly build a "sketch" that will be progressively refined over time. This activity is closely associated with level design and/or level designers.

**DEFINITION** *Level design* is the discipline of planning and creating scenes in the game (or levels). A level designer is a practitioner of level design.

As game development teams have grown in size and team members have become more specialized, a common level-building workflow is for the level designer to create a first version of the level through whiteboxing. This rough level is then handed over to the art team for visual polish. But even on a tiny team, where the same person is both designing levels and creating art for the game, this workflow of first doing whiteboxing and then polishing the visuals generally works best; you have to start somewhere, after all, and whiteboxing gives a clear foundation on which to build up the visuals.

A second purpose served by whiteboxing is that the level reaches a playable state very quickly. It may not be finished (indeed, a level right after whiteboxing is *far* from finished) but this rough version is functional and can support gameplay. At a minimum, the player can walk around the scene (think of the demo from chapter 2). In this way you can test to make sure the level is coming together well (for example, are the rooms the right size for this game?) before investing a lot of time and energy in detailed work. If something is off (say you realize the spaces need to be bigger), then it's much easier to change and retest while you're at the stage of whiteboxing.

Moreover, being able to play the under-construction level is a huge morale boost. Don't discount this benefit: building all the visuals for a scene can take a great deal of time, and it can start to feel like a slog if you have to wait a long time before you can experience any of that work in the game. Whiteboxing builds a complete (if primitive) level right away, and it's exciting to then play the game as it continually improves.

All right, so you understand why levels start with whiteboxing; now let's actually build a level!

### 4.2.2 Drawing a floor plan for the level

Building a level on the computer follows designing the level on paper. We're not going to get into a huge discussion about level design; just as chapter 2 noted about game design, level design (which is a subset of game design) is a large discipline that could fill up an entire book by itself. For our purposes we're going to draw a basic level with little "design" going into the plan, in order to give us a target to work toward.

Figure 4.1 is a top-down drawing of a simple layout with four rooms connected by a central hallway. That's all we need for a plan right now: a bunch of separated areas and interior walls to place. In a real game, your plan would be more extensive and include things like enemies and items.

You could practice whiteboxing by building this floor plan, or you could draw

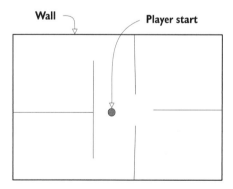

**Figure 4.1   Floor plan for the level: four rooms and a central corridor**

your own simple level to practice that step, too. The specifics of the room layout matters little for this exercise. The important thing for our purposes is to have a floor plan drawn so that we can move forward with the next step.

### 4.2.3  *Laying out primitives according to the plan*

Building the whitebox level in accordance with the drawn floor plan involves positioning and scaling a bunch of blank boxes to be the walls in the diagram. As described in section 2.2.1, select GameObject > 3D Object > Cube to create a blank box that you can position and scale as needed.

> **NOTE**  It isn't required, but instead of cube objects you may want to use the QuadsBox object in the project download. This object is a cube constructed of six separate pieces to give you more flexibility when applying materials. Whether or not you use this object depends on your desired workflow; for example, I don't bother with QuadsBox because all the whitebox geometry will be replaced by new art later anyway.

The first object will be the floor of the scene; in the Inspector, rename the object and lower it to -.5 Y in order to account for the height of the box itself (figure 4.2 depicts this). Then stretch the object along the X- and Z-axes.

Repeat these steps to create the walls of the scene. You probably want to clean up the Hierarchy view by making walls as children of a common base object (remember, position the root object at 0, 0, 0, and then drag objects onto it in Hierarchy), but that's not required. Also put a few simple lights around the scene so that you can see it; referring back to chapter 2, create

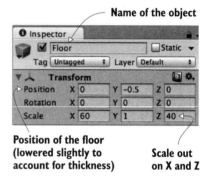

Name of the object

Position of the floor (lowered slightly to account for thickness)

Scale out on X and Z

Figure 4.2   Inspector view of the box positioned and scaled for the floor

lights by selecting them in the Light submenu of the GameObject menu. The level should look something like figure 4.3 once you're done with whiteboxing.

Set up your player object or camera to move around (create the player with a character controller and movement scripts; refer to chapter 2 if you need a full explanation). Now you can walk around the primitive scene in order to experience your work

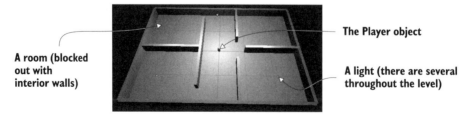

A room (blocked out with interior walls)

The Player object

A light (there are several throughout the level)

Figure 4.3   Whitebox level of the floor plan in figure 4.1

and test it out. And that's how you do whiteboxing! Pretty simple—but all you have right now is blank geometry, so let's dress up the geometry with pictures on the walls.

---

**Exporting whitebox geometry to external art tools**

Much of the work when adding visual polish to the level is done in external 3D art applications like Blender. Because of this, you may want to have the whitebox geometry in your art tool to refer to. By default there's no export option for primitives laid out within Unity. But third-party scripts are available that add this functionality to the editor. Most such scripts allow you to select the geometry in the scene and then hit an Export button (chapter 1 mentioned that scripts can customize the editor).

These custom scripts usually export geometry as an OBJ file (OBJ is one of several file types discussed later in this chapter). On the Unity3D website, click the search button and type `obj exporter`. Or you can go here for one example:

http://wiki.unity3d.com/index.php?title=ObjExporter

---

## 4.3 Texture the scene with 2D images

The level at this point is a rough sketch. It's playable, but clearly a lot more work needs to be done on the visual appearance of the scene. The next step in improving the look of the level is applying textures.

> **DEFINITION** A *texture* is a 2D image being used to enhance 3D graphics. That's literally the totality of what the term means; don't confuse yourself by thinking that any of the various uses of textures are part of how the term is defined. No matter how the image is being used, it's still referred to as a texture.

> **NOTE** The word *texture* is routinely used as both a verb and a noun. In addition to the noun definition, the word describes the action of using 2D images in 3D graphics.

Textures have a number of uses in 3D graphics, but the most straightforward use is to be displayed on the surface of 3D models. Later in the chapter we'll discuss how this works for more complex models, but for our whiteboxed level, the 2D images will act as wallpaper covering the walls (see figure 4.4).

Before texturing
(only shading from lights)

After applying textures
(1 floor texture, 1 on all walls)

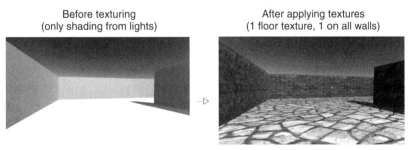

**Figure 4.4  Comparing the level before and after textures**

As you can see from the comparison in figure 4.4, textures turn what was an obviously unreal digital construct into a brick wall. Other uses for textures include masks to cut out shapes and normal maps to make surfaces bumpy; later you may want to look up more information about textures in resources mentioned in appendix D.

### 4.3.1 Choosing a file format

A variety of file formats is available for saving 2D images, so which should you use? Unity supports the use of many different file formats, so you could choose any of the ones shown in table 4.2.

Table 4.2    2D image file formats supported by Unity

| File type | Pros and cons |
| --- | --- |
| PNG | Commonly used on the web. Lossless compression; has an alpha channel. |
| JPG | Commonly used on the web. Lossy compression; no alpha channel. |
| GIF | Commonly used on the web. Lossy compression; no alpha channel. (Technically the loss isn't from compression; rather, data is lost when the image is converted to 8-bit. Ultimately it amounts to the same thing.) |
| BMP | Default image format on Windows. No compression; no alpha channel. |
| TGA | Commonly used for 3D graphics; obscure everywhere else. No or lossless compression; has an alpha channel. |
| TIFF | Commonly used for digital photography and publishing. No or lossless compression; no alpha channel. |
| PICT | Default image format on old Macs. Lossy compression; no alpha channel. |
| PSD | Native file format for Photoshop. No compression; has an alpha channel. The main reason to use this file format would be the advantage of using Photoshop files directly. |

> **DEFINITION**    The *alpha channel* is used to store transparency information in an image. The visible colors come in three "channels" of information: Red, Green, and Blue. Alpha is an additional channel of information that isn't visible but controls the visibility of the image.

Although Unity will accept any of the images shown in table 4.2 to import and use as a texture, the various file formats vary considerably in what features they support. Two factors in particular are important for 2D images imported as textures: how is the image compressed, and does it have an alpha channel? The alpha channel is a straightforward consideration: because the alpha channel is used often in 3D graphics, it's better when the image has an alpha channel. Image compression is a slightly more complicated consideration, but it boils down to "lossy compression is bad": both no compression and lossless compression preserve the image quality, whereas lossy compression reduces the image quality (hence the term *lossy*) as part of reducing the file size.

Between these two considerations, the two file formats I recommend for Unity textures are either PNG or TGA. Targas (TGA) used to be the favorite file format for texturing 3D graphics, before PNG had become widely used on the internet; these days PNG is almost equivalent technologically but is much more widespread, because it's useful both on the web and as a texture. PSD is also commonly recommended for Unity textures, because it's an advanced file format and it's convenient that the same file you work on in Photoshop also works in Unity. But I tend to prefer keeping work files separate from "finished" files that are exported over to Unity (this same mind-set comes up again later with 3D models).

The upshot is that all the images I provide in the example projects are PNG, and I recommend that you work with that file format as well. With this decision made, it's time to bring some images into Unity and apply them to the blank scene.

### 4.3.2 Importing an image file

Let's start creating/preparing the textures we'll use. The images used to texture levels are usually tileable so that they can be repeated across large surfaces like the floor.

> **DEFINITION** A *tileable* image (sometimes referred to as a *seamless tile*) is an image where opposite edges match up when placed side by side. This way the image can be repeated without any visible seams between the repeats. The concept for 3D texturing is just like wallpapers on web pages.

You can obtain tileable images in several different ways, such as manipulating photographs or even painting them by hand. Tutorials and explanations of these techniques can be found in a variety of books and websites, but we don't want to get bogged down with that right now. Instead, let's grab a couple of tileable images from one of the many websites that offer a catalog of such images for 3D artists to use. For example, I obtained a couple of images from www.cgtextures.com (see figure

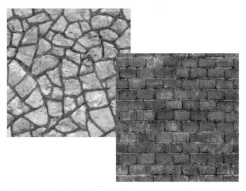

Figure 4.5 Seamlessly tiling stone and brick images obtained from CGTextures.com

4.5) to apply to the walls and floor of the level; find a couple of images you think look good for the floor and walls.

Download the images you want and prepare them for use as textures. Technically, you could use the images directly as they were downloaded, but those images aren't ideal for use as textures. Although they're certainly tileable (the important aspect of why we're using these images), they aren't the right size and they're the wrong file format. Textures should be sized in powers of 2. For reasons of technical efficiency, graphics chips like to handle textures in sizes that are $2^N$: 4, 8, 16, 32, 64, 128, 256,

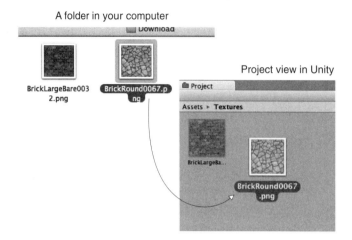

A folder in your computer

Project view in Unity

**Figure 4.6   Drag images from outside Unity to import them into the Project view.**

512, 1024, 2048 (the next number is 4096, but at that point the image is too big to use as a texture). In your image editor (Photoshop, GIMP, or whatever; refer to appendix B) scale the downloaded image to 256x256, and save it as a PNG.

Now drag the files from their location in the computer into the Project view in Unity. This will copy the files into your Unity project (see figure 4.6), at which point they're imported as textures and can be used in the 3D scene. If dragging the file over would be awkward, you could instead right-click in Project and select Import New Asset to get a file picker.

> **TIP**   Organizing your assets into separate folders is probably a good idea as your projects start to get more complex; in the Project view, create folders for Scripts and Textures and then move assets into the appropriate folders. Simply drag files to their new folder.

> **WARNING**   Unity has several keywords that it responds to in folder names, with special ways of handling the contents of these special folders. Those keywords are Resources, Plugins, Editor, and Gizmos. Later in the book we'll go over what some of these special folders do, but for now avoid naming any folders with those words.

Now the images are imported into Unity as textures, ready to use. But how do we apply the textures to objects in the scene?

### 4.3.3   *Applying the image*

Technically, textures aren't applied to geometry directly. Instead, textures can be part of materials, and materials are applied to geometry. As explained in the intro, a material is a set of information defining the properties of a surface; that information can include a texture to display on that surface. This indirection is significant because the same texture can be used with multiple materials. That said, typically each texture

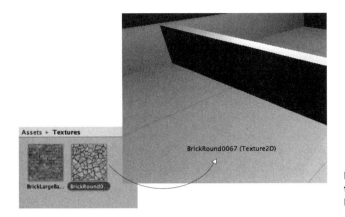

Figure 4.7 One way to apply textures is by dragging them from Project onto Scene objects.

goes with a different material, so for convenience Unity allows you to drop a texture onto an object and then it creates a new material automatically. If you drag a texture from Project view onto an object in the scene, Unity will create a new material and apply the new material to the object; figure 4.7 illustrates the maneuver. Try that now with the texture for the floor.

Besides that convenience method of automatically creating materials, the "proper" way to create a material is through the Create submenu of the Assets menu; the new asset will appear in the Project view. Now select the material to show its properties in the Inspector (you'll see something like figure 4.8) and drag a texture to the main texture slot; the setting is called Albedo (that's a technical term for the base color) and the texture slot is the square to the side of the panel. Meanwhile, drag the material up from Project onto an object in the scene to apply the material to that object. Try these steps now with the texture for the wall: create a new material, drag the wall texture into this material, and drag the material onto a wall in the scene.

You should now see the stone and brick images appearing on the surface of the floor and wall objects, but the images look rather stretched-out and blurry. What's happening is the single image is being stretched out to cover the entire floor. What you want instead is for the image to repeat a few times over the floor surface. You can set this using the Tiling property of the material; select the material in Project and

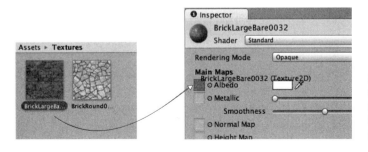

Figure 4.8 Select a material to see it in the Inspector, then drag textures to the material properties.

then change the Tiling number in the Inspector (with separate X and Y values for tiling in each direction). Make sure you're setting the tiling of the main map and not the secondary map (this material supports a secondary texture map for advanced effects). The default tiling is 1 (that's no tiling, with the image being stretched over the entire surface); change the number to something like 8 and see what happens in the scene. Change the numbers in both materials to tiling that looks good.

Great, now the scene has textures applied to the floor and walls! You can also apply textures to the sky of the scene; let's look at that process.

## 4.4    Generating sky visuals using texture images

The brick and stone textures gave a much more natural look to the walls and floor. Yet the sky is currently blank and unnatural; we also want a realistic look for the sky. The most common approach to this task is a special kind of texturing using pictures of the sky.

### 4.4.1    What is a skybox?

By default, the camera's background color is dark blue. Ordinarily that color fills in any empty area of the view (for example, above the walls of this scene), but it's possible to render pictures of the sky as background. This is where the concept of a *skybox* comes in.

> **DEFINITION**    A *skybox* is a cube surrounding the camera with pictures of the sky on each side. No matter what direction the camera is facing, it's looking at a picture of the sky.

Properly implementing a skybox can be tricky; figure 4.9 shows a diagram of how a skybox works. There are a number of rendering tricks needed so that the skybox will appear as a distant background. Fortunately Unity already takes care of all that for you.

New scenes actually come with a very simple skybox already assigned. This is why the sky has a gradient from light to dark blue, rather than being a flat dark blue. If you open the lighting window (Window > Lighting) the first setting is Skybox and the slot for that setting says Default. This setting is in the Environment Lighting panel; this window has a number of settings panels related to the advanced lighting system in Unity, but for now we only care about the first setting.

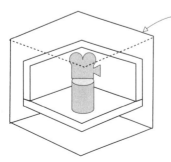

The skybox – functionality needed:

Render behind everything else in the scene.

Stay centered on the camera, so that it will seem too far away for the player's movements to affect it.

Full brightness with no shading applied, to avoid any lighting differences between sides of the cube.

Figure 4.9
Diagram of a skybox

Just like the brick textures earlier, skybox images can be obtained from a variety of websites. Search for *skybox textures*; for example, I obtained several great skyboxes from www.93i.de, including the TropicalSunny-Day set. Once this skybox is applied to the scene, you will see something like figure 4.10.

As with other textures, sky-box images are first assigned to

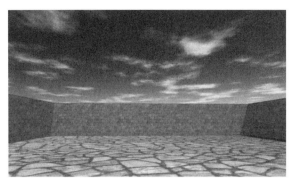

Figure 4.10   Scene with background pictures of the sky

a material, and that gets used in the scene. Let's examine how to create a new skybox material.

### 4.4.2   Creating a new skybox material

First, create a new material (as usual, either right-click and Create, or choose Create from the Assets menu) and select it to see settings in the Inspector. Next you need to change the shader used by this material. The top of the material settings has a Shader menu (see figure 4.11). In section 4.3 we pretty much ignored this menu because the default works fine for most standard texturing, but a skybox requires a special shader.

> **DEFINITION**   A *shader* is a short program that outlines instructions for how to draw a surface, including whether to use any textures. The computer uses these instructions to calculate the pixels when rendering the image. The most common shader takes the color of the material and darkens it according to the light, but shaders can also be used for all sorts of visual effects.

Every material has a shader that controls it (you could kind of think of a material as an instance of a shader). New materials are set to the Standard shader by default. This shader displays the color of the material (including the texture) while applying basic dark and light across the surface.

For skyboxes there's a different shader. Click the menu in order to see the drop-down list (see figure 4.11) of all the available shaders. Move down to the Skybox section and choose 6 Sided in the submenu.

With this shader active, the material now has six large texture slots (instead of just the small Albedo texture slot that the

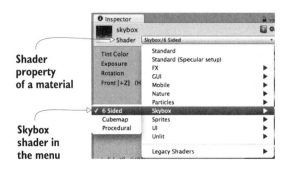

Figure 4.11   The drop-down menu of available shaders

Skybox images from 93i.de:   up,   down,   front,   back,   left,   right

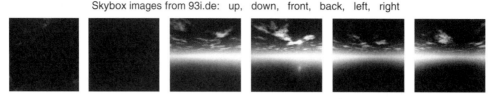

Figure 4.12   Six sides of a skybox—images for top, bottom, front, back, left, and right

standard shader had). These six texture slots correspond to the six sides of a cube, so these images should match up at the edges in order to appear seamless. For example, figure 4.12 shows the images for the sunny skybox.

Import the skybox images into Unity the same way you brought in the brick textures: drag the files into the Project view or right-click in Project and select Import New Asset. There's one subtle import setting to change; click the imported texture to see its properties in the Inspector, and change the Wrap Mode setting (shown in figure 4.13) from Repeat to Clamp (don't forget to click Apply when you're done). Ordinarily textures can be tiled repeatedly over a surface; for this to appear seamless, opposite edges of the image bleed together. But this blending of edges can create faint lines in the sky where images meet, so the Clamp setting (similar to the `Clamp()` function in chapter 2) will limit the boundaries of the texture and get rid of this blending.

Now you can drag these images to the texture slots of the skybox material. The names of the images correspond to the texture slot to assign them to (such as left or front). Once all six textures are linked up, you can use this new material as the skybox for the scene. Open the lighting window again and set this new material to the Skybox slot; either drag the material to that slot, or click the tiny circle icon to bring up a file picker.

> **TIP**   By default, Unity will display the skybox (or at least its main color) in the editor's Scene view. You may find this color distracting while editing objects, so you can toggle the skybox on or off. Across the top of the Scene view's pane are buttons that control what's visible; look for the Effects button to toggle the skybox on or off.

Faint lines may be visible at the edges of the skybox images...

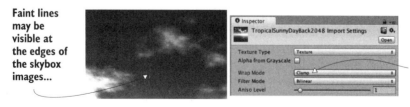

...so change the Wrap Mode of the textures from Repeat to Clamp.

Figure 4.13   Correct faint edge lines by adjusting the Wrap mode.

Woohoo, you've learned how to create sky visuals for your scene! A skybox is an elegant way to create the illusion of a vast atmosphere surrounding the player. The next step in polishing the visuals in your level is to create more complex 3D models.

## 4.5 Working with custom 3D models

In the previous sections we looked at applying textures to the large flat walls and floors of the level. But what about more detailed objects? What if we want, say, interesting furniture in the room? We can accomplish that by building 3D models in external 3D art apps. Recall the definition from the introduction to this chapter: 3D models are the mesh objects in the game (that is, the three-dimensional shapes). Well, we're going to import a 3D mesh of a simple bench.

Applications widely used for modeling 3D objects include Autodesk's Maya and 3ds Max. Those are both expensive commercial tools, so the sample for this chapter uses the open source app Blender. The sample download includes a .blend file that you can use; figure 4.14 depicts the bench model in Blender. If you're interested in learning how to model your own objects, you'll find an exercise in appendix C about modeling this bench in Blender.

This includes both the 3D mesh geometry and a texture applied to the mesh.

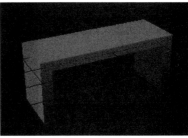

**Figure 4.14  The bench model in Blender**

Besides custom-made models created by yourself or an artist you're working with, many 3D models are available for download from game art websites. One great resource for 3D models is Unity's Asset Store here: https://www.assetstore.unity3d.com

### 4.5.1  Which file format to choose?

Now that you've made the model in Blender, you need to export the asset out from that software. Just as with 2D images, a number of different file formats are available for you to use when exporting out the 3D model, and these file types have various pros and cons. Table 4.3 lists the 3D file formats that Unity supports.

**Table 4.3  3D Model file formats supported by Unity**

| File type | Pros and cons |
|---|---|
| FBX | Mesh and Animation; recommended option when available. |
| Collada (DAE) | Mesh and Animation; another good option when FBX isn't available. |
| OBJ | Mesh only; this is a text format, so sometimes useful for streaming over the internet. |
| 3DS | Mesh only; a pretty old and primitive model format. |
| DXF | Mesh only; a pretty old and primitive model format. |
| Maya | Works via FBX; requires this application to be installed. |

Table 4.3   3D Model file formats supported by Unity *(continued)*

| File type | Pros and cons |
| --- | --- |
| 3ds Max | Works via FBX; requires this application to be installed. |
| Blender | Works via FBX; requires this application to be installed. |

Choosing between these options boils down to whether or not the file supports animation. Because Collada and FBX are the only two options that include animation data, those are the two options to choose. Whenever it's available (not all 3D tools have it as an export option), FBX export tends to work best, but if you're using a tool without FBX export, then Collada works well, too. In our case, Blender supports FBX export so we'll use that file format.

Note that the bottom of table 4.3 lists several 3D art applications. Unity allows you to directly drop those application's files into your project, which seems handy at first, but that functionality has several caveats. For starters, Unity doesn't load those application files directly; instead, it exports the model behind the scenes and loads that exported file. Because the model is being exported to FBX or Collada anyway, it's preferable to do that step explicitly. Furthermore, this export requires that you have the relevant application installed. This requirement is a big hassle if you plan to share files among multiple computers (for example, a team of developers working together). I don't recommend using Blender (or Maya or whatever) files directly in Unity.

### 4.5.2   *Exporting and importing the model*

All right, it's time to export the model from Blender and then import it into Unity. First open the bench in Blender and then choose File > Export > FBX. Once the file is saved, import it into Unity the same way that you import images. Drag the FBX file from the computer into Unity's Project view or right-click in Project and choose Import New Asset. The 3D model will be copied into the Unity project and show up ready to be put in the scene.

> **NOTE**   The sample download includes the .blend file so that you can practice exporting the FBX file from Blender; even if you don't end up modeling anything yourself, you may need to convert downloaded models into a format Unity accepts. If you want to skip all steps involving Blender, use the provided FBX file.

There are a few default settings used to import the model that you want to change immediately. First, Unity defaults imported models to a very small scale (refer to figure 4.15, which shows what you see in the Inspector when you select the model); change the Scale Factor to 100 to partially counteract the .01 File Scale. You may also want to click the Generate Colliders check box, but that's optional; without a collider you can walk through the bench. Then switch to the Animation tab in the import settings and deselect Import Animation (you didn't animate this model).

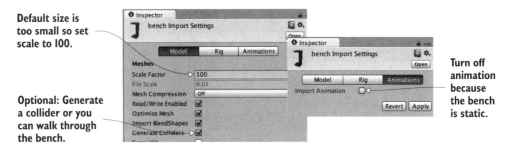

Default size is too small so set scale to 100.

Optional: Generate a collider or you can walk through the bench.

Turn off animation because the bench is static.

**Figure 4.15   Adjust import settings for the 3D model.**

That takes care of the imported mesh. Now for the texture; when Unity imported the FBX file, it also created a material for the bench. This material defaults to blank (just like any new material), so assign the bench texture (the image in figure 4.16) in the same way that you assigned bricks to the walls earlier: drag the texture image into Project to import it into Unity, and then drag the imported texture onto the texture slot of the bench material. The image looks somewhat odd, with different parts of the image appearing on different parts of the bench; the model's texture coordinates were edited to define this mapping of image-to-mesh.

> **DEFINITION** *Texture coordinates* are an extra set of values for each vertex that assigns polygons to areas of the texture image. Think about it like wrapping paper; the 3D model is the box being wrapped, the texture is the wrapping paper, and the texture coordinates represent where on the wrapping paper each side of the box will go.

> **NOTE** Even if you don't want to model the bench, you may want to read the detailed explanation of *texture coordinates* in appendix C. The concept of texture coordinates (as well as other related terms like UVs and mapping) can be useful to know when programming games.

New materials are often too shiny, so you may want to reduce the Smoothness setting (smoother surfaces are more shiny) to 0. Finally, having adjusted everything as needed, you can put the bench in the scene. Drag the model up from the Project view

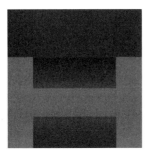

This image relates to the model using "texture coordinates."

To understand the concept of texture coordinates, refer to appendix C.

**Figure 4.16   The 2D image for the bench texture**

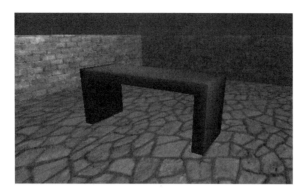

Figure 4.17   The imported
bench in the level

and place it in one room of the level; as you drag the mouse, you should see it in the scene. Once you drop it in place, you should see something like figure 4.17. Congratulations; you created a textured model for the level!

> **NOTE**   We're not going to do it in this chapter, but typically you'd also replace the whitebox geometry with models created in an external tool. The new geometry might look essentially identical, but you'll have much more flexibility to set UVs for the texture.

---

### Animating characters with Mecanim

The model we created is static, sitting still where placed. You can also animate in Blender and then play the animation in Unity. The process of creating 3D animation is long and involved, but this isn't a book about animation so we're not going to discuss that here. As had already been mentioned for modeling, there are a lot of existing resources if you want to learn more about 3D animation. But be warned: it is a *huge* topic. There's a reason "animator" is a specialized role within game development.

Unity has a sophisticated system for managing animations on models, a system called Mecanim. The special name Mecanim identifies the newer, more advanced animation system that was recently added to Unity as a replacement for the older animation system. The older system is still around, identified as legacy animation. But the legacy animation system may be phased out in a future version of Unity, at which point Mecanim will be *the* animation system.

Although we don't work with any animations in this chapter, we'll play animations on a character model in chapter 7.

---

## 4.6   *Creating effects using particle systems*

Besides 2D images and 3D models, the remaining type of visual content that game artists create are particle systems. The definition in this chapter's introduction explained that particle systems are orderly mechanisms for creating and controlling large numbers of moving objects. Particle systems are useful for creating visual effects, such as fire, smoke, or spraying water. For example, the fire effect in figure 4.18 was created using a particle system.

Whereas most other art assets are created in external tools and imported into the project, particle systems are created within Unity itself. Unity provides some flexible and powerful tools for creating particle effects.

> **NOTE** Much like the situation with the Mecanim animation system, there used to be an older legacy particle system and the newer system had a special name, Shuriken. At this point the legacy particle system is entirely phased out, so the separate name is no longer necessary.

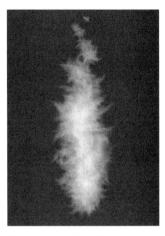

**Figure 4.18 Fire effect created using a particle system**

To begin, create a new particle system and watch the default effect play. From the GameObject menu, choose Particle System, and you'll see basic white puffballs spraying upward from the new object. Or rather, you'll see particles spraying upward while you have the object selected; when you select a particle system, the particle playback panel is displayed in the corner of the screen and indicates how much time has elapsed (see figure 4.19).

The default effect looks pretty neat already, but let's go through the extensive list of parameters you can use to customize the effect.

**Pause or reset the particle effect playing in the scene.**

Particle Effect
Pause | Stop
Playback Speed | 1.00
Playback Time | 6.29

**Click and drag the label "Playback Time" to play back and forth.**

**Figure 4.19 Playback panel for a particle system**

### 4.6.1 Adjusting parameters on the default effect

Figure 4.20 shows the entire list of settings for a particle system. We're not going to go through every single setting in that list; instead, we'll look at the settings relevant to making the fire effect. Once you understand how a few of the settings work, the rest should be fairly self-explanatory. Each of the settings labels is in fact a whole information panel. Initially only the first information panel is expanded; the rest of the panels are collapsed. Click on the setting label to expand that information panel.

> **TIP** Many of the settings are controlled by a curve displayed at the bottom of the Inspector. That curve represents how the value changes over time: the left side of the graph is when the particle first appears, the right side is when the particle is gone, the bottom is a value of 0, and the top is the maximum value. Drag points around the graph, and double-click or right-click on the curve to insert new points.

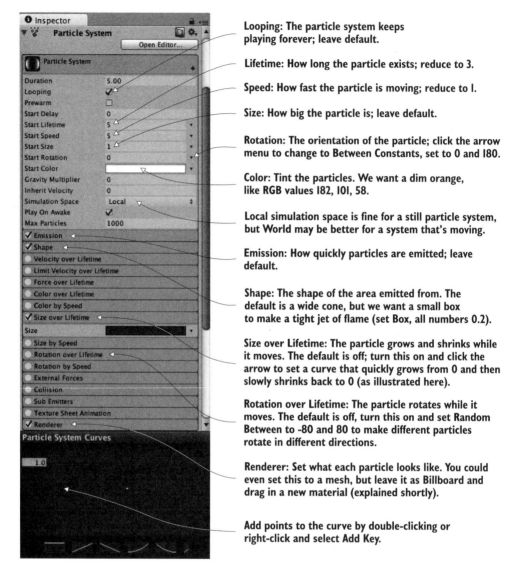

Looping: The particle system keeps playing forever; leave default.

Lifetime: How long the particle exists; reduce to 3.

Speed: How fast the particle is moving; reduce to 1.

Size: How big the particle is; leave default.

Rotation: The orientation of the particle; click the arrow menu to change to Between Constants, set to 0 and 180.

Color: Tint the particles. We want a dim orange, like RGB values 182, 101, 58.

Local simulation space is fine for a still particle system, but World may be better for a system that's moving.

Emission: How quickly particles are emitted; leave default.

Shape: The shape of the area emitted from. The default is a wide cone, but we want a small box to make a tight jet of flame (set Box, all numbers 0.2).

Size over Lifetime: The particle grows and shrinks while it moves. The default is off; turn this on and click the arrow to set a curve that quickly grows from 0 and then slowly shrinks back to 0 (as illustrated here).

Rotation over Lifetime: The particle rotates while it moves. The default is off, turn this on and set Random Between to -80 and 80 to make different particles rotate in different directions.

Renderer: Set what each particle looks like. You could even set this to a mesh, but leave it as Billboard and drag in a new material (explained shortly).

Add points to the curve by double-clicking or right-click and select Add Key.

**Figure 4.20  The Inspector displays settings for a particle system (pointing out settings for the fire effect).**

Adjust parameters of the particle system as indicated in figure 4.20 and it'll look more like a jet of flame.

### 4.6.2  Applying a new texture for fire

Now the particle system looks more like a jet of flame, but the effect still needs the particles to look like flame, not white blobs. That requires importing a new image into Unity. Figure 4.21 depicts the image I painted; I made an orange dot and used the

Smudge tool to draw out the tendrils of flame (and then I drew the same thing in yellow). Whether you use this image from the sample project, draw your own, or download a similar one, you need to import the image file into Unity. As explained before, drag image files into the Project view, or choose Assets > Import New Asset.

**Figure 4.21  The image used for fire particles**

Just like with 3D models, textures aren't applied to particle systems directly; you add the texture to a material and apply that material to the particle system. Create a new material and then select it to see its properties in the Inspector. Drag the fire image from Project up to the texture slot. That linked the fire texture to the fire material, so now you want to apply the material to the particle system. Figure 4.22 shows how to do this; select the particle system, expand Renderer at the bottom of the settings, and drag the material onto the Material slot.

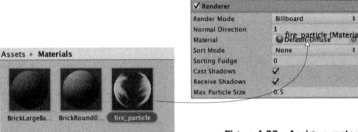

**Figure 4.22  Assign a material to the particle system**

As you did for the skybox material, you need to change the shader for a particle material. Click the Shader menu near the top of the material settings to see the list of available shaders. Instead of the standard default, a material for particles needs one of the shaders under the Particles submenu. As shown in figure 4.23, in this case we want Additive (Soft). This will make the particles appear to be hazy and brighten the scene, just like a fire.

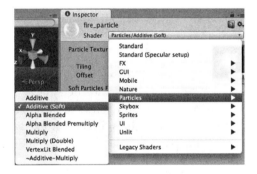

**Figure 4.23  Setting the shader for the fire particle material**

> **DEFINITION** *Additive* is a shader that adds the color of the particle to the color behind it, as opposed to replacing the pixels. This makes the pixels brighter and makes black on the particle turn invisible. The opposite is *Multiply*, which makes everything darker; these shaders have the same visual effect as the Additive and Multiply layer effects in Photoshop.

With the fire material assigned to the fire particle effect, it'll now look like the effect shown earlier in figure 4.18. This looks like a pretty convincing jet of flame, but the effect doesn't only work when sitting still; next let's attach it to an object that moves around.

### 4.6.3   *Attaching particle effects to 3D objects*

Create a sphere (remember, GameObject > 3D Object > Sphere). Create a new script called BackAndForth, as shown in the following listing, and attach it to the new sphere.

#### Listing 4.1   Moving an object back and forth along a straight path

```
using UnityEngine;
using System.Collections;

public class BackAndForth : MonoBehaviour {
    public float speed = 3.0f;                    These are the positions the
    public float maxZ = 16.0f;                    object moves between.
    public float minZ = -16.0f;
                                                  Which direction is the
    private int _direction = 1;                   object currently moving in?

    void Update() {
        transform.Translate(0, 0, _direction * speed * Time.deltaTime);

        bool bounced = false;
        if (transform.position.z > maxZ || transform.position.z < minZ) {
            _direction = -_direction;
            bounced = true;                       Toggle the direction back and forth.
        }
        if (bounced) {
            transform.Translate(0, 0, _direction * speed * Time.deltaTime);
        }
    }
}
```

*Make an extra movement this frame if the object switched directions.*

Run this script and the sphere glides back and forth in the central corridor of the level. Now you can make the particle system a child of the sphere and the fire will move with the sphere. Just like with the walls of the level, in the Hierarchy view drag the particle object onto the sphere object.

> **WARNING**   You usually have to reset the position of an object after making it the child of another object. For example, we want the particle system at 0, 0, 0 (this is relative to the parent). Unity will preserve the placement of an object from before it was linked as a child.

Now the particle system moves along with the sphere; the fire isn't deflecting from the movement, though, which looks unnatural. That's because by default particles move correctly only in the local space of the particle system. To complete the flaming sphere, find Simulation Space in the particle system settings (it's in the top panel of figure 4.20) and switch from Local to World.

> **NOTE** In this script the object moves back and forth in a straight line, but video games commonly have objects moving around complex paths. Unity comes with support for complex navigation and paths; see https://docs.unity3d.com/Manual/Navigation.html to read about it.

I'm sure that at this point you're itching to apply your own ideas and add more content to this sample game. You should do that—you could create more art assets, or even test your skills by bringing in shooting mechanics developed in chapter 3. In the next chapter we'll switch gears to a different game genre and start over with a new game. Even though future chapters will switch to different game genres, everything from these first four chapters will still apply and will be useful.

## 4.7 Summary

In this chapter you've learned that

- Art asset is the term for all individual graphics.
- Whiteboxing is a useful first step for level designers to block out spaces.
- Textures are 2D images displayed on the surface of 3D models.
- 3D models are created outside Unity and imported as FBX files.
- Particle systems are used to create many visual effects (fire, smoke, water, and so on).

# Part 2

## Getting comfortable

You've built your first game prototypes in Unity, so now you're ready to stretch yourself by tackling some other game genres. At this point the rhythms of working within Unity should feel familiar: create a script with such and such function, drag this object to that slot in the Inspector, and so forth. You're not tripping over details of the interface so much anymore, which means the remaining chapters don't need to rehash the basics.

Let's run through a succession of additional projects that will progressively teach you more and more about developing games in Unity.

# Building a Memory game using Unity's new 2D functionality

**This chapter covers**

- Displaying 2D graphics in Unity
- Making objects clickable
- Loading new images programmatically
- Maintaining and displaying state using UI text
- Loading levels and restarting the game

Up to now we've been working with 3D graphics. But you can also work with 2D graphics in Unity, so in this chapter you'll build a 2D game to learn about that. We're going to develop the classic children's game Memory: we'll display a grid of card backs, reveal the card front when it's clicked, and score matches. These mechanics cover the basics you need to know in order to develop 2D games in Unity.

Although Unity originated as a tool for 3D games, it's used often for 2D games as well. Recent versions of Unity (starting with version 4.3, released near the end of 2013) have added the ability to display 2D graphics, but even before then 2D games were already being developed in Unity (especially mobile games that took advantage of Unity's cross-platform nature). In prior versions of Unity, game developers required a third-party framework (such as 2D Toolkit from Unikron Software) to emulate 2D graphics within Unity's 3D scenes. Eventually the core editor and game engine were modified to incorporate 2D graphics, and this chapter will teach you about that newer functionality.

The 2D workflow in Unity is more or less the same as the workflow to develop a 3D game: import art assets, drag them into a scene, and write scripts to attach to the objects. The primary kind of art asset in 2D graphics is called a sprite.

> **DEFINITION**   *Sprites* are 2D images displayed directly on the screen, as opposed to images displayed on the surface of 3D models (that is, textures).

You can import 2D images into Unity as sprites in much the same way you can import images as textures (see chapter 4). Technically these sprites will be objects in 3D space, but they'll be flat surfaces all oriented along the Z-axis. Because they'll all face the same direction, you can point the camera straight at the sprites and players will only be able to discern their movements along the X- and Y-axes (that is, two dimensions).

In chapter 2 we discussed the coordinate axes: having three dimensions adds a Z-axis perpendicular to the X- and Y-axes you were already familiar with. Two dimensions are just those X- and Y-axes (that's what your teacher was talking about in math class!).

## 5.1   *Setting everything up for 2D graphics*

We're going to create the classic game of Memory. For those unfamiliar with this game, a series of cards will be dealt out facedown. Every card will have a matching card located somewhere else, but the player can't tell what the various cards are. The player can turn over two cards at a time, attempting to find matching cards; if the two cards chosen aren't a match, they'll flip back and then the player can guess again.

Figure 5.1 shows a mockup of the game we're going to build; compare this to the roadmap diagram from chapter 2.

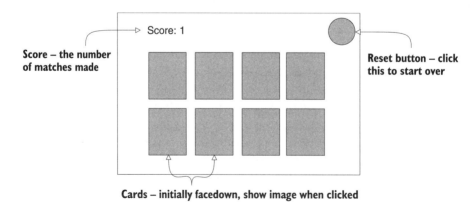

**Figure 5.1   Mockup of what the Memory game will look like**

Note that the mockup this time depicts exactly what the player will see (whereas the mockup for a 3D scene depicted the space around the player and then where the camera went for the player to see through). Now that you know what we'll be building, it's time to get to work!

### 5.1.1 Preparing the project

The first step is to gather up and display graphics for our game. In much the same way as building the 3D demo previously, you want to start the new game by putting together the minimum set of graphics for the game to operate, and after that's in place you can start programming the functionality.

That means we'll need to create everything depicted in figure 5.1: card backs for hidden cards, a series of card fronts for when they turn over, a score display in one corner, and a reset button in the opposite corner. We also need a background for the screen, so all together our art requirements sum up to figure 5.2.

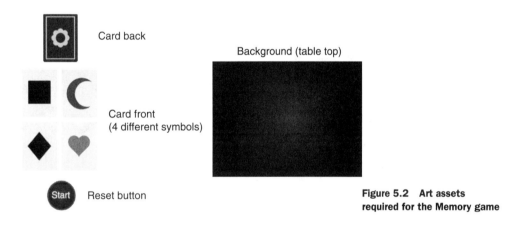

Card back

Background (table top)

Card front
(4 different symbols)

Start Reset button

**Figure 5.2 Art assets required for the Memory game**

TIP As always, a finished version of the project, including all necessary art assets, can be downloaded from www.manning.com/hocking, this book's website. You can copy the images from there to use in your own project.

Gather together the needed images, and then create a new project in Unity. In the New Project window that comes up you'll notice a couple of buttons at the bottom (shown in figure 5.3) that let you switch between 2D and 3D mode. In previous chapters we've worked with 3D graphics, and because that's the default value we haven't

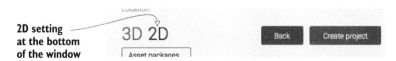

2D setting
at the bottom
of the window

**Figure 5.3 Create new projects in either 2D or 3D mode with these buttons.**

been concerned with this setting. In this chapter, though, you'll want to switch to 2D mode when creating a new project.

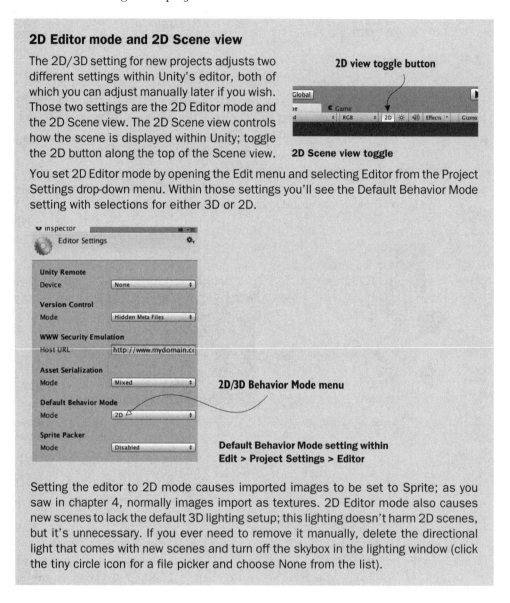

**2D Editor mode and 2D Scene view**

The 2D/3D setting for new projects adjusts two different settings within Unity's editor, both of which you can adjust manually later if you wish. Those two settings are the 2D Editor mode and the 2D Scene view. The 2D Scene view controls how the scene is displayed within Unity; toggle the 2D button along the top of the Scene view.

**2D view toggle button**

**2D Scene view toggle**

You set 2D Editor mode by opening the Edit menu and selecting Editor from the Project Settings drop-down menu. Within those settings you'll see the Default Behavior Mode setting with selections for either 3D or 2D.

**2D/3D Behavior Mode menu**

Default Behavior Mode setting within
Edit > Project Settings > Editor

Setting the editor to 2D mode causes imported images to be set to Sprite; as you saw in chapter 4, normally images import as textures. 2D Editor mode also causes new scenes to lack the default 3D lighting setup; this lighting doesn't harm 2D scenes, but it's unnecessary. If you ever need to remove it manually, delete the directional light that comes with new scenes and turn off the skybox in the lighting window (click the tiny circle icon for a file picker and choose None from the list).

With the new project for this chapter created and set for 2D, we can start putting our images into the scene.

### 5.1.2   *Displaying 2D images (aka sprites)*

Drag all the image files into the Project view to import them; make sure the images are imported as sprites and not textures. (This is automatic if the editor is set to 2D.

Select an asset to see its import settings in the Inspector.) Now drag the `table_top` sprite (our background image) up from the Project view into the empty scene, and then save the scene. As with mesh objects, in the Inspector there's a Transform component for the sprite; type `0, 0, 5` to position the background image.

> **TIP** Another import setting to take note of is Pixels-To-Units. Because Unity was previously a 3D engine that recently had 2D graphics grafted in, one unit in Unity isn't necessarily one pixel in the image. You could set the Pixels-To-Units setting to 1:1 but I recommend leaving it at the default of 100:1 (because the physics engine doesn't work properly at 1:1, and the default is better for compatibility with others' code).

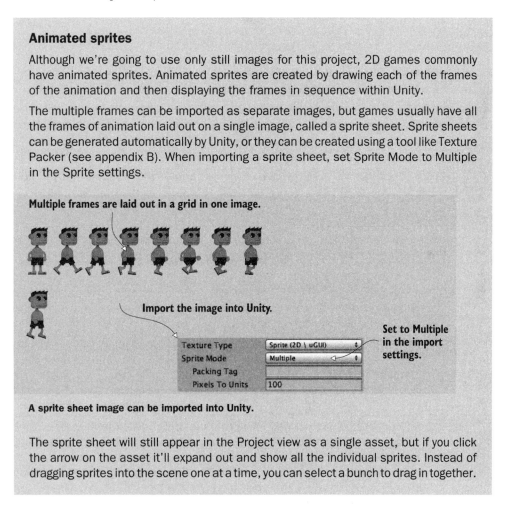

**Animated sprites**

Although we're going to use only still images for this project, 2D games commonly have animated sprites. Animated sprites are created by drawing each of the frames of the animation and then displaying the frames in sequence within Unity.

The multiple frames can be imported as separate images, but games usually have all the frames of animation laid out on a single image, called a sprite sheet. Sprite sheets can be generated automatically by Unity, or they can be created using a tool like Texture Packer (see appendix B). When importing a sprite sheet, set Sprite Mode to Multiple in the Sprite settings.

**Multiple frames are laid out in a grid in one image.**

**Import the image into Unity.**

**Set to Multiple in the import settings.**

| | |
|---|---|
| Texture Type | Sprite (2D \ uGUI) |
| Sprite Mode | Multiple |
| Packing Tag | |
| Pixels To Units | 100 |

*A sprite sheet image can be imported into Unity.*

The sprite sheet will still appear in the Project view as a single asset, but if you click the arrow on the asset it'll expand out and show all the individual sprites. Instead of dragging sprites into the scene one at a time, you can select a bunch to drag in together.

The 0 for X and Y position are straightforward (this sprite will fill the entire screen, so you want it at the center), but that 5 for Z position might seem odd. For 2D graphics, shouldn't only X and Y matter? Well, X and Y are the only coordinates that matter for

Stacked sprites seen in 2D ————————▷ 3D (Perspective) view
(Orthographic) view

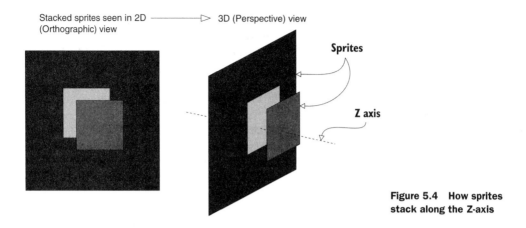

**Sprites**

**Z axis**

**Figure 5.4  How sprites stack along the Z-axis**

positioning the object on the 2D screen; Z coordinates still matter for stacking objects on top of each other, though. Lower Z values are closer to the camera, so sprites with lower Z values are displayed on top of other sprites (refer to figure 5.4). Accordingly, the background sprite should have the highest Z value. We'll set our background to a positive Z position, and then give everything else a 0 or negative Z position.

Other sprites will be positioned with values up to two decimal places because of the Pixels-To-Units setting mentioned earlier. A ratio of 100:1 means that 100 pixels in the image are 1 unit in Unity; put another way, 1 pixel is .01 units. But before we put any more sprites into the scene, let's set up the camera for this game.

---

**Creating atlases using Sprite Packer**

As mentioned in the sidebar "Animated Sprites," you can have multiple sprites laid out in a single image. The image is usually called a sprite sheet when multiple frames of a single 2D animation are combined into one, but the more general term for multiple images combined into one is an *atlas*.

Sprite sheets are useful in order to keep frames of animation together, but sprite atlases are also often used for still images. That's because atlases can optimize the performance of sprites in two ways: 1) by reducing the amount of wasted space in images by packing them tightly, and 2) by reducing the draw calls of the video card (every new image that's loaded causes a bit more work for the video card).

Sprite atlases can be created using external tools (switch to Multiple in the Sprite settings) and that approach certainly will work. But Unity includes a Sprite Packer that will pack together multiple sprites automatically. To use this feature, enable Sprite Packer in Editor settings (found under Edit > Project Settings). Now write a name in Packing Tag option when looking at the Import settings of a sprite image; Unity will pack together sprites with the same packing tag into one atlas. For more information, look at Unity's documentation:

http://docs.unity3d.com/Manual/SpritePacker.html

### 5.1.3   Switching the camera to 2D mode

Now let's adjust settings on the main camera in the scene. You might think that because the Scene view is set to 2D, what you see in Unity is what you'll see in the game. Somewhat non-intuitively, though, that isn't the case.

> **WARNING**   Whether or not the Scene view is set to 2D has nothing to do with the camera view in the running game.

It turns out that regardless of whether the Scene view is set to 2D mode, the camera in the game is set independently. This can be handy in many situations so that you can toggle the Scene view back to 3D in order to work on certain effects within the scene. This disconnect does mean that what you see in Unity isn't necessarily what you see in the game, and it can be easy for beginners to forget this.

The most important camera setting to adjust is Projection. The camera projection is probably already correct because you created the new project in 2D mode, but this is still important to know about and worth double-checking. Select the camera in Hierarchy to show its settings in the Inspector, and then look for the Projection setting (see figure 5.5). For 3D graphics the setting should be Perspective, but for 2D graphics the camera projection should be Orthographic.

> **DEFINITION**   *Orthographic* is the term for a flat camera view that has no perspective apparent. This is the opposite of a Perspective camera, where closer objects appear larger and lines recede into the distance.

Although the Projection mode is the most important camera setting for 2D graphics, there are a few other settings for us to adjust as well. Next we'll look at Size; that setting is under Projection. The camera's orthographic size determines the size of the camera view from the center of the screen up to the top of the screen. In other words, set Size to half the pixel dimensions of the screen you want. If you later set the resolution of the deployed game to the same pixel dimensions, you'll get pixel-perfect graphics.

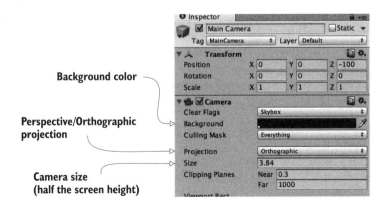

**Figure 5.5
Camera settings to
adjust for 2D graphics**

> **DEFINITION**   *Pixel-perfect* means one pixel on the screen corresponds to one pixel in the image (otherwise, the video card will make the images subtly blurry while scaling up to fit the screen).

For example, let's say you want a pixel-perfect 1024x768 screen. That means the camera height should be 384 pixels. Divide that by 100 (because of the pixels-to-units scale) and you get 3.84 for the camera size. Again, that math is SCREEN_SIZE / 2 / 100f (f as in float, rather than an int value). Given that the background image is 1024x768 (select the asset to check its dimensions), then clearly this value of 3.84 is what we want for our camera.

The two remaining adjustments to make in the Inspector are the camera's background color and Z position. As mentioned previously for sprites, higher Z positions are further away into the scene. Thus the camera should have a pretty low Z position; set the position of the camera to 0, 0, -100. The camera's background color should probably be black; the default color is blue, and that'll look odd displayed along the sides if the screen is wider than the background image (which is likely). Click the color swatch next to Background and set the color picker to black.

Now save the scene as Scene and hit Play; you'll see the Game view filled with our tabletop sprite. As you saw, getting to this point wasn't completely obvious (again, that's because Unity was a 3D game engine that recently had 2D graphics grafted in). But the tabletop is completely bare, so our next step is to put a card on the table.

## 5.2   Building a card object and making it react to clicks

Now that the images are all imported and ready to use, let's build the card objects that form the core of this game. In Memory, all the cards are initially face down, and they're only face up temporarily when you choose a pair of cards to turn over. To implement this functionality, we're going to create objects that consist of multiple sprites stacked on top of one another. Then we'll write code that makes the cards reveal themselves when clicked with the mouse.

### 5.2.1   Building the object out of sprites

Drag one of the card images into the scene. Use one of the card fronts, because you'll add a card back on top to hide the image. Technically the position right now doesn't matter, but eventually it will matter so you may as well position the card at -3, 1, 0. Now drag the card_back sprite into the scene. Make this new sprite a child of the previous card sprite (remember, in the Hierarchy drag the child object onto the parent object) and then set its position to 0, 0, -.1 (Keep in mind that this position is relative to the parent, so this means "Put it at the same X Y but move it closer on Z.")

> **TIP**   Instead of the Move, Rotate, and Scale tools that we used in 3D, in 2D mode we use a single manipulation tool called the Rect Tool. In 2D mode this tool is selected automatically, or you can click the rightmost navigation button in the top-left corner of Unity. With this tool active, click and drag objects to do all three operations (move/rotate/scale) in two dimensions.

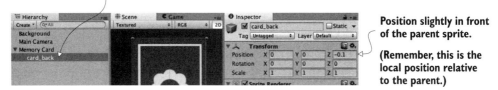

Figure 5.6  Hierarchy linking and position for the card back sprite

With the card back in place as depicted in figure 5.6, the graphics are in place for a reactive card that can be revealed.

### 5.2.2 Mouse input code

In order to respond when the player clicks on them, the card sprites need to have a collider component. New sprites don't have a collider by default, so they can't be clicked on. We're going to attach a collider to the root card object, but not to the card back, so that only the card front and not the card back will receive mouse clicks. To do this, select the root card object in Hierarchy (don't click the card in the scene, because the card back is on top and you'll select that part instead) and then click the Add Component button in the Inspector. Select Physics 2D (not Physics, because that system is for 3D physics and this is a 2D game), and then choose a box collider.

Besides a collider, the card needs a script in order to be reactive to the player clicking on it, so let's write some code. Create a new script called MemoryCard.cs and attach this script to the root card object (again, not the card back). The following listing shows the code that makes the card emit debug messages when clicked.

---

**Listing 5.1   Emitting debug messages when clicked**

```
using UnityEngine;
using System.Collections;

public class MemoryCard : MonoBehaviour {
    public void OnMouseDown() {
        Debug.Log("testing 1 2 3");
    }
}
```

**This function is called when the object is clicked.**

**Just emit a test message to the console for now.**

> **TIP**  If you're not in this habit yet, organizing your assets into separate folders is probably a good idea; create folders for scripts and drag files within the Project view. Just be careful to avoid the special folder names Unity responds to: Resources, Plugins, Editor, and Gizmos. Later in the book we'll go over what some of these special folders do, but for now avoid naming any folders with those words.

Nice, we can click on the card now! Just like `Update()`, `OnMouseDown()` is another function provided by `MonoBehaviour`, this time responding when the object is clicked on. Play the game and watch messages appear in the console. But this only prints to the console for testing; we want the card to be *revealed*.

### 5.2.3   Revealing the card on click

Rewrite the code to match what's shown in the next listing (the code won't run quite yet but don't worry).

> **Listing 5.2   Script that hides the back when the card is clicked**

```
using UnityEngine;
using System.Collections;

public class MemoryCard : MonoBehaviour {
    [SerializeField] private GameObject cardBack;        Variable that appears
                                                         in the Inspector

    public void OnMouseDown() {
        if (cardBack.activeSelf) {                       Only run deactivate code if the
            cardBack.SetActive(false);                   object is currently active/visible.
        }
                                                         Set the object to
    }                                                    inactive/invisible.
}
```

There are two key additions to the script: a reference to an object in the scene, and the SetActive() method that deactivates that object. The first part, the reference to an object in the scene, is similar to what we've done in previous chapters: mark the variable as serialized, and then drag the object from Hierarchy over to the variable in the Inspector. With the object reference set, the code will now affect the object in the scene.

The second key addition to the code is the SetActive command. That command will deactivate any GameObject, making that object invisible. If we now drag card_back in the scene to this script's variable in the Inspector, when you play the game the card back disappears when you click the card. Hiding the card back will reveal the card front; we've accomplished yet another important task for the Memory game! But this is still only one card, so now let's create a bunch of cards.

## 5.3   Displaying the various card images

We've programmed a card object that initially shows the card back but reveals itself when clicked. That was a single card, but the game needs a whole grid of cards, with different images on most cards. We'll implement the grid of cards using a couple concepts seen in previous chapters, along with some new concepts you haven't seen before. Chapter 3 included both the notions of 1) using an invisible SceneController component and 2) instantiating clones of an object. This time the SceneController will apply different images to different cards.

### 5.3.1   Loading images programmatically

There are four card images in the game we're creating. All eight cards on the table (two for each symbol) will be created by cloning the same original, so initially all cards will have the same symbol. We'll have to change the image on the card in the script, loading different images programmatically.

To examine how images can be assigned programmatically, let's write some simple test code (that will be replaced later) to demonstrate the technique. First add the code from the following listing to the MemoryCard script.

---

**Listing 5.3    Test code to demonstrate changing the sprite image**

```
...
[SerializeField] private Sprite image;          Reference to the Sprite
void Start() {                                    asset that will be loaded
    GetComponent<SpriteRenderer>().sprite = image;
}                                                Set the sprite for this
...                                              SpriteRenderer component.
```

After you save this script, the new `image` variable will appear in the Inspector because it has been set as serialized. Drag a sprite up from the Project view (pick one of the card images, and not the same as the image already in the scene) and drop it on the Image slot. Now run the scene, and you'll see the new image on the card.

The key to understanding this code is to know about the SpriteRenderer component. You'll notice in figure 5.7 that the card back object has just two components, the standard Transform component on all objects in the scene, and a new component called Sprite Renderer. This component makes it a sprite object and determines which sprite asset will be displayed. Note that the first property in the component is called Sprite and links to one of the sprites in the Project view; the property can be manipulated in code, and that's precisely what this script does.

Sprite asset displayed
on this Sprite object

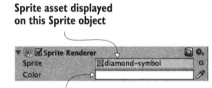

Color that tints this Sprite object
(default is white for no tint)

Figure 5.7    A sprite object in the scene
has the SpriteRenderer component
attached to it.

As it did with CharacterController and custom scripts in previous chapters, the `GetComponent()` method returns other components on the same object, so we use it to reference the `SpriteRenderer` object. The `sprite` property of `SpriteRenderer` can be set to any sprite asset, so this code sets that property to the `Sprite` variable declared at the top (which we filled with a sprite asset in the editor).

Well, that wasn't too hard! But it's only a single image; we have four different images to use, so now delete the new code from listing 5.3 (it was only a quick demonstration of how the technique works) to prepare for the next section.

### 5.3.2    *Setting the image from an invisible SceneController*

Recall in chapter 3 how we created an invisible object in the scene to control spawning objects. We're going to take that approach here as well, using an invisible object to control more abstract features that aren't tied to any specific object in the scene. First create an empty GameObject (remember, select menu GameObject > Create Empty). Then create a new script SceneController.cs in the Project view, and drag this script asset onto the controller GameObject. Before writing code in the new script, first add the contents of the next listing to the MemoryCard script instead of what you saw in listing 5.3.

**Listing 5.4  New public methods in MemoryCard.cs**

```
...
[SerializeField] private SceneController controller;

private int _id;
public int id {                          Added getter function (an
    get {return _id;}                    idiom common in languages
}                                        like C# and Java)

                                         Public method that other scripts can
public void SetCard(int id, Sprite image) {   use to pass new sprites to this object
    _id = id;
    GetComponent<SpriteRenderer>().sprite = image;
}                                        SpriteRenderer code line just like
...                                      in the deleted example code
```

The primary change from previous listings is that we're now setting the sprite image in SetCard() instead of Start(). Because that's a public method that takes a sprite as a parameter, you can call this function from other scripts and set the image on this object. Note that SetCard() also takes an ID number as a parameter, and the code stores that number. Although we don't need the ID quite yet, soon we'll write code that compares cards for matches, and that comparison will rely on the IDs of the cards.

> **NOTE** Depending on what programming languages you've used in the past, you may not be familiar with the concept of "getters" and "setters." Long story short, those are functions that run when you attempt to access the property associated with them (for example, retrieving the value of card.id). There are multiple reasons to use getters and setters, but in this case the id property is read-only because there's only a function to get the value and not set it.

Lastly, note that the code has a variable for the controller; even as SceneController starts cloning card objects to fill the scene, the card objects also need a reference back to the controller to call its public methods. As usual, when the code references objects in the scene, drag the controller object in Unity's editor to the variable slot in the Inspector. Do this once for this single card and all of the copies to come later will have the reference as well.

With that additional code now in MemoryCard, write the code from the next listing in SceneController.

**Listing 5.5   First pass at SceneController for the Memory game**

```
using UnityEngine;
using System.Collections;

public class SceneController : MonoBehaviour {
    [SerializeField] private MemoryCard originalCard;
    [SerializeField] private Sprite[] images;

    void Start() {
        int id = Random.Range(0, images.Length);
        originalCard.SetCard(id, images[id]);
    }
}
```

Reference for the card in the scene

An array for references to the sprite assets

Call the public method we added to MemoryCard.

For now this is a short snippet to demonstrate the concept of manipulating cards from SceneController. Most of this should already be familiar to you (for example, in Unity's editor, drag the card object to the variable slot in the Inspector), but the array of images is new. As shown in figure 5.8, in

Type in how many array elements.

Drag sprite assets onto array elements.

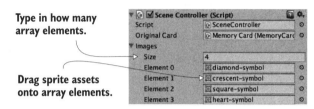

Figure 5.8   The filled-in array of sprites

the Inspector you can set the number of elements. Type in 4 for the array length, and then drag the sprites for card images onto the array slots. Now these sprites can be accessed in the array, like any other object reference.

Incidentally, we used the `Random.Range()` method in chapter 3, so hopefully you recall that. The exact boundary values didn't matter there, but this time it's important to note that the minimum value is inclusive and may be returned, whereas the return value is always below the maximum.

Hit Play to run this new code. You'll see different images being applied to the revealed card each time you run the scene. The next step is to create a whole grid of cards, instead of just one.

### 5.3.3   *Instantiating a grid of cards*

SceneController already has a reference to the card object, so now you'll use the `Instantiate()` method (see the next listing) to clone the object numerous times, like spawning objects in chapter 3.

**Listing 5.6   Cloning the card eight times and positioning in a grid**

```
using UnityEngine;
using System.Collections;

public class SceneController : MonoBehaviour {
    public const int gridRows = 2;
```

Values for how many grid spaces to make and how far apart to place them

```
public const int gridCols = 4;
public const float offsetX = 2f;
public const float offsetY = 2.5f;

[SerializeField] private MemoryCard originalCard;
[SerializeField] private Sprite[] images;

void Start() {
    Vector3 startPos = originalCard.transform.position;

    for (int i = 0; i < gridCols; i++) {
        for (int j = 0; j < gridRows; j++) {
            MemoryCard card;
            if (i == 0 && j == 0) {
                card = originalCard;
            } else {
                card = Instantiate(originalCard) as MemoryCard;
            }

            int id = Random.Range(0, images.Length);
            card.SetCard(id, images[id]);

            float posX = (offsetX * i) + startPos.x;
            float posY = -(offsetY * j) + startPos.y;
            card.transform.position = new Vector3(posX, posY, startPos.z);
        }
    }
}
```

**The position of the first card; all other cards will be offset from here.**

**Nested loops to define both columns and rows of the grid**

**A container reference for either the original card or the copies**

**For 2D graphics, you only need to offset X and Y; keep Z the same.**

Although this script is much longer than the previous listing, there's not a lot to explain because most of the additions are straightforward variable declarations and math. The oddest bit of this code is probably the if/else statement that begins if (i == 0 && j == 0). What that conditional does is either choose the original card object for the first grid slot or clone the card object for all other grid slots. Because the original card already exists in the scene, if you copied the card at every iteration of the loop you'd end up with one too many cards in the scene. The cards are then positioned by offsetting them according to the number of iterations through the loop.

> **TIP** Just as when moving 3D objects, 2D objects can be moved by manipulating transform.position to different points on the screen, and this position could be incremented repeatedly in Update(). But as you saw when moving the first-person player, collision detection isn't applied when adjusting transform.position directly. To move 2D objects with collision detection, you'll probably want to adjust rigidbody2D.velocity after assigning Physics2D components.

Run the code now and a grid of eight cards will be created (as depicted in figure 5.9). The last step in preparing the grid of cards is to organize them into pairs, instead of them being random.

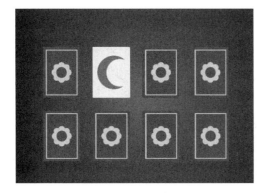

**Figure 5.9** The grid of eight cards that are revealed when you click on them

### 5.3.4 Shuffling the cards

Instead of making every card random, we'll define an array of all the card IDs (numbers 0 through 3 twice, for a pair of each card) and then shuffle that array. We'll then use this array of card IDs when setting cards, rather than making each one random. The following listing shows the code.

**Listing 5.7  Placing cards from a shuffled list**

```
...
void Start() {
    Vector3 startPos = originalCard.transform.position;
    int[] numbers = {0, 0, 1, 1, 2, 2, 3, 3};
    numbers = ShuffleArray(numbers);

    for (int i = 0; i < gridCols; i++) {
        for (int j = 0; j < gridRows; j++) {
            MemoryCard card;
            if (i == 0 && j == 0) {
                card = originalCard;
            } else {
                card = Instantiate(originalCard) as MemoryCard;
            }

            int index = j * gridCols + i;
            int id = numbers[index];
            card.SetCard(id, images[id]);

            float posX = (offsetX * i) + startPos.x;
            float posY = -(offsetY * j) + startPos.y;
            card.transform.position = new Vector3(posX, posY, startPos.z);
        }
    }
}

private int[] ShuffleArray(int[] numbers) {
    int[] newArray = numbers.Clone() as int[];
    for (int i = 0; i < newArray.Length; i++ ) {
```

**Much of this listing is context to show where the additions go.**

**Declare an integer array with a pair of IDs for all four card sprites.**

**Call a function that will shuffle the elements of the array.**

**Retrieve IDs from the shuffled list instead of random numbers.**

**Here's an implementation of the Knuth shuffle algorithm.**

```
            int tmp = newArray[i];
            int r = Random.Range(i, newArray.Length);
            newArray[i] = newArray[r];
            newArray[r] = tmp;
        }
        return newArray;
    }
    ...
```

Now when you hit Play the grid of cards will be a shuffled assortment that reveals exactly two of each card image. The array of cards was run through the Knuth (also known as Fisher-Yates) shuffle algorithm, a simple yet effective way of shuffling the elements of an array. This algorithm loops through the array and swaps every element of the array with a randomly chosen other array position.

You can click on all the cards to reveal them, but the game of Memory is supposed to proceed in pairs; a bit more code is needed.

## 5.4     *Making and scoring matches*

The last step in making a fully functional Memory game is checking for matches. Although we now have a grid of cards that are revealed when clicked, the various cards don't affect each other in any way. In the game of Memory, every time a pair of cards is revealed we should check to see if the revealed cards match.

This abstract logic—checking for matches and responding appropriately—requires that cards notify SceneController when they've been clicked. That requires the additions to SceneController.cs shown in the next listing.

---

**Listing 5.8     SceneController, which must keep track of revealed cards**

```
...
private MemoryCard _firstRevealed;
private MemoryCard _secondRevealed;                    Getter function that returns
                                                       false if there's already a
public bool canReveal {                                second card revealed
    get {return _secondRevealed == null;}    ◁
}
...
public void CardRevealed(MemoryCard card) {
    // initially empty
}
...
```

The CardRevealed() method will be filled in momentarily; we needed the empty scaffolding for now to refer to in MemoryCard.cs without any compiler errors. Note that there is a read-only getter again, this time used to determine whether another card can be revealed; the player can only reveal another card when there aren't already two cards revealed.

We also need to modify MemoryCard.cs to call the (currently empty) method in order to inform SceneController when a card is clicked. Modify the code in Memory-Card.cs according to the following listing.

**Listing 5.9   MemoryCard.cs modifications for revealing cards**

Notify the controller when this card is revealed.

```
...
public void OnMouseDown() {
    if (cardBack.activeSelf && controller.canReveal) {
        cardBack.SetActive(false);
        controller.CardRevealed(this);
    }
}

public void Unreveal() {
    cardBack.SetActive(true);
}
...
```

Check the controller's canReveal property, to make sure only two cards are revealed at a time.

A public method so that SceneController can hide the card again (by turning card_back back on)

If you were to put a debug statement inside `CardRevealed()` in order to test the communication between objects, you'd see the test message appear whenever you click a card. Let's first handle one revealed card.

### 5.4.1   Storing and comparing revealed cards

The card object was passed into `CardRevealed()`, so let's start keeping track of the revealed cards. Write the code from the following listing.

**Listing 5.10   Keeping track of revealed cards in SceneController**

Compare the IDs of the two revealed cards.

```
...
public void CardRevealed(MemoryCard card) {
    if (_firstRevealed == null) {
        _firstRevealed = card;
    } else {
        _secondRevealed = card;
        Debug.Log("Match? " + (_firstRevealed.id == _secondRevealed.id));
    }
}
...
```

Store card objects in one of the two card variables, depending on if the first variable is already occupied.

The listing stores the revealed cards in one of the two card variables, depending on whether the first variable is already occupied. If the first variable is empty, then fill it; if it's already occupied, fill the second variable and check the card IDs for a match. The debug statement prints either `true` or `false` in the console.

At the moment the code doesn't respond to matches—it only checks for them. Now let's program the response.

### 5.4.2   Hiding mismatched cards

We'll use coroutines again because the reaction to mismatched cards should pause to allow the player to see the cards. Refer back to chapter 3 for a full explanation of coroutines; long story short, using a coroutine will allow us to pause when checking for a match. The next listing shows more code for you to add to SceneController.

**Listing 5.11    SceneController, which either scores matches or hides missed matches**

```
...
private int _score = 0;                          ◁┐ Another variable to add to the list
...                                                └  near the top of SceneController
public void CardRevealed(MemoryCard card) {
  if (_firstRevealed == null) {
    _firstRevealed = card;
  } else {
    _secondRevealed = card;
    StartCoroutine(CheckMatch());                ◁┐ The only changed line in this
  }                                                │ function—calls the coroutine
}                                                  └ when both cards are revealed

private IEnumerator CheckMatch() {
  if (_firstRevealed.id == _secondRevealed.id) {
    _score++;                                      ◁┐ Increment the score if the
    Debug.Log("Score: " + _score);                  └ revealed cards have matching IDs.
  }
  else {
    yield return new WaitForSeconds(.5f);

    _firstRevealed.Unreveal();                     ◁┐ Unreveal the cards if
    _secondRevealed.Unreveal();                      └ they do not match.
  }

  _firstRevealed = null;                           ◁┐ Clear out the variables whether
  _secondRevealed = null;                            └ or not a match was made.
}
...
```

First add a _score value to track; then launch a coroutine to CheckMatch() when a second card is revealed. In that coroutine there are two code paths, depending on whether the cards match. If they do match, the coroutine doesn't pause; the yield command gets skipped over. But if the cards don't match, the coroutine pauses for half a second before calling Unreveal() on both cards, hiding them again. Finally, whether or not a match was made, the variables for storing cards are both nulled out, paving the way for revealing more cards.

When you play the game, mismatched cards will display briefly before hiding again. There are debug messages when you score matches, but we want the score displayed as a label on the screen.

### 5.4.3    *Text display for the score*

Displaying information to the player is half of the reason for a UI in a game (the other half is receiving input from the player; UI buttons are discussed in the next section).

> **DEFINITION**    *UI* stand for user interface. Another closely related term is *GUI* (graphical user interface), which refers to the visual part of the interface, such as text and buttons, and which is what a lot of people mean when they say UI.

Unity has multiple ways to create text displays. One way is to create a 3D text object in the scene. This is a special mesh component, so first create an empty object to attach this component to. From the GameObject menu, choose Create Empty. Then click the Add Component button and choose Mesh > Text Mesh.

> **NOTE** That name, *3D* text, might sound incompatible with a 2D game, but don't forget that this is technically a 3D scene that looks flat because it's being seen through an orthographic camera. That means we can put 3D objects into the 2D game if we want—they're just displayed in a flat perspective.

Position this object at -4.75, 3.65, -10; that's 475 pixels to the left and 365 pixels up, putting it in the top-left corner, and nearer to the camera so that it'll appear on top of other game objects. In the Inspector, look for the Font setting toward the bottom; click the little circle button to bring up a file selector, and then pick the Arial font that's available. Enter Score: as the Text setting. Correct positioning also requires Upper Left for the Anchor setting (this controls how letters expand out as they're typed), so change this if needed. By default the text appears blurry, but that's easily fixed by adjusting the settings shown in figure 5.10.

If we imported a new TrueType font into the project we could use that instead, but for our purposes the default font is fine. Oddly enough, a bit of size adjustment is needed to make the default text sharp and clear. First set the TextMesh component's Font Size setting to a very large value (I used 80). Now scale the object down to be very small (like .1, .1, 1). Increasing Font Size added a lot of pixels to the text displayed, and scaling the object compressed those pixels into a smaller space.

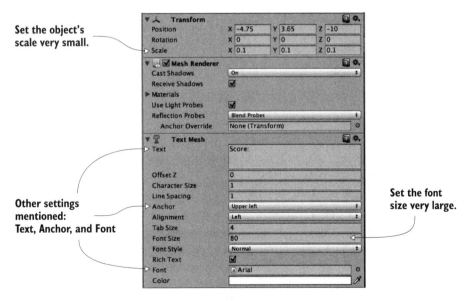

**Figure 5.10** **Inspector settings for a text object to make the text sharp and clear**

Manipulating this text object requires just a few adjustments in the scoring code (see the next listing).

---

**Listing 5.12  Displaying the score on a text object**

```
...
[SerializeField] private TextMesh scoreLabel;
...
private IEnumerator CheckMatch() {
  if (_firstRevealed.id == _secondRevealed.id) {           The text displayed is
    _score++;                                              a property to set
    scoreLabel.text = "Score: " + _score;                  on text objects.
  }
...
```

As you can see, `text` is a property of the object that you can set to a new string. Drag the text in the scene to the variable you just added to SceneController, and then hit Play. Now you should see the score displayed while you play the game and make matches. Huzzah, the game works!

## 5.5  *Restart button*

At this point the Memory game is fully functional. You can play the game, and all the essential features are in place. But this playable core is still lacking the overarching functionality that players expect or need in a finished game. For example, right now you can play the game only once; you need to quit and restart in order to play again. Let's add a control to the screen so that players can start the game over without having to quit.

This functionality breaks down into two tasks: create a UI button, and reset the game when that button is clicked. Figure 5.11 shows what the game will look like with the restart button.

Neither task is specific to 2D games, by the way; all games need UI buttons, and all games need the ability to reset. We'll go over both topics to round out this chapter.

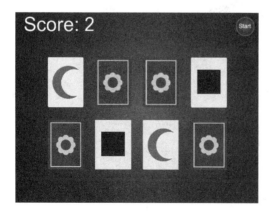

Figure 5.11  Complete Memory game screen, including the Start button

### 5.5.1 Programming a UIButton component using SendMessage

First place the button sprite in the scene; drag it up from the Project view. Give it a position like 4.5, 3.25, -10; that will place the button in the top-right corner (that's 450 pixels to the right and 325 pixels up) and move it nearer to the camera so that it'll appear on top of other game objects. Because we want to be able to click on this object, give it a collider (just as with the card object, select Add Component > Physics 2D > Box Collider).

> **NOTE** As alluded to in the previous section, Unity provides multiple ways to create UI displays, including an advanced UI system introduced in the most recent versions of Unity. For now we'll build the single button out of standard display objects. The next chapter will teach you about the advanced UI functionality; the UI for both 2D and 3D games is ideally built with that system.

Now create a new script called UIButton.cs and assign that script (shown in the following listing) to the button object.

**Listing 5.13   Code to make a generic and reusable UI button**

```
using UnityEngine;
using System.Collections;

public class UIButton : MonoBehaviour {          Reference a target object
  [SerializeField] private GameObject targetObject;   to inform about clicks.
  [SerializeField] private string targetMessage;
  public Color highlightColor = Color.cyan;

  public void OnMouseEnter() {
    SpriteRenderer sprite = GetComponent<SpriteRenderer>();
    if (sprite != null) {
      sprite.color = highlightColor;           Tint the button when the
    }                                          mouse hovers over it.
  }
  public void OnMouseExit() {
    SpriteRenderer sprite = GetComponent<SpriteRenderer>();
    if (sprite != null) {
      sprite.color = Color.white;
    }
  }

  public void OnMouseDown() {                   The button's size pops
    transform.localScale = new Vector3(1.1f, 1.1f, 1.1f);   a bit when it's clicked.
  }
  public void OnMouseUp() {
    transform.localScale = Vector3.one;
    if (targetObject != null) {
      targetObject.SendMessage(targetMessage);   Send a message to the
    }                                            target object when the
  }                                              button is clicked.
}
```

The majority of this code happens inside a series of `OnMouseSomething` functions; like `Start()` and `Update()`, these are a series of functions automatically available to all script components in Unity. `MouseDown` was mentioned back in section 5.2.2, but all these functions respond to mouse interactions if the object has a collider; `MouseEnter` and `MouseExit` are a pair of events used for hovering the mouse cursor over an object: `MouseEnter` is the moment when the mouse cursor first moves over an object, and `MouseExit` is the moment when the mouse cursor moves away. Similarly, `MouseDown` and `MouseUp` are a pair of events for clicking the mouse. `MouseDown` is the moment when the mouse button is physically pressed, and `MouseUp` is the moment when the mouse button is released.

You can see that this code tints the sprite when the mouse hovers over it and scales the sprite when it's clicked on. In both cases you can see that the change (in color or scale) happens when the mouse interaction begins, and then the property returns to default (either white or scale 1) when the mouse interaction ends. For scaling, the code uses the standard transform component that all GameObjects have. For tint, though, the code uses the SpriteRenderer component that sprite objects have; the sprite is set to a color that's defined in Unity's editor through a public variable.

In addition to returning the scale to 1, `SendMessage()` is called when the mouse is released. `SendMessage()` calls the function of the given name in all components of that GameObject. Here the target object for the message, as well as the message to send, are both defined by serialized variables. This way, the same UIButton component can be used for all sorts of buttons, with the target of different buttons set to different objects in the Inspector.

Normally when doing object-oriented programming in a strongly typed language like C#, you need to know the type of a target object in order to communicate with that object (for example, to call a public method of the object, like calling `target-Object.SendMessage()` itself). But scripts for UI elements may have lots of different types of targets, so Unity provides the `SendMessage()` method to communicate specific messages with a target object even if you don't know exactly what type of object it is.

> **WARNING**   Using `SendMessage()` is less efficient for the CPU than calling public methods on known types (that is, using `object.SendMessage("Method")` versus `component.Method()`) so only use `SendMessage()` when it's a big win in terms of making the code simpler to understand and work with. As a general rule of thumb, that will only be the case if there could be lots of different types of objects receiving the message; in situations like that, the inflexibility of inheritance or even interfaces will hinder the game development process and discourage experimentation.

With this code written, wire up the public variables in the button's Inspector. The highlight color can be set to whatever you'd like (although the default cyan looks pretty good on a blue button). Meanwhile, put the SceneController object in the target object slot, and then type `Restart` as the message.

If you play the game now, there's a Reset button in the top-right corner that changes color in response to the mouse, and it makes a slight visual "pop" when clicked on. But an error message was emitted when you clicked the button; in the console you'll see an error about there not being a receiver for the Restart message. That's because we haven't written a `Restart()` method in SceneController, so let's add that next.

### 5.5.2 *Calling LoadLevel from SceneController*

The `SendMessage()` from the button attempts to call `Restart()` in the Scene-Controller, so let's add that (see the next listing).

> **Listing 5.14   SceneController code that reloads the level**

```
...
public void Restart() {
    Application.LoadLevel("Scene");          The scene asset is loaded
}                                            with this command.
...
```

You can see the one thing `Restart()` does is call `Application.LoadLevel()`. That command loads a saved scene asset (that is, the file created when you click Save Scene in Unity). Pass the method the name of the scene you want to load; in my case the scene was saved with the name `Scene`, but if you used a different name, pass that to the method instead.

Hit Play to see what happens. Reveal a few cards and make a few matches; if you then click the Reset button, the game starts over, with all cards hidden and a score of 0. Great, just what we wanted!

As the name `LoadLevel()` implies, this method can load different levels. But what exactly happens when a level loads, and why does this reset the game? What happens is that everything from the current level (all objects in the scene, and thus all scripts attached to those objects) is flushed from memory, and then everything from the new scene is loaded. Because the "new" scene in this case is the saved asset of the current scene, everything is flushed from memory and then reloaded from scratch.

> **TIP**   You can mark specific objects to exclude from the default memory flush when a level is loaded. Unity provides the `DontDestroyOnLoad()` method to keep an object around in multiple scenes; we'll use this method on parts of the code architecture in later chapters.

Another game successfully completed! Well, "completed" is a relative term; you could always implement more features, but everything from the initial plan is done. Many of the concepts from this 2D game apply to 3D games as well, especially the checking of game state and loading levels. Time to switch gears yet again and move away from this Memory game and on to new projects.

## 5.6 *Summary*

In this chapter you've learned that

- Displaying 2D graphics in Unity uses an orthographic camera.
- For pixel-perfect graphics, the camera size should be half the screen height.
- Clicking on sprites requires that you first assign 2D colliders to them.
- New images for the sprites can be loaded programmatically.
- UI text can be made using 3D text objects.
- Loading levels resets the scene.

# Putting a 2D GUI in a 3D game

**This chapter covers**

- Comparing old (pre-Unity 4.6) and new GUI systems
- Creating a canvas for the interface
- Positioning UI elements using anchor points
- Adding interactivity to the UI (buttons, sliders, and so on)
- Broadcasting and listening for events from the UI

In this chapter you'll build a 2D interface display for a 3D game. So far, we've focused on the virtual scene itself while building a first-person demo. But every game needs abstract interaction and information displays in addition to the virtual scene the gameplay takes place in. This is true for all games, whether 2D or 3D, first-person shooter or puzzle game.

These abstract interaction displays are referred to as the UI, or more specifically the GUI. GUI refers to the visual part of the interface, such as text and buttons (see figure 6.1). Technically, the UI includes nongraphical controls, such as the keyboard or gamepad, but people tend to be referring to the graphical parts when they say "user interface."

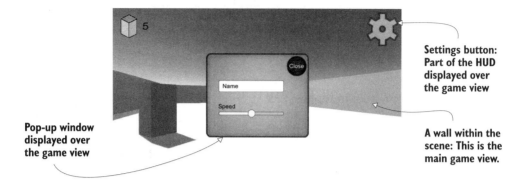

**Figure 6.1   The GUI (a heads-up display, or HUD) you'll create for a game**

Although any software requires some sort of UI in order for the user of that software to control it, games often use their GUI in a slightly different way from other software. In a website, for example, the GUI basically *is* the website (in terms of visual representation). In a game, though, text and buttons are often an additional overlay on top of the game view, a kind of display called a HUD.

> **DEFINITION**   A *heads-up display* (*HUD*) superimposes graphics on top of the view of world. The concept of a HUD originated with military jets so that pilots could see crucial information without having to look down. Similarly, a GUI superimposed on the game view is referred to as the HUD.

This chapter will show how to build the game's HUD using the latest UI tools in Unity. As you saw in chapter 5, Unity provides multiple ways to create UI displays. This chapter demonstrates the new UI system available with Unity 4.6 and later. I'll also discuss the previous UI system and the advantages of the new system.

To learn about the UI tools in Unity, you'll build on top of the first-person shooter (FPS) project from chapter 3. The project in this chapter will involve these steps:

1  Planning the interface
2  Placing UI elements on the display
3  Programming interactions with the UI elements
4  Making the GUI respond to events in the scene
5  Making the scene respond to actions on the GUI

> **NOTE**   This chapter is largely independent of the project you build on top of—it just adds a graphical interface on top of an existing game demo. All the examples in this chapter are built on top of the FPS created in chapter 3, and you could download that sample project, but you're free to use whatever game demo you'd like.

Copy the project from chapter 3 and open the copy to start working on this chapter. As usual, the art assets you need are in the sample download. With those files set up, you're ready to start building the game's UI.

## 6.1 *Before you start writing code...*

To start building the HUD, you first need to understand how the UI system works. Unity provides multiple approaches to building a game's HUD, so we need to go over how those systems work. Then we can briefly plan the UI and prepare the art assets that we'll need.

### 6.1.1 *Immediate mode GUI or advanced 2D interface?*

From its first version, Unity came with an immediate mode GUI system, and that system makes it easy to put a clickable button on the screen. Listing 6.1 shows the code to do that; simply attach this script to any object in the scene. For another example of immediate mode UI, recall the target cursor displayed in chapter 3. This GUI system is entirely based on code, with no work in Unity's editor.

> **DEFINITION** *Immediate mode* refers to explicitly issuing draw commands every frame, versus a system where you define all the visuals once and then for every frame the system knows what to draw without you having to tell it again. The latter approach is called *retained mode*.

**Listing 6.1  Example of a button using the immediate mode GUI**

```
using UnityEngine;
using System.Collections;

public class BasicUI : MonoBehaviour {        Function called every frame
    void OnGUI() {                            after everything else renders
        if (GUI.Button(new Rect(10, 10, 40, 20), "Test")) {
            Debug.Log("Test button");
        }                                     Parameters: position X, pos
    }                                         Y, width, height, text label
}
```

The core of the code in this listing is the `OnGUI()` method. Much like `Start()` and `Update()`, every `MonoBehaviour` automatically responds to `OnGUI()`. That function runs every frame after the 3D scene is rendered, providing a place to put GUI drawing commands. This code draws a button; note that the command for a button is executed every frame (that is, in immediate mode style). The button command is used in a conditional that responds when the button is clicked.

Because the immediate mode GUI makes it easy to get a few buttons onscreen with a minimum of effort, we'll use it for examples in future chapters (especially chapter 8). But making default buttons is about the only thing easy to create with that system, so the latest versions of Unity now have a new interface system based on 2D graphics laid out in the editor. It takes a bit more effort to set up, but you'll probably

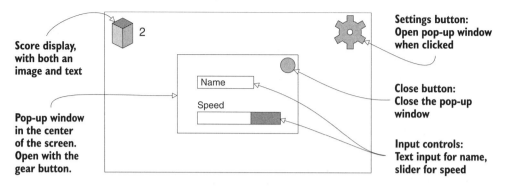

**Figure 6.2   Planned GUI**

want to use the newer interface system in finished games because it produces more polished results.

The new UI system works in retained mode, so the graphics are laid out once and then drawn every frame without needing to be continually redefined. In this system, graphics for the UI are placed in Unity's editor. This provides two advantages over the immediate mode UI: 1) you can see what the UI looks like while placing UI elements, and 2) this system makes it straightforward to customize the UI with your own images.

To use this system you're going to import images and then drag objects into the scene. Next let's plan how this UI will look.

### 6.1.2   Planning the layout

The HUD for most games is only a few different UI controls repeated over and over. That means this project doesn't need to be a terribly complex UI in order for you to learn how to build a game's UI. You're going to put a score display and a settings button in the corners of the screen (see figure 6.2) over the main game view. The settings button will bring up a pop-up window, and that window will have both a text field and a slider.

For this example, those input controls will be used for setting the player's name and movement speed, but ultimately those UI elements could control any settings relevant to your game.

Well, that plan was pretty simple! The next step is bringing in the images that are needed.

### 6.1.3   Importing UI images

This UI requires some images to display for things like buttons. The UI is built from 2D images like the graphics in chapter 5, so you'll follow the same two steps:

1  Import images (if needed, set them to Sprite).
2  Drag the sprites into the scene.

To accomplish these steps, first drag the images into Project view to import them, and then in the Inspector change their Texture Type setting to Sprite (2D And UI).

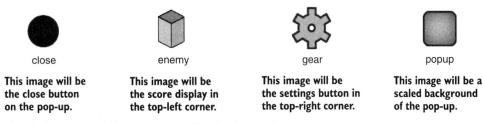

| close | enemy | gear | popup |
|---|---|---|---|
| This image will be the close button on the pop-up. | This image will be the score display in the top-left corner. | This image will be the settings button in the top-right corner. | This image will be a scaled background of the pop-up. |

Figure 6.3   Images that are needed for this chapter's project

> **WARNING**   The Texture Type setting defaults to Texture in 3D projects and to Sprite in 2D projects. If you want sprites in a 3D project, you need to adjust this setting manually.

Get all the needed images from the sample download (see figure 6.3) and then import the images into your project. Make sure all the imported assets are set to Sprite; you'll probably need to adjust Texture Type in the settings displayed after importing.

   These sprites comprise the buttons, score display, and pop-up that you'll create. Now that the images are imported, let's put these graphics onto the screen.

## 6.2   *Setting up the GUI display*

The art assets are the same kind of 2D sprites we used in chapter 5, but the use of those assets in the scene is a bit different. Unity provides special tools to make the images a HUD that's displayed over the 3D scene, rather than displaying the images as part of the scene. The positioning of UI elements also has some special tricks, because of the needs of a display that may change on different screens.

### 6.2.1   *Creating a canvas for the interface*

One of the most fundamental and nonobvious aspects of how the UI system works is that all images must be attached to a canvas object.

> **TIP**   *Canvas* is a special kind of object that Unity renders as the UI for a game.

Open the GameObject menu to see the various kinds of objects you can create; in the UI category, choose Canvas. A canvas object will appear in the scene (it may be clearer to rename the object HUD Canvas). This object represents the entire extent of the screen, and it's huge relative to the 3D scene because it scales one pixel of the screen to one unit in the scene.

> **WARNING**   When you create a canvas object, an EventSystem object is automatically created, too. That object is required for UI interaction but you can otherwise ignore it.

Switch to 2D view mode (refer to figure 6.4) and double-click the canvas in the Hierarchy in order to zoom out and view it fully. The 2D view mode is automatic when the entire project is 2D, but in a 3D project this toggle must be clicked to switch between

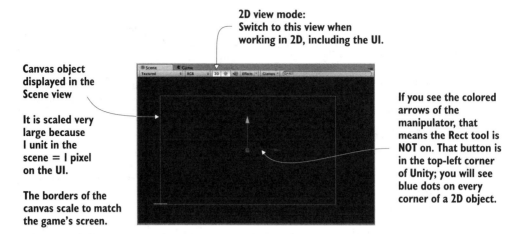

**2D view mode:**
Switch to this view when working in 2D, including the UI.

**Canvas object displayed in the Scene view**

It is scaled very large because I unit in the scene = I pixel on the UI.

The borders of the canvas scale to match the game's screen.

If you see the colored arrows of the manipulator, that means the Rect tool is NOT on. That button is in the top-left corner of Unity; you will see blue dots on every corner of a 2D object.

Figure 6.4  **A blank canvas object in the Scene view**

the UI and the main scene. To return to viewing the 3D scene, toggle the 2D view mode off and then double-click the building to zoom to that object.

> **TIP**  Don't forget this tip from chapter 4: across the top of the Scene view's pane are buttons that control what's visible, so look for the Effects button to turn off the skybox.

The canvas has a number of settings that you can adjust. First is the Render Mode option; leave this at the default setting, but you should know what the three possible settings mean:

- *Screen Space—Overlay*—Renders the UI as 2D graphics on top of the camera view (this is the default setting).
- *Screen Space—Camera*—Also renders the UI on top of the camera view, but UI elements can rotate for perspective effects.
- *World Space*—Places the canvas object within the scene, as if the UI were part of the 3D scene.

The two modes besides the initial default can sometimes be useful for specific effects but are slightly more complicated.

The other important setting is Pixel Perfect. This setting causes the rendering to subtly adjust the position images so that they're always perfectly crisp and sharp (as opposed to blurring them when positioned between pixels). Go ahead and select that check box. Now the HUD canvas is set up, but it's still blank and needs sprites.

### 6.2.2  *Buttons, images, and text labels*

The canvas object defines an area to display as the UI, but it still requires sprites to display. If you refer back to the UI mockup in figure 6.2, there's an image of the block/enemy in the top-left corner, text displaying the score next to that, and a gear-shaped

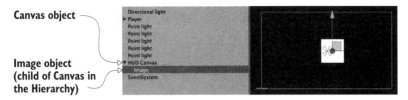

**Canvas object**

**Image object (child of Canvas in the Hierarchy)**

**Figure 6.5   Canvas with an image linked in the Hierarchy view**

button in the top-right corner. Accordingly, in the UI section of the GameObject menu are options to create an image, text, or button. Create one of each.

UI elements need to be a child of the canvas object in order to display correctly. Unity does this automatically, but remember that as usual you can drag objects around the Hierarchy view (see figure 6.5) to make parent-child linkages.

Objects within the canvas can be parented together for positioning purposes, just like any other objects in the scene. For example, you may want to drag the text object onto the image so that the text will move with the image. Similarly, the default button object has a text object as its child; this button doesn't need a text label, so delete the text object.

Roughly position the UI elements into their corners. In the next section we'll make the positions exact; for now, just drag the objects until they're pretty much in position. Click and drag the image object to the top-left of the canvas; the button goes in the top right.

> **TIP** As noted in chapter 5, you use the Rect tool in 2D mode. I described it as a single manipulation tool that encompasses all three transforms: Move, Rotate, and Scale. These operations have to be separate tools in 3D but are combined in 2D because that's one less dimension to worry about. In 2D mode, this tool is selected automatically, or you can click the button in the top-left corner of Unity.

At the moment the images are both blank. If you select a UI object and look at the Inspector, you should see a Source Image slot near the top of the image component. As shown in figure 6.6, drag over sprites (remember, not textures!) from the Project

**I. Drag Sprite from Project view up to Source Image setting...**

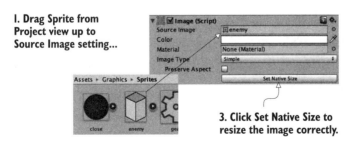

**3. Click Set Native Size to resize the image correctly.**

**2. ...and the image will appear on the UI element.**

**Figure 6.6   Assign 2D sprites to the Image property of UI elements.**

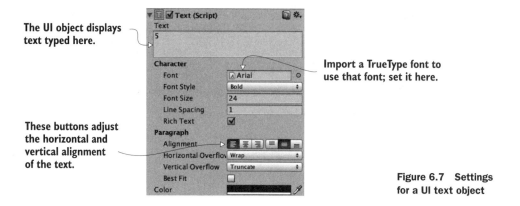

The UI object displays text typed here.

Import a TrueType font to use that font; set it here.

These buttons adjust the horizontal and vertical alignment of the text.

**Figure 6.7   Settings for a UI text object**

view to assign images to the objects. Assign the enemy sprite to the image object, and the gear sprite to the button object (click Set Native Size after assigning sprites to properly size the image object).

That took care of the appearance of both the enemy image and the gear button. As for the text object, there are a bunch of settings in the Inspector. First, type a single number in the large Text box; this text will be overwritten later, but it's useful because it looks like a score display within the editor. The text is small, so increase the Font Size to 24 and make the style Bold. You also want to set this label to left horizontal alignment (see figure 6.7) and middle vertical alignment. For now the remaining settings can be left at their default values.

**NOTE**   Besides the Text box and alignment, the most common property to adjust is the font. You can import a TrueType font into Unity, and then put that font in the Inspector.

Now that sprites have been assigned to the UI images, and the score text is set up, you can hit Play to see the HUD on top of the 3D game. As shown in figure 6.8, the canvas

The Canvas displayed in the editor.

HUD overlays the main game scene when playing.

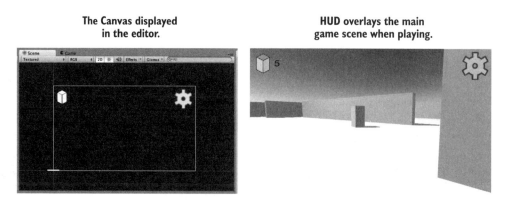

**Figure 6.8   The GUI as seen in the editor (left) and when playing the game (right)**

displayed in Unity's editor shows the bounds of the screen, and UI elements are drawn onto the screen in those positions.

Great, you made a HUD with 2D images displayed over the 3D game! One more complex visual setting remains: positioning UI elements relative to the canvas.

### 6.2.3 *Controlling the position of UI elements*

All UI objects have an anchor, displayed in the editor as a target X (see figure 6.9). An anchor is a flexible way of positioning objects on the UI.

> **DEFINITION**   The *anchor* of an object is the point where an object attaches to the canvas or screen. It determines what that object's position is measured relative to.

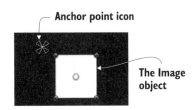

**Figure 6.9   The anchor point of an image object**

Positions are values like "50 pixels on the X-axis." But that leaves the question: 50 pixels from what? This is where anchors come in. The purpose of an anchor is that while the object stays in place relative to the anchor point, the anchor moves around relative to the canvas. The anchor is defined as something like "center of the screen," and then the anchor will stay centered while the screen changes size. Similarly, setting the anchor to the right side of the screen will keep the object rooted to the right side even if the screen changes size (for example, if the game is played on different monitors).

The easiest way to understand what I'm talking about is to see it in action. Select the image object and look over at the Inspector. Anchor settings (see figure 6.10) will appear right below the transform component. By default, UI elements have their anchor set to Center, but you want to set the anchor to Top Left for this image; figure 6.10 shows how to adjust that using the Anchor Presets.

Change the gear button's anchor as well. Set it to Top Right for this object; click the top-right Anchor Preset. Now try scaling the window left and right; click and drag on the side of the Scene view. Thanks to the anchors, the UI objects will stay in their

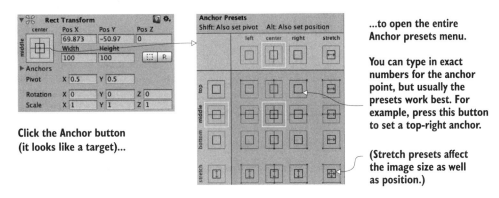

**Figure 6.10   How to adjust anchor settings**

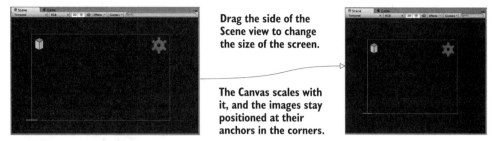

Drag the side of the Scene view to change the size of the screen.

The Canvas scales with it, and the images stay positioned at their anchors in the corners.

**Figure 6.11   Anchors stay in place while the screen changes.**

corners while the canvas changes size. As figure 6.11 shows, these UI elements are now rooted in place while the screen moves.

> **TIP**   Anchor points can adjust scale as well as position. We're not going to explore that functionality in this chapter, but each corner of the image can be rooted to a different corner of the screen. In figure 6.11 the images didn't change size, but we could adjust the anchors so that when the screen changes size, the image stretches with it.

All of the visual setup is done, so it's time to program interactivity.

## 6.3   *Programming interactivity in the UI*

Before you can interact with the UI, you need to have a mouse cursor. If you recall, this game adjusted `Cursor` settings in the `Start()` method of the RayShooter code. Those settings lock and hide the mouse cursor, a behavior that works for the controls in an FPS game but that interferes with using the UI. Remove those lines from Ray-Shooter.cs so that you can click on the HUD.

As long as you have RayShooter.cs open, you could also make sure not to shoot while interacting with the GUI. The following listing shows the code for that.

**Listing 6.2   Adding a GUI check to the code in RayShooter.cs**

```
using UnityEngine.EventSystems;
...
void Update() {
    if (Input.GetMouseButtonDown(0) &&
!EventSystem.current.IsPointerOverGameObject()) {
    Vector3 point = new Vector3(
        camera.pixelWidth/2, camera.pixelHeight/2, 0);
    ...
```

**Include UI system code frameworks**

*Italicized code was already in script; shown for reference*

**Check that GUI isn't being used**

Now you can play the game and click the button, although it doesn't do anything yet. You can watch the tinting of the button change as you mouse over it and click. This mouseover and click behavior is a default tint that can be changed for each button, but the default looks fine for now. You could speed up the default fading behavior;

Fade Duration is a setting in the button component, so try decreasing that to .01 to see how the button changes.

> **TIP** Sometimes the default interaction controls of the UI also interfere with the game. Remember the EventSystem object that was created automatically along with the canvas? That object controls the UI interaction controls, and by default it uses the arrow keys to interact with the GUI. You may need to turn off the arrow keys in EventSystem: in the settings for EventSystem, deselect the check box Send Navigation Event.

But nothing else happens when you click the button because you haven't yet linked it up to any code. Let's take care of that next.

### 6.3.1 Programming an invisible UIController

In general, UI interaction is programmed with a standard series of steps that's the same for all UI elements:

1. Create a UI object in the scene (the button created in the previous section).
2. Write a script to call when the UI is operated.
3. Attach that script to an object in the scene.
4. Link UI elements (such as buttons) to the object with that script.

To follow these steps, first we need to create a controller object to link to the button. Create a script called UIController (shown in the following listing) and drag that script onto the controller object in the scene.

---

**Listing 6.3 UIController script used to program buttons**

```
using UnityEngine;
using UnityEngine.UI;
using System.Collections;                       ⟵ Import UI code framework.

public class UIController : MonoBehaviour {
    [SerializeField] private Text scoreLabel;        ⟵ Reference Text object in
                                                        scene to set text property
    void Update() {
        scoreLabel.text = Time.realtimeSinceStartup.ToString();
    }

    public void OnOpenSettings() {         ⟵ Method called by
        Debug.Log("open settings");           settings button
    }
}
```

> **TIP** You might be wondering why we need separate objects for Scene-Controller and UIController. Indeed, this scene is so simple that you could have one controller handling both the 3D scene and the UI. As the game gets more complex, though, it'll become increasingly useful for the 3D scene and the UI to be separate modules, communicating indirectly. This notion extends well beyond games to software in general; software engineers refer to this principle as *separation of concerns*.

OnClick event panel near
the bottom of settings

Press the + button to add
an entry in the panel.

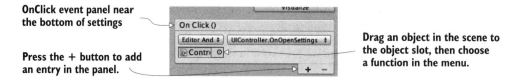

Drag an object in the scene to
the object slot, then choose
a function in the menu.

Figure 6.12   The OnClick panel toward the bottom of the button settings

Now drag objects to component slots in order to wire them up. Drag the score label (the text object we created before) to the UIController's text slot. The code in UIController sets the text displayed on that label. Currently the code displays a timer to test the text display; that will be changed to the score later.

Next, add an OnClick entry to the button to drag the controller object onto. Select the button to see its settings in the Inspector. Toward the bottom you should see an OnClick panel; initially that panel is empty, but (as you can see in figure 6.12) you can click the + button to add an entry to that panel. Each entry defines a single function that gets called when that button is clicked; the listing has both a slot for an object and a menu for the function to call. Drag the controller object to the object slot, and then look for UIController in the menu; select OnOpenSettings() in that section.

### Responding to other mouse events

OnClick is the only event that the button component exposes, but UI elements can respond to a number of different interactions. To go beyond the default interactions, use an EventTrigger component.

Add a new component to the button object and look for the Event section of the component's menu. Select EventTrigger from that menu. Although the button's OnClick responded only to a full click (the mouse button being pressed down and then released), let's try responding to the mouse button being pressed down but not released. Perform the same steps as for OnClick, only responding to a different event. First add another method to UIController:

```
. . .
public void OnPointerDown() {
    Debug.Log("pointer down");
}
. . .
```

Now click Add New Event Type to add a new type to the EventTrigger component. Choose Pointer Down for the event. This will create an empty panel for that event, just like OnClick had. Click the + button to add an event listing, drag the controller object to this entry, and select OnPointerDown() in the menu. There you go!

Play the game and click the button to output debug messages in the console. Again, the code is currently random output in order to test the button's functionality. What we want to do is open a settings pop-up, so let's create that pop-up window next.

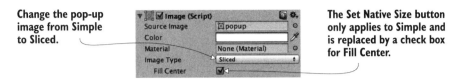

Change the pop-up image from Simple to Sliced.

The Set Native Size button only applies to Simple and is replaced by a check box for Fill Center.

Figure 6.13 Settings for the image component, including Image Type

### 6.3.2 Creating a pop-up window

The UI has a button to open a pop-up window, but there's no pop-up yet. That will be a new image object, along with several controls (such as buttons and sliders) attached to that object. The first step is to create a new image, so choose GameObject > UI > Image. Just as before, the new image has a slot in the Inspector called Source Image. Drag a sprite to that slot to set this image. This time use the sprite called popup.

Ordinarily, the sprite is stretched over the entire image object; this was how the score and gear images worked, and you clicked the Set Native Size button to resize the object to the size of the image. This behavior is the default for image objects, but the pop-up will do something different.

As you can see in figure 6.13, the image component has an Image Type setting. This setting defaults to Simple, which was the correct image type earlier. For the pop-up, though, set Image Type to Sliced.

> **DEFINITION** A *sliced image* is split up into nine sections that scale differently from one another. By scaling the edges of the image separately from the middle, you ensure that the image can scale to any size you want while it maintains its sharp and crisp edges. In other development tools, these kinds of images often have "9" somewhere in the name (such as 9-slice, 9-patch, scale-9) to indicate the 9 sections of the image.

After you switch to a sliced image, Unity may display an error in the component settings, complaining that the image doesn't have a border. That's because the popup sprite doesn't have the nine sections defined yet. To set that up, first select the popup sprite in the Project view. In the Inspector you should see a Sprite Editor button (see figure 6.14); click that button and the Sprite Editor window will appear.

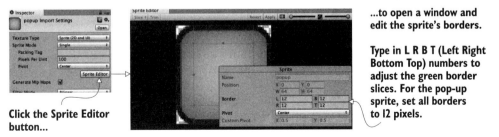

Click the Sprite Editor button...

...to open a window and edit the sprite's borders.

Type in L R B T (Left Right Bottom Top) numbers to adjust the green border slices. For the pop-up sprite, set all borders to 12 pixels.

Figure 6.14 Sprite Editor button in the Inspector and a pop-up window

In the Sprite Editor you can see green lines that indicate how the image will be sliced. Initially the image won't have any border (that is, all of the Border settings are 0). Increase the border width of all four sides, which will result in the border shown in figure 6.14. Because all four sides (Left, Right, Bottom, and Top) have the border set to 12 pixels wide, the border lines will overlap into nine sections. Close the editor window and apply the changes.

Now that the sprite has the nine sections defined, the sliced image will work correctly (and the Image component settings will show Fill Center; make sure that setting is on). Click and drag the blue indicators in the corner of the image to scale it (switch to the Rect tool described in chapter 5 if you don't see any scale indicators). The border sections will maintain their size while the center portion scales.

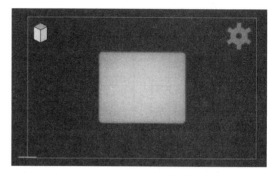

**Figure 6.15   Sliced image scaled to dimensions of the pop-up**

Because the border sections maintain their size, a sliced image can be scaled to any size and still have crisp edges. This is perfect for UI elements—different windows may be different sizes but should still look the same. For this pop-up, enter a width of 250 and a height of 200 to make it look like figure 6.15 (also, center it on position 0, 0, 0).

> **TIP**   How UI images stack on top of each other is determined by their order in the Hierarchy view. In the Hierarchy list, drag the pop-up object above other UI objects (always staying attached to the canvas, of course). Now move the pop-up around within the Scene view; you can see how images overlap the pop-up window. Finally drag the pop-up to the bottom of the canvas hierarchy so that it will display on top of everything else.

The pop-up object is set up now, so write some code for it. Create a script called SettingsPopup (see the next listing) and drag that script onto the pop-up object.

---

**Listing 6.4   SettingsPopup script for the pop-up object**

```
using UnityEngine;
using System.Collections;

public class SettingsPopup : MonoBehaviour {
    public void Open() {
        gameObject.SetActive(true);             Turn the object on to
    }                                           open the window.
    public void Close() {
        gameObject.SetActive(false);            Deactivate this object
    }                                           to close the window.
}
```

Next, open UIController.cs to make a few adjustments, as shown in the following listing.

**Listing 6.5   Adjusting UIController to handle the pop-up**

```
...
[SerializeField] private SettingsPopup settingsPopup;
void Start() {
    settingsPopup.Close();          Close the pop-up when
}                                   the game starts.
...
public void OnOpenSettings() {
    settingsPopup.Open();           Replace the debug text with
}                                   the pop-up's method.
...
```

This code adds a slot for the pop-up object, so drag the pop-up to UIController. Now the pop-up will be closed initially when you play the game, and it'll open when you click the settings button.

At the moment there's no way to close it again, so add a close button to the pop-up. The steps are pretty much the same as for the button created earlier: choose GameObject > UI> Button, position the new button in the top-right corner of the pop-up, drag the close sprite to this UI element's Source Image property, and then click Set Native Size to correctly resize the image. Unlike with the previous button we actually want this text label, so select the text and type Close in the text field, and set Color to white. In the Hierarchy view, drag this button onto the pop-up object so that it will be a child of the pop-up window. And as a final touch of polish, adjust the button transition to a Fade Duration value of .01 and a darker Normal Color setting of 110, 110, 110, 255.

To make the button close the pop-up, it needs an OnClick entry; click the + button on the button's OnClick panel, drag the pop-up window into the object slot, and choose Close() from the function list. Now play the game and this button will close the pop-up window.

The pop-up window has been added to the HUD. The window is currently blank, though, so let's add some controls to it next.

### 6.3.3   *Setting values using sliders and input fields*

Adding some controls to the settings pop-up involves two main steps, like the buttons we made earlier. You create UI elements attached to the canvas, and link those objects to a script. The input controls we need are a slider and a text field, and there will be a static text label to identify the slider. Choose GameObject > UI > Text to create the text object, GameObject > UI > InputField to create the text field, and GameObject > UI > Slider to create the slider object (see figure 6.16).

Make all three objects children of the pop-up by dragging them in the Hierarchy view and then position them as indicated in the figure, lined up in the middle of the pop-up. Set the text to Speed so that it can be a label for the slider. The input field is for typing in text, and *Text* is shown in the box before the player types something else;

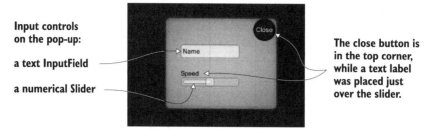

**Input controls on the pop-up:**

a text InputField

a numerical Slider

**The close button is in the top corner, while a text label was placed just over the slider.**

**Figure 6.16  Input controls added to the pop-up window**

set this value to Name. You can leave the options Content Type and Line Type at their defaults; if desired, you can use Content Type to restrict typing to things like only letters or only numbers, whereas you can use Line Type to switch from a single line to multiline text.

> **WARNING**  You won't be able to click the slider if the text label covers it. Make sure the text object appears under the slider by placing it above the slider in the Hierarchy.

As for the slider itself, several settings appear toward the bottom of the component inspector. Min Value is set to 0 by default; leave that. Max Value defaults to 1, but make it 2 for this example. Similarly, both Value and Whole Numbers can be left at their defaults; Value controls the starting value of the slider, and Whole Numbers constrains it to 0 1 2 rather than decimal values (a constraint we don't want).

And that wraps up all the objects. Now you need to write the code that the objects are linked to; add the methods shown in the following listing to SettingsPopup.cs.

**Listing 6.6  SettingsPopup methods for the pop-up's input controls**

```
...
public void OnSubmitName(string name) {
    Debug.Log(name);
}
public void OnSpeedValue(float speed) {
    Debug.Log("Speed: " + speed);
}
...
```

*This will trigger when the user types in the input field.*

*This will trigger when the user adjusts the slider.*

Great, there are methods for the controls to use. Starting with the input field, in settings you'll see an End Edit panel; events listed here are triggered when the user finishes typing. Add an entry to this panel, drag the pop-up to the object slot, and choose OnSubmitName() in the function list.

> **WARNING**  Be sure to select the function in the End Edit panel's top section, Dynamic String, and not the bottom section, Static Parameters. The OnSubmitName() function appears in both sections, but selecting it under

Static Parameters will send only a single string defined ahead of time; *dynamic string* refers to whatever value is typed in the input field.

Follow these same steps for the slider: look for the event panel toward the end of the component settings (in this case, the panel is OnValueChanged), click + to add an entry, drag in the settings pop-up, and choose `OnSpeedValue()` in the list of dynamic value functions.

Now both of the input controls are connected to code in the pop-up's script. Play the game, and watch the console while you move the slider or press Enter after typing input.

---

### Saving settings between plays using PlayerPrefs

A few different methods are available for saving persistent data in Unity, and one of the simplest is called PlayerPrefs. Unity provides an abstracted way (that is, you don't worry about the details) to save small amounts of information that works on all platforms (with their differing filesystems). PlayerPrefs aren't too useful for large amounts of data (in chapter 11 we'll use other methods to save the game's progress), but they're perfect for saving settings.

PlayerPrefs provide simple commands to get and set named values (it works a lot like a hash table or dictionary). For example, you can save the speed setting by adding the line `PlayerPrefs.SetFloat("speed", speed);` inside the `OnSpeedValue()` method of the SettingsPopup script. That method will save the float in a value called `speed`.

Similarly, you'll want to initialize the slider to the saved value. Add the following code to SettingsPopup:

```
using UnityEngine.UI;
...
[SerializeField] private Slider speedSlider;
void Start() {
    speedSlider.value = PlayerPrefs.GetFloat("speed", 1);
}
...
```

Note that the `get` command has both the value to get as well as a default value in case `speed` wasn't previously saved.

---

Although the controls generate debug output, they still don't actually affect the game. Making the HUD affect the game (and vice versa) is the topic of the final section of this chapter.

## 6.4 *Updating the game by responding to events*

Up to now, the HUD and main game have been ignoring each other, but they ought to be communicating back and forth. That could be accomplished via script references as we've done for other sorts of interobject communication, but that approach would have major downsides. In particular, doing so would tightly couple the scene and the HUD; you want to keep them fairly independent from each other so that you can freely edit the game without worrying that you've broken the HUD.

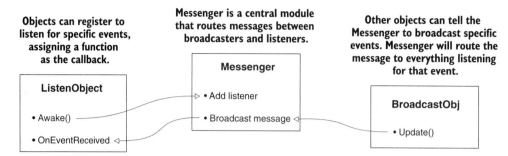

**Figure 6.17**  Diagram of the broadcast event system we'll implement

To alert the UI of actions in the scene, we're going to make use of a broadcast messenger system. Figure 6.17 illustrates how this event messaging system works: scripts can register to listen for an event, other code can broadcast an event, and listeners will be alerted about broadcast messages. Let's go over a messaging system to accomplish that.

> **TIP**  C# does have a built-in system for handling events, so you might wonder why we don't use that. Well, the built-in event system enforces targeted messages, whereas we want a broadcast messenger system. A targeted system requires the code to know exactly where messages originate from; broadcasts can originate from anywhere.

### 6.4.1   Integrating an event system

To alert the UI of actions in the scene, we're going to make use of a broadcast messenger system. Although Unity doesn't have this feature built in, a great script for this purpose exists online. Among the resources listed in appendix D is the Unify community wiki; this is a repository of free code contributed by other developers. Their messenger system is great for providing a decoupled way of communicating events to the rest of the program. When some code broadcasts a message, that code doesn't need to know anything about the listeners, allowing for a great deal of flexibility in switching around or adding objects.

Create a script called `Messenger` and paste in the code from this page on Unify: http://wiki.unity3d.com/index.php/CSharpMessenger_Extended

Then you also need to create a script called `GameEvent` (see the following listing).

**Listing 6.7  GameEvent script to use with Messenger**

```
public static class GameEvent {
    public const string ENEMY_HIT = "ENEMY_HIT";
    public const string SPEED_CHANGED = "SPEED_CHANGED";
}
```

The script in the listing defines a constant for a couple of event messages; the messages are more organized this way, and you don't have to remember and type the message string all over the place.

Now the event messenger system is ready to use, so let's start using it. First we'll communicate from the scene to the HUD, and then we'll go in the other direction.

### 6.4.2 *Broadcasting and listening for events from the scene*

Up to now the score display has displayed a timer as a test of the text display functionality. But we want to display a count of enemies hit, so let's modify the code in UIController. First delete the entire Update() method, because that was the test code. When an enemy dies, it will emit an event, so the following listing makes UIController listen for that event.

**Listing 6.8 Adding event listeners to UIController**

```
...
private int _score;

void Awake() {                                                    Declare which
    Messenger.AddListener(GameEvent.ENEMY_HIT, OnEnemyHit);       method responds to
}                                                                 event ENEMY_HIT.
void OnDestroy() {
    Messenger.RemoveListener(GameEvent.ENEMY_HIT, OnEnemyHit);
}
                                          When an object is destroyed, use
                                          the cleanup listener to avoid errors.
void Start() {
    _score = 0;
    scoreLabel.text = _score.ToString();
                                          Initialize the score to 0.
    settingsPopup.Close();
}

private void OnEnemyHit() {
    _score += 1;
    scoreLabel.text = _score.ToString();    Increment the score in
}                                           response to the event.
...
```

First notice the Awake() and OnDestroy() methods. Much like Start() and Update(), every MonoBehaviour automatically responds when the object awakes or is removed. A listener gets added and removed in Awake()/OnDestroy(). This listener is part of the broadcast messaging system, and it calls OnEnemyHit() when that message is received. OnEnemyHit() increments the score and then puts that value in the score display.

The event listeners are set up in the UI code, so now we need to broadcast that message whenever an enemy is hit. The code to respond to hits is in RayShooter.cs, so emit the message as shown in the following listing.

**Listing 6.9 Broadcast event message from RayShooter**

```
...
if (target != null) {
    target.ReactToHit();                       Message broadcast added
    Messenger.Broadcast(GameEvent.ENEMY_HIT);  to hit response
} else {
...
```

Play the game after adding that message and watch the score display when you shoot an enemy. You should see the count going up every time you make a hit. That covers sending messages from the 3D game to the 2D interface, but we also want an example going in the other direction.

### 6.4.3   *Broadcasting and listening for events from the HUD*

In the previous section, an event was broadcast from the scene and received by the HUD. In a similar way, UI controls can broadcast a message that both players and enemies listen for. In this way, the settings pop-up can affect the settings of the game. Open WanderingAI.cs and add the code from the next listing.

**Listing 6.10   Event listener added to WanderingAI**

```
...
public const float baseSpeed = 3.0f;              Base speed that is adjusted
...                                               by the speed setting
void Awake() {
    Messenger<float>.AddListener(GameEvent.SPEED_CHANGED, OnSpeedChanged);
}
void OnDestroy() {
    Messenger<float>.RemoveListener(GameEvent.SPEED_CHANGED, OnSpeedChanged);
}
...
private void OnSpeedChanged(float value) {         Method that was declared in listener
    speed = baseSpeed * value;                    for event SPEED_CHANGED
}
...
```

`Awake()` and `OnDestroy()` add and remove, respectively, an event listener here, too, but the methods have a value this time. That value is used to set the speed of the wandering AI.

> **TIP**   The code in the previous section just used a generic event, but this messaging system can pass a value along with the message. Supporting a value in the listener is as simple as adding a type definition; note the `<float>` added to the listener command.

Now make the same changes in FPSInput.cs to affect the speed of the player. The code in the next listing is almost exactly the same as that in listing 6.10, except that the player has a different number for `baseSpeed`.

**Listing 6.11   Event listener added to FPSInput**

```
...
public const float baseSpeed = 6.0f;              This value is changed from listing 6.10.
...
void Awake() {
    Messenger<float>.AddListener(GameEvent.SPEED_CHANGED, OnSpeedChanged);
}
void OnDestroy() {
```

```
        Messenger<float>.RemoveListener(GameEvent.SPEED_CHANGED, OnSpeedChanged);
}
...
private void OnSpeedChanged(float value) {
    speed = baseSpeed * value;
}
...
```

Finally, broadcast the speed values from SettingsPopup in response to the slider, as shown in the following listing.

> **Listing 6.12   Broadcast message from SettingsPopup**

```
public void OnSpeedValue(float speed) {
    Messenger<float>.Broadcast(GameEvent.SPEED_CHANGED, speed);        ◁       Send slider value
    ...                                                                         as <float> event
```

Now the enemy and player have their speed changed when you adjust the slider. Hit Play and try it out!

> **Exercise: Changing the speed of spawned enemies**
>
> Currently the speed value is only updated for enemies already in the scene and not for newly spawned enemies; new enemies aren't created at the correct speed setting. I'll leave it as an exercise for you to figure out how to set the speed on spawned enemies. Here's a hint: add a SPEED_CHANGED listener to SceneController, because that script is where enemies are spawned from.

You now know how to build a graphical interface using the new UI tools offered by Unity. This knowledge will come in handy in all future projects, even as we explore different game genres.

## 6.5   Summary

In this chapter you've learned that

- Unity has both an immediate mode GUI system as well as a newer system based on 2D sprites.
- Using 2D sprites for a GUI requires that the scene have a canvas object.
- UI elements can be anchored to relative positions on the adjustable canvas.
- Set the Active property to turn UI elements on and off.
- A decoupled messaging system is a great way to broadcast events between the interface and the scene.

# Creating a third-person 3D game: player movement and animation

**This chapter covers**

- Adding real-time shadows to the scene
- Making the camera orbit around its target
- Changing rotation smoothly using the Lerp algorithm
- Handling ground detection for jumping, ledges, and slopes
- Applying and controlling animation for a lifelike character

In this chapter you'll create another 3D game, but this time you'll be working in a new game genre. If you think back to chapter 2, you built a movement demo for a first-person game. Now you're going to write another movement demo, but this time it'll involve third-person movement. The most important difference is the placement of the camera relative to the player: a player sees through their character's eyes in first-person view, and the camera is placed *outside* the character in third-person view. This view is probably familiar to you from adventure games, like

140

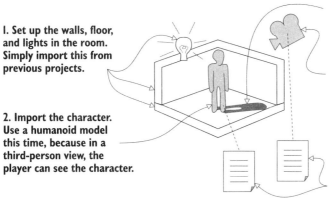

**1. Set up the walls, floor, and lights in the room. Simply import this from previous projects.**

**2. Import the character. Use a humanoid model this time, because in a third-person view, the player can see the character.**

**3. Turn on shadows for this scene. We can see the player now, so shadows are important.**

**4. Position the camera for this demo. The camera should be outside the character, looking down at it.**

**5. Write movement scripts for the camera and player. First write code to orbit the camera around the character, then write code to move the character around (including jumping!).**

**Figure 7.1   Roadmap for the third-person movement demo**

the long-lived Legend of Zelda series, or the more recent Uncharted series of games (refer ahead to figure 7.3 if you want to see a comparison of first-person and third-person views).

The project in this chapter is one of the more visually exciting prototypes we'll build in this book. Figure 7.1 shows how the scene will be constructed. Compare this with the diagram (figure 2.2) of the first-person scene we created in chapter 2.

You can see that the room construction is the same, and the use of scripts is much the same. But the look of the player, as well as the placement of the camera, are different in each case. Again, what defines this as a "third-person" view is that the camera is outside the player's character and looking inward at that character. We'll use a model that looks like a humanoid character (rather than a primitive capsule) because now players can actually see themselves.

Recall that two of the types of art assets discussed in chapter 4 were 3D models and animations. The term *3D model* is almost a synonym for mesh object; the 3D model is the static shape defined by vertices and polygons (that is, mesh geometry). For a humanoid character, this mesh geometry is shaped into a head, arms, legs, and so forth (see figure 7.2).

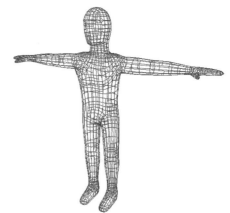

**Figure 7.2   Wireframe view of the model we'll use in this chapter**

As usual, we'll focus on the last step in the roadmap: programming objects in the scene. Here's a recap of our plan of action:

1   Import a character model into the scene.
2   Implement camera controls to look at the character.
3   Write a script that enables the player to run around on the ground.
4   Add the ability to jump to the movement script.
5   Play animations on the model based on its movements.

Copy the project from chapter 2 to modify it, or create a new Unity project (be sure it's set to 3D, not the 2D project from chapter 5) and copy over the scene file from chapter 2's project; either way, also grab the scratch folder from this chapter's download to get the character model we'll use.

> **NOTE**   We're going to build this chapter's project in the walled area from chapter 2. We'll keep the walls and lights but replace the player and all scripts. If you need them, download the sample files from that chapter.

Assuming you're starting with the completed project from chapter 2 (the movement demo, not later projects), let's delete everything we don't need for this chapter. First disconnect the camera from the player in the Hierarchy list (drag the camera object off the player object). Now delete the player object; if you hadn't disconnected the camera first then that would be deleted too, but what you want is to delete only the player capsule and leave the camera. Alternatively, if you already deleted the camera by accident, create a new camera object by selecting GameObject > Camera.

Delete all the scripts as well (which involves removing the script component from the camera as well as deleting the files in the Project view), leaving only the walls, floor, and lights.

## 7.1    Adjusting the camera view for third-person

Before we can write code to make the player move around, we need to put a character in the scene and set up the camera to look at that character. We'll import a faceless humanoid model to use as the player character, and then place the camera above at an angle to look down at the player obliquely. Figure 7.3 compares what the scene looks like in first-person view with what the scene will look like in third-person view (shown with a few large blocks that we'll add in this chapter).

We prepared the scene already, so now let's put a character model into the scene.

### 7.1.1    Importing a character to look at

The scratch folder for this chapter's download includes both the model and the texture; as you'll recall from chapter 4, FBX is the model and TGA is the texture. Import the FBX file into the project; either drag the file into the Project view, or right-click in the Project view and select Import New Asset. Then look in the Inspector to adjust import settings for the model. Later in the chapter you'll adjust imported animations,

First-person demo    Third-person demo

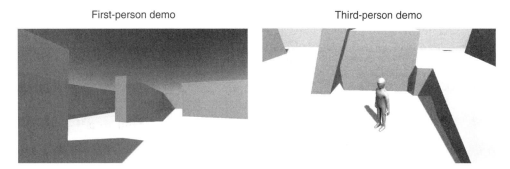

**Figure 7.3   Side-by-side comparison of first-person and third-person views**

but for now you need to make only a couple of adjustments in the Model tab. First change the Scale Factor value to 10 (to partially counteract the File Scale value of .01) so that the model will be the correct size.

A bit farther down you'll find the Normals option (see figure 7.4). This setting controls how lighting and shading appear on the model, using a 3D math concept known as, well, normals.

**DEFINITION**   *Normals* are direction vectors sticking out of polygons that tell the computer which direction the polygon is facing. This facing direction is used for lighting calculations.

The default setting for Normals is Import, which will use the normals defined in the imported mesh geometry. But this particular model doesn't have correctly defined normals and will react in odd ways to lights. Instead, change the setting to Calculate so that Unity will calculate a vector for the facing direction of every polygon.

Once you've adjusted these two settings, click the Apply button in the Inspector. Next import the TGA file into the project and then assign this image as the texture in a material. Select the player material in the Materials folder. Drag the texture image onto the empty texture slot in the Inspector. Once the texture is applied you won't see a dramatic change in the model's color (this texture image is mostly white), but there are shadows painted into the texture that'll improve the look of the model.

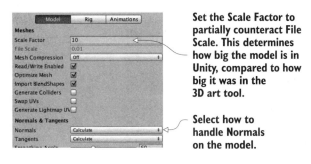

Set the Scale Factor to partially counteract File Scale. This determines how big the model is in Unity, compared to how big it was in the 3D art tool.

Select how to handle Normals on the model.

**Figure 7.4   Import settings for the character model**

With the texture applied, drag the player model from the Project view up into the scene. Position the character at 0, 1.1, 0 so that it'll be in the center of the room and raised up to stand on the floor. Great, we have a third-person character in the scene!

> **NOTE** The imported character has his arms stuck straight out to the sides, rather than the more natural arms-down pose. That's because animations haven't been applied yet; that arms-out position is referred to as the *T-pose* and the standard is for animated characters to default to a T-pose before they're animated.

### 7.1.2    *Adding shadows to the scene*

Before we move on, I want to explain a bit about the shadow being cast by the character. We take shadows for granted in the real world, but shadows aren't guaranteed in the game's virtual world. Fortunately Unity can handle this detail, and shadows are turned on for the default light that comes with new scenes. Select the directional light in your scene and then look in the Inspector for the Shadow Type option. That setting (shown in figure 7.5) is already on Soft Shadows for the default light, but notice the menu also has a No Shadows option.

That's all you need to do to set up shadows in this project, but there's a lot more you should know about shadows in games. Calculating the shadows in a scene is a particularly time-consuming part of computer graphics, so games often cut corners and fake things in various ways in order to achieve the visual look desired. The kind of shadow cast from the character is referred to as *real-time* shadow because the shadow is calculated while the game is running and moves around with moving objects. A perfectly realistic lighting setup would have all objects casting and receiving shadows in real time, but in order for the shadow calculations to run fast enough, real-time shadows are limited in how the shadows look or which lights can even cast shadows. Note that only the directional light is casting shadows in this scene.

Another common way of handling shadows in games is with a technique called *lightmapping*.

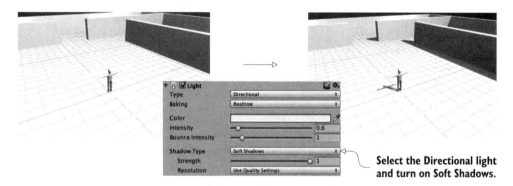

**Figure 7.5   Before and after casting shadows from the directional light**

**DEFINITION** *Lightmaps* are textures applied to the level geometry, with pictures of the shadows baked into the texture image.

**DEFINITION** Drawing shadows onto a model's texture is referred to as *baking* the shadows.

Because these images are generated ahead of time (rather than while the game is running), they can be very elaborate and realistic. On the downside, because the shadows are generated ahead of time, they won't move. Thus, lightmaps are great to use for static level geometry, but they aren't useful for dynamic objects like characters. Lightmaps are generated automatically rather than being painted by hand. The computer calculates how the lights in the scene will illuminate the level while subtle darkness builds up in corners. In Unity, the system for rendering lightmaps is called Enlighten, so you can look up that keyword in Unity's manual.

Whether or not to use real-time shadows or lightmaps isn't an all-or-nothing choice. You can set the Culling Mask property on a light so that real-time shadows are used only for certain objects, allowing you to use the higher-quality lightmaps for other objects in the scene. Similarly, though you almost always want the main character to cast shadows, sometimes you don't want the character to receive shadows; all mesh objects have settings to cast and receive shadows (see figure 7.6).

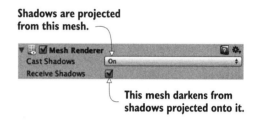

Shadows are projected from this mesh.

This mesh darkens from shadows projected onto it.

**Figure 7.6 The Cast Shadows and Receive Shadows settings in the Inspector**

**DEFINITION** *Culling* is a general term for removing unwanted things. The word comes up a lot in computer graphics in many different contexts, but in this case *culling mask* is the set of objects you want to remove from shadow casting.

All right, now you understand the basics of how to apply shadows to your scenes. Lighting and shading a level can be a big topic unto itself (books about level editing will often spend multiple chapters on lightmapping), but here we restrict ourselves to turning on real-time shadows on one light. And with that, let's turn our attention to the camera.

### 7.1.3 Orbiting the camera around the player character

In the first-person demo, the camera was linked to the player object in Hierarchy view so that they'd rotate together. In third-person movement, though, the player character will be facing different directions independently of the camera. Therefore, you don't want to drag the camera onto the player character in the Hierarchy view this time. Instead, the camera's code will move its position along with the character but will rotate independently of the character.

First, place the camera where you want it to be relative to the player; I went with position 0, 3.5, -3.75 to put the camera above and behind the character (reset rotation to 0, 0, 0 if needed). Then create a script called OrbitCamera (see the next listing). Attach the script component to the camera and then drag the player character into the Target slot of the script. Now you can play the scene to see the camera code in action.

---

**Listing 7.1   Camera script for rotating around a target while looking at it**

```
using UnityEngine;
using System.Collections;

public class OrbitCamera : MonoBehaviour {
    [SerializeField] private Transform target;          ◁ Serialized reference to the
                                                          object to orbit around
    public float rotSpeed = 1.5f;

    private float _rotY;
    private Vector3 _offset;

    void Start() {
        _rotY = transform.eulerAngles.y;                 Store the starting position
        _offset = target.position - transform.position;  ◁ offset between the camera
    }                                                       and the target.

    void LateUpdate() {
        float horInput = Input.GetAxis("Horizontal");    Either rotate the camera
        if (horInput != 0) {                           ◁ slowly using arrow keys...
            _rotY += horInput * rotSpeed;
        } else {                                         ...or rotate quickly
            _rotY += Input.GetAxis("Mouse X") * rotSpeed * 3;  ◁ with the mouse.
        }

        Quaternion rotation = Quaternion.Euler(0, _rotY, 0);
        transform.position = target.position - (rotation * _offset);
        transform.LookAt(target);                        ◁
    }
}
```

Maintain the starting offset, shifted according to the camera's rotation.

No matter where the camera is relative to the target, always face the target.

---

As you're reading through the listing, note the serialized variable for target. The code needs to know what object to orbit the camera around, so this variable is serialized in order to appear within Unity's editor and have the player character linked to it. The next couple of variables are rotation values that are used in the same way as in the camera control code from chapter 2. And there's an _offset value declared; _offset is set within Start() to store the position difference between the camera and target. This way, the relative position of the camera can be maintained while the script runs. In other words, the camera will stay at the initial distance from the character regardless of which way it rotates. The remainder of the code is inside the Late-Update() function.

**TIP** LateUpdate() is another method provided by MonoBehaviour and it's very similar to Update(); it's a method run every frame. The difference, as the name implies, is that LateUpdate() is called on all objects after Update() has run on all objects. This way, we can ensure that the camera updates after the target has moved.

First, the code increments the rotation value based on input controls. This code looks at two different input controls—horizontal arrow keys and horizontal mouse movement—so a conditional is used to switch between them. The code checks if horizontal arrow keys are being pressed; if they are, then it uses that input, but if not, it checks the mouse. By checking the two inputs separately, the code can rotate at different speeds for each type of input.

Next, the code positions the camera based on the position of the target and the rotation value. The transform.position line is probably the biggest "aha!" in this code, because it provides some crucial math that you haven't seen before in previous chapters. Multiplying a position vector by a quaternion (note that the rotation angle was converted to a quaternion using Quaternion.Euler) results in a position that's shifted over according to that rotation. This rotated position vector is then added as the offset from the character's position in order to calculate the position for the camera. Figure 7.7 illustrates the steps of the calculation and provides a detailed breakdown of this rather conceptually dense line of code.

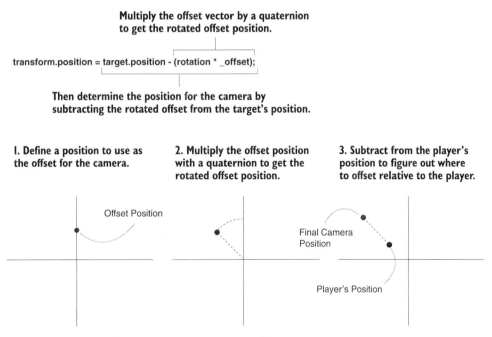

**Figure 7.7 The steps for calculating the camera's position**

**NOTE**   The more mathematically astute among you may be thinking "Hmm, that transforming-between-coordinate-systems thing in chapter 2...can't we do that here, too?" The answer is, yes, we could transform the offset position using a rotated coordinate system to get the rotated offset. But that'd require setting up the rotated coordinate system first, and it's more straightforward not to need that step.

Finally, the code uses the LookAt() method to point the camera at the target; this function points one object (not just cameras) at another object. The rotation value calculated before was used to position the camera at the correct angle around the target, but in that step the camera was only positioned and not rotated. Thus without the final LookAt line, the camera position would orbit around the character but wouldn't necessarily be looking at it. Go ahead and comment out that line to see what happens.

The camera has its script for orbiting around the player character; next up is code that moves the character around.

## 7.2   *Programming camera-relative movement controls*

Now that the character model is imported into Unity and we've written code to control the camera view, it's time to program controls for moving around the scene. Let's program camera-relative controls that'll move the character in various directions when arrow keys are pressed, as well as rotate the character to face those different directions.

> ### What does "camera-relative" mean?
>
> The whole notion of "camera-relative" is a bit nonobvious but very crucial to understand. This is similar to the local versus global distinction mentioned in previous chapters: "left" points in different directions when you mean "left of the local object" or "left of the entire world." In a similar way, when you "move the character to the left," do you mean toward the character's left, or the left side of the screen?
>
> The camera in a first-person game is placed inside the character and moves with it, so no distinction exists between the character's left and the camera's left. A third-person view places the camera outside the character, though, and thus the camera's left may be pointed in a different direction from the character's left. For example, they're literally opposite directions if the camera is looking at the front of the character. Thus we have to decide what we want to have happen in our specific game and controls setup.
>
> Although occasionally games do it the other way, most third-person games make their controls camera-relative. When the player presses the left button, the character moves to the left of the screen, not the character's left. Over time and through experiments with trying out different control schemes, game designers have figured out that players find the controls more intuitive and easier to understand when "left" means "left side of the screen" (which, not coincidentally, is also the player's left).

Implementing camera-relative controls involves two primary steps: first rotate the player character to face the direction of the controls, and then move the character forward. Let's write the code for these two steps next.

### 7.2.1 Rotating the character to face movement direction

First we'll write code to make the character face in the direction of the arrow keys. Create a C# script called RelativeMovement (see listing 7.2). Drag that script onto the player character, and then link the camera to the `target` property of the script component (just like you'd linked the character to the target of the camera script). Now the character will face different directions when you press the controls, facing directions relative to the camera, or stand still when you're not pressing any arrow keys (that is, when rotating using the mouse).

**Listing 7.2  Rotating the character relative to the camera**

```
using UnityEngine;
using System.Collections;

public class RelativeMovement : MonoBehaviour {          This script needs a
    [SerializeField] private Transform target;           reference to the object
                                                         to move relative to.
    void Update() {
        Vector3 movement = Vector3.zero;

        float horInput = Input.GetAxis("Horizontal");    Only handle movement while
        float vertInput = Input.GetAxis("Vertical");     arrow keys are pressed.
        if (horInput != 0 || vertInput != 0) {
            movement.x = horInput;
            movement.z = vertInput;
                                                         Keep the initial rotation to restore
                                                         after finishing with the target object.
            Quaternion tmp = target.rotation;
            target.eulerAngles = new Vector3(0, target.eulerAngles.y, 0);
            movement = target.TransformDirection(movement);
            target.rotation = tmp;

            transform.rotation = Quaternion.LookRotation(movement);
        }
    }
}
```

**Start with vector (0, 0, 0) and add movement components progressively.**

**Transform movement direction from Local to Global coordinates.**

**LookRotation() calculates a quaternion facing in that direction.**

The code in this listing starts the same way as listing 7.1 did, with a serialized variable for `target`. Just as the previous script needed a reference to the object it'd orbit around, this script needs a reference to the object it'll move relative to. Then we get to the `Update()` function. The first line of the function declares a `Vector3` value of 0, 0, 0. It's important to create a zeroed vector and fill in the values later rather than simply create a vector later with the movement values calculated, because the vertical and horizontal movement values will be calculated in different steps and yet they all need to be part of the same vector.

Next we check the input controls, just as we have in previous scripts. Here's where X and Z values are set in the movement vector, for horizontal movement around the scene. Remember that `Input.GetAxis()` returns 0 if no button is pressed, and it varies between 1 and −1 when those keys are being pressed; putting that value in the movement vector sets the movement to the positive or negative direction of that axis (the X-axis is left-right, and the Z-axis is forward-backward).

The next several lines are where the movement vector is adjusted to be camera-relative. Specifically, `TransformDirection()` is used to transform from Local to Global coordinates. This is the same thing we did with `TransformDirection()` in chapter 2, except this time we're transforming from the target's coordinate system instead of from the player's coordinate system. Meanwhile, the code just before and after the `TransformDirection()` line is aligning the coordinate system for our needs: first store the target's rotation to restore later, and then adjust the rotation so that it's only around the Y-axis and not all three axes. Finally perform the transformation and restore the target's rotation.

All of that code was for calculating the movement direction as a vector. The final line of code applies that movement direction to the character by converting the `Vector3` into a `Quaternion` using `Quaternion.LookRotation()` and assigning that value. Try running the game now to see what happens!

---

### Smoothly rotating (interpolating) by using Lerp

Currently, the character's rotation snaps instantly to different facings, but it'd look better if the character smoothly rotated to different facings. We can do so using a mathematical operation called *Lerp*. First add this variable to the script:

```
public float rotSpeed = 15.0f;
```

Then replace the existing `transform.rotation...` line at the end of listing 7.2 with the following code:

```
    ...
    Quaternion direction = Quaternion.LookRotation(movement);
    transform.rotation = Quaternion.Lerp(transform.rotation,
        direction, rotSpeed * Time.deltaTime);
  }
 }
}
```

Now instead of snapping directly to the `LookRotation()` value, that value is used indirectly as the target direction to rotate toward. The `Quaternion.Lerp()` method smoothly rotates between the current and target rotations (with the third parameter controlling how quickly to rotate).

Incidentally, the term for smoothly changing between values is *interpolate*; you can interpolate between two of any kind of value, not just rotation values. Lerp is a quasi-acronym for "linear interpolation," and Unity provides Lerp methods for vectors and float values, too (to interpolate positions, colors, or anything). Quaternions also have a closely related alternative method for interpolation called *Slerp* (for spherical linear interpolation). For slower turns, Slerp rotations may look better than Lerp.

Currently the character is rotating in place without moving; in the next section we'll add code for moving the character around.

> **NOTE** Because sideways facing uses the same keyboard controls as orbiting the camera, the character will slowly rotate while the movement direction points sideways. This doubling up of the controls is desired behavior in this project.

### 7.2.2 *Moving forward in that direction*

As you'll recall from chapter 2, in order to move the player around the scene, we need to add a character controller component to the player object. Select the character and then choose Components > Physics > Character Controller. In the Inspector you should slightly reduce the controller's radius to .4, but otherwise the default settings are all fine for this character model.

The next listing shows what you need to add in the RelativeMovement script.

**Listing 7.3 Adding code to change the player's position**

```
using UnityEngine;
using System.Collections;                          The surrounding lines are
                                                   context for placing the
[RequireComponent(typeof(CharacterController))]    RequireComponent() method.
public class RelativeMovement : MonoBehaviour {
...
public float moveSpeed = 6.0f;
                                                   Here's a pattern you've seen in
private CharacterController _charController;        previous chapters, used for getting
                                                   access to other components.
void Start() {
    _charController = GetComponent<CharacterController>();
}

    void Update() {                                Overwrite the existing X and Z
        ...                                        lines to apply movement speed.
        movement.x = horInput * moveSpeed;
        movement.z = vertInput * moveSpeed;
        movement = Vector3.ClampMagnitude(movement, moveSpeed);
        ...
    }
                                                   Remember to always multiply
        movement *= Time.deltaTime;                movements by deltaTime to make
        _charController.Move(movement);            them frame rate-independent.
    }
}
```

*Limit diagonal movement to the same speed as movement along an axis.*

If you play the game now, you can see the character (stuck in a T-pose) moving around in the scene. Pretty much the entirety of this listing is code you've already seen before, so I'll just review everything briefly.

First, there's a RequireComponent() method at the top of the code. As explained in chapter 2, RequireComponent() will force Unity to make sure the GameObject has a component of the type passed into the command. This line is optional; you don't have to require it, but without this component the script will have errors.

Next there's a movement value declared, followed by getting this script a reference to the character controller. As you'll recall from previous chapters, GetComponent() returns other components attached to the given object, and if the object to search on isn't explicitly defined, then it's assumed to be this.GetComponent() (that is, the same object as this script).

Movement values are assigned based on the input controls. This was in the previous listing, too; the change here is that we also account for the movement speed. Multiply both movement axes by the movement speed, and then use Vector3.Clamp-Magnitude() to limit the vector's magnitude to the movement speed; the clamp is needed because otherwise diagonal movement would have a greater magnitude than movement directly along an axis (picture the sides and hypotenuse of a right triangle).

Finally, at the end we multiply the movement values by deltaTime in order to get frame rate–independent movement (recall that "frame rate-independent" means the character moves at the same speed on different computers with different frame rates). Pass the movement values to CharacterController.Move() to make the movement.

This handles all the horizontal movement; next let's take care of vertical movement.

## 7.3  *Implementing the jump action*

In the previous section we wrote code to make the character run around on the ground. In the chapter introduction, though, I also mentioned making the character jump, so let's do that now. Most third-person games do have a control for jumping. And even if they don't, they almost always have vertical movement from the character falling off ledges. Our code will handle both jumping and falling. Specifically, this code will have gravity pulling the player down at all times, but occasionally an upward jolt will be applied when the player jumps.

Before we write this code, let's add a few raised platforms to the scene. There's currently nothing to jump on or fall off of! Create a couple more cube objects, and then modify their positions and scale to give the player platforms to jump on. In the sample project, I added two cubes and used these settings: Position 5, .75, 5 and Scale 4, 1.5, 4; Position 1, 1.5, 5.5 and Scale 4, 3, 4. Figure 7.8 shows the raised platforms.

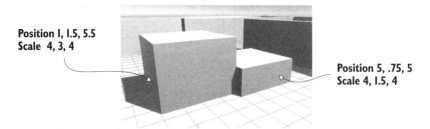

**Figure 7.8   A couple of raised platforms added to the sparse scene**

### 7.3.1 *Applying vertical speed and acceleration*

As mentioned when we first started writing the RelativeMovement script in listing 7.2, the movement values are calculated in separate steps and added to the movement vector progressively. The next listing adds vertical movement to the existing vector.

**Listing 7.4  Adding vertical movement to the RelativeMovement script**

```
...
public float jumpSpeed = 15.0f;
public float gravity = -9.8f;
public float terminalVelocity = -10.0f;
public float minFall = -1.5f;

private float _vertSpeed;
...
void Start() {                          Initialize the vertical speed
    _vertSpeed = minFall;               to the minimum falling speed at
    ...                                 the start of the existing function.
}

    void Update() {                         CharacterController has an
        ...                                 isGrounded property to check if
        if (_charController.isGrounded) {   the controller is on the ground.
            if (Input.GetButtonDown("Jump")) {
                _vertSpeed = jumpSpeed;
            } else {                             If not on the ground, then
                _vertSpeed = minFall;            apply gravity until terminal
            }                                    velocity is reached.
        } else {
            _vertSpeed += gravity * 5 * Time.deltaTime;
            if (_vertSpeed < terminalVelocity) {
                _vertSpeed = terminalVelocity;
            }
        }
        movement.y = _vertSpeed;            The end of listing 7.3, so
                                            that you can see where
        movement *= Time.deltaTime;         this new code goes
        _charController.Move(movement);
    }
}
```

React to the Jump button while on the ground.

As usual we start by adding a few new variables to the top of the script for various movement values, and initialize the values correctly. Then we skip down to just after the big `if` statement for horizontal movement, where we'll add another big `if` statement for vertical movement. Specifically, the code will check if the character is on the ground, because the vertical speed will be adjusted differently depending on whether the character is on the ground. `CharacterController` includes `isGrounded` for checking whether the character is on the ground; this value is `true` if the bottom of the character controller collided with anything in the last frame.

If the character is on the ground, then the vertical speed value (the private variable `_vertSpeed`) should be reset to essentially nothing. The character isn't falling while on the ground, so obviously its vertical speed is 0; if the character then steps off a ledge, we're going to get a nice, natural-looking motion because the falling speed will accelerate from nothing.

> **NOTE**    Well, not *exactly* 0; we're actually setting the vertical speed to `minFall`, a slight downward movement, so that the character will always be pressing down against the ground while running around horizontally. There needs to be some downward force in order to run up and down on uneven terrain.

The exception to this grounded speed value is if the jump button is clicked. In that case, the vertical speed should be set to a high number. The `if` statement checks `GetButtonDown()`, a new input function that works much like `GetAxis()` does, returning the state of the indicated input control. And much like Horizontal and Vertical input axes, the exact key assigned to Jump is defined by going to Input settings under Edit > Project Settings (the default key assignment is Space—that is, the spacebar).

Getting back to the larger `if` condition, if the character is not on the ground, then the vertical speed should be constantly reduced by gravity. Note that this code doesn't simply set the speed value but rather decrements it; this way, it's not a constant speed but rather a downward acceleration, resulting in a realistic falling movement. Jumping will happen in a natural arc, as the character's upward speed gradually reduces to 0 and it starts falling instead.

Finally, the code makes sure the downward speed doesn't exceed terminal velocity. Note that the operator is "less than" and not "greater than," because downward is a negative speed value. Then after the big `if` statement, assign the calculated vertical speed to the Y-axis of the movement vector.

And that's all you need for realistic vertical movement! By applying a constant downward acceleration when the character isn't on the ground, and adjusting the speed appropriately when the character is on the ground, the code creates nice falling behavior. But this all depends on detecting the ground correctly, and there's a subtle glitch we need to fix.

### 7.3.2    *Modifying the ground detection to handle edges and slopes*

As explained in the previous section, the `isGrounded` property of `CharacterController` indicates whether the bottom of the character controller collided with anything in the last frame. Although this approach to detecting the ground works the majority of the time, you'll probably notice that the character seems to float in the air while stepping off edges. That's because the collision area of the character is a surrounding capsule (you can see it when you select the character object) and the bottom of this capsule will still be in contact with the ground when the player steps off the edge of the platform. Figure 7.9 illustrates the problem. This won't do at all!

Similarly, if the character stands on a slope, the current ground detection will cause problematic behavior. Try it now by creating a sloped block against the raised platforms. Create a new cube object and set its transform values to Position -1.5, 1.5, 5 Rotation 0, 0, -25 Scale 1, 4, 4.

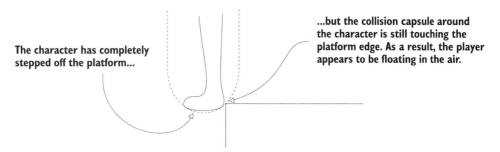

The character has completely stepped off the platform...

...but the collision capsule around the character is still touching the platform edge. As a result, the player appears to be floating in the air.

**Figure 7.9** Diagram showing the character controller capsule touching the platform edge

If you jump onto the slope from the ground, you'll find that you can jump again from midway up the slope and thereby ascend to the top. That's because the slope does touch the bottom of the capsule obliquely and the code currently considers any collision on the bottom to be solid footing. Again, this won't do; the character should slide back down, not have solid footing to jump from.

> **NOTE** Sliding back down is only desired on steep slopes. On shallow slopes, such as uneven ground, we want the player to run around unaffected. If you want one to test on, make a shallow ramp by creating a cube and set it to Position 5.25, .25, .25 Rotation 0, 90, 75 Scale 1, 6, 3.

All these problems have the same root cause: checking for collisions on the bottom of the character isn't a great way of determining if the character is on the ground. Instead, let's use raycasting to detect the ground. In chapter 3 the AI used raycasting to detect obstacles in front of it; let's use the same approach to detect surfaces below the character. Cast a ray straight down from the player's position. If it registers a hit just below the character's feet, that means the player is standing on the ground.

This does introduce a new situation to handle: when the raycast doesn't detect ground below the character but the character controller is colliding with the ground. As in figure 7.9, the capsule still collides with the platform while the character is walking off the edge. Figure 7.10 adds raycasting to the diagram in order to show what will

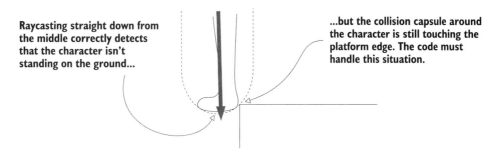

Raycasting straight down from the middle correctly detects that the character isn't standing on the ground...

...but the collision capsule around the character is still touching the platform edge. The code must handle this situation.

**Figure 7.10** Diagram of raycasting downward while stepping off a ledge

happen now: the ray doesn't hit the platform, but the capsule does touch the edge. The code needs to handle this special situation.

In this case, the code should make the character slide off the ledge. The character will still fall (because it's not standing on the ground), but it'll also push away from the point of collision (because it needs to move the capsule away from the platform it's hitting). Thus the code will detect collisions with the character controller and respond to those collisions by nudging away.

The following listing adjusts the vertical movement with everything we just discussed.

---

**Listing 7.5  Using raycasting to detect the ground**

```
...
private ControllerColliderHit _contact;                    Needed to store collision
...                                                        data between functions
        bool hitGround = false;
        RaycastHit hit;
        if (_vertSpeed < 0 &&
            Physics.Raycast(transform.position, Vector3.down, out hit)) {
            float check =
                (_charController.height + _charController.radius) / 1.9f;
            hitGround = hit.distance <= check;
        }

        if (hitGround) {
            if (Input.GetButtonDown("Jump")) {                Instead of using isGrounded,
                _vertSpeed = jumpSpeed;                        check the raycasting result.
            } else {
                _vertSpeed = minFall;
            }
        } else {
            _vertSpeed += gravity * 5 * Time.deltaTime;
            if (_vertSpeed < terminalVelocity) {
                _vertSpeed = terminalVelocity;
            }
            if (_charController.isGrounded) {                 Raycasting didn't detect
                if (Vector3.Dot(movement, _contact.normal) < 0) {   ground, but the capsule
                    movement = _contact.normal * moveSpeed;   is touching the ground.
                } else {
                    movement += _contact.normal * moveSpeed;
                }
            }
        }
        movement.y = _vertSpeed;

        movement *= Time.deltaTime;                          Store the collision data
        _charController.Move(movement);                      in the callback when a
    }                                                        collision is detected.

    void OnControllerColliderHit(ControllerColliderHit hit) {
        _contact = hit;
    }
}
```

**Check if the player is falling.**

**The distance to check against (extend slightly beyond the bottom of the capsule)**

**Respond slightly differently depending on whether the character is facing the contact point.**

This listing contains much of the same code as the previous listing; the new code is interspersed throughout the existing movement script and this listing needed the existing code for context. The first line adds a new variable to the top of the RelativeMovement script. This variable is used to store data about collisions between functions.

The next several lines do raycasting. This code also goes below horizontal movement but before the `if` statement for vertical movement. The actual `Physics.Raycast()` call should be familiar from previous chapters, but the specific parameters are different this time. Although the position to cast a ray from is the same (the character's position), the direction will be down this time instead of forward. Then we check how far away the raycast was when it hit something; if the distance of the hit is at the distance of the character's feet, then the character is standing on the ground, so set `hitGround` to `true`.

> **WARNING** It's a little nonobvious how the check distance is calculated, so let's go over that in detail. First take the height of the character controller (which is the height without the rounded ends) and then add the rounded ends. Divide this value in half because the ray was cast from the middle of the character (that is, already halfway down) to get the distance to the bottom of the character. But we really want to check a little beyond the bottom of the character to account for tiny inaccuracies in the raycasting, so divide by 1.9 instead of 2 to get a distance that's slightly too far.

Having done this raycasting, use `hitGround` instead of `isGrounded` in the `if` statement for vertical movement. Most of the vertical movement code will remain the same, but add code to handle when the character controller collides with the ground even though the player isn't over the ground (that is, when the player walks off the edge of the platform). There's a new `isGrounded` conditional added, but note that it's nested inside the `hitGround` conditional so that `isGrounded` is only checked when `hitGround` doesn't detect the ground.

The collision data includes a `normal` property (again, a normal vector says which way something is facing) that tells us the direction to move away from the point of collision. But one tricky thing is that we want the nudge away from the contact point to be handled differently depending on which direction the player is already moving: when the previous horizontal movement is toward the platform, we want to replace that movement so that the character won't keep moving in the wrong direction; but when facing away from the edge, we want to add to the previous horizontal movement in order to keep the forward momentum away from the edge. The movement vector's facing relative to the point of collision can be determined using the dot product.

> **DEFINITION** The *dot product* is one kind of mathematical operation that can be done on two vectors. Long story short, the dot product of two vectors ranges between -1 and 1, with 1 meaning they point in exactly the same direction, and -1 when they point in exactly opposite directions. Don't confuse "dot product" and "cross product"; the cross product is a different but also commonly seen vector math operation.

Vector3 includes a Dot() function to calculate the dot product of two given vectors. If we calculate the dot product between the movement vector and the collision normal, that will return a negative number when the two directions face away from each other and a positive number when the movement and the collision face the same direction.

Finally, the very end of listing 7.5 adds a new method to the script. In the previous code we were checking the collision normal, but where did that information come from? It turns out that collisions with the character controller are reported through a callback function called OnControllerColliderHit() that MonoBehaviour provides; in order to respond to the collision data anywhere else in the script, that data must be stored in an external variable. That's all the method is doing here: storing the collision data in _contact so that this data can be used within the Update() method.

Now the errors are corrected around platform edges and on slopes. Go ahead and play to test it out by stepping over edges and jumping onto the steep slope. This movement demo is almost complete. The character is moving around the scene correctly, so only one thing remains: animating the character out of the T-pose.

## 7.4 Setting up animations on the player character

Besides the more complex shape defined by mesh geometry, a humanoid character needs animations. In chapter 4 you learned that an animation is a packet of information that defines movement of the associated 3D object. The concrete example I gave was of a character walking around, and that situation is exactly what you're going to be doing now! The character is going to run around the scene, so you'll assign animations that make the arms and legs swing back and forth. Figure 7.11 shows what it'll look like when the character has an animation playing while it moves around the scene.

A good analogy with which to understand 3D animation is to think about puppeteering: 3D models are the puppets, the animator is the puppeteer, and an animation is a recording of the puppet's movements. Animations can be created with a few different approaches; most character animation in modern games (certainly all the animations on this chapter's character) uses a technique called *skeletal animation*.

> **DEFINITION** *Skeletal animation* is a kind of animation where a series of bones are set up inside the model, and then the bones are moved around during the animation. When a bone moves, the model's surface linked to that bone moves along with it.

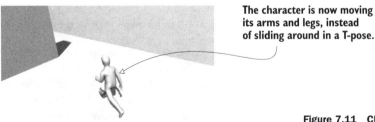

The character is now moving its arms and legs, instead of sliding around in a T-pose.

Figure 7.11  Character moving around with a run animation playing

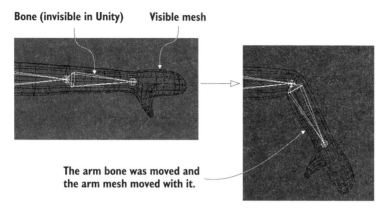

**Bone (invisible in Unity)**     **Visible mesh**

**The arm bone was moved and the arm mesh moved with it.**

**Figure 7.12   Skeletal animation of a humanoid character**

As the name implies, skeletal animation makes the most intuitive sense when simulating the skeleton inside a character (figure 7.12 illustrates this), but the "skeleton" is an abstraction that's useful any time you want a model to bend and flex while still having a definite structure to how it moves (for example, a tentacle that waves around). Although the bones move rigidly, the model surface around the bones can bend and flex.

Achieving the result illustrated in figure 7.11 involves several steps: first define animation clips in the imported file, then set up the controller to play those animation clips, and finally incorporate that animation controller in your code. The animations on the character model will be played back according to the movement scripts you'll write.

Of course the very first thing you need to do, before any of those steps, is turn on the animation system. Select the player model in the Project view to see its Import settings in the Inspector. Select the Animations tab and make sure Import Animation is checked. Then go to the Rig tab and switch Animation Type from Generic to Humanoid (this is a humanoid character, naturally). Note that this last menu also has a Legacy setting; Generic and Humanoid are both settings within the umbrella term Mecanim.

### Explaining Unity's Mecanim animation system

Unity has a sophisticated system for managing animations on models, called Mecanim. Mecanim is based on skeletal animation, the style of animation defined in this chapter. The special name Mecanim identifies the newer, more advanced animation system that was recently added to Unity as a replacement for the older animation system. The older system is still around, identified as Legacy animation, but it may be phased out in a future version of Unity, at which point Mecanim will simply be *the* animation system.

Although the animations we're going to use are all included in the same FBX file as our character model, one of the major advantages of Mecanim's approach is that you

> **(continued)**
>
> can apply animations from other FBX files to a character. For example, all of the human enemies can share a single set of animations. This has a number of advantages, including keeping all your data organized (models can go in one folder, whereas animations go in another folder) as well as saving time spent animating each separate character.

Click the Apply button at the bottom of the Inspector in order to lock these settings onto the imported model and then continue defining animation clips.

> **WARNING**   You may notice a warning (not an error) in the console that says "conversion warning: spine3 is between humanoid transforms." That specific warning isn't a cause for worry; it indicates that the skeleton in the imported model has extra bones beyond the skeleton that Mecanim expects.

### 7.4.1   *Defining animation clips in the imported model*

The first step in setting up animations for our character is defining the various animation clips that'll be played. If you think about a lifelike character, different movements can happen at different times: sometimes the player is running around, sometimes the player is jumping on platforms, and sometimes the character is just standing there with its arms down. Each of these movements is a separate "clip" that can play individually.

Often imported animations come as a single long clip that can be cut up into shorter individual animations. To split up the animation clips, first select the Animations tab in the Inspector. You'll see a Clips panel, shown in figure 7.13; this lists all the defined animation clips, which initially are one imported clip. You'll notice + and – buttons at the bottom of the list; you use these buttons to add and remove clips on the list. Ultimately we need four clips for this character, so add and remove clips as necessary while you work.

When you select a clip, information about that clip (shown in figure 7.14) will appear in the area below the list. The top of this information area shows the name of this clip, and you can type in a new name. Name our first clip `idle`. Define Start and End frames for this animation clip; this allows you to slice a chunk out of the longer imported animation. For the idle animation enter Start 3 and End 141. Next up are the Loop settings.

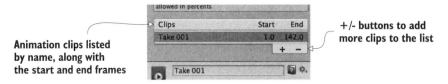

Animation clips listed by name, along with the start and end frames

+/- buttons to add more clips to the list

**Figure 7.13   The Clips list in Animation settings**

The name of the
animation clip;
type a new one here.

Set Start and End
frames for this clip.

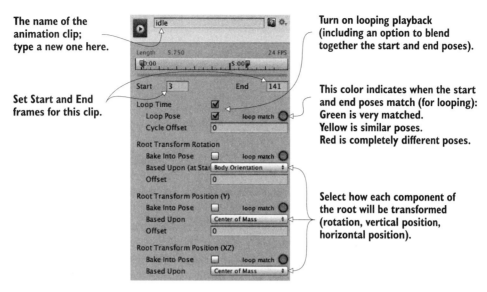

Turn on looping playback
(including an option to blend
together the start and end poses).

This color indicates when the start
and end poses match (for looping):
Green is very matched.
Yellow is similar poses.
Red is completely different poses.

Select how each component of
the root will be transformed
(rotation, vertical position,
horizontal position).

**Figure 7.14　Information about the selected animation clip**

**DEFINITION**　*Loop* refers to a recording that plays over and over repeatedly. A looping animation clip is one that plays again from the start as soon as playback reaches the end.

The idle animation loops, so select both Loop Time and Loop Pose. Incidentally, the green indicator dot tells you when the pose at the beginning of the clip matches the pose at the end for correct looping; this indicator turns yellow when the poses are somewhat off, and it turns red when the start and end poses are completely different.

Below the Loop settings are a series of settings related to the root transform. The word *root* means the same thing for skeletal animation as it does for a hierarchy connected within Unity: the root object is the base object that everything else is connected to. Thus the *animation root* can be thought of as the base of the character, and everything else moves relative to that base. There are a few different settings here for setting up that base, and you may want to experiment here when working with your own animations. For our purposes, though, the settings should be Body Orientation, Center Of Mass, and Center Of Mass, in that order.

Now click Apply and you've added an idle animation clip to your character. Do the same for two more clips: walk starts at frame 144 and ends at 169, and run starts at 171 and ends at 190. All the other settings should be the same as for idle because they're also animation loops.

The fourth animation clip is jump, and the settings for that clip differ a bit. First, this isn't a loop but rather a still pose, so don't select Loop Time. Set the Start and End to 190.5 and 191; this is a single-frame pose, but Unity requires that Start and End be different. The animation preview below won't look quite right because of these tricky numbers, but this pose will look fine in the game.

Click Apply to confirm the new animation clips, and then move on to the next step: creating the animation controller.

### 7.4.2   *Creating the animator controller for these animations*

The next step is to create the animator controller for this character. This step allows us to set up animation states and create transitions between those states. Various animation clips are played during different animation states, and then our scripts will cause the controller to shift between animation states.

This might seem like an odd bit of indirection—putting the abstraction of a controller between our code and the actual playing of animations. You may be familiar with systems where you directly play animations from your code; indeed, the old Legacy animation system worked in exactly that way, with calls like `Play("idle")`. But this indirection enables us to share animations between models, rather than only being able to play animations that are internal to this model. In this chapter we won't take advantage of this ability, but keep in mind that it can be helpful when you're working on a larger project. You can obtain your animations from several sources, including multiple animators, or you can buy individual animations from stores online (such as Unity's Asset Store).

Begin by creating a new animator controller asset (Assets > Create> Animator Controller—not Animation, a different sort of asset). In the Project view you'll see an icon with a funny-looking network of lines on it (see figure 7.15); rename this asset to `player`. Select the character in the scene and you'll notice this object has a component called Animator; any model that can be animated has this component, in addition to the Transform component and whatever else you've added. The Animator component has a Controller slot for you to link a specific animator controller, so drag and drop your new controller asset (and be sure to uncheck Root Motion).

The animator controller is a tree of connected nodes (hence the icon on that asset) that you can see and manipulate by opening the Animator view. This is another view just like Scene or Project (shown in figure 7.16) except this view isn't open by default. Select Animator from the Window menu (be careful not to get confused with the Animation window; that's a separate selection from Animator). The node network displayed here is whichever animator controller is currently selected (or the animator controller on the selected character).

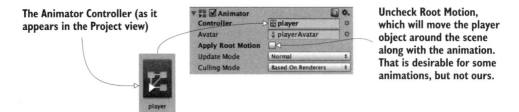

The Animator Controller (as it appears in the Project view)

Uncheck Root Motion, which will move the player object around the scene along with the animation. That is desirable for some animations, but not ours.

player

**Figure 7.15   Animator controller and Animator component**

A series of number or Boolean values can be created here to
control the animations. The currently active state transitions
between states on the graph when these values change.

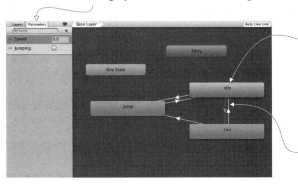

Each node on the graph is an animation
state. The named animation clip plays
when the controller is in that state.

(The orange node is the default
animation state, before any
transitions happen.)

The lines connecting nodes are
"transitions." Transitions have a
direction for transitioning from A to B.

**Figure 7.16   The Animator view with our completed animator controller**

**TIP**   Remember that you can move tabs around in Unity and dock them
wherever you like in order to organize the interface. I like to dock the Animator right next to the Scene and Game windows.

Initially there are only two default nodes, for Entry and Any State. You're not going to
use the Any State node. Instead, you'll drag in animation clips to create new nodes. In
the Project view, click the arrow on the side of the model asset to expand that asset
and see what it contains. Among the contents of this asset are the animation clips you
defined (see figure 7.17), so drag those clips into the Animator view. Don't bother
with the walking animation (that could be useful for other projects) and drag in idle,
run, and jump.

Right-click on the Idle node and select Set As Layer Default State. That node will
turn orange while the other nodes stay gray; the default animation state is where the
network of nodes starts before the game has made any changes. You'll need to link the
nodes together with lines indicating transitions between animation states; right-click
on a node and select Make Transition in order to start dragging out an arrow that you
can click on another node to connect. Connect nodes in the pattern shown in figure
7.16 (be sure to make transitions in both directions for most nodes, but not from
jump to run). These transition lines determine how the animation states connect to
each other, and control the changes from one state to another during the game.

Click the arrow to
expand an asset
and see its contents.

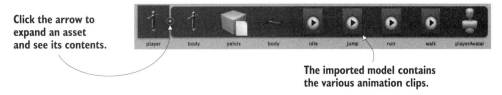

The imported model contains
the various animation clips.

**Figure 7.17   Expanded model asset in Project view**

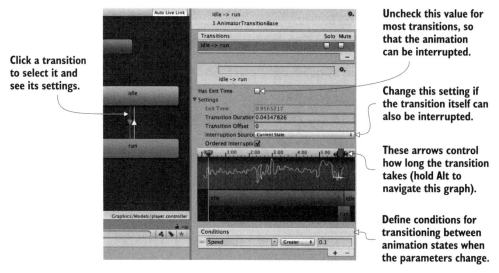

**Figure 7.18 Transition settings in the Inspector**

**WARNING** While working in the Animator view, you may see an error about AnimationStateMachine.TransitionEditionContext.BuildNames. Simply restart Unity; this seems to be a harmless bug.

The transitions rely on a set of controlling values, so let's create those parameters. In the top left of figure 7.16 is a tab called Parameters; click that to see a panel with a + button for adding parameters. Add a float called Speed and a Boolean called Jumping. Those values will be adjusted by our code, and they'll trigger transitions between animation states.

Click on the transition lines to see their settings in the Inspector (see figure 7.18). Here's where we'll adjust how the animation states change when the parameters change. For example, click on the Idle-to-Run transition to adjust the conditions of that transition. Under Conditions, choose Speed, Greater, and 0.1. Turn off Has Exit Time (that would force playing the animation all the way through, as opposed to cutting short immediately when the transition happens). Then click the arrow next to the Settings label in order to see that entire menu; other transitions should be able to interrupt this one, so change the Interruption Source menu from None to Current State. Repeat this for all the transitions in table 7.1.

**Table 7.1 Conditions for all transitions in this animation controller**

| Transition | Condition | Interruption |
|---|---|---|
| Idle-to-Run | Speed greater than .1 | Current State |
| Run-to-Idle | Speed less than .1 | None |

**Table 7.1  Conditions for all transitions in this animation controller** *(continued)*

| Transition | Condition | Interruption |
|---|---|---|
| Idle-to-Jump | Jumping is true | None |
| Run-to-Jump | Jumping is true | None |
| Jump-to-Idle | Jumping is false | None |

In addition to these menu-based settings, there's a complex visual interface shown in figure 7.18 just above the Condition setting. This graph allows you to visually adjust the length in time of a transition. The default transition time looks fine for both transitions between Idle and Run, but all of the transitions to and from Jump should be shorter so that the character will snap faster between the jump animation. The shaded area of the graph indicates how long the transition takes; to see more detail, use Alt+left-click to pan across the graph and Alt+right-click to scale it (these are the same controls as navigating in the Scene view). Use the arrows on top of the shaded area to shrink it to under 4 milliseconds for all three Jump transitions.

Finally, you can perfect the animation network by selecting the animation nodes one at a time and adjusting the ordering of transitions. The Inspector will show a list of all transitions to and from that node; you can drag items in the list (their drag handles are the icon on the left side) to reorder them. Make sure the Jump transition is on top for both the Idle and Run nodes so that the Jump transition has priority over the other transitions. While you're looking at these settings you can also change the playback speed if the animation looks too slow (Run looks better at 1.5 speed).

The animation controller is set up, so now we can operate the animations from the movement script.

### 7.4.3  *Writing code that operates the animator*

Finally, you'll add methods to the RelativeMovement script. As explained earlier, most of the work of setting up animation states is done in the animation controller; only a small amount of code is needed to operate a rich and fluid animation system (see the following listing).

**Listing 7.6  Code for setting values in the Animator component**

```
...
private Animator _animator;
...
_animator = GetComponent<Animator>();          ⟵  Added inside the Start() function
...

        _animator.SetFloat("Speed", movement.sqrMagnitude);   ⟵

        if (hitGround) {                              Just below the entire if
            if (Input.GetButtonDown("Jump")) {        statement for horizontal
                _vertSpeed = jumpSpeed;               movement
```

```
                } else {
                    _vertSpeed = -0.1f;
                    _animator.SetBool("Jumping", false);
                }
            } else {
                _vertSpeed += gravity * 5 * Time.deltaTime;
                if (_vertSpeed < terminalVelocity) {
                    _vertSpeed = terminalVelocity;
                }
                if (_contact != null ) {
                    _animator.SetBool("Jumping", true);
                }

                if (_charController.isGrounded) {
                    if (Vector3.Dot(movement, _contact.normal) < 0) {
                        movement = _contact.normal * moveSpeed;
                    } else {
                        movement += _contact.normal * moveSpeed;
                    }
                }
            }
        }
    ...
```

**Don't trigger this value right at the beginning of the level.**

Again, much of this listing is repeated from previous listings; the animation code is a handful of lines interspersed throughout the existing movement script. Pick out the _animator lines in order to find additions to make in your code.

The script needs a reference to the Animator component, and then the code sets values (either floats or Booleans) on the animator. The only somewhat nonobvious bit of code is the condition (_contact != null) before setting the Jumping Boolean. That condition prevents the animator from playing the jump animation right from the start. Even though the character is technically falling for a split second, there won't be any collision data until the character touches the ground for the first time.

And there you have it! Now we have a nice third-person movement demo, with camera-relative controls and character animation playing.

## 7.5    *Summary*

In this chapter you've learned that

- Third-person view means the camera moves around the character instead of inside the character.
- Simulated shadows, like real-time shadows and lightmaps, improve the graphics.
- Controls can be relative to the camera instead of relative to the character.
- You can improve on Unity's ground detection by casting a ray downward.
- Sophisticated animation set up with Unity's animator controller results in life-like characters.

# Adding interactive devices
# and items within the game

8

---

**This chapter covers**

- Programming doors that the player can open (triggered with a keypress or collision)
- Enabling physics simulations that scatter a stack of boxes
- Building collectible items that players store in their inventory
- Using code to manage game state, such as inventory data
- Equipping and using inventory items

---

Implementing functional items is the next topic we're going to focus on. Previous chapters covered a number of different elements of a complete game: movement, enemies, the user interface, and so forth. But our projects have lacked anything to interact with other than enemies, nor have they had much in the way of game state. In this chapter, you'll learn how to create functional devices like doors. We'll also discuss collecting items, which involves both interacting with objects in the level and tracking game state. Games often have to track state like the player's current stats, progress through objectives, and so on. The player's inventory is an example of this sort of state, so you'll build a code architecture that can keep track of items collected by the player. By the end of this chapter, you'll have built a dynamic space that really feels like a game!

We'll start by exploring devices (such as doors) that are operated with keypresses from the player. After that, you'll write code to detect when the player collides with objects in the level, enabling interactions like pushing objects around or collecting inventory items. Then you'll set up a robust MVC (Model-View-Controller)-style code architecture to manage data for the collected inventory. Finally, you'll program interfaces to make use of the inventory for gameplay, such as requiring a key to open a door.

> **WARNING**  Previous chapters were relatively self-contained and didn't technically require projects from earlier chapters, but this time some of the code listings make edits to scripts from chapter 7. If you skipped directly to this chapter, download the sample project for chapter 7 in order to build on that.

The example project will have these devices and items strewn about the level randomly. A polished game would have a lot of careful design behind the placement of items, but there's no need to carefully plan out a level that only tests functionality. Even so, though the placement of objects will be haphazard, the chapter opening bullets lay out the order in which we'll implement things.

As usual, the explanations build up the code step by step, but if you want to see all the finished code in one place, you can download the sample project.

## 8.1    *Creating doors and other devices*

Although levels in games mostly consist of static walls and scenery, they also usually incorporate a lot of functional devices as well. I'm talking about objects that the player can interact with and operate—things like lights that turn on or a fan that starts turning. The specific devices can vary a lot and are mostly limited only by your imagination, but they almost all use the same sort of code to have the player activate the device. We'll implement a couple of examples in this chapter, and then you should be able to adapt this same code to work with all sorts of other devices.

### 8.1.1    *Doors that open and close on a keypress*

The first kind of device we'll program is a door that opens and closes, and we're going to start with operating the door by pressing a key. There are lots of different kinds of devices you could have in a game, and lots of different ways of operating those devices. We're eventually going to look at a couple of variations, but doors are the most common interactive devices found in games, and using items with a keypress is the most straightforward approach to start with.

The scene has a few spots where a gap exists between walls, so place a new object that blocks the gap. I created a new cube object and then set its transform to Position 2.5 1.5 17 and Scale 5 3 .5, creating the door shown in figure 8.1.

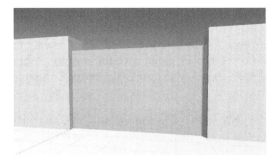

**Figure 8.1   Door object fit into a gap in the wall**

Create a C# script, call it DoorOpenDevice, and put that script on the door object. This code (shown in the next listing) will cause the object to operate as a door.

**Listing 8.1   Script that opens and closes the door on command**

```
using UnityEngine;
using System.Collections;

public class DoorOpenDevice : MonoBehaviour {
    [SerializeField] private Vector3 dPos;

    private bool _open;

    public void Operate() {
        if (_open) {
            Vector3 pos = transform.position - dPos;
            transform.position = pos;
        } else {
            Vector3 pos = transform.position + dPos;
            transform.position = pos;
        }
        _open = !_open;
    }
}
```

> **The position to offset to when the door opens**

> **A Boolean to keep track of the open state of the door**

> **Open or close the door depending on the open state.**

The first variable defines the offset that's applied when the door opens. The door will move this amount when it opens, and then it will subtract this amount when it closes. The second variable is a private Boolean for tracking whether the door is open or closed. In the Operate() method, the object's transform is set to a new position, adding or subtracting the offset depending on whether the door is already open; then _open is toggled on or off.

As with other serialized variables, dPos appears in the Inspector. But this is a Vector3 value, so instead of one input box there are three, all under the one variable name. Type in the relative position of the door when it opens; I decided to have the door slide down to open, so the offset was 0 -2.9 0 (because the door object has a height of 3, moving down 2.9 leaves just a tiny sliver of the door sticking up out of the floor).

> **NOTE**   The transform is applied instantly, but you may prefer seeing the movement when the door opens. As mentioned back in chapter 3, you can use tweens to make objects move smoothly over time. The word *tween* means different things in different contexts, but in game programming it refers to code commands that cause objects to move around; appendix D mentions tweening systems for Unity.

Now other code needs to call `Operate()` to make the door open and close (the single function call handles both cases). We don't yet have that other script on the player; writing that is the next step.

### 8.1.2   *Checking distance and facing before opening the door*

Create a new script and name it DeviceOperator. The following listing implements a control key that operates nearby devices.

**Listing 8.2   Device control key for the player**

```
using UnityEngine;
using System.Collections;

public class DeviceOperator : MonoBehaviour {          How far away from the
  public float radius = 1.5f;                          player to activate devices

  void Update() {                                       Respond to the input button
    if (Input.GetButtonDown("Fire3")) {                defined in Unity's input settings.
      Collider[] hitColliders =
          Physics.OverlapSphere(transform.position, radius);
      foreach (Collider hitCollider in hitColliders) {
        hitCollider.SendMessage("Operate",
          SendMessageOptions.DontRequireReceiver);
      }
    }                                                   SendMessage() tries to call the named
  }                                                     function, regardless of the target's type.
}
```

OverlapSphere() returns a list of nearby objects.

The majority of the script in this listing should look familiar, but a crucial new method is at the center of this code. First, establish a value for how far away to operate devices from. Then, in the `Update()` function, look for keyboard input; since the Jump key is already being used by the RelativeMovement script, this time we'll respond to Fire3 (which is defined in the project's input settings as the left Command key).

Now we get to the crucial new method: `OverlapSphere()`. This method returns an array of all objects that are within a given distance of a given position. By passing in the position of the player and the `radius` variable, this detects all objects near the player. What you actually do with this list can vary (for example, perhaps you just set off a bomb and want to apply an explosive force), but in this situation we want to attempt to call `Operate()` on all nearby objects.

That method is called via `SendMessage()` instead of the typical dot notation, an approach you also saw with UI buttons in previous chapters. As was the case there, the reason to use SendMessage() is because we don't know the exact type of the target object and that command works on all GameObjects. But this time we're going to pass the option DontRequireReceiver to the method. This is because most of the objects returned by OverlapSphere() won't have an Operate() method; normally Send-Message() prints an error message if nothing in the object received the message, but in this case the error messages would be distracting because we already know most objects will ignore the message.

Once the code is written, you can attach this script to the player object. Now you can open and close the door by standing near it and pressing the key.

There's one little detail we can fix. Currently it doesn't matter which way the player is facing, as long as the player is close enough. But we could also adjust the script to only operate devices the player is facing, so let's do that. Recall from chapter 7 that you can calculate the dot product for checking facing. That's a mathematical operation done on a pair of vectors that returns a range between -1 and 1, with 1 meaning they point in exactly the same direction and -1 when they point in exactly opposite directions. The next listing shows the new code in the DeviceOperator script.

**Listing 8.3 Adjusting DeviceOperator to only operate devices that the player is facing**

```
...
foreach (Collider hitCollider in hitColliders) {
    Vector3 direction = hitCollider.transform.position - transform.position;
    if (Vector3.Dot(transform.forward, direction) > .5f) {        <-
        hitCollider.SendMessage("Operate",
            SendMessageOptions.DontRequireReceiver);
    }
}
...
```

Only send the message when facing the right direction

To use the dot product, we first determine the direction to check against. That would be the direction from the player to the object; make a direction vector by subtracting the position of the player from the position of the object. Then call Vector3.Dot() with both that direction vector and the forward direction of the player. When the dot product is close to 1 (specifically, this code checks greater than .5), that means the two vectors are close to pointing in the same direction.

With this adjustment made, the door won't open and close when the player faces away from it, even if the player is close. And this same approach to operating devices can be used with any sort of device. To demonstrate that flexibility, let's create another example device.

### 8.1.3 *Operating a color-changing monitor*

We've created a door that opens and closes, but that same device-operating logic can be used with any sort of device. We're going to create another device that's operated in the same way; this time, we'll create a color-changing display on the wall.

Create a new cube and place it so that one side is barely sticking out of the wall. For example, I went with Position 10.9 1.5 -5. Now create a new script called `ColorChangeDevice` and attach that script (shown in the next listing) to the wall display. Now run up to the wall monitor and hit the same "operate" key as used with the door; you should see the display change color, as figure 8.2 illustrates.

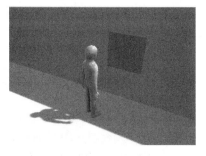

**Figure 8.2   Color-changing display embedded in the wall**

---

**Listing 8.4   Script for a device that changes color**

```
using UnityEngine;
using System.Collections;

public class ColorChangeDevice : MonoBehaviour {      ◁── Declare a method with the
    public void Operate() {                                same name as the door script.
        Color random = new Color(Random.Range(0f,1f),
            Random.Range(0f,1f), Random.Range(0f,1f));
        GetComponent<Renderer>().material.color = random;   ◁── The color is set in
    }                                                           the material attached
}                                                               to the object.
```

The numbers are RGB values that range from 0 to 1.

To start with, declare the same function name as the door script used. "Operate" is the function name that the device operator script uses, so we need to use that name in order for it to be triggered. Inside this function, the code assigns a random color to the object's material (remember, color isn't an attribute of the object itself, but rather the object has a material and that material can have a color).

> **NOTE**   Although the color is defined with Red, Blue, and Green components as is standard in most computer graphics, the values in Unity's `Color` object vary between 0 and 1, instead of 0 and 255, as is common in most places (including Unity's color picker UI).

All right, so we've gone over one approach to interacting with devices in the game and have even implemented a couple of different devices to demonstrate. Another way of interacting with items is by bumping into them, so let's go over that next.

## 8.2   *Interacting with objects by bumping into them*

In the previous section, devices were operated by keyboard input from the player, but that's not the only way players can interact with items in the level. Another very straightforward approach is to respond to collisions with the player. Unity handles most of that for you, by having collision detection and physics built into the game engine. Unity will detect collisions for you, but you still need to program the object to respond.

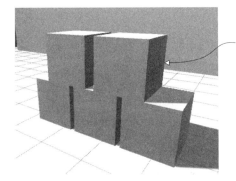

**Each box has a RigidBody
component. Their positions are:**

-4.2  .5  -2.3
-4.2  .5  -1.2
-4.2  .5  -.1
-4.2  1.5  -1.9
-4.2  1.5  -.7

**Figure 8.3   Stack of five
boxes to collide with**

We'll go over three collision responses that are useful for games:

- Push away and fall over
- Trigger a device in the level
- Disappear on contact (for item pickups)

### 8.2.1   *Colliding with physics-enabled obstacles*

To start, we're going to create a pile of boxes and then cause the pile to collapse when the player runs into it. Although the physics calculations involved are complicated, Unity has all of that built in and will scatter the boxes in a realistic way for us.

By default Unity doesn't use its physics simulation to move objects around. That can be enabled by adding a Rigidbody component to the object. This concept was first discussed back in chapter 3, because the enemy's fireballs also needed a Rigidbody component. As I explained in that chapter, Unity's physics system will act only on objects that have a Rigidbody component. Click Add Component and look for Rigidbody under the Physics menu.

Create a new cube object and then add a Rigidbody component to it. Create several such cubes and position them in a neat stack. For example, in the sample download I created five boxes and stacked them into two tiers (see figure 8.3).

The boxes are now ready to react to physics forces. To have the player apply a force to the boxes, make the small addition shown in the following listing to the Relative-Movement script (this is one of the scripts written in the previous chapter) that's on the player.

**Listing 8.5   Adding physics force to the RelativeMovement script**

```
...
public float pushForce = 3.0f;                        Amount of force to apply
...
void OnControllerColliderHit(ControllerColliderHit hit) {
  _contact = hit;

                                                       Check if the collided
                                                       object has a Rigidbody to
  Rigidbody body = hit.collider.attachedRigidbody;     receive physics forces.
```

```
    if (body != null && !body.isKinematic) {
        body.velocity = hit.moveDirection * pushForce;
    }
}
...
```

◁— **Apply velocity to the physics body.**

There's not a ton to explain about this code: whenever the player collides with something, check if the collided object has a Rigidbody component. If so, apply a velocity to that Rigidbody.

Play the game and then run into the pile of boxes; you should see them scatter around realistically. And that's all you had to do to activate physics simulation on a stack of boxes in the scene! Unity has physics simulation built in, so we didn't have to write much code. That simulation can cause objects to move around in response to collisions, but another possible response is firing trigger events, so let's use those trigger events to control the door.

### 8.2.2  *Triggering the door with a pressure plate*

Whereas previously the door was operated by a keypress, this time the door will open and close in response to the character colliding with another object in the scene. Create yet another door and place it in another wall gap (I duplicated the previous door and moved the new door to -2.5 1.5 -17). Now create a new cube to use for the trigger object, and select the Is Trigger  check box for the collider (this step was illustrated when making the fireball in chapter 3). In addition, set the object to the Ignore Raycast layer; the top-right corner of the Inspector has a Layer menu. Finally, you should turn off shadow casting from this object (remember, this setting is under Mesh Renderer when you select the object).

> **WARNING**  These tiny steps are easy to miss but very important: to use an object as a trigger, be sure to turn on Is Trigger. In the Inspector, look for the check box in the Collider component. Also, change the layer to Ignore Raycast so that the trigger object won't show up in raycasting.

> **NOTE**  When trigger objects were first introduced in chapter 3, the object needed to have a Rigidbody component added. Rigidbody wasn't required for the trigger this time because the trigger would be responding to the player (versus colliding with a wall, the earlier situation). In order for triggers to work, either the trigger or the object entering the trigger need to have Unity's physics system enabled; a Rigidbody component fulfills this requirement, but so does the player's CharacterController.

Position and scale the trigger object so that it both encompasses the door and surrounds an area around the door; I used Position -2.5 1.5 -17 (same as the door) and Scale 7.5 3 6. Additionally, you may want to assign a semitransparent material to the object so that you can visually distinguish trigger volumes from solid objects. Create a new material using the Assets menu, and select the new material in the Project view. Looking at the Inspector, the top setting is Rendering Mode (currently set to the default value of Opaque); select Transparent in this menu.

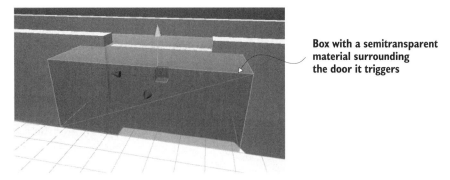

Box with a semitransparent material surrounding the door it triggers

**Figure 8.4   Trigger volume surrounding the door it will trigger**

Now click its color swatch to bring up the Color Picker window. Pick green in the main part of the window, and lower the alpha using the bottom slider. Drag this material from Project onto the object; figure 8.4 shows the trigger with this material.

**DEFINITION**   *Triggers* are often referred to as volumes rather than objects in order to conceptually differentiate solid objects from objects you can move through.

Play the game now and you can freely move through the trigger volume; Unity still registers collisions with the object, but those collisions don't affect the player's movement anymore. To react to the collisions, we need to write code. Specifically, we want this trigger to control the door. Create a new script called DeviceTrigger (see the following listing).

**Listing 8.6   Code for a trigger that controls a device**

```
using UnityEngine;
using System.Collections;

public class DeviceTrigger : MonoBehaviour {
   [SerializeField] private GameObject[] targets;

   void OnTriggerEnter(Collider other) {
      foreach (GameObject target in targets) {
         target.SendMessage("Activate");
      }
   }

   void OnTriggerExit(Collider other) {
      foreach (GameObject target in targets) {
         target.SendMessage("Deactivate");
      }
   }
}
```

List of target objects that this trigger will activate

OnTriggerEnter() is called when another object enters the trigger volume…

…whereas OnTriggerExit() is called when an object leaves the trigger volume.

This listing defines an array of target objects for the trigger; even though it'll only be a list of one most of the time, it's possible to have multiple devices controlled by a single trigger. Loop through the array of targets to send a message to all the targets. This loop happens inside the OnTriggerEnter() and OnTriggerExit() methods. These functions are called once when another object first enters and exits the trigger (as opposed to being called over and over while the object is inside the trigger volume).

Notice that the messages being sent are different than before; now we need to define the functions Activate() and Deactivate() on the door. Add the code in the next listing to the door script.

> **Listing 8.7  Adding activate and deactivate functions to the DoorOpenDevice script**

```
...
public void Activate() {
    if (!_open) {
        Vector3 pos = transform.position + dPos;      Only open the door if it
        transform.position = pos;                     isn't already open.
        _open = true;
    }
}
public void Deactivate() {                            Similarly, only close the door
    if (_open) {                                      if it isn't already closed.
        Vector3 pos = transform.position - dPos;
        transform.position = pos;
        _open = false;
    }
}
...
```

The new Activate() and Deactivate() methods are much the same code as the Operate() method from earlier, except now there are separate functions to open and close the door instead of only one function that handles both cases.

With all the needed code in place you can now use the trigger volume to open and close the door. Put the DeviceTrigger script on the trigger volume and then link the door to the targets property of that script; in the Inspector, first set the size of the array and then drag objects from the Hierarchy view over to slots in the targets array. Because we have only one door that we want to control with this trigger, type 1 in the array's Size field and then drag that door into the target slot.

With all of this done, play the game and watch what happens to the door when the player walks toward and away from it. It'll open and close automatically as the player enters and leaves the trigger volume.

That's another great way to put interactivity into levels! But this trigger volume approach doesn't only work with devices like doors; you can also use this approach to make collectible items.

### 8.2.3  Collecting items scattered around the level

Many games include items that can be picked up by the player. These items include equipment, health packs, and power-ups. The basic mechanism of colliding with items to pick them up is simple; most of the complicated stuff happens after items are picked up, but we'll get to that a bit later.

Create a sphere object and place it hovering at about waist height in an open area of the scene. Make the object small, like Scale .5 .5 .5, but otherwise prepare it like you did with the large trigger volume. Select the Is Trigger setting in the collider, set the object to the Ignore Raycast layer, and then create a new material to give the object a distinct color. Because the object is small, you don't want to make it semitransparent this time, so don't turn down the alpha slider at all. Also, as mentioned in chapter 7, there are settings for removing the shadows cast from this object; whether or not to use the shadows is a judgment call, but for small pickup items like this I prefer to turn them off.

Now that the object in the scene is ready, create a new script to attach to that object. Call the script CollectibleItem (see the following listing).

**Listing 8.8   Script that makes an item delete itself on contact with the player**

```
using UnityEngine;
using System.Collections;

public class CollectibleItem : MonoBehaviour {
    [SerializeField] private string itemName;          Type the name of this
                                                       item in the Inspector.
    void OnTriggerEnter(Collider other) {
        Debug.Log("Item collected: " + itemName);
        Destroy(this.gameObject);
    }
}
```

This script is extremely short and simple. Give the item a name value so that there can be different items in the scene. OnTriggerEnter() destroys itself. There's also a debug message being printed to the console; eventually it will be replaced with useful code.

> **WARNING**  Be sure to call Destroy() on this.gameObject and not this! Don't get confused between the two; this only refers to this script component, whereas this.gameObject refers to the object the script is attached to.

Back in Unity, the variable you added to the code should become visible in the Inspector. Type in a name to identify this item; I went with energy for my first item. Then duplicate the item a few times and change the name of the copies; I also created ore, health, and key (these names must be exact because they'll be used in code later on). Also create separate materials for each item in order to give them distinct colors: I did light blue energy, dark gray ore, pink health, and yellow key.

> **TIP**  Rather than a name like we've done here, items in more complex games often have an identifier used to look up further data. For example, one item might be assigned id 301, and id 301 correlates to such-and-such display name, image, description, and so forth.

Now make prefabs of the items so that you can clone them throughout the level. In chapter 3 I explained that dragging an object from the Hierarchy view down to the Project view will turn that object into a prefab; do that for all four items.

> **NOTE**  The object's name will turn blue in the Hierarchy list; blue names indicate objects that are instances of a prefab. Right-click a prefab instance to pick Select Prefab and select the prefab that the object is an instance of.

Drag out instances of the prefabs and place the items in open areas of the level; even drag out multiple copies of the same item to test with. Play the game and run into items to "collect" them. That's pretty neat, but at the moment nothing happens when you collect an item. We're going to start keeping track of the items collected; to do that, we need to set up the inventory code structure.

## 8.3    *Managing inventory data and game state*

Now that we've programmed the features of collecting items, we need background data managers (similar to web coding patterns) for the game's inventory. The code we'll write will be similar to the MVC architectures behind many web applications. Their advantage is in decoupling data storage from the objects that are displayed on screen, allowing for easier experimentation and iterative development. Even when the data and/or displays are complex, changes in one part of the application don't affect other parts of the application.

That said, such structures vary a lot between different games. Not every game has the same data-management needs, so it wouldn't make sense for Unity to enforce a rule that "Every game must use such-and-such design pattern." It would've been counterproductive to introduce those sorts of concepts too soon, because people would be misled into thinking they need that before they can make any game.

For example, a roleplaying game will have very high data-management needs, so you probably want to implement something like an MVC architecture. A puzzle game, though, has little data to manage, so building a complex decoupled structure of data managers would be overkill. Instead, the game state can be tracked in the scene-specific controller objects (indeed, that's how we handled game state in previous chapters).

In this project we need to manage the player's inventory. Let's set up the code structure for that.

### 8.3.1    *Setting up player and inventory managers*

The general idea here is to split up all the data management into separate, well-defined modules that each manages its own area of responsibility. We're going to create separate modules to maintain player state in `PlayerManager` (things like the player's health) and maintain the inventory list in `InventoryManager`. These data managers will behave like the Model in MVC; the Controller is an invisible object in most scenes (it wasn't needed here, but recall SceneController in previous chapters), and the rest of the scene is analogous to the View.

There will be a higher-level "manager of managers" that keeps track of all the separate modules. Besides keeping a list of all the various managers, this higher-level manager will control the lifecycle of the various managers, especially initializing them at the start. All the other scripts in the game will be able to access these centralized modules by going through the main manager. Specifically, other code can use a number of static properties in the main manager in order to connect with the specific module desired.

### Design patterns for accessing centralized shared modules

Over the years a variety of design patterns have emerged to solve the problem of connecting parts of a program to centralized modules that are shared throughout the program. For example, the Singleton pattern was enshrined in the original "Gang of Four" book about design patterns.

But that pattern has fallen out of favor with many software engineers, so they use alternative patterns like service locator and dependency injection. In my code I use a compromise between the simplicity of static variables and the flexibility of a service locator.

This design leaves the code simple to use while also allowing for swapping in different modules. For example, requesting `InventoryManager` using a singleton will always refer to the exact same class and thus will tightly couple your code to that class; on the other hand, requesting Inventory from a service locator leaves the option to return either `InventoryManager` or `DifferentInventoryManager`. Sometimes it's handy to be able to switch between a number of slightly different versions of the same module (deploying the game on different platforms, for example).

In order for the main manager to reference other modules in a consistent way, these modules must all inherit properties from a common base. We're going to do that with an interface; many programming languages (including C#) allow you to define a sort of blueprint that other classes need to follow. Both `PlayerManager` and `InventoryManager` will implement a common interface (called `IGameManager` in this case) and then the main `Managers` object can treat both `PlayerManager` and `InventoryManager` as type `IGameManager`. Figure 8.5 illustrates the setup I'm describing.

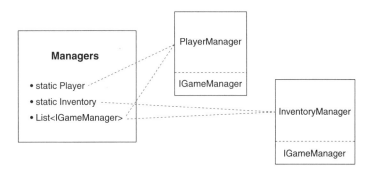

**Figure 8.5  Diagram of the various modules and how they're related**

Incidentally, whereas all of the code architecture I've been talking about consists of invisible modules that exist in the background, Unity still requires scripts to be linked to objects in the scene in order to run that code. As we've done with the scene-specific controllers in previous projects, we're going to create an empty GameObject to link these data managers to.

### 8.3.2   Programming the game managers

All right, so that explained all the concepts behind what we'll do; it's time to write the code. To start with, create a new script called IGameManager (see the next listing).

> **Listing 8.9   Base interface that the data managers will implement**

```
public interface IGameManager {
   ManagerStatus status {get;}

   void Startup();
}
```
⟵ **This is an enum we need to define.**

Hmm, there's barely any code in this file. Note that it doesn't even inherit from `MonoBehaviour`; an interface doesn't do anything on its own and exists only to impose structure on other classes. This interface declares one property (a variable that has a getter function) and one method; both need to be implemented in any class that implements this interface. The `status` property tells the rest of the code whether this module has completed its initialization. The purpose of `Startup()` is to handle initialization of the manager, so initialization tasks happen there and the function sets the manager's status.

Notice that the property is of type `ManagerStatus`; that's an enum we haven't written yet, so create the script ManagerStatus.cs (see the next listing).

> **Listing 8.10   ManagerStatus: possible states for `IGameManager` status**

```
public enum ManagerStatus {
   Shutdown,
   Initializing,
   Started
}
```

This is another file with barely any code in it. This time we're listing the different possible states that managers can be in, thereby enforcing that the `status` property will always be one of these listed values.

Now that IGameManager is written, we can implement it in other scripts. Listings 8.11 and 8.12 contain code for PlayerManager and InventoryManager.

> **Listing 8.11   InventoryManager**

```
using UnityEngine;
using System.Collections;
using System.Collections.Generic;
```
**Import new data structures (used in listing 8.14).**

```
public class InventoryManager : MonoBehaviour, IGameManager {
   public ManagerStatus status {get; private set;}
```
Any long-running startup tasks go here.
> Property can be read from anywhere but only set within this script.
```
   public void Startup() {
      Debug.Log("Inventory manager starting...");
      status = ManagerStatus.Started;
   }
}
```
> For long-running tasks, use status 'Initializing' instead.

**Listing 8.12   PlayerManager**

```
using UnityEngine;
using System.Collections;
using System.Collections.Generic;

public class PlayerManager : MonoBehaviour, IGameManager {
   public ManagerStatus status {get; private set;}
```
> Inherit a class and implement an interface.
```
   public int health {get; private set;}
   public int maxHealth {get; private set;}

   public void Startup() {
      Debug.Log("Player manager starting...");

      health = 50;
      maxHealth = 100;
```
These values could be initialized with saved data.
```
      status = ManagerStatus.Started;
   }

   public void ChangeHealth(int value) {
```
> Other scripts can't set health directly but can call this function.
```
      health += value;
      if (health > maxHealth) {
         health = maxHealth;
      } else if (health < 0) {
         health = 0;
      }

      Debug.Log("Health: " + health + "/" + maxHealth);
   }
}
```

For now, InventoryManager is a shell that will be filled in later, whereas Player-Manager has all the functionality needed for this project. These managers both inherit from the class MonoBehaviour and implement the interface IGameManager. That means the managers both gain all the functionality of MonoBehaviour while also needing to implement the structure imposed by IGameManager. The structure in IGame-Manager was one property and one method, so the managers define those two things.

The status property was defined so that the status could be read from anywhere (the getter is public) but only set within this script (the setter is private). The method in the interface is Startup(), so both managers define that function. In both managers initialization completes right away (InventoryManager doesn't do anything yet, whereas `PlayerManager` sets a couple of values), so the status is set to `Started`. But data modules may have long-running tasks as part of their initialization (such as loading saved data), in which case `Startup()` will launch those tasks and set the manager's status to `Initializing`. Change `status` to `Started` after those tasks complete.

Great—we're finally ready to tie everything together with a main manager-of-managers! Create one more script and call it Managers (see the following listing).

**Listing 8.13  The Manager-of-Managers!**

```
using UnityEngine;
using System.Collections;
using System.Collections.Generic;                    Ensure that the various
                                                     managers exist.
[RequireComponent(typeof(PlayerManager))]
[RequireComponent(typeof(InventoryManager))]
                                                            Static properties that
public class Managers : MonoBehaviour {                     other code uses to
   public static PlayerManager Player {get; private set;}   access managers
   public static InventoryManager Inventory {get; private set;}

   private List<IGameManager> _startSequence;      The list of managers to loop
                                                   through during startup sequence
   void Awake() {
      Player = GetComponent<PlayerManager>();
      Inventory = GetComponent<InventoryManager>();

      _startSequence = new List<IGameManager>();
      _startSequence.Add(Player);
      _startSequence.Add(Inventory);                  Launch the startup
                                                      sequence asynchronously.
      StartCoroutine(StartupManagers());
   }

   private IEnumerator StartupManagers() {
      foreach (IGameManager manager in _startSequence) {
         manager.Startup();
      }

      yield return null;

      int numModules = _startSequence.Count;
      int numReady = 0;
                                                Keep looping until all
                                                managers are started.
      while (numReady < numModules) {
         int lastReady = numReady;
         numReady = 0;

         foreach (IGameManager manager in _startSequence) {
            if (manager.status == ManagerStatus.Started) {
               numReady++;
            }
         }

         if (numReady > lastReady)
            Debug.Log("Progress: " + numReady + "/" + numModules);
```

```
      yield return null;
   }

   Debug.Log("All managers started up");
 }
}
```

→ **Pause for one frame before checking again.**

The most important parts of this pattern are the static properties at the very top. Those enable other scripts to use syntax like `Managers.Player` or `Managers.Inventory` to access the various modules. Those properties are initially empty, but they're filled immediately when the code runs in the `Awake()` method.

> **TIP** Just like `Start()` and `Update()`, `Awake()` is another method automatically provided by `MonoBehaviour`. It's similar to `Start()`, running once when the code first starts running. But in Unity's code-execution sequence, `Awake()` is even sooner than `Start()`, allowing for initialization tasks that absolutely must run before any other code modules.

The `Awake()` method also lists the startup sequence, and then launches the coroutine to start all the managers. Specifically, the function creates a `List` object and then uses `List.Add()` to add the managers.

> **DEFINITION** `List` is a collection data structure provided by C#. List objects are similar to arrays: they're declared with a specific type and store a series of entries in sequence. But a `List` can change size after being created, whereas arrays are created at a static size that can't change later.

> **WARNING** The collection data structures are contained in a new namespace that you must include in the script; notice the additional `using` statement at the top of the script. Don't forget this detail in your scripts!

Because all the managers implement `IGameManager`, this code can list them all as that type and can call the `Startup()` method defined in each. The startup sequence is run as a coroutine so that it will run asynchronously, with other parts of the game proceeding too (for example, a progress bar animated on a startup screen).

The startup function first loops through the entire list of managers and calls `Startup()` on each one. Then it enters a loop that keeps checking whether the managers have started up and won't proceed until they all have. Once all the managers are started, the startup function finally alerts us to this fact before finally completing.

> **TIP** The managers we wrote earlier have such simple initialization that there's no waiting, but in general this coroutine-based startup sequence can elegantly handle long-running asynchronous startup tasks like loading saved data.

Now all of the code structure has been written. Go back to Unity and create a new empty GameObject; as usual with these sorts of empty code objects, position it at 0,0,0 and give the object a descriptive name like `Game Managers`. Attach the script components `Managers`, `PlayerManager`, and `InventoryManager` to this new object.

When you play the game now there should be no visible change in the scene, but in the console you should see a series of messages logging the progress of the startup sequence. Assuming the managers are starting up correctly, it's time to start programming the inventory manager.

### 8.3.3   *Storing inventory in a collection object: List vs. Dictionary*

The actual list of items collected could also be stored as a `List` object. The next listing adds a `List` of items to `InventoryManager`.

> **Listing 8.14   Adding items to InventoryManager**

```
...
private List<string> _items;

public void Startup() {
    Debug.Log("Inventory manager starting...");

    _items = new List<string>();              ◁⌐ Initialize the empty item list.

    status = ManagerStatus.Started;
}

private void DisplayItems() {
    string itemDisplay = "Items: ";           ◁⌐ Print console message
    foreach (string item in _items) {              of the current inventory.
        itemDisplay += item + " ";
    }
    Debug.Log(itemDisplay);
}

public void AddItem(string name) {
    _items.Add(name);                         ◁⌐ Other scripts can't manipulate the
                                                   item list directly but can call this.
    DisplayItems();
}
...
```

Two key additions were made to InventoryManager. One, we added a `List` object to store items in. Two, we added a public method, `AddItem()`, that other code can call. This function adds the item to the list and then prints the list to the console. Now let's make a slight adjustment in the CollectibleItem script to call the new `AddItem()` method (see the following list).

> **Listing 8.15   Using the new `InventoryManager` in CollectibleItem**

```
...
void OnTriggerEnter(Collider other) {
    Managers.Inventory..AddItem(itemName);
    Destroy(this.gameObject);
}
...
```

Now when you run around collecting items, you should see your inventory growing in the console messages. This is pretty cool, but it does expose one limitation of List data structures: as you collect multi-

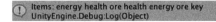

Items: energy health ore health energy ore key
UnityEngine.Debug:Log(Object)

**Figure 8.6   Console message with multiples of the same item listed multiple times**

ples of the same type of item (such as collecting a second Health item), you'll see both copies listed, instead of aggregating all items of the same type (refer to figure 8.6). Depending on your game, you may want the inventory to track each item separately, but in most games the inventory should aggregate multiple copies of the same item. It's possible to accomplish this using List, but it's done more naturally and efficiently using Dictionary instead.

> **DEFINITION**   Dictionary is another collection data structure provided by C#. Entries in the dictionary are accessed by an identifier (or key) rather than by their position in the list. This is similar to a hash table but more flexible, because the keys can be literally any type (for example, "Return the entry for this GameObject").

Change the code in InventoryManager to use Dictionary instead of List. Replace everything from listing 8.14 with the code from the following listing.

**Listing 8.16   Dictionary of items in InventoryManager**

```
...
private Dictionary<string, int> _items;          Dictionary is declared with two
                                                 types: the key and the value.
public void Startup() {
   Debug.Log("Inventory manager starting...");

   _items = new Dictionary<string, int>();

   status = ManagerStatus.Started;
}

private void DisplayItems() {
   string itemDisplay = "Items: ";
   foreach (KeyValuePair<string, int> item in _items) {
      itemDisplay += item.Key + "(" + item.Value + ") ";
   }
   Debug.Log(itemDisplay);
}

public void AddItem(string name) {
   if (_items.ContainsKey(name)) {
      _items[name] += 1;                          Check for existing entries
   } else {                                        before entering new data.
      _items[name] = 1;
   }

   DisplayItems();
}
...
```

Overall this code looks the same as before, but a few tricky differences exist. If you aren't already familiar with `Dictionary` data structures, note that it was declared with two types. Whereas `List` was declared with only one type (the type of values that'll be listed), a `Dictionary` declares both the type of keys (that is, what the identifiers will be) and the type of values.

A bit more logic exists in the `AddItem()` method. Whereas before every item was appended to the `List`, now we need to check if the `Dictionary` already contains that item; that's what the `ContainsKey()` method is for. If it's a new entry, then we'll start the count at 1, but if the entry already exists, then increment the stored value.

Play with the new code and you'll see the inventory messages have an aggregated count of each item (refer to figure 8.7).

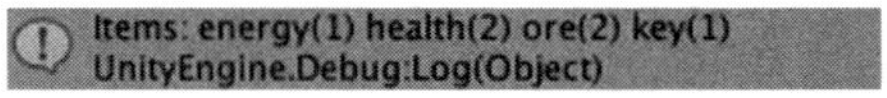

Whew, finally, collected items are managed in the player's inventory! This probably seems like a lot of code to handle a relatively simple problem, and if this were the entire purpose then, yeah, it was over-engineered. The point of this elaborate code architecture, though, is to keep all the data in separate flexible modules, a useful pattern once the game gets more complex. For example, now we can write UI displays and the separate parts of the code will be much easier to handle.

**Figure 8.7   Console message with multiples of the same item aggregated**

## 8.4   *Inventory UI for using and equipping items*

The collection of items in your inventory can be used in multiple ways within the game, but all of those uses first rely on some sort of inventory UI so that players can see their collected items. Then, once the inventory is being shown to the player, you can program interactivity into the UI by enabling players to click on their items. Again, we'll program a couple of specific examples (equipping a key and consuming health packs), and then you should be able to adapt this code to work with other types of items.

> **NOTE**   As mentioned in chapter 6, Unity has both an older immediate mode GUI and a newer sprite-based UI system. We'll use the immediate mode GUI in this chapter because that system is faster to implement and requires less setup; less setup is great for practice exercises. The sprite-based UI system is more polished, though, and for an actual game you'd want a more polished interface.

### 8.4.1   *Displaying inventory items in the UI*

To show the items in a UI display, we first need to add a couple more methods to InventoryManager. Right now the item list is private and only accessible within the manager; in order to display the list, though, that information must have public methods for accessing the data. Add two methods shown in the following listing to InventoryManager.

**Listing 8.17   Adding data access methods to InventoryManager**

```
...
public List<string> GetItemList() {
   List<string> list = new List<string>(_items.Keys);         Returns a List of all
   return list;                                                the Dictionary keys
}

public int GetItemCount(string name) {                 Returns how many of that
   if (_items.ContainsKey(name)) {                     item are in inventory
      return _items[name];
   }
   return 0;
}
...
```

The GetItemList() method returns a list of items in the inventory. You might be thinking, "Wait a minute, didn't we just spend lots of effort to convert the inventory away from a List?" The difference now is that each type of item will only appear once in the list. If the inventory contains two health packs, for example, the name "health" will still only appear once in the list. That's because the List was created from the keys in the Dictionary, not from every individual item.

The GetItemCount() method returns a count of how many of a given item are in the inventory. For example, call GetItemCount("health") to ask "How many health packs are in the inventory?" This way, the UI can display a number of each item along with displaying each item.

With these methods added to InventoryManager, we can create the UI display. Let's display all the items in a horizontal row across the top of the screen. The items will be displayed using icons, so we need to import those images into the project. Unity handles assets in a special way if those assets are in a folder called Resources.

> **TIP**   Assets placed into the Resources folder can be loaded in code using the method Resources.Load(). Otherwise, assets can only be placed in scenes through Unity's editor.

Figure 8.8 shows the four icon images, along with the directory structure showing where to put those images. Create a folder called Resources and then create a folder called Icons inside it.

The icons are all set up, so create a new empty GameObject named Controller and then assign it a new script called BasicUI (see the next listing).

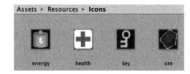

**Figure 8.8   Image assets for equipment icons placed inside the Resources folder**

**Listing 8.18   BasicUI displays the inventory**

```
using UnityEngine;
using System.Collections;
using System.Collections.Generic;
```

```
public class BasicUI : MonoBehaviour {
    void OnGUI() {
        int posX = 10;
        int posY = 10;
        int width = 100;
        int height = 30;
        int buffer = 10;

        List<string> itemList = Managers.Inventory.GetItemList();
        if (itemList.Count == 0) {
            GUI.Box(new Rect(posX, posY, width, height), "No Items");
        }
        foreach (string item in itemList) {
            int count = Managers.Inventory.GetItemCount(item);
            Texture2D image = Resources.Load<Texture2D>("Icons/"+item);
            GUI.Box(new Rect(posX, posY, width, height),
                    new GUIContent("(" + count + ")", image));
            posX += width+buffer;
        }
    }
}
```

**Display a message if the inventory is empty.**

**The method that loads assets from the Resources folder**

**Shift sideways each time through the loop.**

This listing displays the collected items in a horizontal row (see figure 8.9) along with displaying the number collected. As mentioned in chapter 3, every `MonoBehaviour` automatically responds to an `OnGUI()` method. That function runs every frame right after the 3D scene is rendered.

Inside `OnGUI()`, first define a bunch of values for positioning UI elements. These values are incremented when we loop through all the items in order to position UI elements in a row.

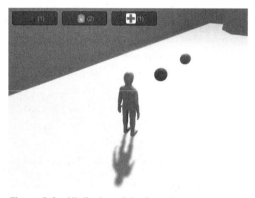

**Figure 8.9  UI display of the inventory**

The specific UI element drawn is `GUI.Box`; those are noninteractive displays that show text and images inside boxes.

The method `Resources.Load()` is used to load assets from the Resources folder. This method is a handy way to load assets by name; notice that the name of the item is passed as a parameter. We have to specify a type to load; otherwise, the return value for that method is a generic object.

The UI shows us what items have been collected. Now we can actually use the items.

### 8.4.2 *Equipping a key to use on locked doors*

Let's go over a couple of examples of using inventory items so that you can extrapolate out to any type of item you want. The first example involves equipping a key required to open the door.

At the moment, the DeviceTrigger script doesn't pay attention to your items (because that script was written before the inventory code). The next listing shows how to adjust that script.

> **Listing 8.19  Requiring a key in DeviceTrigger**

```
...
public bool requireKey;

void OnTriggerEnter(Collider other) {
   if (requireKey && Managers.Inventory.equippedItem != "key") {
      return;
   }
...
```

As you can see, all that's needed is a new public variable in the script and a condition that looks for an equipped key. The requireKey Boolean appears as a check box in the Inspector so that you can require a key from some triggers but not others. The condition at the beginning of OnTriggerEnter() checks for an equipped key in InventoryManager; that requires that you add the code from the next listing to InventoryManager.

> **Listing 8.20  Equipping code for InventoryManager**

```
...
public string equippedItem {get; private set;}
...
public bool EquipItem(string name) {
   if (_items.ContainsKey(name) && equippedItem != name) {      ◁  Check that inventory
      equippedItem = name;                                          has the item and it
      Debug.Log("Equipped " + name);                               isn't already equipped.
      return true;
   }

   equippedItem = null;
   Debug.Log("Unequipped");
   return false;
}
...
```

At the top add the equippedItem property that gets checked by other code. Then add the public method EquipItem() to allow other code to change which item is equipped. That method equips an item if it isn't already equipped, or *unequips* if that item is already equipped.

Finally, in order for the player to equip an item, add that functionality to the UI. The following listing will add a row of buttons for that purpose.

> **Listing 8.21  Equip functionality added to BasicUI**

```
...
   foreach (string item in itemList) {      ◁  Italicized code was already in the
                                                script, shown here for reference.
```

```
        int count = Managers.Inventory.GetItemCount(item);
        GUI.Box(new Rect(posX, posY, width, height), item +
                "(" + count + ")");
        posX += width+buffer;
    }

    string equipped = Managers.Inventory.equippedItem;      Display the currently
    if (equipped != null) {                                 equipped item.
        posX = Screen.width - (width+buffer);
        Texture2D image = Resources.Load("Icons/"+equipped) as Texture2D;
        GUI.Box(new Rect(posX, posY, width, height),
                new GUIContent("Equipped", image));
    }

    posX = 10;
    posY += height+buffer;                                  Loop through all items
                                                            to make buttons.
    foreach (string item in itemList) {
        if (GUI.Button(new Rect(posX, posY, width, height),
                "Equip "+item)) {                           Run the contained code
            Managers.Inventory.EquipItem(item);             if the button is clicked.
        }
        posX += width+buffer;
    }
  }
}
```

`GUI.Box()` is used again to display the equipped item. But that element is noninteractive, so the row of Equip buttons is drawn using `GUI.Button()` instead. That method creates a button that executes the code inside the `if` statement when clicked.

With all the needed code in place, select the `requireKey` option in DeviceTrigger and then play the game. Try running into the trigger volume before equipping a key; nothing happens. Now collect a key and click the button to equip it; running into the trigger volume opens the door.

Just for fun, you could put a key at Position -11 5 -14 to add a simple gameplay challenge to see if you can figure out how to reach the key. Whether or not you try that, let's move on to using health packs.

### 8.4.3   *Restoring the player's health by consuming health packs*

Using items to restore the player's health is another generally useful example. That requires two code changes: a new method in InventoryManager and a new button in the UI (see listings 8.22 and 8.23, respectively).

**Listing 8.22   New method in InventoryManager**

```
...
public bool ConsumeItem(string name) {          Check if the item is in inventory.
    if (_items.ContainsKey(name)) {
        _items[name]--;
        if (_items[name] == 0) {                Remove the entry if
            _items.Remove(name);                the count goes to 0.
```

```
        }
    } else {
        Debug.Log("cannot consume " + name);
        return false;
    }

    DisplayItems();
    return true;
}
...
```

Response if that item
isn't in inventory

**Listing 8.23   Adding a health item to Basic UI**

```
...
        foreach (string item in itemList) {
            if (GUI.Button(new Rect(posX, posY, width, height),
                    "Equip "+item)) {
                Managers.Inventory.EquipItem(item);
            }

            if (item == "health") {
                if (GUI.Button(new Rect(posX, posY + height+buffer, width,
                        height), "Use Health")) {
                    Managers.Inventory.ConsumeItem("health");
                    Managers.Player.ChangeHealth(25);
                }
            }

            posX += width+buffer;
        }
    }
}
```

Italicized code was
already in script, shown
here for reference.

Start of
new code

Run the contained
code if the button
is clicked.

The new `ConsumeItem()` method is pretty much the reverse of `AddItem()`; it checks for an item in the inventory and decrements if the item is found. It has responses to a couple of tricky cases, such as if the item count decrements to 0. The UI code calls this new inventory method, and it calls the `ChangeHealth()` method that `PlayerManager` has had from the beginning.

If you collect some health items and then use them, you'll see health messages appear in the console. And there you go—multiple examples of how to use inventory items!

## 8.5   Summary

In this chapter you've learned that

- Both keypresses and collision triggers can be used to operate devices.
- Objects with physics enabled can respond to collision forces or trigger volumes.
- Complex game state is managed via special objects that can be accessed globally.
- Collections of objects can be organized in List or Dictionary data structures.
- Tracking the equip state of items can be used to affect other parts of the game.

# Part 3

## Strong finish

Y ou know a fair amount about Unity by now. You know how to program the player's controls, how to create enemies that wander around, and how to add interactive devices to the game. You even know how to build a game using both 2D and 3D graphics! That's *almost* everything you need to know in order to develop a complete game, but not quite. You still need to learn about a few final tasks like putting audio in the game, and you need to understand how to put together all the disparate pieces we've been working with.

This is the home stretch, with just four chapters left!

# Connecting your
# game to the internet

---

**This chapter covers**

- Generating visuals for the sky using a skybox
- Downloading data using WWW objects in coroutines
- Parsing common data formats like XML and JSON
- Displaying images downloaded from the internet
- Sending data to a web server

---

In this chapter you'll learn how to send and receive data over a network. The projects built in previous chapters represented a variety of game genres, but all have been isolated to the player's machine. As you know, connecting to the internet and exchanging data is increasingly important for games in all genres. Many games exist almost entirely over the internet, with constant connection to a community of other players; games of this sort are referred to as MMOs (massively multiplayer online) and are most widely known through MMORPGs (MMO role-playing games). Even when a game doesn't require such constant connectivity, modern video games usually incorporate features like reporting scores to a global list of high scores. Unity provides support for such networking, so we'll be going over those features.

Unity supports multiple approaches to network communication, since different approaches are better suited to different needs. However, this chapter will mostly cover the most general sort of internet communication: issuing HTTP requests.

### What are HTTP requests?

I assume most readers know what HTTP requests are, but here's a quick primer just in case: HTTP is a communication protocol for sending requests to and receiving responses from web servers. For example, when you click a link on a web page, your browser (the client) sends out a request to a specific address, and then that server responds with the new page. HTTP requests can be set to a variety of methods, in particular either GET or POST to retrieve or to send data.

HTTP requests are reliable, and that's why the majority of the internet is built around them. The requests themselves, as well as the infrastructure for handling such requests, are designed to be robust and handle a wide range of failures in the network.

In an online game built around HTTP requests, the game developed in Unity is essentially a thick client that communicates with the server in an Ajax style. As a good comparison, imagine how a modern single-page web application works (as opposed to old-school web development based on web pages generated server-side). The familiarity of this approach can be misleading for experienced web developers. Video games often have much more stringent performance requirements than web applications, and these differences can affect design decisions.

> **WARNING**  Time scales can be vastly different between web apps and video-games. Half a second can seem like a short wait for updating a website, but pausing even just a fraction of that time can be excruciating in the middle of a high-intensity action game. The concept of "fast" is definitely relative to the situation.

Online games usually connect to a server specifically intended for that game; for learning purposes, however, we'll connect to some freely available internet data sources, including both weather data and images we can download. The last section of this chapter does require you to set up a custom web server; that section is optional because of that requirement, although I'll explain an easy way to do it with open-source software.

The plan for this chapter is to go over multiple uses of HTTP requests so that you can learn how they work within Unity:

1  Set up an outdoor scene (in particular, build a sky that can react to the weather data).
2  Write code to request weather data from the internet.
3  Parse the response and then modify the scene based on the data.

4  Download and display an image from the internet.
5  Post data to your own server (in this case, a log of what the weather was).

The actual game that you'll use for this chapter's project matters little. Everything in this chapter will add new scripts to an existing project and won't modify any of the existing code. For the sample code, I used the movement demo from chapter 2, mostly so that we can see the sky in first-person view when it gets modified. The project for this chapter isn't directly tied into the gameplay, but obviously for most games you create you would want the networking tied to the gameplay (for example, spawning enemies based on responses from the server).

On to the first step!

## 9.1 Creating an outdoor scene

Because we're going to be downloading weather data, we'll first set up an outdoor area where the weather will be visible. The trickiest part of that will be the sky, but first let's take a moment to apply outdoors-looking textures on the level geometry.

Just as in chapter 4, I obtained a couple images from www.cgtextures.com to apply to the walls and floor of the level. Remember to change the size of the downloaded images to a power of 2, such as 256x256. Then import the images into the Unity project, create materials, and assign the images to the materials (that is, drag an image into the texture slot of the material). Drag the materials onto the walls or floor in the scene, and increase tiling in the material (try numbers like 8 or 9 in one or both directions) so that the image won't be stretched in an ugly way.

Once the ground and walls are taken care of, it's time to address the sky.

### 9.1.1 Generating sky visuals using a skybox

Start by importing the skybox images as you did in chapter 4: go to www.93i.de to download skybox images. This time get the images for the DarkStormy set in addition to TropicalSunnyDay (the sky will be more complex in this project). Import these textures into the Project view, and (as explained in chapter 4) set their Wrap Mode to Clamp.

Now create a new material to use for this skybox. At the top of the settings for this material, click the Shader menu in order to see the drop-down list with all the available shaders. Move down to the Skybox section and choose 6-Sided in that submenu. With this shader active, the material now has six texture slots (instead of only the small Albedo texture slot that the standard shader had).

Drag the SunnyDay skybox images to the texture slots of the new material. The names of the images correspond to the texture slot to assign them to (top, front, and so on) Once all six textures are linked up, you can use this new material as the skybox for the scene.

Assign this skybox material in the Lighting window (Window > Lighting). Assign the material for your skybox to the Skybox slot at the top of the window (either drag the material over or click the little circle button next to the slot). Hit Play and you should see something like figure 9.1.

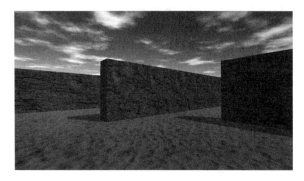

**Figure 9.1   Scene with background pictures of the sky**

Great, now you have an outdoors scene! A skybox is an elegant way to create the illusion of a vast atmosphere surrounding the player. But the skybox shader built into Unity does have one significant limitation: the images can never change, resulting in a sky that appears completely static. We'll address that limitation by creating a new custom shader.

### 9.1.2   *Setting up an atmosphere that's controlled by code*

The images in the TropicalSunnyDay set look great for a sunny day, but what if we want to transition between sunny and overcast weather? This will require a second set of sky images (some pictures of a cloudy sky) so we need a new shader for the skybox.

As explained in chapter 4, a shader is a short program with instructions for how to render the image. That implies that you can program new shaders, and that is in fact the case. We're going to create a new shader that takes two sets of skybox images and transitions between them. Fortunately a shader for this purpose already exists in the Unify Community wiki's collection of scripts: http://wiki.unity3d.com/index.php ?title=SkyboxBlended

In Unity create a new shader script: go to the Create menu just like when you create a new C# script, but select a standard Shader instead. Name the asset `Skybox-Blended` and then double-click the shader to open the script. Copy the code from that wiki page and paste it into the shader script. The top line says `Shader  "Skybox/Blended"`, which tells Unity to add the new shader into the shader list under the Skybox category (the same category as the regular skybox).

> **NOTE**   We're not going to go over all the details of the shader program right now. Shader programming is a pretty advanced computer graphics topic and thus outside the scope of this book. You may want to look that up after you've finished this book; if so, start here: http://docs.unity3d.com/Manual/Shaders Overview.html

Now you can set your material to the Skybox Blended shader. There are 12 texture slots, in two sets of six images. Assign TropicalSunnyDay images to the first six textures just as before; for the remaining textures, use the DarkStormy set of skybox images.

This new shader also added a Blend slider near the top of the settings. The Blend value controls how much of each set of skybox images you want to display; when you adjust the slider from one side to the other, the skybox transitions from sunny to overcast. You can test by adjusting the slider and playing the game, but manually adjusting the sky isn't terribly helpful while the game is running, so let's write some code to transition the sky.

Create an empty object in the scene and name it `Controller`. Create a new script and name it WeatherController. Drag that script onto the empty object, and then write the following listing in that script.

---

**Listing 9.1  WeatherController script that transitions from sunny to overcast**

```
using UnityEngine;
using System.Collections;

public class WeatherController : MonoBehaviour {         Reference the material in Project
   [SerializeField] private Material sky;                 view, not only objects in the scene.
   [SerializeField] private Light sun;

   private float _fullIntensity;

   private float _cloudValue = 0f;

   void Start() {                          Initial intensity of the light is
      _fullIntensity = sun.intensity;      considered "full" intensity.
   }

   void Update() {                         Increment the value every frame
      SetOvercast(_cloudValue);            for a continuous transition.
      _cloudValue += .005f;
   }                                       Adjust both the material's Blend
                                           value and the light's intensity.
   private void SetOvercast(float value) {
      sky.SetFloat("_Blend", value);
      sun.intensity = _fullIntensity - (_fullIntensity * value);
   }
}
```

---

I'll point out a number of things in this code, but the key new method is `SetFloat()`, which appears almost at the bottom. Everything up to that point should be fairly familiar, but that one is new. The method sets a number value on the material. *Which* value specifically is the first parameter to that method. In this case, the material has a property called `Blend` (note that material properties in code start with an underscore).

As for the rest of the code, a few variables are defined, including both the material and a light. For the material you want to reference the blended skybox material we just created, but what's with the light? That's so that the scene will also darken when transitioning from sunny to overcast; as the Blend value increases, we'll turn down the light. The directional light in the scene acts as the main light and provides illumination everywhere; drag that light into the Inspector.

> **NOTE**   The advanced lighting system (called Enlighten) in Unity takes the sky-box into account in order to achieve realistic results. However, this lighting approach won't work right with a changing skybox, so you may want to turn it off. In the Lighting window you can turn off Continuous Baking (this term was defined in chapter 7) at the bottom; now it will only update when you click the button. Set the Blend of the skybox to the middle for an average look, and then click Build at the bottom of the Lighting window to bake lightmaps (lighting information was saved in a new folder that's named after the scene).

When the script starts, it initializes the intensity of the light. The script will store the starting value and consider that to be "full" intensity. This full intensity will be used later in the script when dimming the light.

Then the code increments a value every frame and uses that value to adjust the sky. Specifically, it calls `SetOvercast()` every frame, and that function encapsulates the multiple adjustments made to the scene. I've already explained what `SetFloat()` is doing so we won't go over that again, and the last line adjusts the intensity of the light.

Now play the scene to watch the code running. You'll see what figure 9.2 depicts: over a couple of seconds you'll see the scene transition from a sunny day to dark and overcast.

> **WARNING**   One unexpected quirk about Unity is that the "Blend" change on the material is permanent. Unity resets objects in the scene when the game stops running, but assets that were linked directly from the Project view (such as the skybox material) are changed permanently. This only happens within Unity's editor (changes don't carry over between plays after the game is deployed outside the editor) and thus can result in frustrating bugs if you forget about it.

It's pretty cool watching the scene transition from sunny to overcast. But this was all just a setup for the actual goal: having the weather in the game sync up to real-world weather conditions. For that, we need to start downloading weather data from the internet.

Sunny before transition                                   Overcast after transition

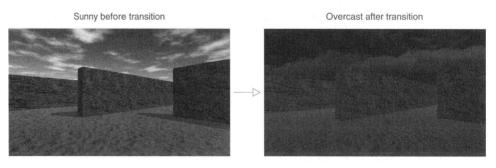

**Figure 9.2   Before and after: scene transition from sunny to overcast**

## 9.2   Downloading weather data from an internet service

Now that we have the outdoors scene set up, we can write code that will download weather data and modify the scene based on that data. This task will provide a good example of retrieving data using HTTP requests. A web service for free weather data is OpenWeatherMap; you'll use their API (application programming interface, a way to access their service using code commands instead of a graphical interface) located at http://openweathermap.org/api

> **DEFINITION**   A *web service* or *web API* is a server connected to the internet that returns data upon request. There's no technical difference between a web API and a website; a website is a web service that happens to return the data for a web page, and browsers interpret HTML data as a visible document.

The code you'll write will be structured around the same Managers architecture from chapter 8. This time you'll have a WeatherManager class that gets initialized from the central manager-of-managers. WeatherManager will be in charge of retrieving and storing weather data, but to do so it'll need the ability to communicate with the internet.

To accomplish that, you'll create a utility class called NetworkService. NetworkService will handle the details of connecting to the internet and making HTTP requests. WeatherManager can then tell NetworkService to make those requests and pass back the response. Figure 9.3 shows how this code structure will operate.

For this to work, obviously WeatherManager will need to have access to the NetworkService object. You're going to address this by creating the object in Managers and then injecting the NetworkService object into the various managers when they're initialized. In this way not only will WeatherManager have a reference to the NetworkService, but so will any other managers you create later.

To start bringing over the Managers code architecture from chapter 8, first copy over ManagerStatus and IGameManager (remember that IGameManager is the interface that all managers must implement, whereas ManagerStatus is an enum that IGameManager uses). You'll need to modify IGameManager slightly to accommodate the new NetworkService class, so create a new script called NetworkService (leave it empty for now; you'll fill it in later) and then adjust IGameManager as shown in listing 9.2.

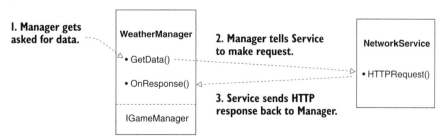

**Figure 9.3   Diagram showing how the networking code will be structured**

**Listing 9.2   Adjusting `IGameManager` to include `NetworkService`**

```
public interface IGameManager {
   ManagerStatus status {get;}

   void Startup(NetworkService service);
}
```
The Startup function now takes one parameter: the injected object.

Next let's create WeatherManager to implement this slightly adjusted interface. Create a new C# script (see the following listing).

**Listing 9.3   Initial script for `WeatherManager`**

```
using UnityEngine;
using System.Collections;
using System.Collections.Generic;

public class WeatherManager : MonoBehaviour, IGameManager {
   public ManagerStatus status {get; private set;}

   // Add cloud value here (listing 9.8)
   private NetworkService _network;

   public void Startup(NetworkService service) {
      Debug.Log("Weather manager starting...");

      _network = service;

      status = ManagerStatus.Started;
   }
}
```
Store the injected NetworkService object.

This initial pass at WeatherManager doesn't really do anything. For now it's just the minimum amount that IGameManager requires that the class implements: declare the status property from the interface, as well as implement the Startup() function. You'll fill in this empty framework over the next few sections. Finally, copy over Managers from chapter 8 and adjust it to start up WeatherManager (see the next listing).

**Listing 9.4   Managers.cs adjusted to initialize `WeatherManager`**

```
using UnityEngine;
using System.Collections;
using System.Collections.Generic;

[RequireComponent(typeof(WeatherManager))]

public class Managers : MonoBehaviour {
   public static WeatherManager Weather {get; private set;}

   private List<IGameManager> _startSequence;

   void Awake() {
      Weather = GetComponent<WeatherManager>();

      _startSequence = new List<IGameManager>();
      _startSequence.Add(Weather);
```
Require the new manager instead of player and inventory.

```
        StartCoroutine(StartupManagers());
    }

    private IEnumerator StartupManagers() {                      Instantiate NetworkService
        NetworkService network = new NetworkService();    ◁     to inject in all managers.

        foreach (IGameManager manager in _startSequence) {
            manager.Startup(network);                     ◁      Pass the network service to
        }                                                        managers during startup.

        yield return null;

        int numModules = _startSequence.Count;
        int numReady = 0;

        while (numReady < numModules) {
            int lastReady = numReady;
            numReady = 0;

            foreach (IGameManager manager in _startSequence) {
                if (manager.status == ManagerStatus.Started) {
                    numReady++;
                }
            }

            if (numReady > lastReady)
                Debug.Log("Progress: " + numReady + "/" + numModules);

            yield return null;
        }

        Debug.Log("All managers started up");
    }
}
```

And that's everything needed codewise for the Managers code architecture. As you
have in previous chapters, create the game managers object in the scene and then
attach both Managers and WeatherManager to the empty object. Even though the
manager isn't doing anything yet, you can see startup messages in the console when
it's set up correctly.

Whew, there were quite a few "boilerplate" things to get out of the way! Now we
can get on with writing the networking code.

### 9.2.1 *Requesting WWW data using coroutines*

NetworkService is currently an empty script, so you can write code in it to make HTTP
requests. The primary class you need to know about is WWW. Unity provides the WWW
class to communicate with the internet. Instantiating a WWW object using a URL will
send a request to that URL.

Coroutines can work with the WWW class to wait for the request to complete. Coroutines were first introduced back in chapter 3, where we used them to pause some code
for a set period of time. Recall the explanation given there: coroutines are special
functions that seemingly run in the background of a program, in a repeated cycle of
running partway and then returning to the rest of the program. When used along with

the StartCoroutine() method, the yield keyword causes the coroutine to temporarily pause, handing back the program flow and picking up again from that point next frame.

In chapter 3 the coroutines yielded at WaitForSeconds(), an object that caused the function to pause for a specific number of seconds. Yielding a coroutine with WWW will pause the function until that network request completes. The program flow here is similar to making asynchronous Ajax calls in a web application: first you send a request, then you continue with the rest of the program, and after some time you receive a response.

**THAT WAS THE THEORY; NOW LET'S WRITE THE CODE**

All right, let's implement this stuff in our code. First open the NetworkService script and replace the default template with the contents of the following listing.

**Listing 9.5   Making HTTP requests in NetworkService**

```
using UnityEngine;
using System.Collections;
using System;

public class NetworkService {                          URL to send request to
    private const string xmlApi =
"http://api.openweathermap.org/data/2.5/weather?q=Chicago,us&mode=xml";

    private bool IsResponseValid(WWW www) {
        if (www.error != null) {                       Check for errors in the response.
            Debug.Log("bad connection");
            return false;
        }
        else if (string.IsNullOrEmpty(www.text)) {
            Debug.Log("bad data");
            return false;
        }
        else {   // all good
            return true;
        }
    }

    private IEnumerator CallAPI(string url, Action<string> callback) {
        WWW www = new WWW(url);                         HTTP request sent by
        yield return www;                              creating a WWW object

        if (!IsResponseValid(www))
            yield break;                               Delegate can be called just
                                                       like the original function
        callback(www.text);
    }

    public IEnumerator GetWeatherXML(Action<string> callback) {
        return CallAPI(xmlApi, callback);
    }                                                  yield cascades through coroutine
}                                                      methods that call each other.
```

Pause while downloading.

Break out of the coroutine if error

Remember the code design explained earlier: WeatherManager will tell Network-Service to go fetch data. Thus all this code doesn't actually run yet; you're setting up code that will be called by WeatherManager a bit later. To explore this code listing, let's start at the bottom and work our way up.

### WRITING COROUTINE METHODS THAT CASCADE THROUGH EACH OTHER

GetWeatherXML() is the coroutine method that outside code can use to tell Network-Service to make an HTTP request. Notice that this function has IEnumerator for its return type; methods used in coroutines must have IEnumerator declared as the return type.

It might look odd at first that GetWeatherXML() doesn't have a yield statement. Coroutines are paused by the yield statement, which implies that every coroutine must yield somewhere. It turns out that the yielding can cascade through multiple methods. If the initial coroutine method itself calls another method, and that other method yields part of the way through, then the coroutine will pause inside that second method and resume there. Thus the yield statement in CallAPI() pauses the coroutine that was started in GetWeatherXML(); figure 9.4 shows this code flow.

The next potential head-scratcher is the callback parameter of type Action.

### UNDERSTANDING HOW THE CALLBACK WORKS

When the coroutine is started, the method is called with a parameter called callback, and callback has the type Action. But what is an Action?

> **DEFINITION** The type Action is a delegate (C# has a few approaches to delegates, but this one is the simplest). Delegates are references to some other method/function. They allow you to store the function (or rather a pointer to the function) in a variable and to pass that function as a parameter to another function.

If you're unfamiliar with the concept of delegates, realize that they enable you to pass around functions just as you do numbers and strings. Without delegates, you can't pass around functions to call later—you can only directly call the function then. With delegates you can tell code about other methods to call later. This is useful for many purposes, especially for implementing callback functions.

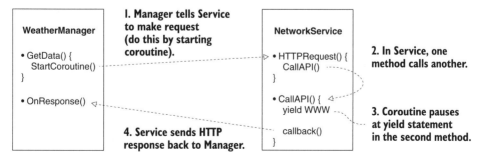

**Figure 9.4** Diagram showing how the network coroutine works

> **DEFINITION** A *callback* is a function used to communicate back to the calling object. Object A could tell Object B about one of the methods in A. B could later call A's method to communicate back to A.

For example, in this case the callback is used to communicate the response data back after waiting for the HTTP request to complete. In `CallAPI()` the code first makes an HTTP request, then yields until that request completes, and finally uses `callback()` to send back the response.

Note the `<>` syntax used with the `Action` keyword; the type written in the angle brackets declares the parameters required to fit this `Action`. In other words, the function this `Action` points to must take parameters matching the declared type. In this case the parameter is a single string, so the callback method must have a signature like this:

```
MethodName(string value)
```

The concept of a callback may make more sense after you've seen it in action, which you will in listing 9.6; this initial explanation is so that you'll recognize what's going on when you see that additional code.

The rest of listing 9.5 is pretty straightforward. `IsResponseValid()` checks for errors in the HTTP response. There are two kinds of errors: the request could've failed due to a bad internet connection, or the data returned could be malformed in some way. A `const` value is declared with the URL to make the request to. (Incidentally, you can change this URL to get weather for different locations.)

### MAKING USE OF THE NETWORKING CODE

That wraps up the code in `NetworkService`. Now let's use `NetworkService` in WeatherManager; the next listing shows the additions to that script.

---

**Listing 9.6  Adjusting WeatherManager to use `NetworkService`**

```
...
public void Startup(NetworkService service) {
   Debug.Log("Weather manager starting...");

   _network = service;                                          Start loading data
   StartCoroutine(_network.GetWeatherXML(OnXMLDataLoaded));     from the internet.

   status = ManagerStatus.Initializing;          Instead of Started, make
}                                                 the status Initializing.

public void OnXMLDataLoaded(string data) {        Callback method once
   Debug.Log(data);                               the data is loaded

   status = ManagerStatus.Started;
}
...
```

Three primary changes are made to the code in this manager: starting a coroutine to download data from the internet, setting a different startup status, and defining a callback method to receive the response.

Starting the coroutine is simple. Most of the complexity behind coroutines was already handled in `NetworkService`, so calling `StartCoroutine()` is all you need to do here. Then you set a different startup status, because the manager isn't actually finished initializing; it needs to receive data from the internet before startup is complete.

> **WARNING** Always start networking methods using `StartCoroutine()`; don't just call the function normally. This can be easy to forget because creating `WWW` objects outside of a coroutine doesn't generate any sort of compiler error.

When you call the `StartCoroutine()` method, you need to invoke the method. That is, actually type the parentheses—()—and don't just provide the name of the function. In this case, the coroutine method needs a callback function as its one parameter, so let's define that function. We'll use `OnXMLDataLoaded()` for the callback; notice that this method has a string parameter, which fits the `Action<string>` declaration from `NetworkService`. The callback function doesn't do a lot right now; the debug line simply prints the received data to the console to verify that the data was received correctly. Then the last line of the function changes the startup status of the manager to say that it's completely started up.

Hit Play to run the code. Assuming you have a solid internet connection, you should see a bunch of data appear in the console. This data is simply a long string, but the string is formatted in a specific way that we can make use of.

### 9.2.2 Parsing XML

Data that exists as a long string usually has individual bits of information embedded within the string. You extract those bits of information by parsing the string.

> **DEFINITION** *Parsing* means analyzing a chunk of data and dividing it up into separate pieces of information.

In order to parse the string, it needs to be formatted in a way that allows you (or rather, the parser code) to identify separate pieces. There are a couple of standard formats commonly used to transfer data over the internet; the most common standard format is XML.

> **DEFINITION** *XML* stands for Extensible Markup Language. It's a set of rules for encoding documents in a structured way, similar to HTML web pages.

Fortunately, Unity (or rather Mono, the code framework built into Unity) provides functionality for parsing XML. The weather data we requested is formatted in XML, so we're going to add code to `WeatherManager` to parse the response and extract the cloudiness. Put the URL into a web browser in order to see the code; there's a lot there, but we're only interested in the node that contains something like `<clouds value="40" name="scattered clouds"/>`.

In addition to adding code to parse XML, we're going to make use of the same messenger system we did in chapter 6. That's because once the weather data is downloaded and parsed, we still need to inform the scene about that. Create a script called `Messenger` and paste in the code from this page on the Unify wiki: http://wiki.unity3d.com/index.php/CSharpMessenger_Extended

Then you need to create a script called GameEvent (see the next listing). As explained in chapter 6, this messenger system is great for providing a decoupled way of communicating events to the rest of the program.

### Listing 9.7    GameEvent code

```
public static class GameEvent {
    public const string WEATHER_UPDATED = "WEATHER_UPDATED";
}
```

Once the messenger system is in place, adjust WeatherManager as shown in the following listing.

### Listing 9.8    Parsing XML in WeatherManager

```
...
using System;                          Be sure to add needed
using System.Xml;                      using statements.
...
public float cloudValue {get; private set;}     Cloudiness is modified internally
...                                             but read-only elsewhere.
public void OnXMLDataLoaded(string data) {
    XmlDocument doc = new XmlDocument();
    doc.LoadXml(data);                          Parse XML into a
    XmlNode root = doc.DocumentElement;         searchable structure.

    XmlNode node = root.SelectSingleNode("clouds");
    string value = node.Attributes["value"].Value;      Pull out a single
    cloudValue = Convert.ToInt32(value) / 100f;         node from the data.
    Debug.Log("Value: " + cloudValue);

    Messenger.Broadcast(GameEvent.WEATHER_UPDATED);     Broadcast message to
                                                        inform the other scripts.
    status = ManagerStatus.Started;
}
...
```

Convert the value to a 0-1 float.

You can see that the most important changes were made inside `OnXMLDataLoaded()`. Previously this method simply logged the data to the console to verify that data was coming through correctly. This listing adds a lot of code to parse the XML.

First create a new empty XML document; this is an empty container that you can fill with a parsed XML structure. The next line parses the data string into a structure contained by the XML document. Then we start at the root of the XML tree so that everything can search up the tree in subsequent code.

At this point you can search for nodes within the XML structure in order to pull out individual bits of information. In this case, `<clouds>` is the only node we're interested in. First find that node in the XML document, and then extract the `value` attribute from that node. This data defines the cloud value as a 0-100 integer, but we're going to need it as a 0-1 float in order to adjust the scene later. Converting that is a simple bit of math added to the code.

Finally, after extracting out the cloudiness value from the full data, broadcast a message that the weather data has been updated. Currently nothing is listening for that message, but the broadcaster doesn't need to know anything about listeners (indeed, that's the entire point of a decoupled messenger system). Later we'll add a listener to the scene.

Great—we've written code to parse XML data! But before we move on to applying this value to the visible scene, I want to go over another option for data transfer.

### 9.2.3 *Parsing JSON*

Before continuing to the next step in the project, let's explore an alternative format for transferring data. XML is one common format for data transferred over the internet, but another common format is called JSON.

> **DEFINITION** *JSON* stands for JavaScript Object Notation. Similar in purpose to XML, JSON was designed to be a lightweight alternative. Although the syntax for JSON was originally derived from JavaScript, the format is not language-specific and is readily used with a variety of programming languages.

Unlike XML, Mono doesn't come with a parser for this format. There are a number of good JSON parsers available that you could download, such as MiniJSON (https://gist.github.com/darktable/1411710). Create a script called MiniJSON and paste in that code. Now you can use this library to parse JSON data. We've been getting XML from the OpenWeatherMap API, but as it happens they can also send the same data formatted as JSON. To do that, modify `NetworkService` according to the next listing.

> **Listing 9.9   Making `NetworkService` request JSON instead of XML**

```
...
private const string jsonApi =
"http://api.openweathermap.org/data/2.5/weather?q=Chicago,us";
...                                                                    The URL is slightly
public IEnumerator GetWeatherJSON(Action<string> callback) {          different this time.
    return CallAPI(jsonApi, callback);
}
...
```

This is pretty much the same as the code to download XML data, except that the URL is slightly different. The data returned from this request has the same values, but it's formatted differently. This time we're looking for a chunk like `"clouds":{"all":40}`.

There wasn't a ton of additional code required this time. That's because we set up the code for requests into nicely parceled separate functions, so every subsequent

HTTP request will be easy to add. Nice! Now let's modify `WeatherManager` to request JSON data instead of XML (see the following listing).

---

**Listing 9.10   Modifying `WeatherManager` to request JSON instead**

```
...
using MiniJSON;                                        Be sure to add needed
...                                                    using statement.
public void Startup(NetworkService service) {
   Debug.Log("Weather manager starting...");

   _network = service;                                          Network
   StartCoroutine(_network.GetWeatherJSON(OnJSONDataLoaded));   request
                                                                changed
   status = ManagerStatus.Initializing;
}
...
public void OnJSONDataLoaded(string data) {        Instead of custom XML container,
   Dictionary<string, object> dict;                parse into Dictionary
   dict = Json.Deserialize(data) as Dictionary<string,object>;

   Dictionary<string, object> clouds =
      (Dictionary<string,object>)dict["clouds"];
   cloudValue = (long)clouds["all"] / 100f;      The syntax has changed,
   Debug.Log("Value: " + cloudValue);            but this code is still doing
                                                 the same things.
   Messenger.Broadcast(GameEvent.WEATHER_UPDATED);

   status = ManagerStatus.Started;
}
...
```

---

As you can see, the code for working with JSON looks similar to the code for XML. The only real difference is that this JSON parser works with a standard `Dictionary` instead of a custom document container like XML did. There's a command to deserialize, and that may be an unfamiliar word.

> **DEFINITION**   *Deserialize* means pretty much the same thing as parse. This is the reverse of *serialize*, which means to encode a batch of data into a form that can be transferred and stored, such as a JSON string.

Aside from the different syntax, all the steps are exactly the same. Extract the value from the data chunk (for some reason the value is called `all` this time, but that's just a quirk of the API) and do some simple math to convert the value to a 0-1 float.

With that done, it's time to apply the value to the visible scene.

### 9.2.4   *Affecting the scene based on Weather Data*

Regardless of exactly how the data is formatted, once the cloudiness value is extracted from the response data, we can use that value in the `SetOvercast()` method of `WeatherController`. Whether XML or JSON, the data string ultimately gets parsed into a series of words and numbers. The `SetOvercast()` method takes a number as a parameter. In section 9.1.2 we used a number incremented every frame, but we could just as easily use the number returned by the weather API.

The next listing shows the full WeatherController script again after modifications.

**Listing 9.11  WeatherController that reacts to downloaded weather data**

```
using UnityEngine;
using System.Collections;

public class WeatherController : MonoBehaviour {
    [SerializeField] private Material sky;
    [SerializeField] private Light sun;

    private float _fullIntensity;
                                          ┌ Add/Remove event listeners.
    void Awake() {                     ⤺
        Messenger.AddListener(GameEvent.WEATHER_UPDATED, OnWeatherUpdated);
    }
    void OnDestroy() {
        Messenger.RemoveListener(GameEvent.WEATHER_UPDATED, OnWeatherUpdated);
    }

    void Start() {
        _fullIntensity = sun.intensity;
    }
                                               Use the cloudiness value
    private void OnWeatherUpdated() {           from WeatherManager.
        SetOvercast(Managers.Weather.cloudValue);   ⤺
    }

    private void SetOvercast(float value) {
        sky.SetFloat("_Blend", value);
        sun.intensity = _fullIntensity - (_fullIntensity * value);
    }
}
```

Notice that the changes aren't only additions; several bits of test code got removed. Specifically, we removed the local cloudiness value that was incremented every frame; we don't need that anymore, because we'll use the value from `WeatherManager`.

A listener gets added and removed in `Awake()`/`OnDestroy()` (these are `MonoBehaviour`'s functions called when the object awakes or is removed). This listener is part of the broadcast messaging system, and it calls `OnWeatherUpdated()` when that message is received. `OnWeatherUpdated()` retrieves the cloudiness value from `WeatherManager` and calls `SetOvercast()` using that value. In this way, the appearance of the scene is controlled by downloaded weather data.

Run the scene now and you'll see the sky update according to the cloudiness in the weather data. You may see it take time to request the weather; in a real game, you'd probably want to hide the scene behind a loading screen until the sky updates.

**Game networking beyond HTTP**

HTTP requests are robust and reliable, but the latency between making a request and receiving a response can be a little slow for many games. HTTP requests are therefore a good way of doing relatively slow-paced messages to a server (such as moves in a turn-based game, or submission of high scores for any game), but something like a multiplayer FPS would need a different approach to networking.

These different approaches involve various communication technologies, as well as techniques to compensate for lag. For example, Unity uses the RakNet networking library through a system called remote procedure calls (RPCs).

The cutting edge for networked action games is a complex topic that goes beyond the scope of this book. You can look up more information on your own, starting here: http://docs.unity3d.com/Manual/NetworkReferenceGuide.html.

Now that you know how to get numerical and string data from the internet, let's do the same thing with an image.

## 9.3    *Adding a networked billboard*

Although the responses from a web API are almost always text strings formatted in XML or JSON, many other sorts of data are transferred over the internet. Besides text data, the most common kind of data requested is images. Unity's WWW object can be used to download images, too.

You're going to learn about this task by creating a billboard that displays an image downloaded from the internet. You need to code two steps: downloading an image to display, and applying that image to the billboard object. Then, as a third step, you'll improve the code so that the image will be stored to use on multiple billboards.

### 9.3.1    *Loading images from the internet*

First let's write the code to download an image. You're going to download some public domain landscape photography (see figure 9.5) to test with. The downloaded image won't be visible on the billboard yet; I'll show you a script to display the image in the next section, but before that, let's get code in place that will retrieve the image.

The code architecture for downloading an image looks much the same as the architecture

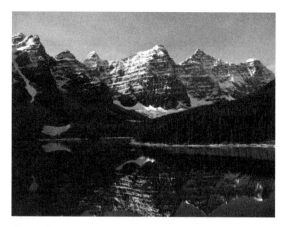

**Figure 9.5   Image of Moraine Lake in Banff National Park, Canada**

for downloading data. A new manager module (called `ImagesManager`) will be in charge of downloaded images to be displayed. Once again, the details of connecting to the internet and sending HTTP requests will be handled in `NetworkService`, and `ImagesManager` will call upon `NetworkService` to download images for it.

The first addition to code is in NetworkService. The following listing adds image downloading to that script.

**Listing 9.12    Downloading an image in NetworkService**

```
...
private const string webImage =
"http://upload.wikimedia.org/wikipedia/commons/c/c5/
    Moraine_Lake_17092005.jpg";
...
public IEnumerator DownloadImage(Action<Texture2D> callback) {
    WWW www = new WWW(webImage);
    yield return www;
    callback(www.texture);
}
...
```

> ◁ **Put this const up near the top with the other URLs.**

> ◁ **This callback takes a Texture2D instead of a string.**

The code that downloads an image looks almost identical to the code for downloading data. The primary difference is the type of callback method; note that the callback takes a Texture2D this time instead of a string. That's because you're sending back the relevant response: you downloaded a string of data before—now you're downloading an image. The next listing contains code for the new `ImagesManager`. Create a new script and enter that code.

**Listing 9.13    Creating `ImagesManager` to retrieve and store images**

```
using UnityEngine;
using System.Collections;
using System.Collections.Generic;
using System;

public class ImagesManager : MonoBehaviour, IGameManager {
   public ManagerStatus status {get; private set;}

   private NetworkService _network;

   private Texture2D _webImage;

   public void Startup(NetworkService service) {
      Debug.Log("Images manager starting...");

      _network = service;

      status = ManagerStatus.Started;
   }
```

> ⌐ **Variable to store downloaded image**

**Check if the image is already stored.**

```
public void GetWebImage(Action<Texture2D> callback) {
    if (_webImage == null) {
        StartCoroutine(_network.DownloadImage(callback));
    }
    else {
        callback(_webImage);
    }
}
```

**Invoke callback right away (don't download) if there's a stored image.**

The most interesting part of this code is `GetWebImage()`; everything else in this script consists of standard properties and methods that implement the manager interface. When `GetWebImage()` is called, it'll return (via a callback function) the web image. First it'll check if `_webImage` already has a stored image: if not, it'll invoke the network call to download the image. If `_webImage` already has a stored image, `GetWebImage()` will send back the stored image (rather than downloading the image anew).

> **NOTE** Currently the downloaded image is never being stored, which means `_webImage` will always be empty. Code that specifies what to do when `_webImage` is *not* empty is already in place, so you'll adjust the code to store that image in the following sections. This adjustment is in a separate section because it involves some tricky code wizardry.

Of course, just like all manager modules, `ImagesManager` needs to be added to `Managers`; the following listing details the additions to Managers.cs.

> **Listing 9.14  Adding the new manager to Managers.cs**

```
...
[RequireComponent(typeof(ImagesManager))]
...
public static ImagesManager Images {get; private set;}
...
void Awake() {
    Weather = GetComponent<WeatherManager>();
    Images = GetComponent<ImagesManager>();

    _startSequence = new List<IGameManager>();
    _startSequence.Add(Weather);
    _startSequence.Add(Images);

    StartCoroutine(StartupManagers());
}
...
```

Unlike how we set up `WeatherManager`, `GetWebImage()` in `ImagesManager` isn't called automatically on startup. Instead, the code waits until invoked; that'll happen in the next section.

### 9.3.2   *Displaying images on the billboard*

The `ImagesManager` you just wrote doesn't do anything until it's called upon, so now we'll create a billboard object that will call methods in `ImagesManager`. First create a

Billboard without image          Billboard with downloaded image

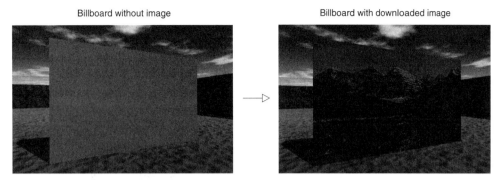

**Figure 9.6  The billboard object, before and after displaying the downloaded image**

new cube and then place it in the middle of the scene, at something like Position 0 1.5 -5 and Scale 5 3 .5 (see figure 9.6).

You're going to create a device that operates just like the color-changing monitor in chapter 8. Copy the DeviceOperator script and put it on the player. As you may recall, that script will operate nearby devices when the Fire3 button is pressed (which is defined in the project's input settings as the left Command key). Also create a script for the billboard device called WebLoadingBillboard, put that script on the billboard object, and enter the code from the next listing.

**Listing 9.15  WebLoadingBillboard device script**

```
using UnityEngine;
using System.Collections;

public class WebLoadingBillboard : MonoBehaviour {          Call the method in
   public void Operate() {                                  ImagesManager.
      Managers.Images.GetWebImage(OnWebImage);
   }
                                                            Downloaded
   private void OnWebImage(Texture2D image) {               image is applied
      GetComponent<Renderer>().material.mainTexture = image;  to the material
   }                                                        in the callback
}
```

This code does two primary things: it calls `ImagesManager.GetWebImage()` when the device is operated, and it applies the image from the callback function. Textures are applied to materials so you can change the texture in the material that's on the billboard. Figure 9.6 shows what the billboard will look like after you play the game.

**AssetBundles: How to download other kinds of assets**

Downloading an image is fairly straightforward using the WWW object, but what about other kinds of assets, like mesh objects and prefabs? WWW has properties for text and images, but other assets are a bit more complicated.

*(continued)*

Unity can download any kind of asset through a mechanism called AssetBundles. Long story short, you first package up some assets into a bundle, and then Unity can extract the assets after downloading the bundle. The details of both creating and downloading AssetBundles are beyond the scope of this book; if you want to learn more, start by reading this section of Unity's manual:

http://docs.unity3d.com/Manual/AssetBundlesIntro.html

Great, the downloaded image is displayed on the billboard! But this code could be optimized further to work with multiple billboards. Let's tackle that optimization in the next section.

### 9.3.3    *Caching the downloaded image for reuse*

As noted in section 9.3.1, `ImagesManager` doesn't yet store the downloaded image. That means the image will be downloaded over and over for multiple billboards. This is inefficient, because it'll be the same image each time. To address this, we're going to adjust `ImagesManager` to cache images that have been downloaded.

> **DEFINITION**    *Cache* means to keep stored locally. The most common (but not only!) context involves images downloaded from the internet.

The key is to provide a callback function in `ImagesManager` that first saves the image, and then calls the callback from `WebLoadingBillboard`. This is tricky to do (as opposed to the current code that uses the callback from `WebLoadingBillboard`) because the code doesn't know ahead of time what the callback from `WebLoading-Billboard` will be. Put another way, there's no way to write a method in `Images-Manager` that calls a specific method in `WebLoadingBillboard` because the code doesn't know what that specific method will be. The way around this conundrum is to use lambda functions.

> **DEFINITION**    A *lambda function* (also called an *anonymous function*) is a function that doesn't have a name. Such functions are usually created on the fly inside other functions.

Lambda functions are a tricky code feature supported in a number of programming languages, including C#. By using a lambda function for the callback in `Images-Manager`, the code can create the callback function on the fly using the method passed in from `WebLoadingBillboard`. Thus you don't need to know the method to call ahead of time, because this lambda function doesn't exist ahead of time! The following listing shows how to do this voodoo in `ImagesManager`.

**Listing 9.16  Lambda function for callback in `ImagesManager`**

```
...
using System;
...
public void GetWebImage(Action<Texture2D> callback) {
    if (_webImage == null) {
        StartCoroutine(_network.DownloadImage((Texture2D image) => {
            _webImage = image;
            callback(_webImage);
        }));
    }
    else {
        callback(_webImage);
    }
}
...
```

Store downloaded image → `_webImage = image;` `callback(_webImage);`

← **Callback is used in lambda function instead of sent directly to NetworkService**

The main change was in the function passed to `NetworkService.DownloadImage()`. Previously the code was passing through the same callback method from `WebLoadingBanner`. After the change, though, the callback sent to `NetworkService` was a separate lambda function declared on the spot that called the method from `WebLoadingBanner`. Take note of the syntax to declare a lambda method: `() => {}`.

Making the callback a separate function made it possible to do more than call the method in `WebLoadingBanner`; specifically, the lambda function also stores a local copy of the downloaded image. Thus `GetWebImage()` only has to download the image the first time; all subsequent calls will use the locally stored image.

Because this optimization applies to subsequent calls, the effect will be noticeable only on multiple billboards. Let's duplicate the billboard object so that there will be a second billboard in the scene. Select the billboard object, hit Duplicate (look under the Edit menu or right-click), and move the duplicate over (for example, change the X position to 18).

Now play the game and watch what happens. When you operate the first billboard, there will be a noticeable pause while the image downloads from the internet. But when you then walk over to the second billboard, the image will appear immediately because it has already been downloaded.

This is an important optimization for downloading images (there's a reason web browsers cache images by default). There's one more major networking task remaining to go over: sending data back to the server.

## 9.4  Posting data to a web server

We've gone over multiple examples of downloading data, but we still need to see an example of *sending* data. This last section does require you to have a server to send requests to, so this section is optional. But it's easy to download open-source software to set up a server to test on.

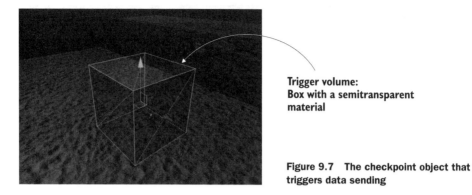

Trigger volume:
**Box with a semitransparent material**

**Figure 9.7   The checkpoint object that triggers data sending**

I recommend XAMPP for a test server. Go to www.apachefriends.org to download XAMPP. Once that's installed and the server is running, you can access XAMPP's htdocs folder with the address http://localhost/ just like you would a server on the internet. Once you have XAMPP up and running, create a folder called ch9 in htdocs; that's where you'll put the server-side script.

Whether you use XAMPP or your own existing web server, the actual task will be to post weather data to the server when the player reaches a checkpoint in the scene. This checkpoint will be a trigger volume, just like the door trigger in chapter 8. You need to create a new cube object, position the object off to one side of the scene, set the collider to Trigger, and apply a semitransparent material like you did in the previous chapter (remember, set the material's Rendering Mode). Figure 9.7 shows the checkpoint object with a green semitransparent material applied.

Now that the trigger object is in the scene, let's write the code that it invokes.

### 9.4.1  *Tracking current weather: sending post requests*

The code that's invoked by the checkpoint object will cascade through several scripts. As with the code for downloading data, the code for sending data will involve WeatherManager telling NetworkService to make the request, while NetworkService handles the details of HTTP communication. The next listing shows the adjustments you need to make to NetworkService.

**Listing 9.17   Adjusting NetworkService to post data**

**Address of the server-side script; change this if needed.**

```
...
private const string localApi = "http://localhost/ch9/api.php";
...
private IEnumerator CallAPI(string url, Hashtable args, Action<string>
    callback) {
    WWW www;
```

**Added arguments to CallAPI() parameters**

```
    if (args == null) {
      www = new WWW(url);
    } else {                                    Send arguments along with
      WWWForm form = new WWWForm();             WWW using WWWForm.
      foreach(DictionaryEntry arg in args) {
         form.AddField(arg.Key.ToString(), arg.Value.ToString());
      }
      www = new WWW(url, form);                 WWWForm automatically changes
    }                                           the request from GET to POST.

    yield return www;
    ...                                         Calls modified
}                                               because of
                                                changed
                                                parameters
public IEnumerator GetWeatherXML(Action<string> callback) {
    return CallAPI(xmlApi, null, callback);
}
public IEnumerator GetWeatherJSON(Action<string> callback) {
    return CallAPI(jsonApi, null, callback);
}

public IEnumerator LogWeather(string name, float cloudValue, Action<string>
      callback) {
    Hashtable args = new Hashtable();
    args.Add("message", name);                  Define a table of
    args.Add("cloud_value", cloudValue);        arguments to send.
    args.Add("timestamp", DateTime.UtcNow.Ticks);
                                                Send timestamp along
    return CallAPI(localApi, args, callback);   with the cloudiness.
}
...
```

First, notice that `CallAPI()` has a new parameter. This is a table of arguments to send along with the HTTP request. Within `CallAPI()` a `WWWForm` object may be created according to that table of arguments. Normally `WWW` sends a GET request, but `WWWForm` will change it to a POST request to send data. All the other changes in the code react to that central change (for example, modifying `GetWhatever()` code because of the `CallAPI()` parameters).

The next listing shows what you need to add in `WeatherManager`.

**Listing 9.18  Adding code to `WeatherManager` that sends data**

```
...
public void LogWeather(string name) {
    StartCoroutine(_network.LogWeather(name, cloudValue, OnLogged));
}
private void OnLogged(string response) {
    Debug.Log(response);
}
...
```

Finally, make use of that code by adding a checkpoint script to the trigger volume in the scene. Create a script called CheckpointTrigger, put that script on the trigger volume, and enter the contents of the next listing.

**Listing 9.19   CheckpointTrigger script for the trigger volume**

```
using UnityEngine;
using System.Collections;

public class CheckpointTrigger : MonoBehaviour {
    public string identifier;

    private bool _triggered;

    void OnTriggerEnter(Collider other) {
        if (_triggered) {return;}

        Managers.Weather.LogWeather(identifier);
        _triggered = true;
    }
}
```

Track if the checkpoint has already been triggered.

Call to send data

An Identifier slot will appear in the Inspector; name it something like checkpoint1. Run the code and data will be sent when you enter the checkpoint. The response will indicate an error, though, because there's no script on the server to receive the request. That's the last step in this section.

### 9.4.2   Server-side code in PHP

The server needs to have a script to receive data sent from the game. Coding server scripts is beyond the scope of this book, so we won't go into detail here. We'll just whip up a PHP script because that's the easiest approach. Create a text file in htdocs (or wherever your web server is located) and name the file api.php (see listing 9.20).

**Listing 9.20   Server script written in PHP that receives our data**

```
<?php

$message = $_POST['message'];
$cloudiness = $_POST['cloud_value'];
$timestamp = $_POST['timestamp'];
$combined = $message." cloudiness=".$cloudiness." time=".$timestamp."\n";

$filename = "data.txt";
file_put_contents($filename, $combined, FILE_APPEND | LOCK_EX);

echo "Logged";

?>
```

Extract post data into variables.

Write the file.

Define the filename to write to.

Note that this script writes received data into data.txt, so you also need to put a text file with that name on the server. Once api.php is in place, you'll see weather logs appear in data.txt when triggering checkpoints in the game. Great!

## 9.5 *Summary*

In this chapter you've learned that

- Skybox is designed for sky visuals that render behind everything else.
- Unity provides WWW to download data.
- Common data formats like XML and JSON can be parsed easily.
- Materials can display images downloaded from the internet.
- WWW can also post data to a web server.

# *Playing audio:*
## *sound effects and music*

Although graphics get most of the attention when it comes to content in video games, audio is crucial, too. Most games play background music and have sound effects. Accordingly, Unity has audio functionality so that you can put sound effects and music into your games. Unity can import and play a variety of audio file formats, adjust the volume of sounds, and even handle sounds playing from a specific position within the scene.

This chapter starts with sound effects rather than music. Sound effects are short clips that play along with actions in the game (such as a gunshot that plays when the player fires), whereas the sound clips for music are longer (often running into minutes) and playback isn't directly tied to events in the game. Ultimately, both boil down to the same kind of audio files and playback code, but the simple fact that the sound files for music are usually much larger than the short clips used for sound effects (indeed, files for music are often the largest files in the game!) merits covering them in a separate section.

The complete roadmap for this chapter will be to take a game without sound and do the following:

1  Import audio files for sound effects.
2  Play sound effects for the enemy and for shooting.
3  Program an audio manager to control volume.
4  Optimize the loading of music.
5  Control music volume separately from sound effects, including cross-fading tracks.

> **NOTE**   This chapter is largely independent of the project you build; it simply adds audio capabilities on top of an existing game demo. All of the examples in this chapter are built on top of the FPS created in chapter 3 and you could download that sample project, but you're free to use whatever game demo you'd like.

Once you have an existing game demo copied to use for this chapter, you can tackle the first step: importing sound effects.

## 10.1  Importing sound effects

Before you can play any sounds, you obviously need to import the sound files into your Unity project. First you'll collect sound clips in the desired file format, and then you'll bring the files into Unity and adjust them for your purposes.

### 10.1.1  Supported file formats

Much as you saw with art assets in chapter 4, Unity supports a variety of audio formats with different pros and cons. Table 10.1 lists the audio file formats that Unity supports.

**Table 10.1   Audio file formats supported by Unity**

| File type | Pros and cons |
|---|---|
| WAV | Default audio format on Windows. Uncompressed sound file. |
| AIF | Default audio format on Mac. Uncompressed sound file. |
| MP3 | Compressed sound file; sacrifices a bit of quality for much smaller files. |
| OGG | Compressed sound file; sacrifices a bit of quality for much smaller files. |

**Table 10.1   Audio file formats supported by Unity *(continued)***

| File type | Pros and cons |
| --- | --- |
| MOD | Music tracker file format. A specialized kind of efficient digital music. |
| XM | Music tracker file format. A specialized kind of efficient digital music. |

The primary consideration differentiating audio files is the compression applied. Compression reduces the file's size but accomplishes that by throwing out a bit of information in the file. Audio compression is clever about only throwing out the least important information so that the compressed sound still sounds good. Nevertheless, it's a small loss of quality, so you should choose uncompressed audio when the sound clip is short and thus wouldn't be a large file. Longer sound clips (especially music) should use compressed audio, because the audio clip would be prohibitively large otherwise.

Unity adds a small wrinkle to this decision, though…

**TIP**   Although music should be compressed in the final game, Unity can compress the audio after you've imported the file. Thus, when developing a game in Unity you usually want to use uncompressed file formats even for lengthy music, as opposed to importing compressed audio.

### How digital audio works

In general, audio files store the waveform that'll be created in the speakers when the sound plays. Sound is a series of waves that travel through the air, and different sounds are made with different sizes and frequencies of sound waves. Audio files record these waves by sampling the wave repeatedly at short time intervals and saving the state of the wave at each sample.

Recordings that sample the wave more frequently get a more accurate recording of the wave changing over time—there's less gap between changes. But more frequent samples mean more data to save, resulting in a larger file. Compressed sound files reduce the file size through a number of tricks, including tossing out data at sound frequencies that aren't noticeable to listeners.

Music trackers are a special type of sequencer software used to create music. Whereas traditional audio files store the raw waveform for the sound, sequencers store something more akin to sheet music: the tracker file is a sequence of notes, with information like intensity and pitch stored with each note. These "notes" consist of little waveforms, but the total amount of data stored is reduced because the same note is used repeatedly throughout the sequence. Music composed this way can be efficient, but this is a fairly specialized sort of audio.

Because Unity will compress the audio after it's been imported, you should always choose either WAV or AIF file format. You'll probably need to adjust the import settings differently for short sound effects and longer music (in particular, to tell Unity when to apply compression), but the original files should always be uncompressed.

There are various ways to create sound files (for example, appendix B mentions tools like Audacity that can record sounds from a microphone), but for our purposes we'll download some sounds from one of the many free sound websites. We're going to use a number of clips downloaded from www.freesound.org and get the clips in WAV file format.

> **WARNING** "Free" sounds are offered under a variety of licensing schemes, so always make sure that you're allowed to use the sound clip in the way you intend. For example, many free sounds are for noncommercial use only.

The sample project uses the following public domain sound effects (of course, you can choose to download your own sounds; look for a 0 license listed on the side):

- "thump" by hy96
- "ding" by Daphne_in_Wonderland
- "swish bamboo pole" by ra_gun
- "fireplace" by leosalom

Once you have the sound files to use in your game, the next step is to import the sounds into Unity.

### 10.1.2 *Importing audio files*

After gathering together some audio files, you need to bring them into Unity. Just as you did with art assets in chapter 4, you have to import audio assets into the project before they can be used in the game.

The actual mechanics of importing files are simple and are the same as with other assets: drag the files from their location on the computer to the Project view within Unity (create a folder called Sound FX to drag the files into). Well, that was easy! But just like other assets, there are import settings (shown in figure 10.1) to adjust in the Inspector.

Leave Force To Mono unchecked. That refers to mono versus stereo sound; often sounds are recorded in stereo, where there are actually two waveforms in the file, one

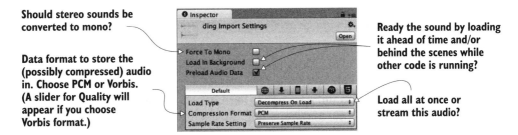

**Figure 10.1 Import settings for audio files**

each for the left and right ears/speakers. To save on file size, you might want to halve the audio information so that the same waveform is sent to both speakers rather than separate waves sent to the left and right speakers.

Next are check boxes for Load In Background and Preload Audio Data. The preload setting relates to balancing playback performance and memory usage; preloading audio will consume memory while the sound waits to be used but will avoid having to wait to load. Loading audio in the background of the program will allow the program to keep running while the audio is loading; this is generally a good idea for long music clips so that the program won't freeze. But this means the audio won't start playing right away; usually you want to keep this setting off for short sound clips to ensure that they load completely before they play. Because the imported clips are short sound effects, you should leave Load In Background off.

Finally, the most important settings are Load Type and Compression Format. Compression Format controls the formatting of the audio data that's stored. As discussed in the previous section, music should be compressed; choose Vorbis (it's the name of a compressed audio format) in that case. Short sound clips don't need to be compressed, so choose PCM (Pulse Code Modulation, the technical term for the raw, sampled sound wave) for these clips. The third setting, ADPCM, is a variation on PCM and occasionally results in slightly better sound quality.

Load Type controls how the data from the file will be loaded by the computer. Because computers have limited memory and audio files can be large, sometimes you want the audio to play while it's streaming into memory, saving the computer from needing to have the entire file loaded at once. But there's a bit of computing overhead when streaming audio like this, so audio plays fastest when it's loaded into memory first. Even then you can choose whether the loaded audio data will be in compressed form or if it will be decompressed for faster playback. Because these sound clips are short, they don't need to stream and can be set to Decompress On Load.

At this point, the sound effects are all imported and ready to use.

## 10.2  Playing sound effects

Now that you have some sound files added to the project, you naturally want to play the sounds. The code for triggering sound effects isn't terribly hard to understand, but the audio system in Unity does have a number of different parts that must work in concert.

### 10.2.1  Explaining what's involved: audio clip vs. source vs. listener

Although you might expect that playing a sound is simply a matter of telling Unity which clip to play, it turns out that you must define three different parts in order to play sounds in Unity: AudioClip, AudioSource, and AudioListener. The reason for breaking apart the sound system into multiple components has to do with Unity's support for 3D sounds: the different components tell Unity positional information that it uses for manipulating 3D sounds.

## 2D vs. 3D sound

Sounds in games can be either 2D or 3D. 2D sounds are what you're already familiar with: standard audio that plays normally. The moniker "2D sound" mostly means "not 3D sound."

3D sounds are specific to 3D simulations and may not already be familiar to you; these are sounds that have a specific location within the simulation. Their volume and pitch are influenced by the movement of the listener. For example, a sound effect triggered in the distance will sound very faint.

Unity supports both kinds of audio, and you decide if an audio source should play audio as 2D sounds or 3D sounds. Things like music should be 2D sounds, but using 3D sounds for most sound effects will create immersive audio in the scene.

As an analogy, imagine a room in the real world. The room has a stereo playing a CD. If a man comes into the room, he hears it clearly. When he leaves the room he hears it more quietly, and eventually not at all. Similarly, if we move the stereo around the room, he'll hear the music changing volume as it moves. As figure 10.2 illustrates, in this analogy the CD is an AudioClip, the stereo is an AudioSource, and the man is the AudioListener.

The first of the three different parts is an Audio Clip. That refers to the actual sound file that we imported in the last section. This raw waveform data is the foundation for everything else the audio system does, but audio clips don't do anything by themselves.

The next kind of object is an Audio Source. This is the object that plays audio clips. This is an abstraction over what the audio system is actually doing, but it's a useful abstraction that makes 3D sounds easier to understand. A 3D sound played from a specific audio source is located at the position of that audio source; 2D sounds also must be played from an audio source, but the location doesn't matter.

The third kind of object involved in Unity's audio system is an Audio Listener. As the name implies, this is the object that hears sounds projected from audio sources. This is another abstraction on top of what the audio system is doing (obviously the actual listener is the player of the game!), but—much like how the position of the

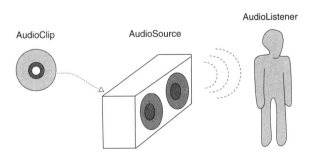

**Figure 10.2  Diagram of the three things you control in Unity's audio system**

audio source gives the position that the sound is projected from—the position of the audio listener gives the position that the sound is heard from.

> **Advanced sound control using Audio Mixers**
>
> Audio Mixers are a new feature added in Unity 5. Rather than playing audio clips directly, audio mixers enable you to process audio signals and apply various effects to your clips. Learn more about AudioMixer in Unity's documentation; for example, watch this tutorial video: https://unity3d.com/learn/tutorials/modules/beginner/5-pre-order-beta/audiomixer-and-audiomixer-groups

Although both audio clips and AudioSource components have to be assigned, an AudioListener component is already on the default camera when you create a new scene. Typically you want 3D sounds to react to the position of the viewer.

### 10.2.2  Assigning a looping sound

All right, now let's set our first sound in Unity! The audio clips were already imported, and the default camera has an AudioListener component, so we only need to assign an AudioSource component. We're going to put a crackling fire sound on the Enemy prefab, the enemy character that wanders around.

> **NOTE**  Because the enemy will sound like it's on fire, you might want to give it a particle system so that it looks like it's on fire. You can copy over the particle system created in chapter 4 by making the particle object into a prefab and then choosing Export Package from the Asset menu. Alternatively, you could redo the steps from chapter 4 here to create a new particle object from scratch (drag the Enemy prefab into the scene to edit it and then choose GameObject > Apply Changes To Prefab).

Usually you need to drag a prefab into the scene in order to edit it, but you can edit the prefab asset directly when you're just adding a component onto the object. Select the Enemy prefab so that its properties appear in the Inspector. Now add a new component; choose Audio > Audio Source. An AudioSource component will appear in the Inspector.

Tell the audio source what sound clip to play. Drag an audio file from the Project view up to the Audio Clip slot in the Inspector; we're going to use the "fireplace" sound effect for this example (refer to figure 10.3).

Skip down a bit in the settings and select both Play On Awake and Looping (of course, make sure that Mute isn't checked). Play On Awake tells the audio source to begin playing as soon as the scene starts (in the next section you'll learn how to trigger sounds manually while the scene is running). Looping tells the audio source to keep playing continuously, repeating the audio clip when playback is over.

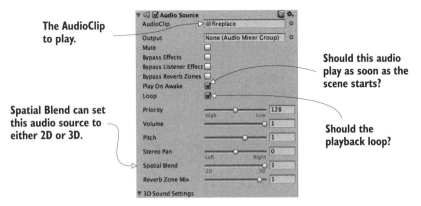

The AudioClip to play.

Should this audio play as soon as the scene starts?

Spatial Blend can set this audio source to either 2D or 3D.

Should the playback loop?

**Figure 10.3    Settings for the AudioSource component**

You want this audio source to project 3D sounds. As explained earlier, 3D sounds have a distinct position within the scene. That aspect of the audio source is adjusted using the Spatial Blend setting. That setting is a slider between 2D and 3D; set it to 3D for this audio source.

Now play the game and make sure your speakers are turned on. You can hear a crackling fire coming from the enemy, and the sound becomes faint if you move away because you used a 3D audio source.

### 10.2.3  *Triggering sound effects from code*

Setting the AudioSource component to play automatically is handy for some looping sounds, but for the majority of sound effects you'll want to trigger the sound with code commands. That approach still requires an AudioSource component, but now the audio source will only play sound clips when told to by the program, instead of automatically all the time.

Add an AudioSource component to the player object (not the camera object). You don't have to link in a specific audio clip because the audio clips will be defined in code. You can turn off Play On Awake because sounds from this source will be triggered in code. Also, adjust Spatial Blend to 3D because this sound is located in the scene.

Now make the additions shown in the next listing to RayShooter, the script that handles shooting.

**Listing 10.1    Sound effects added in the RayShooter script**

```
...
[SerializeField] private AudioSource soundSource;       References the two sound
[SerializeField] private AudioClip hitWallSound;        files you want to play
[SerializeField] private AudioClip hitEnemySound;
...
```

```
if (target != null) {                    If target is not null, the
    target.ReactToHit();                 player has hit an enemy, so...
    soundSource.PlayOneShot(hitEnemySound);
} else {                                            ...call PlayOneShot() to play the
    StartCoroutine(SphereIndicator(hit.point));     Hit An Enemy sound, or...
    soundSource.PlayOneShot(hitWallSound);
}                                                   ...call PlayOneShot() to play the Hit
...                                                 A Wall sound if the player missed.
```

The new code includes several new serialized variables at the top of the script. Drag the player object (the object with an AudioSource component) to the soundSource slot in the Inspector. Then drag the audio clips to play onto the sound slots; "swish" is for hitting the wall and "ding" is for hitting the enemy.

The other two lines added are PlayOneShot() methods. That method causes an audio source to play a given audio clip. Add those methods inside the target conditional in order to play sounds when different objects are hit.

> **NOTE**  You could set the clip in the AudioSource and call Play() to play the clip. Multiple sounds would cut each other off, though, so we used Play-OneShot() instead. Replace PlayOneShot() with this code and shoot a bunch rapidly to see (er, hear) the problem:

```
soundSource.clip=hitEnemySound; soundSource.Play();
```

All right, play the game and shoot around. You now have several different sound effects in the game. These same basic steps can be used to add all sorts of sound effects. A robust sound system in a game requires a lot more than just a bunch of disconnected sounds, though; at a minimum, all games should offer volume control. You'll implement that control next through a central audio module.

## 10.3  Audio control interface

Continuing the code architecture established in previous chapters, you're going to create an AudioManager. Recall that the Managers object has a master list of various code modules used by the game, such as a manager for the player's inventory. This time you'll create an audio manager to stick into the list. This central audio module will allow you to modulate the volume of audio in the game and even mute it. Initially you'll only worry about sound effects, but in later sections you'll extend the Audio-Manager to handle music as well.

### 10.3.1  Setting up the central AudioManager

The first step in setting up AudioManager is to put in place the Managers code framework. From the chapter 9 project, copy over IGameManager, ManagerStatus, and NetworkService; we won't change them. (Remember that IGameManager is the interface that all managers must implement, whereas ManagerStatus is an enum that IGameManager uses. NetworkService provides calls to the internet and won't be used in this chapter.)

**NOTE** Unity will probably issue a warning because `NetworkService` is assigned but not used. You can just ignore Unity's warning; we want to enable the code framework to access the internet, even though we don't use that functionality in this chapter.

Also copy over the Managers file, which will be adjusted for the new AudioManager. Leave it be for now (or comment out the erroneous sections if the sight of compiler errors drives you crazy!). Create a new script called AudioManager that the `Managers` code can refer to (see the following listing).

**Listing 10.2   Skeleton code for AudioManager**

```
using UnityEngine;
using System.Collections;
using System.Collections.Generic;

public class AudioManager : MonoBehaviour, IGameManager {
   public ManagerStatus status {get; private set;}

   private NetworkService _network;

   // Add volume controls here (listing 10.4)

   public void Startup(NetworkService service) {
      Debug.Log("Audio manager starting...");

      _network = service;

      // Initialize music sources here (listing 10.10)      ◁── Any long-running
                                                                  startup tasks go here.
      status = ManagerStatus.Started;          ◁── Set status to Initializing if there
   }                                                 are long-running startup tasks.
}
```

This initial code looks just like managers from previous chapters; this is the minimum amount that `IGameManager` requires that the class implements. The Managers script can now be adjusted with the new manager (see the next listing).

**Listing 10.3   Managers script adjusted with AudioManager**

```
using UnityEngine;
using System.Collections;
using System.Collections.Generic;

[RequireComponent(typeof(AudioManager))]

public class Managers : MonoBehaviour {
   public static AudioManager Audio {get; private set;}

   private List<IGameManager> _startSequence;
```

```
void Awake() {
    Audio = GetComponent<AudioManager>();          Only list AudioManager in
                                                    this project, instead of
    _startSequence = new List<IGameManager>();      PlayerManager, and so on.
    _startSequence.Add(Audio);

    StartCoroutine(StartupManagers());
}

private IEnumerator StartupManagers() {
    NetworkService network = new NetworkService();

    foreach (IGameManager manager in _startSequence) {
        manager.Startup(network);
    }

    yield return null;

    int numModules = _startSequence.Count;
    int numReady = 0;

    while (numReady < numModules) {
        int lastReady = numReady;
        numReady = 0;

        foreach (IGameManager manager in _startSequence) {
            if (manager.status == ManagerStatus.Started) {
                numReady++;
            }
        }

        if (numReady > lastReady)
            Debug.Log("Progress: " + numReady + "/" + numModules);

        yield return null;
    }

    Debug.Log("All managers started up");
}
}
```

As you have in previous chapters, create the Game Managers object in the scene and then attach both Managers and AudioManager to the empty object. Playing the game will show the managers startup messages in the console, but the audio manager doesn't do anything yet.

### 10.3.2   *Volume control UI*

With the bare-bones AudioManager set up, it's time to give it volume control functionality. These volume control methods will then be used by UI displays in order to mute the sound effects or adjust the volume.

You'll use the new UI tools that were the focus of chapter 6. Specifically, you're going to create a pop-up window with a button and a slider to control volume settings

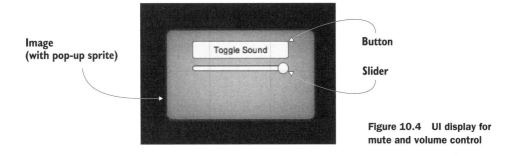

Image
(with pop-up sprite)

Button

Slider

**Figure 10.4   UI display for mute and volume control**

(see figure 10.4). I'll list the steps involved without going into detail; if you need a refresher, refer back to chapter 6:

1  Import popup.png as a sprite (set Texture Type to Sprite).
2  In Sprite Editor, set a 12-pixel border on all sides (remember to apply changes).
3  Create a canvas in the scene (GameObject > UI > Canvas).
4  Turn on the Pixel Perfect setting for the canvas.
5  (Optional) Name the object HUD Canvas and switch to 2D view mode.
6  Create an image connected to that canvas (GameObject > UI > Image).
7  Name the new object Settings Popup.
8  Assign the popup sprite to the image's Source Image.
9  Set Image Type to Sliced and turn on Fill Center.
10  Position the pop-up image at 0, 0 to center it.
11  Scale the pop-up to 250 width and 150 height.
12  Create a button (GameObject > UI > Button).
13  Parent the button to the pop-up (that is, drag it in the Hierarchy).
14  Position the button at 0, 40.
15  Expand the button's hierarchy in order to select its text label.
16  Change the text to say Toggle Sound.
17  Create a slider (GameObject > UI > Slider).
18  Parent the slider to the pop-up and position at 0, 15.

Those were all the steps to create the settings pop-up! Now that the pop-up has been created, let's write code that it'll work with. This will involve both a script on the pop-up object itself, as well as volume control functionality that the pop-up script calls. First adjust the code in AudioManager according to the next listing.

**Listing 10.4   Volume control added to AudioManager**

Property with getter and setter for volume

```
...
public float soundVolume {
    get {return AudioListener.volume;}       Implement the getter/setter
    set {AudioListener.volume = value;}      using AudioListener.
}
```

```
public bool soundMute {
   get {return AudioListener.pause;}
   set {AudioListener.pause = value;}
}
```
◁── **Add a similar property to mute.**

```
public void Startup(NetworkService service) {
   Debug.Log("Audio manager starting...");

   _network = service;

   soundVolume = 1f;

   status = ManagerStatus.Started;
}
...
```
◁── **Italicized code was already in script, shown here for reference.**

◁── **Initialize the value (0 to 1 range; 1 is full volume).**

Properties for `soundVolume` and `soundMute` were added to AudioManager. For both properties, the `get` and `set` functions were implemented using global values on Audio-Listener. The `AudioListener` class can modulate the volume of all sounds received by all `AudioListener` instances. Setting AudioManager's `soundVolume` property has the same effect as setting the volume on `AudioListener`. The advantage here is encapsulation: everything having to do with audio is being handled in a single manager, without code outside the manager needing to know the details of the implementation.

With those methods added to AudioManager, you can now write a script for the pop-up. Create a script called SettingsPopup and add the contents of the following listing.

**Listing 10.5   SettingsPopup script with controls for adjusting the volume**

```
using UnityEngine;
using System.Collections;

public class SettingsPopup : MonoBehaviour {

   public void OnSoundToggle() {
      Managers.Audio.soundMute = !Managers.Audio.soundMute;
   }

   public void OnSoundValue(float volume) {
      Managers.Audio.soundVolume = volume;
   }
}
```
◁── **This button will toggle the mute property of AudioManager.**

◁── **This slider will adjust the volume property of AudioManager.**

This script has two methods that affect the properties of AudioManager: `OnSound-Toggle()` sets the `soundMute` property, and `OnSoundValue()` sets the `soundVolume` property. As usual, link in the SettingsPopup script by dragging it onto the `Settings Popup` object in the UI.

Then, in order to call the functions from the button and slider, link the pop-up object to interaction events in those controls. In the Inspector for the button, look for the panel labeled OnClick. Click the + button to add a new entry to this event. Drag

Settings Popup to the object slot in the new entry and then look for SettingsPopup in the menu; select `OnSoundToggle()` to make the button call that function.

The method used to link the function applies to the slider as well. First look for the interaction event in a panel of the slider's settings; in this case, the panel is called OnValueChanged. Click the + button to add a new entry and then drag Settings Popup to the object slot. In the function menu find the SettingsPopup script and then choose `OnSoundValue()` under Dynamic Float.

> **WARNING** Remember to choose the function under Dynamic Float and not Static Parameter! Although the method appears in both sections of the list, in the latter case it will only receive a single value typed in ahead of time.

The settings controls are now working, but there's one more script we need to address the fact that the pop-up is currently always covering up the screen. A simple fix is to make the pop-up only open when you hit the M key. Create a new script called UIController, link that script to the Controller object in the scene, and write the code shown in the next listing.

**Listing 10.6  UIController that toggles the settings pop-up**

```
using UnityEngine;
using System.Collections;

public class UIController : MonoBehaviour {            References pop-up
    [SerializeField] private SettingsPopup popup;      object in scene

    void Start() {                                     Initializes pop-up hidden
        popup.gameObject.SetActive(false);
    }

    void Update() {                                    Toggles pop-up with M key
        if (Input.GetKeyDown(KeyCode.M)) {
            bool isShowing = popup.gameObject.activeSelf;
            popup.gameObject.SetActive(!isShowing);

            if (isShowing) {
                Cursor.lockState = CursorLockMode.Locked;
                Cursor.visible = false;
            } else {                                   Also toggles cursor
                Cursor.lockState = CursorLockMode.None; along with pop-up
                Cursor.visible = true;
            }
        }
    }
}
```

To wire up this object reference, drag the settings pop-up to the slot on this script. Play now and try changing the slider (remember to activate the UI by hitting M) while shooting around to hear the sound effects; you'll hear the sound effects change volume according to the slider.

### 10.3.3  *Playing UI sounds*

You're going to make another addition to AudioManager now to allow the UI to play sounds when buttons are clicked. This task is more involved than it seems at first, owing to Unity's need for an AudioSource. When sound effects issued from objects in the scene, it was fairly obvious where to attach the AudioSource. But UI sound effects aren't part of the scene, so you'll set up a special AudioSource just for AudioManager to use when there isn't any other audio source.

Create a new empty `GameObject` and parent it to the main `Game Managers` object; this new object is going to have an AudioSource used by AudioManager, so call the new object `Audio`. Add an AudioSource component to this object (leave the Spatial Blend setting at 2D this time, because the UI doesn't have any specific position in the scene) and then add the code shown in the next listing to use this source in AudioManager.

---

**Listing 10.7   Play sound effects in AudioManager**

```
...
[SerializeField] private AudioSource soundSource;          Variable slot in the Inspector to
...                                                         reference the new audio source
public void PlaySound(AudioClip clip) {
    soundSource.PlayOneShot(clip);                Play sounds that don't
}                                                 have any other source.
...
```

A new variable slot will appear in the Inspector; drag the `Audio` object onto this slot. Now add the UI sound effect to the pop-up script (see the following listing).

---

**Listing 10.8   Adding sound effects to SettingsPopup**

```
...
[SerializeField] private AudioClip sound;                  Inspector slot to reference
...                                                         the sound clip
public void OnSoundToggle() {
    Managers.Audio.soundMute = !Managers.Audio.soundMute;
    Managers.Audio.PlaySound(sound);                Play the sound effect when
}                                                   the button is pressed.
...
```

Drag the UI sound effect onto the variable slot; I used the 2D sound "thump." When you press the UI button, that sound effect plays at the same time (well, when the sound isn't muted, of course!). Even though the UI doesn't have any audio source itself, AudioManager has an audio source that plays the sound effect.

Great, we've set up all our sound effects! Now let's turn our attention to music.

## 10.4   *Background music*

You're going to add some background music to the game, and you'll do that by adding music to AudioManager. As explained in the chapter introduction, music clips aren't fundamentally different from sound effects. The way digital audio functions through waveforms is the same, and the commands for playing the audio are largely the same. The main difference is the length of the audio, but that difference cascades out into a number of consequences.

For starters, music tracks tend to consume a large amount of memory on the computer, and that memory consumption must be optimized. You must watch out for two areas of memory issues: having the music loaded into memory before it's needed, and consuming too much memory when loaded.

Optimizing *when* music loads is done using the `Resources.Load()` command introduced in chapter 8. As you learned, this command allows you to load assets by name; though that's certainly one handy feature, that's not the only reason to load assets from the Resources folder. Another key consideration is delaying loading; normally Unity loads all assets in a scene as soon as the scene loads, but assets from Resources aren't loaded until the code manually fetches them. In this case, we want to lazy-load the audio clips for music. Otherwise, the music could consume a lot of memory while it isn't even being used.

> **DEFINITION** *Lazy-loading* is when a file isn't loaded ahead of time but rather is delayed until it's needed. Typically data responds faster (for example, the sound plays immediately) if it's loaded in advance of use, but lazy-loading can save a lot of memory when responsiveness doesn't matter as much.

The second memory consideration is dealt with by streaming music off the disc. As explained in section 10.1.2, streaming the audio saves the computer from ever needing to have the entire file loaded at once. The style of loading was a setting in the Inspector of the imported audio clip.

Ultimately there are several steps to go through for playing background music, including steps to cover these memory optimizations.

### 10.4.1 Playing music loops

The process of playing music involves the same series of steps as UI sound effects did (background music is also 2D sound without a source within the scene), so we're going to go through all the steps again:

1 Import audio clips.
2 Set up an AudioSource for AudioManager to use.
3 Write code to play the audio clips in AudioManager.
4 Add music controls to the UI.

Each step will be modified slightly to work with music instead of sound effects. Let's look at the first step.

#### STEP 1: IMPORT AUDIO CLIPS

Obtain some music by downloading or recording tracks. For the sample project I went to www.freesound.org and downloaded the following public domain music loops:

- "loop" by Xythe/Ville Nousiainen
- "Intro Synth" by noirenex

Drag the files into Unity to import them and then adjust their import settings in the Inspector. As explained earlier, audio clips for music generally have different settings than audio clips for sound effects. First, the audio format should be set to Vorbis, for compressed audio. Remember, compressed audio will have a significantly smaller file size. Compression also degrades the audio quality slightly, but that slight degradation is an acceptable trade-off for long music clips; set Quality to 50% in the slider that appears.

The next import setting to adjust is Load Type. Again, music should stream from the disc rather than being loaded completely. Choose Streaming from the Load Type menu. Similarly, turn on Load In Background so that the game won't pause or slow down while music is loading.

Even after you adjust all the import settings, the asset files must be moved to the correct location in order to load correctly. Remember that the `Resources.Load()` command requires that the assets be in the Resources folder. Create a new folder called Resources, create a folder within that called Music, and drag the audio files into the Music folder (see figure 10.5).

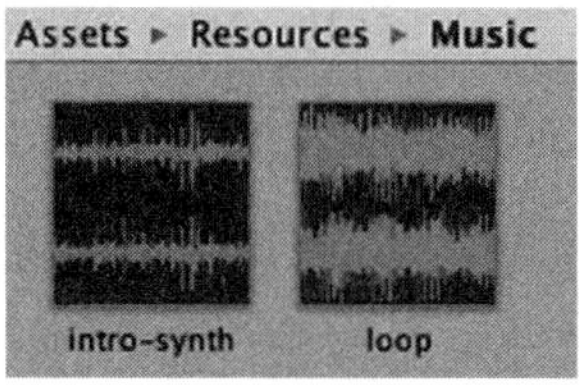

That took care of step number 1.

**Figure 10.5  Music audio clips placed inside the Resources folder**

**STEP 2: SET UP AN AUDIOSOURCE FOR AUDIOMANAGER TO USE**

Step 2 is to create a new AudioSource for music playback. Create another empty GameObject, name this object `Music 1` (instead of just Music because we'll add `Music 2` later in the chapter), and parent it to the Audio object.

Add an AudioSource component to `Music 1` and then adjust the settings in the component. Deselect Play On Awake but turn on the Loop option this time; whereas sound effects usually only play once, music plays over and over in a loop. Leave the Spatial Blend setting at 2D, because music doesn't have any specific position in the scene.

You may want to reduce the Priority value, too. For sound effects, this value didn't matter, so we left the value at the default 128. But for music you probably want to lower this value, so I set the music source to 60. This value tells Unity which sounds are most important when layering multiple sounds; somewhat counterintuitively, lower values are higher priority. When too many sounds are playing simultaneously, the audio system will start discarding sounds; by making music higher priority than sound effects, you ensure the music will keep playing when too many sound effects trigger at the same time.

**STEP 3: WRITE CODE TO PLAY THE AUDIO CLIPS IN AUDIOMANAGER**

The Music audio source has been set up, so add the code shown in the next listing to AudioManager.

**Listing 10.9  Playing music in AudioManager**

```
...
[SerializeField] private AudioSource music1Source;
```

```
[SerializeField] private string introBGMusic;
[SerializeField] private string levelBGMusic;
...
public void PlayIntroMusic() {
    PlayMusic(Resources.Load("Music/"+introBGMusic) as AudioClip);
}
public void PlayLevelMusic() {
    PlayMusic(Resources.Load("Music/"+levelBGMusic) as AudioClip);
}

private void PlayMusic(AudioClip clip) {
    music1Source.clip = clip;
    music1Source.Play();
}

public void StopMusic() {
    music1Source.Stop();
}
...
```

**Write music names in these strings.**

**Load intro music from Resources.**

**Load main music from Resources.**

**Play music by setting AudioSource.clip.**

As usual, the new serialized variables will be visible in the Inspector when you select the object Game Managers. Drag Music 1 into the audio source slot. Then type in the names of the music files in the two string variables: intro-synth and loop.

The remainder of the added code calls commands for loading and playing music (or, in the last added method, stopping the music). The Resources.Load() command loads the named asset from the Resources folder (taking into account that the files are placed in the Music subfolder within Resources). A generic object is returned by that command, but the object can be converted to a more specific type (in this case, an AudioClip) using the as keyword.

The loaded audio clip is then passed into the PlayMusic() method. This function sets the clip in the AudioSource and then calls Play(). As I explained earlier, sound effects are better implemented using PlayOneShot(), but setting the clip in the AudioSource is a more robust approach for music, allowing you to stop or pause the playing music.

**STEP 4: ADD MUSIC CONTROLS TO THE UI**

The new music playback methods in AudioManager won't do anything unless they're called from elsewhere. Let's add more buttons to the audio UI that will play different music when pressed. Here again are the steps enumerated with little explanation (refer back to chapter 6 if needed):

1  Change the pop-up's width to 350 (to fit more buttons).
2  Create a new UI button and parent it to the pop-up.
3  Set the button's width to 100 and position to 0, -20.
4  Expand the button's hierarchy to select the text label and set that to Level Music.
5  Repeat these steps twice more to create two additional buttons.
6  Position one at -105, -20 and the other at 105, -20 (so they appear on either side).
7  Change the first text label to Intro Music and the last text label to No Music.

Now the pop-up has three buttons for playing different music. Write a method (shown in the following listing) in SettingsPopup that will be linked to each button.

---
**Listing 10.10   Adding music controls to SettingsPopup**
---

```
...
public void OnPlayMusic(int selector) {              ◁  This method gets a number
   Managers.Audio.PlaySound(sound);                       parameter from the button.

   switch (selector) {                               ◁  Call a different music function in
   case 1:                                              AudioManager for each button.
      Managers.Audio.PlayIntroMusic();
      break;
   case 2:
      Managers.Audio.PlayLevelMusic();
      break;
   default:
      Managers.Audio.StopMusic();
      break;
   }
}
...
```

Note that the function takes an int parameter this time; normally button methods don't have a parameter and are simply triggered by the button. In this case, we need to distinguish between the three buttons, so the buttons will each send a different number.

Go through the typical steps to connect a button to this code: add an entry to the OnClick panel in the Inspector, drag the pop-up to the object slot, and choose the appropriate function from the menu. This time, there will be a text box for typing in a number, because OnPlayMusic() takes a number for a parameter. Type 1 for Intro Music, 2 for Level Music, and anything else for No Music (I went with 0). The switch statement in OnMusic() plays intro music or level music depending on the number, or stops the music as a default if the number isn't 1 or 2.

When you press the music buttons while the game is playing, you'll hear the music. Great! The code is loading the audio clips from the Resources folder. Music plays efficiently, although there are still two bits of polish we'll add: separate music volume control and cross-fading when changing the music.

### 10.4.2  *Controlling music volume separately*

The game already has volume control, and currently that affects the music, too. Most games have separate volume controls for sound effects and music, though, so let's tackle that now.

The first step is to tell the music AudioSources to ignore settings on AudioListener. We want volume and mute on the global AudioListener to continue to affect all sound effects, but we don't want this volume to apply to music. Listing 10.10 includes code to tell the music source to ignore the volume on AudioListener. The code in the following listing also adds volume control and mute for music, so add it to AudioManager.

**Listing 10.11   Controlling music volume separately in AudioManager**

```
...
private float _musicVolume;
public float musicVolume {
   get {
      return _musicVolume;
   }
   set {
      _musicVolume = value;

      if (music1Source != null) {
         music1Source.volume = _musicVolume;
      }
   }
}
...
public bool musicMute {
   get {
      if (music1Source != null) {
         return music1Source.mute;
      }
      return false;
   }
   set {
      if (music1Source != null) {
         music1Source.mute = value;
      }
   }
}

public void Startup(NetworkService service) {
   Debug.Log("Audio manager starting...");

   _network = service;

   music1Source.ignoreListenerVolume = true;
   music1Source.ignoreListenerPause = true;

   soundVolume = 1f;
   musicVolume = 1f;

   status = ManagerStatus.Started;
}
...
```

◁ **Private variable that won't be accessed directly, only through the property's getter**

◁ **Adjust volume of the AudioSource directly.**

◁ **Default value in case the AudioSource is missing**

◁ **Italicized code was already in script, shown here for reference.**

**These properties tell the AudioSource to ignore AudioListener volume.**

The key to this code is realizing you can adjust the volume of an AudioSource directly, even though that audio source is ignoring the global volume defined in AudioListener. There are properties for both volume and mute that manipulate the individual music source.

The `Startup()` method initializes the music source with both `ignoreListenerVolume` and `ignoreListenerPause` turned on. As the names suggest, those properties cause the audio source to ignore the global volume setting on AudioListener.

You can hit Play now to verify that the music is no longer affected by the existing volume control. Now let's add a second UI control for the music volume; start by adjusting SettingsPopup according to the next listing.

---

**Listing 10.12   Music volume controls in SettingsPopup**

```
...
public void OnMusicToggle() {
    Managers.Audio.musicMute = !Managers.Audio.musicMute;      ⊲  Repeat the mute
    Managers.Audio.PlaySound(sound);                              control, only use
}                                                                 musicMute instead.

public void OnMusicValue(float volume) {
    Managers.Audio.musicVolume = volume;              ⊲  Repeat the volume control,
}                                                        only use musicVolume instead.
...
```

There's not a lot to explain about this code—it's mostly repeating the sound volume controls. Obviously the AudioManager properties used have changed from `sound-Mute`/`soundVolume` to `musicMute`/`musicVolume`.

In the editor, create a button and slider just as you did before. Here are those steps again:

1  Change the pop-up's height to 225 (to fit more controls).
2  Create a UI button.
3  Parent the button to the pop-up.
4  Position the button at 0, -60.
5  Expand the button's hierarchy in order to select its text label.
6  Change the text to `Toggle Music`.
7  Create a slider (from the same UI menu).
8  Parent the slider to the pop-up and position at 0, -85.

Link up these UI controls to the code in SettingsPopup. Find the OnClick/OnValueChanged panel in the UI element's settings, click the + button to add an entry, drag the pop-up object to the object slot, and select the function from the menu. The functions you need to pick are `OnMusicToggle()` and `OnMusicValue()` from the Dynamic Float section of the menu.

Now run this code and you'll see that the controls affect sound effects and music separately. This is getting pretty sophisticated, but there's one more bit of polish remaining: cross-fade between music tracks.

### 10.4.3   *Fading between songs*

As a final bit of polish, let's make AudioManager fade in and out between different background tunes. Currently the switch between different music tracks is pretty jarring, with the sound suddenly cutting off and changing to the new track. We can smooth out that transition by having the volume of the previous track quickly dwindle away while the volume quickly rises from 0 on the new track. This is a simple but clever bit of code that combines both the volume control methods you just saw, along with a coroutine to change the volume incrementally over time.

Listing 10.13 adds a lot of bits to AudioManager, but most revolve around a simple concept: now that we'll have two separate audio sources, play separate music tracks on separate audio sources, and incrementally increase the volume of one source while simultaneously decreasing the volume of the other (as usual, italicized code was already in the script and is shown here for reference).

**Listing 10.13 Cross-fade between music in AudioManager**

```
...
[SerializeField] private AudioSource music2Source;          Second AudioSource
                                                            (keep the first, too)
private AudioSource _activeMusic;
private AudioSource _inactiveMusic;                         Keep track of which
                                                            source is active vs. inactive.
public float crossFadeRate = 1.5f;
private bool _crossFading;                                  A toggle to avoid bugs while
...                                                         a cross-fade is happening
public float musicVolume {
    ...
    set {
        _musicVolume = value;

        if (music1Source != null && !_crossFading) {
            music1Source.volume = _musicVolume;
            music2Source.volume = _musicVolume;            Adjust the volume on
        }                                                   both music sources.
    }
}
...
public bool musicMute {
    ...
    set {
        if (music1Source != null) {
            music1Source.mute = value;
            music2Source.mute = value;
        }
    }
}

public void Startup(NetworkService service) {
    Debug.Log("Audio manager starting...");

    _network = service;

    music1Source.ignoreListenerVolume = true;
    music2Source.ignoreListenerVolume = true;
    music1Source.ignoreListenerPause = true;
    music2Source.ignoreListenerPause = true;
```

```
    soundVolume = 1f;
    musicVolume = 1f;

    _activeMusic = music1Source;          Initialize one as the
    _inactiveMusic = music2Source;        active AudioSource.

    status = ManagerStatus.Started;
}
...
private void PlayMusic(AudioClip clip) {          Call a coroutine when
    if (_crossFading) {return;}                   changing music.
    StartCoroutine(CrossFadeMusic(clip));
}
private IEnumerator CrossFadeMusic(AudioClip clip) {
    _crossFading = true;

    _inactiveMusic.clip = clip;
    _inactiveMusic.volume = 0;
    _inactiveMusic.Play();

    float scaledRate = crossFadeRate * _musicVolume;
    while (_activeMusic.volume > 0) {
        _activeMusic.volume -= scaledRate * Time.deltaTime;
        _inactiveMusic.volume += scaledRate * Time.deltaTime;

        yield return null;                    This yield statement
    }                                         pauses for one frame.

    AudioSource temp = _activeMusic;          Temporary variable to use while
                                              swapping _active and _inactive.
    _activeMusic = _inactiveMusic;
    _activeMusic.volume = _musicVolume;

    _inactiveMusic = temp;
    _inactiveMusic.Stop();

    _crossFading = false;
}

public void StopMusic() {
    _activeMusic.Stop();
    _inactiveMusic.Stop();
}
...
```

The first addition is a variable for the second music source. While keeping the first
AudioSource object, duplicate that object (make sure the settings are the same—select
Loop) and then drag the new object into this Inspector slot. The code also defines
AudioSource variables active and inactive but those are private variables used within
the code and not exposed in the Inspector. Specifically, those variables define which of
the two audio sources is considered "active" or "inactive" at any given time.

The code now calls a coroutine when playing new music. This coroutine sets the
new music playing on one AudioSource while the old music keeps playing on the old

audio source. Then the coroutine incrementally increases the volume of the new music while incrementally decreasing the volume of the old music. Once the cross-fading is complete (that is, the volumes have completely exchanged places), the function swaps which audio source is considered "active" and "inactive."

Great! We've completed the background music for our game's audio system.

---

### FMOD: a tool for game audio

The audio system in Unity is powered by FMOD, a popular audio programming library. The library is available at www.fmod.org, but it's already integrated into Unity. Unity has many features of FMOD integrated, although it lacks the library's most advanced features (you can visit their website to learn about those features).

Such advanced audio features are offered through FMOD Studio (a plug-in that adds more functionality to Unity), but the examples in this chapter will stick to the functionality built into Unity. That core functionality comprises the most important features for a game's audio system. Most game developers have their audio needs served quite well by this core functionality, but the plug-in is useful for those wishing to get even more intricate with their game's audio.

---

## 10.5 Summary

In this chapter you've learned that

- Sound effects should be uncompressed audio and music should be compressed, but use the WAV format for both because Unity applies compression to imported audio.
- Audio clips can be 2D sounds that always play the same or 3D sounds that react to the listener's position.
- The volume of sound effects is easily adjusted globally using Unity's Audio-Listener.
- You can set volume on individual audio sources that play music.
- You can fade background music in and out by setting the volume on individual audio sources.

# Putting the parts together into a complete game

**11**

**This chapter covers**

- Assembling objects and code from other projects
- Programming point-and-click controls
- Upgrading the UI from the old to a new system
- Loading new levels in response to objectives
- Setting up win/loss conditions
- Saving and loading the player's progress

The project in this chapter will tie together everything from previous chapters. Most chapters have been pretty self-contained, and there was never any end-to-end look at the entire game. I'll walk you through pulling together pieces that had been introduced separately so that you know how to build a complete game out of all the pieces. I'll also discuss the encompassing structure of the game, including switching levels and especially ending the game (for example, *Game Over* when you die, *Success* when you reach the exit). And I'll show you how to save the game, because saving the player's progress becomes increasingly important as the game grows in size.

> **WARNING** Much of this chapter will use tasks that were explained in detail in previous chapters, so I'll move through steps quickly. If certain steps confuse you, refer to the relevant previous chapter (for example, chapter 6 about the UI) for a more detailed explanation.

This chapter's project is a demo of an action RPG. In this sort of game, the camera is placed high and looks down sharply (see figure 11.1), and the character is controlled by clicking the mouse where you want to go; you may be familiar with the game *Diablo*, which is an action RPG like this. I'm switching to yet another game genre so that we can squeeze in one more genre before the end of the book!

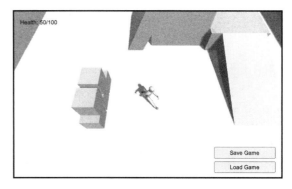

**Figure 11.1   Screenshot of the top-down viewpoint**

In full, the project in this chapter will be the biggest game yet. It'll feature the following:

- A top-down view with point-and-click movement
- The ability to click on devices to operate them
- Scattered items you can collect
- Inventory that's displayed in a UI window
- Enemies wandering around the level
- The ability to save the game and restore your progress
- Three levels that must be completed in sequence

Whew, that's a lot to pack in; good thing this is almost the last chapter!

## 11.1   *Building an action RPG by repurposing projects*

We'll develop the action RPG demo by building on the project from chapter 8. Copy that project's folder and open the copy in Unity to start working. Or, if you skipped directly to this chapter, download the sample project for chapter 8 in order to build on that.

The reason we're building on the chapter 8 project is that it's the closest to our goal for this chapter and thus will require the least modification (when compared to other projects). Ultimately, we'll pull together assets from several chapters, so technically it's not that different than if we started with one of those projects and pulled in assets from chapter 8.

Here's a recap of what's in the project from chapter 8:

- A character with an animation controller already set up
- A third-person camera that follows the character around
- A level with floors, walls, and ramps
- Lights and shadows all placed
- Operable devices, including a color-changing monitor
- Collectible inventory items
- Back-end managers code framework

This hefty list of features covers quite a bit of the action in the RPG demo already, but there's a bit more that we'll either need to modify or add.

### 11.1.1  *Assembling assets and code from multiple projects*

All right, the first modifications will be to update the managers framework and to bring in computer-controlled enemies. For the former task, recall that updates to the framework were made in chapter 9, which means those updates aren't in the project from chapter 8. For the latter task, recall that you programmed an enemy in chapter 3.

#### UPDATING THE MANAGERS FRAMEWORK

Updating the managers is a fairly simple task, so let's get that out of the way first. The IGameManager interface was modified in chapter 9 (see the next listing).

**Listing 11.1   Adjusted `IGameManager`**

```
public interface IGameManager {
   ManagerStatus status {get;}

   void Startup(NetworkService service);
}
```

The code in this listing adds a reference to NetworkService, so also be sure to copy over that additional script; drag the file from its location in the chapter 9 project (remember, a Unity project is a folder on your disc, so get the file from there) and drop it in the new project. Now modify Managers.cs to work with the changed interface (see the following listing).

**Listing 11.2   Changing a bit of code in the Managers script**

```
...
private IEnumerator StartupManagers() {
   NetworkService network = new NetworkService();        ◁──  The adjustments are at the
                                                               beginning of this method.
   foreach (IGameManager manager in _startSequence) {
      manager.Startup(network);
   }
   ...
```

Finally, adjust both InventoryManager and PlayerManager to reflect the changed interface. The next listing shows the modified code from InventoryManager; Player-Manager needs the same code modifications but with different names.

**Listing 11.3 Adjusting InventoryManager to reflect IGameManager**

```
...
private NetworkService _network;

public void Startup(NetworkService service) {
    Debug.Log("Inventory manager starting...");

    _network = service;

    _items = new Dictionary<string, int>();
    ...
```

> Same adjustments in both managers, but change names.

Once all the minor code changes are in, everything should still act as before. This update should work invisibly, and the game still works the same. That adjustment was easy, but the next one will be harder.

**BRING OVER THE AI ENEMY**

Besides the NetworkServices adjustments from chapter 9, you also need the AI enemy from chapter 3. Implementing enemy characters involved a bunch of scripts and art assets, so you need to import all those assets.

First copy over these scripts (remember, WanderingAI and ReactiveTarget were behaviors for the AI enemy, Fireball was the projectile fired, the enemy attacks the PlayerCharacter component, and SceneController handles spawning enemies):

- PlayerCharacter.cs
- SceneController.cs
- WanderingAI.cs
- ReactiveTarget.cs
- Fireball.cs

Similarly, get the Flame material, Fireball prefab, and Enemy prefab by dragging those files in. If you got the enemy from chapter 10 instead of 3, you also need the added fire particle material.

After copying over all the required assets, the links between assets will probably be broken, so you'll need to relink everything in order to get them to work. In particular, scripts are probably not correctly connected to the prefabs. For example, the Enemy prefab has two missing scripts in the Inspector, so click the circle button (indicated in figure 11.2) to choose WanderingAI and ReactiveTarget from the list of scripts.

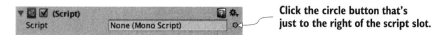

> Click the circle button that's just to the right of the script slot.

**Figure 11.2 Linking a script to a component**

Similarly, check the Fireball prefab and relink that script if needed. Once you're through with the scripts, check the links to materials and textures.

Now add SceneController.cs to the controller object and drag the Enemy prefab onto that component's Enemy slot in the Inspector. You may need to drag the Fireball prefab onto the Enemy's script component (select the Enemy prefab and look at WanderingAI in the Inspector). Also attach PlayerCharacter.cs to the player object so that enemies will attack the player.

Play the game and you'll see the enemy wandering around. The enemy shoots fireballs at the player, although it won't do much damage; select the Fireball prefab and set its Damage value to 10.

> **NOTE** Currently the enemy isn't particularly good at tracking down and hitting the player. In this case, I'd start by giving the enemy a wider field of vision (using the dot product approach from chapter 8). Ultimately, though, you'll spend a lot of time polishing a game, and that includes iterating on the behavior of enemies. Polishing a game to make it more fun, though crucial for a game to be released, isn't something you'll do in this book.

The other issue is that when you wrote this code in chapter 3, the player's health was an ad hoc thing for testing. Now the game has an actual PlayerManager, so modify PlayerCharacter according to the next listing in order to work with health in that manager.

**Listing 11.4  Adjusting PlayerCharacter to use health in PlayerManager**

```
using UnityEngine;
using System.Collections;

public class PlayerCharacter : MonoBehaviour {
    public void Hurt(int damage) {                    Use the value in PlayerManager
        Managers.Player.ChangeHealth(-damage);    ⤶  instead of the variable in
    }                                                 PlayerCharacter.
}
```

At this point you have a game demo with pieces assembled from multiple previous projects. An enemy character has been added to the scene, making the game more threatening. But the controls and viewpoint are still from the third-person movement demo, so let's implement point-and-click controls for an action RPG.

### 11.1.2 *Programming point-and-click controls: movement and devices*

This demo needs a top-down view and mouse control of the player's movement (refer back to figure 11.1). Currently the camera responds to the mouse, whereas the player responds to the keyboard (that is, what was programmed in chapter 7), which is the reverse of what you want in this chapter. In addition, you'll modify the color-changing monitor so that devices are operated by clicking on them. In both cases, the existing code isn't terribly far from what you need; you'll make adjustments to both the movement and device scripts.

## TOP-DOWN VIEW OF THE SCENE

First, you'll raise the camera to 8 Y to position it for an overhead view. You'll also adjust OrbitCamera to remove mouse controls from the camera and only use arrow keys (see the following listing).

**Listing 11.5  Adjusting OrbitCamera to remove mouse controls**

```
...
void LateUpdate() {
    _rotY -= Input.GetAxis("Horizontal") * rotSpeed;        Reverse the direction
    Quaternion rotation = Quaternion.Euler(0, _rotY, 0);    from before.
    transform.position = target.position - (rotation * _offset);
    transform.LookAt(target);
}
...
```

### The camera's Near/Far clipping planes

As long as you're adjusting the camera, I want to point out the Near/Far clipping planes. These settings never came up before because the defaults are fine, but you may need to adjust these in some future project.

Select the camera in the scene and look for the Clipping Planes section in the Inspector; both Near and Far are numbers you'll type here. These values define near and far boundaries within which meshes are rendered: polygons closer than the Near clipping plane or farther than the Far clipping plane aren't drawn.

You want the Near/Far clipping planes as close together as possible while still being far enough apart to render everything in your scene. When those planes are too far apart (Near is too close or Far is too far), the rendering algorithm can no longer tell which polygons are closer. This results in a characteristic rendering error called *z-fighting* (as in the Z-axis for depth) where polygons flicker on top of each other.

With the camera raised even higher, the view when you play the game will be top-down. At the moment, though, the movement controls still use the keyboard, so let's write a script for point-and-click movement.

## WRITING THE MOVEMENT CODE

The general idea for this code (illustrated in figure 11.3) will be to automatically move the player toward its target position. This position is set by clicking in the scene. In this way, the code that moves the player isn't directly reacting to the mouse but the player's movement is being controlled indirectly by clicking.

> **NOTE**  This movement algorithm is useful for AI characters as well. Rather than using mouse clicks, the target position could be on a path that the character follows.

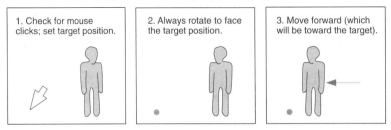

**Figure 11.3   Diagram of how point-and-click controls work**

To implement this, create a new script called PointClickMovement and replace the RelativeMovement component on the player. Start coding PointClickMovement by pasting in the entirety of RelativeMovement (because you still want most of that script for handling falling and animations). Then adjust the code according to the next listing.

**Listing 11.6   New movement code in PointClickMovement script**

```
...
public class PointClickMovement : MonoBehaviour {        ◁   Correct the name
...                                                           after pasting scripts.
public float deceleration = 25.0f;
public float targetBuffer = 1.75f;
private float _curSpeed = 0f;
private Vector3 _targetPos = Vector3.one;
...
void Update() {
    Vector3 movement = Vector3.zero;                         Set target position
                                                             when mouse clicks.
    if (Input.GetMouseButton(0)) {
        Ray ray = Camera.main.ScreenPointToRay(Input.mousePosition);  ◁
        RaycastHit mouseHit;
        if (Physics.Raycast(ray, out mouseHit)) {              Raycast at the
                                                               mouse position.
            _targetPos = mouseHit.point;
            _curSpeed = moveSpeed;
        }
    }
                                                  Move if target
    }                                             position is set.
    if (_targetPos != Vector3.one) {              ◁
        Vector3 adjustedPos = new Vector3(_targetPos.x,
            transform.position.y, _targetPos.z);
        Quaternion targetRot = Quaternion.LookRotation(
            adjustedPos - transform.position);
        transform.rotation = Quaternion.Slerp(transform.rotation,
            targetRot, rotSpeed * Time.deltaTime);             ◁    Rotate toward
                                                                    the target.
        movement = _curSpeed * Vector3.forward;
        movement = transform.TransformDirection(movement);
```

*Set target to position hit.*

```
          if (Vector3.Distance(_targetPos, transform.position) < targetBuffer) {
              _curSpeed -= deceleration * Time.deltaTime;
              if (_curSpeed <= 0) {
                  _targetPos = Vector3.one;
              }
          }
      }
  }
  _animator.SetFloat("Speed", movement.sqrMagnitude);
  ...
```

**Decelerate to 0 when close to target.** *(annotation pointing to first two lines)*

**Everything stays the same from here down.** *(annotation pointing to _animator.SetFloat line)*

Almost everything at the beginning of the Update() method was gutted, because that code was handling keyboard movement. Notice that this new code has two main if statements: one that runs when the mouse clicks, and one that runs when a target is set.

When the mouse clicks, set the target according to where the mouse clicked. Here's yet another great use for raycasting: to determine which point in the scene is under the mouse cursor. The target position is set to where the mouse hits.

As for the second conditional, first rotate to face the target. Quaternion.Slerp() rotates smoothly to face the target, rather than immediately snapping to that rotation. Then, transform the forward direction from the player's local coordinates to global coordinates (in order to move forward). Finally, check the distance between the player and the target: if the player has almost reached the target, decrement the movement speed and eventually end movement by removing the target position.

---

### Exercise: Turn off jump control

Currently this script still has the jump control from RelativeMovement. The player still jumps when the spacebar is pressed, but there shouldn't be a jump button with point-and-click movement. Here's a hint: adjust the code inside the 'if (hitGround)' conditional branch.

---

This takes care of moving the player using mouse controls. Play the game to test it out. Next let's make devices operate when clicked on.

#### OPERATING DEVICES USING THE MOUSE

In chapter 8 (and here until we adjust the code), devices were operated by pressing a button. Instead, they should operate when clicked on. To do this, you'll first create a base script that all devices will inherit from; the base script will have the mouse control, and devices will inherit that. Create a new script called BaseDevice and write the code from the following listing.

**Listing 11.7   BaseDevice script that operates when clicked on**

```
using UnityEngine;
using System.Collections;

public class BaseDevice : MonoBehaviour {
   public float radius = 3.5f;
```

**Function that runs when clicked**

```
void OnMouseDown() {
    Transform player = GameObject.FindWithTag("Player").transform;
    if (Vector3.Distance(player.position, transform.position) < radius) {
        Vector3 direction = transform.position - player.position;
        if (Vector3.Dot(player.forward, direction) > .5f) {
            Operate();
        }
    }
}

public virtual void Operate() {
    // behavior of the specific device
}
}
```

**Call Operate() if player is nearby and facing**

**virtual marks a method that inheritance can override.**

Most of this code happens inside `OnMouseDown()` because `MonoBehaviour` calls that method when the object is clicked on. First, it checks the distance to the player, and then it uses dot product to see if the player is facing the device. `Operate()` is an empty shell to be filled in by devices that inherit this script.

> **NOTE** This code looks in the scene for an object with the `Player` tag, so assign this tag to the player object. Tag is a drop-down menu at the top of the Inspector; you can define custom tags as well, but several tags are defined by default, including `Player`. Select the player object to edit it, and then select the `Player` tag.

Now that BaseDevice is programmed, you can modify ColorChangeDevice to inherit from that script. The following listing shows the new code.

**Listing 11.8   Adjusting ColorChangeDevice to inherit from BaseDevice**

```
using UnityEngine;
using System.Collections;

public class ColorChangeDevice : BaseDevice {
    public override void Operate() {
        Color random = new Color(Random.Range(0f,1f),
            Random.Range(0f,1f), Random.Range(0f,1f));
        GetComponent<Renderer>().material.color = random;
    }
}
```

**Inherit BaseDevice instead of MonoBehaviour.**

Because this script inherits from BaseDevice instead of `MonoBehaviour`, it gets the mouse control functionality. Then it overrides the empty `Operate()` method to program the color changing behavior.

Now the device will operate when you click on it. Also remove the player's Device-Operator script component, because that script operates devices using the control key.

This new device input brings up an issue with the movement controls: currently the movement target is set any time the mouse clicks, but you don't want to set the movement target when clicking on devices. You can fix this issue by using layers; similar to how a tag was set on the player, objects can be set to different layers and the code can check for that. Adjust PointClickMovement to check for the object's layer (see the next listing).

---

**Listing 11.9   Adjusting mouse click code in PointClickMovement**

```
...
Ray ray = Camera.main.ScreenPointToRay(Input.mousePosition);
RaycastHit mouseHit;
if (Physics.Raycast(ray, out mouseHit)) {
   GameObject hitObject = mouseHit.transform.gameObject;          Added code; the
   if (hitObject.layer == LayerMask.NameToLayer("Ground")) {      rest is reference.
      _targetPos = mouseHit.point;
      _curSpeed = moveSpeed;
   }
}
...
```

This listing adds a conditional inside the mouse click code to see if the clicked object is on the Ground layer. Layers (like Tags) is a drop-down menu at the top of the Inspector; click it to see the options. Also like tags, several layers are already defined by default. You want to create a new layer, so choose Edit Layers in the menu. Type Ground in an empty layer slot (probably slot 8; NameToLayer() in the code converts names into layer numbers so that you can say the name instead of the number).

Now that the Ground layer has been added to the menu, set ground objects to the Ground layer—that means the floor of the building, along with the ramps and plat-forms that the player can walk on. Select those objects, and then select Ground in the Layers menu.

Play the game and you won't move when clicking on the color-changing monitor. Great, the point-and-click controls are complete! One more thing to bring into this project from previous projects is the improved UI.

### 11.1.3  *Replacing the old GUI with a new interface*

Chapter 8 used Unity's old immediate-mode GUI because that approach was simpler to code. But the UI from chapter 8 doesn't look as nice as the one from chapter 6, so let's bring over that interface system. The newer UI is more visually polished than the old GUI; figure 11.4 shows the interface you're going to create.

First, you'll set up the UI graphics. Once the UI images are all in the scene, you can attach scripts to the UI objects. I'll list the steps involved without going into detail; if you need a refresher, refer back to chapter 6:

1  Import popup.png as a sprite (choose Texture Type).
2  In the Sprite Editor, set a 12-pixel border on all sides (remember to apply changes).
3  Create a canvas in the scene (GameObject > UI > Canvas).
4  Choose the Pixel Perfect setting of the canvas.
5  Optional: Name the object HUD Canvas and switch to 2D view mode.
6  Create a Text object connected to that canvas (GameObject > UI > Text).

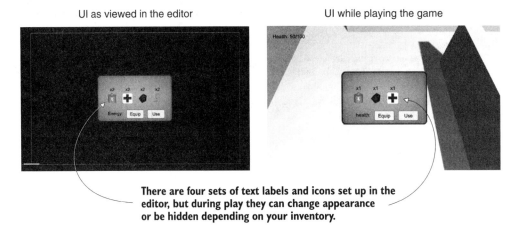

UI as viewed in the editor                    UI while playing the game

There are four sets of text labels and icons set up in the
editor, but during play they can change appearance
or be hidden depending on your inventory.

Figure 11.4   The UI for this chapter's project

7  Set the Text object's anchor to top-left and position 100, -40.

8  Type Health: as the text on the label.

9  Create an image connected to that canvas (GameObject > UI > Image).

10  Name the new object Inventory Popup.

11  Assign the pop-up sprite to the image's Source Image.

12  Set Image Type to Sliced and select Fill Center.

13  Position the pop-up image at 0, 0 and scale the pop-up to 250 width 150 height.

NOTE   Recall how to switch between viewing the 3D scene and the 2D interface: toggle 2D view mode and double-click either the Canvas or the Building
to zoom to that object.

Now you have the Health label in the corner and the large blue pop-up window in the
center. Let's program these parts first before getting deeper into the UI functionality.
The interface code will use the same Messenger system from chapter 6, so copy over
the Messenger script. Then create a GameEvent script (see the following listing).

---

**Listing 11.10   GameEvent script to use with this Messenger system**

```
public static class GameEvent {
   public const string HEALTH_UPDATED = "HEALTH_UPDATED";
}
```

For now only one event is defined; over the course of this chapter you'll add a few
more events. Broadcast this event from PlayerManager.cs (shown in the next listing).

---

**Listing 11.11   Broadcasting the health event from PlayerManager.cs**

```
...
public void ChangeHealth(int value) {
```

```
    health += value;
    if (health > maxHealth) {
        health = maxHealth;
    } else if (health < 0) {
        health = 0;
    }

    Messenger.Broadcast(GameEvent.HEALTH_UPDATED);
}
...
```

Add a line to the end of this function.

The event is broadcast every time `ChangeHealth()` finishes to tell the rest of the program that the health has changed. You want to adjust the health label in response to this event, so create a UIController script (see the next listing).

**Listing 11.12   The script UIController, which handles the interface**

```
using UnityEngine;
using UnityEngine.UI;
using System.Collections;

public class UIController : MonoBehaviour {                 Reference UI object in scene
    [SerializeField] private Text healthLabel;
    [SerializeField] private InventoryPopup popup;

    void Awake() {
        Messenger.AddListener(GameEvent.HEALTH_UPDATED, OnHealthUpdated);
    }
    void OnDestroy() {
        Messenger.RemoveListener(GameEvent.HEALTH_UPDATED, OnHealthUpdated);
    }

    void Start() {
        OnHealthUpdated();

        popup.gameObject.SetActive(false);
    }

    void Update() {
        if (Input.GetKeyDown(KeyCode.M)) {
            bool isShowing = popup.gameObject.activeSelf;
            popup.gameObject.SetActive(!isShowing);
            popup.Refresh();
        }
    }

    private void OnHealthUpdated() {
        string message = "Health: " + Managers.Player.health + "/" +
      Managers.Player.maxHealth;
        healthLabel.text = message;
    }
}
```

Set listener for health update event

Call function manually at startup

Initialize pop-up to be hidden

Toggle pop-up with M key

Event listener calls function to update health label

Attach this script to the Controller object and remove BasicUI. Also, create an InventoryPopup script (add an empty public `Refresh()` method for now; the rest will be filled in later) and attach it to the pop-up window (the Image object). Now you can drag the pop-up to the reference slot in the Controller's component; also link the health label to the Controller.

The health label changes when you get hurt or use health packs, and pressing M toggles the pop-up window. One last detail to adjust is that currently clicking on the pop-up window causes the player to move; just as with devices, you don't want to set the target position when the UI has been clicked on. Make the adjustment shown in the next listing to PointClickMovement.

---

**Listing 11.13  Checking the UI in PointClickMovement**

```
using UnityEngine.EventSystems;
...
void Update() {
  Vector3 movement = Vector3.zero;
  if (Input.GetMouseButton(0) &&
    !EventSystem.current.IsPointerOverGameObject()) {
    ...
```

Note that the conditional checks whether or not the mouse is on the UI. That completes the overall structure of the interface, so now let's deal with the inventory pop-up specifically.

**IMPLEMENTING THE INVENTORY POP-UP**

The pop-up window is currently blank but it should display the player's inventory (depicted in figure 11.5). These steps will create the UI objects:

1  Create four images and parent them to the pop-up (that is, drag objects in the Hierarchy).
2  Create four text labels and parent them to the pop-up.
3  Position all the images at 0 Y and X values -75, -25, 25, and 75.
4  Position the text labels at 50 Y and X values -75, -25, 25, and 75.
5  Set the text (not the anchor!) to Center alignment, Bottom vertical align, and Height 60.
6  In Resources, set all inventory icons as Sprite (instead of Textures).

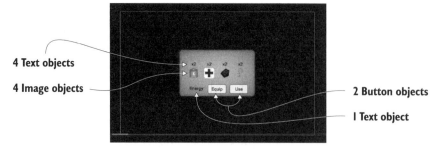

**Figure 11.5  Diagram of the inventory UI**

7 Drag these sprites to the Source Image slot of the Image objects (also set Native Size).

8 Enter x2 for all the text labels.

9 Add another text label and two buttons, all parented to the pop-up.

10 Position this text label at -120, -55 and set Right alignment.

11 Type Energy: for the text on this label

12 Set both buttons to Width 60, then Position at -50 Y and X values 0 or 70.

13 Type Equip on one button and Use on the other.

These are the visual elements for the inventory pop-up; next is the code. Write the contents of the following listing into the InventoryPopup script.

**Listing 11.14  Full script for InventoryPopup**

```
using UnityEngine;
using UnityEngine.UI;
using UnityEngine.EventSystems;
using System.Collections;
using System.Collections.Generic;

public class InventoryPopup : MonoBehaviour {
    [SerializeField] private Image[] itemIcons;        Arrays to reference four
    [SerializeField] private Text[] itemLabels;        images and text labels

    [SerializeField] private Text curItemLabel;
    [SerializeField] private Button equipButton;
    [SerializeField] private Button useButton;

    private string _curItem;

    public void Refresh() {
        List<string> itemList = Managers.Inventory.GetItemList();

        int len = itemIcons.Length;                     Check inventory list while
        for (int i = 0; i < len; i++) {                 looping through all UI images
            if (i < itemList.Count) {
                itemIcons[i].gameObject.SetActive(true);
                itemLabels[i].gameObject.SetActive(true);

                string item = itemList[i];

                Sprite sprite = Resources.Load<Sprite>("Icons/"+item);
                itemIcons[i].sprite = sprite;
                itemIcons[i].SetNativeSize();

                int count = Managers.Inventory.GetItemCount(item);
                string message = "x" + count;
                if (item == Managers.Inventory.equippedItem) {
                    message = "Equipped\n" + message;
                }
                itemLabels[i].text = message;
```

Load sprite from
Resources

Resize image
to native size
of the sprite

Label may say "Equipped"
in addition to item count

```
                          EventTrigger.Entry entry = new EventTrigger.Entry();
                          entry.eventID = EventTriggerType.PointerClick;
                          entry.callback.AddListener((BaseEventData data) => {
                             OnItem(item);
                          });

                          EventTrigger trigger = itemIcons[i].GetComponent<EventTrigger>();
                          trigger.delegates.Clear();
                          trigger.delegates.Add(entry);
                       }
                       else {
                          itemIcons[i].gameObject.SetActive(false);
                          itemLabels[i].gameObject.SetActive(false);
                       }
                    }
                 }

                 if (!itemList.Contains(_curItem)) {
                    _curItem = null;
                 }
                 if (_curItem == null) {
                    curItemLabel.gameObject.SetActive(false);
                    equipButton.gameObject.SetActive(false);
                    useButton.gameObject.SetActive(false);
                 }
                 else {
                    curItemLabel.gameObject.SetActive(true);
                    equipButton.gameObject.SetActive(true);
                    if (_curItem == "health") {
                       useButton.gameObject.SetActive(true);
                    } else {
                       useButton.gameObject.SetActive(false);
                    }

                    curItemLabel.text = _curItem+":";
                 }
              }

              public void OnItem(string item) {
                 _curItem = item;
                 Refresh();
              }

              public void OnEquip() {
                 Managers.Inventory.EquipItem(_curItem);
                 Refresh();
              }

              public void OnUse() {
                 Managers.Inventory.ConsumeItem(_curItem);
                 if (_curItem == "health") {
                    Managers.Player.ChangeHealth(25);
                 }
                 Refresh();
              }
           }
```

**Lambda function to trigger differently for each item** ▷

**Enable clicking on icons.** ◁

**Add this listener function to EventTrigger.** ▷

**Clear listener to refresh from clean slate** ◁

**Hide this image/text if no item to display.**

**Hide buttons if no item selected** ◁

**Display currently selected item** ▷

**Use button only for health item** ◁

**Function called by mouse click listener** ◁

**Refresh inventory display after making changes** ◁

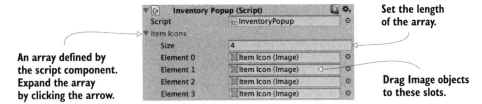

An array defined by the script component. Expand the array by clicking the arrow.

Set the length of the array.

Drag Image objects to these slots.

**Figure 11.6   Arrays displayed in the Inspector**

Whew, that was a long script! And new Unity versions require a small correction; refer to the sample download. The script component now has the various object references, including the two arrays; expand both arrays and set to a length of 4 (see figure 11.6). Drag the four images to the `icons` array, and drag the four text labels to the `labels` array.

**NOTE**   If you aren't sure which object is linked where (they all look the same), click the slot in the Inspector to see that object highlighted in the Hierarchy view.

Similarly, slots in the component reference the text label and buttons at the bottom of the pop-up. After linking those objects, you'll add `OnClick` listeners for both buttons. Link these events to the pop-up object, and choose either `OnEquip()` or `OnUse()` as appropriate.

Finally, add an EventTrigger component to all four of the item images. The InventoryPopup script modifies this component on each icon, so they better have this component! You'll find EventTrigger under Add Component > Event (it may be more convenient to copy/paste the component by clicking the little gear button in the top corner of the component: select Copy Component from one object and then Paste As New on the other). Add this component but don't assign event listeners, because that's done in the InventoryPopup code.

And that completes the inventory UI! Play the game to watch the inventory pop-up respond when you collect items and click buttons. We're now finished assembling parts from previous projects; next I'll explain how to build a more expansive game from this beginning.

## 11.2   *Developing the overarching game structure*

Now that you have a functioning action RPG demo, we're going to build the overarching structure of this game. By that I mean the overall flow of the game through multiple levels and progressing through the game by beating levels. What we got from chapter 8's project was a single level, but the roadmap for this chapter specified three levels.

Doing this will involve decoupling the scene even further from the Managers back end, so you'll broadcast messages about the managers (just as PlayerManager broadcasts health updates). Create a new script called StartupEvent (listing 11.15); define these events in a separate script because these events go with the reusable Managers system, whereas GameEvent is specific to the game.

**Listing 11.15   The StartupEvent script**

```
public static class StartupEvent {
   public const string MANAGERS_STARTED = "MANAGERS_STARTED";
   public const string MANAGERS_PROGRESS = "MANAGERS_PROGRESS";
}
```

Now it's time to start adjusting Managers, including broadcasting these new events!

### 11.2.1  *Controlling mission flow and multiple levels*

Currently the project has only one scene, and the Game Managers object is in that scene. The problem with that is that every scene will have its own set of game managers, whereas you actually want a single set of game managers shared by all scenes. To do that, you'll create a separate Startup scene that initializes the managers and then shares that object with the other scenes of the game.

We're also going to need a new manager to handle progress through the game. Create a new script called MissionManager (as shown in the next listing).

**Listing 11.16   MissionManager**

```
using UnityEngine;
using System.Collections;
using System.Collections.Generic;

public class MissionManager : MonoBehaviour, IGameManager {
   public ManagerStatus status {get; private set;}

   public int curLevel {get; private set;}
   public int maxLevel {get; private set;}

   private NetworkService _network;

   public void Startup(NetworkService service) {
      Debug.Log("Mission manager starting...");

      _network = service;

      curLevel = 0;
      maxLevel = 1;

      status = ManagerStatus.Started;
   }

   public void GoToNext() {                        Send arguments along with
      if (curLevel < maxLevel) {                   WWW using WWWForm.
         curLevel++;
         string name = "Level" + curLevel;
         Debug.Log("Loading " + name);             Check if last level reached
         Application.LoadLevel(name);
```

```
      } else {
        Debug.Log("Last level");
      }
    }
  }
}
```

For the most part, there's nothing unusual going on in this listing, but note the Load-Level() method near the end; although I mentioned that method before (in chapter 5), it wasn't important until now. That's Unity's method for loading a scene file; in chapter 5 you used it to reload the one scene in the game, but you can load any scene by passing in the name of the scene file.

Attach this script to the Game Managers object in the scene. Also add a new component to the Managers script (see the following listing).

**Listing 11.17  Adding a new component to the Managers script**

```
...
[RequireComponent(typeof(MissionManager))]

public class Managers : MonoBehaviour {
  public static PlayerManager Player {get; private set;}
  public static InventoryManager Inventory {get; private set;}
  public static MissionManager Mission {get; private set;}
  ...
  void Awake() {
    DontDestroyOnLoad(gameObject);                        ← Unity's command to persist
                                                             an object between scenes
    Player = GetComponent<PlayerManager>();
    Inventory = GetComponent<InventoryManager>();
    Mission = GetComponent<MissionManager>();

    _startSequence = new List<IGameManager>();
    _startSequence.Add(Player);
    _startSequence.Add(Inventory);
    _startSequence.Add(Mission);

    StartCoroutine(StartupManagers());
  }

  private IEnumerator StartupManagers() {
    ...
      if (numReady > lastReady) {
        Debug.Log("Progress: " + numReady + "/" + numModules);
        Messenger<int, int>.Broadcast(
          StartupEvent.MANAGERS_PROGRESS, numReady, numModules);    ←
      }
                                                    Startup event broadcast with
      yield return null;                             data related to the event
    }
                          Debug.Log("All managers started up");
  Startup event        Messenger.Broadcast(StartupEvent.MANAGERS_STARTED);
  broadcast
  without
  parameters
  }
  ...
```

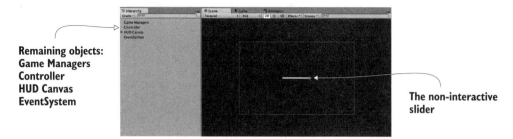

**Remaining objects:**
**Game Managers**
**Controller**
**HUD Canvas**
**EventSystem**

**The non-interactive**
**slider**

Figure 11.7  **The Startup scene with everything unnecessary removed**

Most of this code should already be familiar to you (adding MissionManager is just like adding other managers), but there are two new parts. One is the event that sends two integer values; you saw both generic valueless events and messages with a single number before, but you can send an arbitrary number of values with the same syntax.

The other new bit of code is the DontDestroyOnLoad() method. It's a method provided by Unity for persisting an object between scenes. Normally all objects in a scene are purged when a new scene loads, but by using DontDestroyOnLoad() on an object, you ensure that that object will still be there in the new scene.

**SEPARATE SCENES FOR STARTUP AND LEVEL**

Because the Game Managers object will persist in all scenes, you must separate the managers from individual levels of the game. In Project view, duplicate the scene file (Edit > Duplicate) and then rename the two files appropriately: one Startup and the other Level1. Open Level1 and delete the Game Managers object (it'll be provided by Startup). Open Startup and delete everything other than Game Managers, Controller, HUD Canvas, and EventSystem. Remove the script components on Controller, and delete the UI objects (health label and InventoryPopup) parented to the Canvas.

The UI is currently empty, so create a new slider (see figure 11.7) and then turn off its Interactable setting. The Controller object also has no script components anymore, so create a new StartupController script and attach that to the Controller object (see the following listing).

> Listing 11.18  **The new StartupController script**

```
using UnityEngine;
using UnityEngine.UI;
using System.Collections;

public class StartupController : MonoBehaviour {
   [SerializeField] private Slider progressBar;

   void Awake() {
      Messenger<int, int>.AddListener(StartupEvent.MANAGERS_PROGRESS,
         OnManagersProgress);
```

```
        Messenger.AddListener(StartupEvent.MANAGERS_STARTED,
            OnManagersStarted);
    }
    void OnDestroy() {
        Messenger<int, int>.RemoveListener(StartupEvent.MANAGERS_PROGRESS,
            OnManagersProgress);
        Messenger.RemoveListener(StartupEvent.MANAGERS_STARTED,
            OnManagersStarted);
    }

    private void OnManagersProgress(int numReady, int numModules) {
        float progress = (float)numReady / numModules;
        progressBar.value = progress;                          Update the slider to
    }                                                          show loading progress.

    private void OnManagersStarted() {
        Managers.Mission.GoToNext();               Load the next scene once
    }                                              managers have started.
}
```

Next, link the `Slider` object to the slot in the Inspector. One last thing to do in preparation is add the two scenes to Build Settings. Building the app will be the topic of the next chapter, so for now choose File > Build Settings to see and adjust the list of scenes. Click the Add Current button to add a scene to the list (load both scenes and do this for each).

> **NOTE** You need to add the scenes to Build Settings so that they can be loaded. If you don't, Unity won't know what scenes are available. You didn't need to do this in chapter 5 because you weren't actually switching levels— you were reloading the current scene.

Now you can launch the game by hitting Play from the Startup scene. The `Game Managers` object will be shared in both scenes.

> **WARNING** Because the managers are loaded in the Startup scene, you always need to launch the game from that scene. You could remember to always open that scene before hitting Play, but there's a script on the Unify wiki that will automatically switch to a set scene when you click Play: http://wiki.unity3d.com/index.php/SceneAutoLoader.

This structural change handles the sharing of game managers between different scenes, but you still don't have any success or failure conditions within the level.

### 11.2.2 Completing a level by reaching the exit

To handle level completion, you'll put an object in the scene for the player to touch, and that object will inform MissionManager when the player reaches the objective. This will involve the UI responding to a message about level completion, so add another GameEvent (see the following listing).

**Listing 11.19    Level Complete added to GameEvent.cs**

```
public static class GameEvent {
    public const string HEALTH_UPDATED = "HEALTH_UPDATED";
    public const string LEVEL_COMPLETE = "LEVEL_COMPLETE";
}
```

Now add a new method to MissionManager in order to keep track of mission objectives and broadcast the new event message (see the next listing).

**Listing 11.20    Objective method in MissionManager**

```
...
public void ReachObjective() {
    // could have logic to handle multiple objectives
    Messenger.Broadcast(GameEvent.LEVEL_COMPLETE);
}
...
```

Adjust the UIController script to respond to that event (as shown in the next listing).

**Listing 11.21    New event listener in UIController**

```
...
[SerializeField] private Text levelEnding;
...
void Awake() {
    Messenger.AddListener(GameEvent.HEALTH_UPDATED, OnHealthUpdated);
    Messenger.AddListener(GameEvent.LEVEL_COMPLETE, OnLevelComplete);
}
void OnDestroy() {
    Messenger.RemoveListener(GameEvent.HEALTH_UPDATED, OnHealthUpdated);
    Messenger.RemoveListener(GameEvent.LEVEL_COMPLETE, OnLevelComplete);
}
...
void Start() {
    OnHealthUpdated();

    levelEnding.gameObject.SetActive(false);
    popup.gameObject.SetActive(false);
}
...
private void OnLevelComplete() {
    StartCoroutine(CompleteLevel());
}
private IEnumerator CompleteLevel() {
    levelEnding.gameObject.SetActive(true);
    levelEnding.text = "Level Complete!";

    yield return new WaitForSeconds(2);           ◁  Show message for two seconds
                                                     and then go to next level
    Managers.Mission.GoToNext();
}
...
```

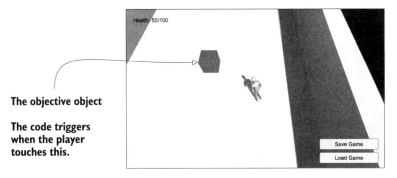

**The objective object**

**The code triggers when the player touches this.**

**Figure 11.8   Objective object that the player touches to complete the level**

You'll notice that this listing has a reference to a text label. Open the Level1 scene to edit it, and create a new UI text object. This label will be a level completion message that appears in the middle of the screen. Set this text to Width 240, Height 60, Center for both Align and Vertical-align, and Font Size 22. Type Level Complete! in the text area and then link this text object to the levelEnding reference of UIController.

Finally, we'll create an object that the player touches to complete the level (figure 11.8 shows what the objective looks like). This will be similar to collectible items: it needs a material and a script, and you'll make the entire thing a prefab.

Create a cube object at Position 18, 1, 0. Select the Is Trigger option of the Box Collider, turn off Cast/Receive Shadows in Mesh Renderer, and set the object to the Ignore Raycast layer. Create a new material called objective; make it bright green and set the shader to Unlit > Color for a flat, bright look.

Next, create the script ObjectiveTrigger (shown in the next listing) and attach that script to the objective object.

**Listing 11.22   Code for ObjectiveTrigger to put on objective objects**

```
using UnityEngine;
using System.Collections;

public class ObjectiveTrigger : MonoBehaviour {        Call the new objective
    void OnTriggerEnter(Collider other) {             method in MissionManager.
        Managers.Mission.ReachObjective();
    }
}
```

Drag this object from the Hierarchy into Project view to turn it into a prefab; in future levels, you could put the prefab in the scene. Now play the game and go reach the objective. The completion message shows when you beat the level.

Next let's have a failure message show when you lose.

### 11.2.3 Losing the level when caught by enemies

The failure condition will be when the player runs out of health (because of the enemy attacking). First add another GameEvent:

```
public const string LEVEL_FAILED = "LEVEL_FAILED";
```

Now adjust PlayerManager to broadcast this message when health drops to 0 (as shown in the next listing).

**Listing 11.23  Broadcast Level Failed from PlayerManager**

```
...
public void Startup(NetworkService service) {
   Debug.Log("Player manager starting...");

   _network = service;                        Call the update method instead
                                              of setting variables directly.
   UpdateData(50, 100);

   status = ManagerStatus.Started;
}

public void UpdateData(int health, int maxHealth) {
   this.health = health;
   this.maxHealth = maxHealth;
}

public void ChangeHealth(int value) {
   health += value;
   if (health > maxHealth) {
      health = maxHealth;
   } else if (health < 0) {
      health = 0;
   }

   if (health == 0) {
      Messenger.Broadcast(GameEvent.LEVEL_FAILED);
   }
   Messenger.Broadcast(GameEvent.HEALTH_UPDATED);
}

public void Respawn() {                        Reset the player
   UpdateData(50, 100);                        to the initial state.
}
...
```

Add a small method to MissionManager for restarting the level (see the next listing).

**Listing 11.24  MissionManager, which can restart the current level**

```
...
public void RestartCurrent() {
   string name = "Level" + curLevel;
   Debug.Log("Loading " + name);
   Application.LoadLevel(name);
}
...
```

With that in place, add another event listener to UIController (shown in the following listing).

---

**Listing 11.25   Responding to Level Failed in UIController**

```
...
Messenger.AddListener(GameEvent.LEVEL_FAILED, OnLevelFailed);
...
Messenger.RemoveListener(GameEvent.LEVEL_FAILED, OnLevelFailed);
...
private void OnLevelFailed() {
    StartCoroutine(FailLevel());
}
private IEnumerator FailLevel() {
    levelEnding.gameObject.SetActive(true);          Reuse the same text label,
    levelEnding.text = "Level Failed";               but set a different message.

    yield return new WaitForSeconds(2);
                                                     Restart the current level
    Managers.Player.Respawn();                       after a 2-second pause.
    Managers.Mission.RestartCurrent();
}
...
```

Play the game and let the enemy shoot you several times; the level failure message will appear. Great job—the player can now complete and fail levels! Building off that, the game must keep track of the player's progress.

## 11.3   *Handling the player's progression through the game*

Right now the individual level operates independently, without any relation to the overall game. You'll add two things that will make progress through the game feel more complete: saving the player's progress and detecting when the game (not just the level) is complete.

### 11.3.1   *Saving and loading the player's progress*

Saving and loading the game is an important part of most games. Unity and Mono provide I/O functionality that you can use for this purpose. Before you can start using that, though, you must add UpdateData() for both MissionManager and Inventory-Manager. That method will work just as it does in PlayerManager and will enable code outside the manager to update data within the manager. Listing 11.26 and listing 11.27 show the changed managers.

---

**Listing 11.26   UpdateData() method in MissionManager**

```
...
public void Startup(NetworkService service) {
    Debug.Log("Mission manager starting...");

    _network = service;                              Modify this line using
                                                     the new method.
    UpdateData(0, 1);
```

```
        status = ManagerStatus.Started;
}

public void UpdateData(int curLevel, int maxLevel) {
    this.curLevel = curLevel;
    this.maxLevel = maxLevel;
}
...
```

**Listing 11.27   UpdateData() method in InventoryManager**

```
...
public void Startup(NetworkService service) {
    Debug.Log("Inventory manager starting...");

    _network = service;

    UpdateData(new Dictionary<string, int>());        ◁—  Initialize an empty list.

    status = ManagerStatus.Started;
}

public void UpdateData(Dictionary<string, int> items) {
    _items = items;
}                                                           Need getter in
public Dictionary<string, int> GetData() {          ◁—     order to save data
    return _items;
}
...
```

Now that the various managers all have `UpdateData()` methods, the data can be saved from a new code module. Saving the data will involve a procedure referred to as *serializing* the data.

> **DEFINITION**   *Serialize* means to encode a batch of data into a form that can be stored.

You'll save the game as binary data, but note that C# is also fully capable of saving text files. For example, the JSON strings you worked with in chapter 9 were data serialized as text. Previous chapters used PlayerPrefs but in this project you're going to save a local file (PlayerPrefs are limited to one megabyte and are only intended to save a handful of values). Create the script DataManager (see the next listing).

> **WARNING**   You can't access the filesystem in a web game. This is a security feature that means a web game can't save a local file. To save data for web games, post the data to your server.

**Listing 11.28   New script for DataManager**

```
using UnityEngine;
using System.Collections;
using System.Collections.Generic;
```

```
using System.Runtime.Serialization.Formatters.Binary;
using System.IO;

public class DataManager : MonoBehaviour, IGameManager {
    public ManagerStatus status {get; private set;}

    private string _filename;

    private NetworkService _network;

    public void Startup(NetworkService service) {
        Debug.Log("Data manager starting...");

        _network = service;

        _filename = Path.Combine(
                Application.persistentDataPath, "game.dat");

        status = ManagerStatus.Started;
    }

    public void SaveGameState() {
        Dictionary<string, object> gamestate = new Dictionary<string,
        object>();
        gamestate.Add("inventory", Managers.Inventory.GetData());
        gamestate.Add("health", Managers.Player.health);
        gamestate.Add("maxHealth", Managers.Player.maxHealth);
        gamestate.Add("curLevel", Managers.Mission.curLevel);
        gamestate.Add("maxLevel", Managers.Mission.maxLevel);

        FileStream stream = File.Create(_filename);
        BinaryFormatter formatter = new BinaryFormatter();
        formatter.Serialize(stream, gamestate);
        stream.Close();
    }

    public void LoadGameState() {
        if (!File.Exists(_filename)) {
            Debug.Log("No saved game");
            return;
        }

        Dictionary<string, object> gamestate;

        BinaryFormatter formatter = new BinaryFormatter();
        FileStream stream = File.Open(_filename, FileMode.Open);
        gamestate = formatter.Deserialize(stream) as Dictionary<string,
        object>;
        stream.Close();

        Managers.Inventory.UpdateData((Dictionary<string,
        int>)gamestate["inventory"]);
        Managers.Player.UpdateData((int)gamestate["health"],
        (int)gamestate["maxHealth"]);
        Managers.Mission.UpdateData((int)gamestate["curLevel"],
        (int)gamestate["maxLevel"]);
        Managers.Mission.RestartCurrent();
    }
}
```

**Construct full path to the game.dat file**

**Dictionary that will be serialized**

**Create a file at the file path.**

**Serialize the Dictionary as contents of the created file.**

**Only continue to load if the file exists.**

**Dictionary to put loaded data in**

**Update managers with deserialized data.**

During `Startup()` the full file path is constructed using `Application.persistent-DataPath`, a location Unity provides to store data in. The exact file path differs on different platforms, but Unity abstracts it behind this static variable (incidentally, this path includes both Company Name and Product Name from Player Settings, so adjust those if needed). The `File.Create()` method will create a binary file; call `File.CreateText()` if you want a text file.

> **WARNING**  When constructing file paths, the path separator is different on different computer platforms. C# has `Path.DirectorySeparatorChar` to account for this.

Open the Startup scene to find Game Managers. Add the `DataManager` script component to the `Game  Managers` object, and then add the new manager to the Managers script (listing 11.29).

---
**Listing 11.29  Adding `DataManager` to Managers.cs**

```
...
[RequireComponent(typeof(DataManager))]
...
public static DataManager Data {get; private set;}
...
void Awake() {
    DontDestroyOnLoad(gameObject);

    Data = GetComponent<DataManager>();
    Player = GetComponent<PlayerManager>();
    Inventory = GetComponent<InventoryManager>();
    Mission = GetComponent<MissionManager>();

    _startSequence = new List<IGameManager>();       ◁
    _startSequence.Add(Player);                          Managers start in this order.
    _startSequence.Add(Inventory);
    _startSequence.Add(Mission);
    _startSequence.Add(Data);

    StartCoroutine(StartupManagers());
}
...
```

> **WARNING**  Because `DataManager` uses other managers (in order to update them), you should make sure that the other managers appear earlier in the startup sequence.

Finally, in Level1 add buttons to use functions in `DataManager` (figure 11.9 shows the buttons). Create two buttons parented to the HUD Canvas (not in the Inventory pop-up).

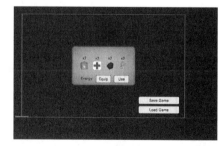

**Figure 11.9   Save and Load buttons on the bottom right of the screen**

Call them (set the attached text objects) `Save Game` and `Load Game`, set Anchor to bottom-right, and position them at -100,65 and -100,30.

These buttons will link to functions in UIController, so write those methods (as shown in the following listing).

---

**Listing 11.30   Save and Load methods in UIController**

```
...
public void SaveGame() {
    Managers.Data.SaveGameState();
}

public void LoadGame() {
    Managers.Data.LoadGameState();
}
...
```

Link these functions to `OnClick` listeners in the buttons (add a listing in the `OnClick` setting, drag in the UIController object, and select functions from the menu). Now play the game, pick up a few items, use a health pack to increase your health, and then save the game. Restart the game and check your inventory to verify that it's empty. Hit Load; you now have the health and items you had when you saved the game!

### 11.3.2   *Beating the game by completing three levels*

As implied by our saving of the player's progress, this game can have multiple levels, not just the one level you've been testing. To properly handle multiple levels, the game must detect not only the completion of a single level, but also the completion of the entire game. First add yet another `GameEvent`:

```
public const string GAME_COMPLETE = "GAME_COMPLETE";
```

Now modify MissionManager to broadcast that message after the last level (see the next listing).

---

**Listing 11.31   Broadcasting Game Complete from MissionManager**

```
...
public void GoToNext() {
    ...
    } else {
        Debug.Log("Last level");
        Messenger.Broadcast(GameEvent.GAME_COMPLETE);
    }
}
```

Respond to that message in UIController (as shown in the following listing).

---

**Listing 11.32   Adding an event listener to UIController**

```
...
Messenger.AddListener(GameEvent.GAME_COMPLETE, OnGameComplete);
...
```

```
Messenger.RemoveListener(GameEvent.GAME_COMPLETE, OnGameComplete);
...
private void OnGameComplete() {
    levelEnding.gameObject.SetActive(true);
    levelEnding.text = "You Finished the Game!";
}
...
```

Try completing the level to watch what happens: move the player to the level objective to complete the level as before. You'll first see the Level Complete message, but after a couple of seconds it'll change to a message about completing the game.

### ADDING MORE LEVELS

At this point you can add an arbitrary number of additional levels, and Mission-Manager will watch for the last level. The final thing you'll do in this chapter is add a few more levels to the project in order to demonstrate the game progressing through multiple levels.

Duplicate the Level1 scene file twice (Unity should automatically increment the numbers to Level2 and Level3) and add the new levels to Build Settings (so that they can be loaded during gameplay). Modify each scene so that you can tell the difference between levels; feel free to rearrange most of the scene, but there are several essential game elements that you must keep: the player object that's tagged Player, the floor object set to the Ground layer, and the objective object, Controller, HUD Canvas, and EventSystem.

> **TIP**   By default, the lighting system regenerates the lightmaps when the level is loaded. But this only works while you are editing the level; lightmaps won't be generated when loading levels while the game is running. As you did in chapter 9, you can turn off Continuous Baking in the lighting window (Window > Lighting) and then click Build to bake lightmaps (remember, don't touch the lighting folder that's created).

You also need to adjust MissionManager to load the new levels. Change maxLevel to 3 by changing the call `UpdateData(0, 1);` to `UpdateData(0, 3);`.

Now play the game and you'll start on Level1 initially; reach the level objective and you'll move on to the next level! Incidentally, you can also save on a later level to see that the game will restore that progress.

---

**Exercise: Integrating audio into the full game**

Chapter 10 was all about implementing audio in Unity. I didn't explain how to integrate that into this chapter's project, but at this point you should understand how. I encourage you to practice your skills by integrating the audio functionality from the previous chapter into this chapter's project. Here's a hint: change the key to toggle the audio settings pop-up so that it doesn't interfere with the inventory pop-up.

You now know how to create a full game with multiple levels. The obvious next task is the final chapter: getting your game into the hands of players.

## 11.4 Summary

In this chapter you've learned that

- Unity makes it easy to repurpose assets and code from a project in a different game genre.
- Another great use for raycasting is to determine where in the scene the player is clicking.
- Unity has simple methods for both loading levels and persisting certain objects between levels.
- You progress through levels in response to various events within the game.
- You can use the I/O methods that come with C# to store data at `Application` `.persistentDataPath`.

# Deploying your game to players' devices

**This chapter covers**

- Building an application package for various platforms
- Assigning build settings, such as the app icon or name
- Interacting with the web page for web games
- Developing plug-ins for apps on mobile platforms

Throughout the book you've learned how to program various games within Unity, but the crucial last step has been missing: deploying those games to players. Until a game is playable outside the Unity editor, it's of little interest to anyone other than the developer. Unity shines at this last step, with the ability to build applications for a huge variety of gaming platforms. This final chapter will go over how to build games for these various platforms.

When I speak of building for a platform, I'm referring to generating an application package that will run on that platform. On every platform (Windows, iOS, and so on) the exact form of a built application differs, but once the executable has

276

been generated, that app package can be played without Unity and can be distributed to players. A single Unity project can be deployed to any platform without needing to be redone for each.

This "build once, deploy anywhere" capability applies to the vast majority of the features in your games, but not to everything. I would estimate that 95% of the code written in Unity (for example, almost everything we've done so far in this book) is platform-agnostic and will work just as well across all platforms. But there are a few specific tasks that differ for different platforms, so we'll go over those platform-specific areas of development.

In total, the basic free version of Unity is capable of building apps for the following platforms:

- Windows PC
- Mac OS X
- Linux
- Web (both the web player and WebGL)
- iOS
- Android
- Blackberry 10

In addition, through specially licensed modules, Unity can build apps for the following:

- XBox 360
- XBox One
- PlayStation 3
- PlayStation 4
- PS Vita
- Wii U
- Windows Phone 8

Whew, that full list is really long! Frankly, that's almost comically long, way more than the supported platforms of almost any other game development tool out there. This chapter will focus on the first six platforms listed because those platforms are of primary interest to the majority of people exploring Unity, but keep in mind how many options are available to you.

To see all these platforms, open the Build Settings window. That's the window you used in the previous chapter to add scenes to be loaded; to access it, choose File > Build Settings. In chapter 11 you only cared about the list at the top, but now you want to pay attention to the buttons at the bottom (see figure 12.1). You'll notice a lot of space taken up by the list of platforms; the currently active platform is indicated with the Unity icon. Select platforms in this list and then click the Switch Platform button.

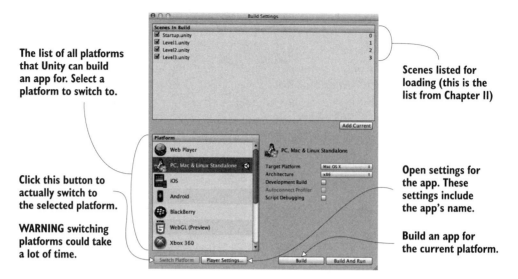

The list of all platforms that Unity can build an app for. Select a platform to switch to.

Scenes listed for loading (this is the list from Chapter 11)

Click this button to actually switch to the selected platform.

**WARNING** switching platforms could take a lot of time.

Open settings for the app. These settings include the app's name.

Build an app for the current platform.

**Figure 12.1  The Build Settings window**

> **WARNING**   When in a big project, switching platforms often takes quite a bit of time to complete; make sure you're ready to wait. This is because Unity recompresses all assets (such as textures) in an optimal way for each platform.

Also across the bottom of this window are the Player Settings and Build buttons. Click Player Settings to view settings for the app in the Inspector, such as the name and icon for the app. Clicking Build launches the build process.

> **TIP**   Build And Run does the same thing as Build, plus it automatically runs the built application. I usually want to do that part manually, so I rarely use Build And Run.

When you click Build, the first thing that comes up is a file selector so that you can tell Unity where to generate the app package. Once you select a file location, the build process starts. Unity creates an executable app package for the currently active platform; let's go over the build process for the most popular platforms: desktop, web, and mobile.

## 12.1  *Start by building for the desktop: Windows, Mac, and Linux*

The simplest place to start when first learning to build Unity games is by deploying to desktop computers—Windows PC, Mac OS X, or Linux. Because Unity runs on desktop computers, that means you'll build an app for the computer you're already using.

> **NOTE**   Open up any project to work with in this section. Seriously, any Unity project will work; in fact, I strongly suggest using a different project in every section to drive home the fact that Unity can build any project to any platform!

### 12.1.1 *Building the application*

First choose File > Build Settings to open the Build Settings window. By default, the current platform will be set to PC, Mac, and Linux, but if that isn't current, select the correct platform from the list and click Switch Platform.

On the right side of the window you'll notice the Target Platform menu. This menu lets you choose between Windows PC, Mac OS X, and Linux. All three are treated as one platform in the list on the left side, but these are very different platforms, so choose the correct one.

Once you've chosen your desktop platform, click Build. A file dialog pops up, allowing you to choose where the built application will go. Then the build process starts; this could take a while for a big project, but the build process should be fast for the tiny demos we've been making.

---

### Custom post-build script

Although the basic build process works fine in most situations, you may want a series of steps to be taken (such as moving help files into the same directory as the application) every time you build your game. You can easily automate such tasks by programming them in a script that will execute after the build process completes.

First, create a new folder in the Project view and name that folder Editor; any scripts that affect Unity's editor (and that includes the build process) must go in the Editor folder. Create a new script in that folder, rename it TestPostBuild, and write the following code in it:

```
using UnityEngine;
using UnityEditor;
using UnityEditor.Callbacks;

public static class TestPostBuild {

    [PostProcessBuild]
    public static void OnPostprocessBuild(BuildTarget target, string
            pathToBuiltProject) {
        Debug.Log("build location: " + pathToBuiltProject);
    }
}
```

The directive `[PostProcessBuild]` tells the script to run the function that's immediately after it. That function will receive the location of the built app; you could then use that location with the various filesystem commands provided by C#.

---

The application will appear in the location you chose; double-click it to run it, like any other program. Congrats, that was easy! Building applications is a snap, but the process can be customized in a number of ways; let's look at how to adjust the build.

**TIP** Quit fullscreen games with Alt+F4 on Windows or Cmd+Q on Mac. Finished games should have a button that calls Application.Quit().

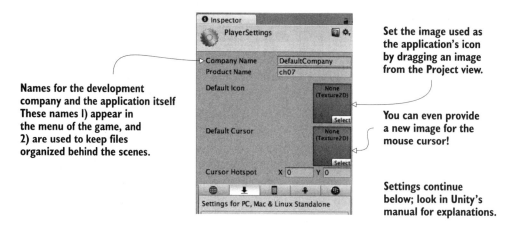

Names for the development company and the application itself These names 1) appear in the menu of the game, and 2) are used to keep files organized behind the scenes.

Set the image used as the application's icon by dragging an image from the Project view.

You can even provide a new image for the mouse cursor!

Settings continue below; look in Unity's manual for explanations.

Figure 12.2   Player settings displayed in the Inspector

### 12.1.2 Adjusting Player Settings: setting the game's name and icon

Go back to the Build Settings window, but this time click Player Settings instead of Build. A huge list of settings will appear in the Inspector (see figure 12.2); these settings control a number of aspects of the built application.

Because of the large number of settings, you'll probably want to look them up in Unity's manual; the relevant doc page is http://docs.unity3d.com/Manual/class-PlayerSettings.html.

The first three settings at the top are easiest to understand: Company Name, Product Name, and Default Icon. Type in values for the first two. Company Name is the name for your development studio, and Product Name is the name of this specific game. Then drag an image from the Project view (import an image into the project if needed) to set that image as the icon; when the app is built, this image will appear as the application's icon.

---

**Quality settings**

The built application is also affected by project settings located under the Edit menu. In particular, the visual quality of the final app can be tuned here. Go to Project Settings in the Edit menu and then choose Quality from the drop-down menu.

Quality settings appear in the Inspector, and the most important settings are the grid of check marks at the top. The different platforms that Unity can target are listed as icons across the top, and the possible quality settings are listed along the side. The boxes are checked for quality settings available for that platform, and the check box is highlighted green for the setting being used. Most of the time these settings default to Fastest (which is the lowest quality) but you can change to Fantastic quality if things look bad; if you click the down arrow underneath a platform's column, a pop-up menu will appear.

It seems a bit redundant that this UI has both check boxes and the Default menu, but there you have it. Different platforms often have different graphical capabilities, so Unity allows you to set different quality levels for different build targets (such as highest quality on desktop and lower quality on mobile).

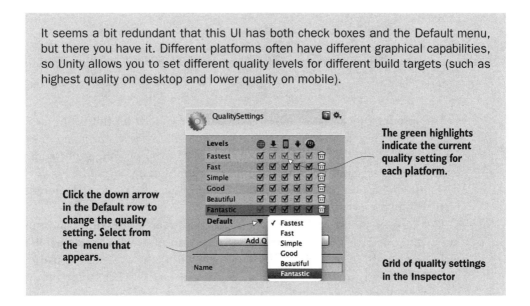

Customizing the icon and name of the application are important for giving it a finished appearance. Another useful way of customizing the behavior of built applications is with platform-dependent code.

### 12.1.3 *Platform-dependent compilation*

By default, all the code you write will run the same way on all platforms. But Unity provides a number of compiler directives (known as *platform defines*) that cause different code to run on different platforms. You'll find the full list of platform defines on this page of the manual: http://docs.unity3d.com/Manual/PlatformDependent-Compilation.html.

As that page indicates, there are directives for every platform that Unity supports, allowing you to run separate code on every platform. Usually the majority of your code doesn't have to be inside platform directives, but occasionally small bits of the code need to run differently on different platforms. Some code assemblies only exist on one platform (for example, chapter 11 mentioned that filesystem access isn't available on the web player), so you need to have platform compiler directives around those commands. The following listing shows how to write such code.

**Listing 12.1 PlatformTest script showing how to write platform-dependent code**

```
using UnityEngine;
using System.Collections;

public class PlatformTest : MonoBehaviour {
    void OnGUI() {
#if UNITY_EDITOR
        GUI.Label(new Rect(10, 10, 200, 20), "Running in Editor");
```

This section only runs within the editor.

**Only in desktop/ stand-alone applications**

```
#elif UNITY_STANDALONE
        GUI.Label(new Rect(10, 10, 200, 20), "Running on Desktop");
#else
        GUI.Label(new Rect(10, 10, 200, 20), "Running on other platform");
#endif
    }
}
```

Create a script called PlatformTest and write the code from this listing in it. Attach that script to an object in the scene (any object will do for testing), and a small message will appear in the top-left of the screen. When you play the game within Unity's editor, the message will say "Running in the Editor," but if you build the game and run the built application, the message will say "Running on Desktop." Different code is being run in each case!

For this test we used the platform define that treats all desktop platforms as one, but as indicated on that doc page, separate platform defines are available for Windows, Mac, and Linux. In fact, there are platform defines for all the platforms supported by Unity so that you can run different code on each. Let's move on to the next important platform: the web.

## 12.2  Building for the web

Although desktop platforms are the most basic targets to build for, another important platform for Unity games is deployment to the web. This refers to games that run within a web browser and can thus be played over the internet.

### 12.2.1  Unity Player vs. HTML5/WebGL

Previously, Unity had to deploy web builds in a form that plays within a custom browser plug-in. This has long been necessary because 3D graphics aren't built-in for web browsers. In the last few years, though, a standard has emerged for 3D graphics on the web called *WebGL*. Technically, WebGL is separate from HTML5, although the two terms are related and are often used interchangeably.

Unity 5 has added WebGL to the platforms list of the Build window, and future versions may even make it the new main avenue for doing web builds. In part, these changes in Unity's web build are being driven by strategic decisions made within Unity (the company). These changes are also being driven by pushes from browser makers, who are moving away from custom plug-ins and embracing HTML5/WebGL as the way to do interactive web applications, including games.

Regardless of the form of the final built app, the process for doing a web build is almost exactly the same for both a web player and WebGL. The following sections will describe the process for the web player, so you should also use that platform. The text will mention spots where the code you write differs slightly for WebGL.

### 12.2.2  Building the Unity file and a test web page

Open a different project (again, this is to emphasize how any project will work) and open the Build Settings window. Switch the platform to Web Player and then click the

Build button. A file selector will come up; type in the name `WebTest` for this application, and change to a safe location if necessary (that is, a location not within the Unity project).

The build process will now create two files: the actual Unity game will have the extension .unity3d, and there will be a bare-bones web page for playing that game. Open this web page and the game should be embedded in the middle of the otherwise blank page.

There's nothing particularly special about this page; it's just an example to test your game with. It's possible to customize the code on that page, or even provide your own web page (with the Unity code copied over). One of the most important customizations to make is enabling communication between Unity and the browser, so let's go over that next.

### 12.2.3 *Communicating with JavaScript in the browser*

A Unity web game can communicate with the browser (or rather with JavaScript running in the browser), and these messages can go in both directions: from Unity to the browser, and from the browser to Unity. Sending messages to the browser is straightforward: Unity has a couple of special commands that directly run code in the browser.

For messages from the browser the methodology is slightly more involved: JavaScript in the browser identifies an object by name, and then Unity passes the message to the named object in the scene. Thus you must have an object in the scene that will receive communications from the browser.

To demonstrate these tasks, create a new script in Unity called WebTestObject. Also create an empty object in the active scene called `Listener` (the object in the scene must have that exact name, because that's the name used in the code). Attach the new script to that object, and then write in the code from the next listing.

**Listing 12.2   WebTestObject script for testing communication with the browser**

```
using UnityEngine;
using System.Collections;

public class WebTestObject : MonoBehaviour {
   private string _message;

   void Start() {                              Initial value for
      _message = "No message yet";             the message
   }

   void Update() {                             On mouse click, call
      if (Input.GetMouseButtonDown(0)) {       function in browser
         Application.ExternalCall("ShowAlert", "Hello out there!");
      }
   }

   void OnGUI() {                              Display message
      GUI.Label(new Rect(10, 10, 200, 20), _message);   in top left of screen
   }
```

```
public void RespondToBrowser(string message) {          ⊲⌐
    _message = message;                                       ⌐ Function for the
}                                                                browser to call
}
```

Now build for web again to update the game with this new code. Unity's web build is ready now, but the web page also needs to be adjusted. You need to add a couple of functions to the JavaScript on the page, as well as add a button to the HTML. Add the JavaScript code and the HTML tag in the following listing; the JavaScript functions go at the end of the `<script>` tag, and the HTML button goes at the end of the page's `<body>`.

---

**Listing 12.3   JavaScript and HTML that enable browser–Unity communication**

```
...
function ShowAlert(arg) {          ⌐ Display an alert box.
    alert(arg);          ⊲⌐
}                                                 SendMessage() calls a
function SendToUnity() {          ⊲⌐          ⌐ function within Unity.
    u.getUnity().SendMessage("Listener", "RespondToBrowser", "Hello from the
        browser!");
}
-->
</script>
...
<input type="button" value="Send to Unity" onclick="SendToUnity();" /> #C
</body>
</html>
```

**Button that calls the JavaScript function** ⟶ (points to `<input type="button"...` line)

Open the web page to test this code out. To test communication from Unity to the browser, the WebTestObject script in Unity will call a function in the browser when you click within Unity; try clicking a few times and you'll see an alert box appear in the browser. The `Application.ExternalCall()` method will run the named JavaScript function. Unity also has `Application.ExternalEval()` for sending messages to the browser; in that case, arbitrary snippets of JavaScript are run in the browser, rather than calling a defined function. Most of the time it's better to call functions (to keep JavaScript and Unity compartmentalized), but sometimes it's useful to run arbitrary snippets, such as this code to reload the page:

```
Application.ExternalEval("location.reload();");
```

JavaScript in the web page can also send a message to Unity; click the button on the web page and you'll see the changed message displayed in Unity. The button's HTML tag links to a JavaScript function, and that function calls `SendMessage()` on the Unity instance. This method calls a named function on a named object within Unity; the first parameter is the name of the object, the second parameter is the name of the method, and the third parameter is a string to pass in while calling the method. Listing 12.3 calls `RespondToBrowser()` from the WebTestObject script.

> **NOTE** WebGL builds can also communicate with JavaScript in the web page, and the code to do so is almost exactly the same. Indeed, it *is* exactly the same for communicating from Unity to the page. As for the other direction—from the page to Unity—the `SendMessage()` method has the same parameters but no longer requires the `u.getUnity()` prefix.

That wraps up browser communication for web builds; there's one more platform (or rather, set of platforms) to discuss building apps for: mobile apps.

## 12.3 *Building for mobile apps: iOS and Android*

Mobile apps are another important build target for Unity. My gut impression (totally not scientific) is that mobile games are the largest number of commercial games created using Unity.

> **DEFINITION** *Mobile* refers to handheld computing devices that people carry around. The designation started with smartphones but now includes tablets. The two most widely used mobile computing platforms are iOS (from Apple) and Android (from Google).

Setting up the build process for mobile apps is more complicated than either desktop or web builds, so this is an optional section—optional as in only read through it and not actually do the steps; I'll still write as if you're working along, but you'd have to buy a developer license for iOS and install all the developer tools for Android.

> **WARNING** Mobile devices are undergoing so much innovation that the exact build process is likely to be slightly different by the time you read this. The high-level concepts are probably still true, but you should look at up-to-date documentation online for an exact rundown on the commands to execute and buttons to push. For starters, here are the doc pages from Apple and Google:
> https://developer.apple.com/library/ios/documentation/IDEs/Conceptual/AppDistributionGuide/Introduction/Introduction.html
> http://developer.android.com/tools/building/index.html

---

**Touch input**

Input on mobile devices works differently than on the desktop or the web. Mobile input is done by touching the screen, rather than with the mouse and keyboard. Unity has input functionality for handling touches, including code like `Input.touchCount` and `Input.GetTouch()`.

You may want to use these commands to write platform-specific code on mobile devices. Handling input that way can be a hassle, though, so a number of code frameworks are available to streamline the use of touch input. For example, I use FingerGestures (http://fingergestures.fatalfrog.com/).

---

All right, with those caveats out of the way, I'll explain the overall build process for both iOS and Android. Keep in mind that these platforms occasionally change the details of the build process.

### 12.3.1   *Setting up the build tools*

Mobile devices are all separate from the computer you're developing on, and that separateness makes the process of building and deploying to devices slightly more complex. You'll need to set up a variety of specialized tools before you can click Build.

#### SETTING UP IOS BUILD TOOLS

At a high level, the process of deploying a Unity game on iOS requires first building an Xcode project from Unity and then building the Xcode project into an IPA (iOS App Package) using Xcode. Unity can't build the final IPA directly because all iOS apps have to go through Apple's build tools. That means you need to install Xcode (Apple's programming IDE), including the iOS SDK.

> **WARNING**   That means you have to be working on a Mac—Xcode only runs on OS X. Developing a game within Unity can be done on either Windows or Mac, but building the iOS app must be done on a Mac.

Get Xcode from Apple's website, in the developer section: https://developer.apple .com/xcode/downloads/.

> **NOTE**   You need membership in the Apple Developer Program in order to sell your iOS game in the App Store. Apple's developer program costs $99/year; enroll at https://developer.apple.com/programs/.

Once Xcode is installed, go back to Unity and switch to iOS. You need to adjust the Player settings for the iOS app (remember, open Build Settings and click Player Settings). You should already be on the iOS tab of the Player settings, but click the iPhone icon tab if needed. Scroll down to Other Settings and then look for Identification. Bundle Identifier needs to be adjusted so that Apple will correctly identify the app.

> **NOTE**   Both iOS and Android use Bundle Identifier the same way, so that setting is important on both platforms. The identifier should follow the same convention as that for any code package: all lowercase in the form `com.companyname.productname`.

Another important setting that applies to both iOS and Android is Bundle Version (this is the version number of the app). Most of the settings beyond that are platform-specific, though; for example, recently iOS added a short version number that will be visible to players, separate from the main bundle version. There's also a setting for Scripting Backend; Mono was always used before, but the new IL2CPP back end can support platform updates, like 64-bit binaries.

Now click Build in Unity. Select the location for the built files, and that'll generate an Xcode project in that location. The Xcode project that results can be modified directly if you want (some simple modifications could be part of the postbuild script).

Regardless, open the Xcode project; the built folder has many files, but double-click the .xcodeproj file (it has an icon of a blueprint). Xcode will open with this project loaded; Unity already took care of most of the needed settings in the project, but you do need to adjust the provisioning profiles being used.

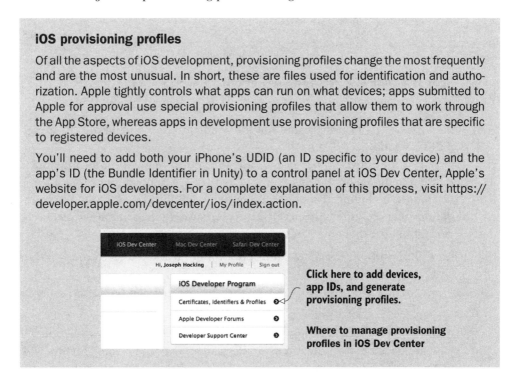

## iOS provisioning profiles

Of all the aspects of iOS development, provisioning profiles change the most frequently and are the most unusual. In short, these are files used for identification and authorization. Apple tightly controls what apps can run on what devices; apps submitted to Apple for approval use special provisioning profiles that allow them to work through the App Store, whereas apps in development use provisioning profiles that are specific to registered devices.

You'll need to add both your iPhone's UDID (an ID specific to your device) and the app's ID (the Bundle Identifier in Unity) to a control panel at iOS Dev Center, Apple's website for iOS developers. For a complete explanation of this process, visit https://developer.apple.com/devcenter/ios/index.action.

Select your app in the project list on the left side of Xcode. Several tabs relevant to the selected project will appear; go to Build Settings and scroll down to Code Signing to set the provisioning profiles (see figure 12.3). Also make sure Scheme Destination at

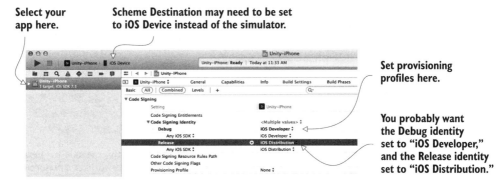

**Figure 12.3   Provisioning profile settings in Xcode**

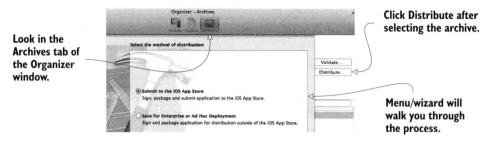

**Figure 12.4   Distribute archived iOS apps from the Organizer window.**

the top is set to iOS Device and not the simulator (some build options are grayed out if this is wrong).

Once the provisioning profiles are set, you're ready to build the app. From the Product menu, choose either Run or Archive. There are a lot of options in the Product menu, including the tantalizingly named Build, but for our purposes the two options that are useful are either Run or Archive. Build generates executable files but doesn't bundle them for iOS, whereas

- Run will test the application on an iPhone connected to the computer with a USB cable.
- Archive will create an application package that can be sent to other registered devices (what Apple refers to as "ad-hoc distribution").

Archive doesn't create the app package directly but rather creates a bundle in an intermediate stage between the raw code files and an IPA. The created archive will be listed in Xcode's Organizer window; in that window, click the Distribute button in order to generate an IPA file from the archive. Figure 12.4 shows this process; after you click Distribute, you'll be asked if you want to distribute the app on the store or ad hoc.

If you choose ad hoc distribution, you'll end up with an IPA file that can be sent to testers. You could send the file directly for them to install through iTunes, but it's more convenient to use TestFlight (https://developer.apple.com/testflight/) to handle distributing and installing ad hoc builds.

### SETTING UP ANDROID BUILD TOOLS

Unlike iOS apps, Unity can generate the APK (Android Application Package) directly. This requires pointing Unity to the Android SDK, which includes the necessary compiler. Download the Android SDK from the Android website; then choose this file location in Unity's preferences (see figure 12.5). You can download the SDK here: http://developer.android .com/sdk/index.html.

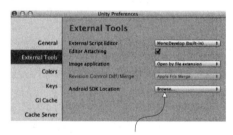

Click this menu in the External Tools section of Unity's preferences.

**Figure 12.5   Unity preference setting to point to Android SDK**

After setting the Android SDK in Unity's preferences, you need to specify the Bundle Identifier just as you did for iOS. You'll find Bundle Identifier in Player Settings; set it to com.companyname.productname (as explained in section 12.3.1). Then click Build to start the process. As with all builds, it'll first ask where to save the file. Then it'll create an APK file in that location.

Now that you have the app package, you must install it on a device. You can get the APK file onto an Android phone by downloading the file from the web or by transferring the file via a USB cable connected to your computer (an approach referred to as *sideloading*). The details of how to transfer files onto your phone vary for every device, but once there it can be installed using a file manager app. I don't know why file managers aren't built into Android, but you can install one for free from the Play Store. Navigate to your APK file within the file manager and then install the app.

As you can see, the basic build process for Android is a lot simpler than the build process for iOS. Unfortunately, the process of customizing the build and implementing plug-ins is more complicated than with iOS; you'll learn how in section 12.3.3. Before that, let's talk about texture compression.

### 12.3.2 *Texture compression*

Assets can add a lot of file size to an app, and this certainly includes textures. To reduce their file size, you can compress assets in some way; mobile apps in particular need to be careful about using too much space, so these apps apply compression to their textures. A variety of methods exist to compress images, with different pros and cons to each method. Because of these pros and cons, you may need to adjust how Unity compresses the textures.

It's essential to manage texture compression on mobile devices, but technically textures are often compressed on other platforms, too. But you don't have to pay as much attention to compression on other platforms for various reasons (the chief reason is that the platform is more technologically mature). On mobile devices, you need to pay closer attention to texture compression because the devices are touchier about this detail.

Unity compresses textures for you; in most development tools you need to compress images yourself, but in Unity you generally import uncompressed images, and then Unity applies image compression in the import settings for the image (see figure 12.6).

Change from Texture to Advanced for advanced texture compression settings.

Click the Android icon to see settings for this platform.

Override settings for Android to change compression on this image.

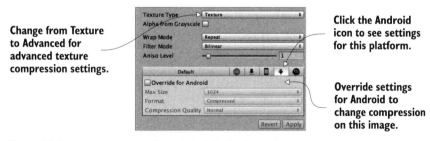

**Figure 12.6  Texture compression settings in the Inspector**

These compression settings are the default, and you may need to adjust them for specific images. In particular, image compression is trickier on Android. This is mostly due to the fragmentation of Android devices: because all iOS devices use pretty much the same video hardware, iOS apps can have texture compression optimized for their graphics chips (the GPU). Android apps don't enjoy the same uniformity of hardware, so their texture compression has to aim for the lowest common denominator.

To be more specific, all iOS devices use PowerVR GPUs; thus, iOS apps can use the optimized PVR texture compression. Some Android devices also use PowerVR chips, but they just as frequently use Adreno chips from Qualcomm, Mali GPUs from ARM, or other options. As a result, Android apps generally rely on Ericsson Texture Compression (ETC), a compression algorithm supported by all Android devices. Unfortunately, ETC (ETC1, anyway; the successor under development is ETC2) doesn't support alpha transparency, so images with alpha transparency can't be compressed using that algorithm.

Unity recompresses images when you switch platforms. On Android, Unity gets around the transparent image limitation by converting images with transparency to 16-bit instead of compressing them. Converting images to 16-bit does lower their file size, but it does so at the cost of reducing image quality. Because of this, on Android you sometimes need to manually reset the compression of individual images, determining image by image which ones need transparency versus which ones can have ETC (better image quality and no transparency), and deciding which transparent images need reduced file size versus which ones can be made uncompressed.

If you need to adjust compression on a texture, adjust the settings shown in figure 12.6. Change Texture Type to Advanced in order to access those settings, and set Android (click the Android icon tab) to override the default compression.

Adjusting texture compression is an important optimization detail on Android. The topic of the next section is important for both iOS and Android: developing native plug-ins.

### 12.3.3  *Developing plug-ins*

Unity has a huge amount of functionality built in, but that functionality is mostly limited to features common across all platforms. Taking advantage of platform-specific toolkits (such as Play Game Services on Android) often requires add-on plug-ins for Unity.

> **TIP**  A variety of premade mobile plug-ins are available for iOS- and Android-specific features; appendix D lists a few places to get mobile plug-ins. These plug-ins operate in the manner described in this section, except that the plug-in code is already written for you.

The process for communicating back and forth with native plug-ins is similar to the process for communicating with the browser. On the Unity side of things, there are special commands that call functions within the plug-in. On the plug-in's side, the plug-in can use `SendMessage()` to send a message to an object in Unity's scene. The exact code looks different on different platforms, but the general idea is always the same.

> **WARNING**  Just as with the initial build process, the process for developing mobile plug-ins tends to change frequently—not the Unity end of the process, but the native code part. I'll cover things at a high level, but you should look for up-to-date documentation online.

Also, plug-ins for both platforms are put in the same place within Unity. Create a folder in the Project view called Plugins; much as with folders like Editor, Unity handles the Plugins folder in a special way. In this case, Unity looks for plug-in files within the Plugins folder. Then, inside Plugins create two folders for Android and iOS; Unity copies the contents of those folders when doing a build.

**IOS PLUG-INS**

The "plug-in" is really just some native code that gets called by Unity. First create a script in Unity to handle the native code; call this script TestPlugin (see the next listing).

---

**Listing 12.4  TestPlugin script that calls iOS native code from Unity**

```
using UnityEngine;
using System;
using System.Collections;
using System.Runtime.InteropServices;

public class TestPlugin : MonoBehaviour {
   private static TestPlugin _instance;

   public static void Initialize() {
      if (_instance != null) {
         Debug.Log("TestPlugin instance was found. Already initialized");
         return;
      }
      Debug.Log("TestPlugin instance not found. Initializing...");

      GameObject owner = new GameObject("TestPlugin_instance");
      _instance = owner.AddComponent<TestPlugin>();
      DontDestroyOnLoad(_instance);
   }

   #region iOS
   [DllImport("__Internal")]
   private static extern float _TestNumber();

   [DllImport("__Internal")]
   private static extern string _TestString(string test);
   #endregion iOS

   public static float TestNumber() {
      float val = 0f;
```

Object is created in this static function, so you don't have to create it in the editor.

Tag that identifies section of code; tag doesn't do anything by itself

Refer to function in the iOS code.

```
      if (Application.platform == RuntimePlatform.IPhonePlayer)
         val = _TestNumber();
      return val;
   }

   public static string TestString(string test) {
      string val = "";
      if (Application.platform == RuntimePlatform.IPhonePlayer)
         val = _TestString(test);
      return val;
   }
}
```

**Call this if platform is IPhonePlayer**

First, note that the static `Initialize()` function creates a permanent object in the scene so that you don't have to do it manually in the editor. You haven't previously seen code to create an object from scratch because it's a lot simpler to use a prefab in most cases, but in this case it's cleaner to create the object in code (so that you can use the plug-in script without editing the scene).

The main wizardry going on here involves the `DLLImport` and `static extern` commands. Those commands tell Unity to link up to functions in the native code you provide. Then you can use those referenced functions in this script's methods (with a check to make sure the code is running on iPhone/iOS).

Next you'll use these plug-in functions to test them. Create a new script called MobileTestObject, create an empty object in the scene, and then attach the script (see the next listing) to the object.

### Listing 12.5   Using the plug-in from MobileTestObject

```
using UnityEngine;
using System.Collections;

public class MobileTestObject : MonoBehaviour {
   private string _message;

   void Awake() {
      TestPlugin.Initialize();
   }

   // Use this for initialization
   void Start() {
      _message = "START: " + TestPlugin.TestString("ThIs Is A tEsT");
   }

   // Update is called once per frame
   void Update() {

      // Make sure the user touched the screen
      if (Input.touchCount==0) {return;}

      Touch touch = Input.GetTouch(0);
      if (touch.phase == TouchPhase.Began) {
```

**Initialize the plug-in at the beginning.**

**Respond to touch input.**

```
            _message = "TOUCH: " + TestPlugin.TestNumber();
        }
    }

    void OnGUI() {                                              Display a message in the
        GUI.Label(new Rect(10, 10, 200, 20), _message);   ◁───  corner of the screen.
    }
}
```

The script in this listing initializes the plug-in object and then calls plug-in methods in response to touch input. Once this is running on the device, you'll see the test message in the corner change whenever you tap the screen.

The final thing left to do is to write the native code that TestPlugin references. Code on iOS devices is written using Objective C and/or C, so we need both a .h header file and a .mm implementation file. As described earlier, they need to go in the folder Plugins/iOS/ in the Project view. Create TestPlugin.h and TestPlugin.mm there; in the .h file write the code from the following listing.

### Listing 12.6  TestPlugin.h header for iOS code

```
#import <Foundation/Foundation.h>

@interface TestObject : NSObject {
NSString* status;
}

@end
```

Look for an explanation about iOS programming to understand what this header is doing; explaining iOS programming is beyond this introductory book. Write the code from the next listing in the .mm file.

### Listing 12.7  TestPlugin.mm implementation

```
#import "TestPlugin.h"

@implementation TestObject
@end

NSString* CreateNSString (const char* string)
{
if (string)
return [NSString stringWithUTF8String: string];
else
return [NSString stringWithUTF8String: ""];
}

char* MakeStringCopy (const char* string)
{
if (string == NULL)
return NULL;
```

```
char* res = (char*)malloc(strlen(string) + 1);
strcpy(res, string);
return res;
}

extern "C" {
    const char* _TestString(const char* string) {
        NSString* oldString = CreateNSString(string);
        NSString* newString = [oldString uppercaseString];
        return MakeStringCopy([newString UTF8String]);
    }

    float _TestNumber() {
        return (arc4random() % 100)/100.0f;
    }
}
```

Again, a detailed explanation of this code is a bit beyond this book. Note that many of the string functions are there to convert between how Unity represents string data and what the native code uses.

> **TIP** This sample only communicates in one direction, from Unity to the plug-in. But the native code could also communicate to Unity by using the UnitySendMessage() method. You can send a message to a named object in the scene; during initialization the plug-in created TestPlugin_instance to send messages to.

With the native code in place, you can build the iOS app and test it on a device. Very cool! That's how to make an iOS plug-in, so let's look at Android, too.

**ANDROID PLUG-INS**

To create an Android plug-in, the Unity side of things is almost exactly the same. We don't need to change MobileTestObject at all. Make the additions shown in the following listing in TestPlugin.

**Listing 12.8   Modifying TestPlugin to use the Android plug-in**

```
...
    #region iOS
    [DllImport("__Internal")]
    private static extern float _TestNumber();

    [DllImport("__Internal")]
    private static extern string _TestString(string test);
    #endregion iOS

#if UNITY_ANDROID
    private static Exception _pluginError;
    private static AndroidJavaClass _pluginClass;
    private static AndroidJavaClass GetPluginClass() {           AndroidJNI functionality
        if (_pluginClass == null && _pluginError == null) {      provided by Unity
            AndroidJNI.AttachCurrentThread();
```

```
            try {
                _pluginClass = new
        AndroidJavaClass("com.companyname.testplugin.TestPlugin");
            } catch (Exception e) {
                _pluginError = e;
            }
        }
        return _pluginClass;
    }

    private static AndroidJavaObject _unityActivity;
    private static AndroidJavaObject GetUnityActivity() {
        if (_unityActivity == null) {
            AndroidJavaClass unityPlayer = new
        AndroidJavaClass("com.unity3d.player.UnityPlayer");
            _unityActivity =
        unityPlayer.GetStatic<AndroidJavaObject>("currentActivity");
        }
        return _unityActivity;
    }
#endif

    public static float TestNumber() {
        float val = 0f;
        if (Application.platform == RuntimePlatform.IPhonePlayer)
            val = _TestNumber();
#if UNITY_ANDROID
        if (!Application.isEditor && _pluginError == null)
            val = GetPluginClass().CallStatic<int>("getNumber");
#endif
        return val;
    }

    public static string TestString(string test) {
        string val = "";
        if (Application.platform == RuntimePlatform.IPhonePlayer)
            val = _TestString(test);
#if UNITY_ANDROID
        if (!Application.isEditor && _pluginError == null)
            val = GetPluginClass().CallStatic<string>("getString", test);
#endif
        return val;
    }
}
```

**Name of the class we programmed; change this name as needed.**

**Unity creates an activity for the Android app.**

**Call to functions in plugin .jar**

You'll notice most of the additions happen inside UNITY_ANDROID platform defines; as explained earlier in the chapter, these compiler directives cause code to apply only to certain platforms and are omitted on other platforms. Whereas the iOS code wasn't doing anything that would break on other platforms (it won't do anything, but it won't cause errors, either), the code for Android plug-ins will only compile when Unity is set to the Android platform.

In particular, note the calls to AndroidJNI. That's the system within Unity for connecting to native Android. The other possibly confusing word that appears is Activity;

in Android apps, an activity is an app process. Unity is an activity of the Android app, so the plug-in code needs access to that activity to pass it around when needed.

Finally, you need the native Android code. Whereas iOS code is written in languages like Objective C and C, Android is programmed in Java. But we can't simply provide the raw Java code for the plug-in; the plug-in must be a JAR packaged from the Java code. Here again, the details of Android programming are out of scope for a Unity intro, but for reference the following listing shows an Ant build file (replace paths with locations on your computer; especially notice Unity's classes.jar to use when building Android plug-ins) and listing 12.10 shows the Java code for the plug-in being used.

**Listing 12.9   Script build.xml that generates a JAR from the Java code**

```xml
<?xml version="1.0" encoding="UTF-8"?>
<project name="TestPluginJava">
    <!-- Change this in order to match your configuration -->
    <property name="sdk.dir"
      value="LOCATION OF ANDROID SDK"/>
    <property name="target" value="android-18"/>
    <property name="unity.androidplayer.jarfile"
       value="/Applications/Unity/Unity.app/Contents/PlaybackEngines/
    AndroidPlayer/development/bin/classes.jar"/>
    <!-- Source directory -->
    <property name="source.dir"
value="LOCATION OF THIS PROJECT/Assets/Plugins/ Android/TestPlugin" />
    <!-- Output directory for .class files-->
    <property name="output.dir"
value="LOCATION OF THIS PROJECT/Assets/Plugins/ Android/TestPlugin/classes"/>
    <!-- Name of the jar to be created. Please note that the name
      should match the name of the class and the name
    placed in the AndroidManifest.xml-->
    <property name="output.jarfile" value="../TestPlugin.jar"/>
      <!-- Creates the output directories if they don't exist yet. -->
    <target name="-dirs"  depends="message">
       <echo>Creating output directory: ${output.dir} </echo>
       <mkdir dir="${output.dir}" />
    </target>
   <!-- Compiles this project's .java files into .class files. -->
    <target name="compile" depends="-dirs"
      description="Compiles project's .java files into .class files">
        <javac encoding="ascii" target="1.6" debug="true"
          destdir="${output.dir}" verbose="${verbose}"
          includeantruntime="false">
            <src path="${source.dir}" />
            <classpath>
                <pathelement
                  location="${sdk.dir}\platforms\${target}\android.jar"/>
                <pathelement location="${unity.androidplayer.jarfile}"/>
            </classpath>
        </javac>
    </target>
```

```
    <target name="build-jar" depends="compile">
        <zip zipfile="${output.jarfile}" basedir="${output.dir}" />
    </target>
    <target name="clean-post-jar">
        <echo>Removing post-build-jar-clean</echo>
        <delete dir="${output.dir}"/>
    </target>
    <target name="clean"
      description="Removes output files created by other targets.">
        <delete dir="${output.dir}" verbose="${verbose}" />
    </target>
    <target name="message">
     <echo>Android Ant Build for Unity Android Plugin</echo>
        <echo>    message:      Displays this message.</echo>
        <echo>    clean:      Removes output files created by other targets.
          </echo>
        <echo>    compile:   Compiles .java files into .class files.</echo>
        <echo>    build-jar: Compiles .class files into .jar file.</echo>
    </target>
</project>
```

---

**Listing 12.10   TestPlugin.java that compiles into a JAR**

```java
package com.companyname.testplugin;

public class TestPlugin {
private static int number = 0;

public static int getNumber() {
number++;
return number;
}

public static String getString(String message) {
return message.toLowerCase();
}
}
```

---

### Android's manifest and resources folder

It wasn't required for this simple test plug-in, but Android plug-ins often must edit the manifest file. All Android apps are controlled by a main configuration file called Android-Manifest.xml; Unity creates a basic manifest file if you don't provide one, but you could provide one manually by putting it in Plugins/Android/ alongside the plug-in JAR.

When an Android app is built, Unity puts the generated manifest file in the Temp folder at StagingArea/AndroidManifest.xml; copy that file to manually edit it (the downloaded code includes a sample manifest file).

Similarly, there's a folder called res where you can put resources like custom icons; you could create res in the Android plugins folder.

The JAR file generated by that build script goes in Plugins/Android (people often put the entire Java project here for clarity, but technically only the JAR matters). Now build the game, and then the message will change whenever you tap the screen. Also, like the iOS plug-in, an Android plug-in could use `UnityPlayer.UnitySendMessage()` to communicate with the object in the scene (the Java code would need to import Unity's Android Player library/JAR).

I know I glossed over a lot in developing Android JARs, but that's because the process is both too complicated and changes frequently. If you become advanced enough to develop plug-ins for your Android games, you're going to have to look up documentation on Android's developer website.

**CONGRATULATIONS, YOU'VE REACHED THE END!**

Congratulations, you now know the steps for deploying a Unity game to mobile devices. The basic build process for all platforms is simple (just a single button), but customizing the app on various platforms can get complicated. Now you're ready to get out there and build your own games!

## 12.4   *Summary*

In this chapter you've learned that

- Unity can build executable applications for a huge variety of platforms, including desktop computers, mobile devices, and websites.
- A host of settings can be applied to builds, including details like the icon for the app and the name that appears.
- Web games can interact with the web page they're embedded in, allowing for all kinds of interesting web apps.
- Unity supports custom plug-ins in order to extend its functionality.

# *afterword*

At this point, you know everything you need to know in order to build a complete game using Unity—everything from a programming standpoint, that is; a top-notch game needs fantastic art and sounds, too. But success as a game developer involves a lot more than technical skills. Let's face it—learning Unity isn't your end goal. Your goal is to create successful games, and Unity is just a tool (granted, a very good tool) to get you to that goal.

Beyond the technical skills to implement everything in the game, you need an additional intangible attribute: grit. I'm talking about the doggedness and confidence to keep working on a challenging project and see it through to the end, what I sometimes refer to as "finishing ability." There's only one way to build up your finishing ability, and that's to complete lots of projects. That seems like a catch-22 (to gain the ability to complete projects, you first need to complete a lot of projects), but the key point to recognize is that small projects are way easier to complete than large projects.

Thus, the path forward is to first build a lot of small projects—because those are easy to complete—and work up to larger projects. Many new game developers make the mistake of tackling a project that's too large. They make this mistake for two main reasons: they want to copy their favorite (big) game, and everyone underestimates how much work it takes to make a game. The project seemingly starts off fine but quickly gets bogged down in too many challenges, and eventually the developer gets dejected and quits.

Instead, someone new to game development should start small. Start with projects so small that they almost seem trivial; the projects in this book are the sort of "small, almost to the point of trivial" projects that you should start with. If you've done all the projects in this book, then you've already gotten a lot of these starter projects out of the way. Try something bigger for your next project, but be wary of making too big a jump. You'll build up your skills and confidence so you can get a little more ambitious each time.

You'll hear this same advice almost any time you ask how to start developing games. For example, Unity asked the web series *Extra Credits* (a great series about game development) to do some videos about starting in game dev, and you'll find those videos here:

http://unity3d.com/learn/tutorials/modules/beginner/your-first-game/

## Game design

The entire *Extra Credits* series goes way beyond this handful of videos sponsored by Unity. It covers a lot of ground but mostly focuses on the discipline of game design.

> **DEFINITION**   *Game design* is the process of defining a game by creating its goals, rules, and challenges. Game design is not to be confused with *visual* design, which is designing appearance, not function; this is a common mistake because the average person is most familiar with "design" in the context of "graphic design."

> **DEFINITION**   One of the most central parts of game design is crafting game *mechanics*; these are individual actions (or systems of actions) within a game. The mechanics in a game are often set up by its rules, whereas the challenges in a game generally come from applying the mechanics to specific situations. For example, walking around the game is a mechanic, whereas a maze is a kind of challenge based on that mechanic.

Thinking about game design can be tricky for newcomers to game development. On the one hand, the most successful (and satisfying to create!) games are built with interesting and innovative game mechanics. On the other hand, worrying too much about the design of your first game can distract you from other aspects of game development, like learning how to program a game. You're better off starting out by aping the design of existing games (remember, I'm only talking about *starting out*; cloning existing games is great for initial practice, but eventually you'll have enough skills and experience to branch out further).

That said, any successful game developer should be curious about game design. There are lots of ways to learn more about game design—you already know about the *Extra Credits* videos, but here are some other websites:

- www.gamasutra.com
- www.lostgarden.com
- www.sloperama.com

There are also a number of great books on the subject, such as the following:

- *Game Design Workshop*, Third Edition, by Tracy Fullerton (A K Peters/CRC Press, 2014)
- *A Theory of Fun for Game Design*, Second Edition, by Raph Koster (O'Reilly Media, 2013)
- *The Art of Game Design*, Second Edition, by Jesse Schell (A K Peters/CRC Press, 2014)

## Marketing your game

In the *Extra Credits* videos the fourth video is about marketing your game. Sometimes game developers put off thinking about marketing. They only want to think about building the game and not marketing it, but that attitude will probably result in a failed game. The best game in the world still won't be successful if nobody knows about it!

The word *marketing* often evokes thoughts of ads, and if you have the budget, then running ads for your game is certainly one way to market it. But there are lots of low-cost or even free ways to get the word out about your game. Specifics tend to change over time, but overall strategies mentioned in that video include tweeting about your game (or posting on social media in general, not just Twitter) and creating a trailer video to share on YouTube with reviewers, bloggers, and so on. Be persistent and get creative!

Now go and create some great games. Unity is an excellent tool for doing just that, and you've learned how to use it. Good luck on your journey!

# appendix A
# Scene navigation and keyboard shortcuts

Operating Unity is done through mouse and keyboard, but it isn't obvious to a newcomer *how* the mouse and keyboard are used in Unity. In particular, the most basic sort of mouse and keyboard input is navigating around the scene and looking around the 3D objects. Unity also has a number of keyboard commands for commonly used operations.

I'll explain the input controls here, but there are also a couple of web pages you could refer to (these are the relevant pages in Unity's online manual):

http://docs.unity3d.com/Documentation/Manual/SceneViewNavigation.html
http://docs.unity3d.com/Documentation/Manual/UnityHotkeys.html

## A.1 Scene navigation using the mouse

Scene navigation is primarily done with three main navigation maneuvers: Move, Orbit, and Zoom. The three different movements involve clicking and dragging while holding down some combination of Alt (or Option on the Mac) and Control. The exact controls vary for one-, two-, and three-button mice; table A.1 lists all the controls.

**Table A.1  Scene navigation controls for various kinds of mice**

| Navigation action | Three-button mouse | Two-button mouse | One-button mouse |
|---|---|---|---|
| Move | Middle button click/drag | Alt+Command+left-click/drag | Alt+Command+click/drag |
| Orbit | Hold Alt+left-click/drag | Alt+left-click/drag | Alt+click/drag |
| Zoom | Hold Alt+right-click/drag | Alt+right-click/drag | Alt+Ctrl+click/drag |

**NOTE** Although Unity can be used with one- or two-button mice, I highly recommend getting a three-button mouse (and yes, a three-button mouse works fine on Mac OS X).

Besides the navigation maneuvers done using the mouse, there are also some view controls based on the keyboard. If you hold down the right button on the mouse, the WASD keys on the keyboard can be used to walk around in the manner common to most first-person games. Hold Shift during any other control to move faster. But most important, if you press F while an object is selected, the view will pan and zoom to focus on that object. If you get lost while navigating your scene, a common "escape hatch" is to select an object listed in the Hierarchy and then press F.

## A.2 Commonly used keyboard shortcuts

Unity has a number of keyboard commands to quickly access important functions. The most important keyboard shortcuts are W, E, R, and T: those buttons activate the transform tools Translate, Rotate, and Scale (refer back to chapter 1 if you don't recall what the transform tools do) as well as the 2D Rect tool. Because those keys are right next to each other, it's common to leave your left hand on those keys while your right hand operates the mouse.

In addition to the transform tools, there are a number of keyboard shortcuts; table A.2 lists many useful keyboard shortcuts in Unity.

**Table A.2   Useful keyboard shortcuts**

| Keystroke | Function |
|---|---|
| W | Translate (move the selected object) |
| E | Rotate (rotate the selected object) |
| R | Scale (resize the selected object) |
| T | Rect tool (manipulate 2D objects) |
| F | Focus view on the selected object |
| V | Snap to vertices |
| Ctrl/Command+Shift+N | New GameObject |
| Ctrl/Command+P | Play game |
| Ctrl/Command+R | Refresh project |
| Ctrl/ Command+1 | Set current window to Scene view |
| Ctrl/Command+2 | Set to Game view |
| Ctrl/Command+3 | Set to Inspector view |
| Ctrl/Command+4 | Set to Hierarchy view |
| Ctrl/Command+5 | Set to Project view |
| Ctrl/Command+6 | Set to Animation view |

Unity responds to a number of other keyboard shortcuts as well, but they get increasingly obscure the further down the list we get.

# appendix B
# External tools used
# alongside Unity

Developing a game using Unity relies on a variety of external software tools for taking care of various tasks. In chapter 1 we already discussed one external tool; MonoDevelop is technically a separate application, even though it's bundled along with Unity. In a similar manner, developers rely on an array of external tools to do work not internal to Unity.

This isn't to say that Unity is lacking capabilities that it ought to have. Rather, the game development process is so complex and multifaceted that any well-designed piece of software with a clear focus and clean separation of concerns will inevitably limit itself to being good at a limited subset of the process. In this case, Unity concentrates on being the glue and the engine that brings together all the content of a game and makes it function. Creating all that content is done with other tools; let's take a look at several categories of software that could be useful to you.

## B.1 Programming tools

We've already looked at MonoDevelop, the most significant programming tool used alongside Unity. But there are a handful of other programming tools to be aware of, as you'll see in this section.

### B.1.1 Visual Studio

As mentioned in chapter 1, although Unity comes with MonoDevelop and you can use that IDE on both Windows and Mac, on Windows you could also choose to use Visual Studio. Recently Microsoft acquired SyntaxTree, a company that has been improving the integration of Visual Studio:

http://unityvs.com

### B.1.2  Xcode

Xcode is the programming environment provided by Apple (in particular an IDE, but also including SDKs for Apple platforms). Although you'd still be doing the vast majority of the work within Unity, you need to use Xcode to deploy a game to iOS. That work often involves debugging or profiling your app using the tools in Xcode:

https://developer.apple.com/xcode/

### B.1.3  Android SDK

Similar to how you need to install Xcode in order to deploy to iOS, you need to download the Android SDK in order to deploy to Android. Unlike when building an iOS game, you don't need to fire up any development tools outside of Unity—you simply have to set preferences in Unity that point to the Android SDK:

http://developer.android.com/sdk/index.html

### B.1.4  SVN, Git, or Mercurial

Any decent-sized software development project will involve a lot of complex revisions to code files, so programmers have developed a class of software called VCS (version control system) to handle this problem. Three of the most popular systems are Subversion (also known as SVN), Git, and Mercurial; if you don't already use a VCS, I highly recommend starting to use one. Unity fills the project folder with temp files and workspace settings, but the only two folders that need to be in version control are Assets (make sure your version control is picking up the meta files generated by Unity) and Project Settings:

- http://subversion.apache.org/
- http://git-scm.com/
- http://mercurial.selenic.com/wiki/Mercurial

## B.2  3D art applications

Although Unity is perfectly capable of handling 2D graphics (and chapters 5 and 6 focus on 2D graphics), it originated as a 3D game engine and continues to have strong 3D graphics features. Many 3D artists work with at least one of the software packages described in this section.

### B.2.1  Maya

Maya is a 3D art and animation package with deep roots in moviemaking. Maya's feature set covers almost every task that comes up for 3D artists, from crafting beautiful cinematic animations to making efficient game-ready models. 3D animation done in Maya (such as a character walking) can be exported over to Unity:

www.autodesk.com/products/autodesk-maya/overview

### B.2.2  *3ds Max*

The other widely used 3D art and animation package, 3ds Max offers an almost identical feature set and is quite comparable in workflow to Maya. 3ds Max runs only on Windows (whereas other tools, including Maya, are cross-platform), but it's used just as often in the game industry:

www.autodesk.com/products/autodesk-3ds-max/overview

### B.2.3  *Blender*

Though not as commonly used in the game industry as either 3ds Max or Maya, Blender is also comparable to those other applications. Blender also covers almost all 3D art tasks, and best of all, Blender is open source. Given that it's available for free on all platforms, Blender is the only 3D art application that's assumed to be available by this book:

www.blender.org

## B.3    *2D image editors*

2D images are crucial to all games, be they displayed directly for 2D games or as textures on the surface of 3D models. Several 2D graphics tools come up often in game development, as you'll see in this section.

### B.3.1  *Photoshop*

Photoshop is easily the most widely used 2D image application there is. The tools in Photoshop can be used for touching up existing images, applying image filters, or even painting pictures from scratch. Photoshop supports dozens of different file formats, including all image formats used in Unity:

www.photoshop.com

### B.3.2  *GIMP*

An acronym standing for GNU Image Manipulation Program, this is the best-known open source 2D graphics application. GIMP trails Photoshop in both features and usability, but it's still a useful image editor, and you can't beat the price!

www.gimp.org

### B.3.3  *TexturePacker*

Whereas the previously mentioned tools are all used beyond just the field of game development, TexturePacker is only useful for game development. But it's very good at the task it was designed for: assembling sprite sheets to use in 2D games. If you're developing a 2D game, then you probably want to try out TexturePacker:

www.codeandweb.com/texturepacker

## B.4    *Audio software*

A dizzying array of audio production tools are available, including both sound editors (that work with raw waveforms) and sequencers (that compose music using a sequence of notes). To give a taste of the audio software available, this section looks at two major sound-editing tools (other examples beyond this list include Logic, Ableton, and Reason).

### B.4.1   Pro Tools

This audio software boasts many useful features and is considered the industry standard by countless music producers and audio engineers. It's frequently used for all sorts of professional audio work, including game development:

www.avid.com/US/products/family/Pro-Tools

### B.4.2   Audacity

Although nowhere near as useful for professional audio work, Audacity is a handy sound editor for small-scale audio work, like preparing short sound files to use as sound effects in a game. This is a popular choice for those looking for open source sound editing software:

http://audacity.sourceforge.net/

# *appendix C*
# *Modeling a bench in Blender*

In chapters 2 and 4 we looked at creating levels with large flat walls and floors. But what about more detailed objects? What if you want, say, interesting furniture in the room? You can accomplish that by building 3D models in external 3D art apps. Recall the definition from the introduction to chapter 4: 3D models are the mesh objects in the game (that is, the three-dimensional shapes). In this appendix I'll show you how to create a mesh object of a simple bench (see figure C.1).

While appendix B lists a number of 3D art tools, we'll use Blender for this exercise because it's open source and thus accessible to all readers. You'll create a mesh object in Blender and export that out to an art asset that works with Unity.

> **TIP** Modeling is a huge topic, but we'll cover only a handful of modeling functions that will allow you to create the bench. If you want to keep learning more about modeling after this chapter, look to some of the many books and tutorials on the subject (to start with, look at the learning resources on www.blender.org).

> **WARNING** I used Blender 2.67, so the explanations and screenshots come from that version of the software. Newer versions of Blender are released frequently, and there may be slight changes to the placement of buttons or names of commands.

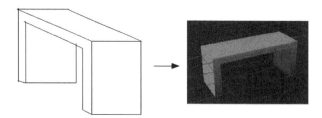

**Figure C.1 Diagram of the simple bench you're going to model**

**The default camera
(delete this)**

**A default cube**

**The default light
(delete this)**

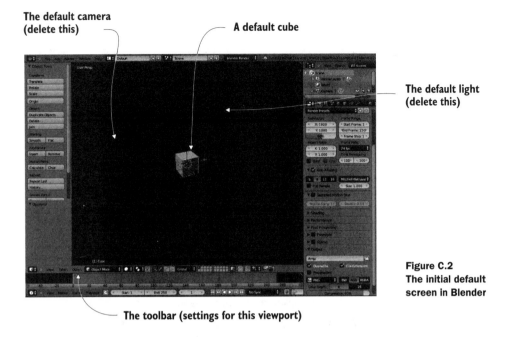

**Figure C.2
The initial default
screen in Blender**

**The toolbar (settings for this viewport)**

## C.1 Building the mesh geometry

Launch Blender; the initial default screen looks like figure C.2, with a cube in the middle of the scene. Use the middle-mouse button to manipulate the camera view: click and drag to tumble, Shift with click-drag to pan, and Control with click-drag to zoom.

Blender starts out in Object mode, which, as the name implies, is when you manipulate entire objects, moving them around the scene. To edit a single object in detail, you must switch to Edit mode; figure C.3 shows the menu you use (Edit appears in this menu only when an object is selected, and Blender starts out with the object selected). Similarly, when

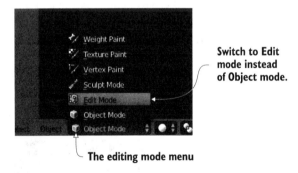

**Switch to Edit
mode instead
of Object mode.**

**The editing mode menu**

**Figure C.3    Menu for switching from Object to Edit mode**

you first switch to Edit mode, Blender is set to Vertex Selection mode, but there are buttons (refer to figure C.4) that let you switch between Vertex, Edge, and Face Selection modes. The various selection modes allow you to select different mesh elements.

Transform tool:
translate, rotate, scale

Selection mode:
vertex, edge, or face

Toggle: select back
of object, too

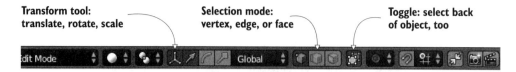

**Figure C.4    Controls along the bottom of the viewport**

**DEFINITION**    *Mesh elements* are the vertices, edges, and faces that comprise the geometry of the mesh—in other words, the individual corner points, the lines connecting the points, and the shapes filled in between connected lines.

### Fundamental mouse and keyboard shortcuts in Blender

Also depicted in figure C.4 are the various transform tools. As in Unity, the transforms are Translate, Rotate, and Scale. The first button toggles the Transform Gizmo (the arrows in the scene) on and off; I recommend leaving that gizmo on, because otherwise you can only access the transform tools via keyboard shortcuts. The keyboard shortcuts in Blender are often unexpected, as is the mouse functionality.

For example, though the use of the middle-mouse to manipulate the camera makes intuitive sense, selecting elements in the scene is done with the right mouse button (in most applications the left mouse button selects things). Even weirder, a box selection is done by pressing B and then left-clicking-and-dragging. You add to the selection (as opposed to replace the selection) by holding Shift while clicking on elements, and you clear the selection by pressing A.

These are the basic controls for using Blender, so now we'll see some functions for editing the model. To start with, scale the cube into a long, thin plank. Select every vertex of the model (be sure to also select vertices on the side of the object facing away) and then switch to the Scale tool. Click-drag the blue arrow for the Z-axis to scale down vertically, and then click-drag the green arrow for Y to scale out sideways (see figure C.5).

Long, thin plank
that will be
top of bench

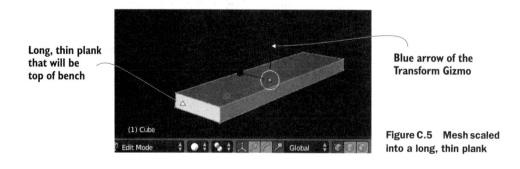

Blue arrow of the
Transform Gizmo

**Figure C.5    Mesh scaled
into a long, thin plank**

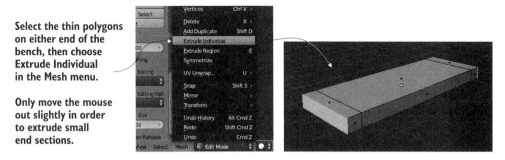

**Select the thin polygons on either end of the bench, then choose Extrude Individual in the Mesh menu.**

**Only move the mouse out slightly in order to extrude small end sections.**

**Figure C.6   In the Mesh menu use Extrude Individual to pull out extra sections.**

Switch to Face Selection mode (use the button indicated in figure C.4) and select both small ends of the plank. Now click on the Mesh menu at the bottom of the viewport and select Extrude Individual (see figure C.6). As you move the mouse you'll see additional sections added to the ends of the plank; move them out slightly and then left-click to confirm. This additional section is only the width of the bench legs, giving you a little additional geometry to work with.

> **DEFINITION**   *Extrude* is when you push out new geometry with a cross-section in the shape of the selected faces. The two different extrude commands define what to do when multiple elements are selected: Extrude Individual treats each element as a separate piece to extrude, whereas Extrude Region treats the entire selection as a single piece.

Now look at the bottom of the plank and select the two thin faces on each end. Use the Extrude Individual command again to pull down legs for the bench (refer to figure C.7).

The shape is complete! But before you export the model over to Unity, you want to take care of texturing the model.

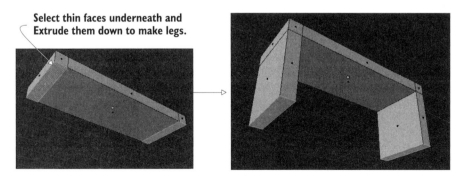

**Select thin faces underneath and Extrude them down to make legs.**

**Figure C.7   Select the thin faces underneath the bench and pull down legs.**

## C.2     *Texture-mapping the model*

3D models can have 2D images (referred to as *textures*) displayed on their surface. How exactly the 2D images relate to the 3D surface is straightforward for a large flat surface like a wall; simply stretch the image across the flat surface. But what about an oddly shaped surface, like the sides of the bench? This is where it becomes important to understand the concept of *texture coordinates*.

Texture coordinates define how parts of the texture relate to parts of the mesh. These coordinates assign mesh elements to areas of the texture. Think about it like wrapping paper (see figure C.8); the 3D model is the box being wrapped, the texture is the wrapping paper, and the texture coordinates represent where on the wrapping paper each side of the box will go. The texture coordinates define points and shapes on the 2D image; those shapes correlate to polygons on the mesh, and that part of the image appears on that part of the mesh.

> **TIP**  Another name for texture coordinates is *UV coordinates*. This name comes from the fact that texture coordinates are defined using the letters U and V, like coordinates on the 3D model are defined using X, Y, and Z.

The technical term for correlating part of one thing to part of another is *mapping*—hence the term *texture mapping* for the process of creating texture coordinates. Coming from the wrapping paper analogy, another name for the process is *unwrapping*. And then there are terms created by mashing up the other terminology, like *UV*

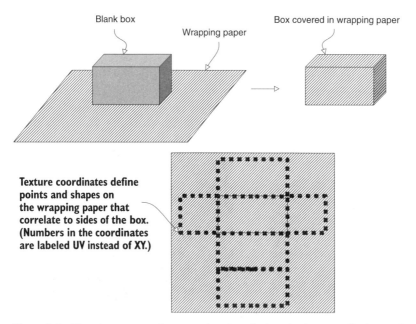

**Figure C.8  Wrapping paper makes a good analogy for how texture coordinates work.**

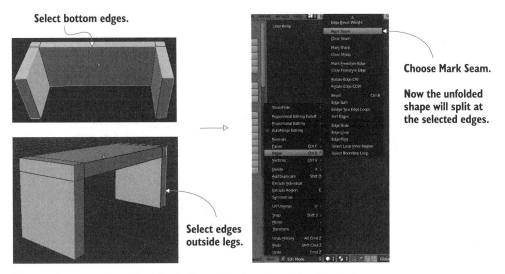

**Figure C.9    Seam edges along the bottom of the bench and along the legs**

*unwrapping*; there are a lot of essentially synonymous terms surrounding texture mapping, so try not to get confused.

Traditionally the process of texture mapping has been wickedly complicated, but fortunately Blender provides tools to make the process fairly simple. First you define seams on the model; if you think further about wrapping around a box (or better yet, think about the other direction, unfolding a box) you'll realize that not every part of a 3D shape can remain seamless when unfolded into two dimensions. There will have to be seams in the 3D form where the sides come apart. Blender enables you to select edges and declare them as seams.

Switch to Edge Selection mode (see the buttons in figure C.4) and select edges along the outside of the bottom of the bench. Now select Mesh > Edges > Mark Seam (see figure C.9). This tells Blender to separate the bottom of the bench for purposes of texture mapping. Do the same thing for the sides of the bench, but don't separate the sides entirely. Instead, only seam edges running up the legs of the bench; this way, the sides will remain connected to the bench while spreading out like wings.

Once all the seams are marked, run the Texture Unwrap command. First select the entire mesh (don't forget the side of the object facing away). Next, choose Mesh > UV Unwrap > Unwrap to create the texture coordinates. But you can't see the texture coordinates in this view; Blender defaults to a 3D view of the scene. To see the texture coordinates you must switch from 3D View to UV Editor, using the Viewports menu located on the far left of the toolbar (not the word *View* but the little icon; see figure C.10).

Now you can see the texture coordinates. You can see the polygons of the bench laid out flat, separated and unfolded according to the seams you marked.  To paint a texture, you have to see these UV coordinates in your image-editing program. Referring

**Export UV Layout menu**

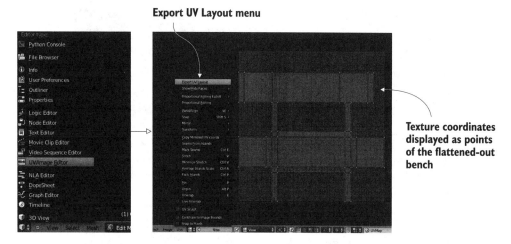

**Texture coordinates displayed as points of the flattened-out bench**

Figure C.10   Switch from 3D View to UV Editor, where the texture coordinates are displayed.

again to figure C.10, under the UVs menu choose Export UV Layout; save the image as bench.png (this name will also be used later when importing into Unity).

Open this image in your image editor and paint colors for the various parts of your texture. Painting different colors for different UVs will put different colors on those faces. For example, figure C.11 shows darker blue where the bottom of the bench was unfolded on the top of the UV layout, and red was painted on the sides of the bench. Now the image can be brought back into Blender to texture the model; select Image > Open Image.

**UV Editor after choosing Open in the Image menu**

**Exported UV layout**          **Texture image painted**

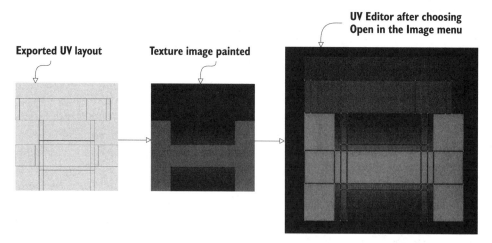

Figure C.11   Paint colors over the exported UVs and then bring the texture into Blender.

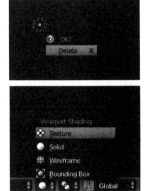

**I. Return to Object mode and delete the light (and the camera). Hit X to delete.**

**2. Then switch Viewport Shading to "Texture."**

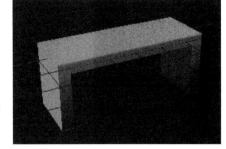

**3. Presto!**

Figure C.12   Delete the default light and view the texture on the model.

At this point you can return to the 3D view (using the same menu you used to switch to UV Editor). You still can't see the texture on the model, but that only requires a couple more steps. You need to delete the default light and then turn on textures in the viewport (see figure C.12).

To delete the light, first switch back to Object mode in order to select it (using the same menu you used to switch to Edit mode). Press X to delete a selected object; delete the camera while you're at it. Finally, go to the Viewport Shading menu to switch to Texture. Now you can see the finished bench, with texture applied!

Go ahead and save the model now. Blender will save the file with the .blend extension, using the native file format for Blender. Use the native file format to work in so that all the features of Blender will be preserved correctly, but later you'll have to export the model to a different file format for importing into Unity. Note that the texture image isn't actually saved in the model file; what's saved is a reference to the image, but you still need the image file that's being referenced.

# appendix D
# Online learning resources

This book is designed to be a complete introduction to game development in Unity, but there's a lot more to learn beyond this introduction. There are lots of great resources online you can use to go further after finishing this book.

## D.1 Additional tutorials

Many sites exist that provide directed information on a variety of topics within Unity. Several of these are even provided officially by the company behind Unity.

### UNITY MANUAL

This is the comprehensive user manual provided by Unity. Not only is the manual useful for looking up information, but the list of topics is useful by itself for giving users a full idea of what Unity is capable of:

  http://docs.unity3d.com/Documentation/Manual/index.html

### SCRIPT REFERENCE

Unity programmers end up reading this resource more than any other (at least, I do!). The user manual covers the capabilities of the engine and use of the editor, but the script reference is a thorough reference to Unity's entire API (application programming interface). Every Unity command is listed here:

  http://docs.unity3d.com/Documentation/ScriptReference/index.html

### UNITY3D STUDENT

This site provides a large library of tutorials covering an array of topics. Most importantly, the tutorials are all videos. This may be good or bad depending on your perspective; if you are someone who likes to watch video tutorials, then this is a good site to check out:

  www.unity3dstudent.com

### LEARN UNITY3D

Part of the same family of websites as Unity 3D Student, the Learn Unity 3D site is similar in purpose but provides slightly different information in a very different format (more of a news site with articles of interest to learners). It's another good site to browse through for tutorials:

http://learnunity3d.com/

### GAME DEVELOPMENT AT STACKEXCHANGE

This is another great information site with a different format from the previous ones listed. Rather than a series of self-contained tutorials, StackExchange presents a mostly text QA that encourages searching. StackExchange has sections about a huge array of topics; this is the area of the site focused on game development. For what it's worth, I look for Unity information here almost as often as I use the script reference:

http://gamedev.stackexchange.com/

### MAYA LT GUIDE

As described earlier in appendix B, external art applications are a crucial part of creating visually stunning games. Many resources are available that teach about Maya, 3ds Max, Blender, or any of the other 3D art applications out there. Appendix C offers a tutorial about Blender. Meanwhile, here's one online guide about using Maya LT (which is a less expensive and game development–oriented version of Maya):

http://steamcommunity.com/sharedfiles/filedetails/?id=242847724

## D.2  *Code libraries*

Although the previously listed resources provide tutorials and/or learning information about Unity, the sites in this section provide code that can be used in your projects. Libraries and plug-ins are another kind of resource that can be useful for new developers, both for using directly but also for learning from (by reading their code).

### UNIFY COMMUNITY WIKI

This wiki is a central database of code contributions from many developers, and the scripts hosted here cover a wide range of functionality. Throughout this book, I sometimes directed you to specific scripts hosted here (the event system and the JSON parser, for example). There are certainly many more useful scripts you can find here:

http://wiki.unity3d.com/index.php/Scripts

### UNITY PATTERNS

The library of scripts here isn't nearly as extensive as at the Unify wiki, but there's some useful code to look through, along with some illuminating tutorials:

http://unitypatterns.com/

### ITWEEN

As mentioned briefly in chapters 3 and 8, a kind of motion effect commonly used in games is referred to as a *tween*. This is a kind of movement where a single code command can set an object moving to a target over a certain amount of time. Tweening functionality can be added using libraries like:

http://dotween.demigiant.com/
https://github.com/dentedpixel/LeanTween
http://itween.pixelplacement.com/

### PRIME[31]

Unity provides deployment to mobile platforms like iOS and Android, but the actual platform-specific features are limited to core features. You can add a lot of more specific features through plug-ins, and prime[31] has many such plug-ins:

https://prime31.com/

### PLAY GAMES SERVICES FROM GOOGLE

On iOS, Unity has GameCenter integration built in so that your games can have platform-native leaderboards and achievements. The equivalent system on Android is called Google Play Games; although this isn't built into Unity, Google maintains a plug-in:

https://github.com/playgameservices/play-games-plugin-for-unity

### FMOD STUDIO

The audio functionality built into Unity works well for simply playing back recordings but can be limited for advanced sound design work. FMOD Studio is an advanced sound design tool that has a free-to-use (but not necessarily publish) Unity plug-in. Scroll down to find it in their Downloads page:

www.fmod.org/download/

### PROBUILDER AND PROTOTYPE

ProBuilder and Prototype are add-ons that enable powerful level editing within Unity. ProBuilder costs money for professional features like flexible texturing, but Prototype is free and ideal for use in the white-boxing workflow from chapter 4:

www.protoolsforunity3d.com/prototype/

### FPS CONTROL

FPS Control is a suite of tools and code designed to ease the creation of FPS (first-person shooter) games. This framework grew out of a popular series of video tutorials:

www.fpscontrol.com/features

# index

## YOU MAY ALSO BE INTERESTED IN

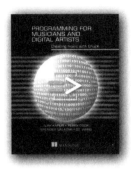

*Programming for Musicians and Digital Artists*
*Creating music with ChucK*

by Ajay Kapur, Perry Cook, Spencer Salazar, Ge Wang

ISBN: 9781617291708
344 pages, $44.99
December 2014


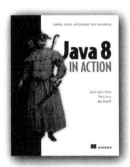

*Java 8 in Action*
*Lambdas, streams, and functional-style programming*

by Raoul-Gabriel Urma, Mario Fusco, Alan Mycroft

ISBN: 9781617291999
424 pages, $49.99
August 2014


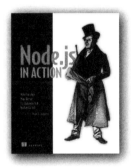

*Node.js in Action*

by Mike Cantelon, Marc Harter,
  T.J. Holowaychuk, Nathan Rajlich

ISBN: 9781617290572
416 pages, $44.99
October 2013


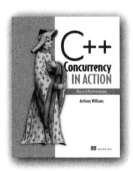

*C++ Concurrency in Action*
*Practical Multithreading*

by Anthony Williams

ISBN: 9781933988771
528 pages, $69.99
February 2012

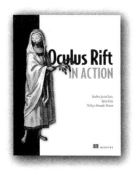

*Oculus Rift in Action*
by Bradley Austin Davis, Karen Bryla,
  Phillips Alexander Benton

  ISBN: 9781617292194
  475 pages, $54.99
  July 2015

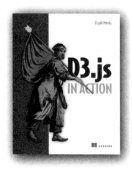

*D3.js in Action*
by Elijah Meeks

  ISBN: 9781617292118
  352 pages, $44.99
  February 2015

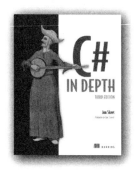

*C# in Depth, Third Edition*
by Jon Skeet

  ISBN: 9781617291340
  616 pages, $49.99
  September 2013

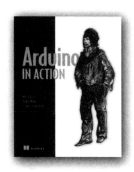

*Arduino in Action*
by Martin Evans, Joshua Noble,
  Jordan Hochenbaum

  ISBN: 9781617290244
  368 pages, $39.99
  May 2013

*For ordering information go to www.manning.com*